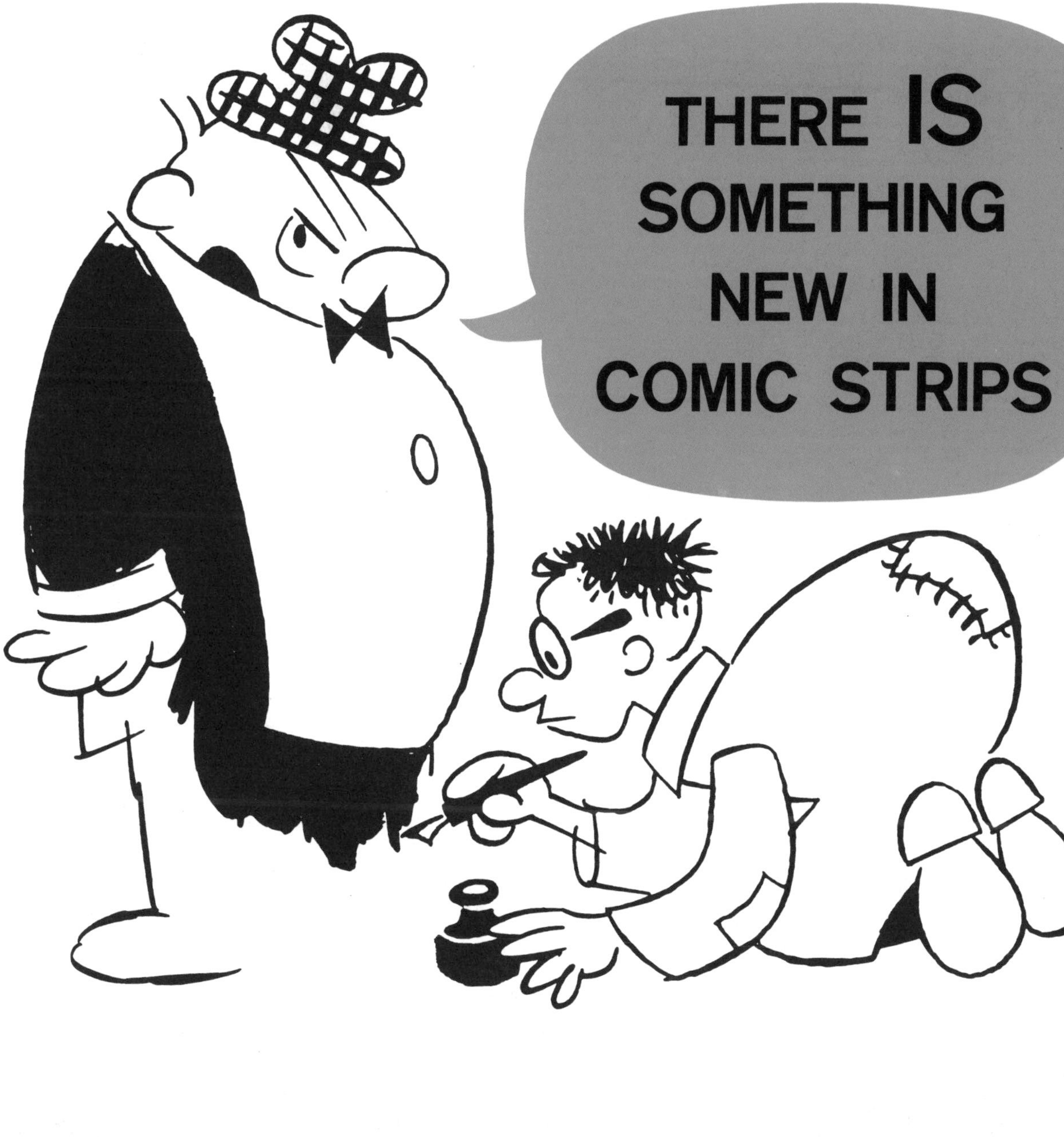
THERE IS SOMETHING NEW IN COMIC STRIPS

FANTAGRAPHICS BOOKS, 7563 Lake City Way NE, Seattle, Washington 98115 | Editor: Brian Walker | Designer: Adam Grano | Strip restoration: Bill Janocha | Production assistance: Paul Baresh and Neal Walker | Promotion: Eric Reynolds | Publishers: Gary Groth and Kim Thompson | *Sam's Strip* is copyright © 2009 Mort Walker and Jerry Dumas. All rights reserved. Permission to reproduce material must be obtained from the authors or the publisher. | Distributed in the U.S. by W.W. Norton and Company, Inc. (212-354-500) | Distributed in Canada by the Canadian Manda Group (416-516-0911) | Distributed in the United Kingdom by Turnaround Distribution (108-829-3009) | ISBN: 978-1-56097-972-2 | First Fantagraphics printing: March, 2009 | Printed in Singapore

SAM'S STRIP

> **READER HERE SAYS HE DOESN'T UNDERSTAND WHO I AM**

6-26

> **I AM A COMIC CHARACTER WHO DWELLS IN THE WORLD OF IDEAS. I CAN DO ANYTHING!**

SAM

> **I'M NOT REAL, SEE? I'M JUST A THOUGHT! I ONLY EXIST IN YOUR MIND!**

> **C'MON! CUT IT OUT!!**

SAM

THE COMIC ABOUT COMICS

by **MORT WALKER** *and* **JERRY DUMAS**

FB

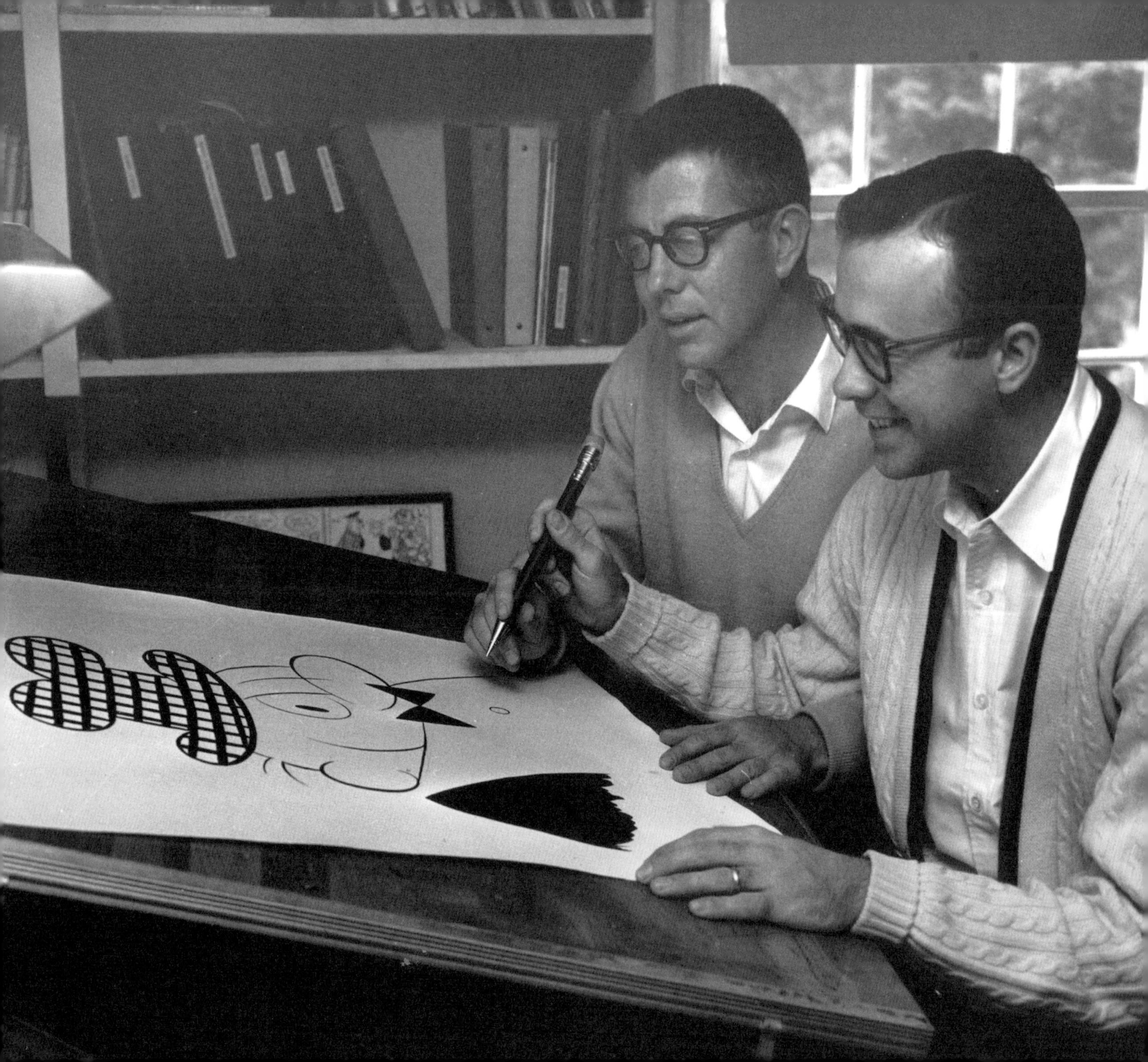

HOW SAM'S STRIP BEGAN

by JERRY DUMAS

All through the late 1950s, Mort Walker and I worked together three or four days a week, however long it took, doing the artwork for the daily and Sunday *Beetle Bailey* strips. The rest of the time I worked in my own home, writing gag ideas for both *Beetle* and *Hi and Lois*. At that time and on into the 1960s, we were the only writers for both strips. Each week we wrote ten gags apiece and on Monday mornings we showed each other our gags, graded them and discussed them. We never did rough sketches of ideas unless we thought they could actually be used, so out of twenty gag sketches it wasn't hard to select the fourteen we needed for the two strips each week.

OPPOSITE: **Mort Walker** (left) has had a guiding hand in nine syndicated comic strips since 1950 and has been drawing *Beetle Bailey* for over 58 years — the longest run by any cartoonist on his original creation. Born in El Dorado, Kansas, Mort was a lieutenant in the army during World War II, studied journalism at the University of Missouri, served as president of the National Cartoonists Society, founded the Museum of Cartoon Art and has been the recipient of numerous awards for his lifetime achievements in the cartooning profession. **Jerry Dumas** (right) was born in Detroit, received a degree in English Literature from Arizona State University, and was in the air force during the Korean War. He is married, has three sons, has published two books, countless magazine articles and newspaper columns, and has worked with Mort Walker in many capacities since 1956.

Jerry remembers: "In this early version of Sam, he seems a little too 'stuffed,' looking as though he is about to explode – the kind of feeling you have when you get up from the Thanksgiving table. Looking as though he over-indulged, he may have made some readers uncomfortable. Eventually, in *Sam and Silo*, I had to lower the face line; I needed more room for expressions."

We both had a fairly thorough knowledge of comic strip history, so just for fun, just for each other, we began doing gags about comic strip characters. We quickly saw how much fun it was to have comic characters from other strips, other times, interact with each other. The idea soon came up: What about having a guy who ran his own comic strip as a business? Mort, who enjoyed alliteration as much as anyone (Beetle Bailey, Sergeant Snorkel) came up with the name: "Sam's Strip."

But what should this character look like? One day Mort was doodling around and I was looking over his shoulder. He drew a face that looked roughly like the short character, Mac, in *Tillie the Toiler*. I said that he didn't look different enough, didn't look unique. We both stared at the paper for a minute or two. I said, "Draw a line across the middle of his face. Let's see what that looks like." Mort penciled a line from Sam's ear to his nose, cutting off the whole lower half. Now he looked different and that's the way, for better or worse, he stayed. Later on, in *Sam and Silo*, I lowered and curved the bottom line of the face to get more room for expressions. Since Sam needed someone to talk to, and since Sam was sort of fat, Mort created a thin guy (the old Laurel and Hardy concept), who never had a name until *Sam and Silo* started seventeen years later.

Mort and I split the gag writing, and I did all the drawing, except for the lettering, which Mort did, just as I did the lettering for *Beetle*. I always admired Mort's lettering enormously. (Some very good artists can't letter at all.)

We had no trouble selling the strip to King Features, which distributed *Beetle* and *Hi and Lois*. We all wondered, briefly, if there would be any problem with copyrights, using all those characters with impunity as we planned to, but no one ever minded, not even the Walt Disney Company, which today threatens lawsuits if anyone uses one of their characters without permission (or maybe paying for the privilege). In those days, other cartoonists were flattered, and even Disney would write to us and ask for the original.

When *Sam's Strip* started, on October 16, 1961, there were no copy machines, or no good ones, anyway. All the *Sam's Strips* were drawn from scratch, laboriously penciled and inked, and research took a great deal of time. I took pride in copying an artist's work exactly, even Tenniel's *Alice in Wonderland* drawings. But doing this strip took way more time than drawing a normal strip. The week we did a comics convention, with dozens of old comic characters in each strip, it took me three weeks to turn out one week of dailies. It was fun, and it felt like an accomplishment, but it was exhausting. Some fellow cartoonists were surprised to discover that I wasn't cutting and pasting.

"What?" I said. "Cut pages out of books? I wouldn't do that."

People have said that *Sam's Strip* came along too soon, that readers weren't ready then for such a radical departure. It certainly was too soon as far as drawing aids were concerned. In 1961 there were

LOOK! REAL PEOPLE!
THE FIRST ONES WE'VE SEEN SINCE ALICE!
In this Style 10/6
10-3
HOW DID THEY GET HERE? I THOUGHT WE BOARDED UP THAT RABBIT HOLE!
IT ALL STARTED WHEN WE MADE A WRONG TURN OFF THE TURNPIKE
© King Features Syndicate, Inc., 1962. World rights reserved.

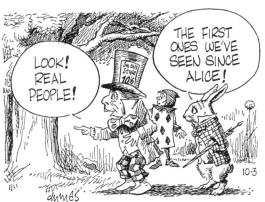

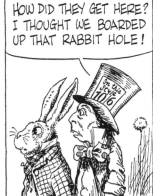

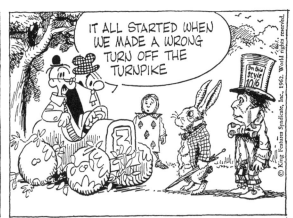

Sam's Strip, October 3, 1962. Jerry was inspired by John Tenniel's illustrations for Lewis Carroll's *Alice in Wonderland*.

HONK
© King Features Syndicate, Inc., 1962. World rights reserved.
I KNEW HAVING THAT BIG AUTOMOBILE ACCOUNT WOULD CHANGE THAT KID
9-5

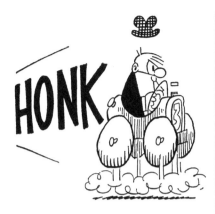

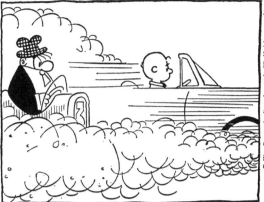

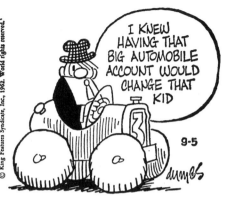

ABOVE: *Sam's Strip*, September 5, 1962. Charles Schulz signed a contract with the Ford Motor Company in 1959, licensing his characters to appear in advertisements for the Ford Falcon. RIGHT: Charles Schulz wrote Jerry this letter thanking him for the *Sam's Strip* orignal art from September 5, 1962.

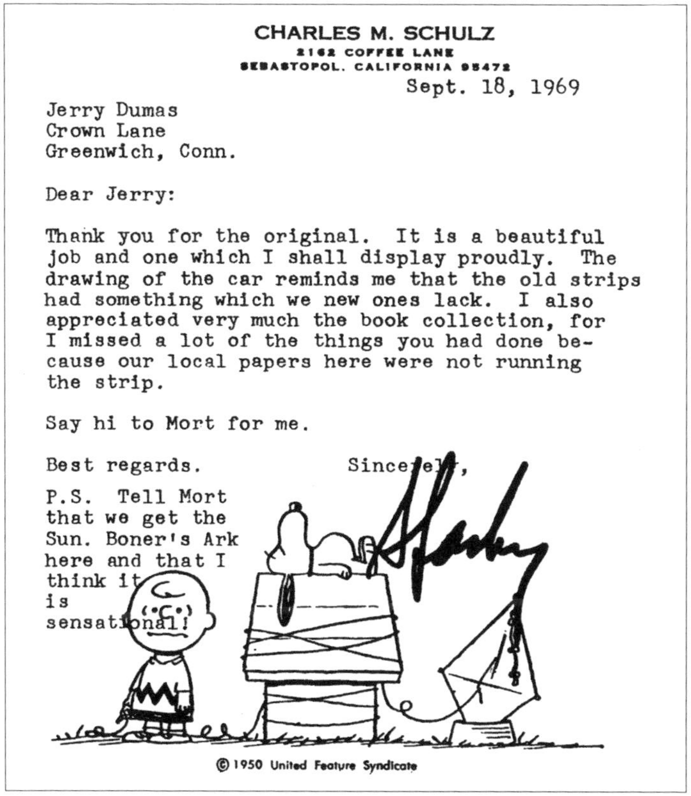

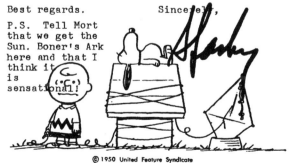

CHARLES M. SCHULZ
2162 COFFEE LANE
SEBASTOPOL, CALIFORNIA 95472

Sept. 18, 1969

Jerry Dumas
Crown Lane
Greenwich, Conn.

Dear Jerry:

Thank you for the original. It is a beautiful job and one which I shall display proudly. The drawing of the car reminds me that the old strips had something which we new ones lack. I also appreciated very much the book collection, for I missed a lot of the things you had done because our local papers here were not running the strip.

Say hi to Mort for me.

Best regards.

Sincerely,

P.S. Tell Mort that we get the Sun. Boner's Ark here and that I think it is sensational!

© 1950 United Feature Syndicate

no shortcuts, which made things hard on the eyes.

Some editors wrote to say that they thought the strip was brilliant, while others said they felt their readers weren't knowledgeable enough to understand it.

"What was there to understand?" we wondered. When an old comic strip character, like Krazy Kat or Happy Hooligan, comes along, someone yells, "Hey, there's an old comic strip character!" So we never felt that only a cartoonist could understand and love it. Still, it was always good to get complimentary letters from people like Charles M. Schulz, whose own *Peanuts* had been in existence for only ten years at that point.

Later, other comic strips would occasionally do *Sam's Strip* type of inside gags, but not very often. That's the kind of heavy labor most cartoonists try to avoid. During its brief existence, *Sam's Strip* gave Mort and me deep satisfaction, and if anybody didn't like it, that was all right, and if anybody, on the other hand, really liked it, that was all right too. •

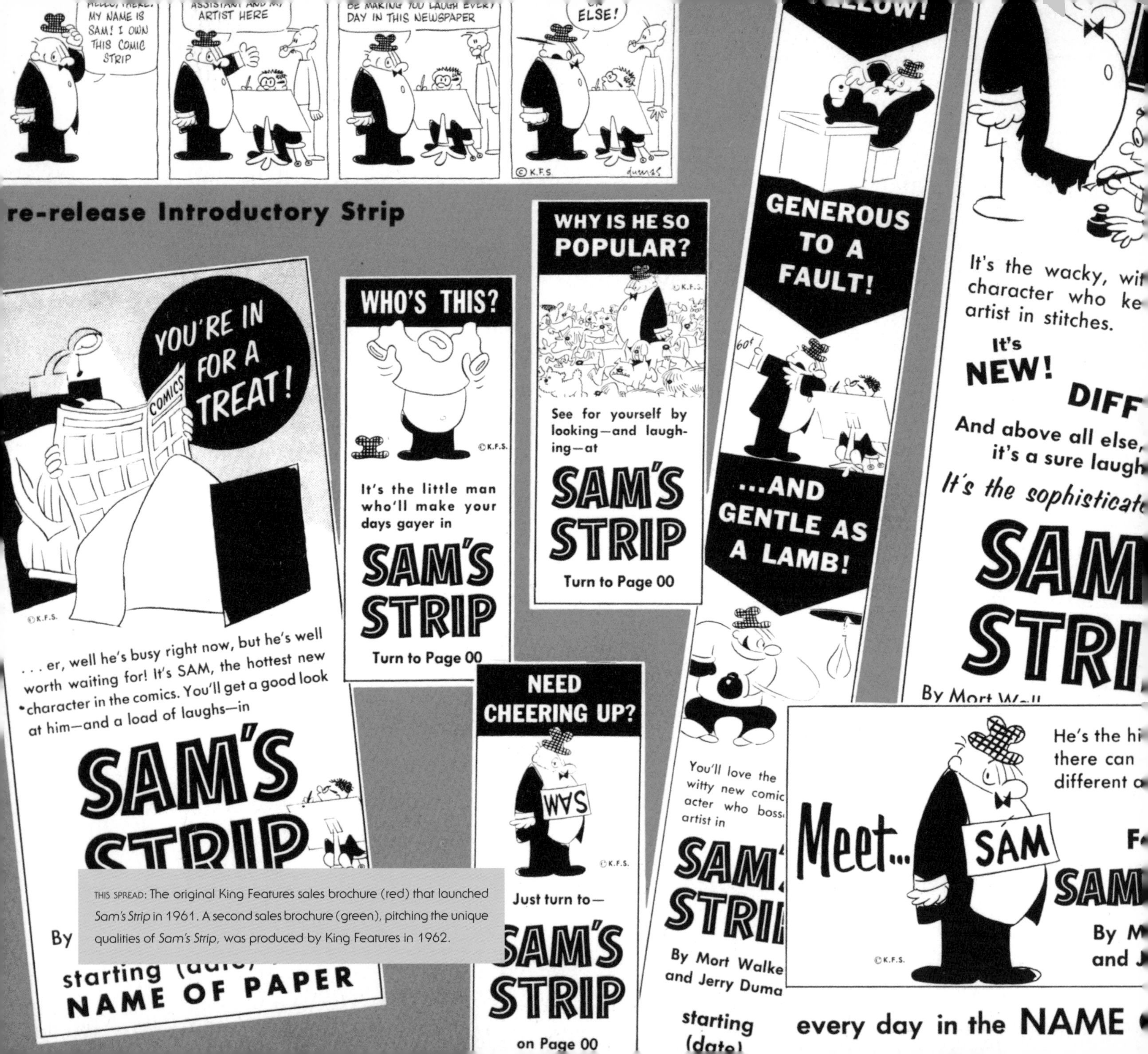

MY NAME IS SAM! I OWN THIS COMIC STRIP
ARTIST HERE
DAY IN THIS NEWSPAPER
ELSE!
© K.F.S.
re-release Introductory Strip
YOU'RE IN FOR A TREAT!
COMICS
© K.F.S.
. . . er, well he's busy right now, but he's well worth waiting for! It's SAM, the hottest new character in the comics. You'll get a good look at him—and a load of laughs—in
SAM'S STRIP
By
starting (date)
NAME OF PAPER
WHO'S THIS?
© K.F.S.
It's the little man who'll make your days gayer in
SAM'S STRIP
Turn to Page 00
WHY IS HE SO POPULAR?
© K.F.S.
See for yourself by looking—and laughing—at
SAM'S STRIP
Turn to Page 00
NEED CHEERING UP?
SAM
© K.F.S.
Just turn to—
SAM'S STRIP
on Page 00
GENEROUS TO A FAULT!
60¢
...AND GENTLE AS A LAMB!
You'll love the witty new comic acter who boss artist in
SAM
STRI
By Mort Walke and Jerry Duma
starting (date)
It's the wacky, wit character who ke artist in stitches.
It's NEW!
DIFF
And above all else, it's a sure laugh
It's the sophisticat
SAM
STRI
By Mort W
He's the hi there can different a
Meet...
SAM
© K.F.S.
SAM
By M and J
every day in the NAME

THIS SPREAD: The original King Features sales brochure (red) that launched *Sam's Strip* in 1961. A second sales brochure (green), pitching the unique qualities of *Sam's Strip*, was produced by King Features in 1962.

ning
Way!

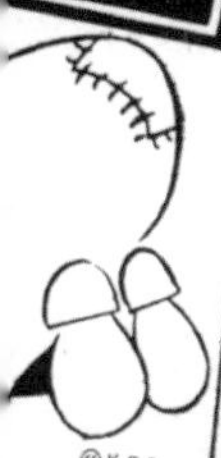

©K.F.S.

strip
n his

T!
ay!
c—

oof that
eshingly
in comics

TRIP
lker
mas

APER

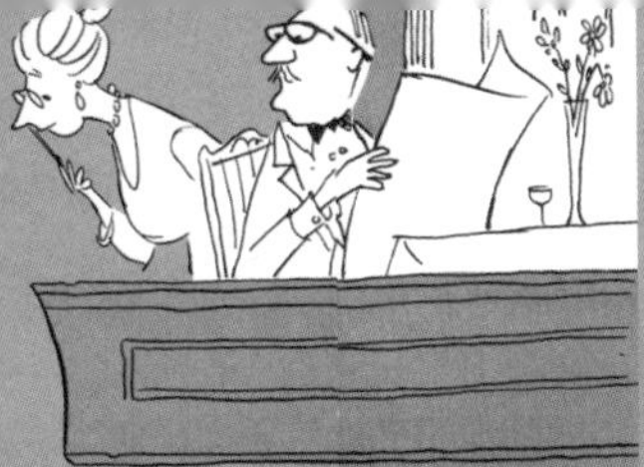

ATTRACT HIGH INCOME READERSHIP to Your Newspaper— with a COMIC STRIP?

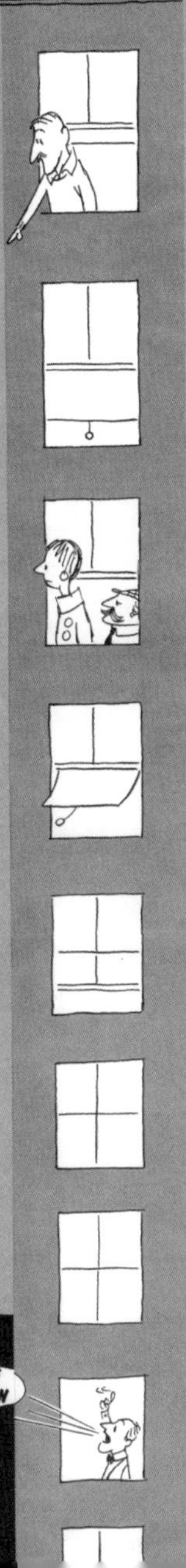

YES! With SAM'S STRIP

by Mort Walker and Jerry Dumas

• (Mort Walker is the creator-artist-writer of one of the world's most successful comic strips, the fabulous BEETLE BAILEY, appearing in nearly 900 newspapers)

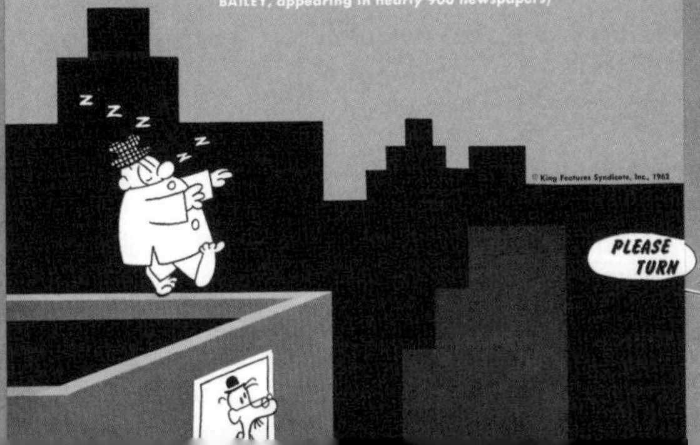
Z Z Z
PLEASE TURN

SAM'S STRIP—a Landmark in the Art of the Comic Strip—Destined to Take Its Place as One of the Very Few "Breakthrough" Comic Strips—Now Helping These Leading Papers (and many more) Make Comic Page History:

New York, N. Y., JOURNAL-AMERICAN
St. Louis, Mo., POST-DISPATCH
Chicago, Ill., CHICAGO'S AMERICAN
Seattle, Wash., POST-INTELLIGENCER
Houston, Tex., CHRONICLE
Honolulu, Hawaii, STAR-BULLETIN
Milwaukee, Wisc., SENTINEL
Salt Lake City, Utah, TRIBUNE
Charleston, W. Va., GAZETTE
Memphis, Tenn., PRESS-SCIMITAR
Portland, Me., PRESS HERALD
Phoenix, Ariz., GAZETTE
Tulsa, Okla., TRIBUNE
Dayton, Ohio, JOURNAL HERALD
Vancouver, B.C., PROVINCE
Dublin, Ireland, EVENING HERALD
Copenhagen, Denmark, EKSTRA BLADET
Manila, P.I., THE MANILA TIMES
Helsinki, Finland, SANOMA OY
Stockholm, Sweden, AFTONBLADET

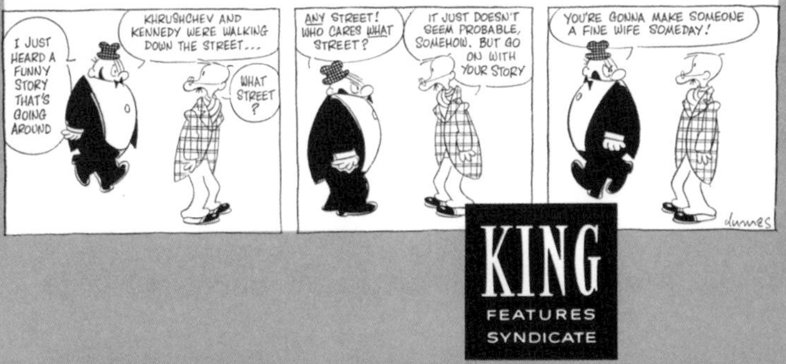
SAM'S STRIP ® By Mort Walker and Jerry Dumas
I JUST HEARD A FUNNY STORY THAT'S GOING AROUND
KHRUSHCHEV AND KENNEDY WERE WALKING DOWN THE STREET...
WHAT STREET?
ANY STREET! WHO CARES WHAT STREET?
IT JUST DOESN'T SEEM PROBABLE, SOMEHOW. BUT GO ON WITH YOUR STORY
YOU'RE GONNA MAKE SOMEONE A FINE WIFE SOMEDAY!
dumas

KING FEATURES SYNDICATE

DON'T WAIT ANOTHER DAY TO MAKE THIS GREAT NEW CONCEPT IN COMIC PAGE ENTERTAINMENT A PART OF YOUR NEWSPAPER!

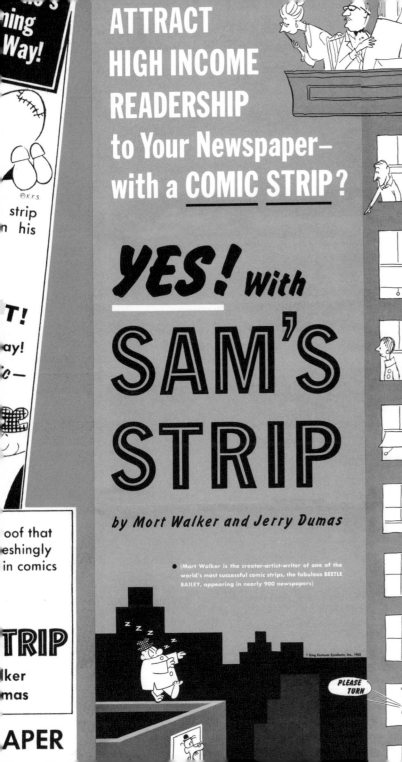

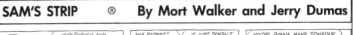

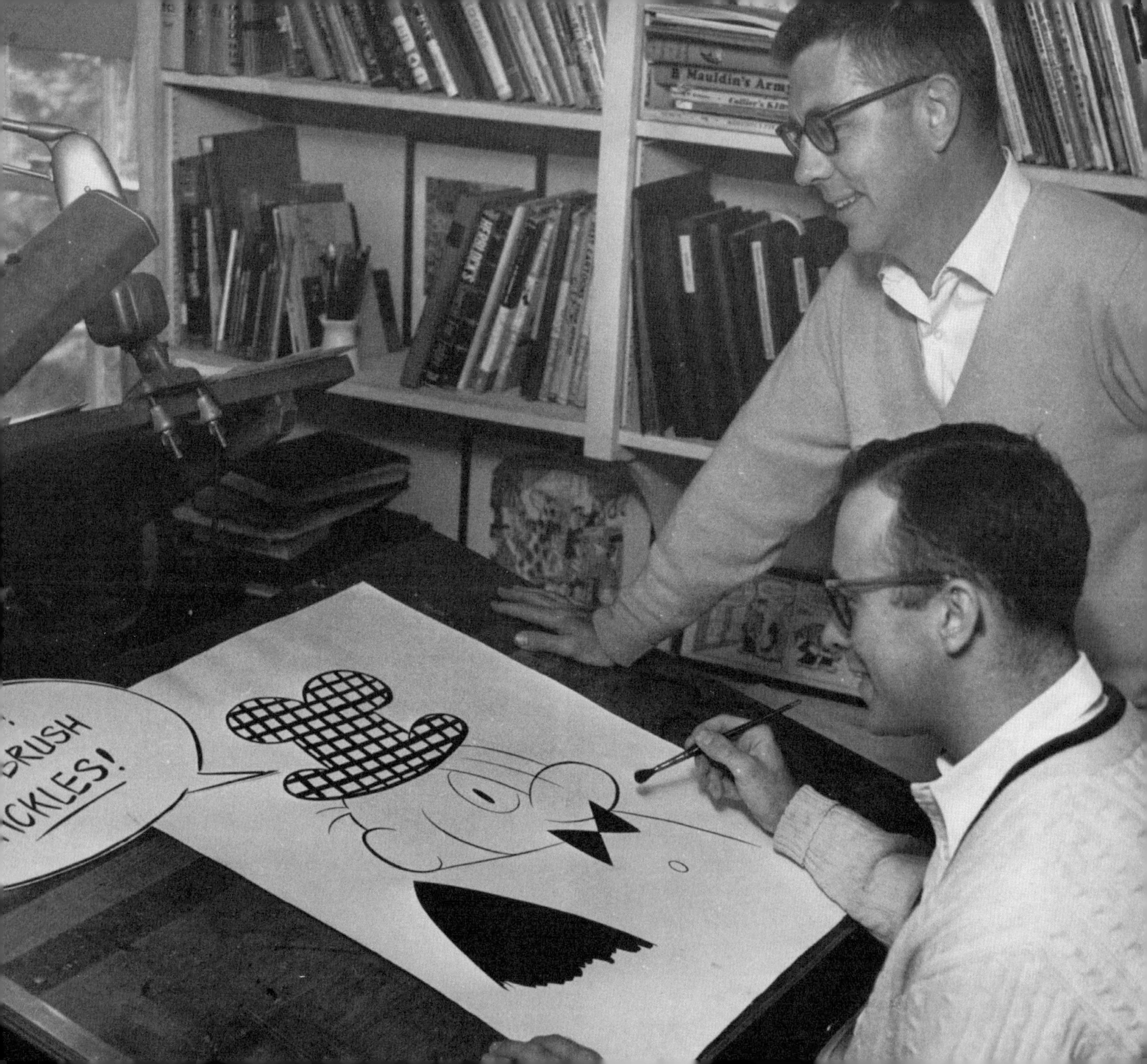
BRUSH

MY TIME WITH SAM'S STRIP

by MORT WALKER

There were problems in doing *Sam's Strip*. It was a satirical strip using characters from contemporary strips as well as old-time comic characters. Satire requires that readers have previous knowledge of the subject matter to understand what's going on. With *Sam's Strip*, the readers had to be familiar with the various characters we were satirizing before they could get the gag. It's a tough sell. In show business the saying goes, "Satire dies on Saturday night."

An insurance salesman once asked me what I did for a living. I showed him the comic page for that day and pointed to *Sam's Strip*. It was the episode where Blondie is passing by and Sam says, "They're so different in real life." The salesman looked at it and seemed puzzled. "What's Blondie doing in your strip? She belongs at the top of the page." I wonder how many readers suffered the same puzzlement that day.

Even when I went to sell the strip to King Features, I had trouble. Four executives sat there reading the strip and asking questions like, "Why are you making fun of Snuffy Smith?" "Would Mickey Mouse really do this?" "Why does Sam have a closet full of exclamation marks?" They seemed bent on killing the idea but there was enough laughter going on so that the editor finally said, "Oh, go ahead and do the strip if you really want to."

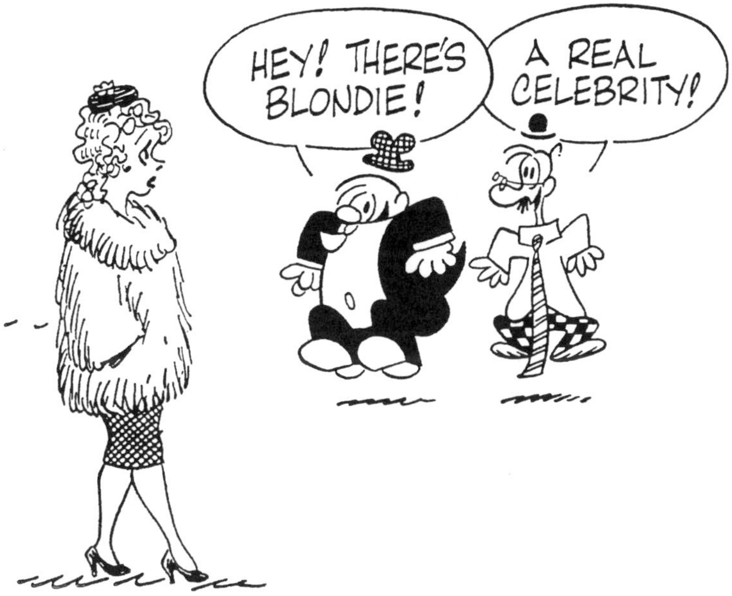
HEY! THERE'S BLONDIE!
A REAL CELEBRITY!

Sam's Strip, September 26, 1962. "What is Blondie doing in your strip?" a reader asked Mort.

OPPOSITE: Mort watches Jerry put the finishing touches on a portrait of Sam for a King Features publicity photo from 1961.

Selling it to the newspapers was another problem. A lot of editors didn't understand it while others thought it was hilarious. The editor of the *Washington Star* wrote us that it was his favorite strip, but sales were very slow around the country.

BOY! THE MIDDLE OF THE MONTH AND I'M ALMOST BROKE
ME TOO.. BUT IT COULD BE WORSE
Menu
2-25
WHAT COULD BE WORSE THAN BEING BROKE AND IN THE ARMY?
MORT WALKER
NOT BEING IN THE ARMY AND BEING BROKE
10¢
© King Features Syndicate, Inc., 1967. World rights reserved.

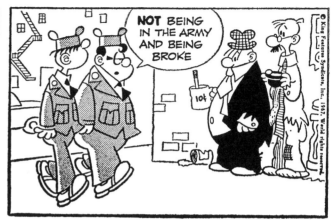

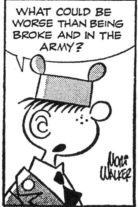

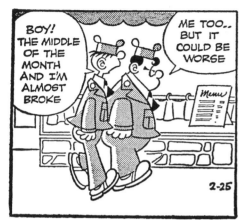

Beetle Bailey daily strip, February 25, 1967. Sam and his sidekick, now out of work, make a guest appearance.

SAY! OH YOU YELLOW KID

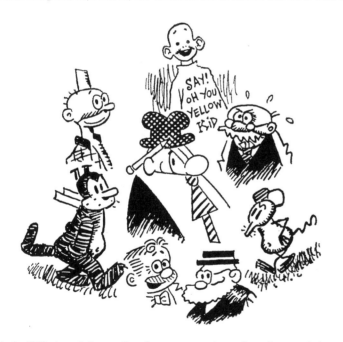

April, 1962. Artwork from a King Features press release. From the top, clockwise surrounding Sam, are: The Yellow Kid, Paw from *Polly and Her Pals*, Ignatz, Si from *And Her Name was Maude*, Casper from *Toots and Casper*, Krazy Kat and Happy Hooligan.

Of course, the cartoonists all loved it. They understood it and howled at the familiar comic gimmicks. But most of the cartoonists lived in the New York area and read it in the *Journal-American*. When competition for TV hit the newspaper business in the 1960s, the *Journal* folded and so did our informed audience. We didn't hear from the cartoonists any more and the joy went out of doing it. Eventually, the problems convinced us to kill the strip on June 1, 1963.

Years later, I got a call from the NEA Syndicate wanting to revive *Sam's Strip*. They felt that readers were now ready to get the gags. I went to King Features to see if they'd release it. The president of King got out the old sales records to show me why it wouldn't sell. He said, "But, if you want to revive it using the same characters with a different theme, we'll try it." I went to Sylvan Byck's office, the comics editor, and we sat around for a few hours pondering what new roles Sam and his buddy could play. Nothing seemed right until I said, "How about them being small-town cops?"

That was thirty years ago and Sam and Silo are still screwing up as small-town cops in roles that everyone understands. •

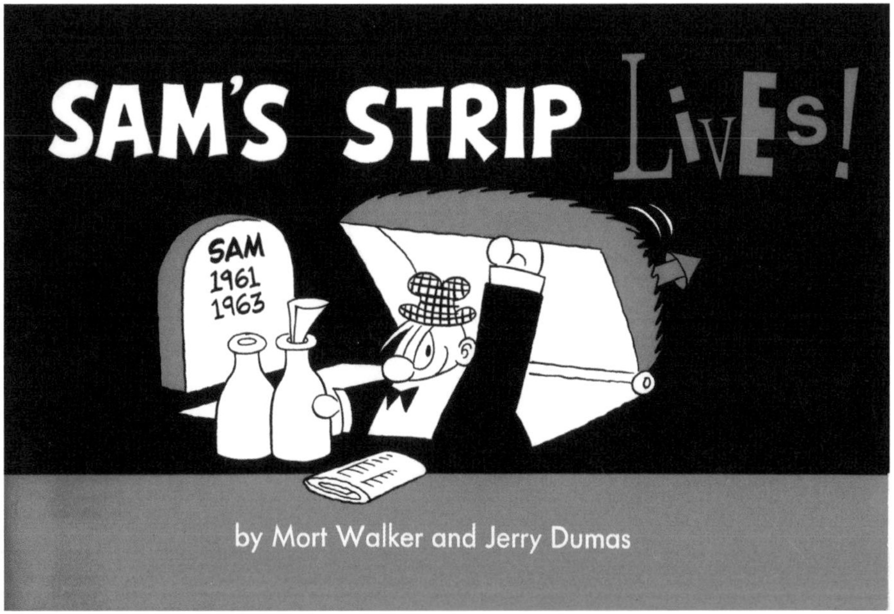
SAM'S STRIP LivEs!
SAM
1961
1963
by Mort Walker and Jerry Dumas

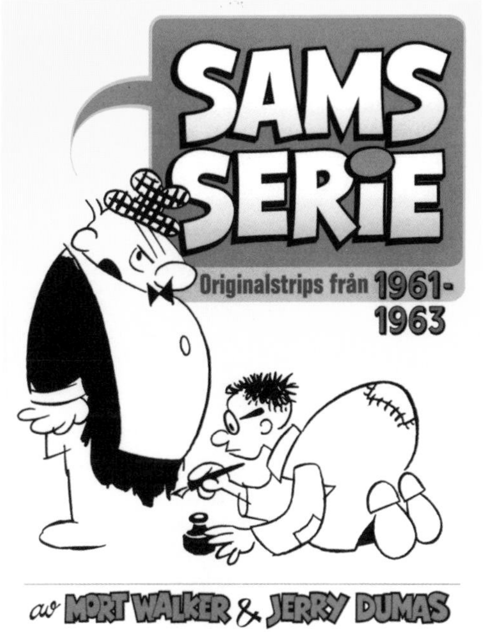
SAMS SERiE
Originalstrips från 1961-1963
av MORT WALKER & JERRY DUMAS

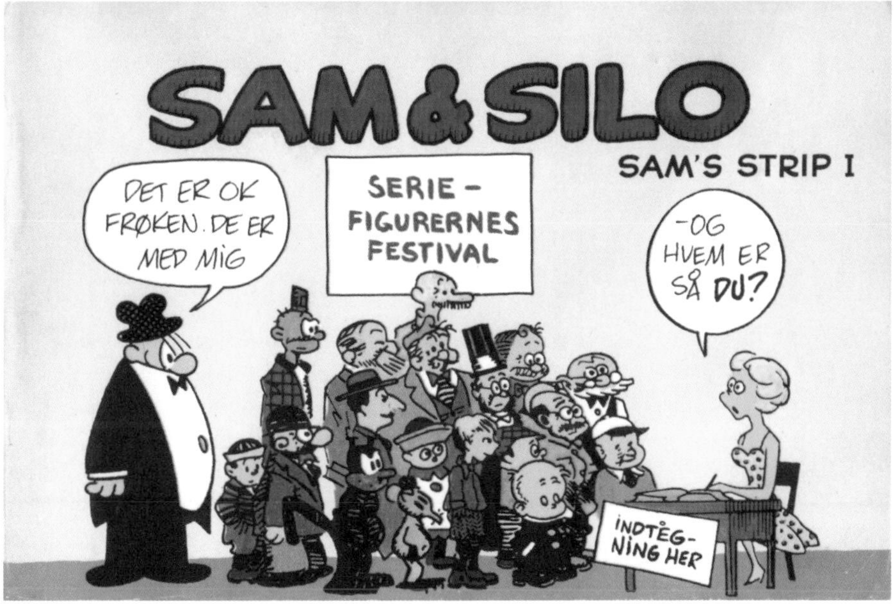
SAM&SILO
SAM'S STRIP I
DET ER OK FRØKEN. DE ER MED MIG
SERIE-FIGURERNES FESTIVAL
-OG HVEM ER SÅ DU?
INDTEG-NING HER

Reprint books, shown here, include *Sam's Strip Lives*, self-published by Mort Walker and Jerry Dumas in the late 1960s, *Sams Serie*, published by Semic Press in Sweden, 1986, and *Sam & Silo – Sam's Strip 1*, published by Interpresse in Denmark, 1979.

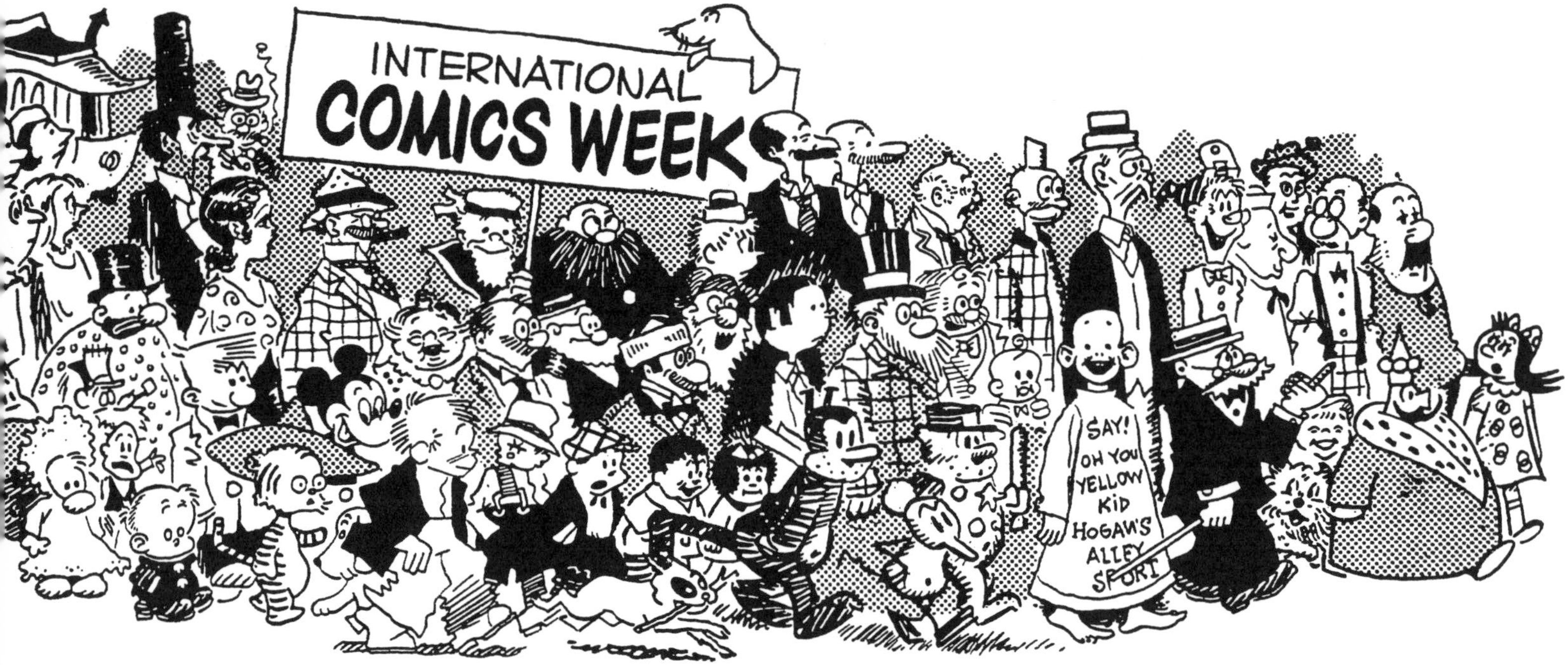
INTERNATIONAL
COMICS WEEK
SAY! OH YOU YELLOW KID HOGAN'S ALLEY SPORT

From *Sam's Strip*, April 30, 1962. A crowd of cartoon characters showed up in *Sam's Strip* to celebrate International Comics Week. Included are: Tillie the Toiler and Mac, John Q. Public, Mr. Dry, Bunky and Fagan, the Toonerville Folks, Jerry on the Job, Just Kids, Krazy Kat, Ignatz, Officer Pupp, Mr. Nebb, The Timid Soul, Reg'lar Fellars, Casper and Buttercup, Happy Hooligan, Si from *Maud*, The Yellow Kid, Harold Teen and Pop, Mickey Mouse, Smokey Stover, Alfred, Tuffy and Pop, The Little King, Tippie and Cap Stubbs, Nancy, The Gumps, Snuffy Smith and Barney Google, The Katzenjammer Kids, the Journal Tigers, Mr. and Mrs., Paw from *Polly and Her Pals* and characters from James Thurber and John Held cartoons.

The symbols below indicate that a strip is annotated in the section following the *Sam's Strip* comics.

: *Annotated by* JERRY DUMAS, *beginning on page 173.*   : *Annotated by* BRIAN WALKER, *beginning on page 181.*

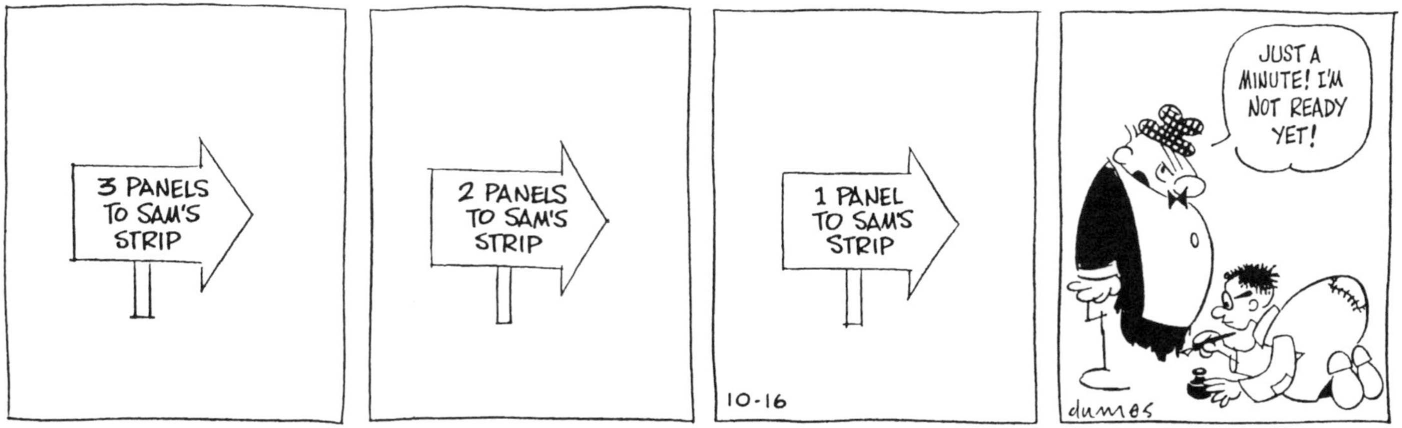
3 PANELS TO SAM'S STRIP
2 PANELS TO SAM'S STRIP
1 PANEL TO SAM'S STRIP
10-16
JUST A MINUTE! I'M NOT READY YET!
dumas

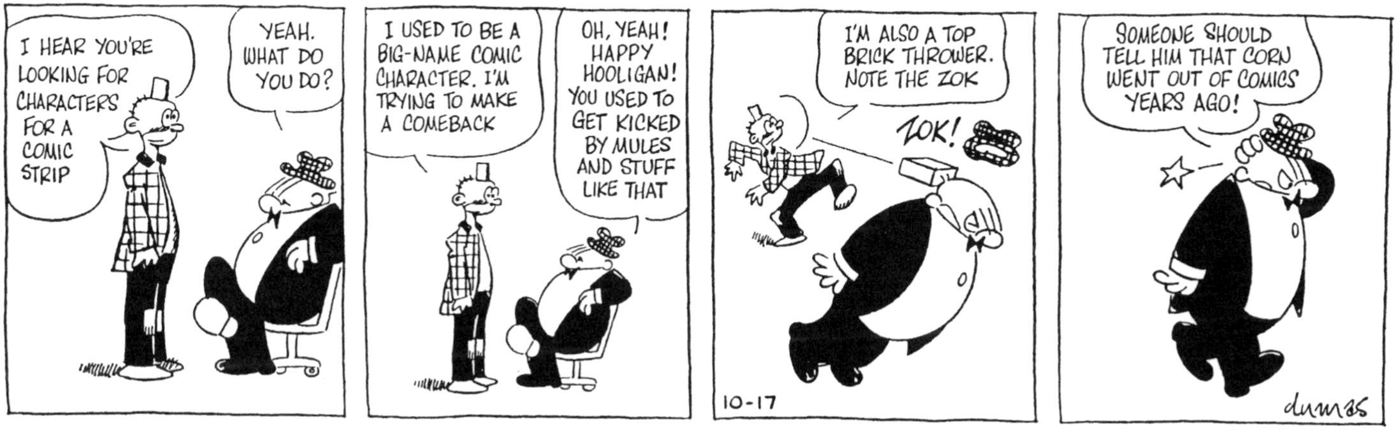
I HEAR YOU'RE LOOKING FOR CHARACTERS FOR A COMIC STRIP
YEAH. WHAT DO YOU DO?
I USED TO BE A BIG-NAME COMIC CHARACTER. I'M TRYING TO MAKE A COMEBACK
OH, YEAH! HAPPY HOOLIGAN! YOU USED TO GET KICKED BY MULES AND STUFF LIKE THAT
I'M ALSO A TOP BRICK THROWER. NOTE THE ZOK
ZOK!
10-17
SOMEONE SHOULD TELL HIM THAT CORN WENT OUT OF COMICS YEARS AGO!
dumas

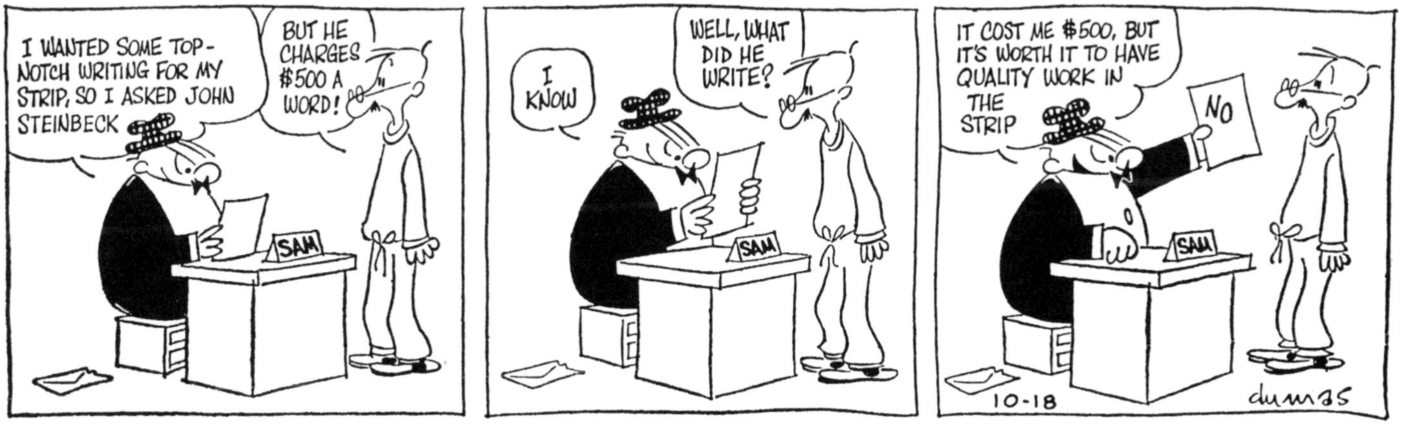
I WANTED SOME TOP-NOTCH WRITING FOR MY STRIP, SO I ASKED JOHN STEINBECK
BUT HE CHARGES $500 A WORD!
SAM
I KNOW
WELL, WHAT DID HE WRITE?
SAM
IT COST ME $500, BUT IT'S WORTH IT TO HAVE QUALITY WORK IN THE STRIP
NO
SAM
10-18
dumas

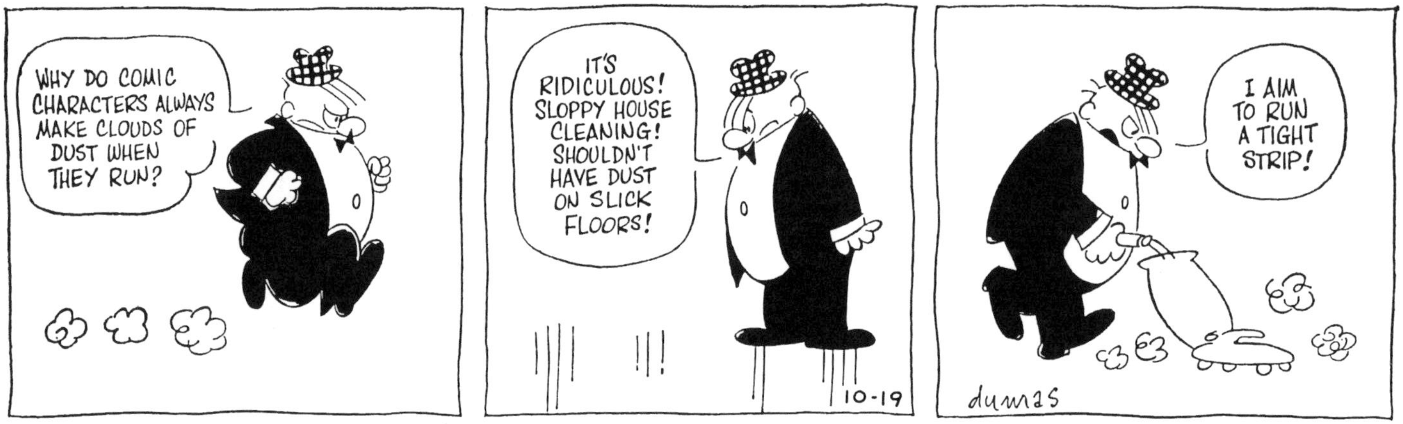
WHY DO COMIC CHARACTERS ALWAYS MAKE CLOUDS OF DUST WHEN THEY RUN?
IT'S RIDICULOUS! SLOPPY HOUSE CLEANING! SHOULDN'T HAVE DUST ON SLICK FLOORS!
10-19
I AIM TO RUN A TIGHT STRIP!
dumas

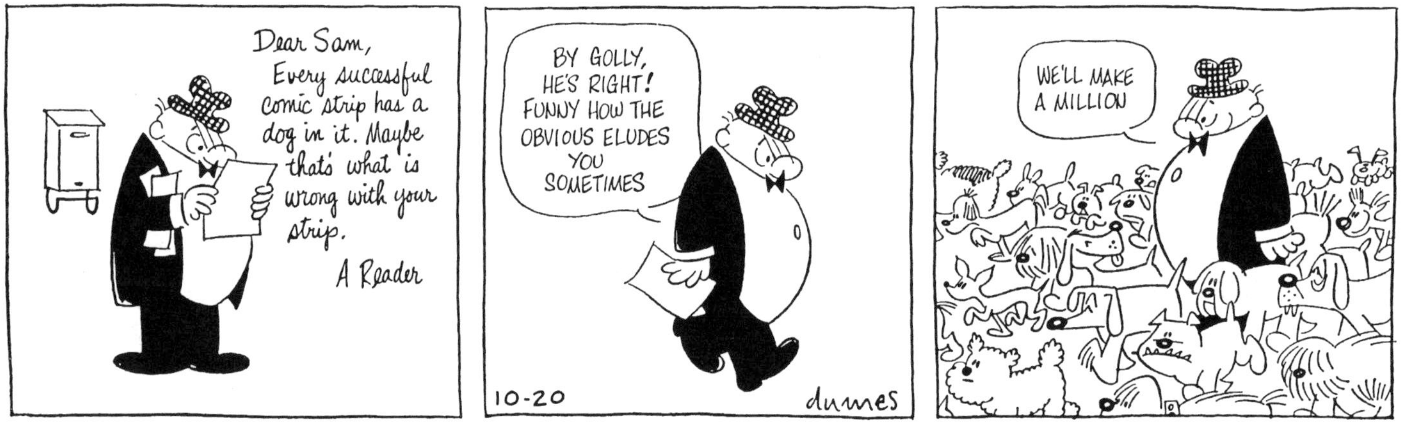
Dear Sam,
Every successful comic strip has a dog in it. Maybe that's what is wrong with your strip.
A Reader
BY GOLLY, HE'S RIGHT! FUNNY HOW THE OBVIOUS ELUDES YOU SOMETIMES
10-20
dumas
WE'LL MAKE A MILLION

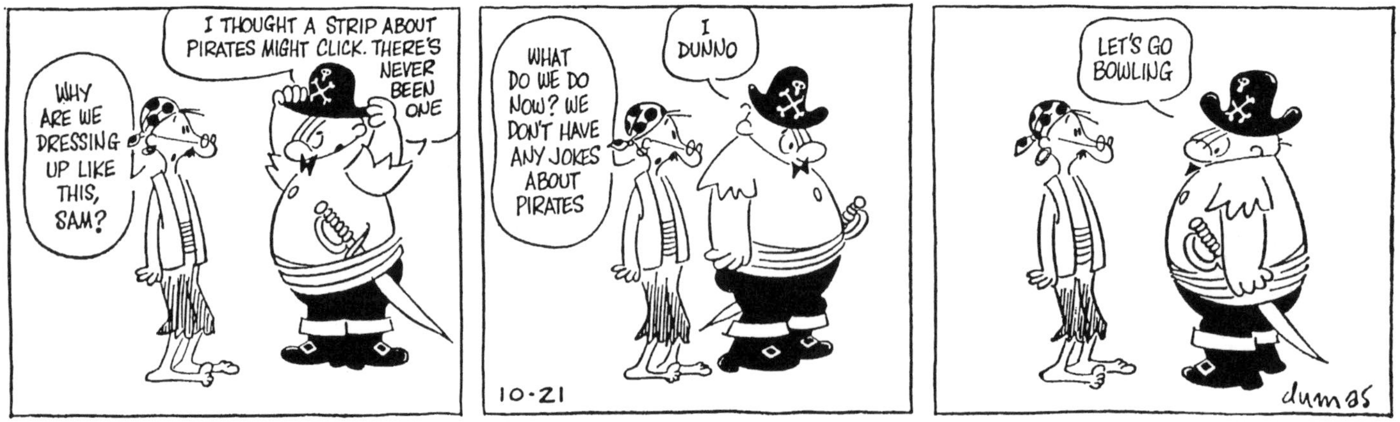
WHY ARE WE DRESSING UP LIKE THIS, SAM?
I THOUGHT A STRIP ABOUT PIRATES MIGHT CLICK. THERE'S NEVER BEEN ONE
WHAT DO WE DO NOW? WE DON'T HAVE ANY JOKES ABOUT PIRATES
I DUNNO
10-21
LET'S GO BOWLING
dumas

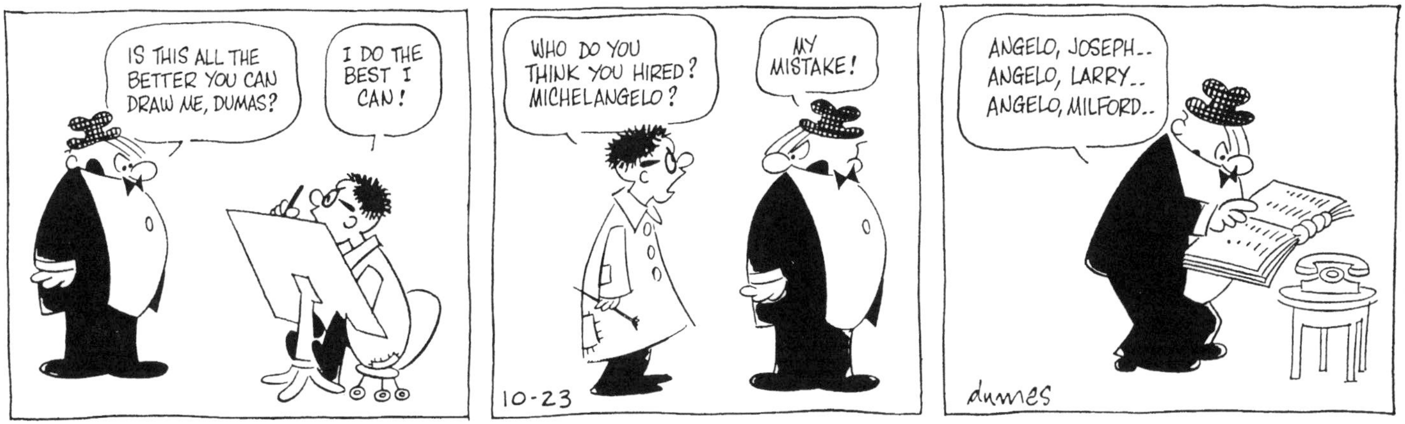
IS THIS ALL THE BETTER YOU CAN DRAW ME, DUMAS?
I DO THE BEST I CAN!
WHO DO YOU THINK YOU HIRED? MICHELANGELO?
MY MISTAKE!
ANGELO, JOSEPH.. ANGELO, LARRY.. ANGELO, MILFORD..
10-23
dumas

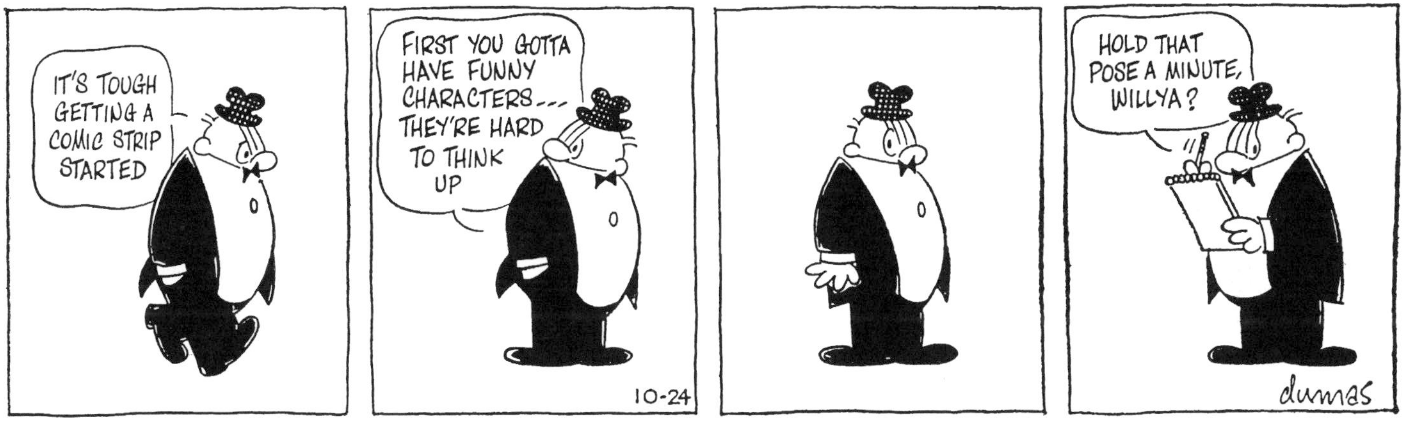
IT'S TOUGH GETTING A COMIC STRIP STARTED
FIRST YOU GOTTA HAVE FUNNY CHARACTERS... THEY'RE HARD TO THINK UP
10-24
HOLD THAT POSE A MINUTE, WILLYA?
dumas

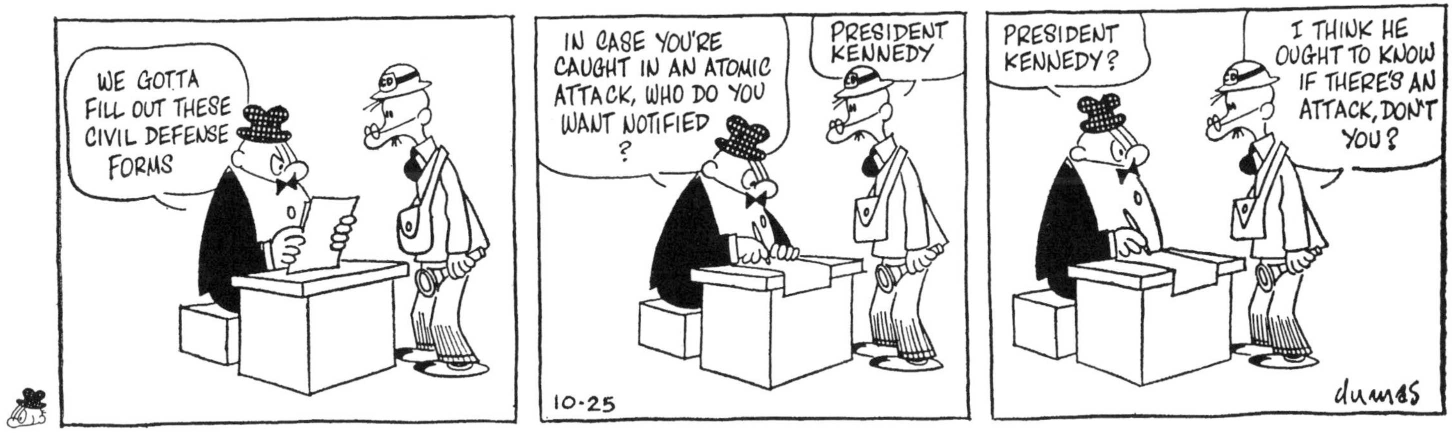
WE GOTTA FILL OUT THESE CIVIL DEFENSE FORMS
IN CASE YOU'RE CAUGHT IN AN ATOMIC ATTACK, WHO DO YOU WANT NOTIFIED?
PRESIDENT KENNEDY
10-25
PRESIDENT KENNEDY?
I THINK HE OUGHT TO KNOW IF THERE'S AN ATTACK, DON'T YOU?
dumas

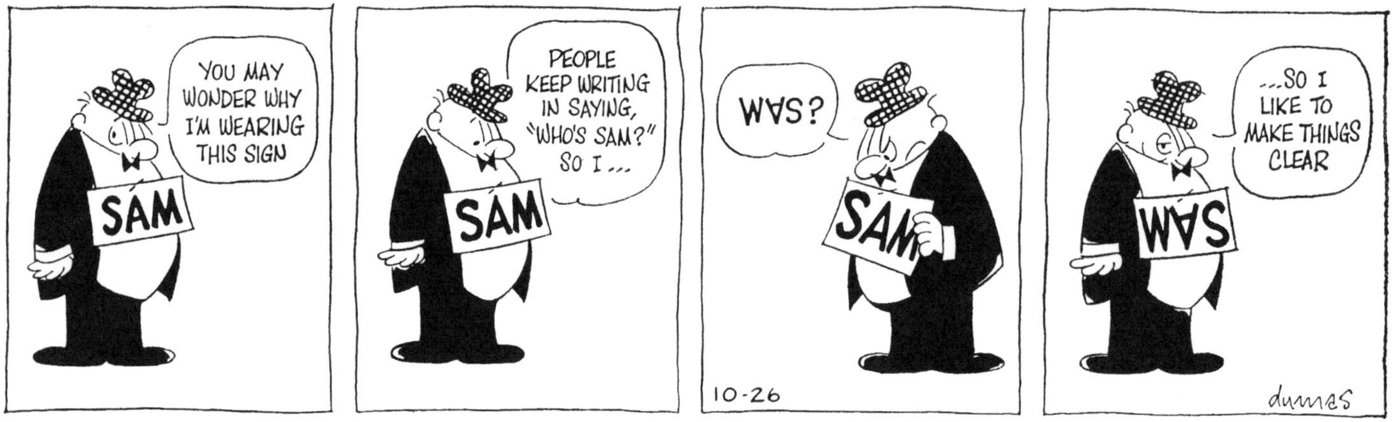
YOU MAY WONDER WHY I'M WEARING THIS SIGN
SAM
PEOPLE KEEP WRITING IN SAYING, "WHO'S SAM?" SO I...
SAM
WAS?
SAM
...SO I LIKE TO MAKE THINGS CLEAR
WAS
10-26
dumas

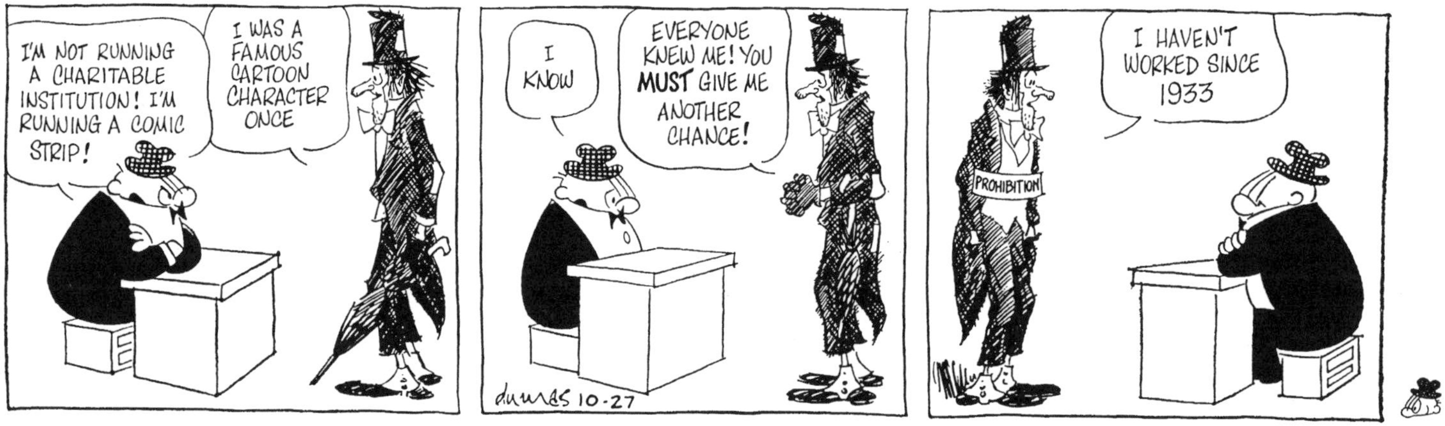
I'M NOT RUNNING A CHARITABLE INSTITUTION! I'M RUNNING A COMIC STRIP!
I WAS A FAMOUS CARTOON CHARACTER ONCE
I KNOW
EVERYONE KNEW ME! YOU MUST GIVE ME ANOTHER CHANCE!
dumas 10-27
PROHIBITION
I HAVEN'T WORKED SINCE 1933

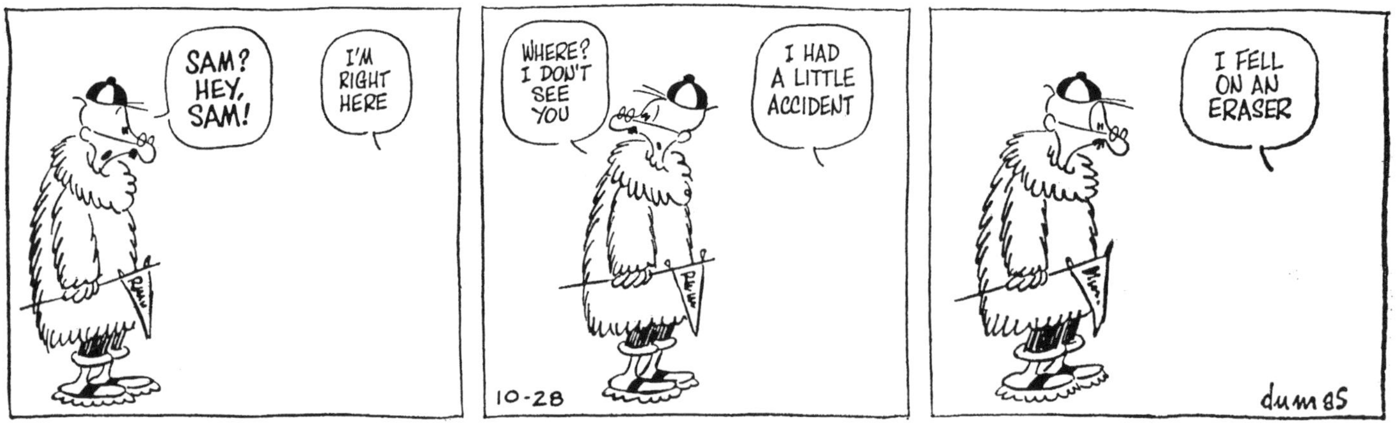
SAM? HEY, SAM!
I'M RIGHT HERE
WHERE? I DON'T SEE YOU
I HAD A LITTLE ACCIDENT
10-28
I FELL ON AN ERASER
dumas

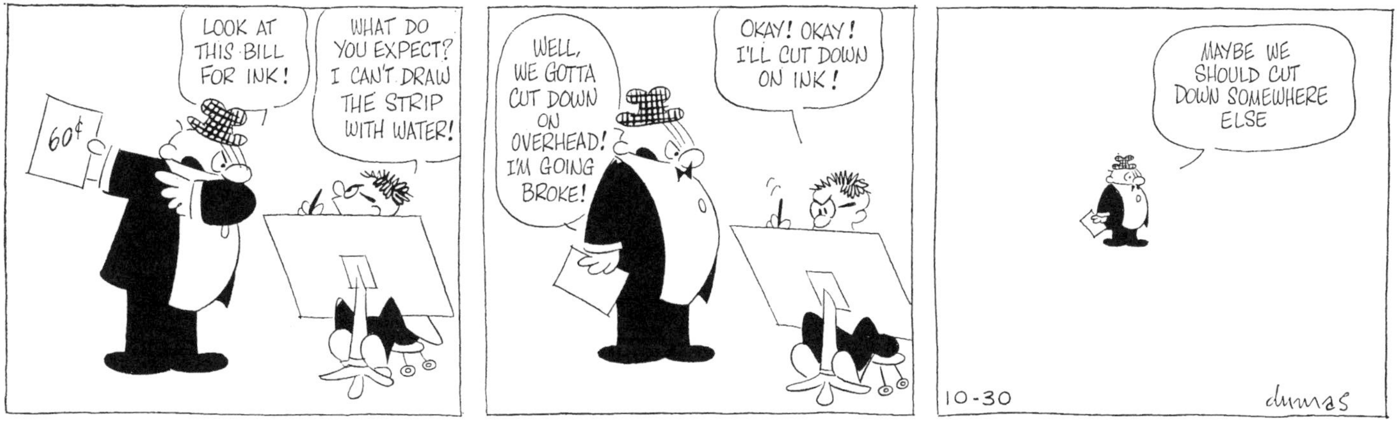
LOOK AT THIS BILL FOR INK!
60¢
WHAT DO YOU EXPECT? I CAN'T DRAW THE STRIP WITH WATER!
WELL, WE GOTTA CUT DOWN ON OVERHEAD! I'M GOING BROKE!
OKAY! OKAY! I'LL CUT DOWN ON INK!
MAYBE WE SHOULD CUT DOWN SOMEWHERE ELSE
10-30
dumas

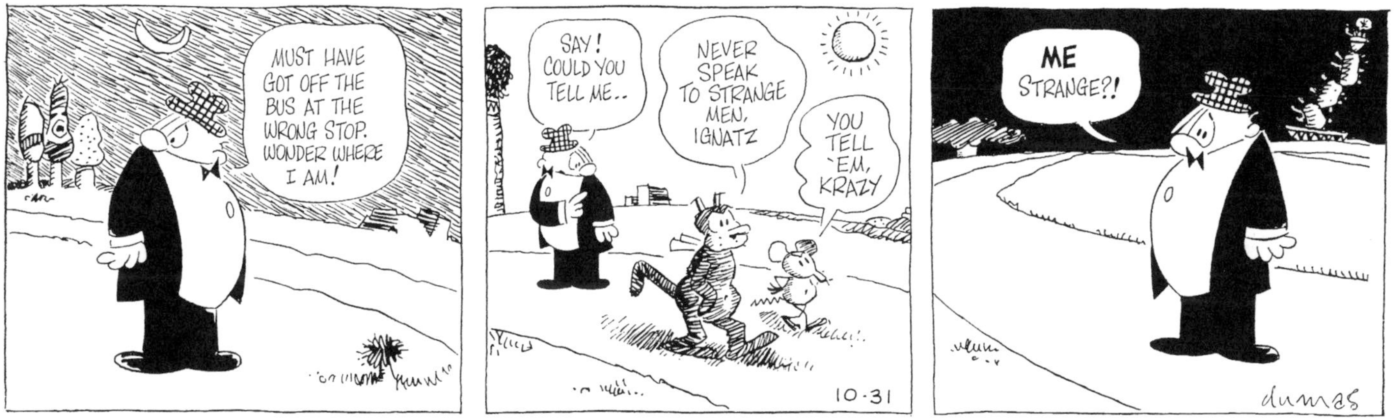
MUST HAVE GOT OFF THE BUS AT THE WRONG STOP. WONDER WHERE I AM!
SAY! COULD YOU TELL ME..
NEVER SPEAK TO STRANGE MEN, IGNATZ
YOU TELL 'EM, KRAZY
10-31
ME STRANGE?!
dumas

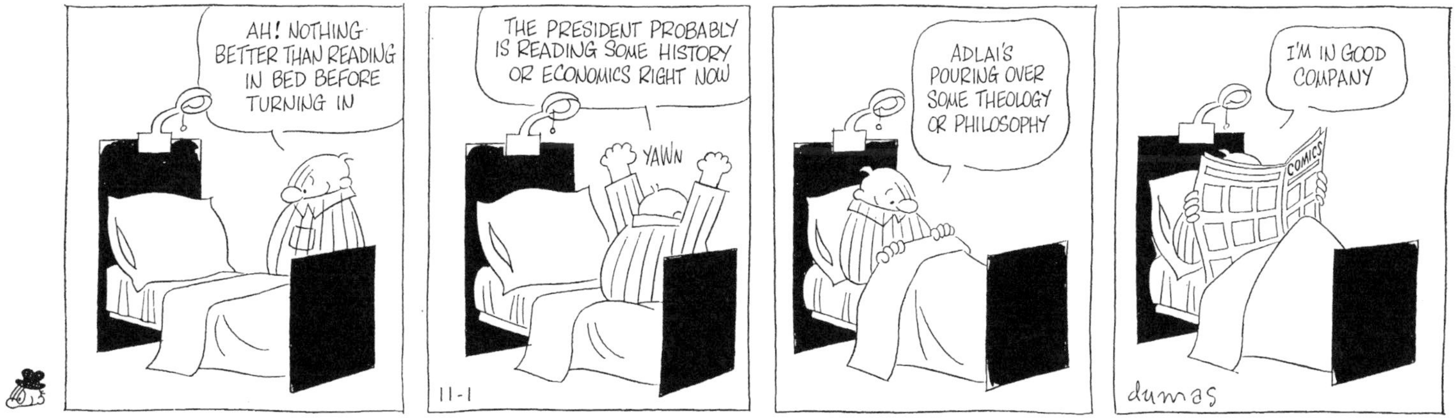
AH! NOTHING BETTER THAN READING IN BED BEFORE TURNING IN
THE PRESIDENT PROBABLY IS READING SOME HISTORY OR ECONOMICS RIGHT NOW
YAWN
11-1
ADLAI'S POURING OVER SOME THEOLOGY OR PHILOSOPHY
COMICS
I'M IN GOOD COMPANY
dumas

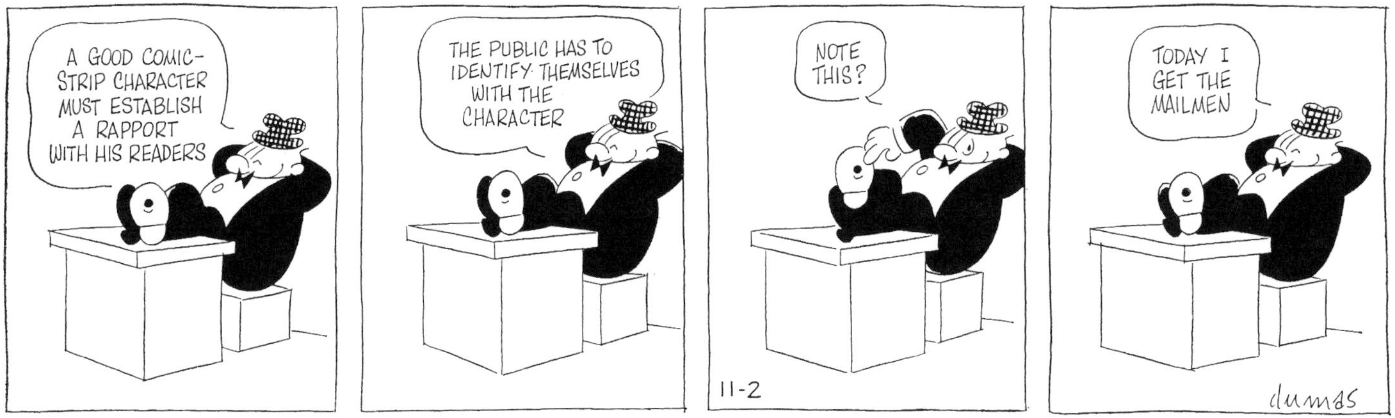

A GOOD COMIC-STRIP CHARACTER MUST ESTABLISH A RAPPORT WITH HIS READERS
THE PUBLIC HAS TO IDENTIFY THEMSELVES WITH THE CHARACTER
NOTE THIS?
TODAY I GET THE MAILMEN
11-2
dumas

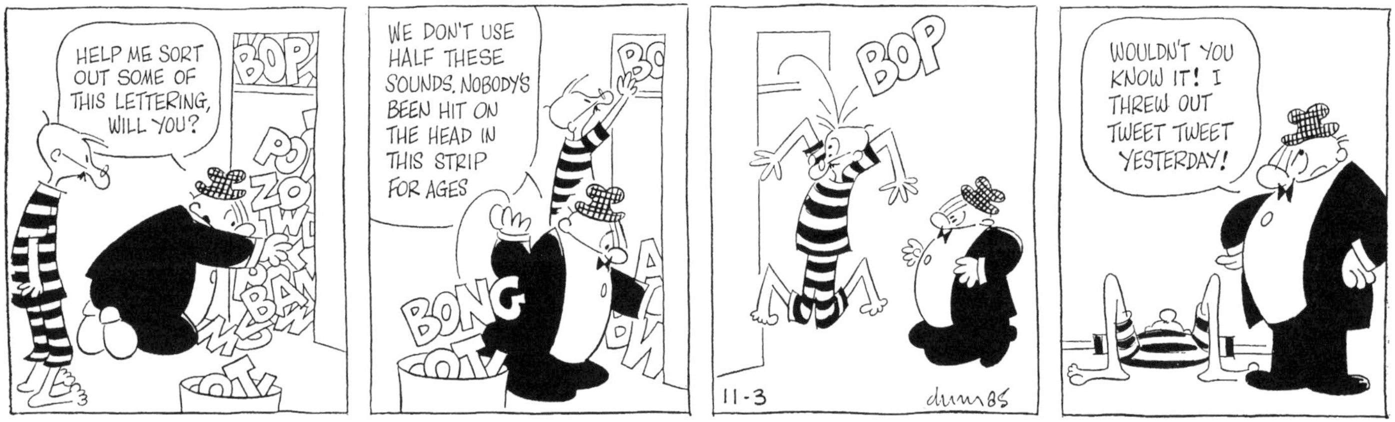

HELP ME SORT OUT SOME OF THIS LETTERING, WILL YOU?
BOP
WE DON'T USE HALF THESE SOUNDS. NOBODY'S BEEN HIT ON THE HEAD IN THIS STRIP FOR AGES
BONG
BOP
11-3
dumas
WOULDN'T YOU KNOW IT! I THREW OUT TWEET TWEET YESTERDAY!

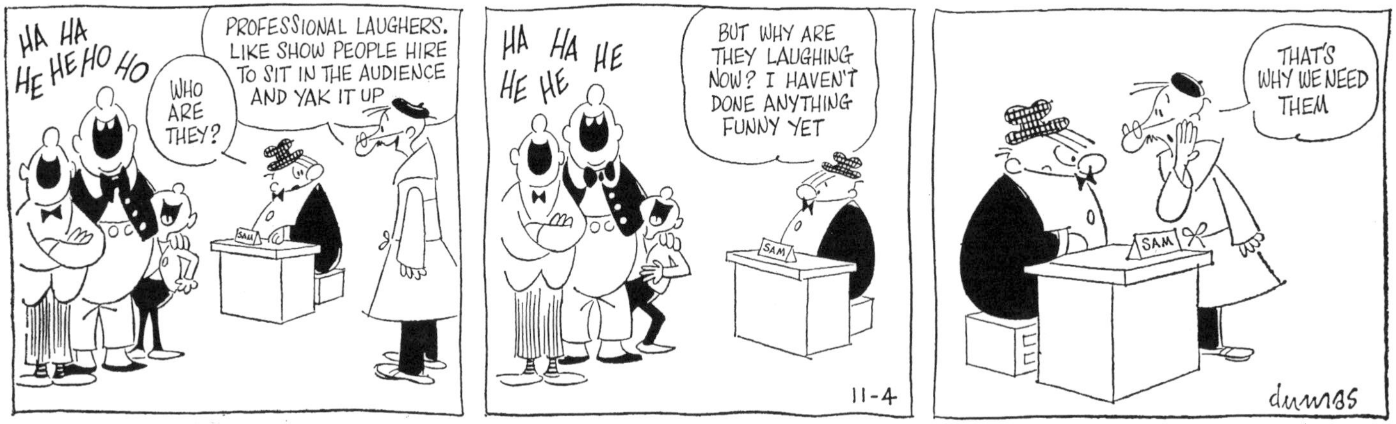

HA HA HE HE HO HO
WHO ARE THEY?
PROFESSIONAL LAUGHERS. LIKE SHOW PEOPLE HIRE TO SIT IN THE AUDIENCE AND YAK IT UP
SAM
HA HA HE HE HE
BUT WHY ARE THEY LAUGHING NOW? I HAVEN'T DONE ANYTHING FUNNY YET
SAM
11-4
THAT'S WHY WE NEED THEM
SAM
dumas

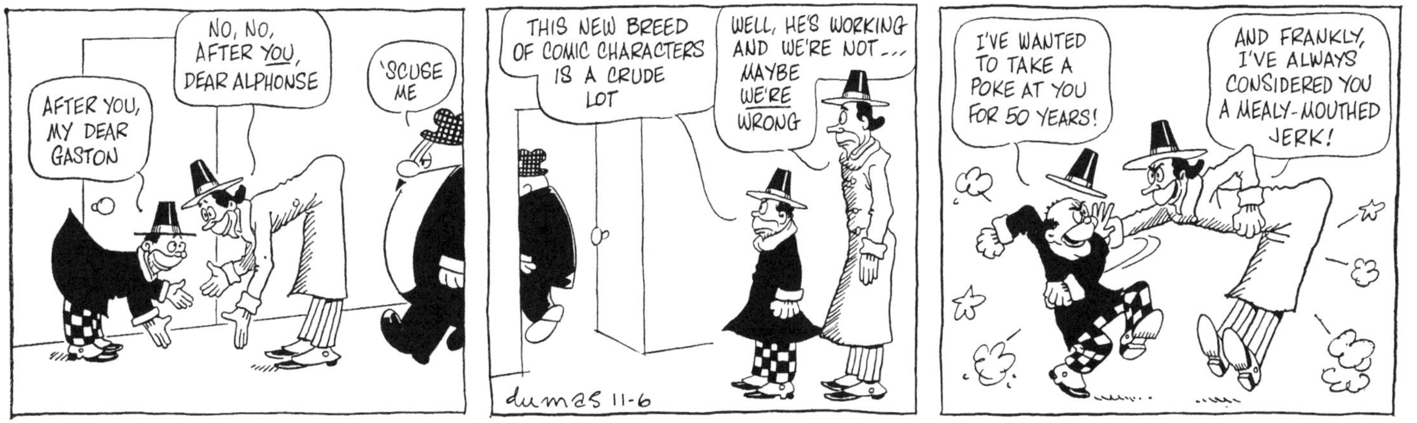
AFTER YOU, MY DEAR GASTON
NO, NO, AFTER YOU, DEAR ALPHONSE
'SCUSE ME
THIS NEW BREED OF COMIC CHARACTERS IS A CRUDE LOT
WELL, HE'S WORKING AND WE'RE NOT... MAYBE WE'RE WRONG
dumas 11-6
I'VE WANTED TO TAKE A POKE AT YOU FOR 50 YEARS!
AND FRANKLY, I'VE ALWAYS CONSIDERED YOU A MEALY-MOUTHED JERK!

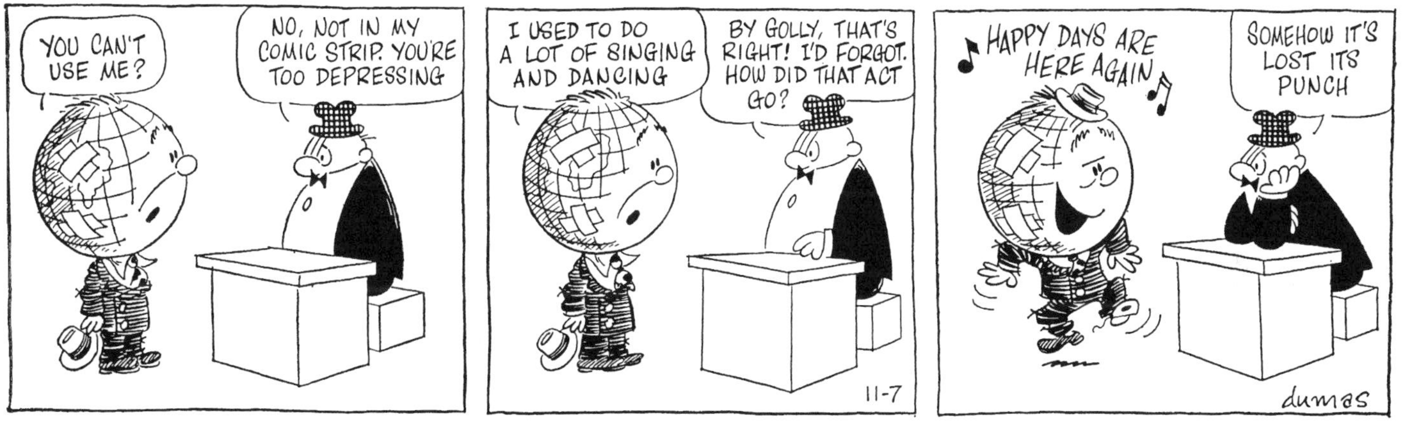
YOU CAN'T USE ME?
NO, NOT IN MY COMIC STRIP. YOU'RE TOO DEPRESSING
I USED TO DO A LOT OF SINGING AND DANCING
BY GOLLY, THAT'S RIGHT! I'D FORGOT. HOW DID THAT ACT GO?
11-7
HAPPY DAYS ARE HERE AGAIN
SOMEHOW IT'S LOST ITS PUNCH
dumas

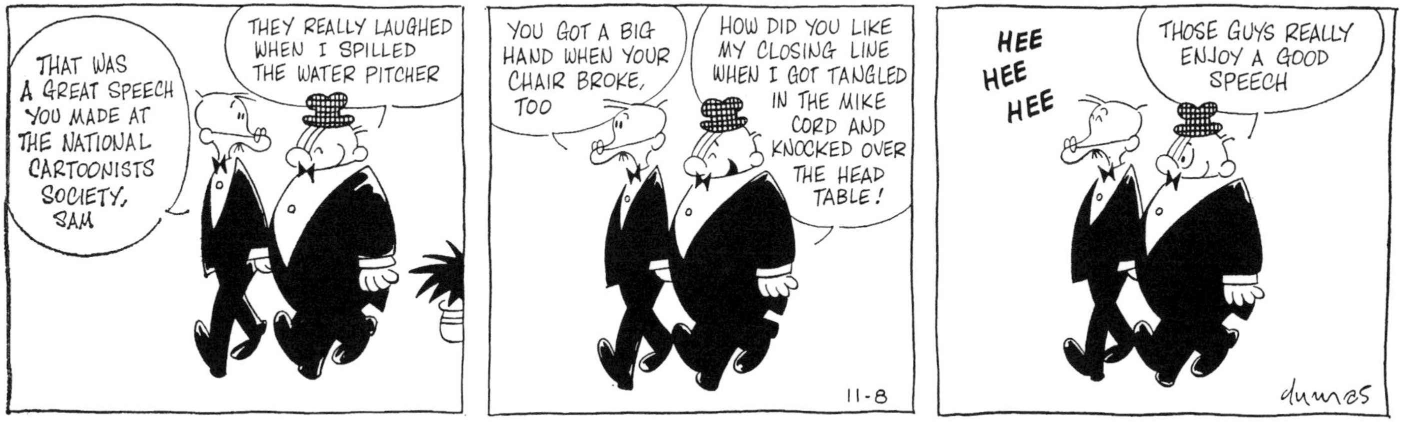
THAT WAS A GREAT SPEECH YOU MADE AT THE NATIONAL CARTOONISTS SOCIETY, SAM
THEY REALLY LAUGHED WHEN I SPILLED THE WATER PITCHER
YOU GOT A BIG HAND WHEN YOUR CHAIR BROKE, TOO
HOW DID YOU LIKE MY CLOSING LINE WHEN I GOT TANGLED IN THE MIKE CORD AND KNOCKED OVER THE HEAD TABLE!
11-8
HEE HEE HEE
THOSE GUYS REALLY ENJOY A GOOD SPEECH
dumas

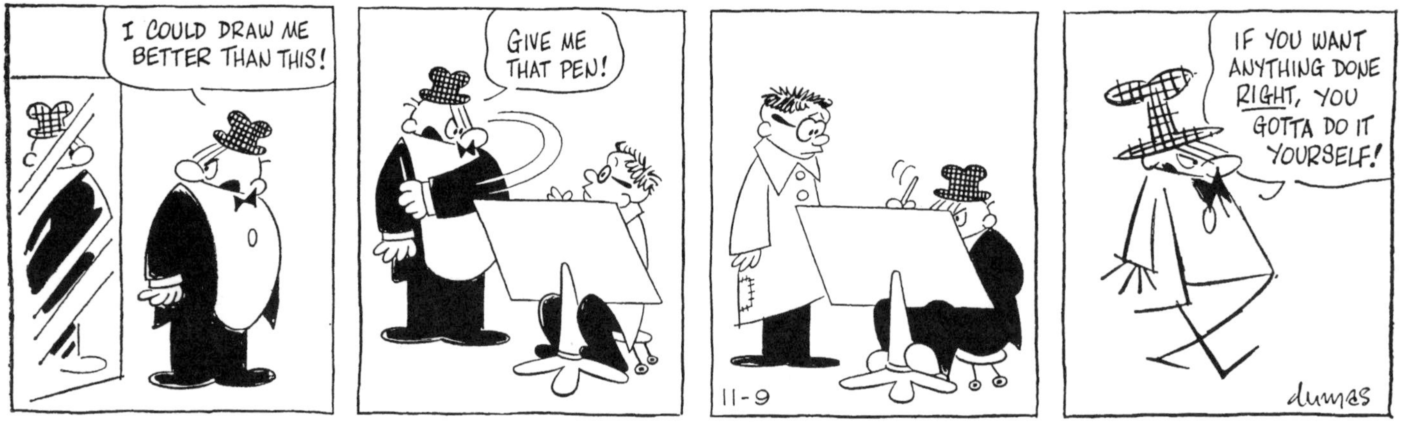
I COULD DRAW ME BETTER THAN THIS!
GIVE ME THAT PEN!
11-9
IF YOU WANT ANYTHING DONE RIGHT, YOU GOTTA DO IT YOURSELF!
dumas

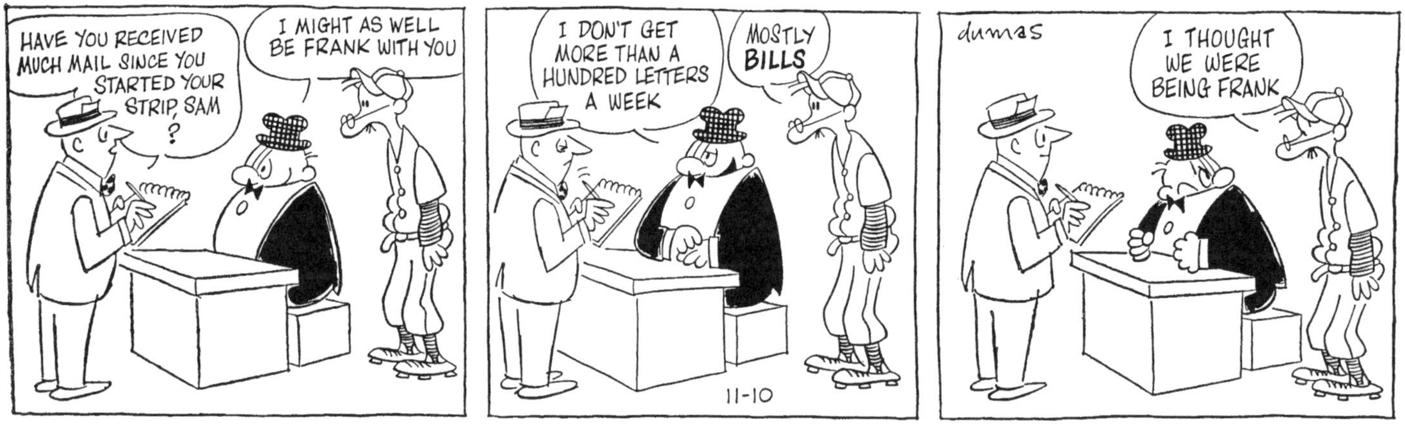
HAVE YOU RECEIVED MUCH MAIL SINCE YOU STARTED YOUR STRIP, SAM?
I MIGHT AS WELL BE FRANK WITH YOU
I DON'T GET MORE THAN A HUNDRED LETTERS A WEEK
MOSTLY **BILLS**
11-10
dumas
I THOUGHT WE WERE BEING FRANK

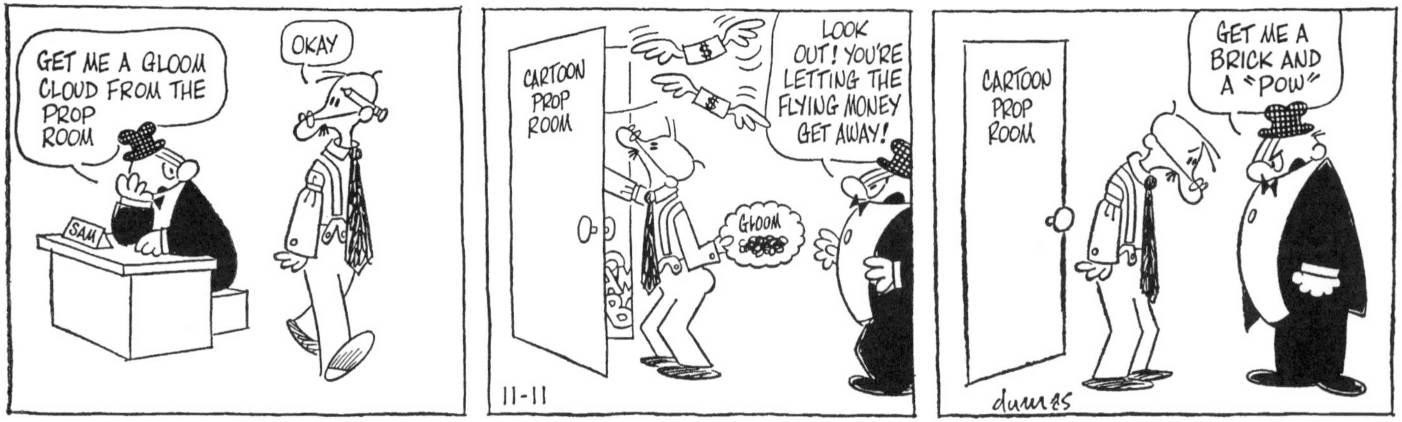
GET ME A GLOOM CLOUD FROM THE PROP ROOM
SAM
OKAY
CARTOON PROP ROOM
LOOK OUT! YOU'RE LETTING THE FLYING MONEY GET AWAY!
GLOOM
11-11
CARTOON PROP ROOM
GET ME A BRICK AND A "POW"
dumas

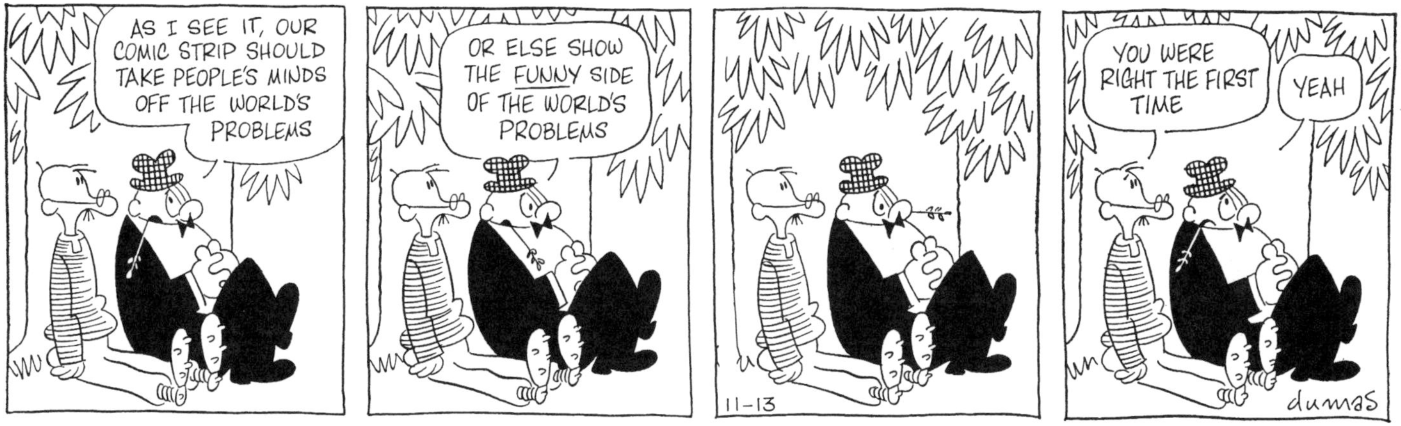
AS I SEE IT, OUR COMIC STRIP SHOULD TAKE PEOPLE'S MINDS OFF THE WORLD'S PROBLEMS
OR ELSE SHOW THE FUNNY SIDE OF THE WORLD'S PROBLEMS
11-13
YOU WERE RIGHT THE FIRST TIME
YEAH
dumas

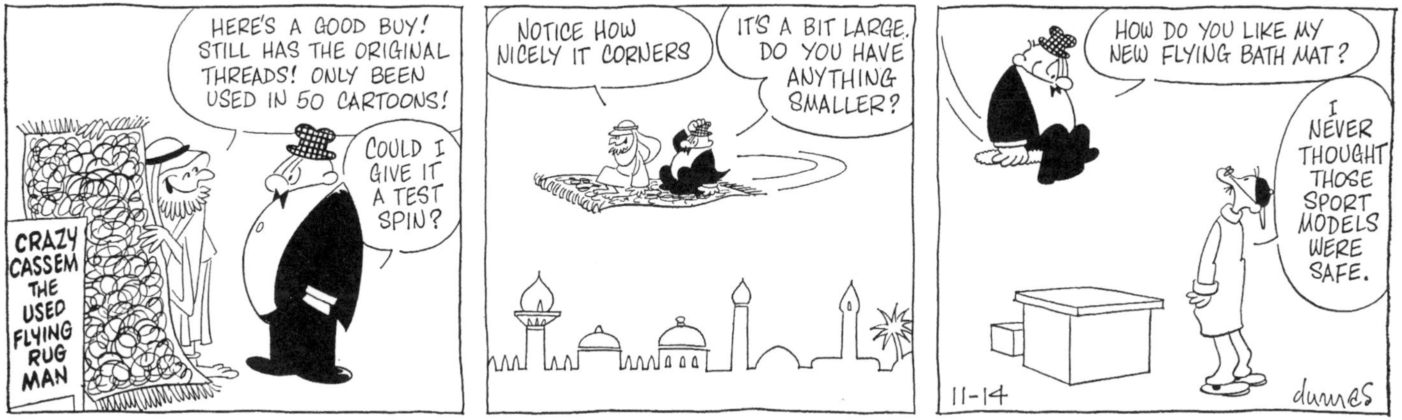
HERE'S A GOOD BUY! STILL HAS THE ORIGINAL THREADS! ONLY BEEN USED IN 50 CARTOONS!
COULD I GIVE IT A TEST SPIN?
CRAZY CASSEM THE USED FLYING RUG MAN
NOTICE HOW NICELY IT CORNERS
IT'S A BIT LARGE. DO YOU HAVE ANYTHING SMALLER?
HOW DO YOU LIKE MY NEW FLYING BATH MAT?
I NEVER THOUGHT THOSE SPORT MODELS WERE SAFE.
11-14
dumas

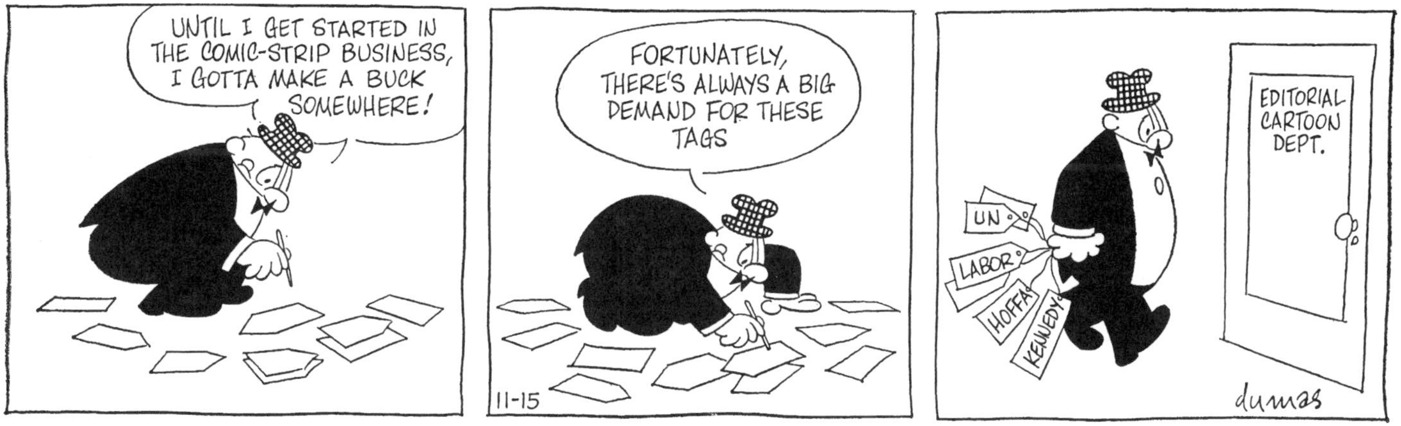
UNTIL I GET STARTED IN THE COMIC-STRIP BUSINESS, I GOTTA MAKE A BUCK SOMEWHERE!
FORTUNATELY, THERE'S ALWAYS A BIG DEMAND FOR THESE TAGS
11-15
UN
LABOR
HOFFA
KENNEDY
EDITORIAL CARTOON DEPT.
dumas

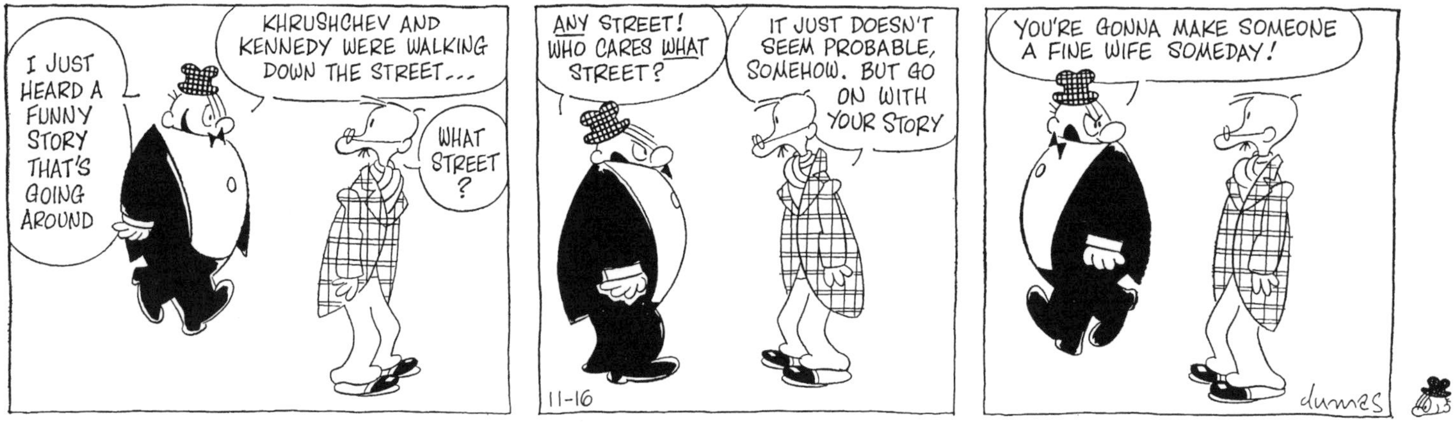
I JUST HEARD A FUNNY STORY THAT'S GOING AROUND
KHRUSHCHEV AND KENNEDY WERE WALKING DOWN THE STREET...
WHAT STREET ?
ANY STREET! WHO CARES WHAT STREET ?
IT JUST DOESN'T SEEM PROBABLE, SOMEHOW. BUT GO ON WITH YOUR STORY
11-16
YOU'RE GONNA MAKE SOMEONE A FINE WIFE SOMEDAY!
dumas

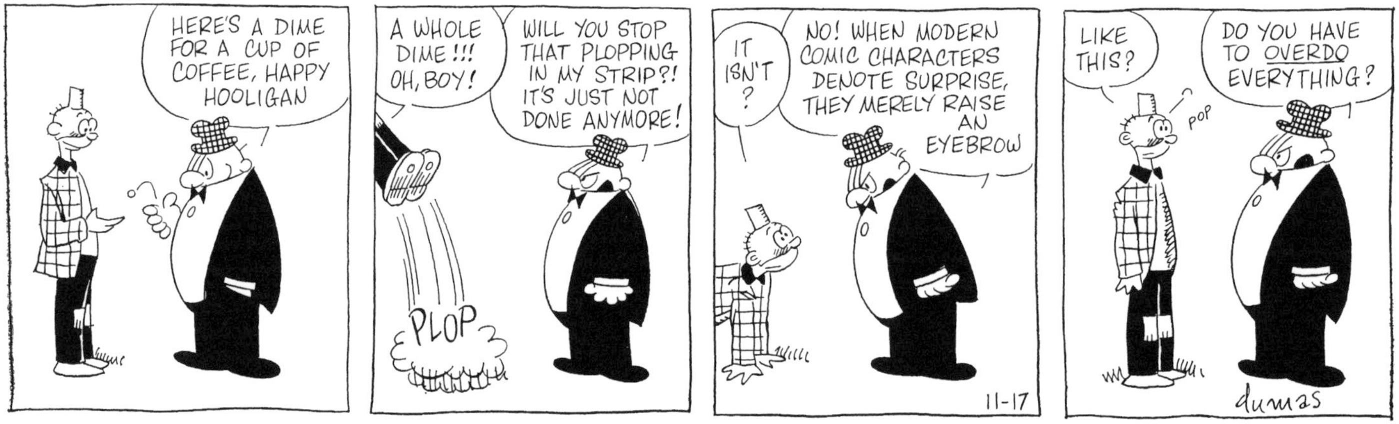
HERE'S A DIME FOR A CUP OF COFFEE, HAPPY HOOLIGAN
A WHOLE DIME!!! OH, BOY!
WILL YOU STOP THAT PLOPPING IN MY STRIP?! IT'S JUST NOT DONE ANYMORE!
PLOP
IT ISN'T ?
NO! WHEN MODERN COMIC CHARACTERS DENOTE SURPRISE, THEY MERELY RAISE AN EYEBROW
11-17
LIKE THIS?
POP
DO YOU HAVE TO OVERDO EVERYTHING?
dumas

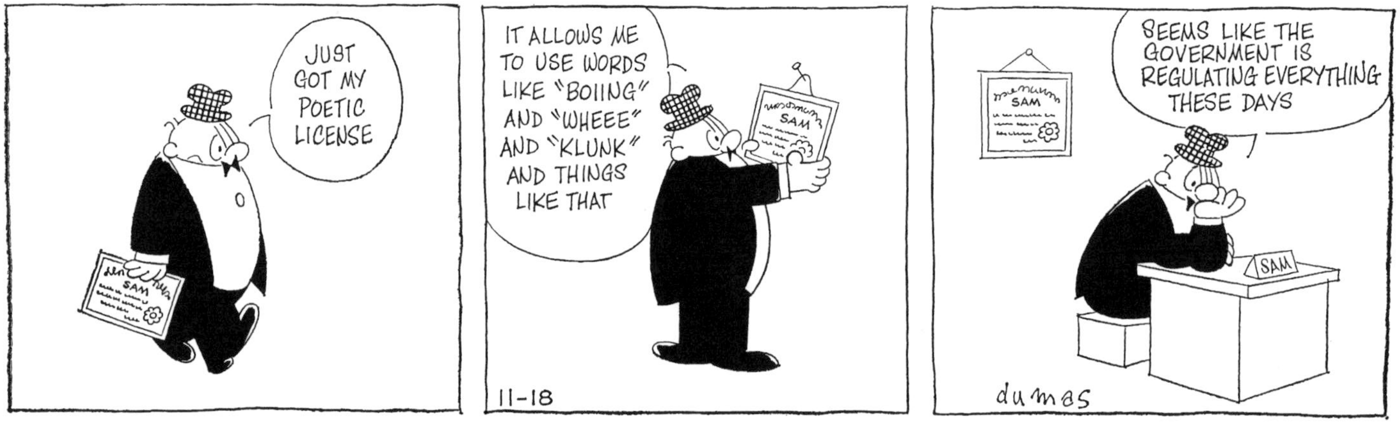
JUST GOT MY POETIC LICENSE
SAM
IT ALLOWS ME TO USE WORDS LIKE "BOIING" AND "WHEEE" AND "KLUNK" AND THINGS LIKE THAT
SAM
11-18
SAM
SEEMS LIKE THE GOVERNMENT IS REGULATING EVERYTHING THESE DAYS
SAM
dumas

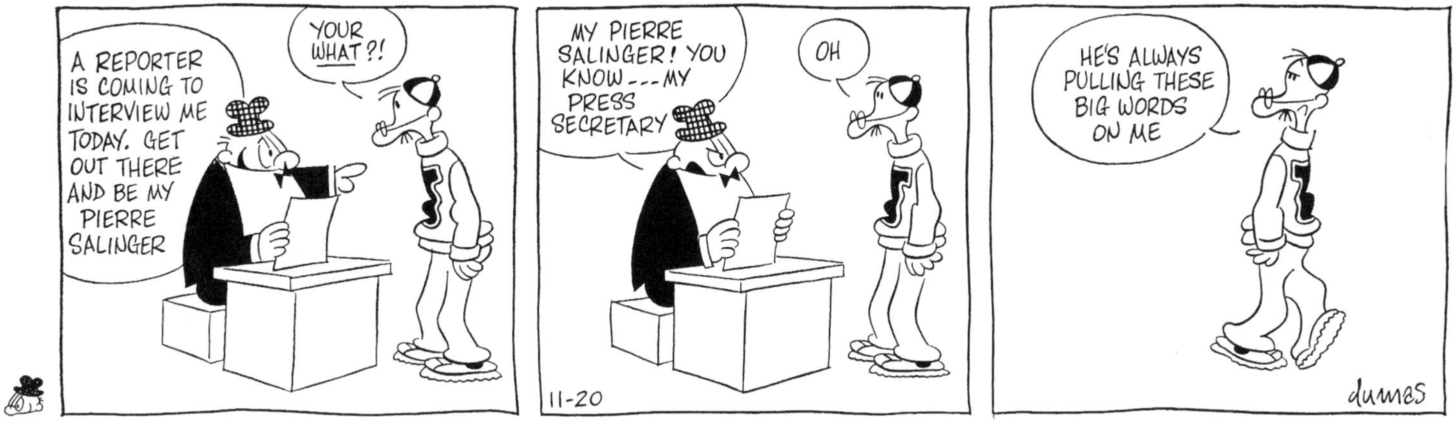
A REPORTER IS COMING TO INTERVIEW ME TODAY. GET OUT THERE AND BE MY PIERRE SALINGER
YOUR WHAT?!
MY PIERRE SALINGER! YOU KNOW---MY PRESS SECRETARY
OH
HE'S ALWAYS PULLING THESE BIG WORDS ON ME
11-20
dumas

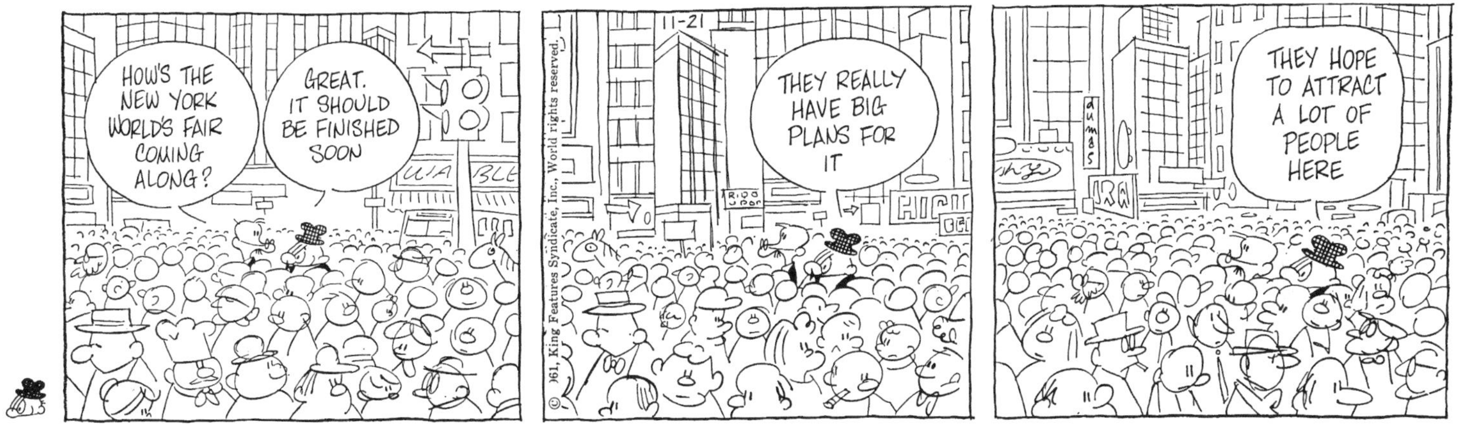
HOW'S THE NEW YORK WORLD'S FAIR COMING ALONG?
GREAT. IT SHOULD BE FINISHED SOON
11-21
THEY REALLY HAVE BIG PLANS FOR IT
THEY HOPE TO ATTRACT A LOT OF PEOPLE HERE

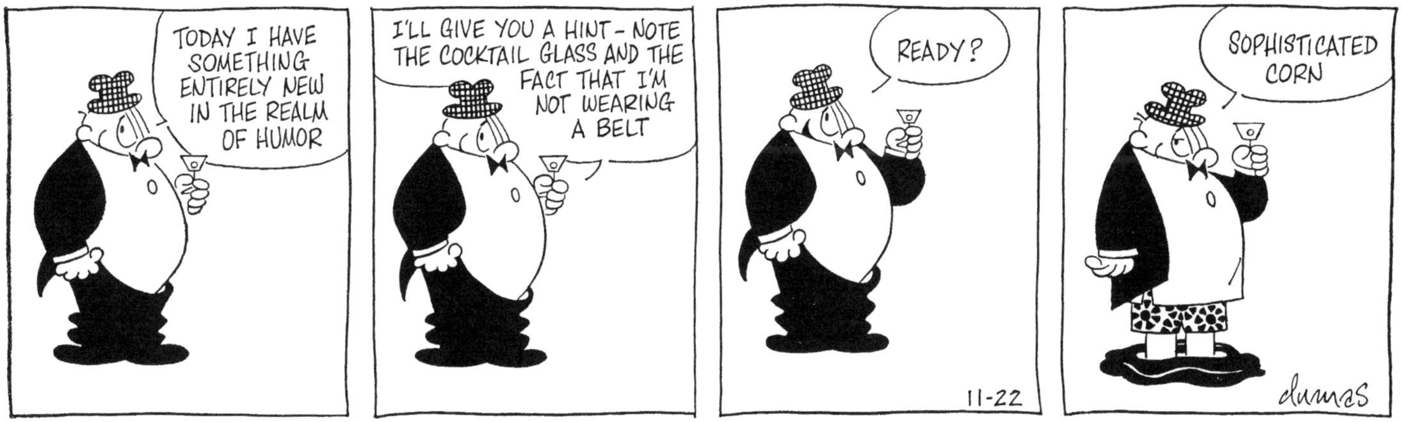
TODAY I HAVE SOMETHING ENTIRELY NEW IN THE REALM OF HUMOR
I'LL GIVE YOU A HINT- NOTE THE COCKTAIL GLASS AND THE FACT THAT I'M NOT WEARING A BELT
READY?
11-22
SOPHISTICATED CORN
dumas

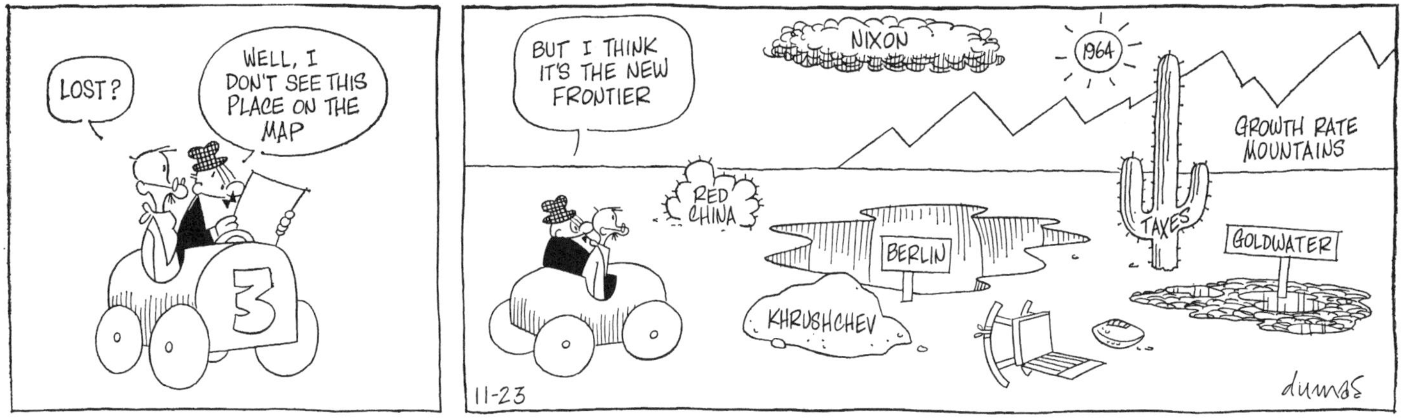
LOST?
WELL, I DON'T SEE THIS PLACE ON THE MAP
BUT I THINK IT'S THE NEW FRONTIER
NIXON
1964
GROWTH RATE MOUNTAINS
RED CHINA
BERLIN
TAXES
GOLDWATER
KHRUSHCHEV
11-23
dumas

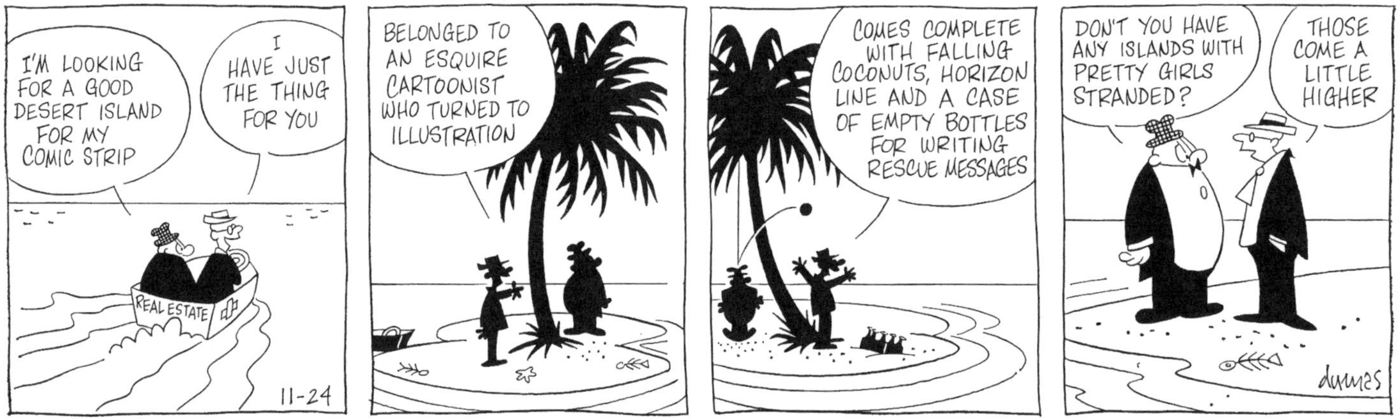
I'M LOOKING FOR A GOOD DESERT ISLAND FOR MY COMIC STRIP
I HAVE JUST THE THING FOR YOU
REAL ESTATE
11-24
BELONGED TO AN ESQUIRE CARTOONIST WHO TURNED TO ILLUSTRATION
COMES COMPLETE WITH FALLING COCONUTS, HORIZON LINE AND A CASE OF EMPTY BOTTLES FOR WRITING RESCUE MESSAGES
DON'T YOU HAVE ANY ISLANDS WITH PRETTY GIRLS STRANDED?
THOSE COME A LITTLE HIGHER
dumas

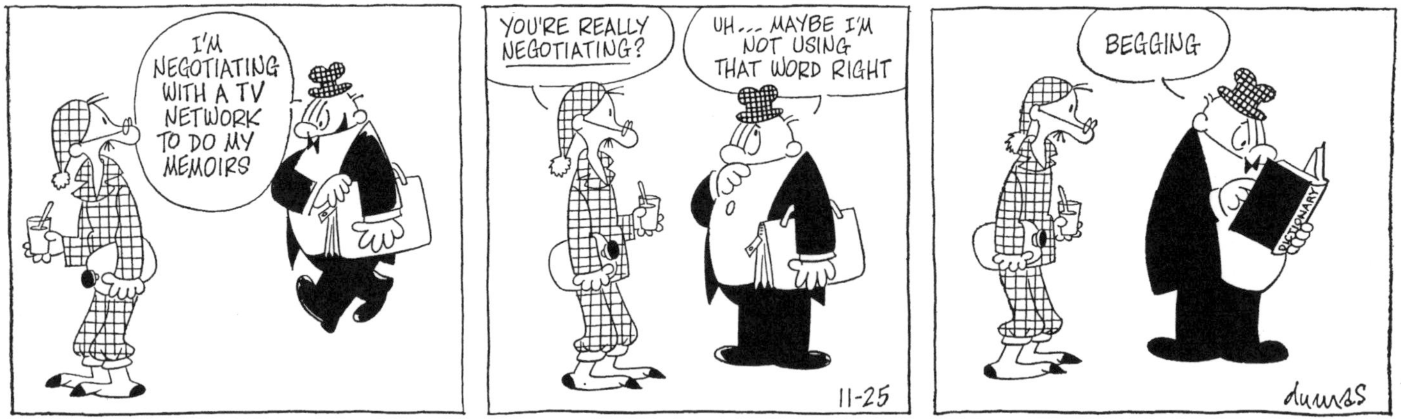
I'M NEGOTIATING WITH A TV NETWORK TO DO MY MEMOIRS
YOU'RE REALLY NEGOTIATING?
UH... MAYBE I'M NOT USING THAT WORD RIGHT
11-25
BEGGING
DICTIONARY
dumas

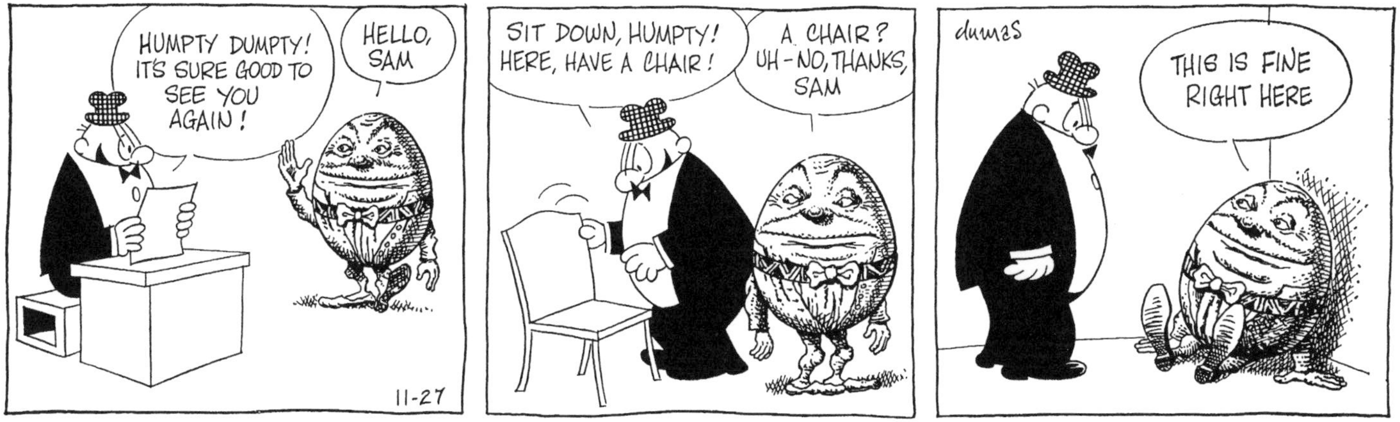
HUMPTY DUMPTY! IT'S SURE GOOD TO SEE YOU AGAIN!
HELLO, SAM
11-27
SIT DOWN, HUMPTY! HERE, HAVE A CHAIR!
A CHAIR? UH-NO, THANKS, SAM
dumas
THIS IS FINE RIGHT HERE

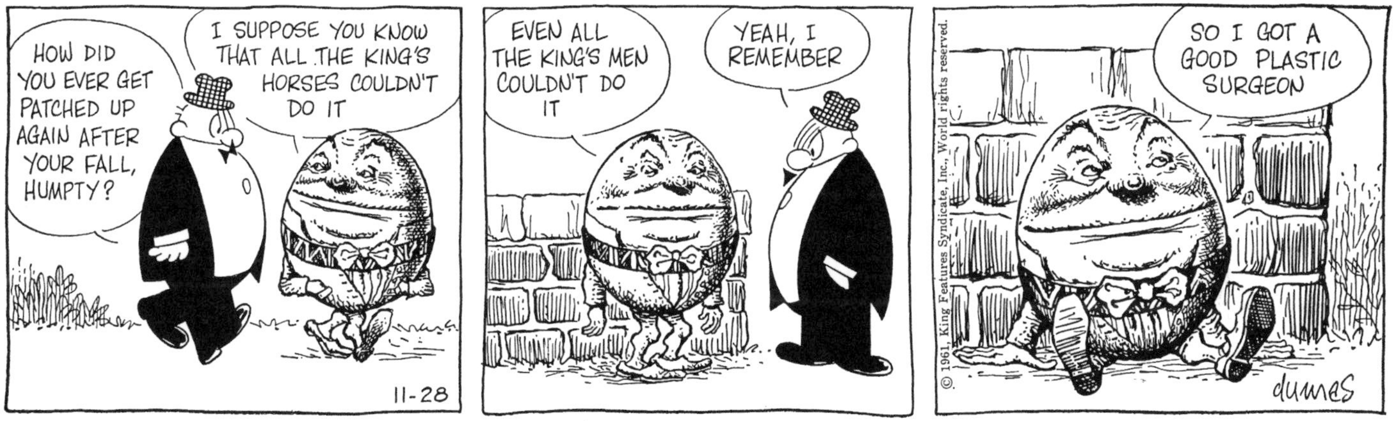
HOW DID YOU EVER GET PATCHED UP AGAIN AFTER YOUR FALL, HUMPTY?
I SUPPOSE YOU KNOW THAT ALL THE KING'S HORSES COULDN'T DO IT
11-28
EVEN ALL THE KING'S MEN COULDN'T DO IT
YEAH, I REMEMBER
© 1961, King Features Syndicate, Inc., World rights reserved.
SO I GOT A GOOD PLASTIC SURGEON
dumas

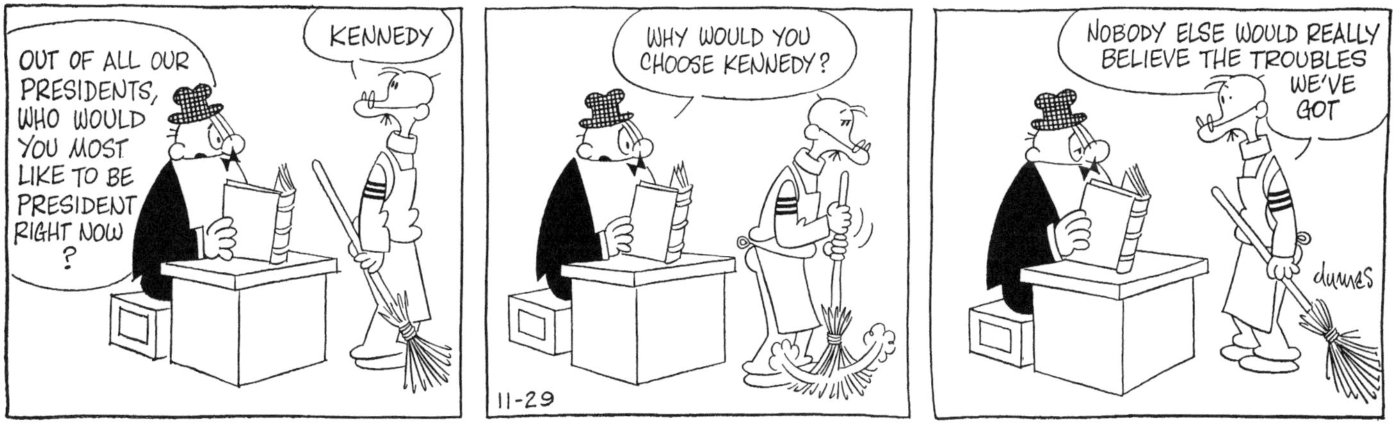
OUT OF ALL OUR PRESIDENTS, WHO WOULD YOU MOST LIKE TO BE PRESIDENT RIGHT NOW?
KENNEDY
WHY WOULD YOU CHOOSE KENNEDY?
11-29
NOBODY ELSE WOULD REALLY BELIEVE THE TROUBLES WE'VE GOT
dumas

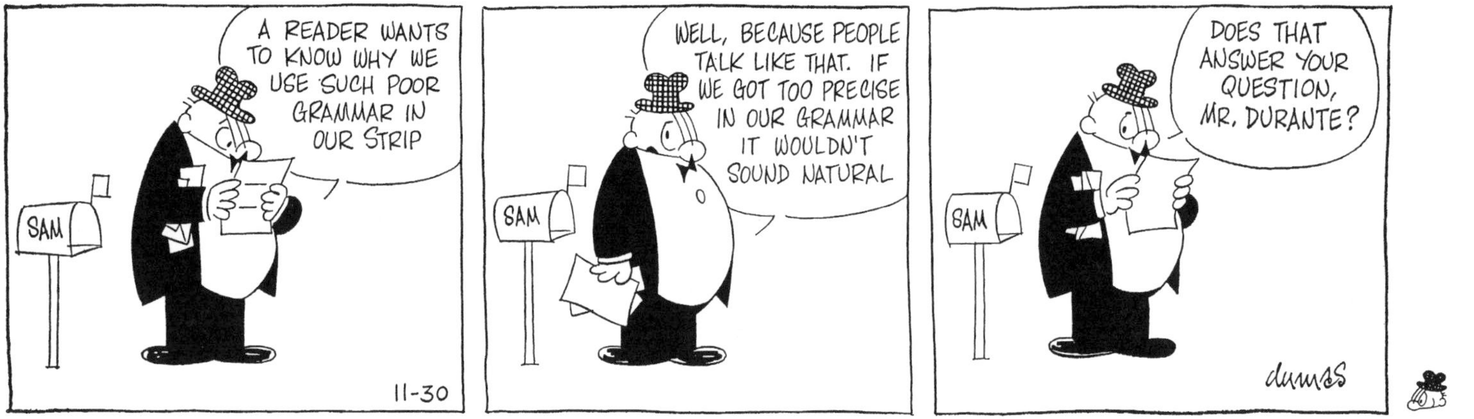
SAM
A READER WANTS TO KNOW WHY WE USE SUCH POOR GRAMMAR IN OUR STRIP
11-30
SAM
WELL, BECAUSE PEOPLE TALK LIKE THAT. IF WE GOT TOO PRECISE IN OUR GRAMMAR IT WOULDN'T SOUND NATURAL
SAM
DOES THAT ANSWER YOUR QUESTION, MR. DURANTE?
dumas

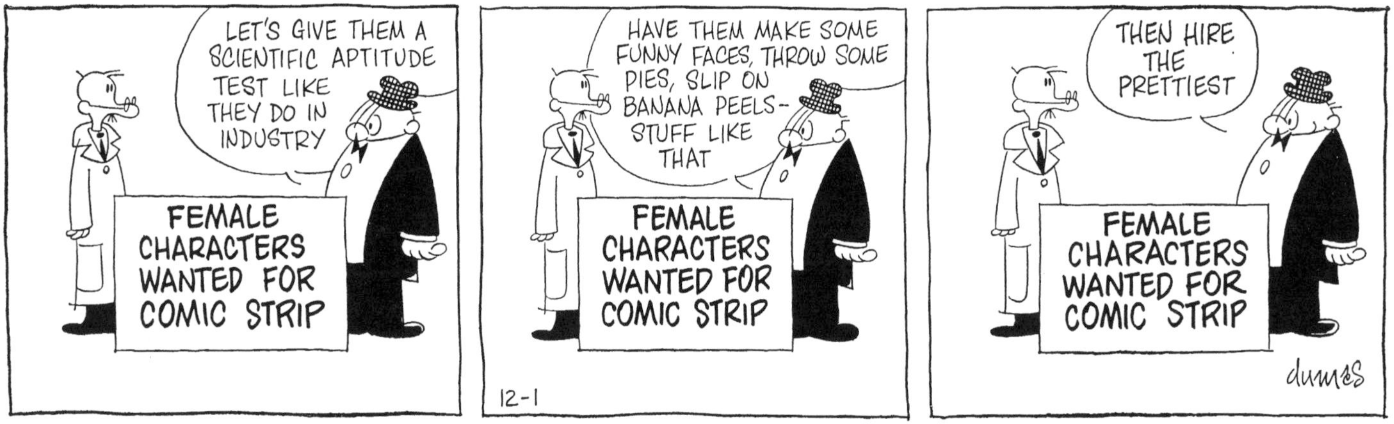
LET'S GIVE THEM A SCIENTIFIC APTITUDE TEST LIKE THEY DO IN INDUSTRY
FEMALE CHARACTERS WANTED FOR COMIC STRIP
HAVE THEM MAKE SOME FUNNY FACES, THROW SOME PIES, SLIP ON BANANA PEELS- STUFF LIKE THAT
FEMALE CHARACTERS WANTED FOR COMIC STRIP
12-1
THEN HIRE THE PRETTIEST
FEMALE CHARACTERS WANTED FOR COMIC STRIP
dumas

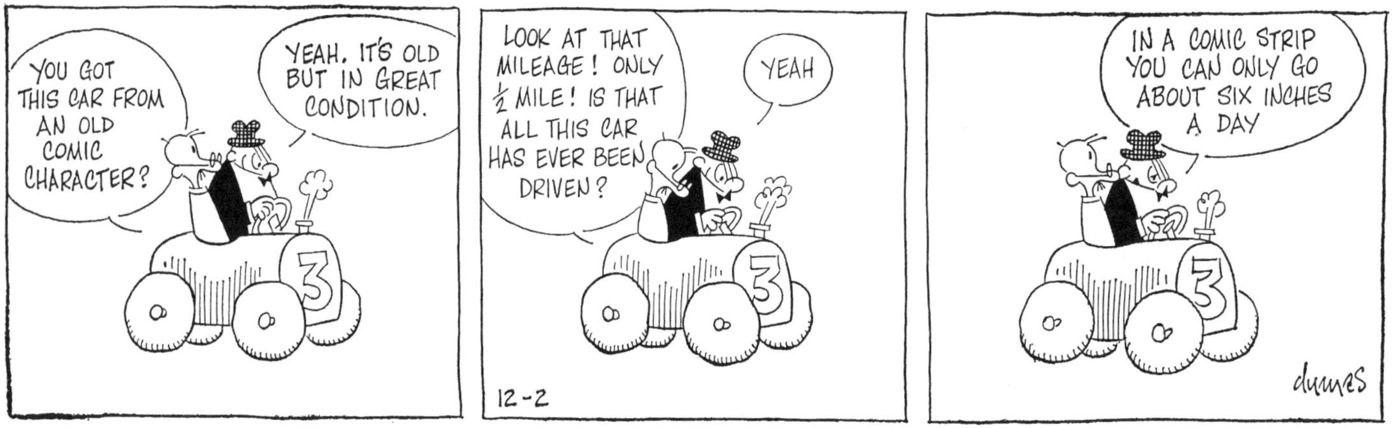
YOU GOT THIS CAR FROM AN OLD COMIC CHARACTER?
YEAH. IT'S OLD BUT IN GREAT CONDITION.
LOOK AT THAT MILEAGE! ONLY ½ MILE! IS THAT ALL THIS CAR HAS EVER BEEN DRIVEN?
YEAH
12-2
IN A COMIC STRIP YOU CAN ONLY GO ABOUT SIX INCHES A DAY
dumas

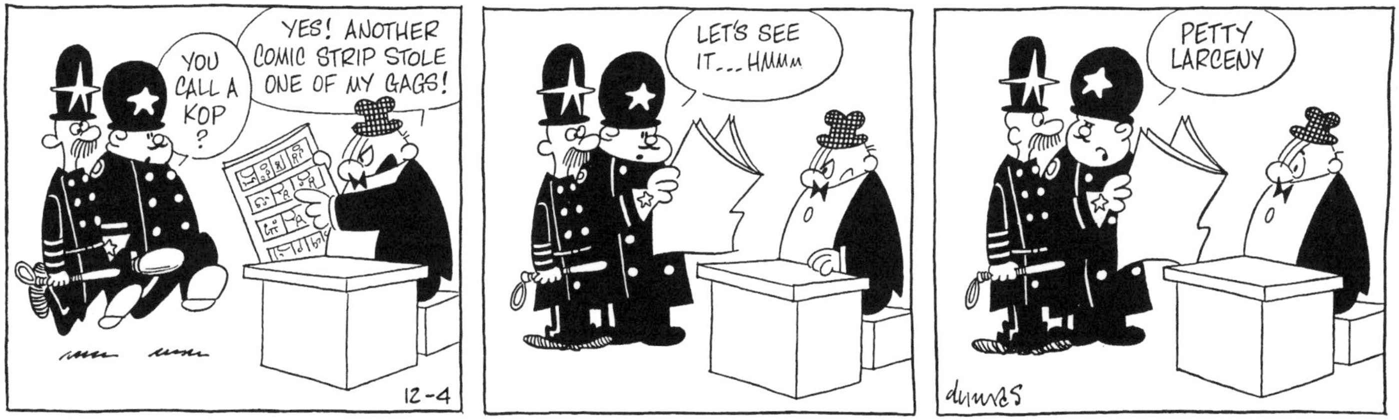
YOU CALL A KOP ?
YES! ANOTHER COMIC STRIP STOLE ONE OF MY GAGS!
12-4
LET'S SEE IT... HMMM
PETTY LARCENY
dumas

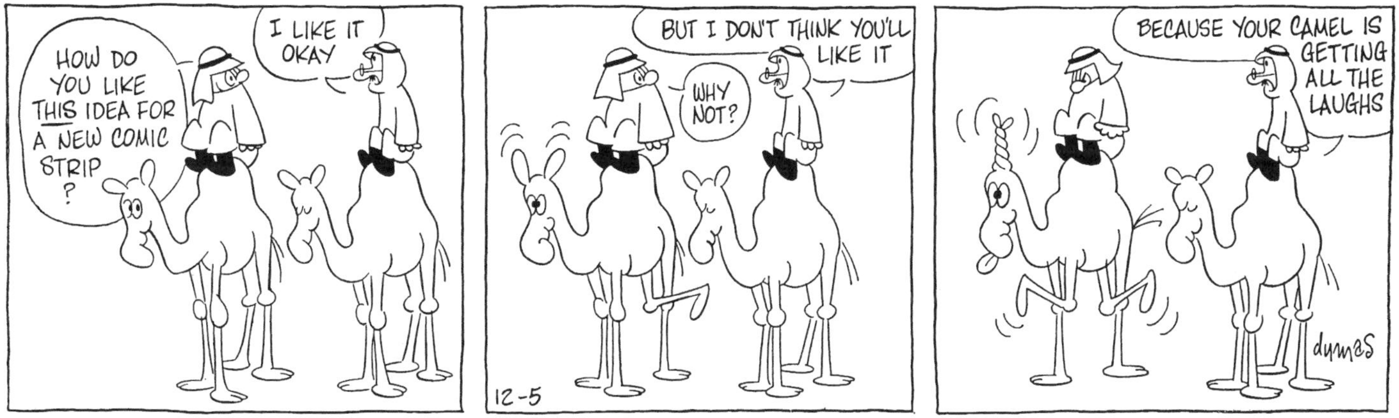
HOW DO YOU LIKE THIS IDEA FOR A NEW COMIC STRIP ?
I LIKE IT OKAY
BUT I DON'T THINK YOU'LL LIKE IT
WHY NOT?
12-5
BECAUSE YOUR CAMEL IS GETTING ALL THE LAUGHS
dumas

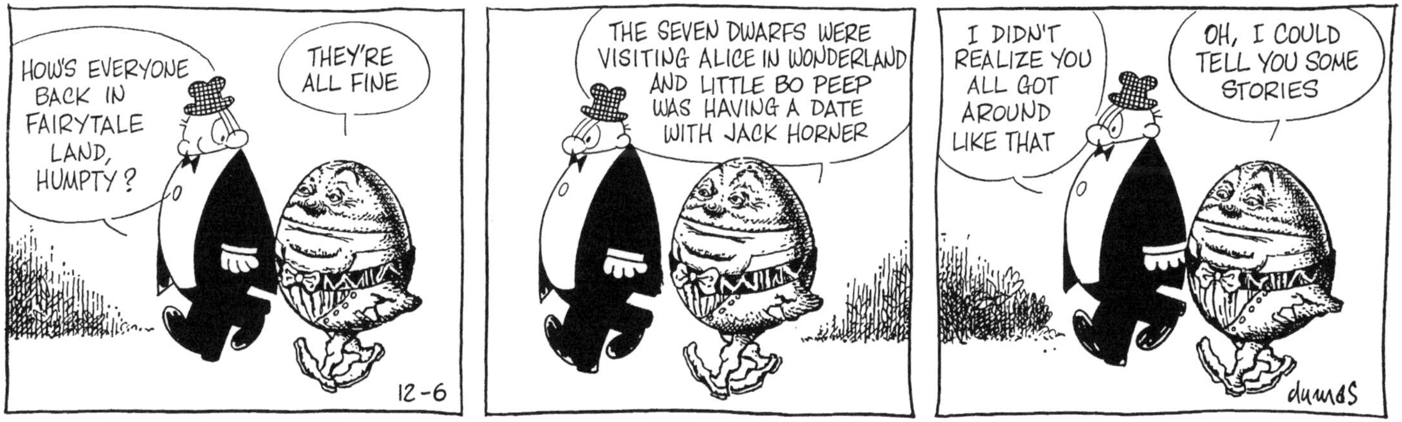
HOW'S EVERYONE BACK IN FAIRYTALE LAND, HUMPTY ?
THEY'RE ALL FINE
12-6
THE SEVEN DWARFS WERE VISITING ALICE IN WONDERLAND AND LITTLE BO PEEP WAS HAVING A DATE WITH JACK HORNER
I DIDN'T REALIZE YOU ALL GOT AROUND LIKE THAT
OH, I COULD TELL YOU SOME STORIES
dumas

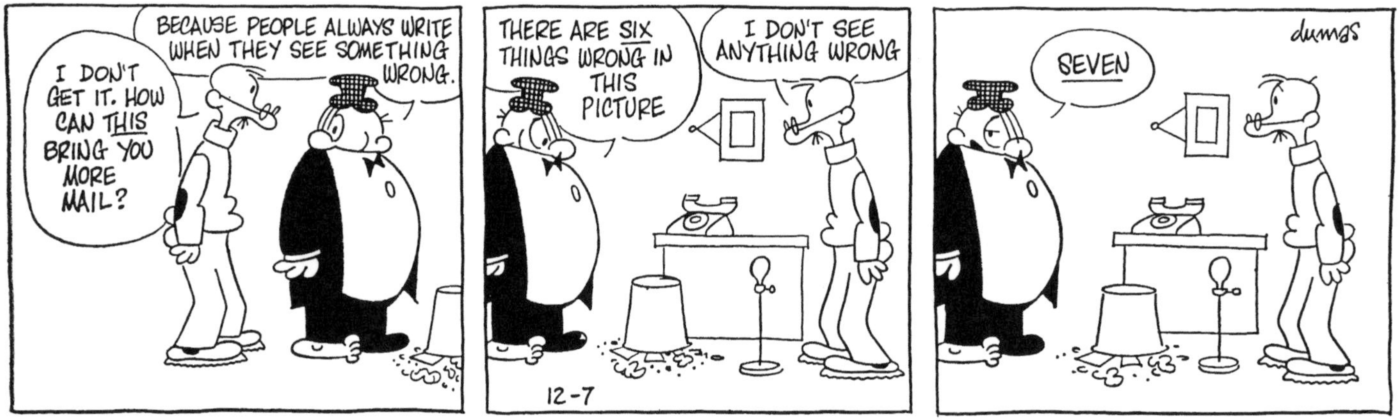
I DON'T GET IT. HOW CAN THIS BRING YOU MORE MAIL?
BECAUSE PEOPLE ALWAYS WRITE WHEN THEY SEE SOMETHING WRONG.
THERE ARE SIX THINGS WRONG IN THIS PICTURE
I DON'T SEE ANYTHING WRONG
12-7
dumas
SEVEN

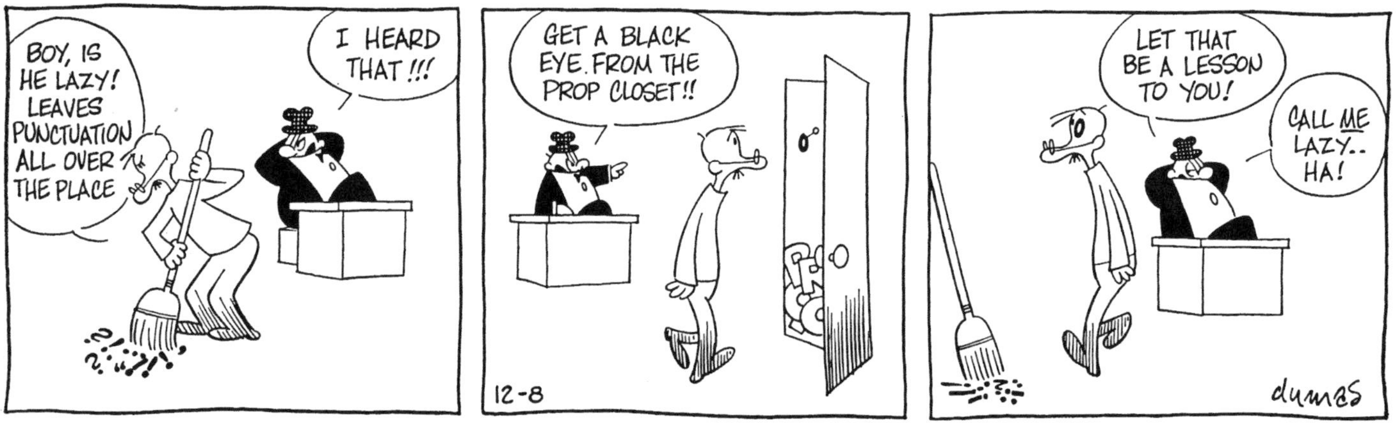
BOY, IS HE LAZY! LEAVES PUNCTUATION ALL OVER THE PLACE
I HEARD THAT !!!
GET A BLACK EYE FROM THE PROP CLOSET!!
12-8
LET THAT BE A LESSON TO YOU!
CALL ME LAZY.. HA!
dumas

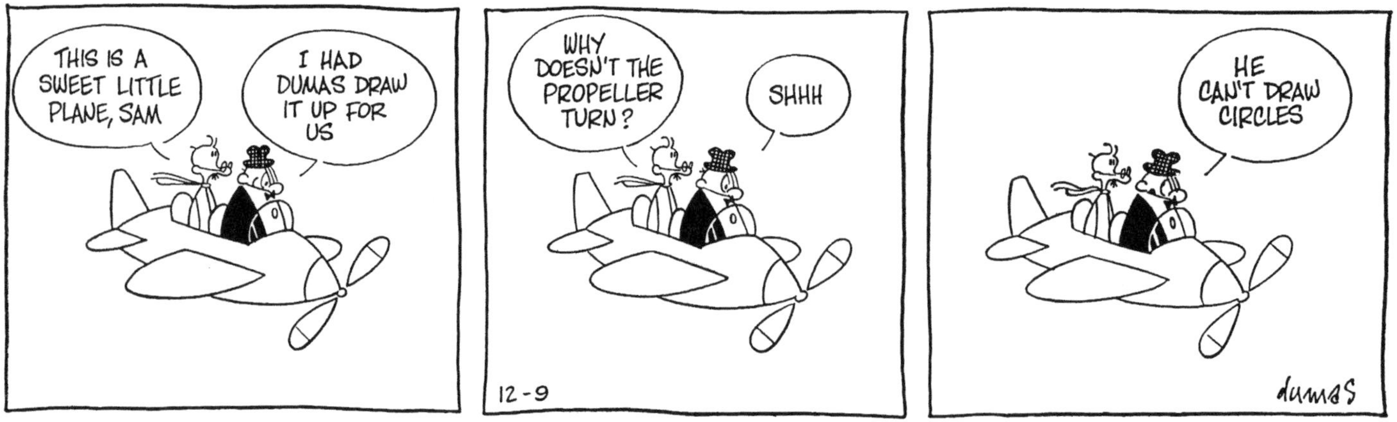
THIS IS A SWEET LITTLE PLANE, SAM
I HAD DUMAS DRAW IT UP FOR US
WHY DOESN'T THE PROPELLER TURN?
SHHH
12-9
HE CAN'T DRAW CIRCLES
dumas

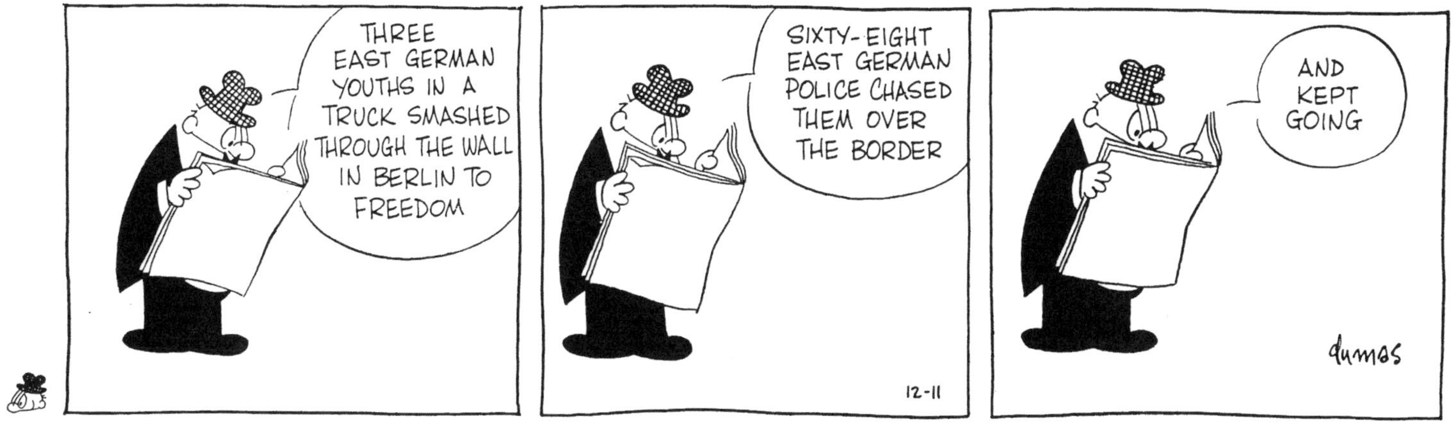
THREE EAST GERMAN YOUTHS IN A TRUCK SMASHED THROUGH THE WALL IN BERLIN TO FREEDOM
SIXTY-EIGHT EAST GERMAN POLICE CHASED THEM OVER THE BORDER
12-11
AND KEPT GOING
dumas

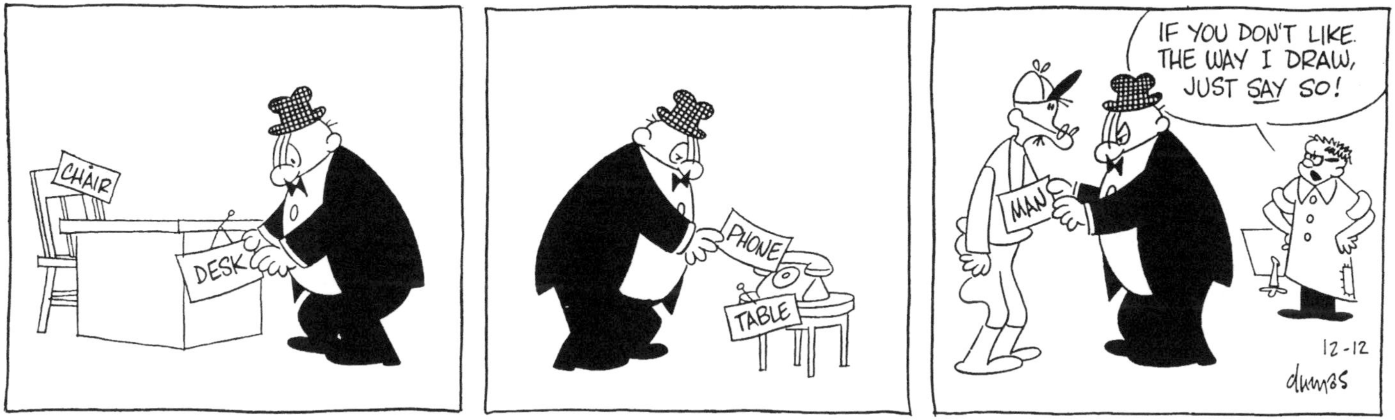
CHAIR
DESK
PHONE
TABLE
IF YOU DON'T LIKE THE WAY I DRAW, JUST SAY SO!
MAN
12-12
dumas

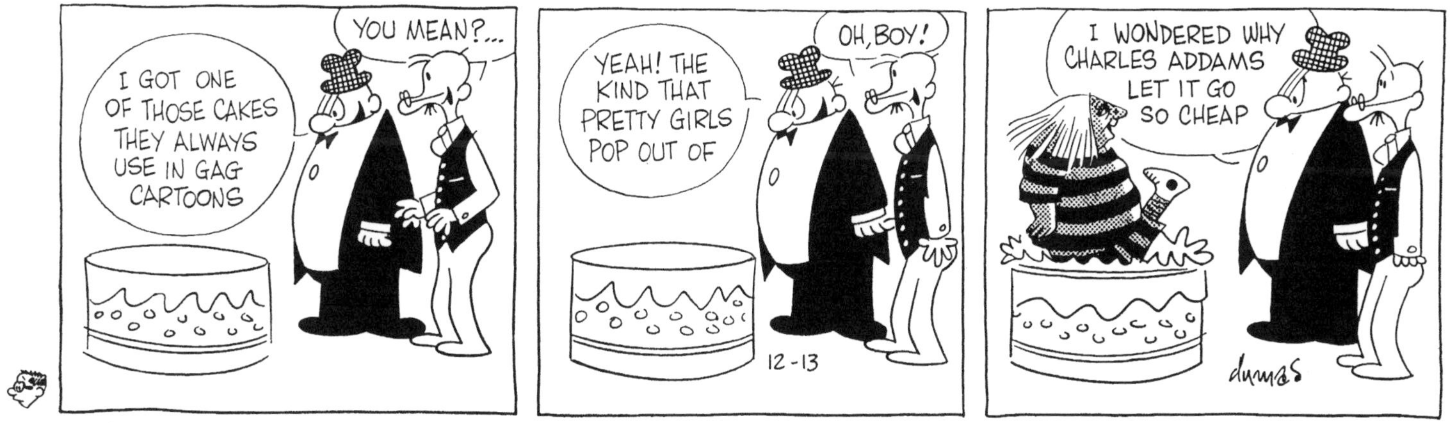
YOU MEAN?...
I GOT ONE OF THOSE CAKES THEY ALWAYS USE IN GAG CARTOONS
OH, BOY!
YEAH! THE KIND THAT PRETTY GIRLS POP OUT OF
12-13
I WONDERED WHY CHARLES ADDAMS LET IT GO SO CHEAP
dumas

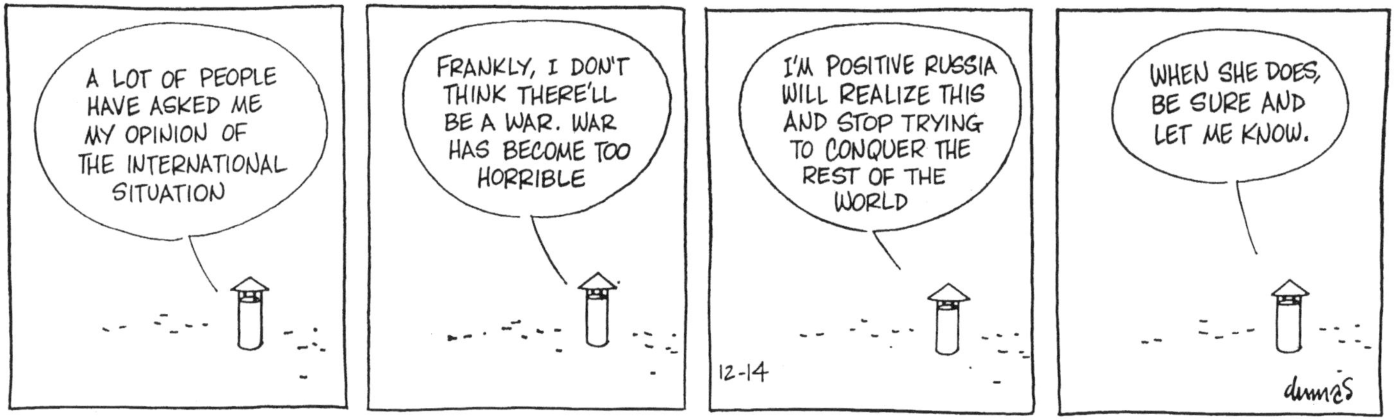
A LOT OF PEOPLE HAVE ASKED ME MY OPINION OF THE INTERNATIONAL SITUATION
FRANKLY, I DON'T THINK THERE'LL BE A WAR. WAR HAS BECOME TOO HORRIBLE
I'M POSITIVE RUSSIA WILL REALIZE THIS AND STOP TRYING TO CONQUER THE REST OF THE WORLD
12-14
WHEN SHE DOES, BE SURE AND LET ME KNOW.
dumas

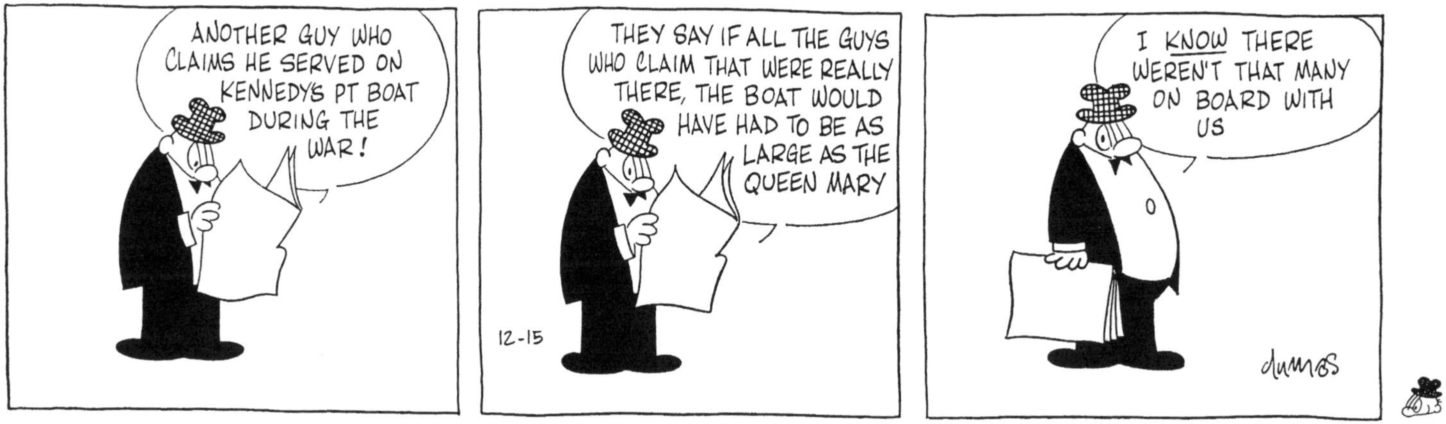
ANOTHER GUY WHO CLAIMS HE SERVED ON KENNEDY'S PT BOAT DURING THE WAR!
THEY SAY IF ALL THE GUYS WHO CLAIM THAT WERE REALLY THERE, THE BOAT WOULD HAVE HAD TO BE AS LARGE AS THE QUEEN MARY
12-15
I KNOW THERE WEREN'T THAT MANY ON BOARD WITH US
dumas

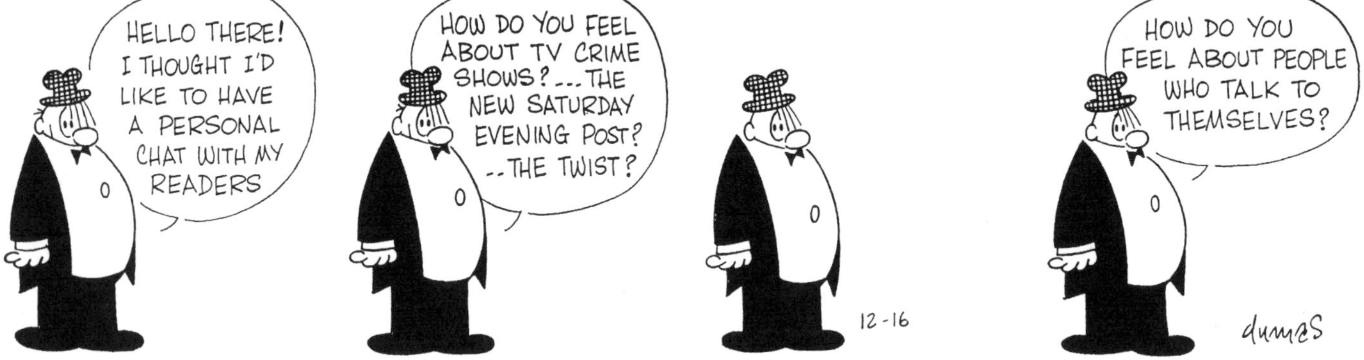
HELLO THERE! I THOUGHT I'D LIKE TO HAVE A PERSONAL CHAT WITH MY READERS
HOW DO YOU FEEL ABOUT TV CRIME SHOWS?... THE NEW SATURDAY EVENING POST? --THE TWIST?
12-16
HOW DO YOU FEEL ABOUT PEOPLE WHO TALK TO THEMSELVES?
dumas

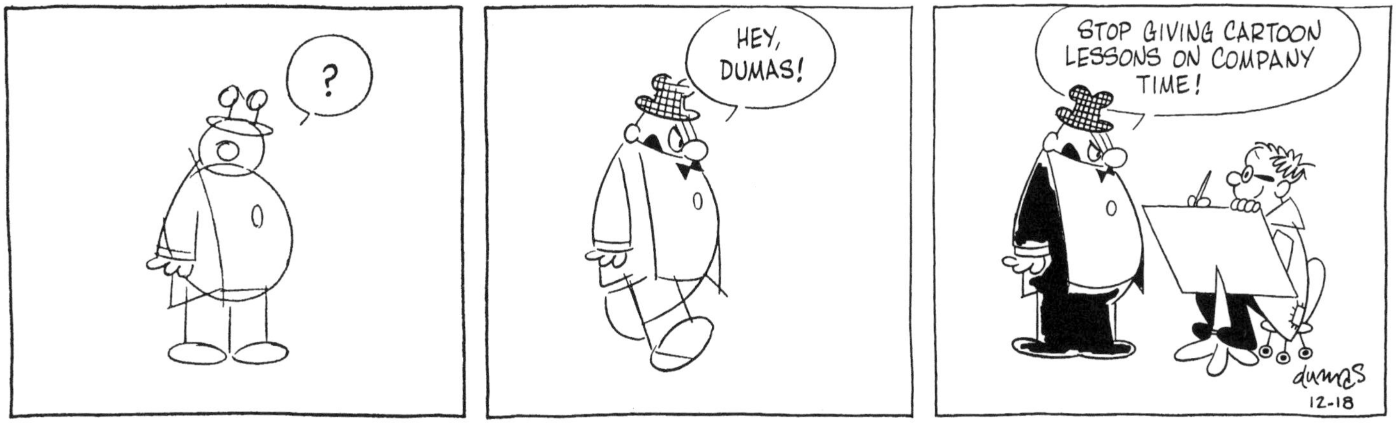
?
HEY, DUMAS!
STOP GIVING CARTOON LESSONS ON COMPANY TIME!
dumas
12-18

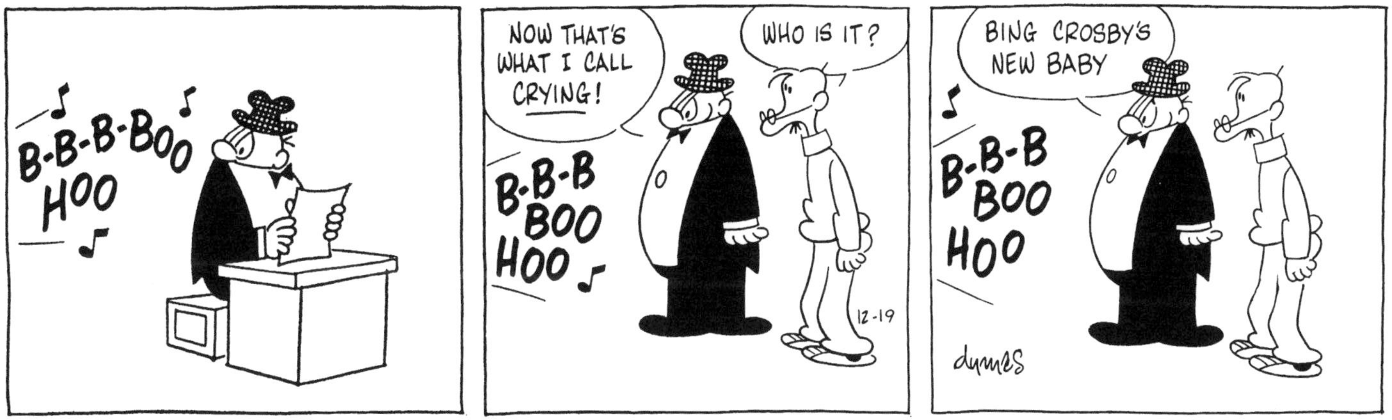
B-B-B-BOO HOO
NOW THAT'S WHAT I CALL CRYING!
B-B-B BOO HOO
WHO IS IT?
12-19
BING CROSBY'S NEW BABY
B-B-B BOO HOO
dumas

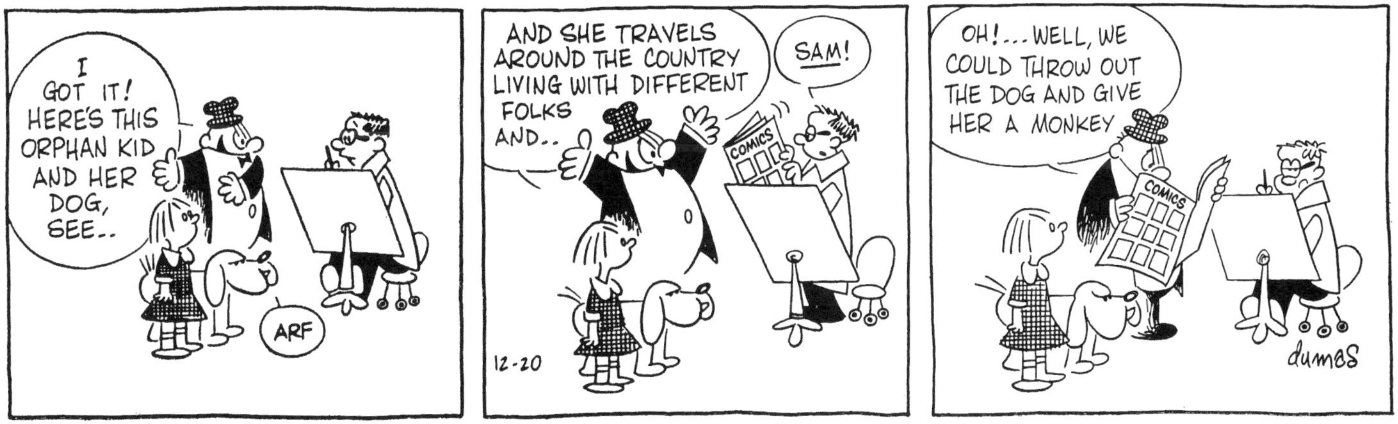
I GOT IT! HERE'S THIS ORPHAN KID AND HER DOG, SEE..
ARF
AND SHE TRAVELS AROUND THE COUNTRY LIVING WITH DIFFERENT FOLKS AND..
SAM!
COMICS
12-20
OH!...WELL, WE COULD THROW OUT THE DOG AND GIVE HER A MONKEY
COMICS
dumas

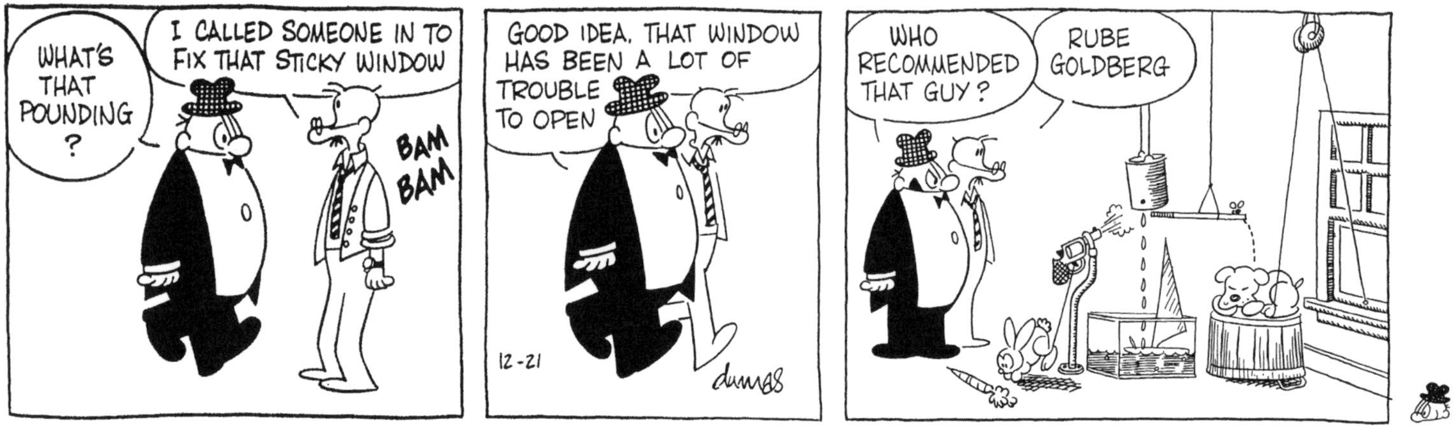
WHAT'S THAT POUNDING ?
I CALLED SOMEONE IN TO FIX THAT STICKY WINDOW
BAM BAM
GOOD IDEA. THAT WINDOW HAS BEEN A LOT OF TROUBLE TO OPEN
12-21
dumas
WHO RECOMMENDED THAT GUY ?
RUBE GOLDBERG

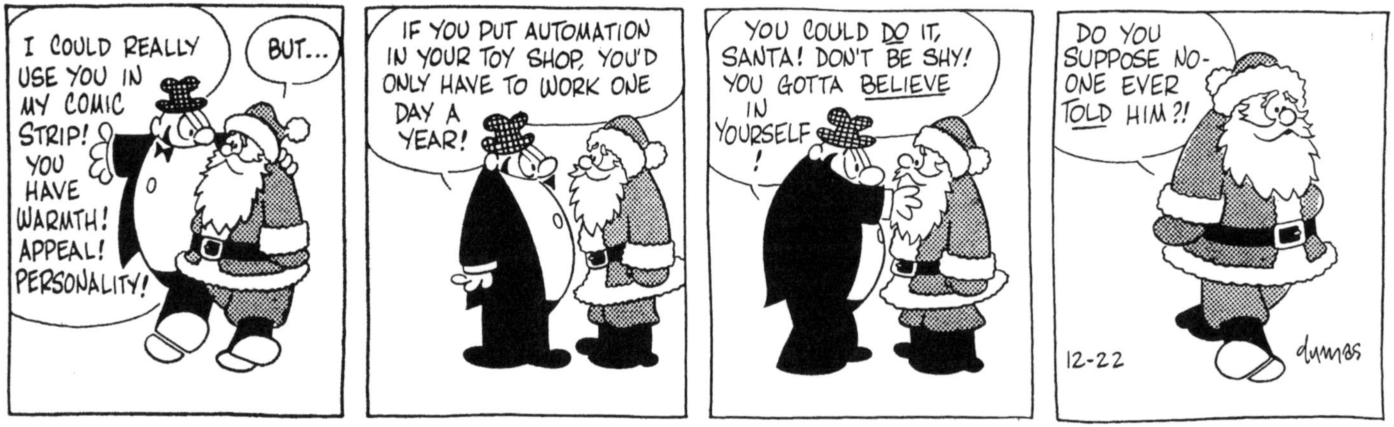
I COULD REALLY USE YOU IN MY COMIC STRIP! YOU HAVE WARMTH! APPEAL! PERSONALITY!
BUT...
IF YOU PUT AUTOMATION IN YOUR TOY SHOP, YOU'D ONLY HAVE TO WORK ONE DAY A YEAR!
YOU COULD DO IT, SANTA! DON'T BE SHY! YOU GOTTA BELIEVE IN YOURSELF !
DO YOU SUPPOSE NO-ONE EVER TOLD HIM ?!
12-22
dumas

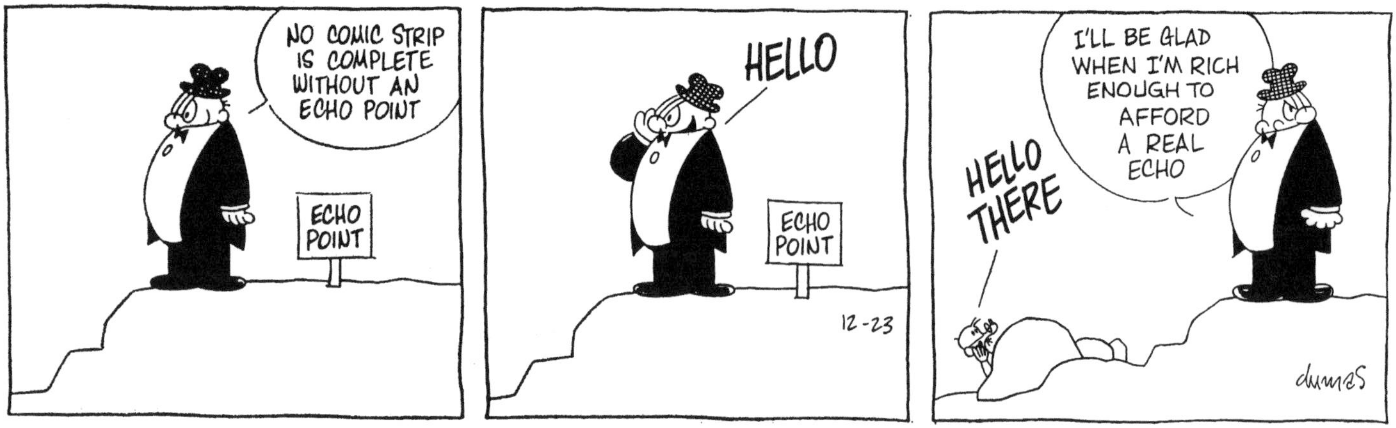
NO COMIC STRIP IS COMPLETE WITHOUT AN ECHO POINT
ECHO POINT
HELLO
ECHO POINT
12-23
HELLO THERE
I'LL BE GLAD WHEN I'M RICH ENOUGH TO AFFORD A REAL ECHO
dumas

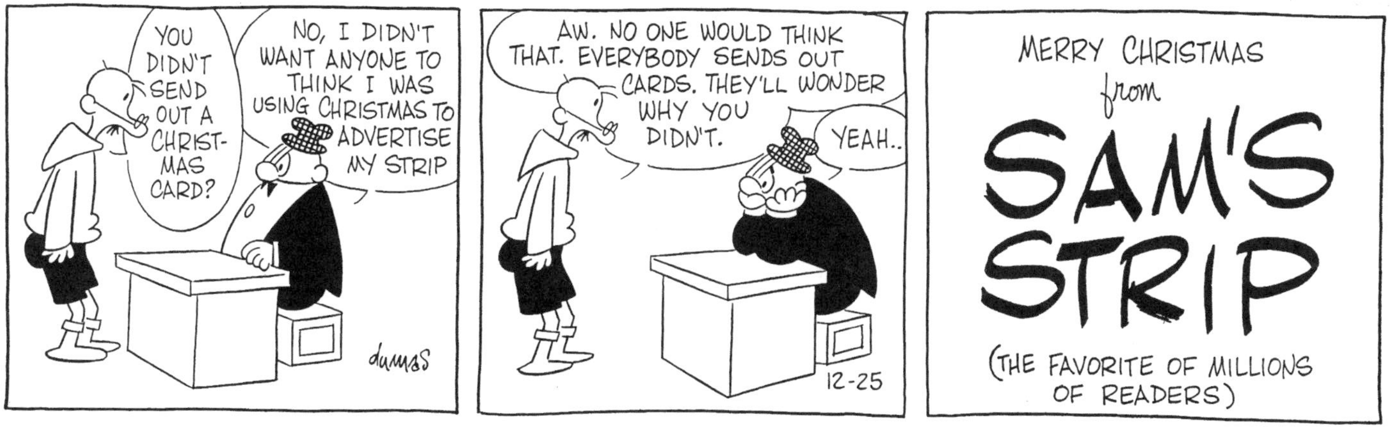
YOU DIDN'T SEND OUT A CHRISTMAS CARD?
NO, I DIDN'T WANT ANYONE TO THINK I WAS USING CHRISTMAS TO ADVERTISE MY STRIP
dumas
AW. NO ONE WOULD THINK THAT. EVERYBODY SENDS OUT CARDS. THEY'LL WONDER WHY YOU DIDN'T.
YEAH..
12-25
MERRY CHRISTMAS
from
SAM'S STRIP
(THE FAVORITE OF MILLIONS OF READERS)

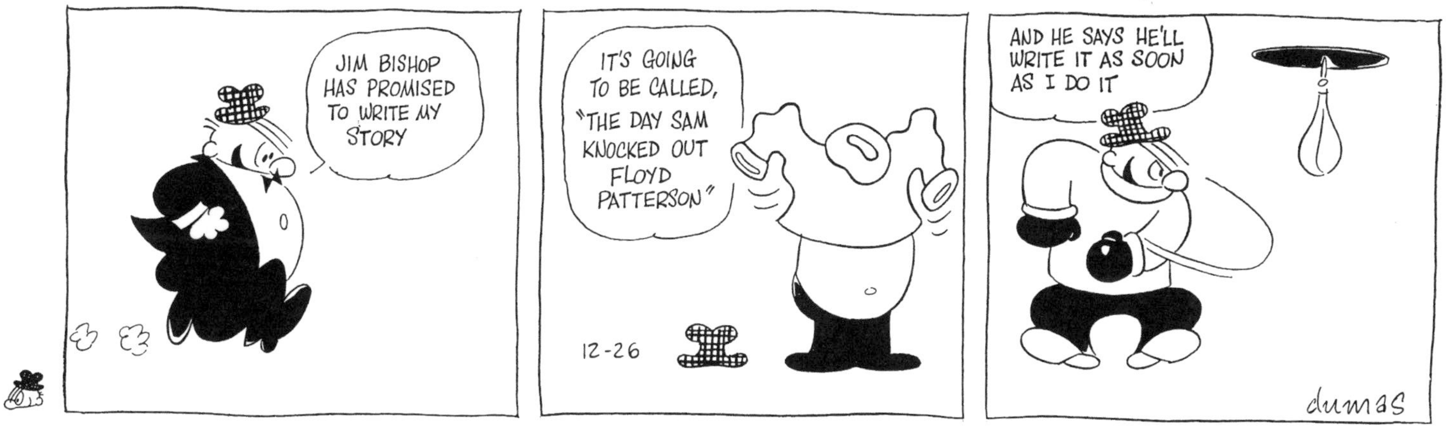
JIM BISHOP HAS PROMISED TO WRITE MY STORY
IT'S GOING TO BE CALLED, "THE DAY SAM KNOCKED OUT FLOYD PATTERSON"
12-26
AND HE SAYS HE'LL WRITE IT AS SOON AS I DO IT
dumas

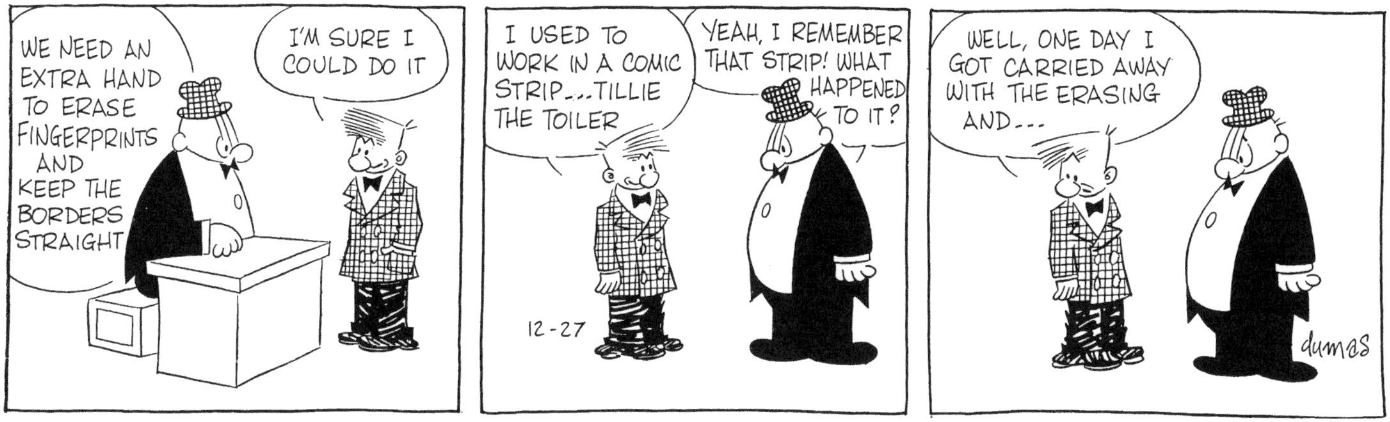
WE NEED AN EXTRA HAND TO ERASE FINGERPRINTS AND KEEP THE BORDERS STRAIGHT
I'M SURE I COULD DO IT
I USED TO WORK IN A COMIC STRIP....TILLIE THE TOILER
YEAH, I REMEMBER THAT STRIP! WHAT HAPPENED TO IT?
12-27
WELL, ONE DAY I GOT CARRIED AWAY WITH THE ERASING AND...
dumas

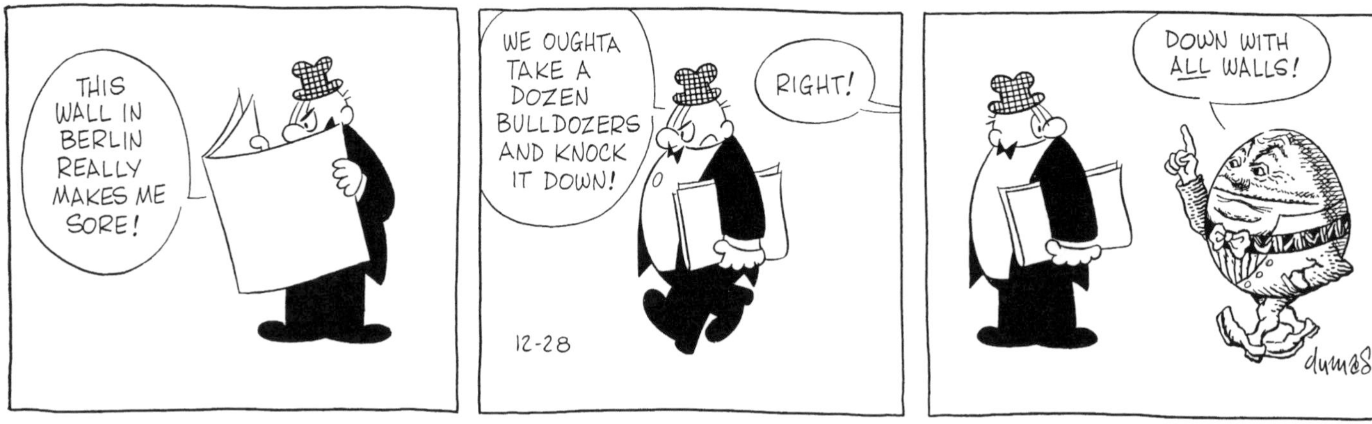
THIS WALL IN BERLIN REALLY MAKES ME SORE!
WE OUGHTA TAKE A DOZEN BULLDOZERS AND KNOCK IT DOWN!
RIGHT!
12-28
DOWN WITH ALL WALLS!
dumas

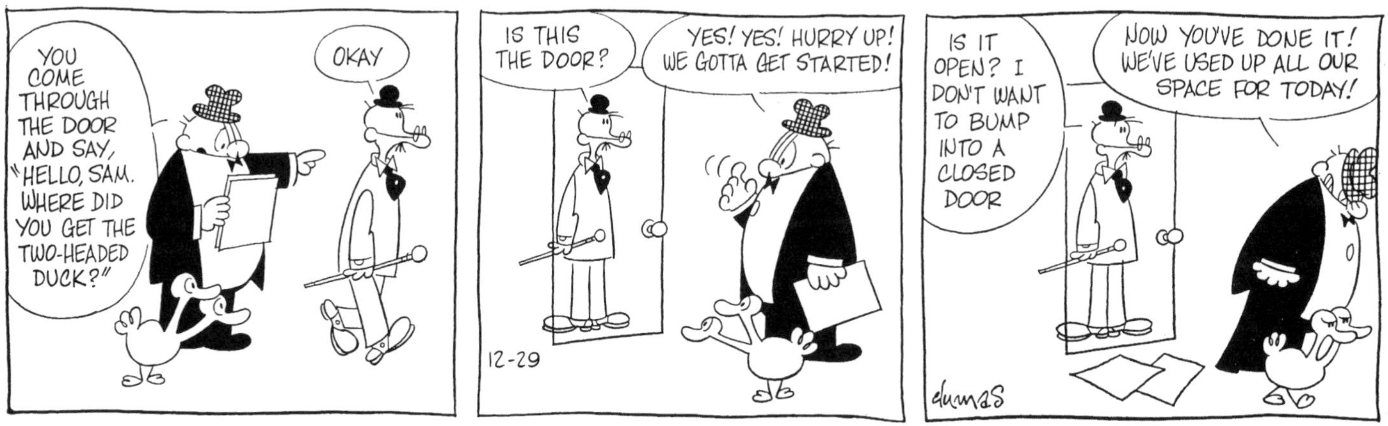
YOU COME THROUGH THE DOOR AND SAY, "HELLO, SAM. WHERE DID YOU GET THE TWO-HEADED DUCK?"
OKAY
IS THIS THE DOOR?
YES! YES! HURRY UP! WE GOTTA GET STARTED!
12-29
IS IT OPEN? I DON'T WANT TO BUMP INTO A CLOSED DOOR
NOW YOU'VE DONE IT! WE'VE USED UP ALL OUR SPACE FOR TODAY!
dumas

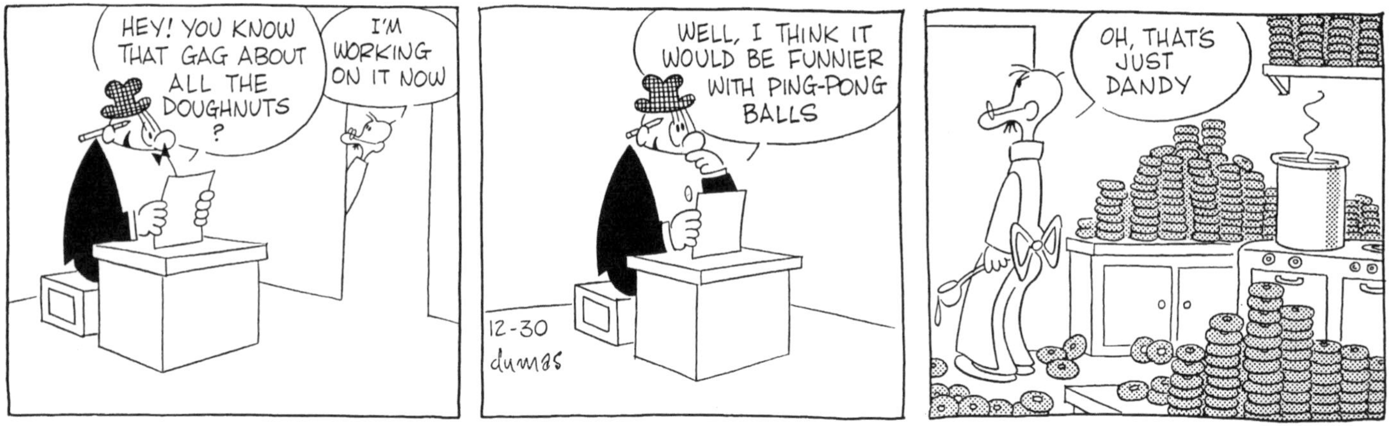
HEY! YOU KNOW THAT GAG ABOUT ALL THE DOUGHNUTS ?
I'M WORKING ON IT NOW
WELL, I THINK IT WOULD BE FUNNIER WITH PING-PONG BALLS
12-30
dumas
OH, THAT'S JUST DANDY

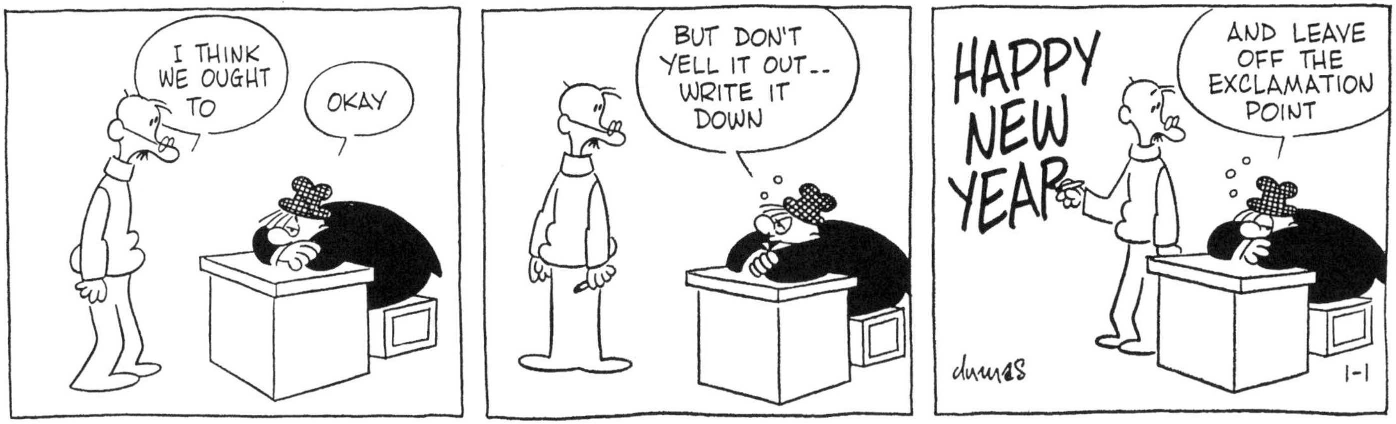
I THINK WE OUGHT TO
OKAY
BUT DON'T YELL IT OUT.. WRITE IT DOWN
HAPPY NEW YEAR
AND LEAVE OFF THE EXCLAMATION POINT
dumas
1-1

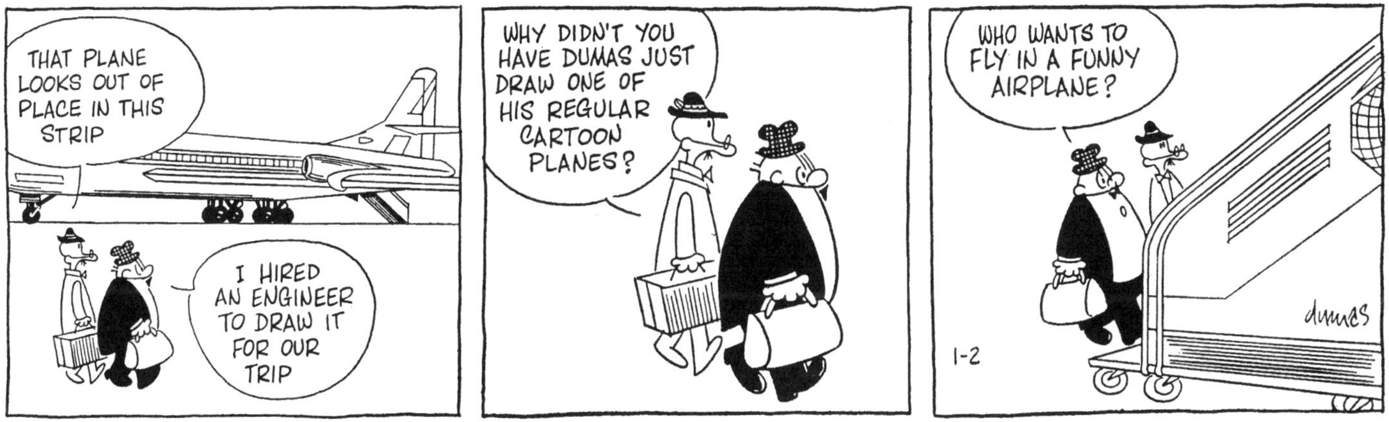
THAT PLANE LOOKS OUT OF PLACE IN THIS STRIP
I HIRED AN ENGINEER TO DRAW IT FOR OUR TRIP
WHY DIDN'T YOU HAVE DUMAS JUST DRAW ONE OF HIS REGULAR CARTOON PLANES?
WHO WANTS TO FLY IN A FUNNY AIRPLANE?
1-2
dumas

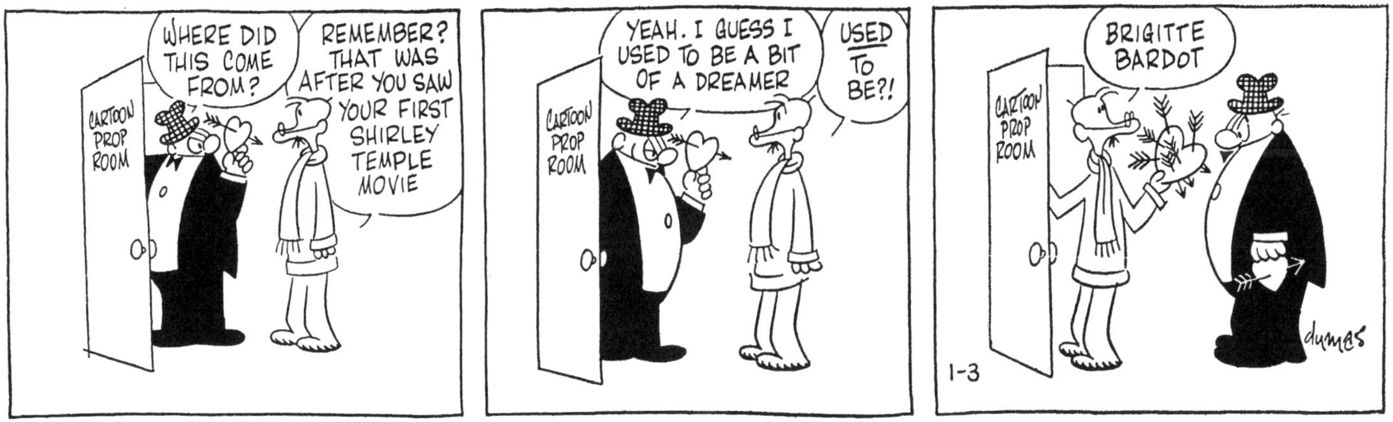
CARTOON PROP ROOM
WHERE DID THIS COME FROM?
REMEMBER? THAT WAS AFTER YOU SAW YOUR FIRST SHIRLEY TEMPLE MOVIE
CARTOON PROP ROOM
YEAH. I GUESS I USED TO BE A BIT OF A DREAMER
USED TO BE?!
CARTOON PROP ROOM
BRIGITTE BARDOT
1-3
dumas

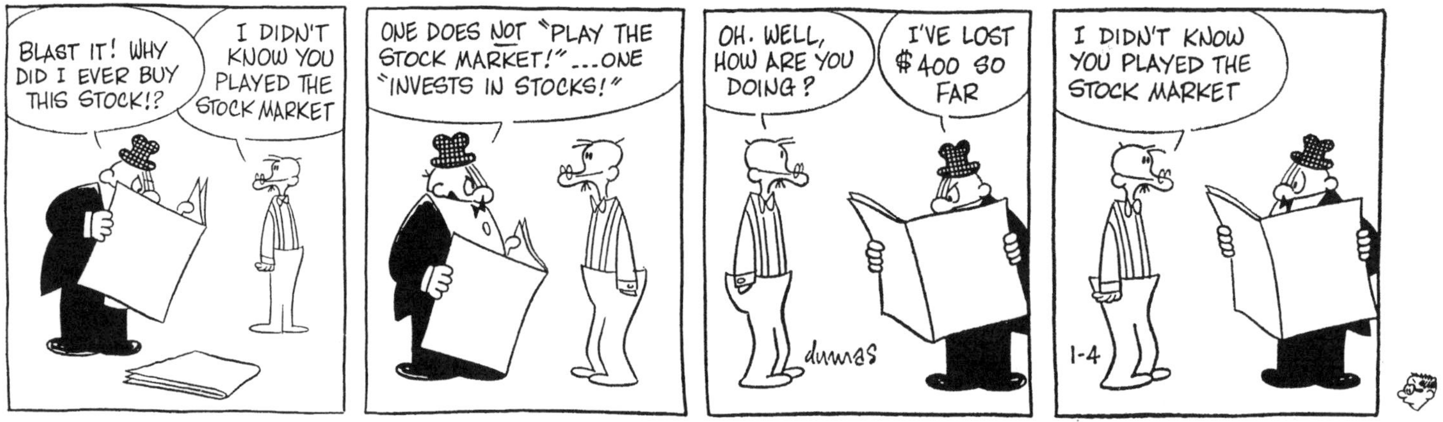
BLAST IT! WHY DID I EVER BUY THIS STOCK!?
I DIDN'T KNOW YOU PLAYED THE STOCK MARKET
ONE DOES NOT "PLAY THE STOCK MARKET!" ...ONE "INVESTS IN STOCKS!"
OH. WELL, HOW ARE YOU DOING?
I'VE LOST $400 SO FAR
I DIDN'T KNOW YOU PLAYED THE STOCK MARKET
dumas
1-4

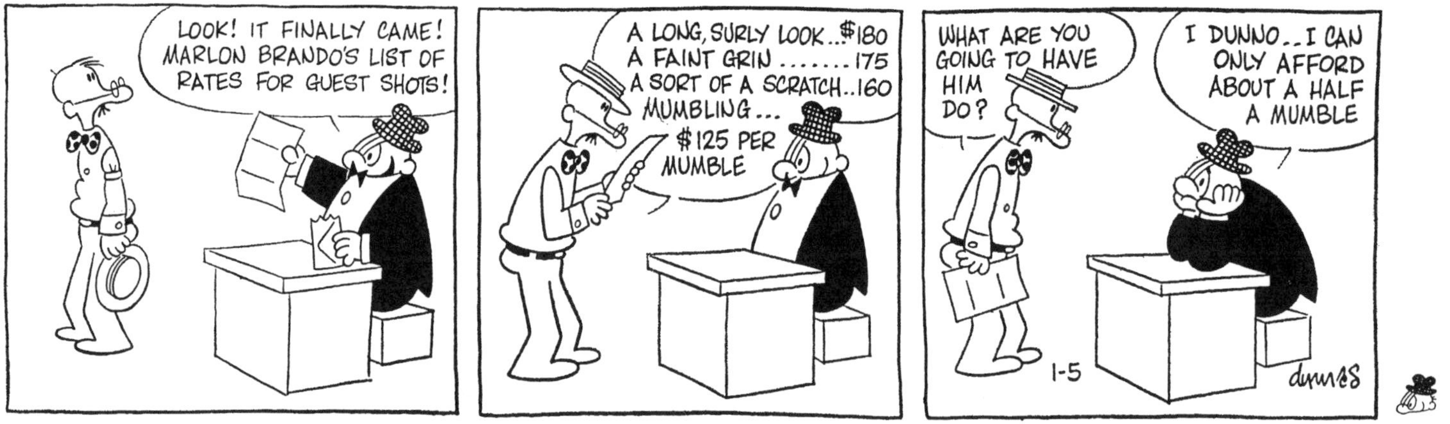
LOOK! IT FINALLY CAME! MARLON BRANDO'S LIST OF RATES FOR GUEST SHOTS!
A LONG, SURLY LOOK..$180
A FAINT GRIN 175
A SORT OF A SCRATCH..160
MUMBLING... $125 PER MUMBLE
WHAT ARE YOU GOING TO HAVE HIM DO?
I DUNNO..I CAN ONLY AFFORD ABOUT A HALF A MUMBLE
1-5
dumas

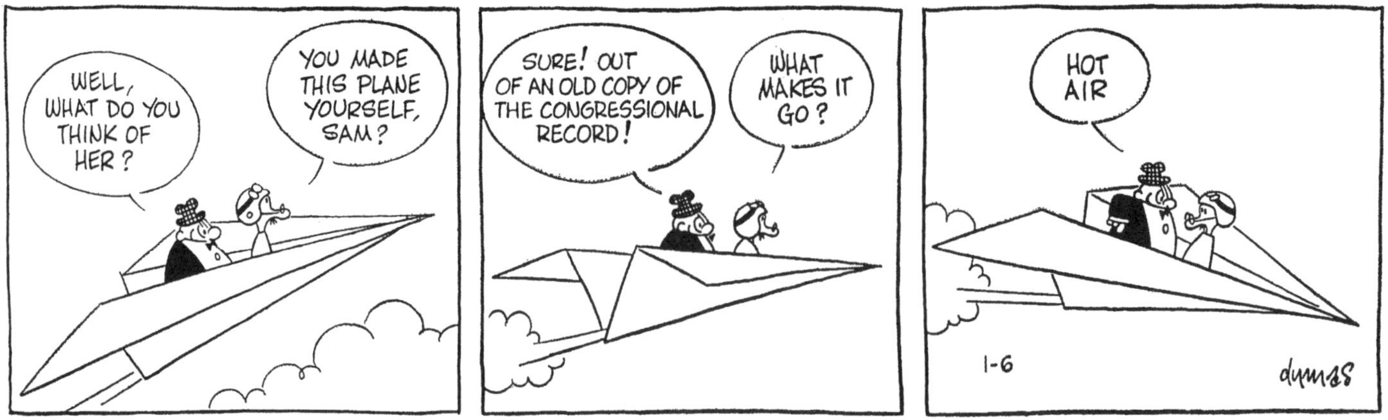
WELL, WHAT DO YOU THINK OF HER?
YOU MADE THIS PLANE YOURSELF, SAM?
SURE! OUT OF AN OLD COPY OF THE CONGRESSIONAL RECORD!
WHAT MAKES IT GO?
HOT AIR
1-6
dumas

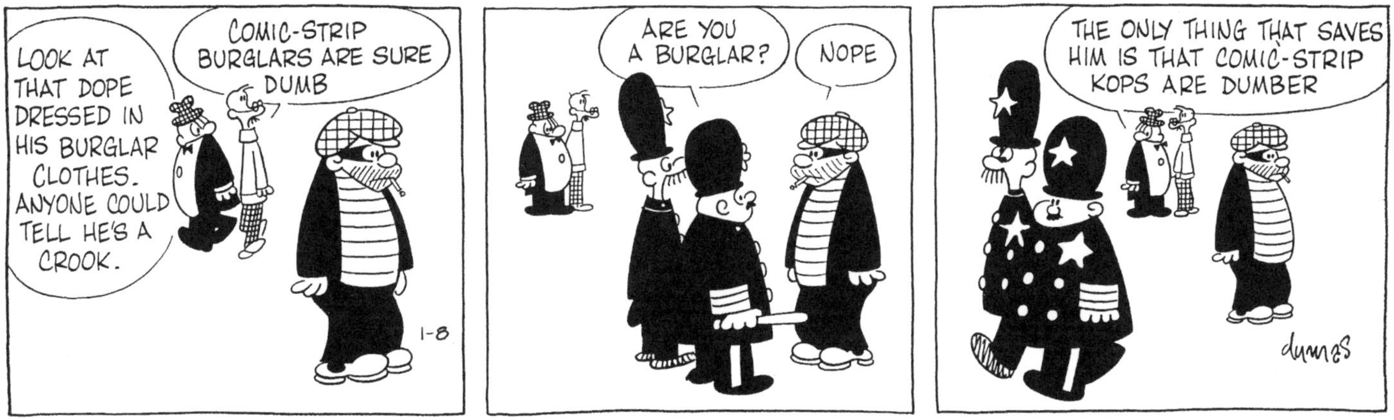
LOOK AT THAT DOPE DRESSED IN HIS BURGLAR CLOTHES. ANYONE COULD TELL HE'S A CROOK.
COMIC-STRIP BURGLARS ARE SURE DUMB
1-8
ARE YOU A BURGLAR?
NOPE
THE ONLY THING THAT SAVES HIM IS THAT COMIC-STRIP KOPS ARE DUMBER
dumas

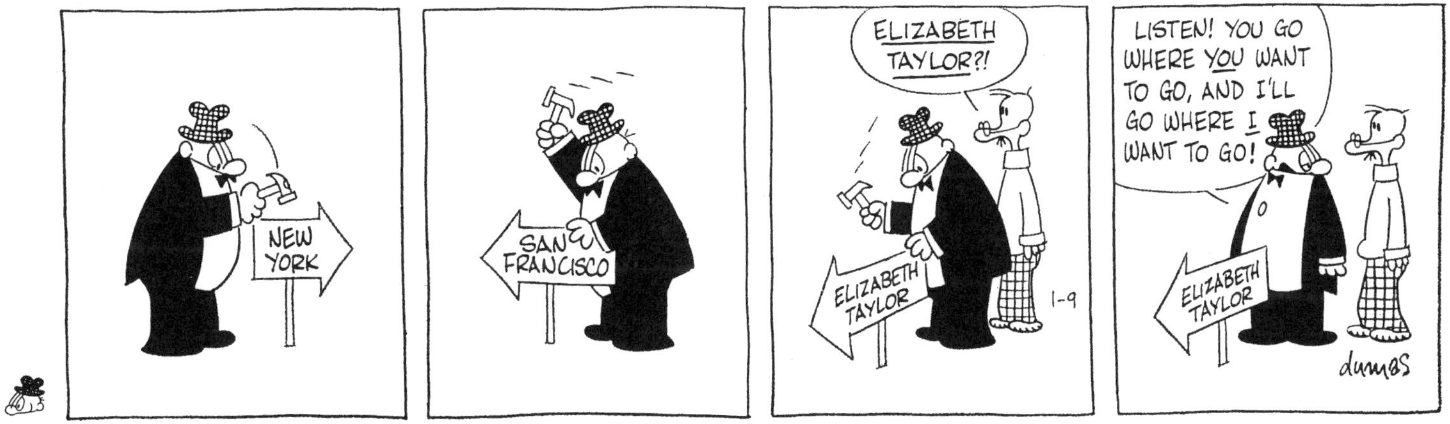
NEW YORK
SAN FRANCISCO
ELIZABETH TAYLOR?!
ELIZABETH TAYLOR
1-9
LISTEN! YOU GO WHERE YOU WANT TO GO, AND I'LL GO WHERE I WANT TO GO!
ELIZABETH TAYLOR
dumas

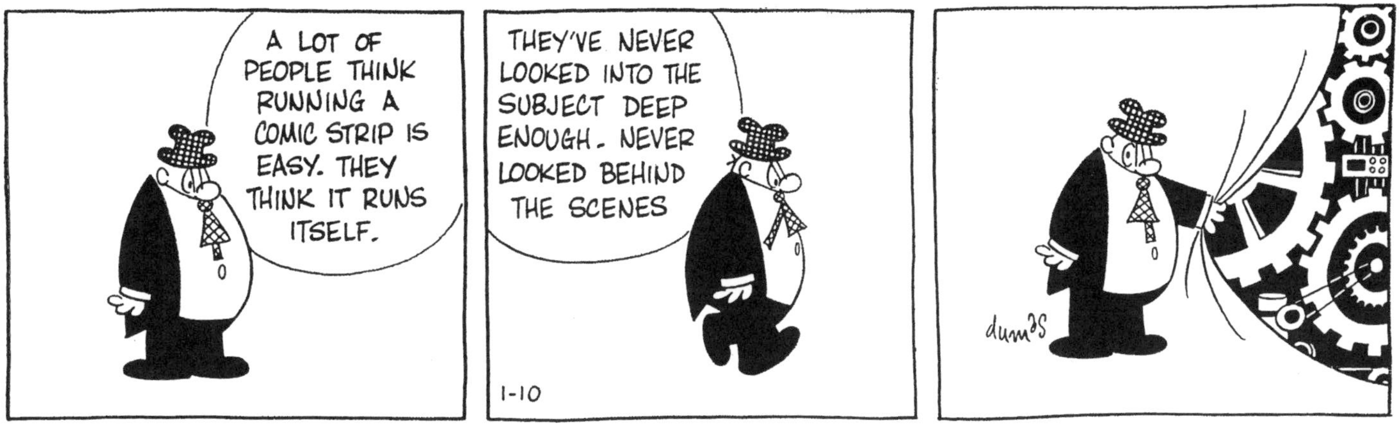
A LOT OF PEOPLE THINK RUNNING A COMIC STRIP IS EASY. THEY THINK IT RUNS ITSELF.
THEY'VE NEVER LOOKED INTO THE SUBJECT DEEP ENOUGH. NEVER LOOKED BEHIND THE SCENES
1-10
dumas

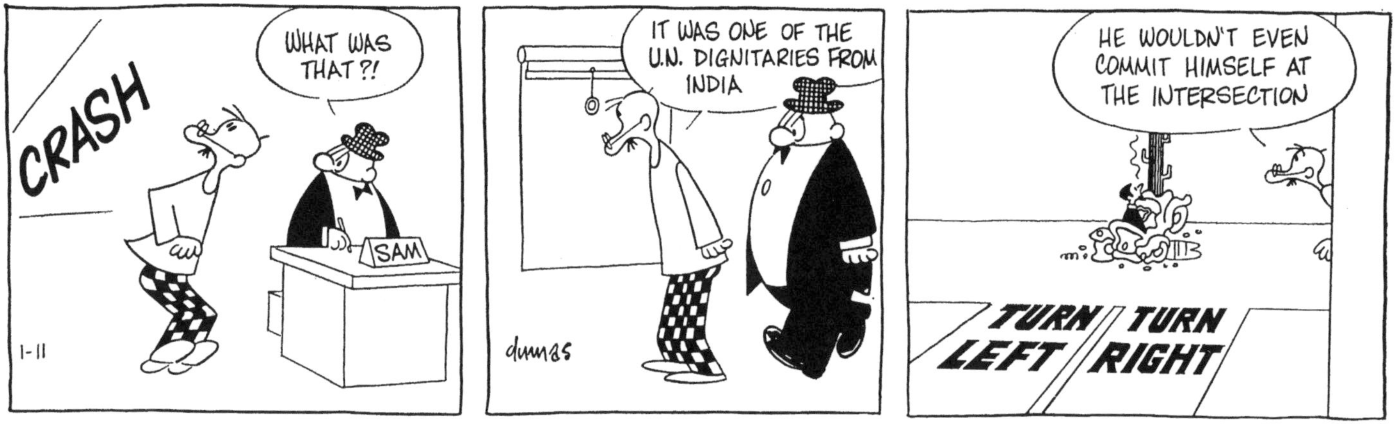
CRASH
WHAT WAS THAT?!
SAM
1-11
IT WAS ONE OF THE U.N. DIGNITARIES FROM INDIA
dumas
HE WOULDN'T EVEN COMMIT HIMSELF AT THE INTERSECTION
TURN LEFT
TURN RIGHT

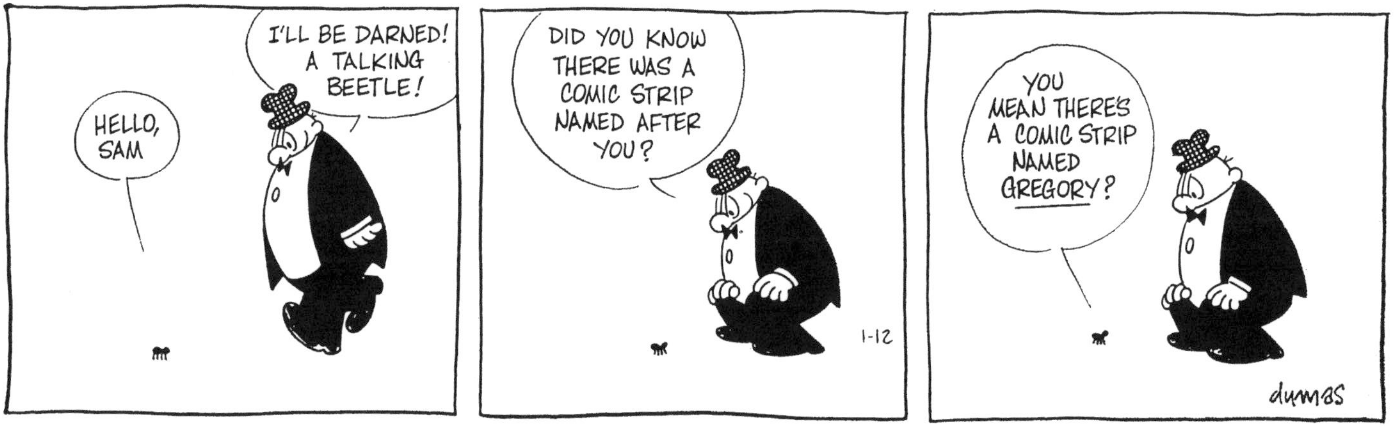
HELLO, SAM
I'LL BE DARNED! A TALKING BEETLE!
DID YOU KNOW THERE WAS A COMIC STRIP NAMED AFTER YOU?
1-12
YOU MEAN THERE'S A COMIC STRIP NAMED GREGORY?
dumas

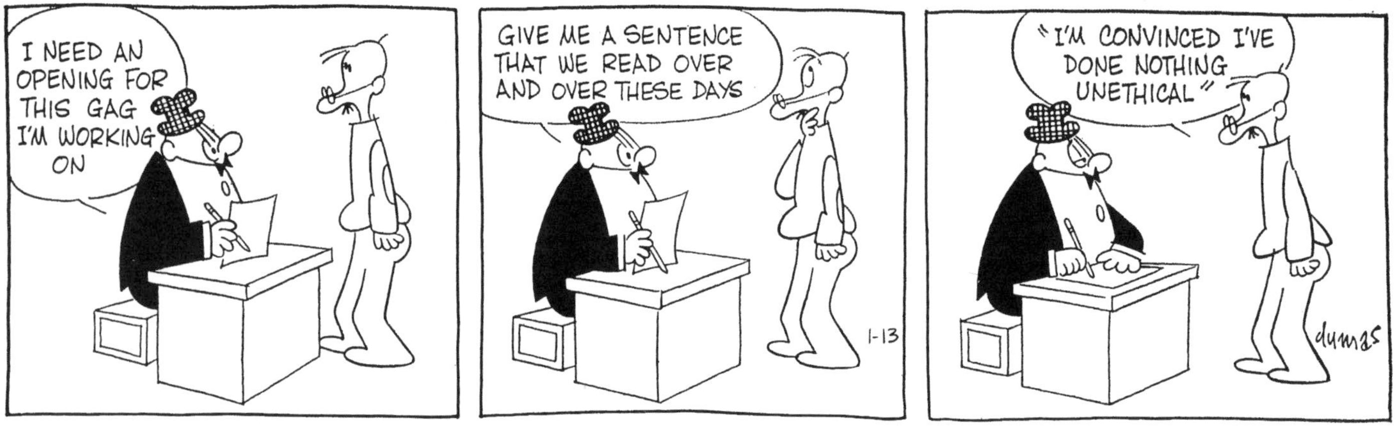
I NEED AN OPENING FOR THIS GAG I'M WORKING ON
GIVE ME A SENTENCE THAT WE READ OVER AND OVER THESE DAYS
1-13
"I'M CONVINCED I'VE DONE NOTHING UNETHICAL"
dumas

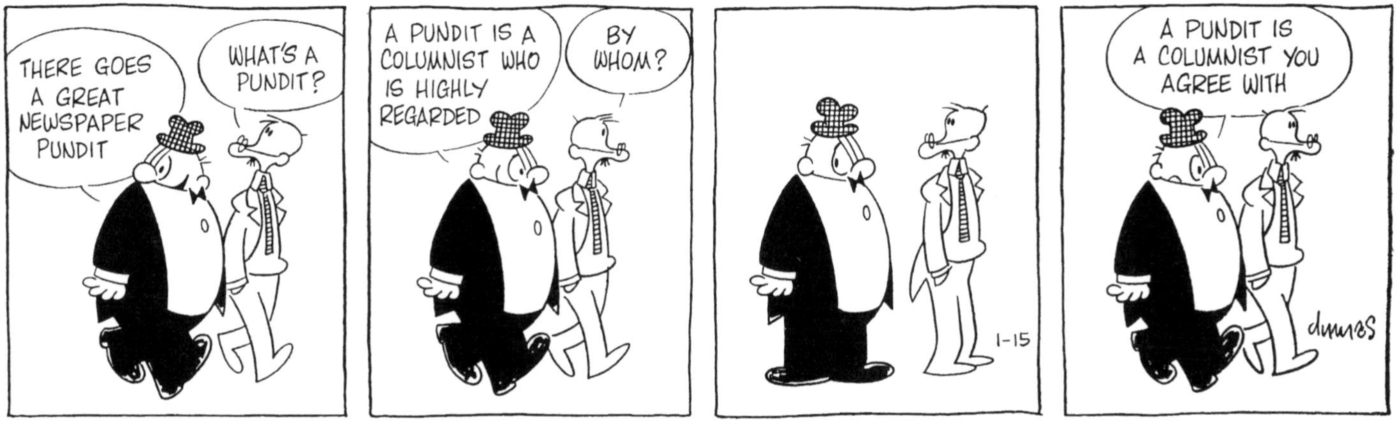
THERE GOES A GREAT NEWSPAPER PUNDIT
WHAT'S A PUNDIT?
A PUNDIT IS A COLUMNIST WHO IS HIGHLY REGARDED
BY WHOM?
1-15
A PUNDIT IS A COLUMNIST YOU AGREE WITH
dumas

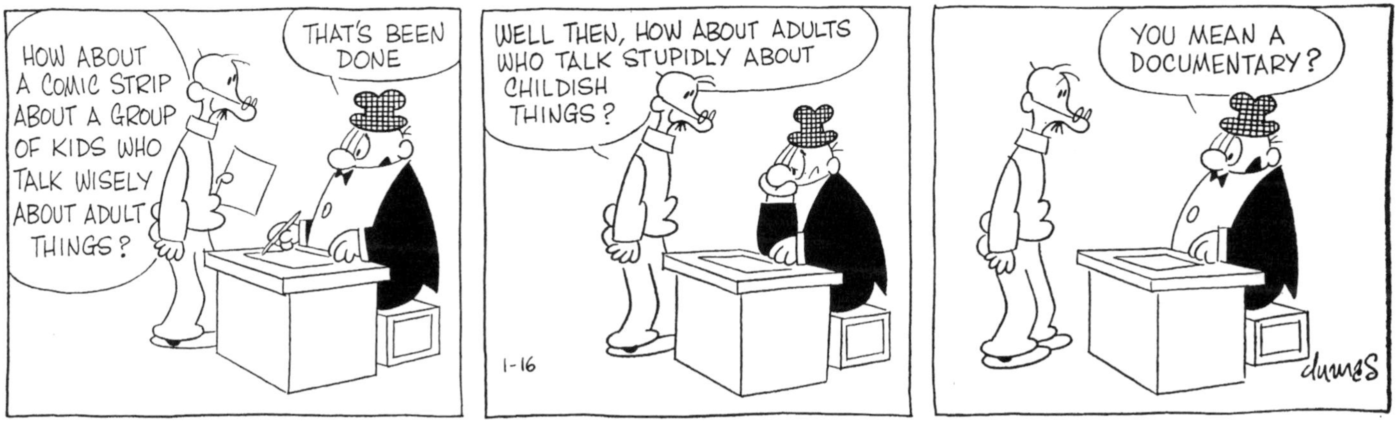
HOW ABOUT A COMIC STRIP ABOUT A GROUP OF KIDS WHO TALK WISELY ABOUT ADULT THINGS?
THAT'S BEEN DONE
WELL THEN, HOW ABOUT ADULTS WHO TALK STUPIDLY ABOUT CHILDISH THINGS?
1-16
YOU MEAN A DOCUMENTARY?
dumas

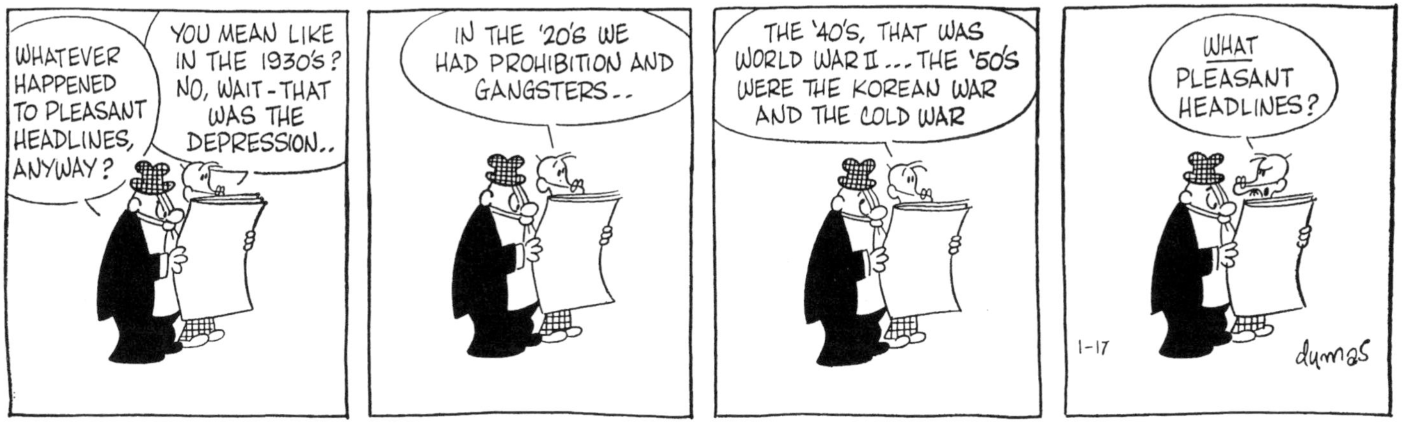
WHATEVER HAPPENED TO PLEASANT HEADLINES, ANYWAY?
YOU MEAN LIKE IN THE 1930'S? NO, WAIT-THAT WAS THE DEPRESSION..
IN THE '20'S WE HAD PROHIBITION AND GANGSTERS..
THE '40'S, THAT WAS WORLD WAR II ... THE '50'S WERE THE KOREAN WAR AND THE COLD WAR
1-17
WHAT PLEASANT HEADLINES?
dumas

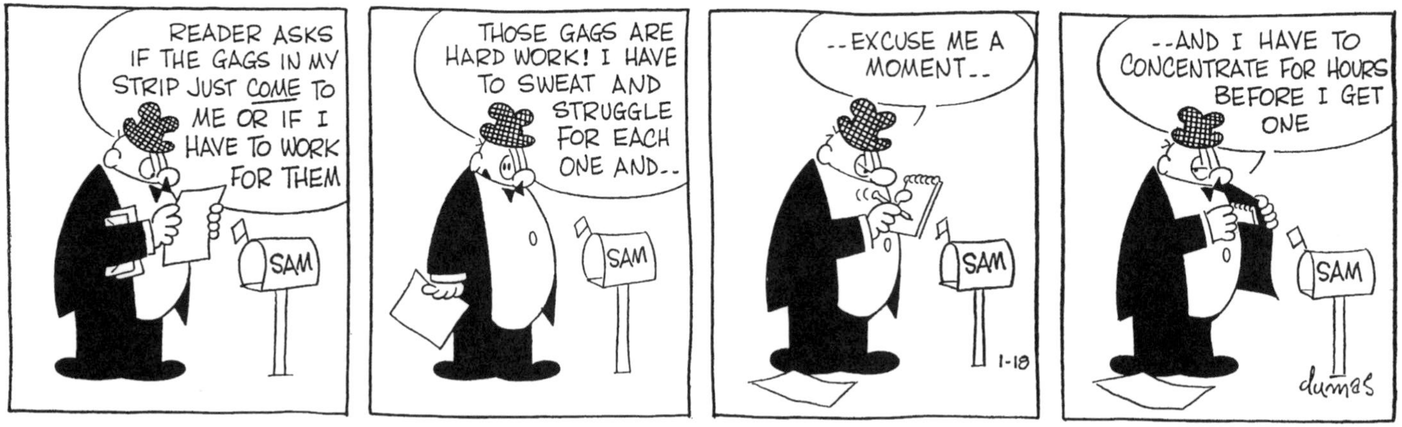
READER ASKS IF THE GAGS IN MY STRIP JUST COME TO ME OR IF I HAVE TO WORK FOR THEM
SAM
THOSE GAGS ARE HARD WORK! I HAVE TO SWEAT AND STRUGGLE FOR EACH ONE AND--
SAM
--EXCUSE ME A MOMENT--
SAM
1-18
--AND I HAVE TO CONCENTRATE FOR HOURS BEFORE I GET ONE
SAM
dumas

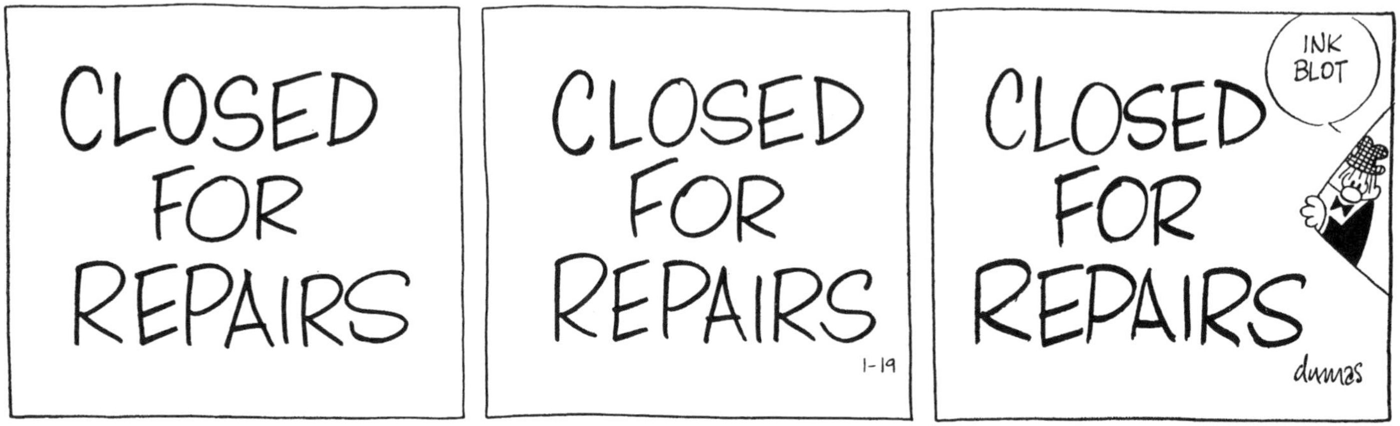
CLOSED FOR REPAIRS
CLOSED FOR REPAIRS
1-19
CLOSED FOR REPAIRS
INK BLOT
dumas

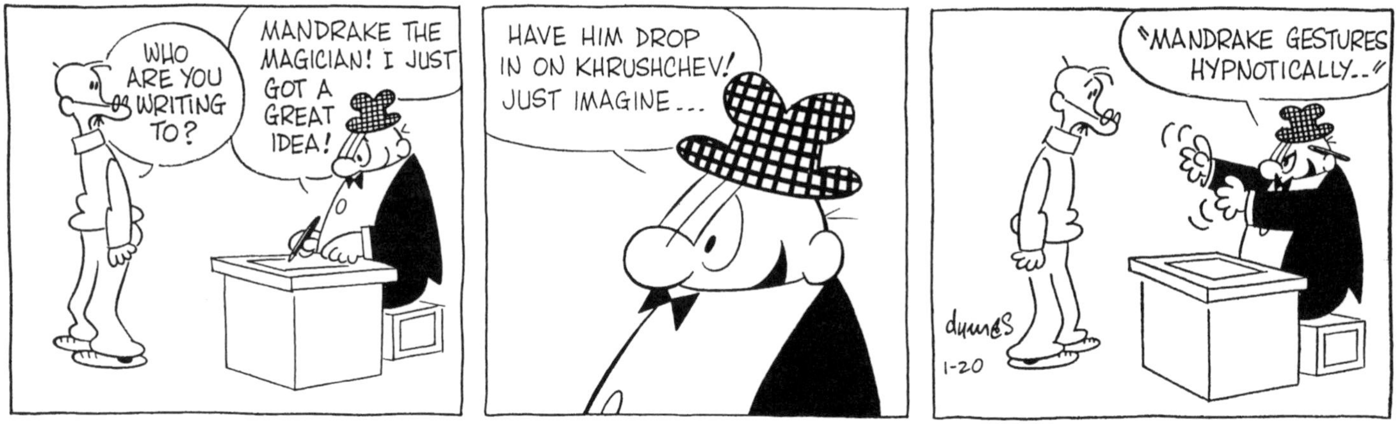
WHO ARE YOU WRITING TO?
MANDRAKE THE MAGICIAN! I JUST GOT A GREAT IDEA!
HAVE HIM DROP IN ON KHRUSHCHEV! JUST IMAGINE...
dumas
1-20
"MANDRAKE GESTURES HYPNOTICALLY--"

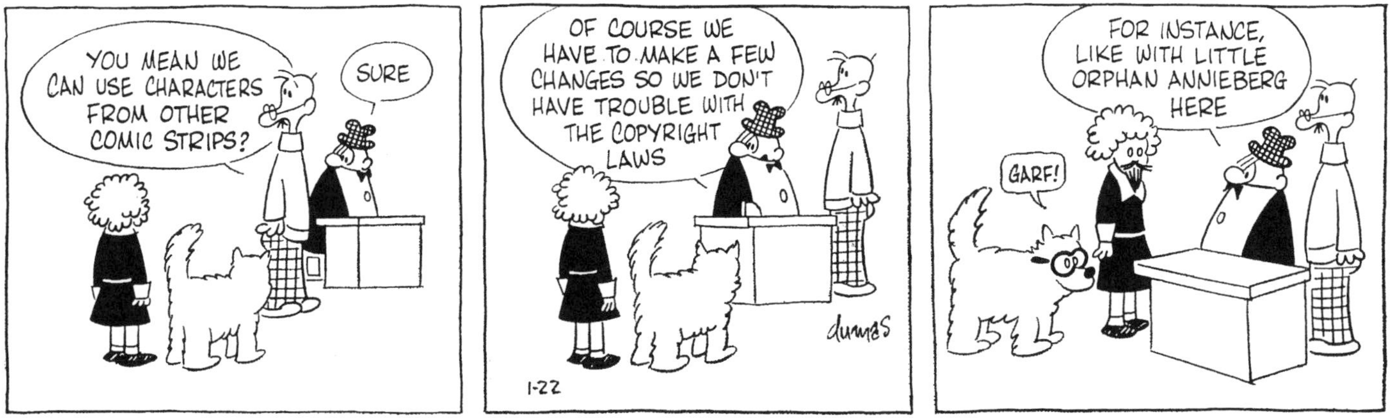
YOU MEAN WE CAN USE CHARACTERS FROM OTHER COMIC STRIPS?
SURE
OF COURSE WE HAVE TO MAKE A FEW CHANGES SO WE DON'T HAVE TROUBLE WITH THE COPYRIGHT LAWS
dumas
1-22
FOR INSTANCE, LIKE WITH LITTLE ORPHAN ANNIEBERG HERE
GARF!

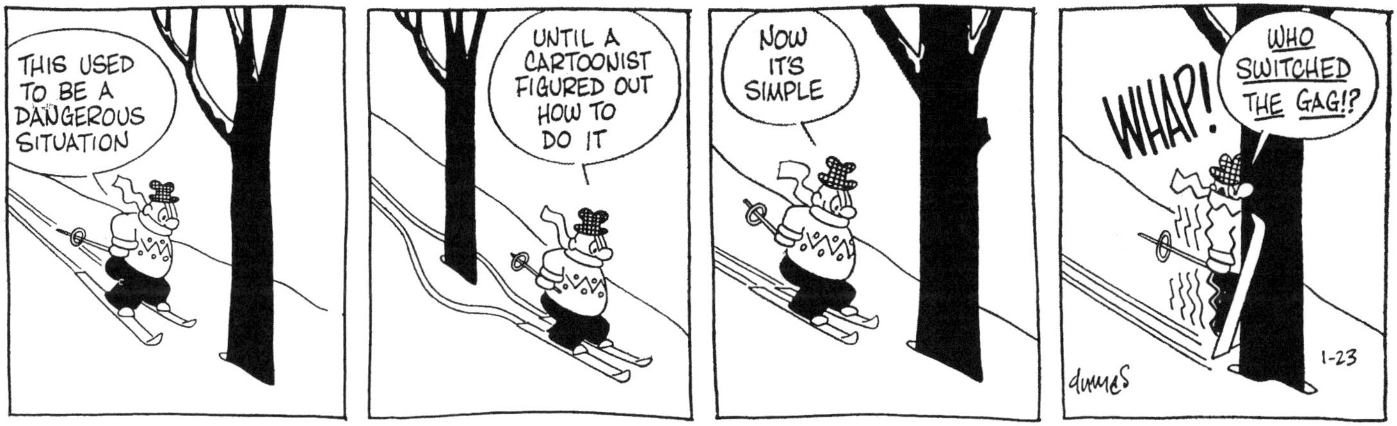
THIS USED TO BE A DANGEROUS SITUATION
UNTIL A CARTOONIST FIGURED OUT HOW TO DO IT
NOW IT'S SIMPLE
WHAP!
WHO SWITCHED THE GAG!?
dumas
1-23

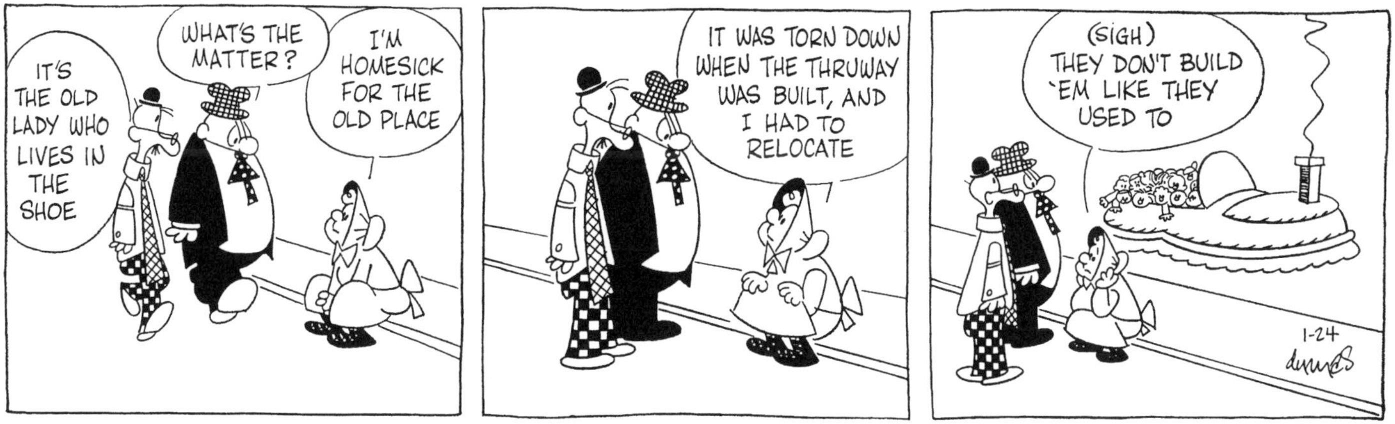
IT'S THE OLD LADY WHO LIVES IN THE SHOE
WHAT'S THE MATTER?
I'M HOMESICK FOR THE OLD PLACE
IT WAS TORN DOWN WHEN THE THRUWAY WAS BUILT, AND I HAD TO RELOCATE
(SIGH) THEY DON'T BUILD 'EM LIKE THEY USED TO
1-24
dumas

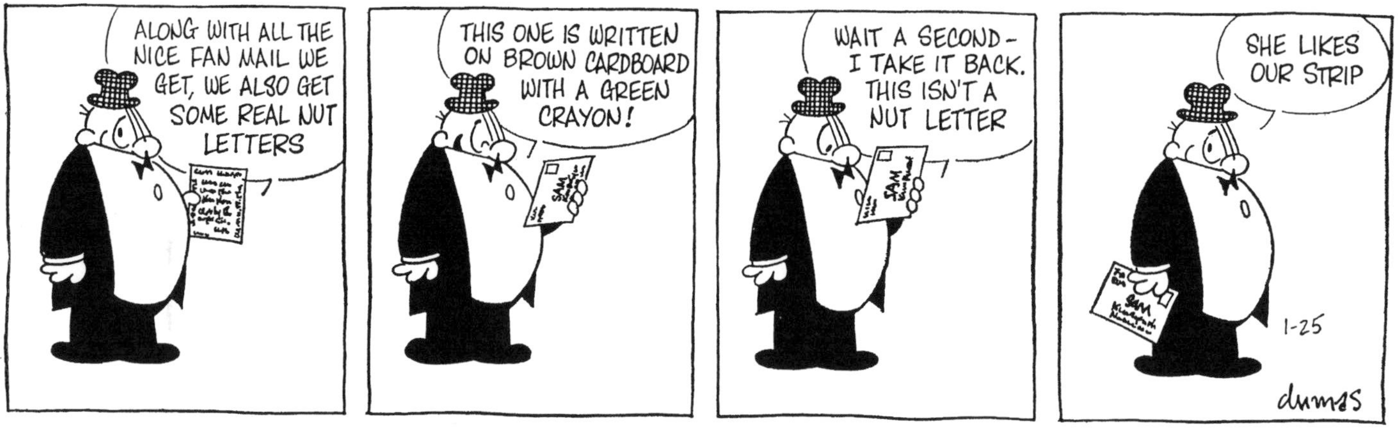
ALONG WITH ALL THE NICE FAN MAIL WE GET, WE ALSO GET SOME REAL NUT LETTERS
THIS ONE IS WRITTEN ON BROWN CARDBOARD WITH A GREEN CRAYON!
WAIT A SECOND - I TAKE IT BACK. THIS ISN'T A NUT LETTER
SHE LIKES OUR STRIP
1-25
dumas

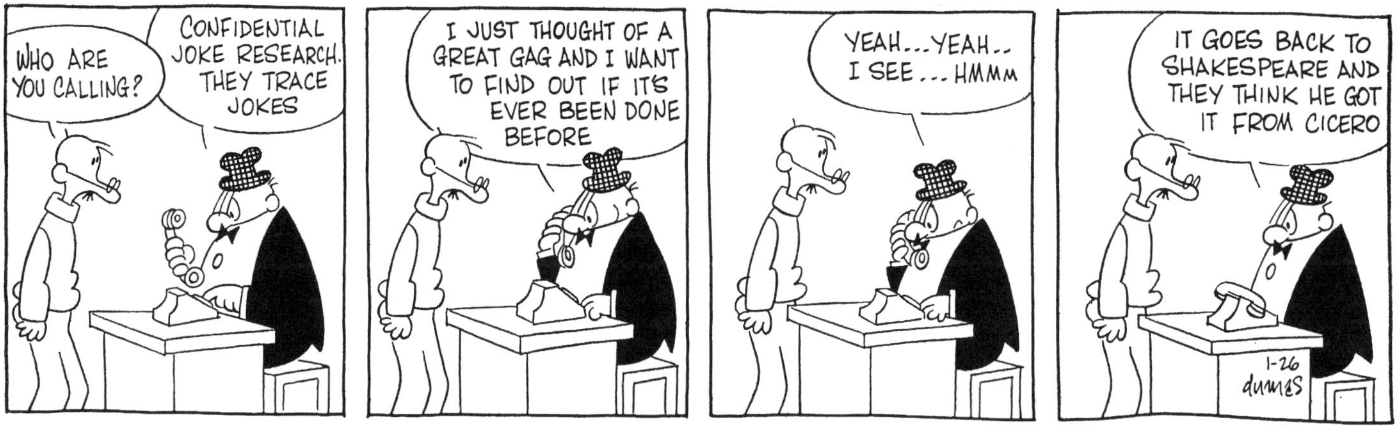
WHO ARE YOU CALLING?
CONFIDENTIAL JOKE RESEARCH. THEY TRACE JOKES
I JUST THOUGHT OF A GREAT GAG AND I WANT TO FIND OUT IF IT'S EVER BEEN DONE BEFORE
YEAH... YEAH.. I SEE... HMMM
IT GOES BACK TO SHAKESPEARE AND THEY THINK HE GOT IT FROM CICERO
1-26
dumas

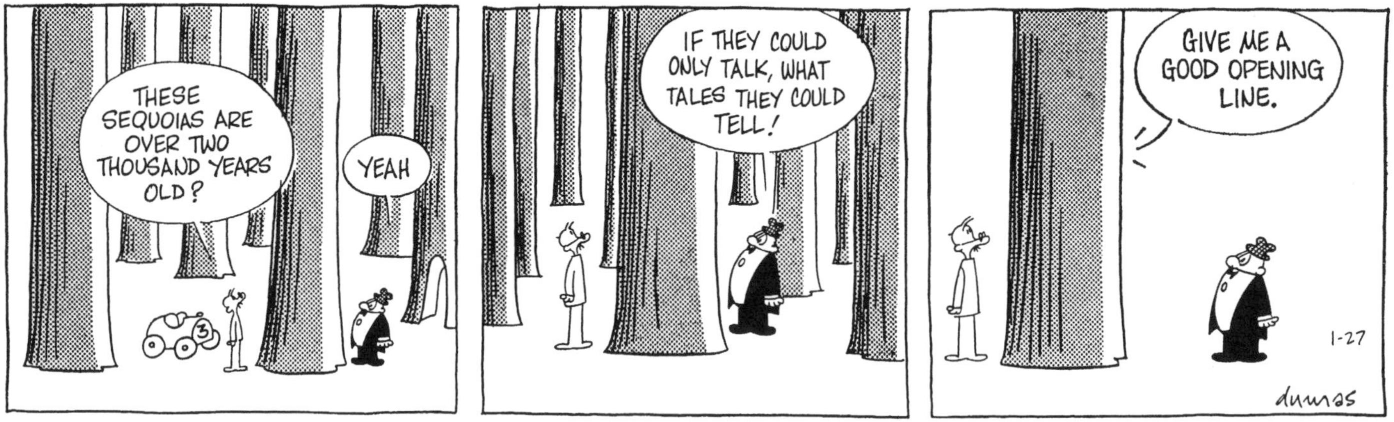
THESE SEQUOIAS ARE OVER TWO THOUSAND YEARS OLD?
YEAH
IF THEY COULD ONLY TALK, WHAT TALES THEY COULD TELL!
GIVE ME A GOOD OPENING LINE.
1-27
dumas

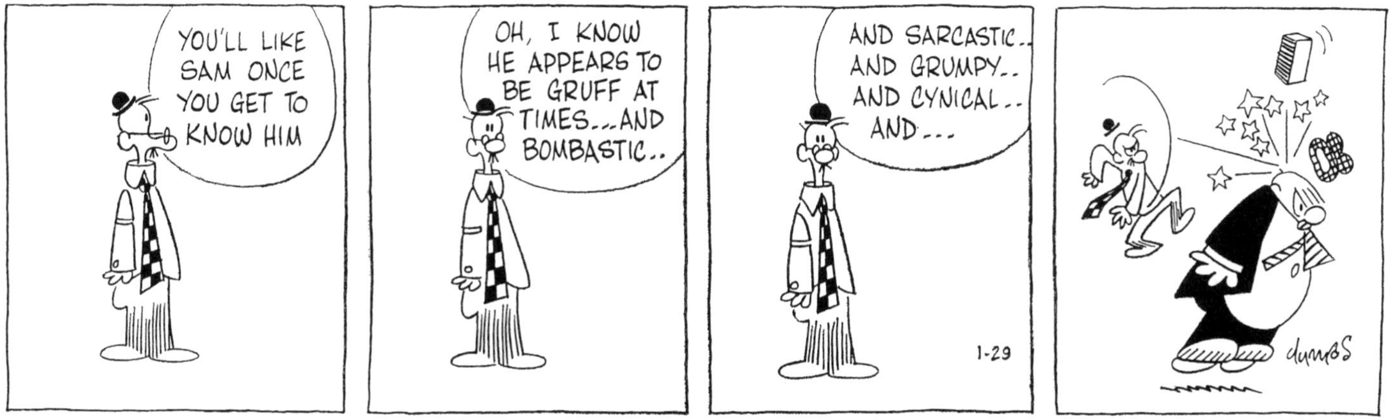
YOU'LL LIKE SAM ONCE YOU GET TO KNOW HIM
OH, I KNOW HE APPEARS TO BE GRUFF AT TIMES...AND BOMBASTIC..
AND SARCASTIC.. AND GRUMPY.. AND CYNICAL.. AND...
1-29
dumas

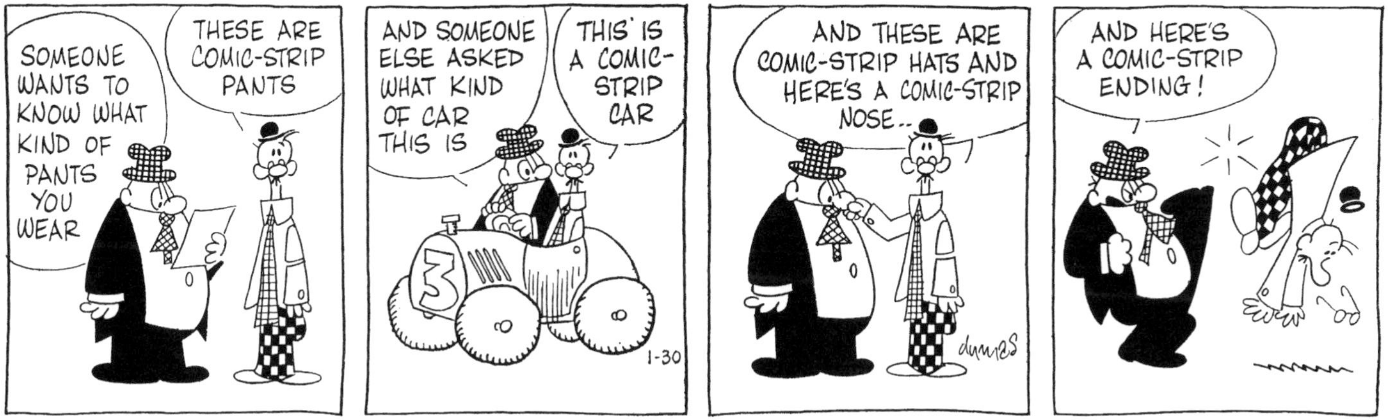
SOMEONE WANTS TO KNOW WHAT KIND OF PANTS YOU WEAR
THESE ARE COMIC-STRIP PANTS
AND SOMEONE ELSE ASKED WHAT KIND OF CAR THIS IS
THIS IS A COMIC-STRIP CAR
3
1-30
AND THESE ARE COMIC-STRIP HATS AND HERE'S A COMIC-STRIP NOSE..
dumas
AND HERE'S A COMIC-STRIP ENDING!

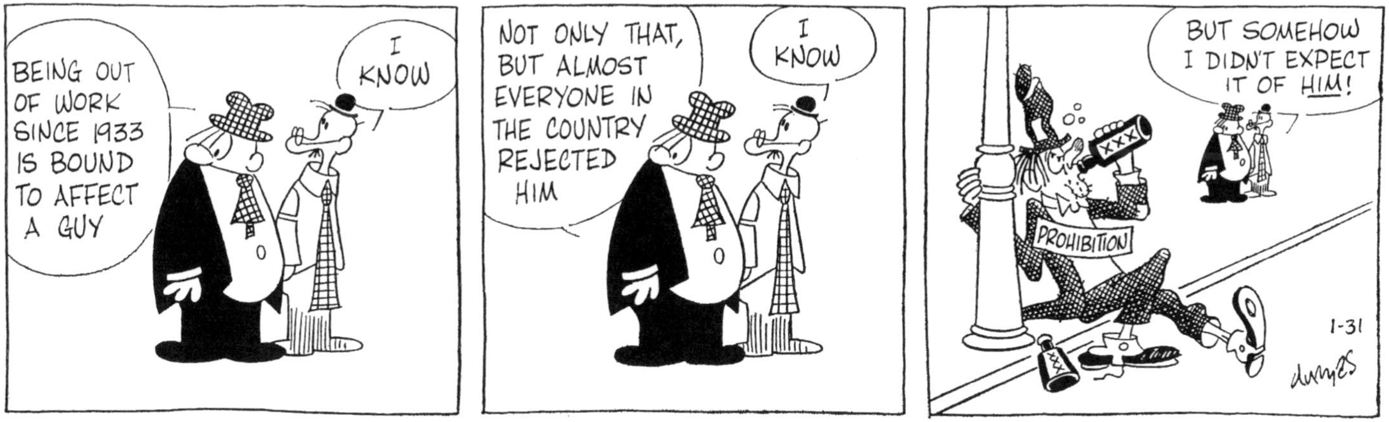
BEING OUT OF WORK SINCE 1933 IS BOUND TO AFFECT A GUY
I KNOW
NOT ONLY THAT, BUT ALMOST EVERYONE IN THE COUNTRY REJECTED HIM
I KNOW
BUT SOMEHOW I DIDN'T EXPECT IT OF HIM!
XXX
PROHIBITION
XXX
1-31
dumas

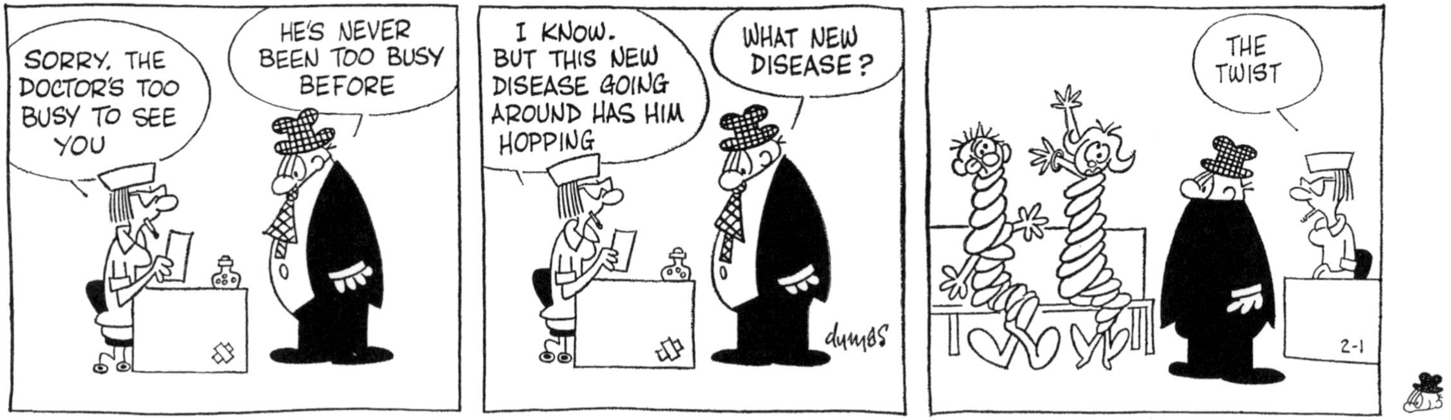
SORRY. THE DOCTOR'S TOO BUSY TO SEE YOU
HE'S NEVER BEEN TOO BUSY BEFORE
I KNOW. BUT THIS NEW DISEASE GOING AROUND HAS HIM HOPPING
WHAT NEW DISEASE?
dumas
THE TWIST
2-1

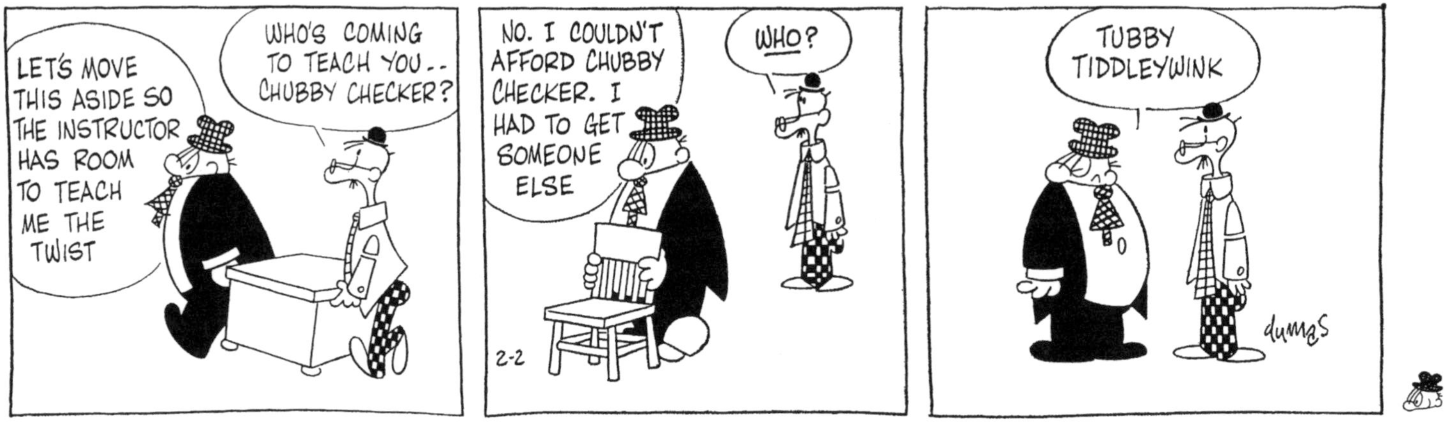
LET'S MOVE THIS ASIDE SO THE INSTRUCTOR HAS ROOM TO TEACH ME THE TWIST
WHO'S COMING TO TEACH YOU.. CHUBBY CHECKER?
NO. I COULDN'T AFFORD CHUBBY CHECKER. I HAD TO GET SOMEONE ELSE
WHO?
2-2
TUBBY TIDDLEYWINK
dumas

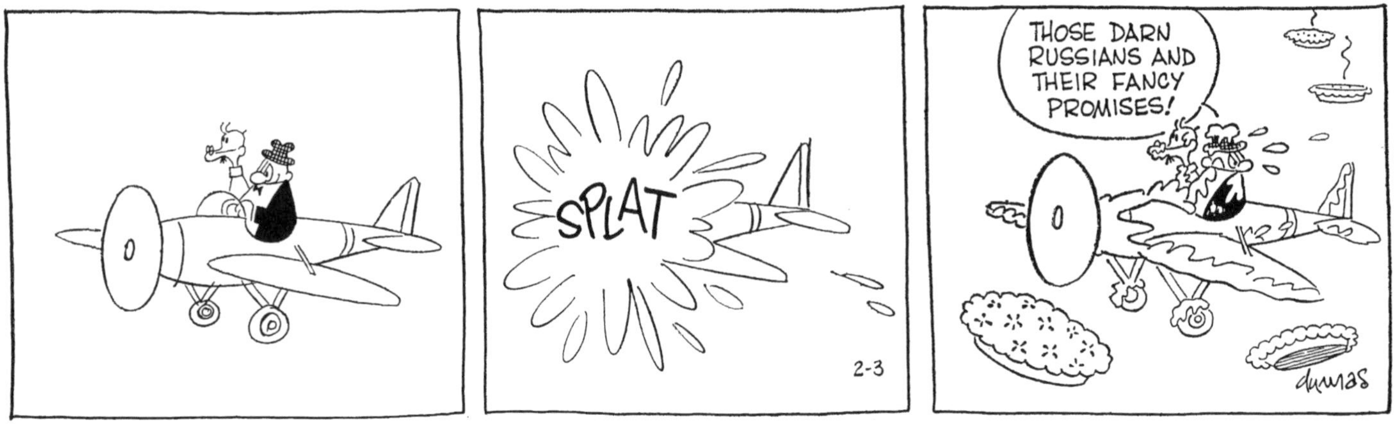
SPLAT
2-3
THOSE DARN RUSSIANS AND THEIR FANCY PROMISES!
dumas

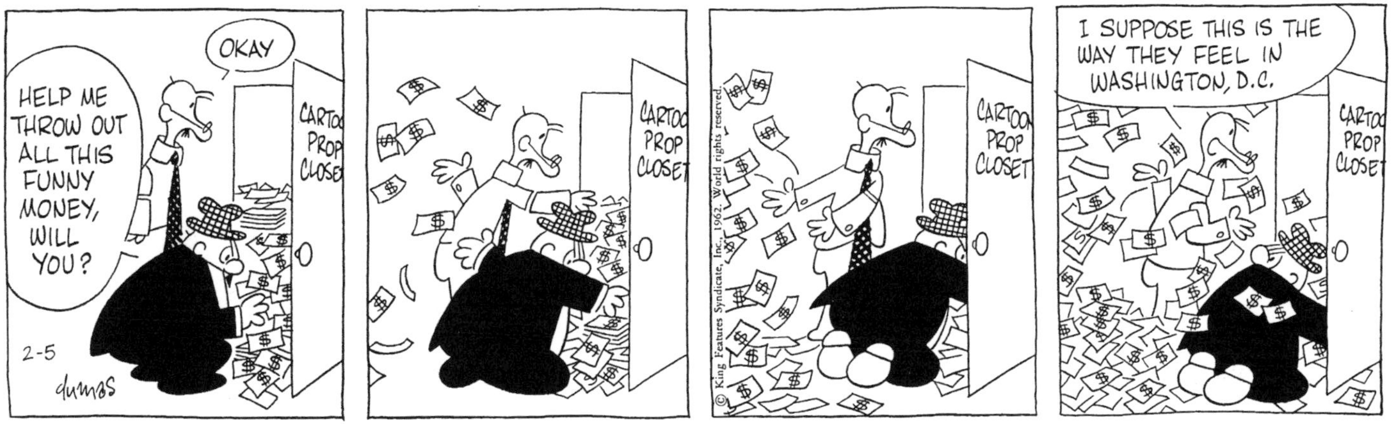
OKAY
HELP ME THROW OUT ALL THIS FUNNY MONEY, WILL YOU?
CARTOON PROP CLOSET
2-5
dumas
© King Features Syndicate, Inc., 1962. World rights reserved.
I SUPPOSE THIS IS THE WAY THEY FEEL IN WASHINGTON, D.C.

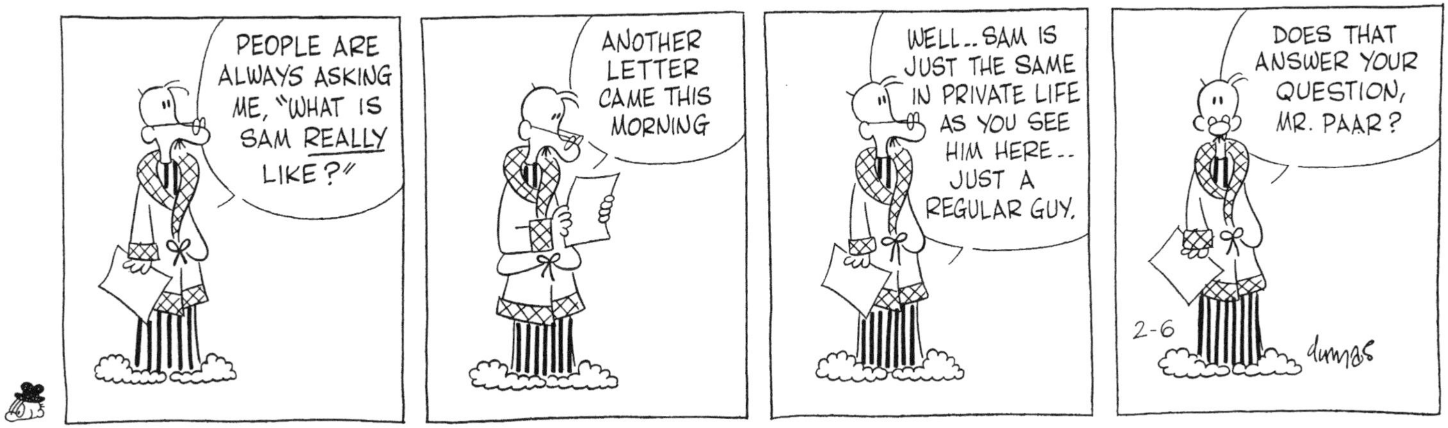
PEOPLE ARE ALWAYS ASKING ME, "WHAT IS SAM REALLY LIKE?"
ANOTHER LETTER CAME THIS MORNING
WELL.. SAM IS JUST THE SAME IN PRIVATE LIFE AS YOU SEE HIM HERE.. JUST A REGULAR GUY.
DOES THAT ANSWER YOUR QUESTION, MR. PAAR?
2-6
dumas

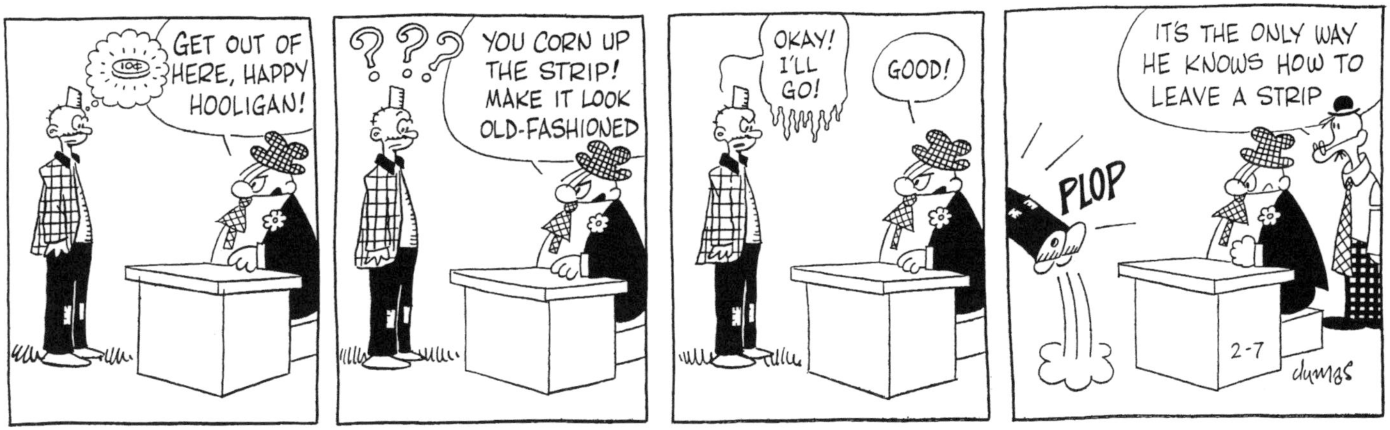
10¢
GET OUT OF HERE, HAPPY HOOLIGAN!
YOU CORN UP THE STRIP! MAKE IT LOOK OLD-FASHIONED
OKAY! I'LL GO!
GOOD!
PLOP
IT'S THE ONLY WAY HE KNOWS HOW TO LEAVE A STRIP
2-7
dumas

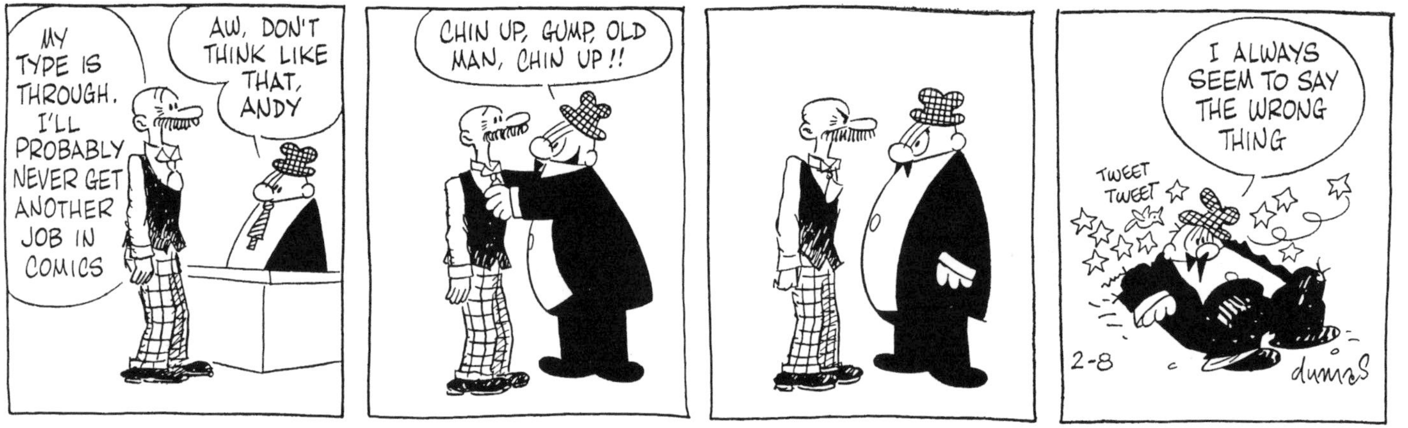
MY TYPE IS THROUGH. I'LL PROBABLY NEVER GET ANOTHER JOB IN COMICS
AW, DON'T THINK LIKE THAT, ANDY
CHIN UP, GUMP, OLD MAN, CHIN UP!!
I ALWAYS SEEM TO SAY THE WRONG THING
TWEET TWEET
2-8
dumas

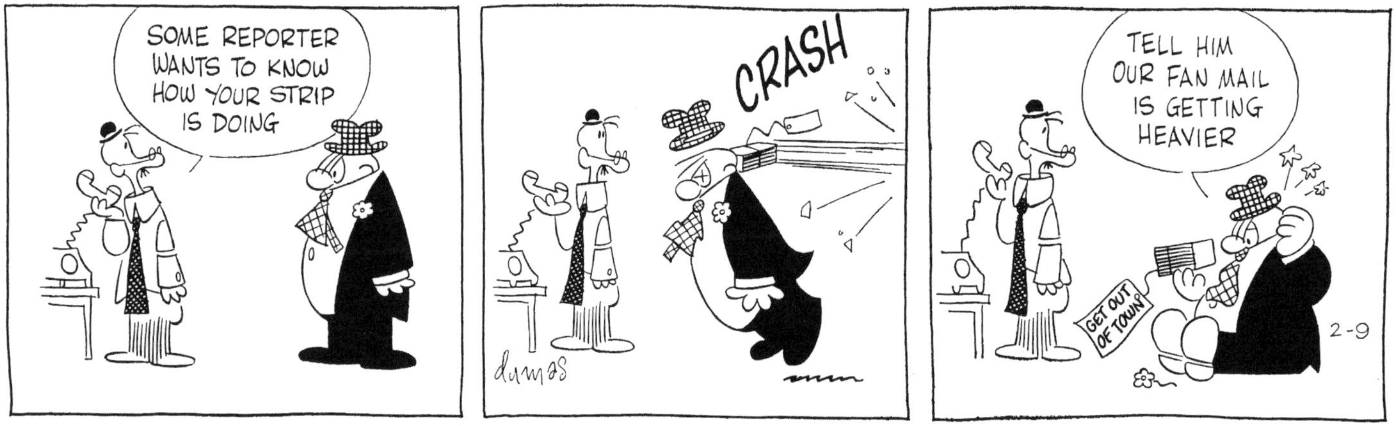
SOME REPORTER WANTS TO KNOW HOW YOUR STRIP IS DOING
CRASH
dumas
TELL HIM OUR FAN MAIL IS GETTING HEAVIER
GET OUT OF TOWN
2-9

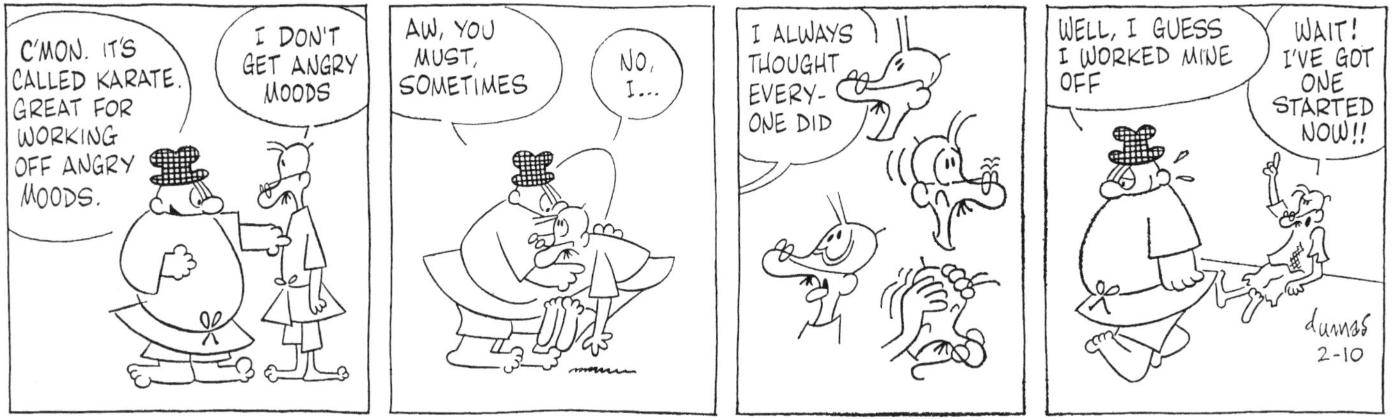
C'MON. IT'S CALLED KARATE. GREAT FOR WORKING OFF ANGRY MOODS.
I DON'T GET ANGRY MOODS
AW, YOU MUST, SOMETIMES
NO, I...
I ALWAYS THOUGHT EVERY-ONE DID
WELL, I GUESS I WORKED MINE OFF
WAIT! I'VE GOT ONE STARTED NOW!!
dumas
2-10

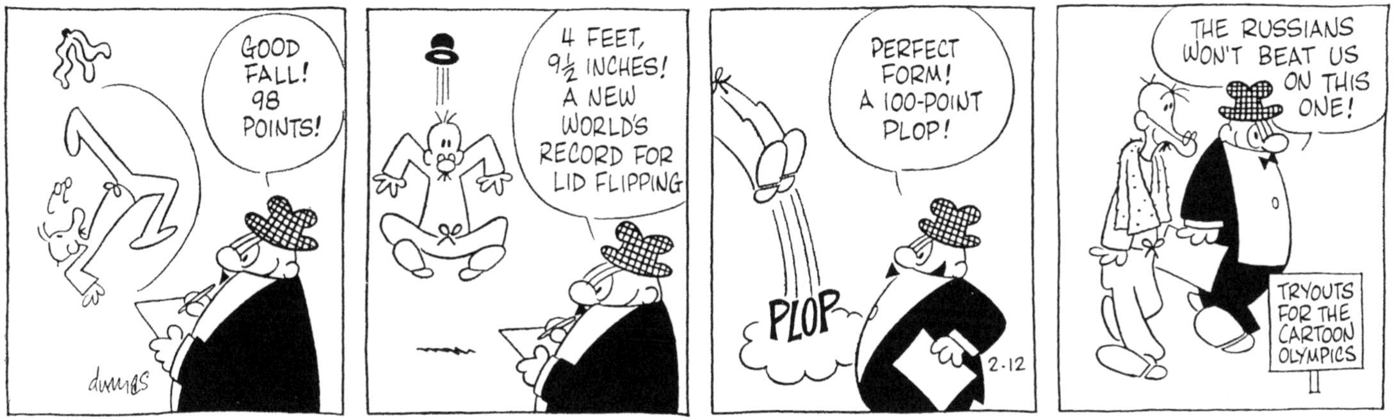
GOOD FALL! 98 POINTS!
4 FEET, 9½ INCHES! A NEW WORLD'S RECORD FOR LID FLIPPING
PERFECT FORM! A 100-POINT PLOP!
PLOP
2-12
THE RUSSIANS WON'T BEAT US ON THIS ONE!
TRYOUTS FOR THE CARTOON OLYMPICS

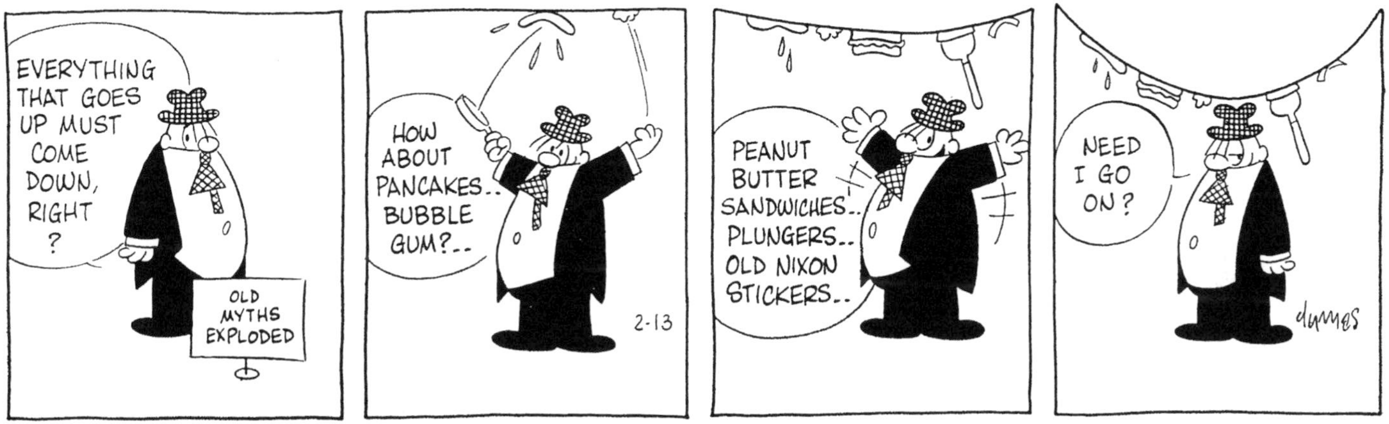
EVERYTHING THAT GOES UP MUST COME DOWN, RIGHT ?
OLD MYTHS EXPLODED
HOW ABOUT PANCAKES.. BUBBLE GUM?..
2-13
PEANUT BUTTER SANDWICHES.. PLUNGERS.. OLD NIXON STICKERS..
NEED I GO ON ?

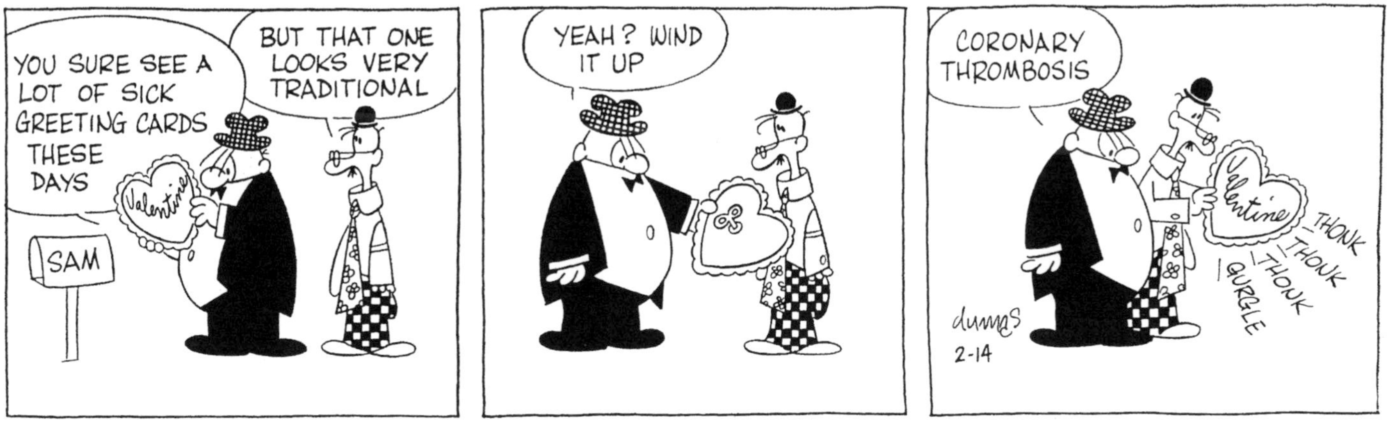
YOU SURE SEE A LOT OF SICK GREETING CARDS THESE DAYS
BUT THAT ONE LOOKS VERY TRADITIONAL
Valentine
SAM
YEAH? WIND IT UP
CORONARY THROMBOSIS
Valentine
THONK
THONK
THONK
GURGLE
2-14

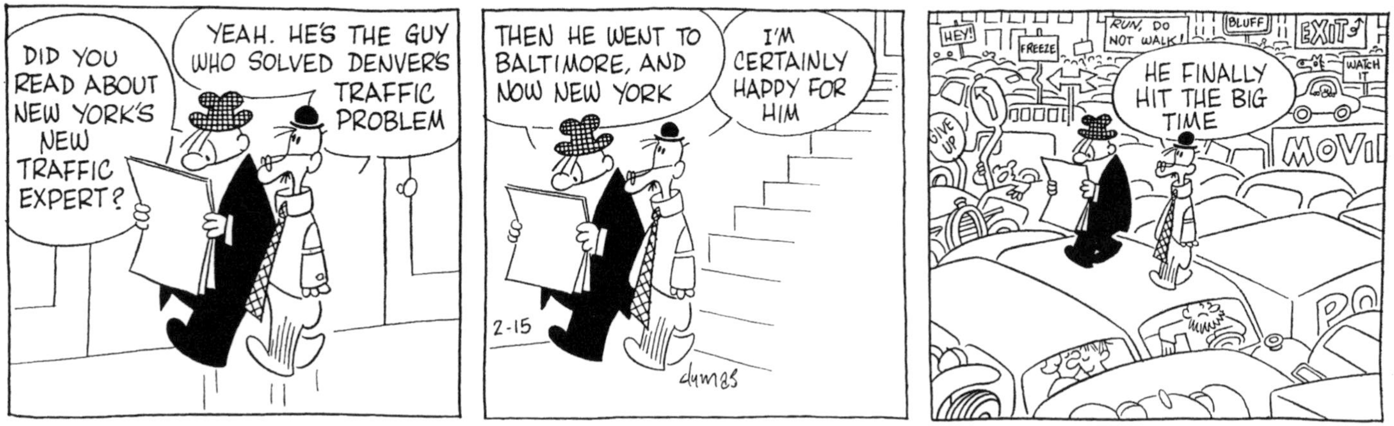
DID YOU READ ABOUT NEW YORK'S NEW TRAFFIC EXPERT?
YEAH. HE'S THE GUY WHO SOLVED DENVER'S TRAFFIC PROBLEM
THEN HE WENT TO BALTIMORE, AND NOW NEW YORK
I'M CERTAINLY HAPPY FOR HIM
2-15
dumas
HEY!
FREEZE
RUN, DO NOT WALK!
BLUFF
EXIT
WATCH IT
GIVE UP
HE FINALLY HIT THE BIG TIME
MOVI
PO

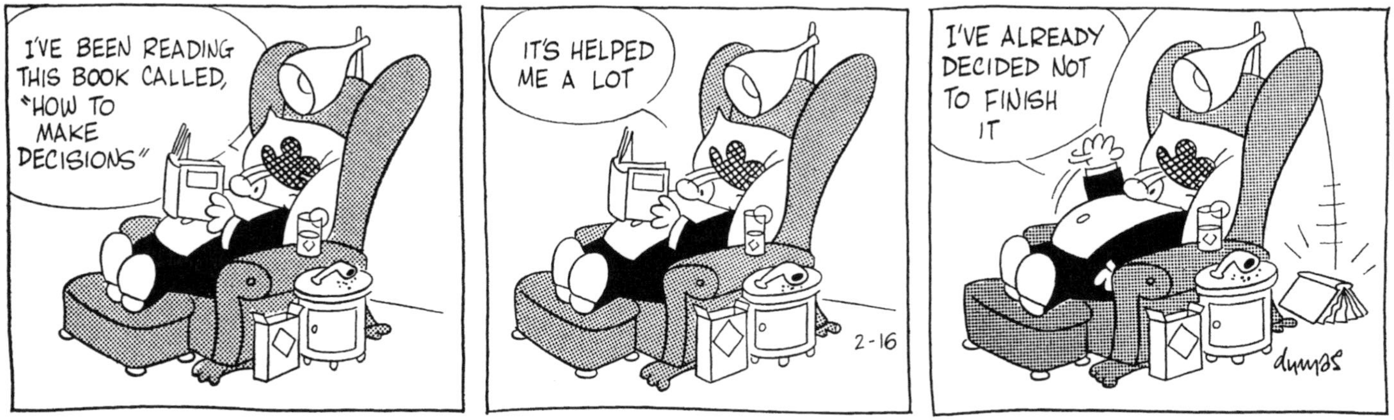
I'VE BEEN READING THIS BOOK CALLED, "HOW TO MAKE DECISIONS"
IT'S HELPED ME A LOT
2-16
I'VE ALREADY DECIDED NOT TO FINISH IT
dumas

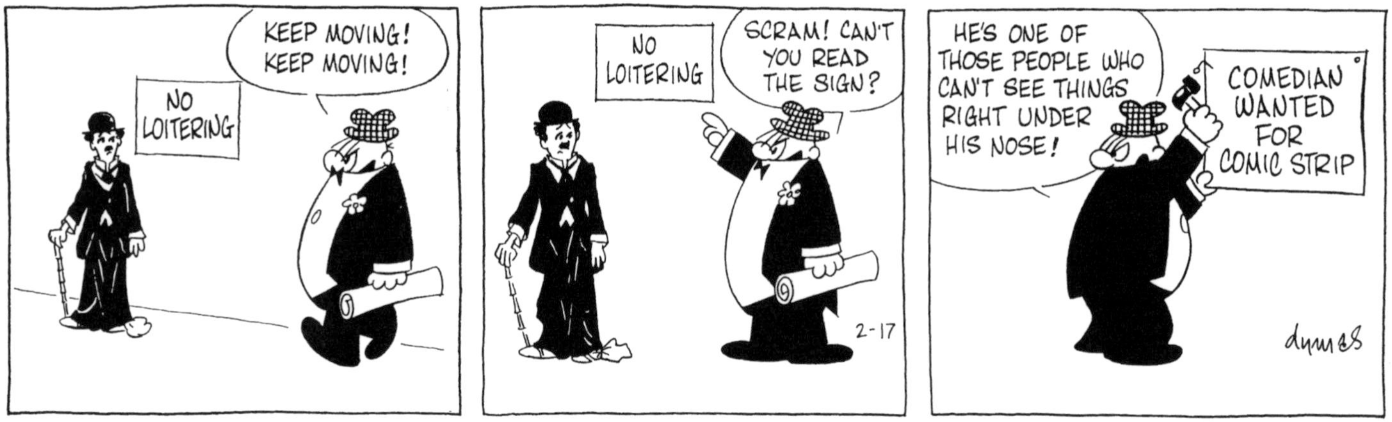
NO LOITERING
KEEP MOVING! KEEP MOVING!
NO LOITERING
SCRAM! CAN'T YOU READ THE SIGN?
2-17
HE'S ONE OF THOSE PEOPLE WHO CAN'T SEE THINGS RIGHT UNDER HIS NOSE!
COMEDIAN WANTED FOR COMIC STRIP
dumas

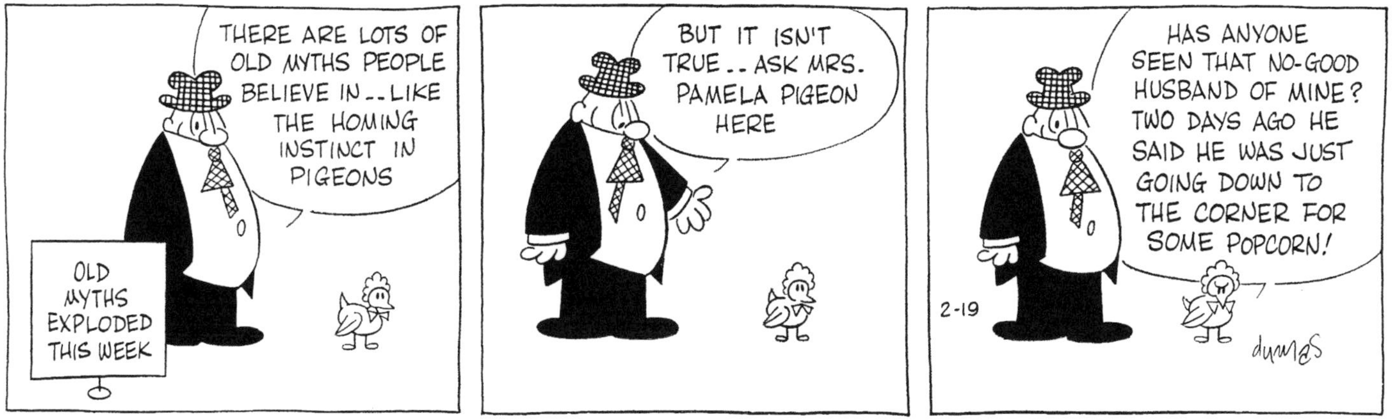
THERE ARE LOTS OF OLD MYTHS PEOPLE BELIEVE IN..LIKE THE HOMING INSTINCT IN PIGEONS
OLD MYTHS EXPLODED THIS WEEK
BUT IT ISN'T TRUE.. ASK MRS. PAMELA PIGEON HERE
HAS ANYONE SEEN THAT NO-GOOD HUSBAND OF MINE? TWO DAYS AGO HE SAID HE WAS JUST GOING DOWN TO THE CORNER FOR SOME POPCORN!
2-19
dumas

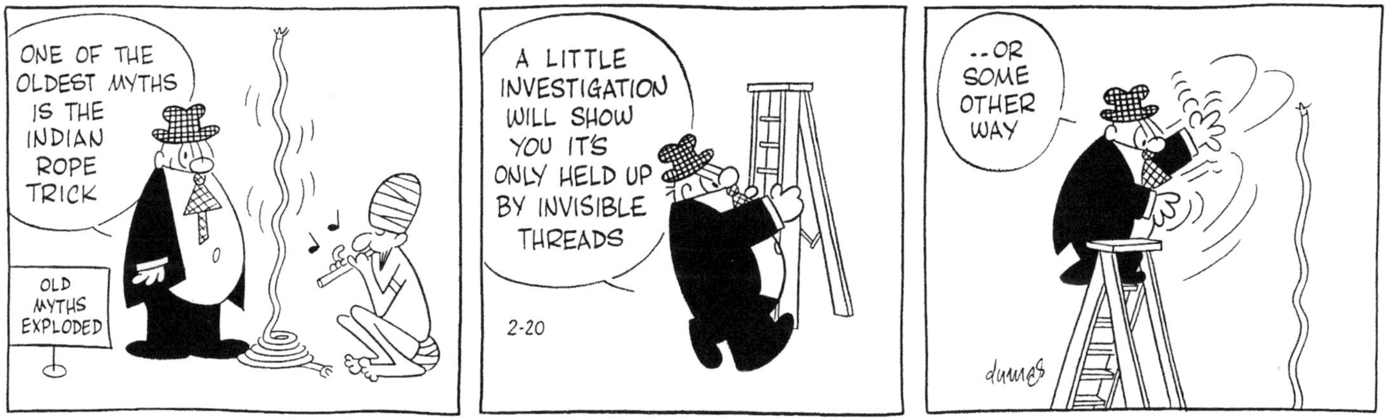
ONE OF THE OLDEST MYTHS IS THE INDIAN ROPE TRICK
OLD MYTHS EXPLODED
A LITTLE INVESTIGATION WILL SHOW YOU IT'S ONLY HELD UP BY INVISIBLE THREADS
2-20
..OR SOME OTHER WAY
dumas

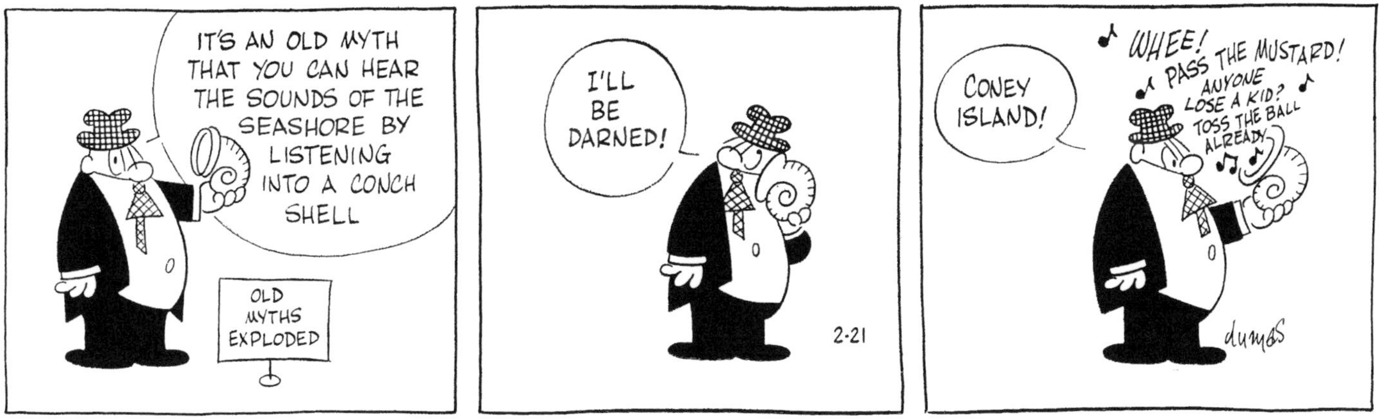
IT'S AN OLD MYTH THAT YOU CAN HEAR THE SOUNDS OF THE SEASHORE BY LISTENING INTO A CONCH SHELL
OLD MYTHS EXPLODED
I'LL BE DARNED!
2-21
CONEY ISLAND!
WHEE! PASS THE MUSTARD! ANYONE LOSE A KID? TOSS THE BALL ALREADY
dumas

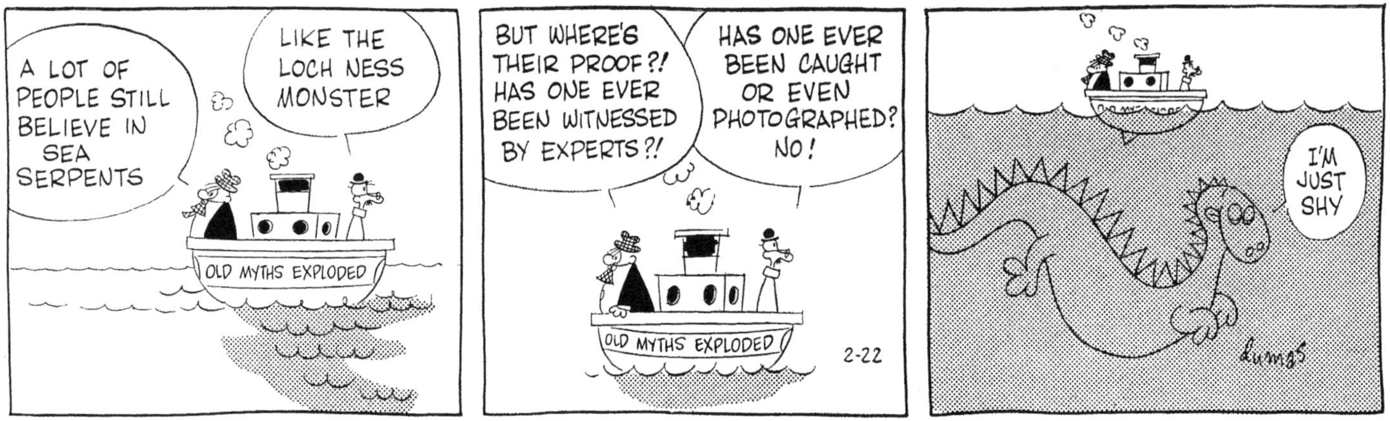
A LOT OF PEOPLE STILL BELIEVE IN SEA SERPENTS
LIKE THE LOCH NESS MONSTER
OLD MYTHS EXPLODED
BUT WHERE'S THEIR PROOF?! HAS ONE EVER BEEN WITNESSED BY EXPERTS?!
HAS ONE EVER BEEN CAUGHT OR EVEN PHOTOGRAPHED? NO!
OLD MYTHS EXPLODED
2-22
I'M JUST SHY
dumas

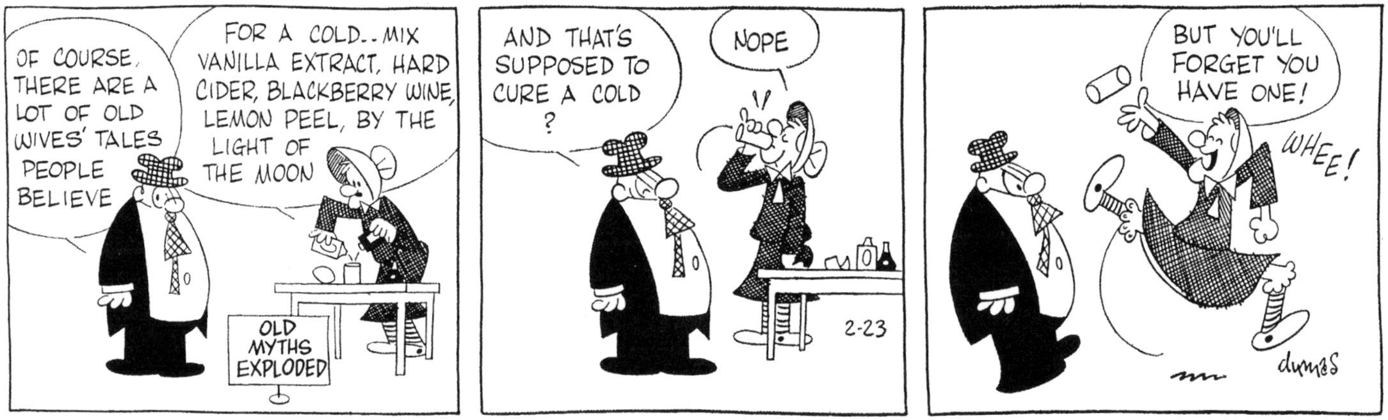
OF COURSE, THERE ARE A LOT OF OLD WIVES' TALES PEOPLE BELIEVE
FOR A COLD..MIX VANILLA EXTRACT, HARD CIDER, BLACKBERRY WINE, LEMON PEEL, BY THE LIGHT OF THE MOON
OLD MYTHS EXPLODED
AND THAT'S SUPPOSED TO CURE A COLD ?
NOPE
2-23
BUT YOU'LL FORGET YOU HAVE ONE!
WHEE!
dumas

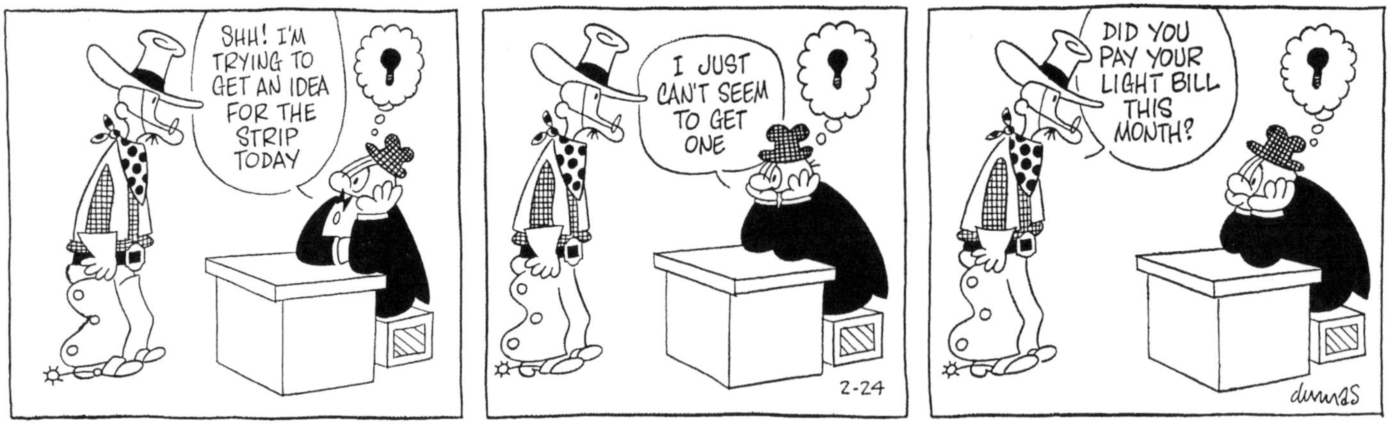
SHH! I'M TRYING TO GET AN IDEA FOR THE STRIP TODAY
I JUST CAN'T SEEM TO GET ONE
2-24
DID YOU PAY YOUR LIGHT BILL THIS MONTH?
dumas

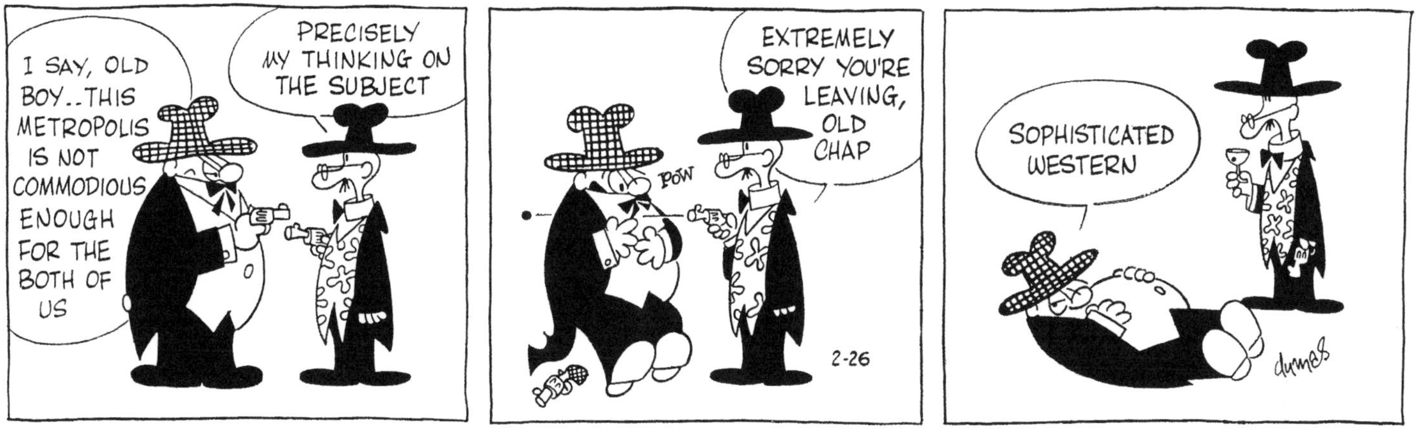
I SAY, OLD BOY..THIS METROPOLIS IS NOT COMMODIOUS ENOUGH FOR THE BOTH OF US
PRECISELY MY THINKING ON THE SUBJECT
POW
EXTREMELY SORRY YOU'RE LEAVING, OLD CHAP
2-26
SOPHISTICATED WESTERN
dumas

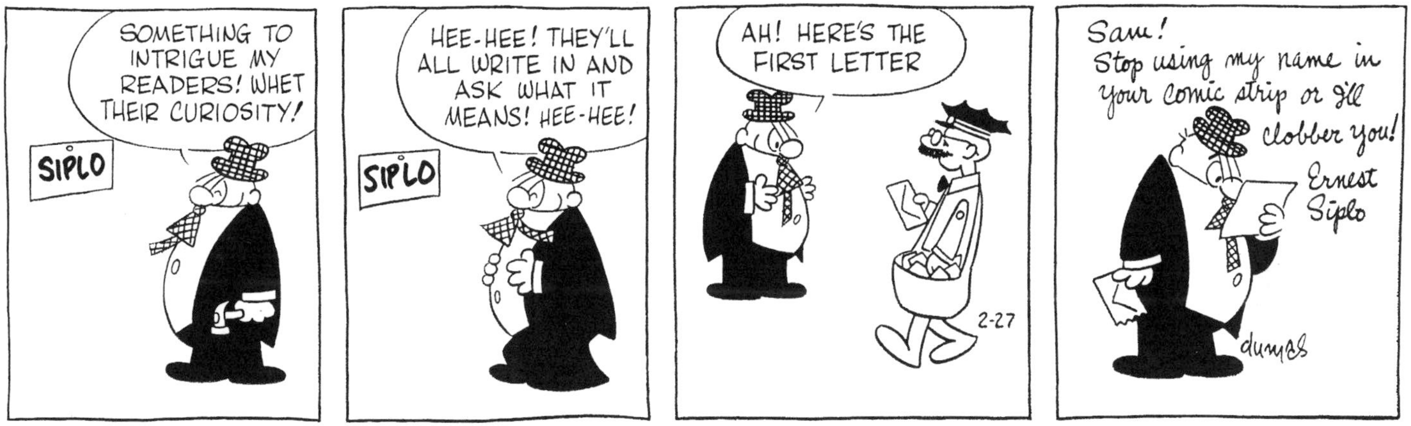
SOMETHING TO INTRIGUE MY READERS! WHET THEIR CURIOSITY!
SIPLO
HEE-HEE! THEY'LL ALL WRITE IN AND ASK WHAT IT MEANS! HEE-HEE!
SIPLO
AH! HERE'S THE FIRST LETTER
2-27
Sam! Stop using my name in your comic strip or I'll clobber you! Ernest Siplo
dumas

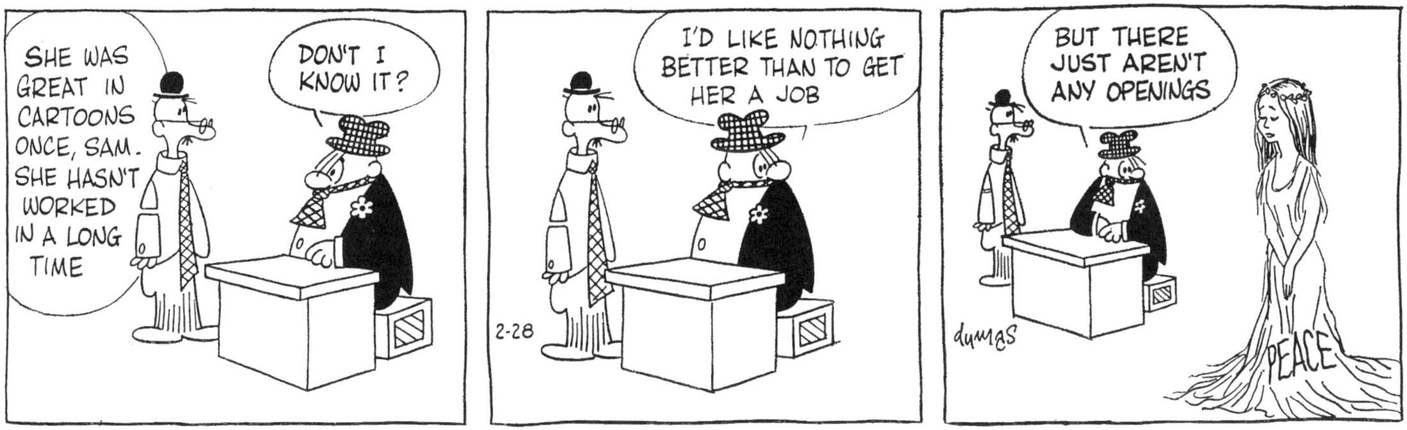
SHE WAS GREAT IN CARTOONS ONCE, SAM. SHE HASN'T WORKED IN A LONG TIME
DON'T I KNOW IT?
I'D LIKE NOTHING BETTER THAN TO GET HER A JOB
2-28
BUT THERE JUST AREN'T ANY OPENINGS
PEACE
dumas

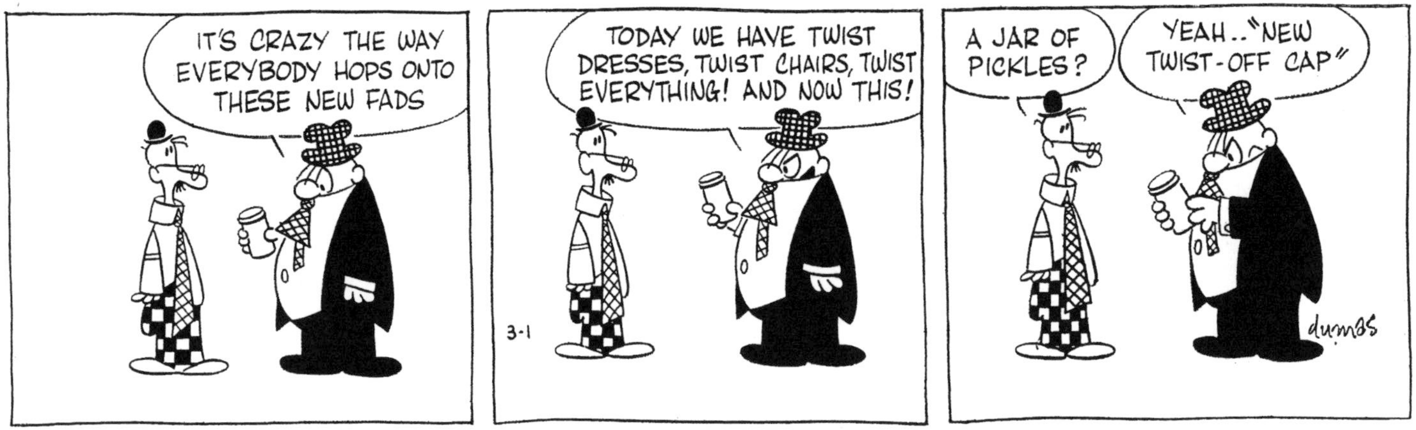
IT'S CRAZY THE WAY EVERYBODY HOPS ONTO THESE NEW FADS
TODAY WE HAVE TWIST DRESSES, TWIST CHAIRS, TWIST EVERYTHING! AND NOW THIS!
3-1
A JAR OF PICKLES?
YEAH.."NEW TWIST-OFF CAP"
dumas

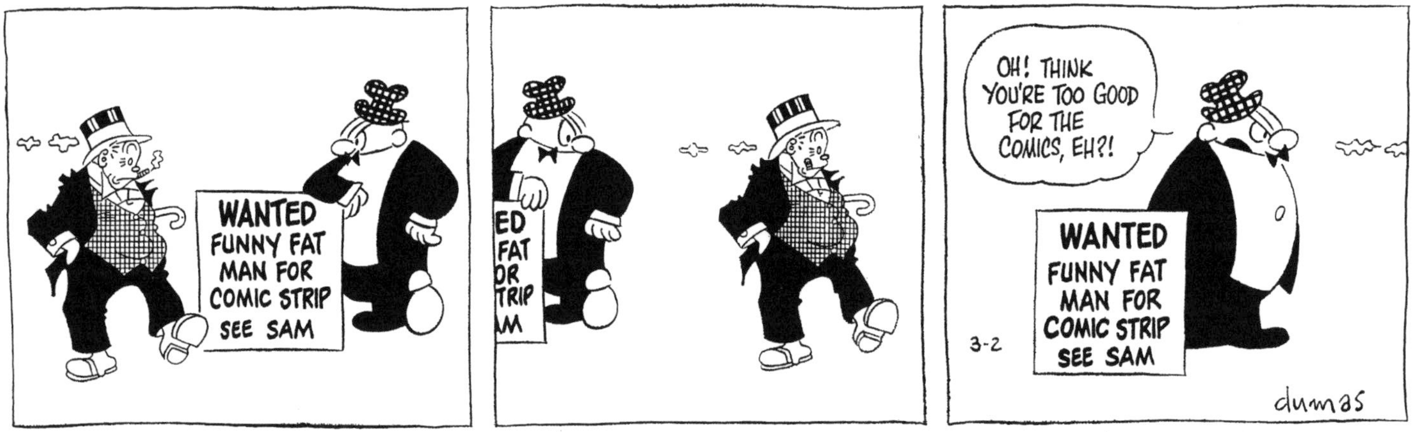
WANTED FUNNY FAT MAN FOR COMIC STRIP SEE SAM
OH! THINK YOU'RE TOO GOOD FOR THE COMICS, EH?!
WANTED FUNNY FAT MAN FOR COMIC STRIP SEE SAM
3-2
dumas

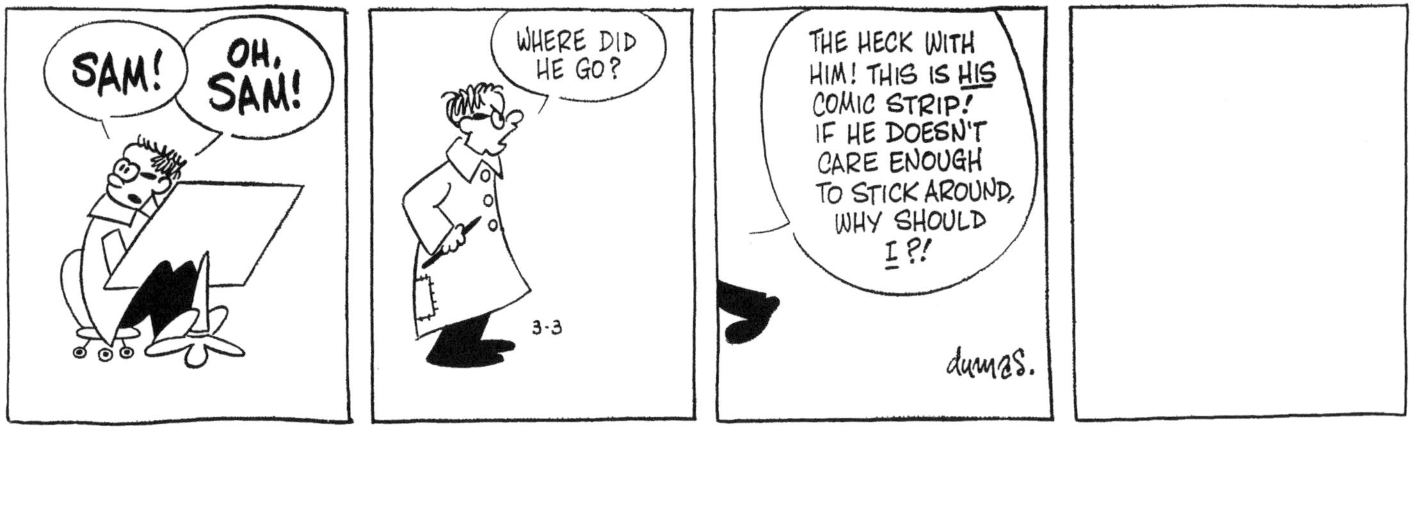
SAM!
OH, SAM!
WHERE DID HE GO?
3-3
THE HECK WITH HIM! THIS IS HIS COMIC STRIP! IF HE DOESN'T CARE ENOUGH TO STICK AROUND, WHY SHOULD I?!
dumas.

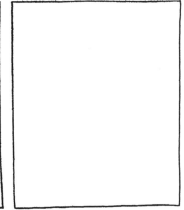

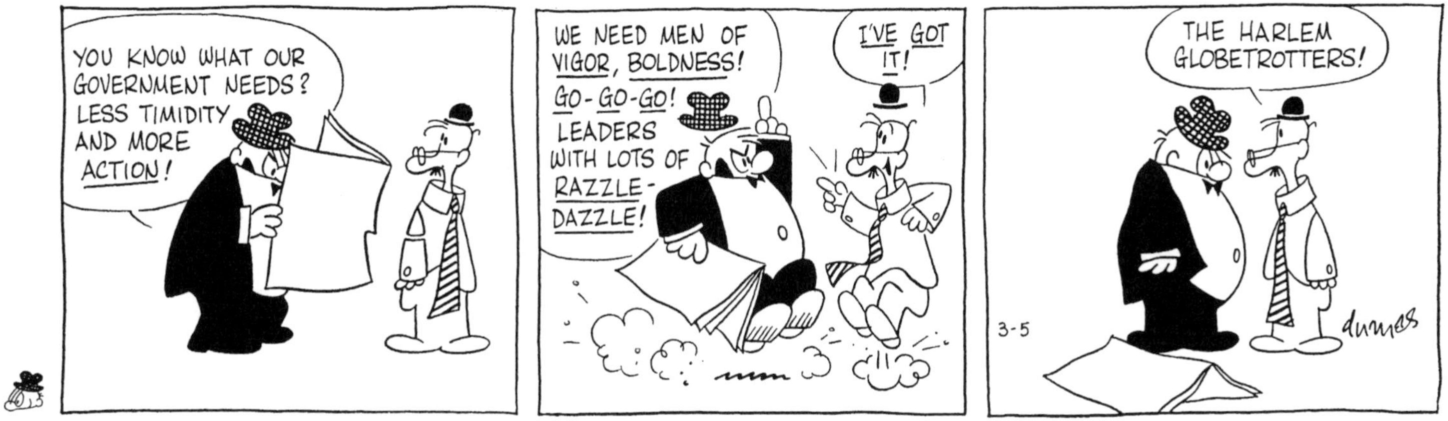
YOU KNOW WHAT OUR GOVERNMENT NEEDS? LESS TIMIDITY AND MORE ACTION!
WE NEED MEN OF VIGOR, BOLDNESS! GO-GO-GO! LEADERS WITH LOTS OF RAZZLE-DAZZLE!
I'VE GOT IT!
THE HARLEM GLOBETROTTERS!
3-5

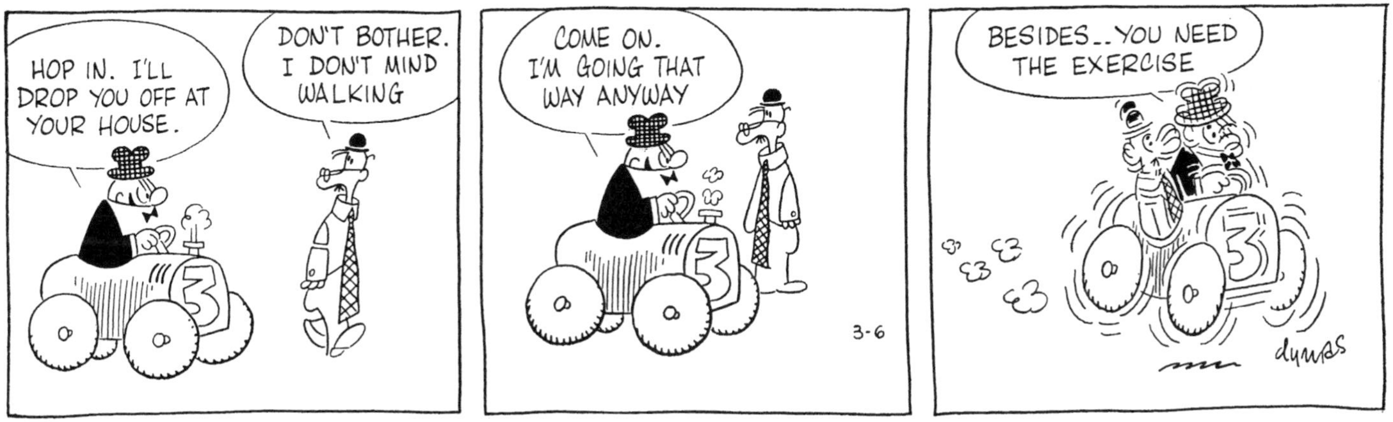
HOP IN. I'LL DROP YOU OFF AT YOUR HOUSE.
DON'T BOTHER. I DON'T MIND WALKING
COME ON. I'M GOING THAT WAY ANYWAY
3-6
BESIDES..YOU NEED THE EXERCISE

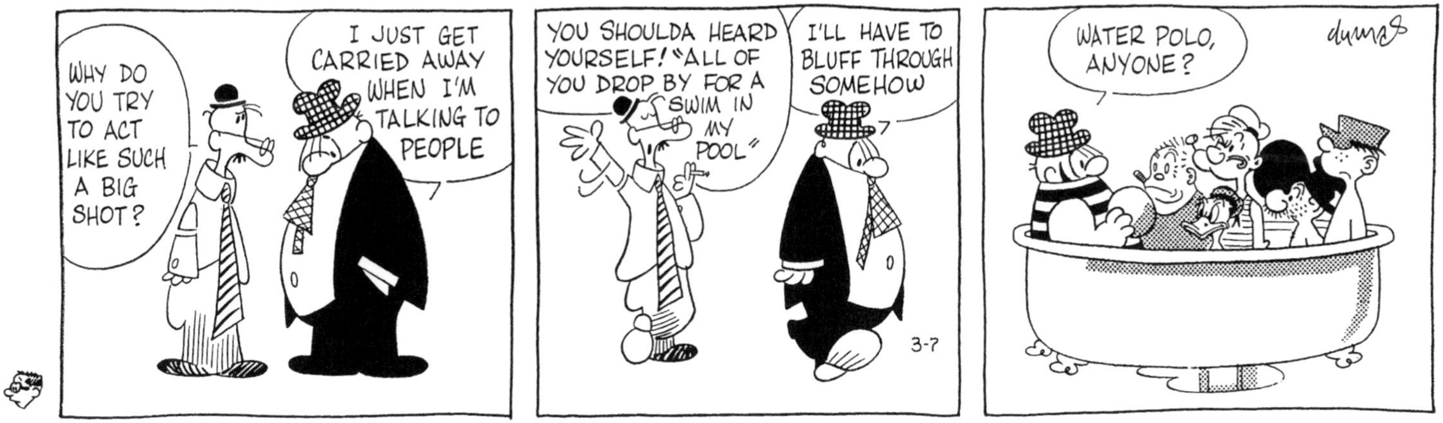
WHY DO YOU TRY TO ACT LIKE SUCH A BIG SHOT?
I JUST GET CARRIED AWAY WHEN I'M TALKING TO PEOPLE
YOU SHOULDA HEARD YOURSELF! "ALL OF YOU DROP BY FOR A SWIM IN MY POOL"
I'LL HAVE TO BLUFF THROUGH SOMEHOW
3-7
WATER POLO, ANYONE?

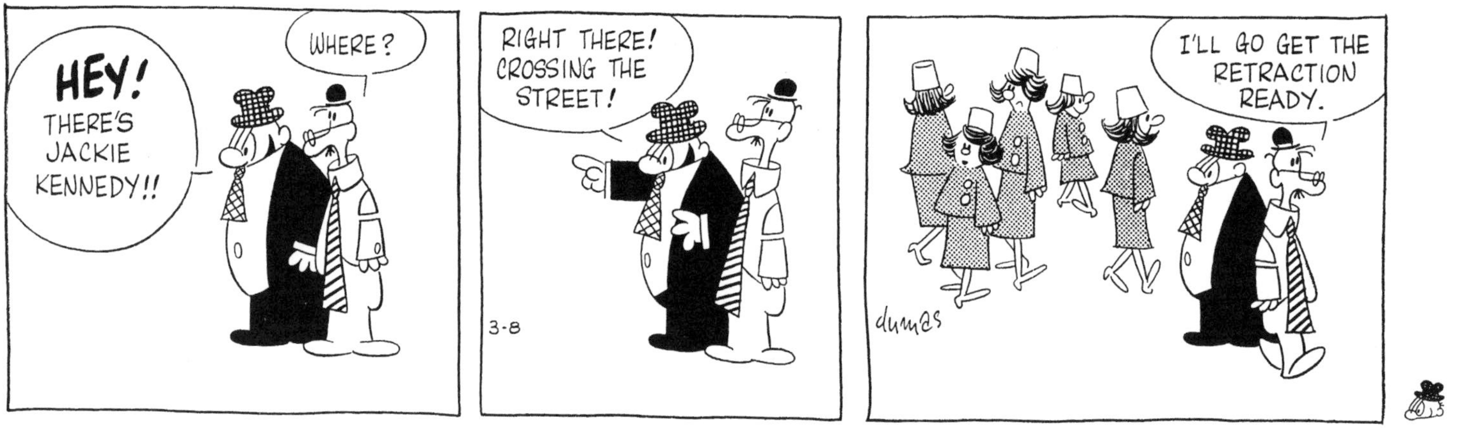
HEY! THERE'S JACKIE KENNEDY!!
WHERE?
RIGHT THERE! CROSSING THE STREET!
3-8
I'LL GO GET THE RETRACTION READY.
dumas

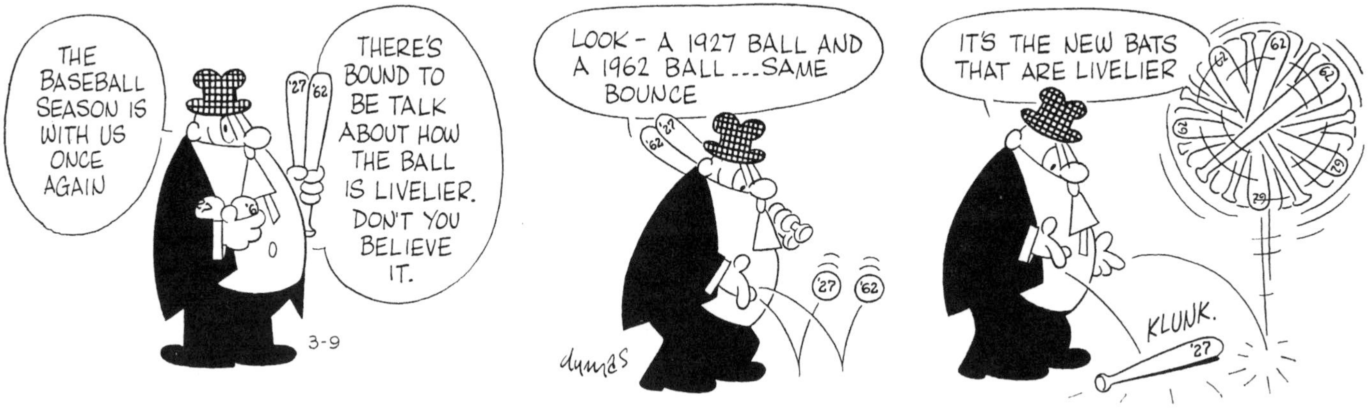
THE BASEBALL SEASON IS WITH US ONCE AGAIN
'27 '62
THERE'S BOUND TO BE TALK ABOUT HOW THE BALL IS LIVELIER. DON'T YOU BELIEVE IT.
3-9
LOOK - A 1927 BALL AND A 1962 BALL ... SAME BOUNCE
'27 '62
dumas
IT'S THE NEW BATS THAT ARE LIVELIER
KLUNK.
'27

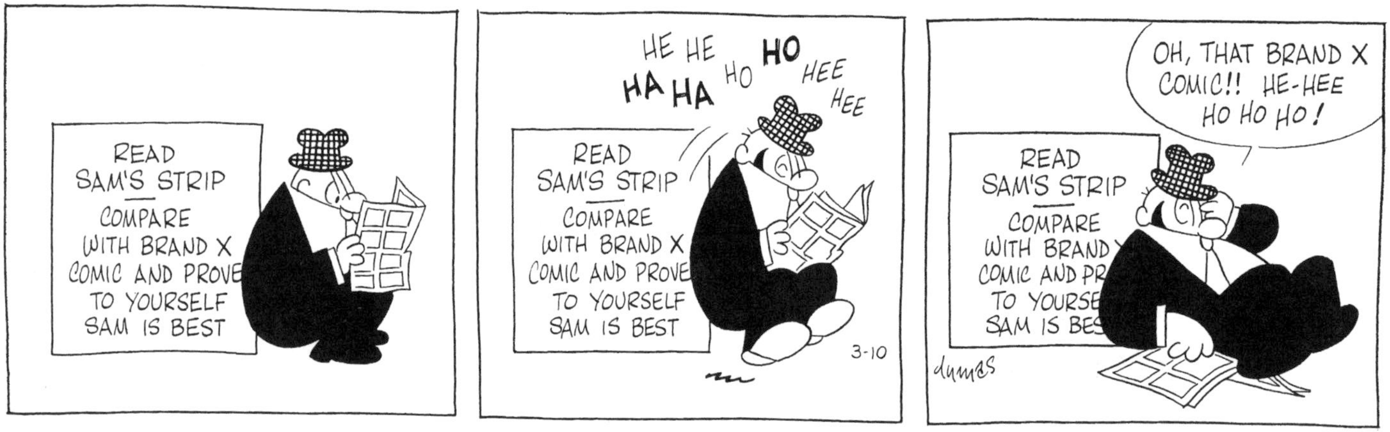
READ SAM'S STRIP
COMPARE WITH BRAND X COMIC AND PROVE TO YOURSELF SAM IS BEST
HE HE HA HA HO HO HEE HEE
READ SAM'S STRIP
COMPARE WITH BRAND X COMIC AND PROVE TO YOURSELF SAM IS BEST
3-10
OH, THAT BRAND X COMIC!! HE-HEE HO HO HO!
READ SAM'S STRIP
COMPARE WITH BRAND COMIC AND PR TO YOURSE SAM IS BES
dumas

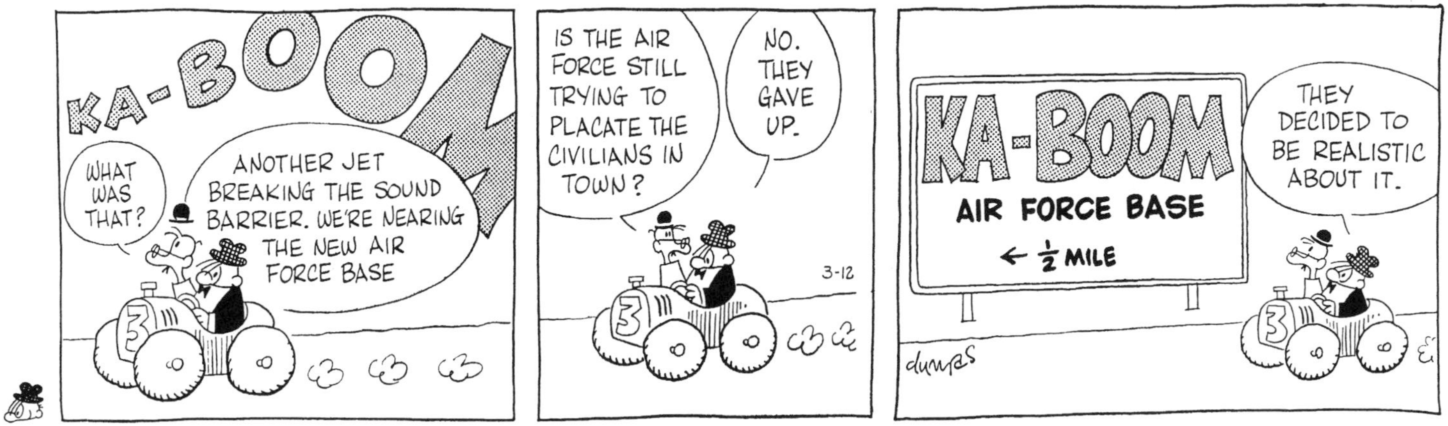
KA-BOOM
WHAT WAS THAT?
ANOTHER JET BREAKING THE SOUND BARRIER. WE'RE NEARING THE NEW AIR FORCE BASE
IS THE AIR FORCE STILL TRYING TO PLACATE THE CIVILIANS IN TOWN?
NO. THEY GAVE UP.
3-12
KA-BOOM
AIR FORCE BASE
← ½ MILE
THEY DECIDED TO BE REALISTIC ABOUT IT.
dumas

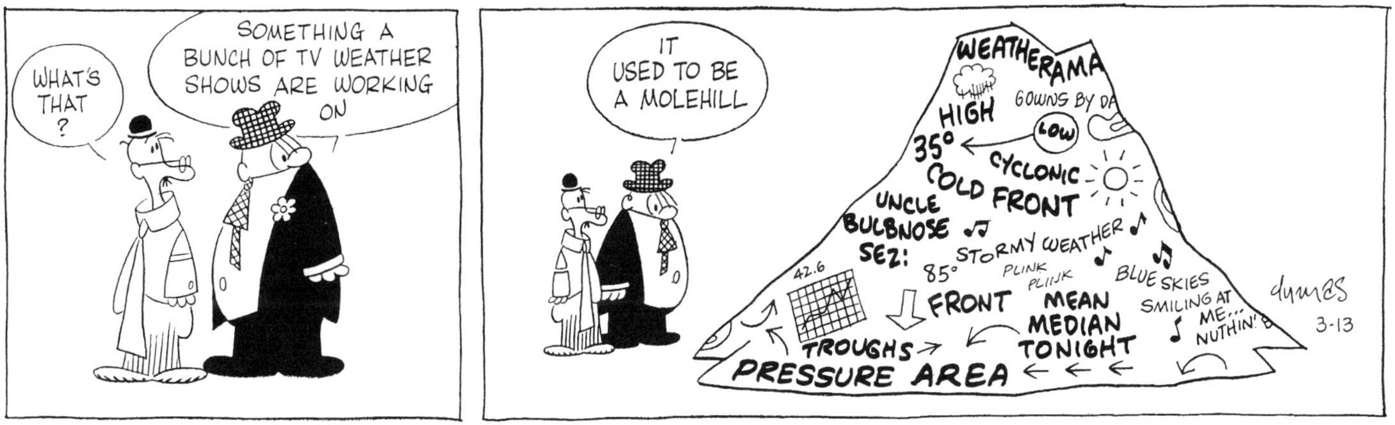
WHAT'S THAT?
SOMETHING A BUNCH OF TV WEATHER SHOWS ARE WORKING ON
IT USED TO BE A MOLEHILL
WEATHERAMA
GOWNS BY DA
HIGH
LOW
35°
CYCLONIC
COLD FRONT
UNCLE BULBNOSE SEZ:
STORMY WEATHER
85°
PLINK PLINK
BLUE SKIES SMILING AT ME... NUTHIN'!
42.6
FRONT
MEAN MEDIAN TONIGHT
TROUGHS
PRESSURE AREA
dumas
3-13

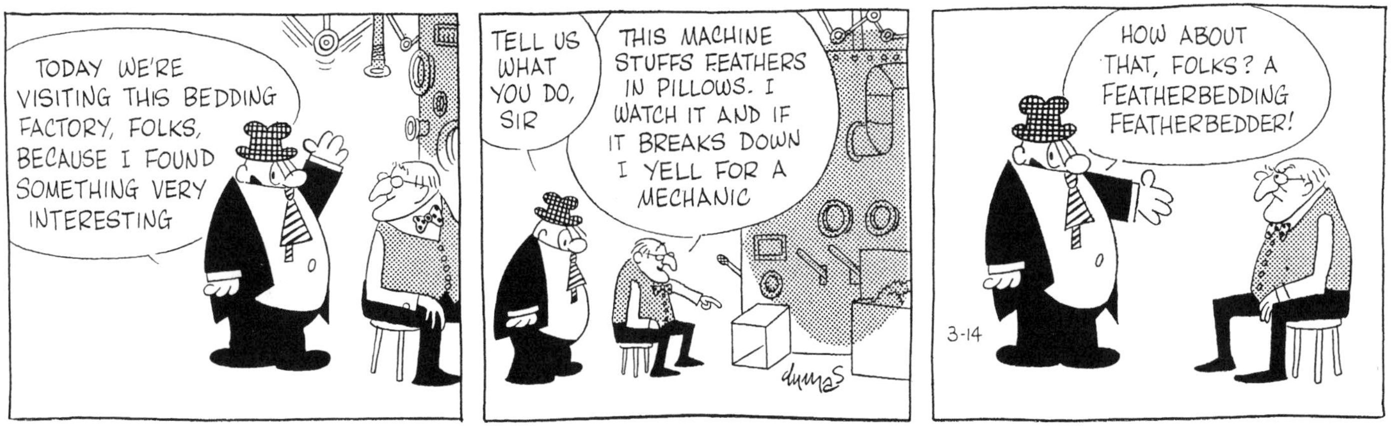
TODAY WE'RE VISITING THIS BEDDING FACTORY, FOLKS, BECAUSE I FOUND SOMETHING VERY INTERESTING
TELL US WHAT YOU DO, SIR
THIS MACHINE STUFFS FEATHERS IN PILLOWS. I WATCH IT AND IF IT BREAKS DOWN I YELL FOR A MECHANIC
dumas
3-14
HOW ABOUT THAT, FOLKS? A FEATHERBEDDING FEATHERBEDDER!

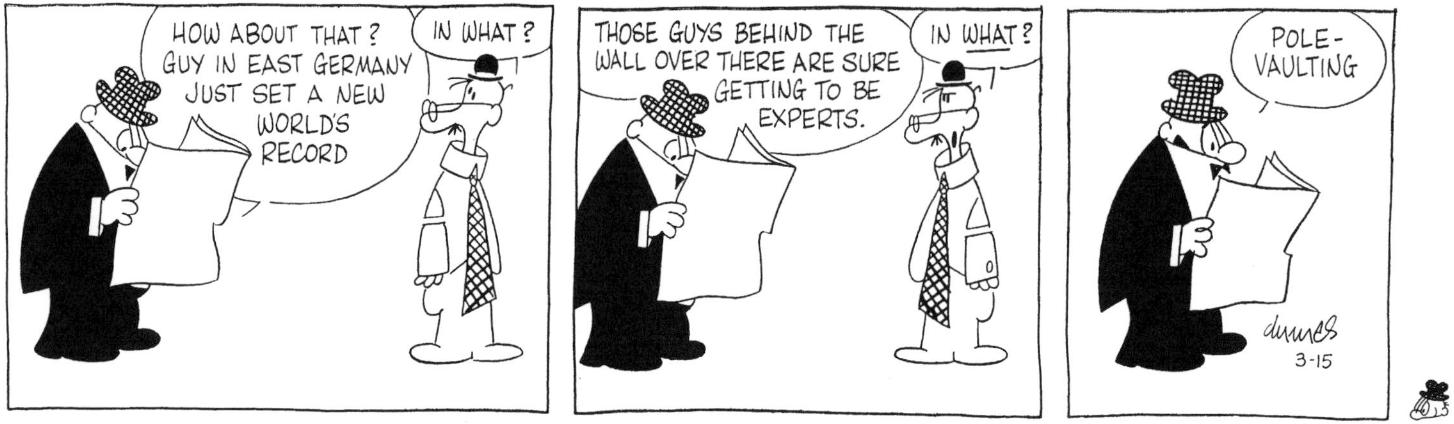
HOW ABOUT THAT? GUY IN EAST GERMANY JUST SET A NEW WORLD'S RECORD
IN WHAT?
THOSE GUYS BEHIND THE WALL OVER THERE ARE SURE GETTING TO BE EXPERTS.
IN WHAT?
POLE-VAULTING
3-15

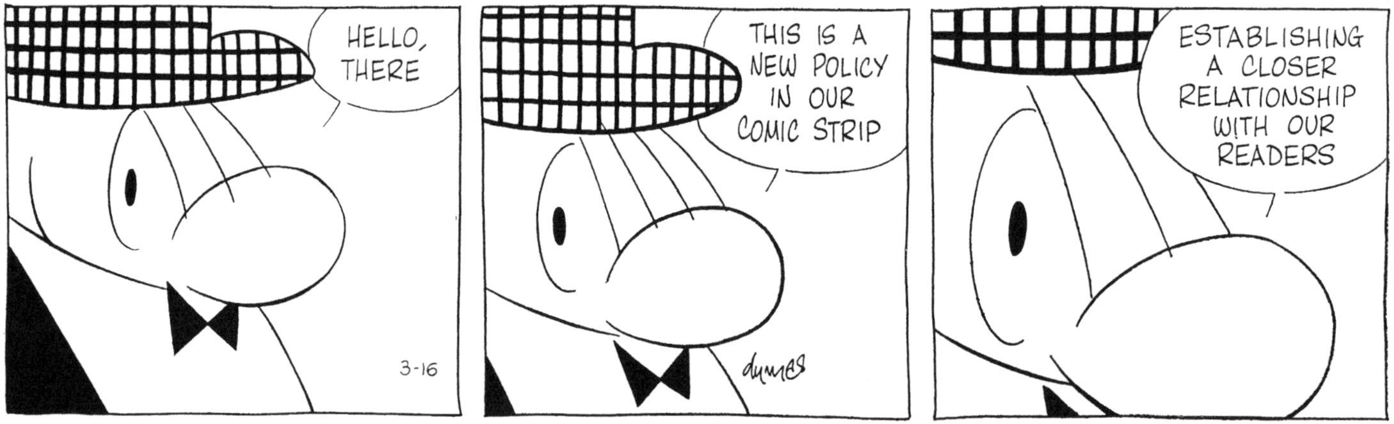
HELLO, THERE
3-16
THIS IS A NEW POLICY IN OUR COMIC STRIP
ESTABLISHING A CLOSER RELATIONSHIP WITH OUR READERS

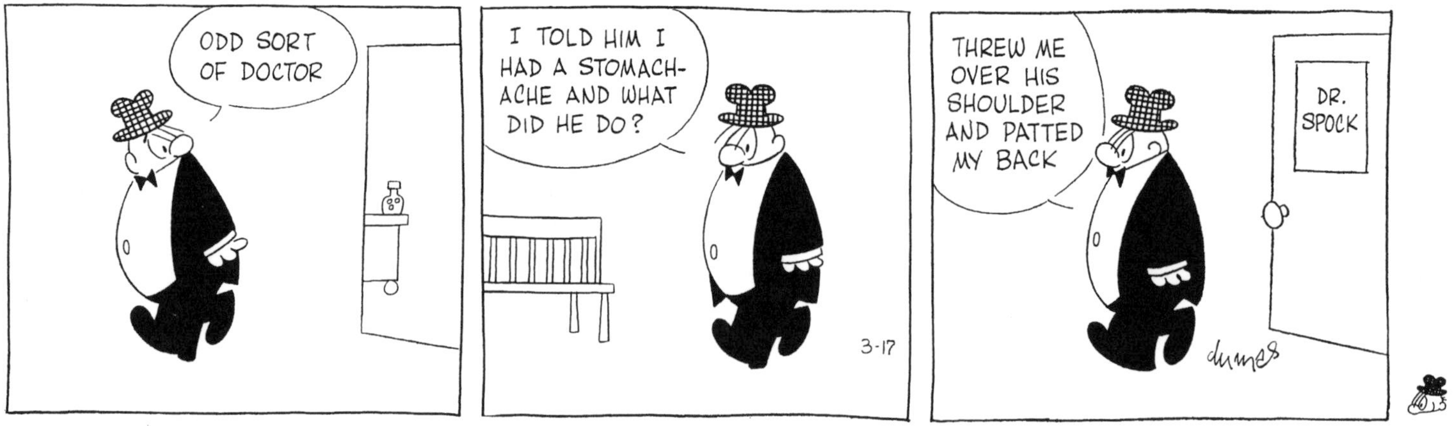
ODD SORT OF DOCTOR
I TOLD HIM I HAD A STOMACH-ACHE AND WHAT DID HE DO?
3-17
THREW ME OVER HIS SHOULDER AND PATTED MY BACK
DR. SPOCK

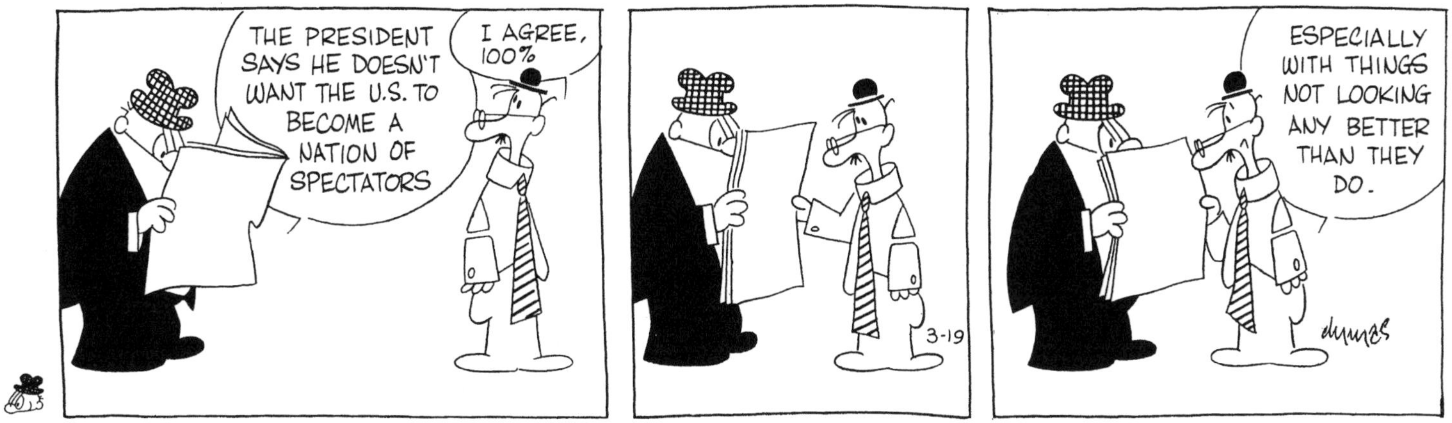
THE PRESIDENT SAYS HE DOESN'T WANT THE U.S. TO BECOME A NATION OF SPECTATORS
I AGREE, 100%
ESPECIALLY WITH THINGS NOT LOOKING ANY BETTER THAN THEY DO.
3-19

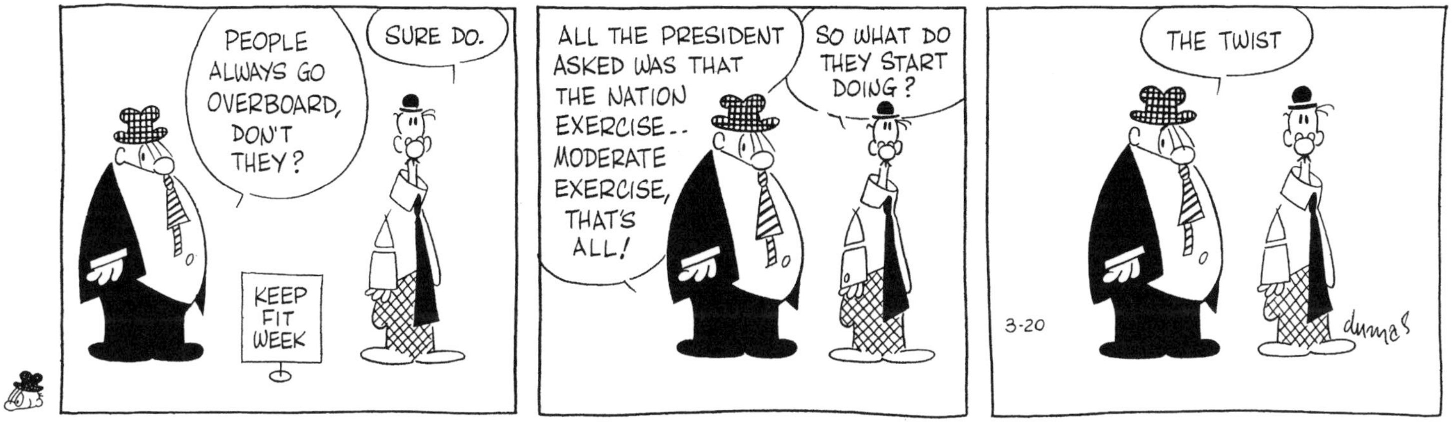
PEOPLE ALWAYS GO OVERBOARD, DON'T THEY?
SURE DO.
KEEP FIT WEEK
ALL THE PRESIDENT ASKED WAS THAT THE NATION EXERCISE.. MODERATE EXERCISE, THAT'S ALL!
SO WHAT DO THEY START DOING?
THE TWIST
3-20

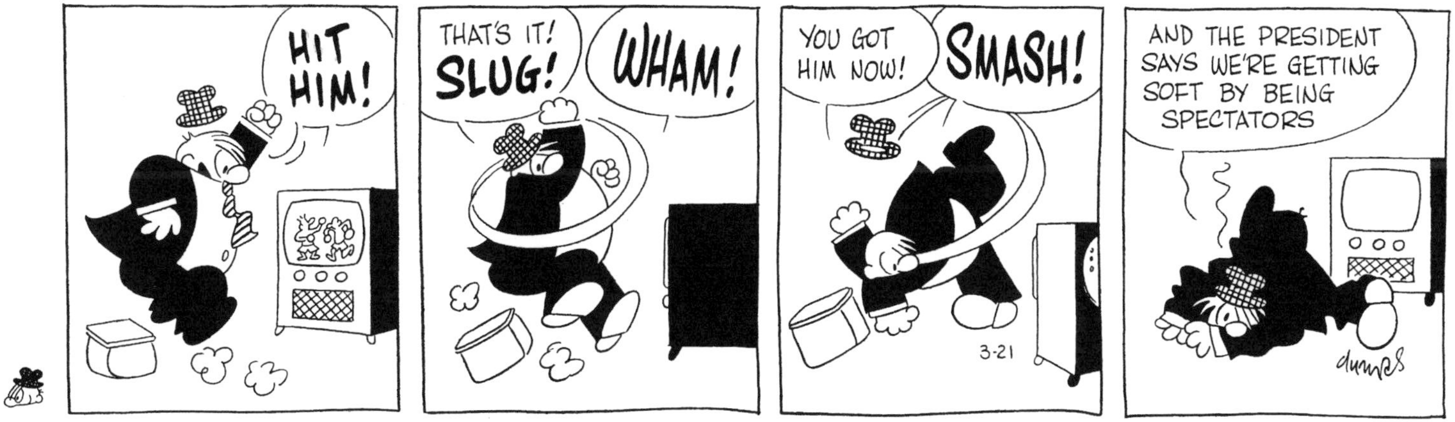
HIT HIM!
THAT'S IT! SLUG!
WHAM!
YOU GOT HIM NOW!
SMASH!
AND THE PRESIDENT SAYS WE'RE GETTING SOFT BY BEING SPECTATORS
3-21

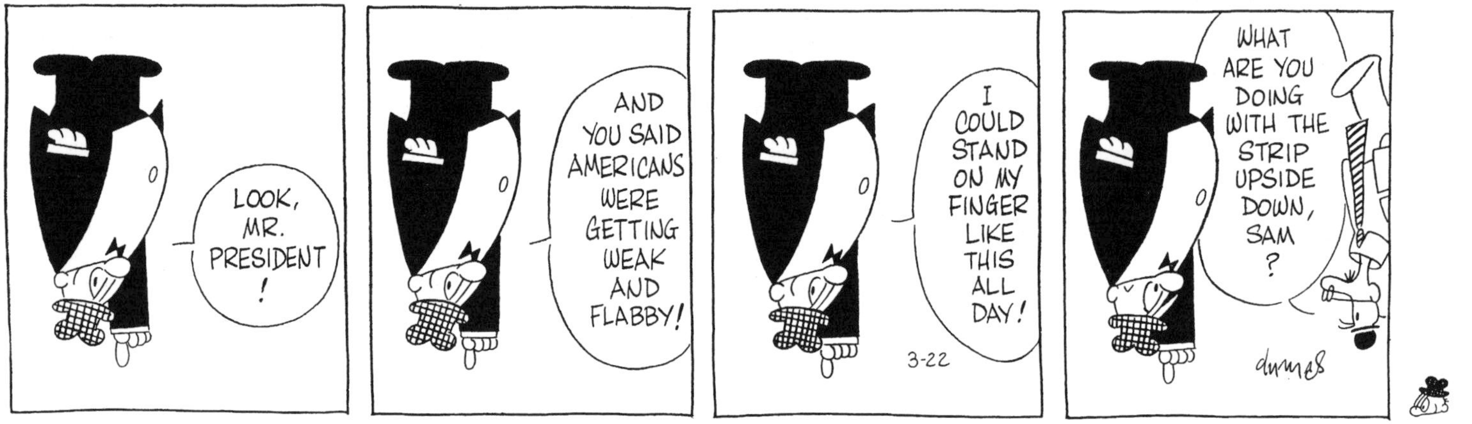
LOOK, MR. PRESIDENT!
AND YOU SAID AMERICANS WERE GETTING WEAK AND FLABBY!
I COULD STAND ON MY FINGER LIKE THIS ALL DAY!
3-22
WHAT ARE YOU DOING WITH THE STRIP UPSIDE DOWN, SAM?

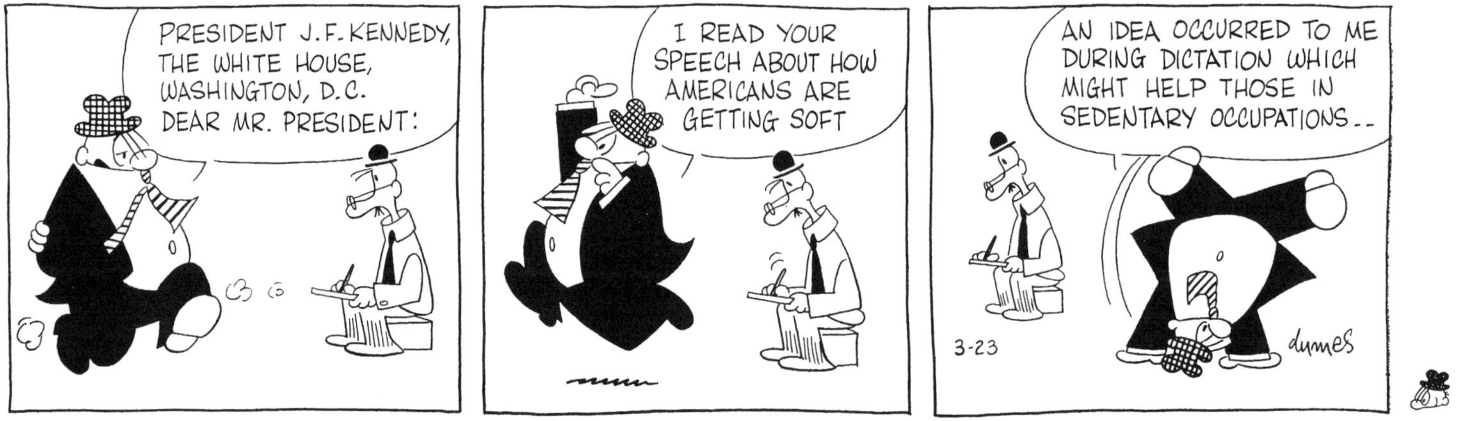
PRESIDENT J.F. KENNEDY, THE WHITE HOUSE, WASHINGTON, D.C. DEAR MR. PRESIDENT:
I READ YOUR SPEECH ABOUT HOW AMERICANS ARE GETTING SOFT
AN IDEA OCCURRED TO ME DURING DICTATION WHICH MIGHT HELP THOSE IN SEDENTARY OCCUPATIONS..
3-23

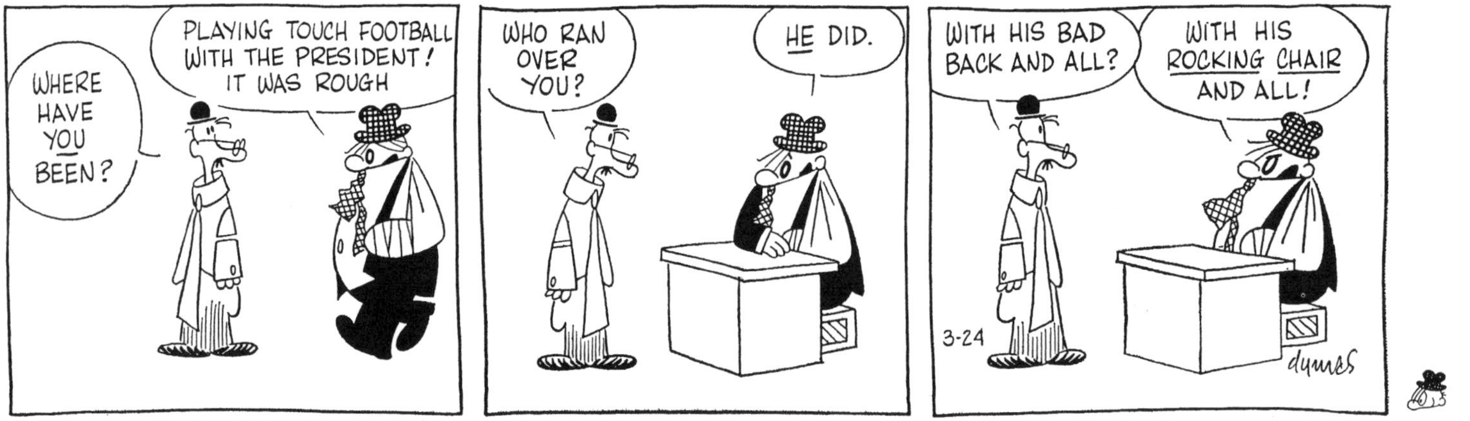
WHERE HAVE YOU BEEN?
PLAYING TOUCH FOOTBALL WITH THE PRESIDENT! IT WAS ROUGH
WHO RAN OVER YOU?
HE DID.
WITH HIS BAD BACK AND ALL?
WITH HIS ROCKING CHAIR AND ALL!
3-24

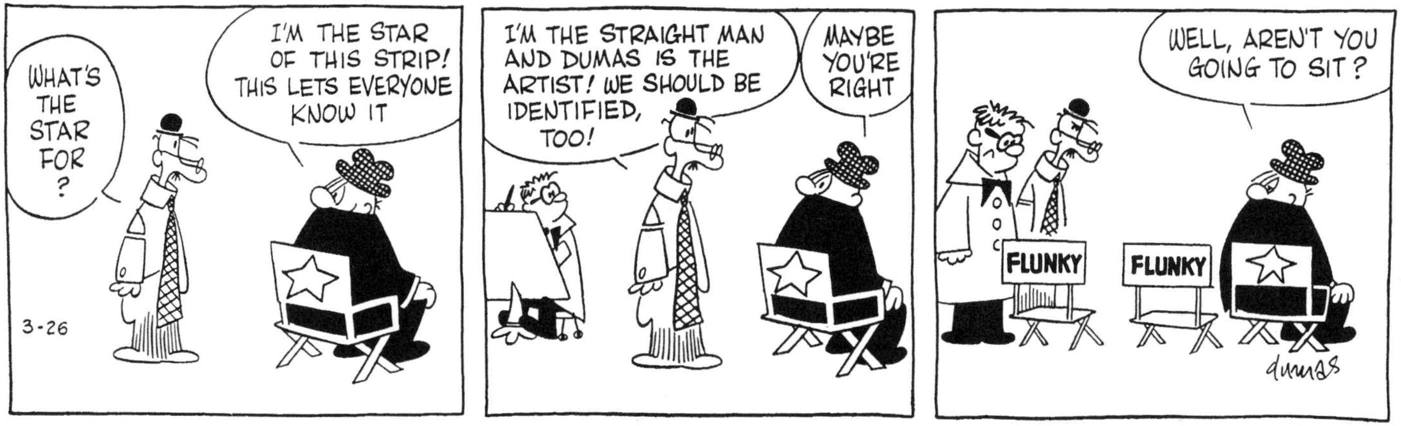
WHAT'S THE STAR FOR ?
I'M THE STAR OF THIS STRIP! THIS LETS EVERYONE KNOW IT
3-26
I'M THE STRAIGHT MAN AND DUMAS IS THE ARTIST! WE SHOULD BE IDENTIFIED, TOO!
MAYBE YOU'RE RIGHT
WELL, AREN'T YOU GOING TO SIT?
FLUNKY
FLUNKY
dumas

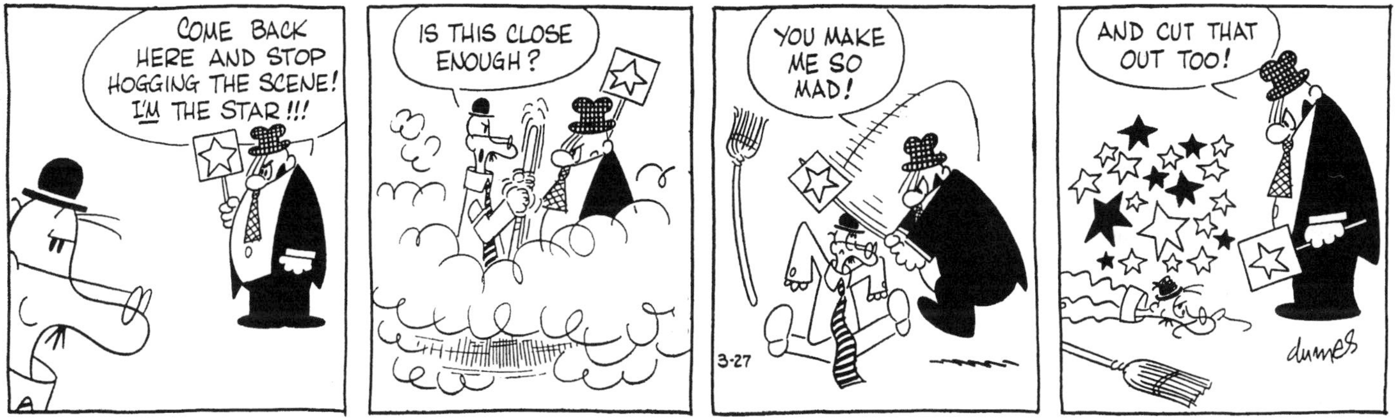
COME BACK HERE AND STOP HOGGING THE SCENE! I'M THE STAR!!!
IS THIS CLOSE ENOUGH?
YOU MAKE ME SO MAD!
3-27
AND CUT THAT OUT TOO!
dumas

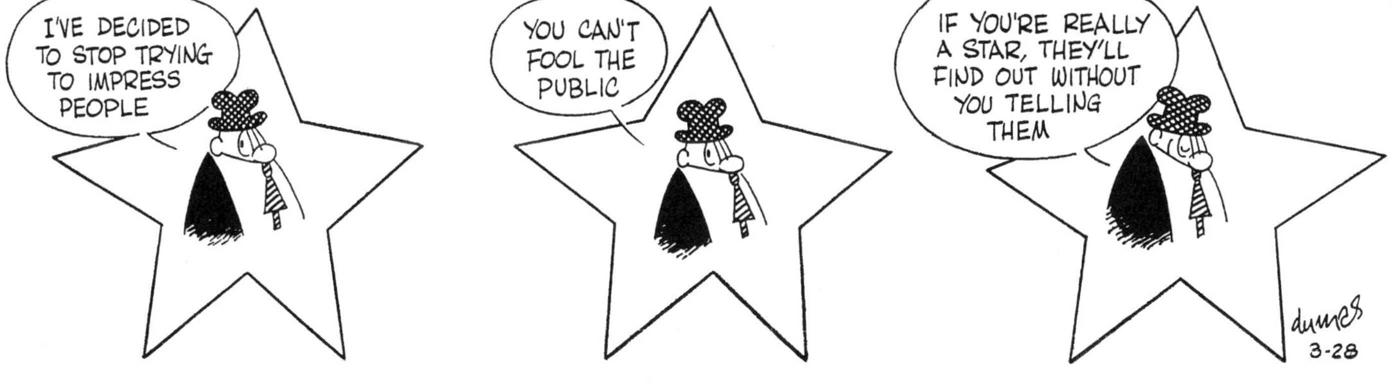
I'VE DECIDED TO STOP TRYING TO IMPRESS PEOPLE
YOU CAN'T FOOL THE PUBLIC
IF YOU'RE REALLY A STAR, THEY'LL FIND OUT WITHOUT YOU TELLING THEM
dumas
3-28

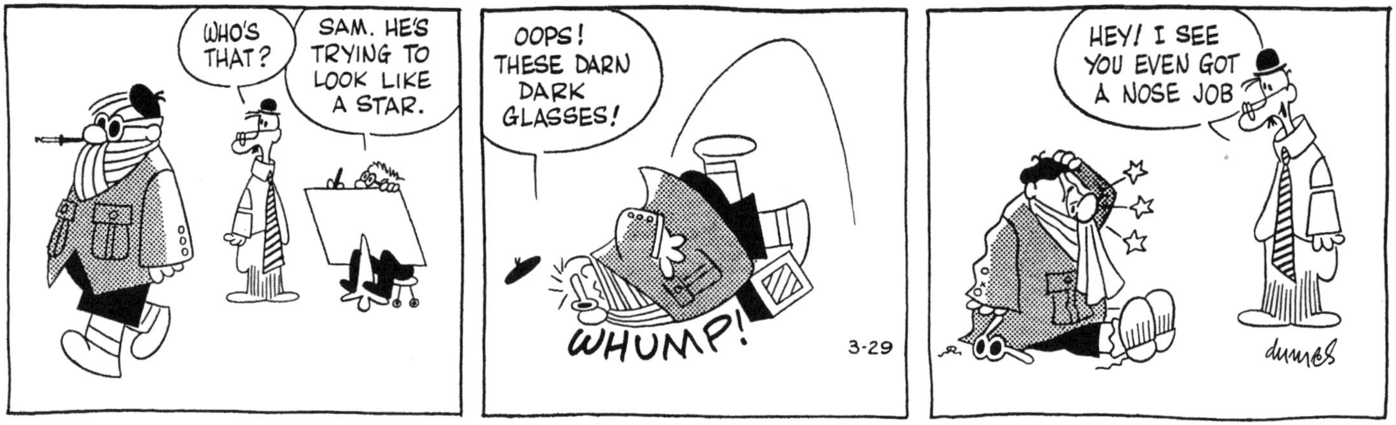
WHO'S THAT?
SAM. HE'S TRYING TO LOOK LIKE A STAR.
OOPS! THESE DARN DARK GLASSES!
WHUMP!
3-29
HEY! I SEE YOU EVEN GOT A NOSE JOB

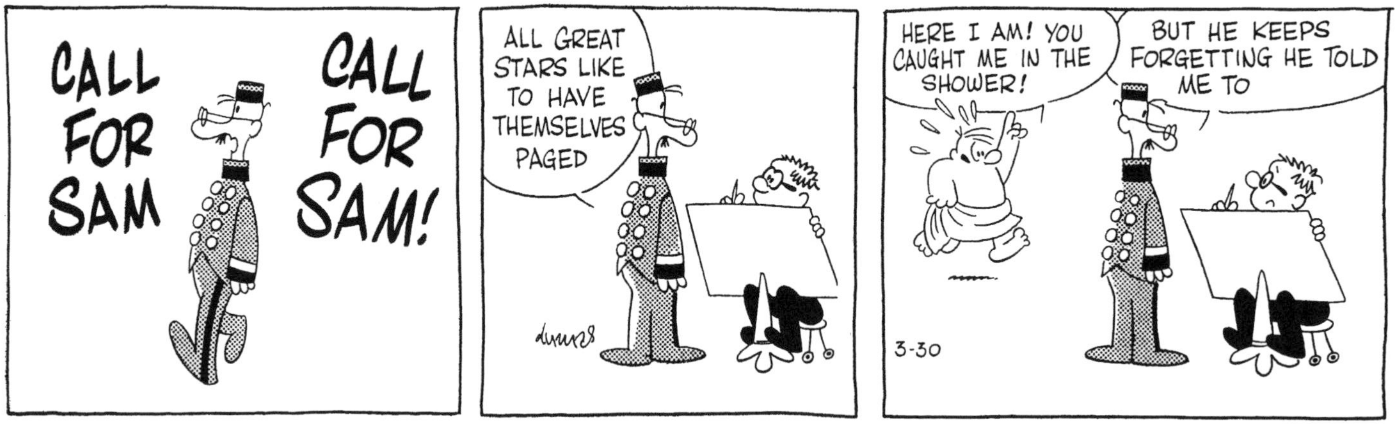
CALL FOR SAM
CALL FOR SAM!
ALL GREAT STARS LIKE TO HAVE THEMSELVES PAGED
HERE I AM! YOU CAUGHT ME IN THE SHOWER!
BUT HE KEEPS FORGETTING HE TOLD ME TO
3-30

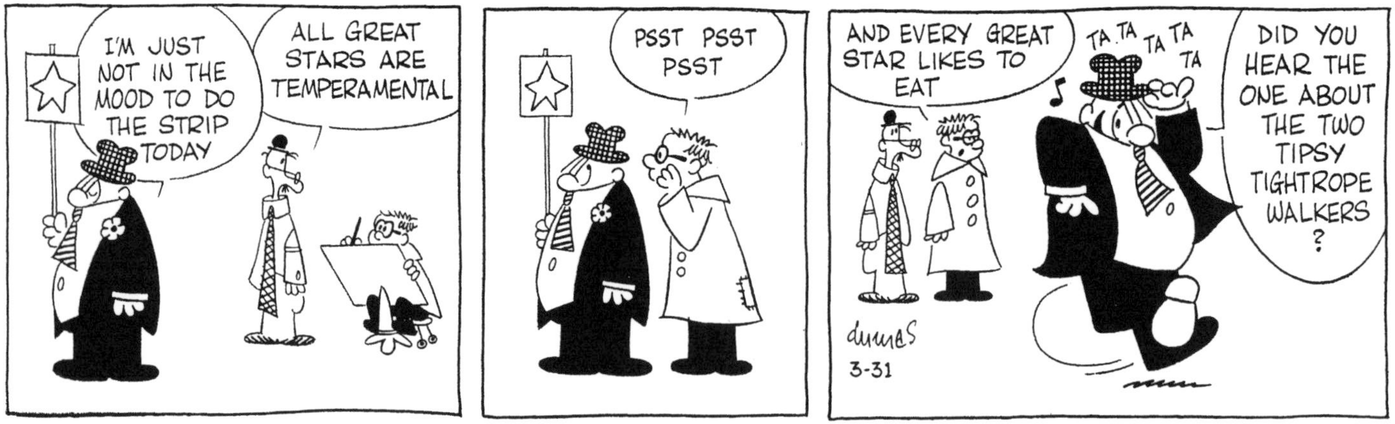
I'M JUST NOT IN THE MOOD TO DO THE STRIP TODAY
ALL GREAT STARS ARE TEMPERAMENTAL
PSST PSST PSST
AND EVERY GREAT STAR LIKES TO EAT
TA TA TA TA TA
DID YOU HEAR THE ONE ABOUT THE TWO TIPSY TIGHTROPE WALKERS ?
3-31

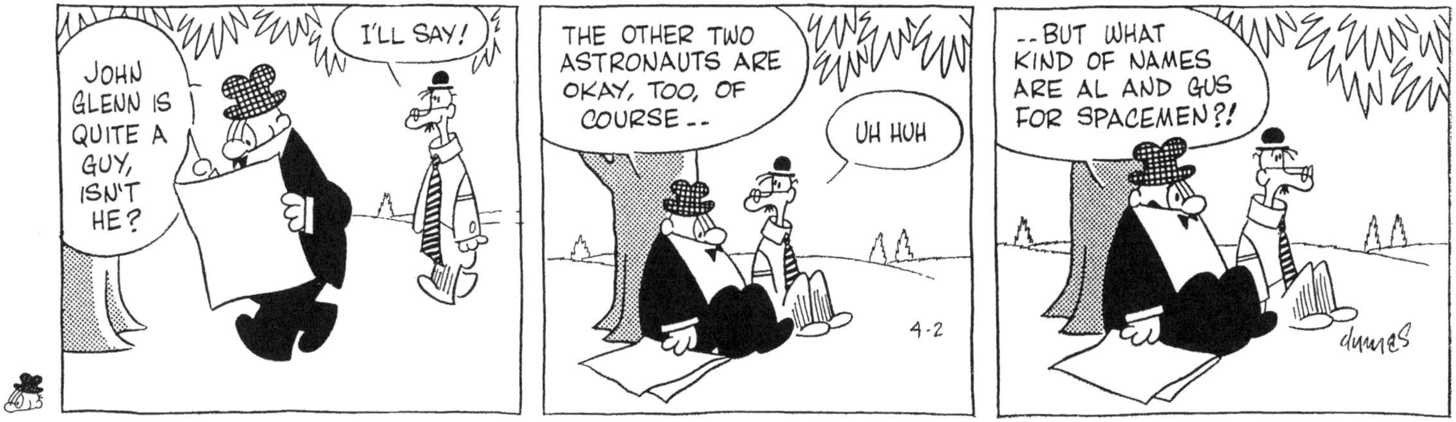
JOHN GLENN IS QUITE A GUY, ISN'T HE?
I'LL SAY!
THE OTHER TWO ASTRONAUTS ARE OKAY, TOO, OF COURSE --
UH HUH
4-2
-- BUT WHAT KIND OF NAMES ARE AL AND GUS FOR SPACEMEN?!

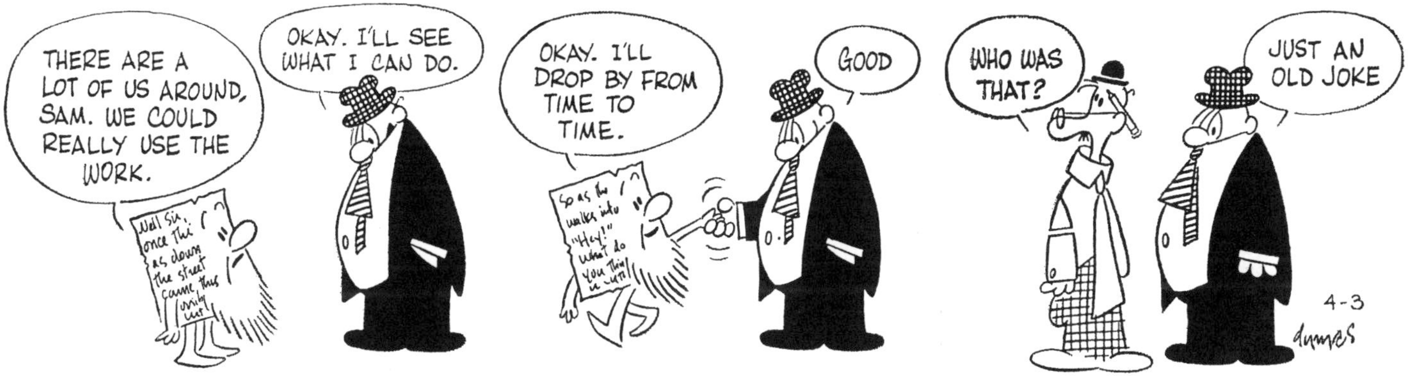
THERE ARE A LOT OF US AROUND, SAM. WE COULD REALLY USE THE WORK.
OKAY. I'LL SEE WHAT I CAN DO.
OKAY. I'LL DROP BY FROM TIME TO TIME.
GOOD
WHO WAS THAT?
JUST AN OLD JOKE
4-3

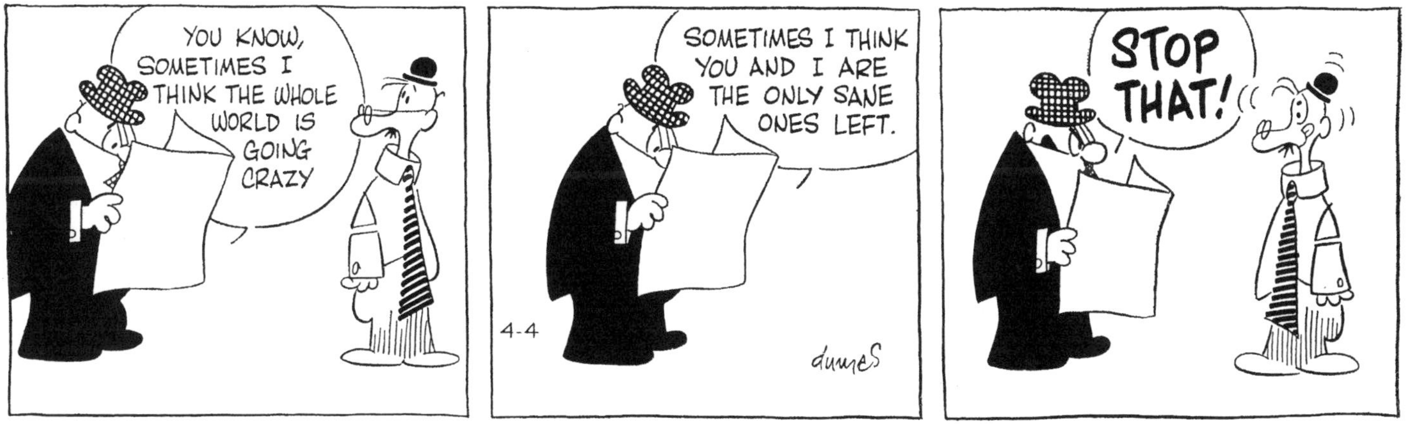
YOU KNOW, SOMETIMES I THINK THE WHOLE WORLD IS GOING CRAZY
SOMETIMES I THINK YOU AND I ARE THE ONLY SANE ONES LEFT.
4-4
STOP THAT!

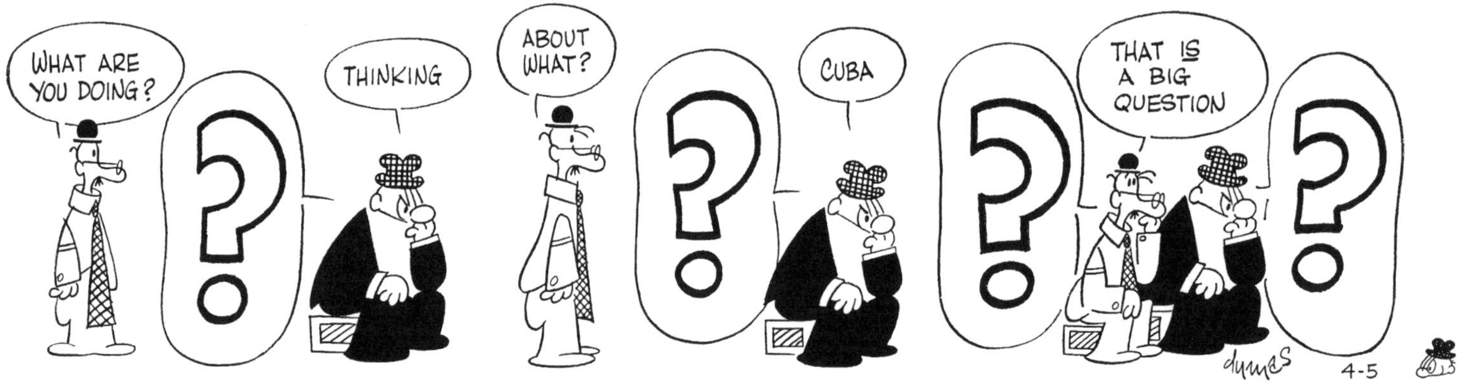
WHAT ARE YOU DOING?
THINKING
ABOUT WHAT?
CUBA
THAT IS A BIG QUESTION
4-5

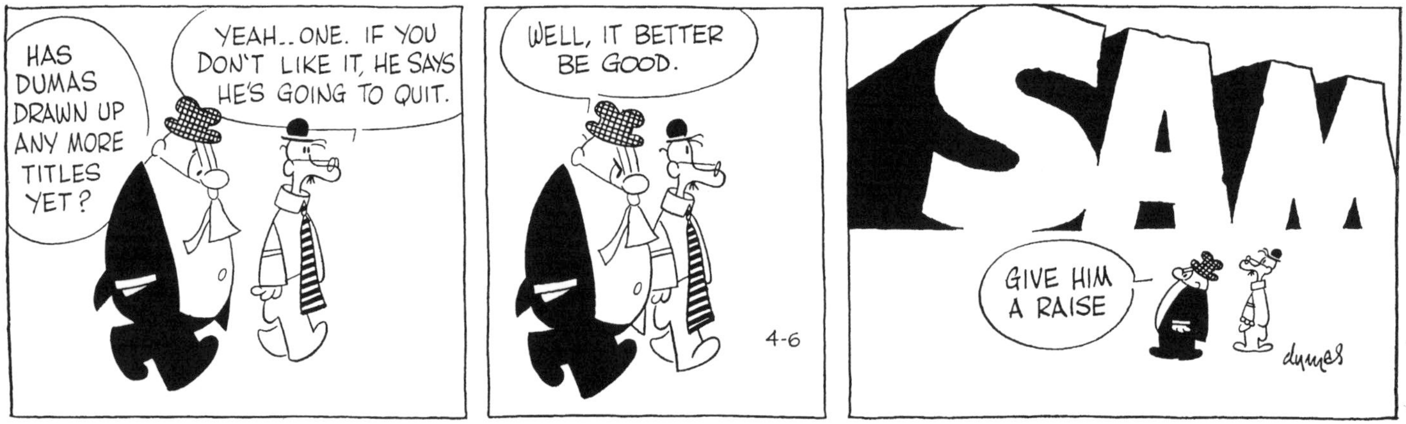
HAS DUMAS DRAWN UP ANY MORE TITLES YET?
YEAH..ONE. IF YOU DON'T LIKE IT, HE SAYS HE'S GOING TO QUIT.
4-6
WELL, IT BETTER BE GOOD.
SAM
GIVE HIM A RAISE

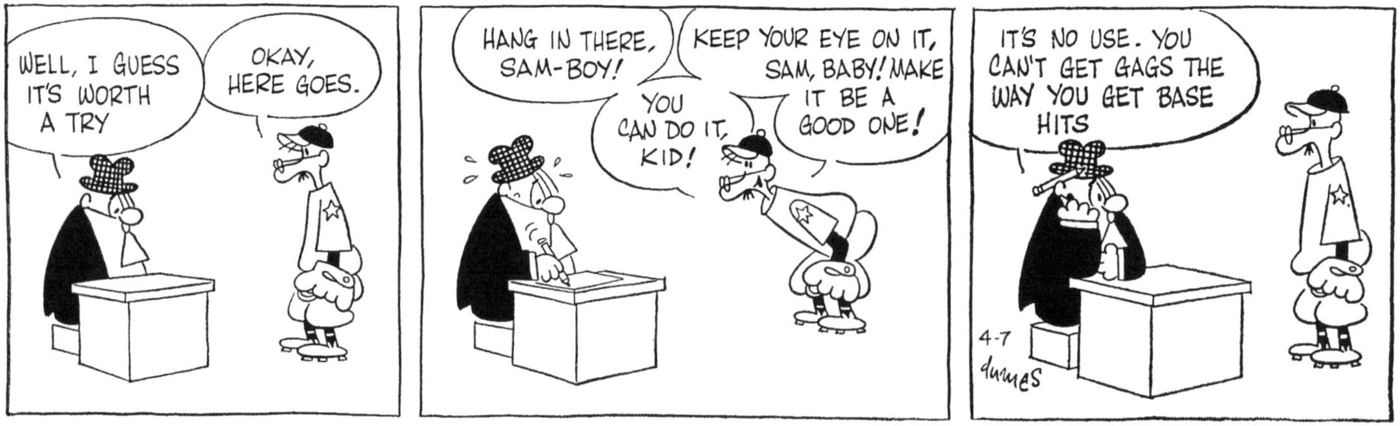
WELL, I GUESS IT'S WORTH A TRY
OKAY, HERE GOES.
HANG IN THERE, SAM-BOY!
KEEP YOUR EYE ON IT, SAM, BABY! MAKE IT BE A GOOD ONE!
YOU CAN DO IT, KID!
IT'S NO USE. YOU CAN'T GET GAGS THE WAY YOU GET BASE HITS
4-7

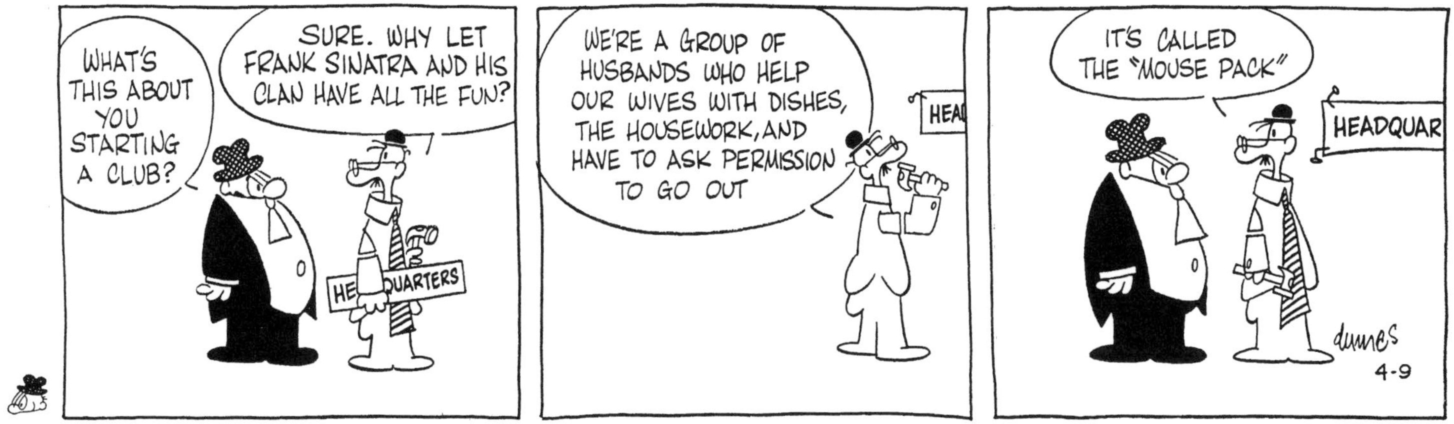
WHAT'S THIS ABOUT YOU STARTING A CLUB?
SURE. WHY LET FRANK SINATRA AND HIS CLAN HAVE ALL THE FUN?
HE QUARTERS
WE'RE A GROUP OF HUSBANDS WHO HELP OUR WIVES WITH DISHES, THE HOUSEWORK, AND HAVE TO ASK PERMISSION TO GO OUT
HEA
IT'S CALLED THE "MOUSE PACK"
HEADQUAR
dumas
4-9

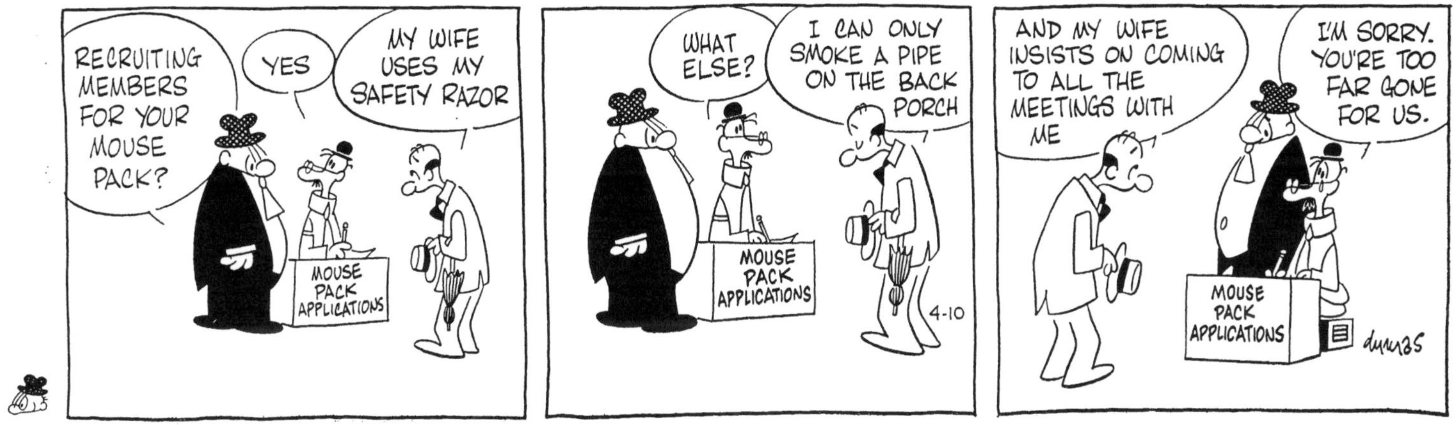
RECRUITING MEMBERS FOR YOUR MOUSE PACK?
YES
MY WIFE USES MY SAFETY RAZOR
MOUSE PACK APPLICATIONS
WHAT ELSE?
I CAN ONLY SMOKE A PIPE ON THE BACK PORCH
MOUSE PACK APPLICATIONS
4-10
AND MY WIFE INSISTS ON COMING TO ALL THE MEETINGS WITH ME
I'M SORRY. YOU'RE TOO FAR GONE FOR US.
MOUSE PACK APPLICATIONS
dumas

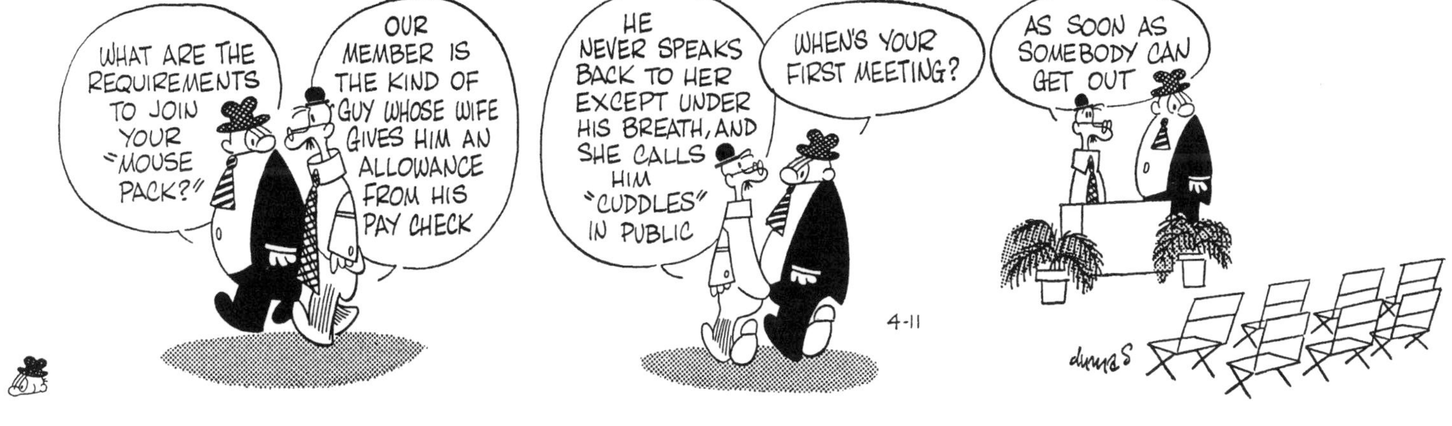
WHAT ARE THE REQUIREMENTS TO JOIN YOUR "MOUSE PACK?"
OUR MEMBER IS THE KIND OF GUY WHOSE WIFE GIVES HIM AN ALLOWANCE FROM HIS PAY CHECK
HE NEVER SPEAKS BACK TO HER EXCEPT UNDER HIS BREATH, AND SHE CALLS HIM "CUDDLES" IN PUBLIC
WHEN'S YOUR FIRST MEETING?
4-11
AS SOON AS SOMEBODY CAN GET OUT
dumas

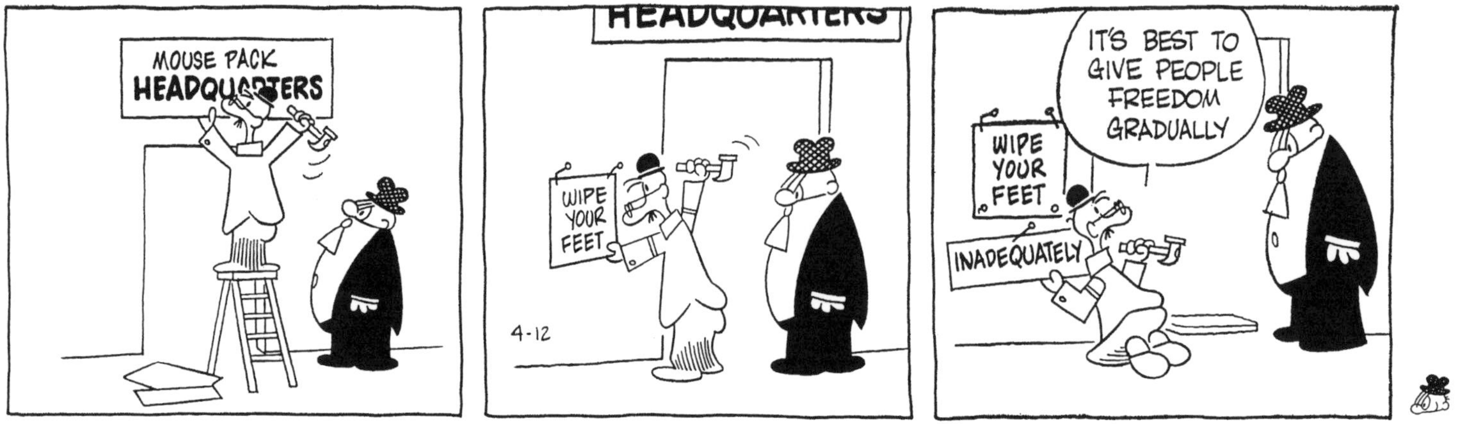
MOUSE PACK
HEADQUARTERS
WIPE YOUR FEET
4-12
IT'S BEST TO GIVE PEOPLE FREEDOM GRADUALLY
WIPE YOUR FEET
INADEQUATELY

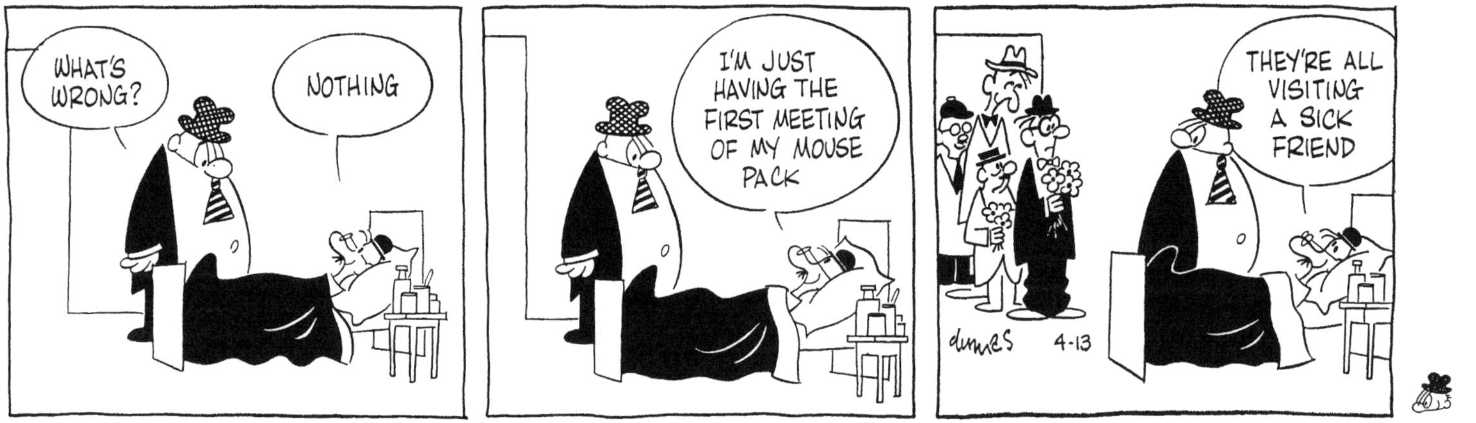
WHAT'S WRONG?
NOTHING
I'M JUST HAVING THE FIRST MEETING OF MY MOUSE PACK
dumas 4-13
THEY'RE ALL VISITING A SICK FRIEND

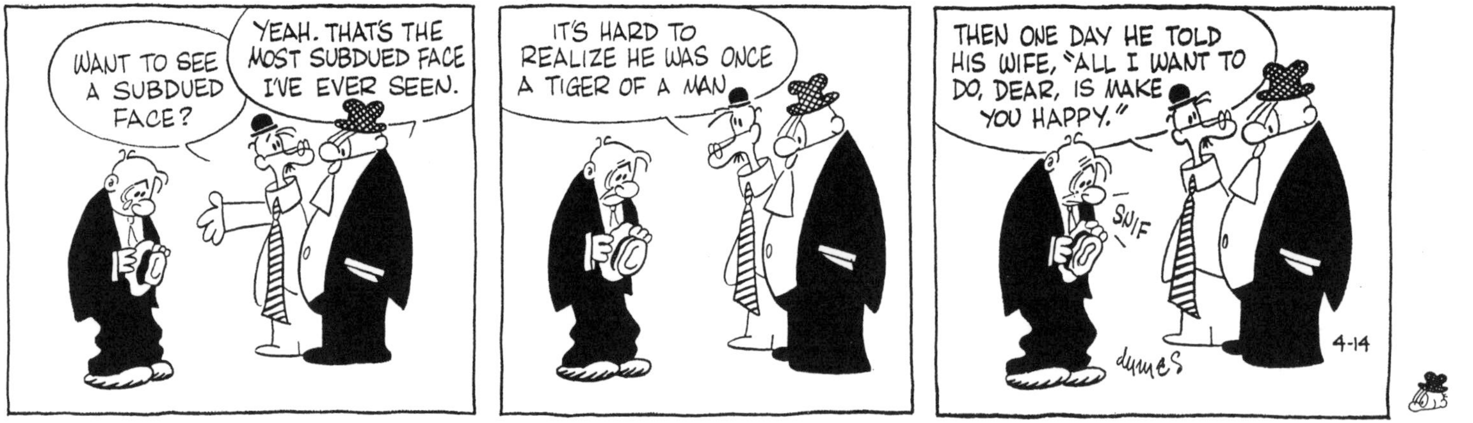
WANT TO SEE A SUBDUED FACE?
YEAH. THAT'S THE MOST SUBDUED FACE I'VE EVER SEEN.
IT'S HARD TO REALIZE HE WAS ONCE A TIGER OF A MAN
THEN ONE DAY HE TOLD HIS WIFE, "ALL I WANT TO DO, DEAR, IS MAKE YOU HAPPY."
SNIF
4-14
dumas

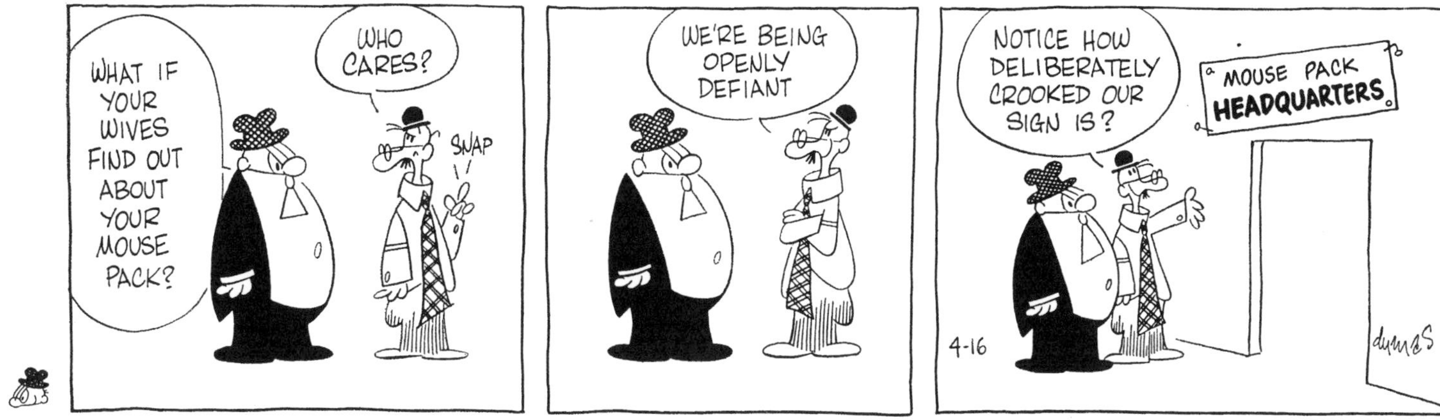
WHAT IF YOUR WIVES FIND OUT ABOUT YOUR MOUSE PACK?
WHO CARES?
SNAP
WE'RE BEING OPENLY DEFIANT
NOTICE HOW DELIBERATELY CROOKED OUR SIGN IS?
MOUSE PACK HEADQUARTERS
4-16
dumas

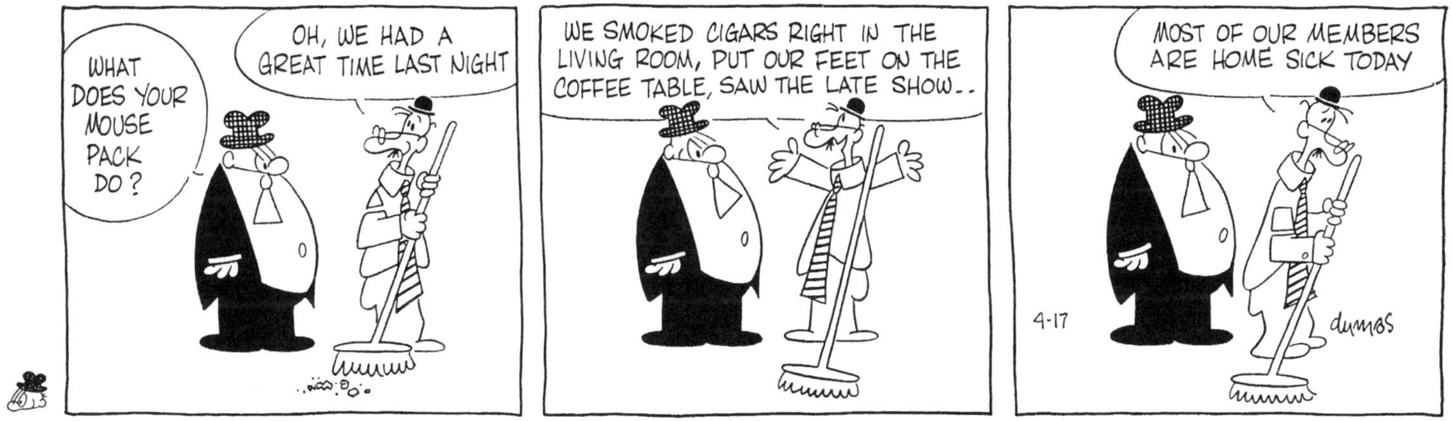
WHAT DOES YOUR MOUSE PACK DO?
OH, WE HAD A GREAT TIME LAST NIGHT
WE SMOKED CIGARS RIGHT IN THE LIVING ROOM, PUT OUR FEET ON THE COFFEE TABLE, SAW THE LATE SHOW..
MOST OF OUR MEMBERS ARE HOME SICK TODAY
4-17
dumas

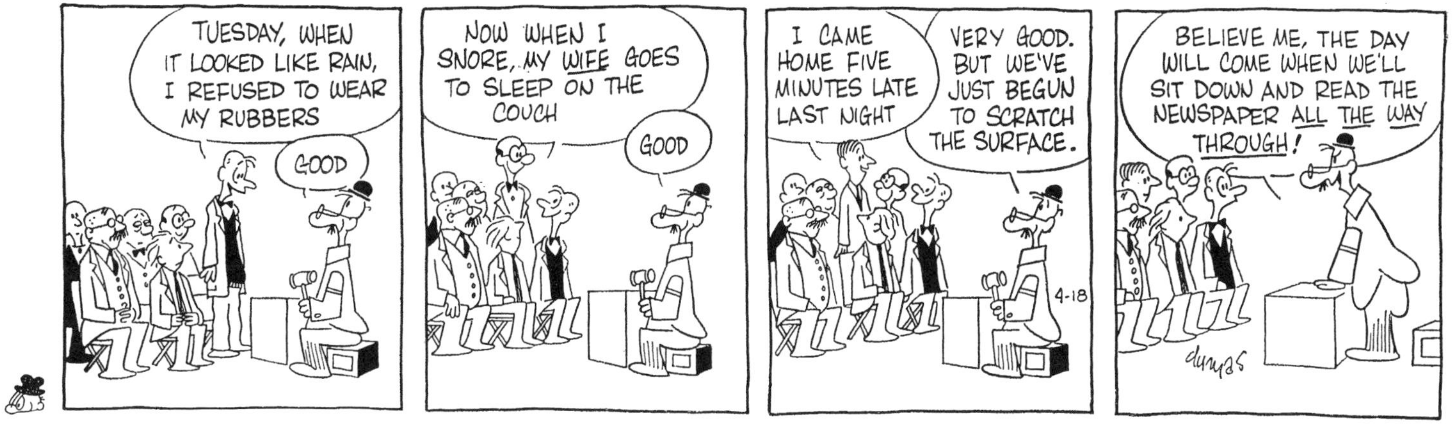
TUESDAY, WHEN IT LOOKED LIKE RAIN, I REFUSED TO WEAR MY RUBBERS
GOOD
NOW WHEN I SNORE, MY WIFE GOES TO SLEEP ON THE COUCH
GOOD
I CAME HOME FIVE MINUTES LATE LAST NIGHT
VERY GOOD. BUT WE'VE JUST BEGUN TO SCRATCH THE SURFACE.
4-18
BELIEVE ME, THE DAY WILL COME WHEN WE'LL SIT DOWN AND READ THE NEWSPAPER ALL THE WAY THROUGH!
dumas

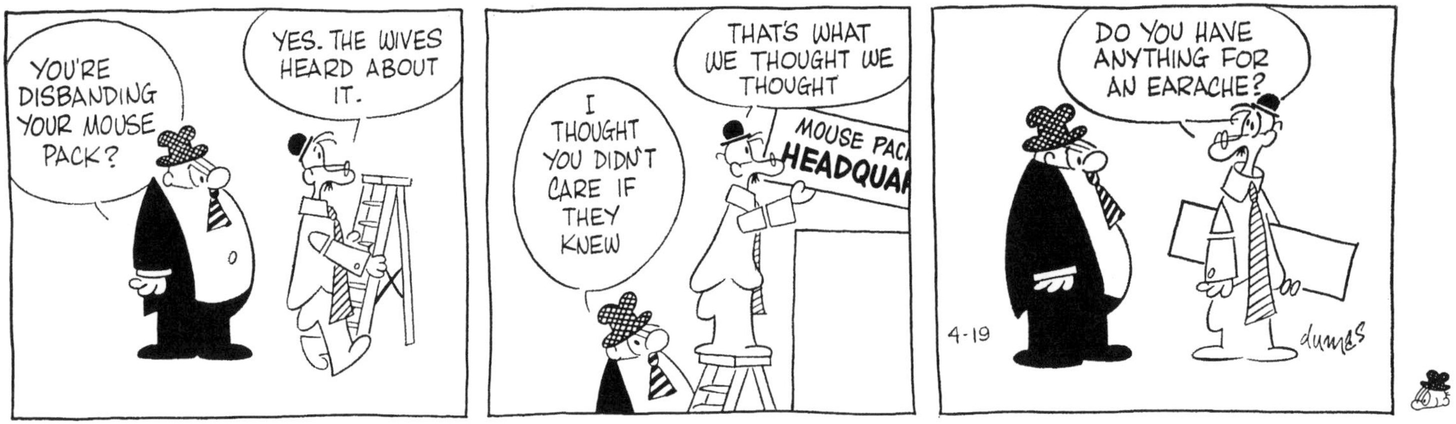
YOU'RE DISBANDING YOUR MOUSE PACK?
YES. THE WIVES HEARD ABOUT IT.
THAT'S WHAT WE THOUGHT WE THOUGHT
MOUSE PAC
HEADQUA
I THOUGHT YOU DIDN'T CARE IF THEY KNEW
DO YOU HAVE ANYTHING FOR AN EARACHE?
4-19
dumas

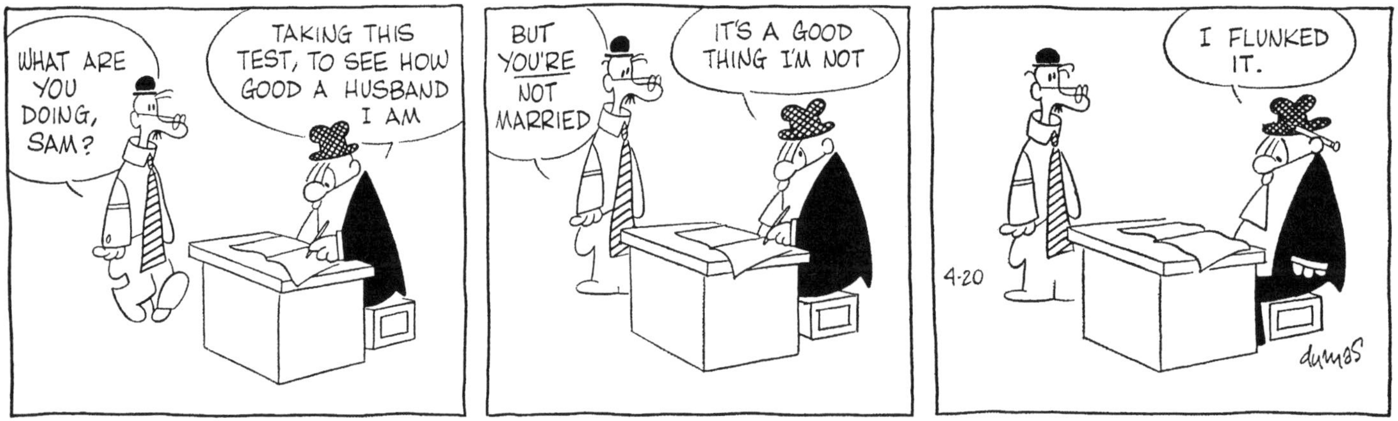
WHAT ARE YOU DOING, SAM?
TAKING THIS TEST, TO SEE HOW GOOD A HUSBAND I AM
BUT YOU'RE NOT MARRIED
IT'S A GOOD THING I'M NOT
I FLUNKED IT.
4-20
dumas

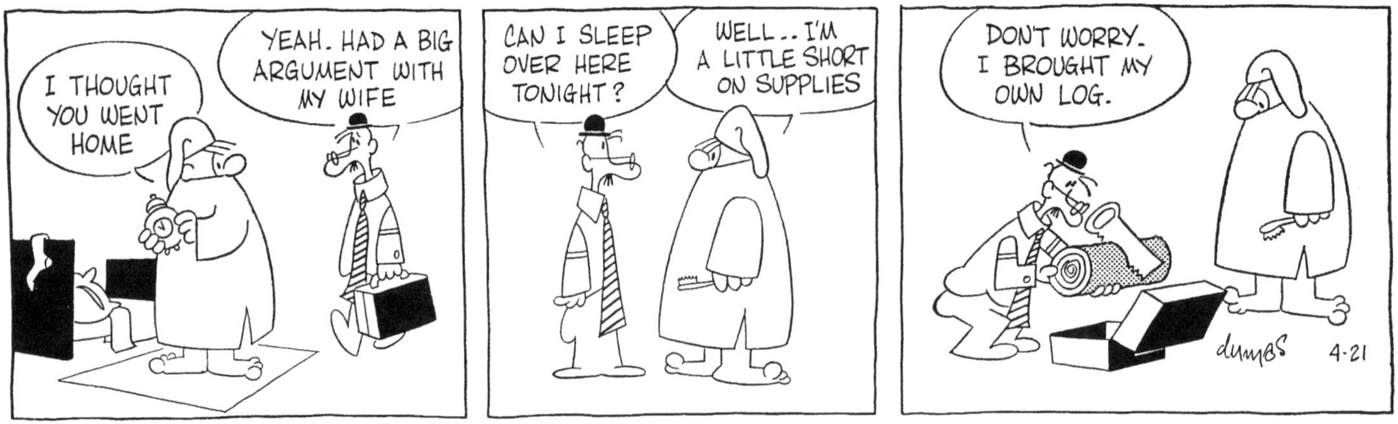
I THOUGHT YOU WENT HOME
YEAH. HAD A BIG ARGUMENT WITH MY WIFE
CAN I SLEEP OVER HERE TONIGHT?
WELL.. I'M A LITTLE SHORT ON SUPPLIES
DON'T WORRY. I BROUGHT MY OWN LOG.
dumas
4-21

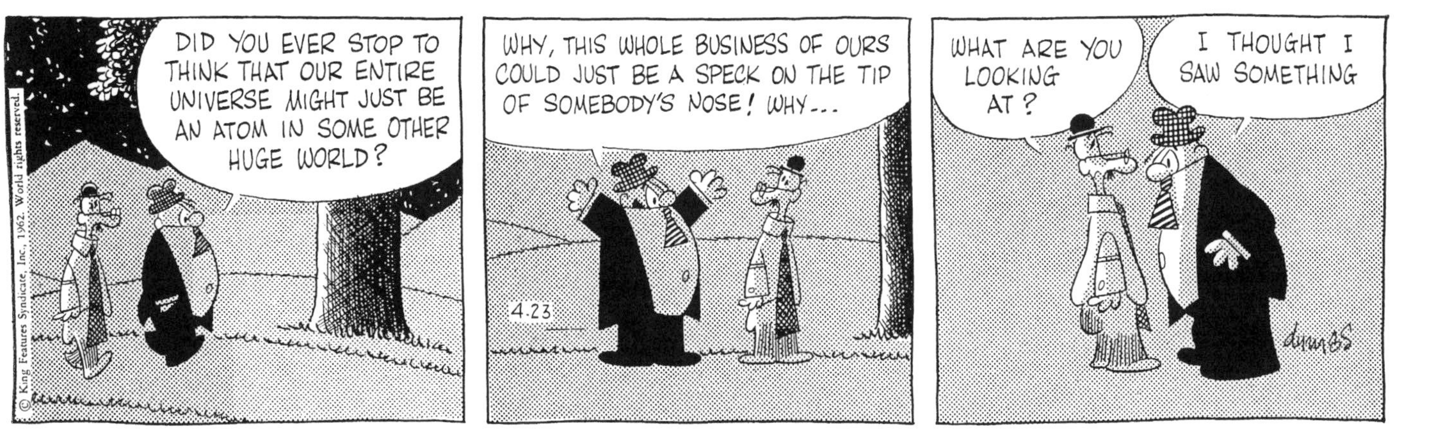
© King Features Syndicate, Inc., 1962. World rights reserved.
DID YOU EVER STOP TO THINK THAT OUR ENTIRE UNIVERSE MIGHT JUST BE AN ATOM IN SOME OTHER HUGE WORLD?
WHY, THIS WHOLE BUSINESS OF OURS COULD JUST BE A SPECK ON THE TIP OF SOMEBODY'S NOSE! WHY...
4.23
WHAT ARE YOU LOOKING AT?
I THOUGHT I SAW SOMETHING

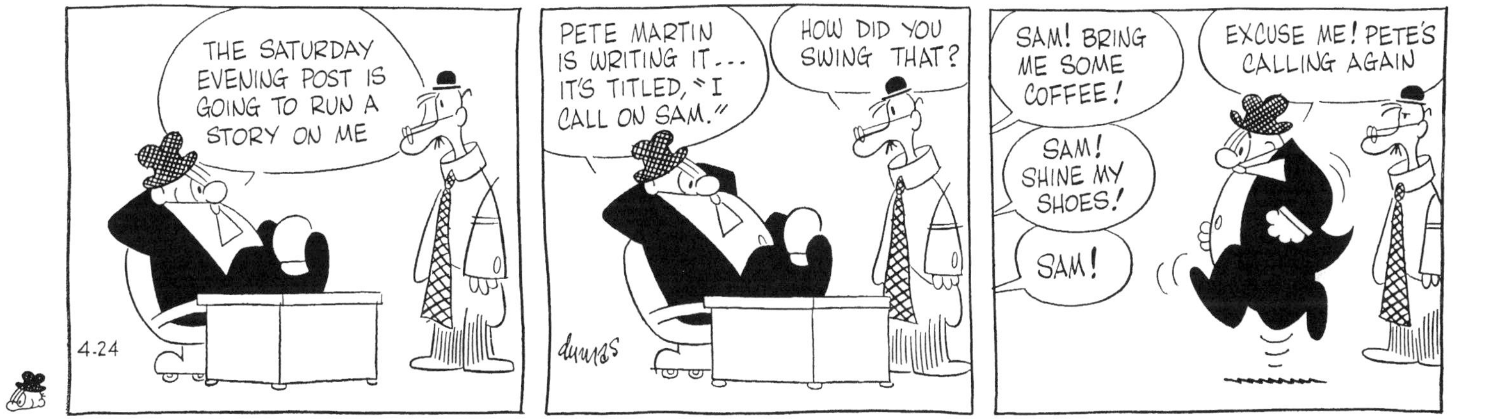
THE SATURDAY EVENING POST IS GOING TO RUN A STORY ON ME
4.24
PETE MARTIN IS WRITING IT... IT'S TITLED, "I CALL ON SAM."
HOW DID YOU SWING THAT?
SAM! BRING ME SOME COFFEE!
SAM! SHINE MY SHOES!
SAM!
EXCUSE ME! PETE'S CALLING AGAIN

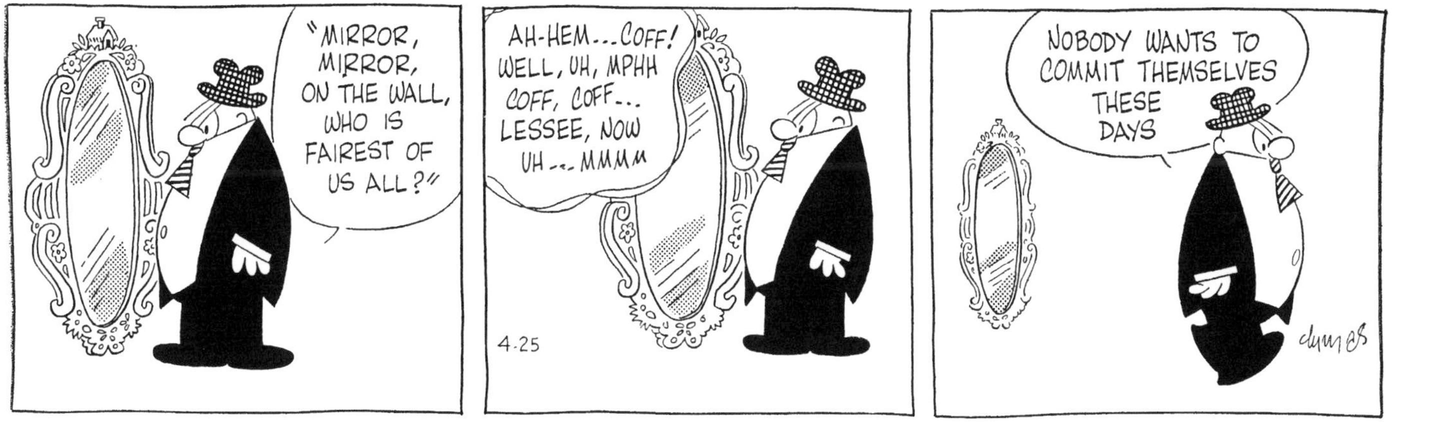
"MIRROR, MIRROR, ON THE WALL, WHO IS FAIREST OF US ALL?"
AH-HEM...COFF! WELL, UH, MPHH COFF, COFF... LESSEE, NOW UH...MMMM
4.25
NOBODY WANTS TO COMMIT THEMSELVES THESE DAYS

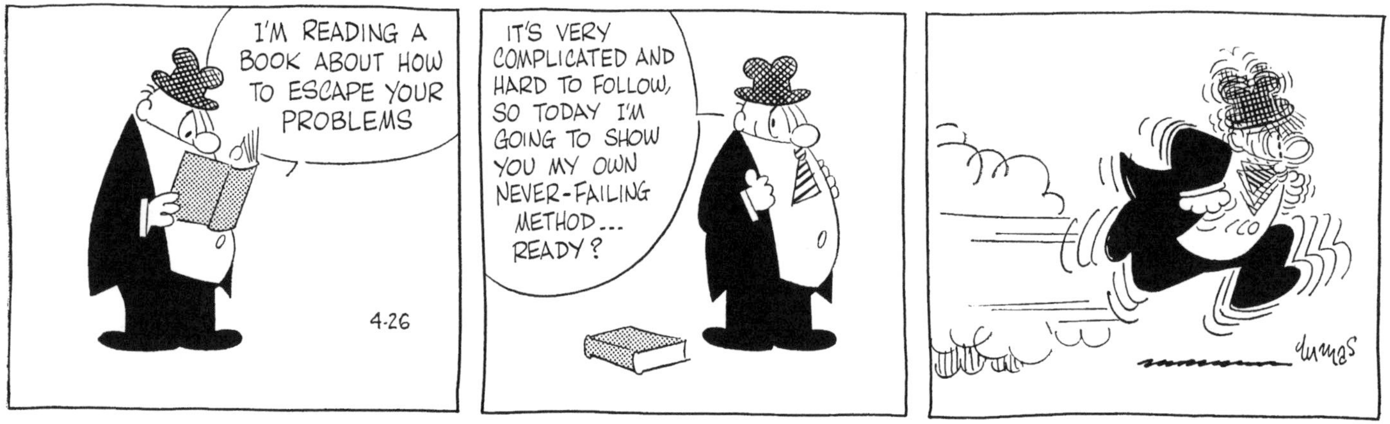
I'M READING A BOOK ABOUT HOW TO ESCAPE YOUR PROBLEMS
4-26
IT'S VERY COMPLICATED AND HARD TO FOLLOW, SO TODAY I'M GOING TO SHOW YOU MY OWN NEVER-FAILING METHOD... READY?
dumas

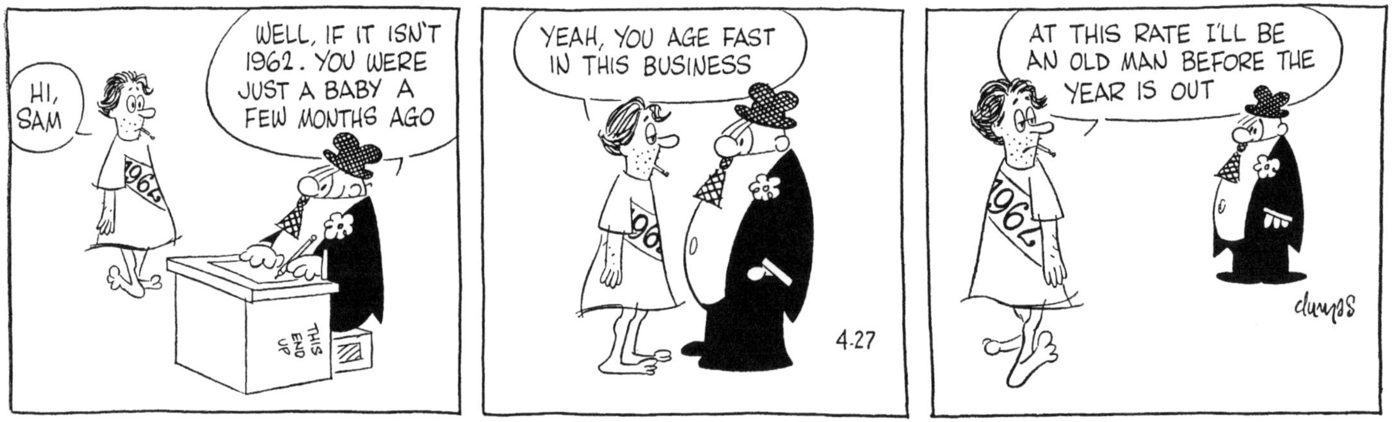
HI, SAM
WELL, IF IT ISN'T 1962. YOU WERE JUST A BABY A FEW MONTHS AGO
1962
THIS END UP
YEAH, YOU AGE FAST IN THIS BUSINESS
4-27
AT THIS RATE I'LL BE AN OLD MAN BEFORE THE YEAR IS OUT
dumas

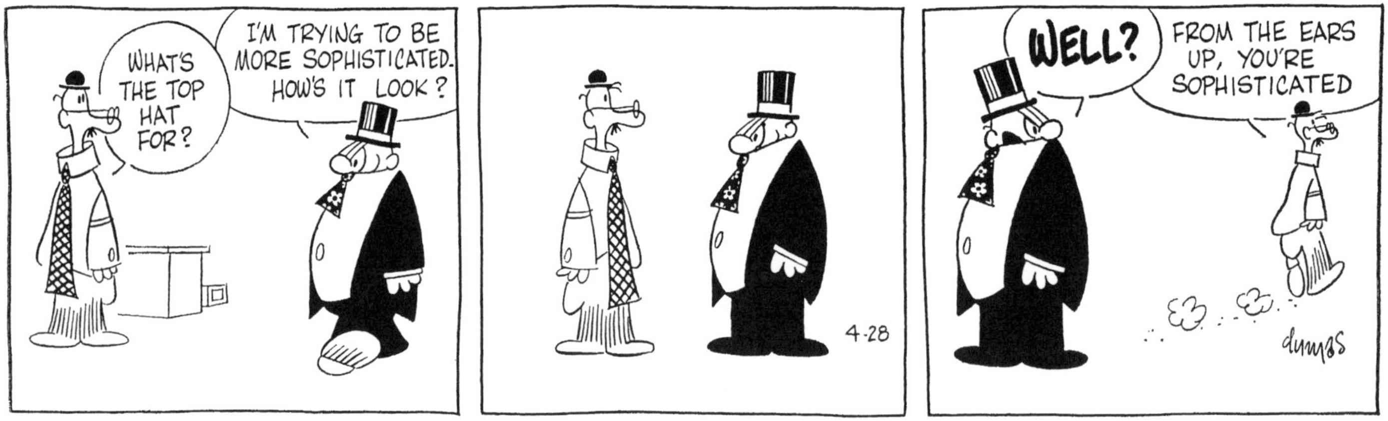
WHAT'S THE TOP HAT FOR?
I'M TRYING TO BE MORE SOPHISTICATED. HOW'S IT LOOK?
4-28
WELL?
FROM THE EARS UP, YOU'RE SOPHISTICATED
dumas

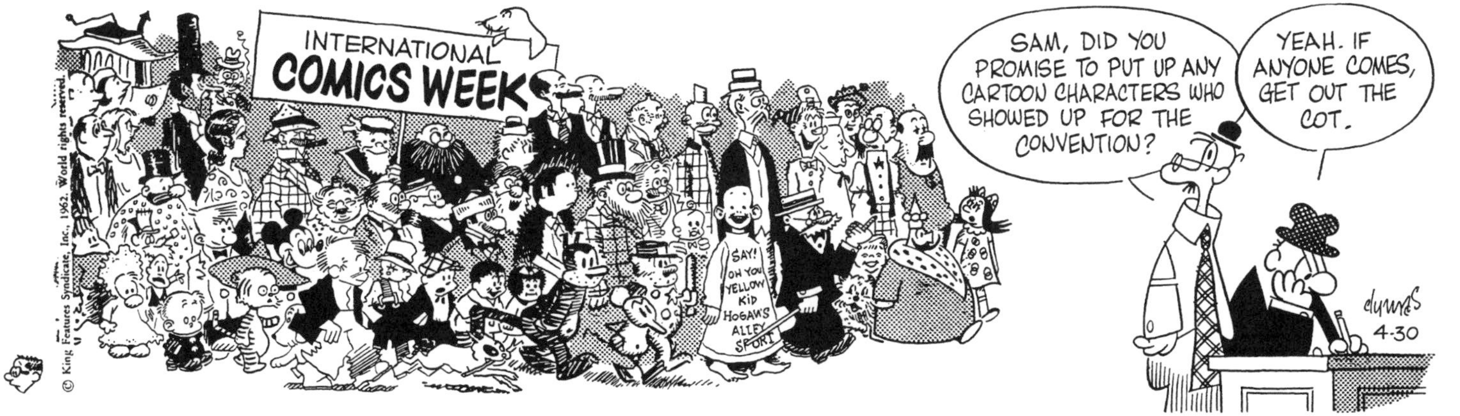

© King Features Syndicate, Inc., 1962. World rights reserved.
INTERNATIONAL COMICS WEEK
SAY! OH YOU YELLOW KID HOGAN'S ALLEY SPORT
SAM, DID YOU PROMISE TO PUT UP ANY CARTOON CHARACTERS WHO SHOWED UP FOR THE CONVENTION?
YEAH. IF ANYONE COMES, GET OUT THE COT.
dumas
4-30

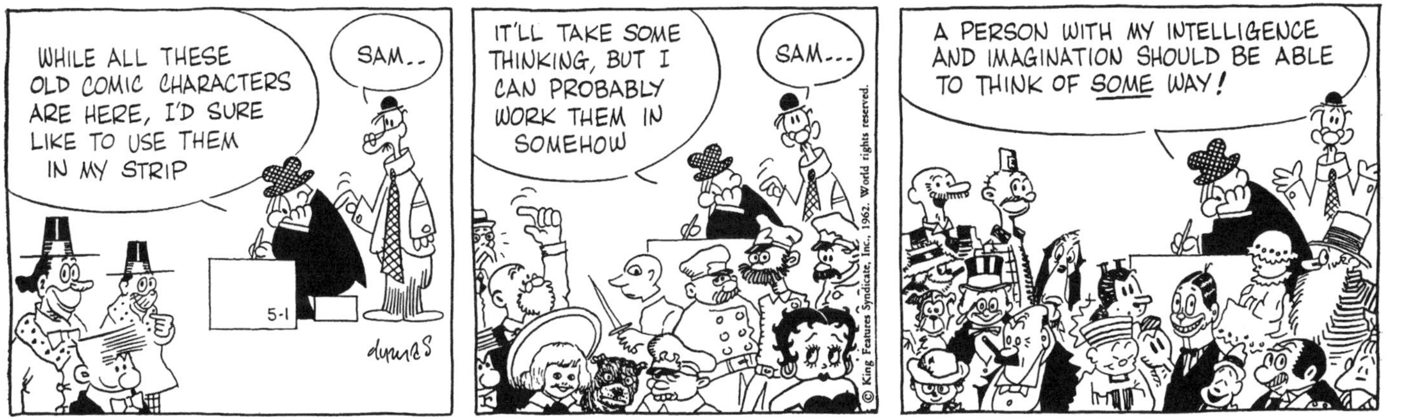

WHILE ALL THESE OLD COMIC CHARACTERS ARE HERE, I'D SURE LIKE TO USE THEM IN MY STRIP
SAM..
5-1
dumas
IT'LL TAKE SOME THINKING, BUT I CAN PROBABLY WORK THEM IN SOMEHOW
SAM...
© King Features Syndicate, Inc., 1962. World rights reserved.
A PERSON WITH MY INTELLIGENCE AND IMAGINATION SHOULD BE ABLE TO THINK OF SOME WAY!

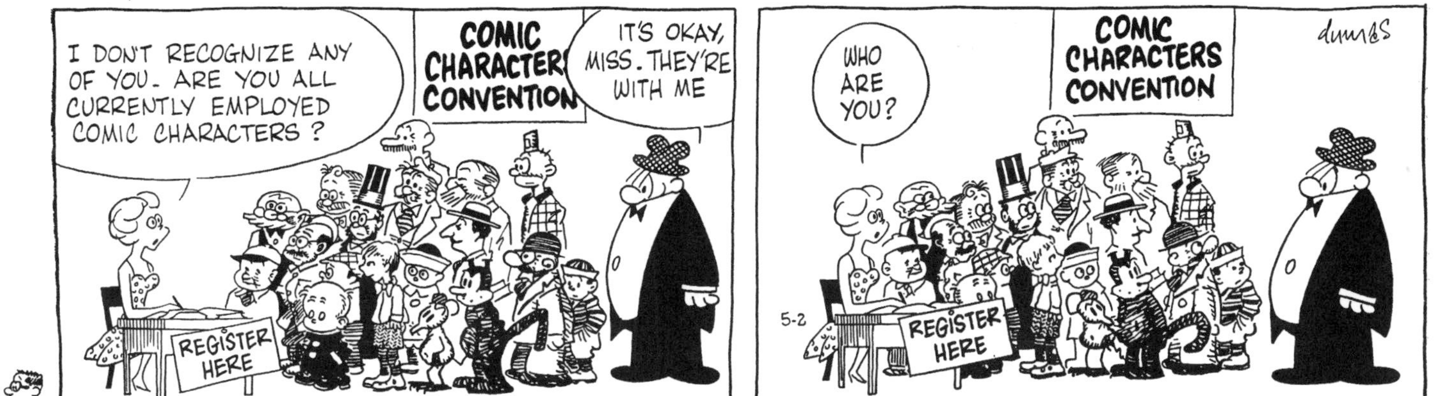

I DON'T RECOGNIZE ANY OF YOU. ARE YOU ALL CURRENTLY EMPLOYED COMIC CHARACTERS?
COMIC CHARACTERS CONVENTION
IT'S OKAY, MISS. THEY'RE WITH ME
REGISTER HERE
WHO ARE YOU?
COMIC CHARACTERS CONVENTION
dumas
5-2
REGISTER HERE

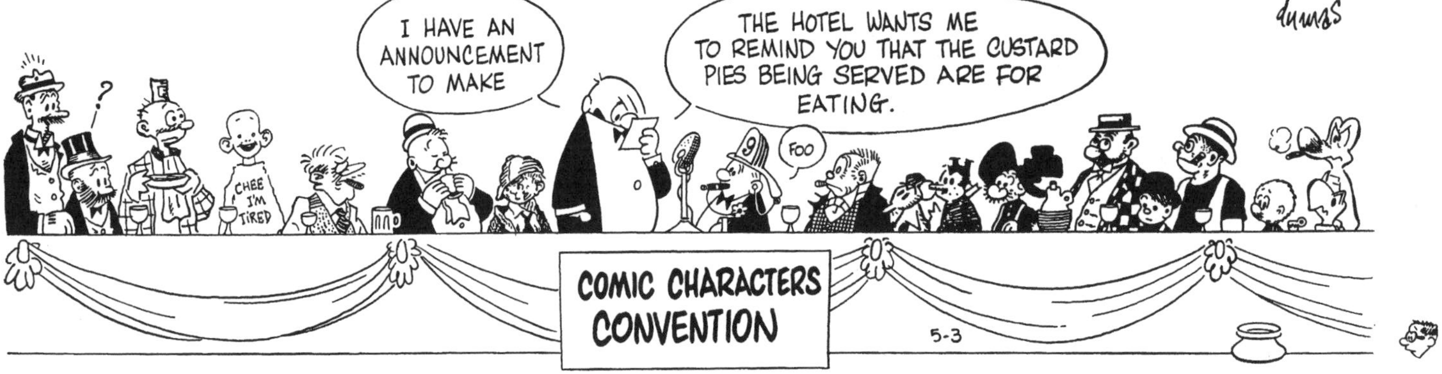
I HAVE AN ANNOUNCEMENT TO MAKE
THE HOTEL WANTS ME TO REMIND YOU THAT THE CUSTARD PIES BEING SERVED ARE FOR EATING.
CHEE I'M TIRED
FOO
COMIC CHARACTERS CONVENTION
5-3

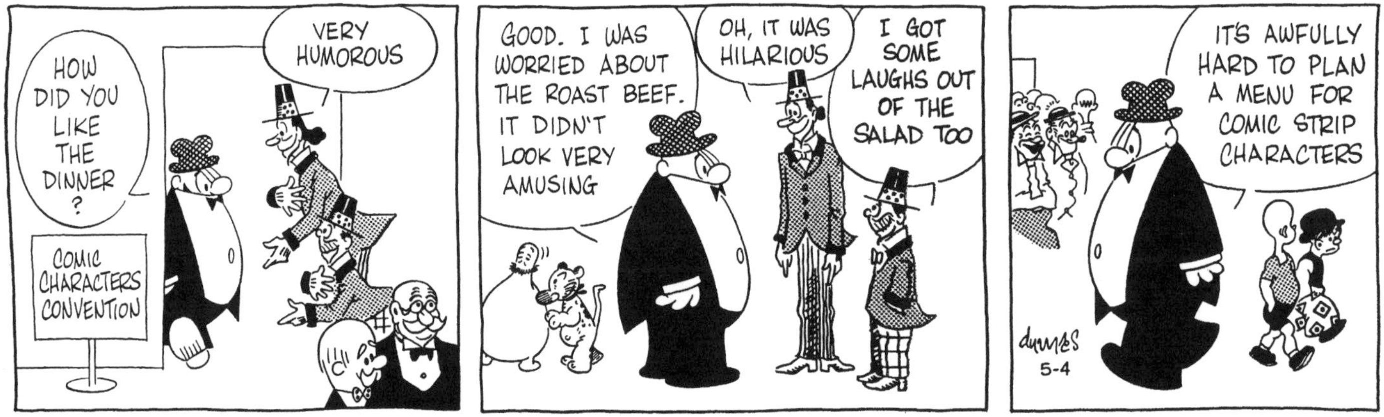
HOW DID YOU LIKE THE DINNER ?
VERY HUMOROUS
COMIC CHARACTERS CONVENTION
GOOD. I WAS WORRIED ABOUT THE ROAST BEEF. IT DIDN'T LOOK VERY AMUSING
OH, IT WAS HILARIOUS
I GOT SOME LAUGHS OUT OF THE SALAD TOO
IT'S AWFULLY HARD TO PLAN A MENU FOR COMIC STRIP CHARACTERS
5-4

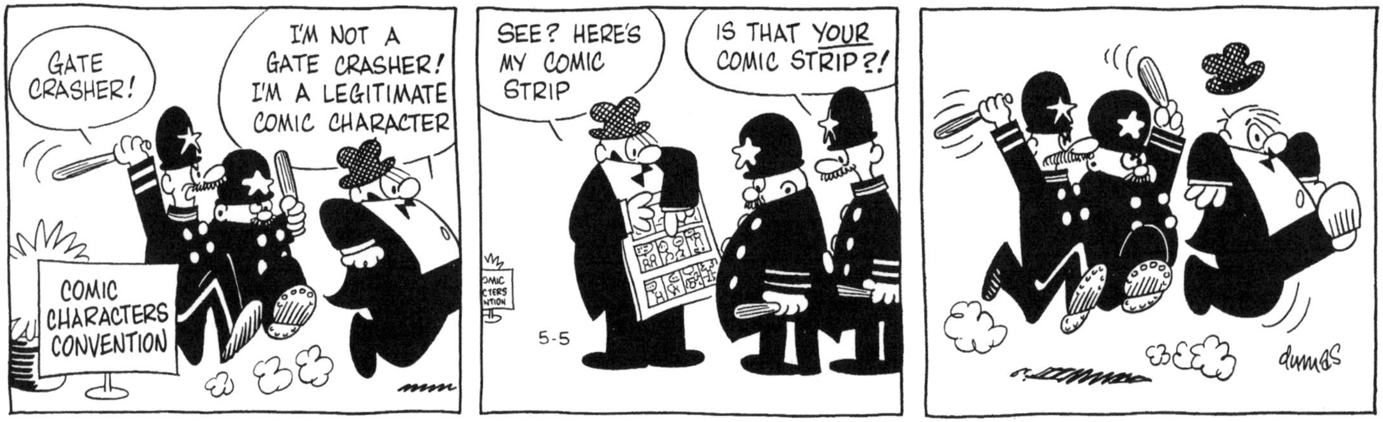
GATE CRASHER!
I'M NOT A GATE CRASHER! I'M A LEGITIMATE COMIC CHARACTER
COMIC CHARACTERS CONVENTION
SEE? HERE'S MY COMIC STRIP
IS THAT YOUR COMIC STRIP?!
5-5

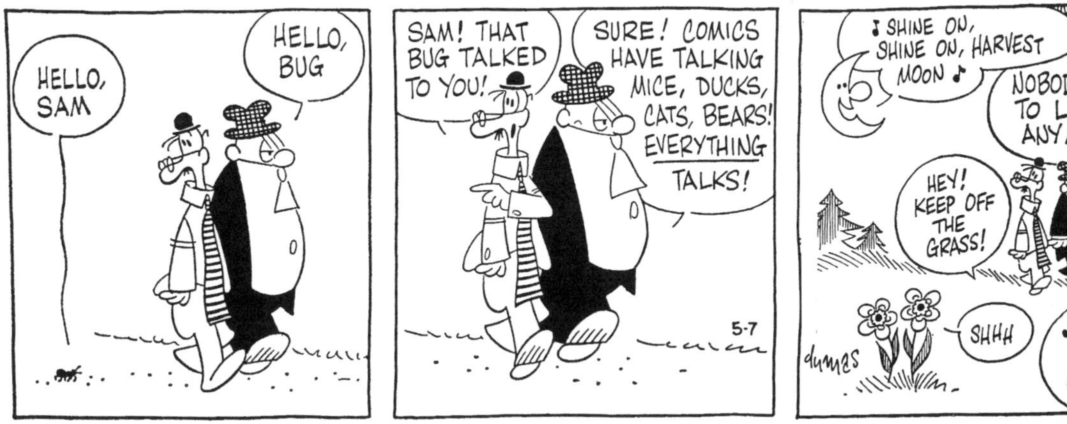
HELLO, SAM
HELLO, BUG
SAM! THAT BUG TALKED TO YOU!
SURE! COMICS HAVE TALKING MICE, DUCKS, CATS, BEARS! EVERYTHING TALKS!
5-7
♪ SHINE ON, SHINE ON, HARVEST MOON ♪
NOBODY WANTS TO LISTEN ANYMORE
SO LONG, DAD
HEY! KEEP OFF THE GRASS!
OUCH!
HIS HEAD LOOKS LIKE UNCLE HENRY'S
SHHH
♪ ROCK-A-BYE YOUR BA-BEE WITH A DIXIE.. ♫
dumas

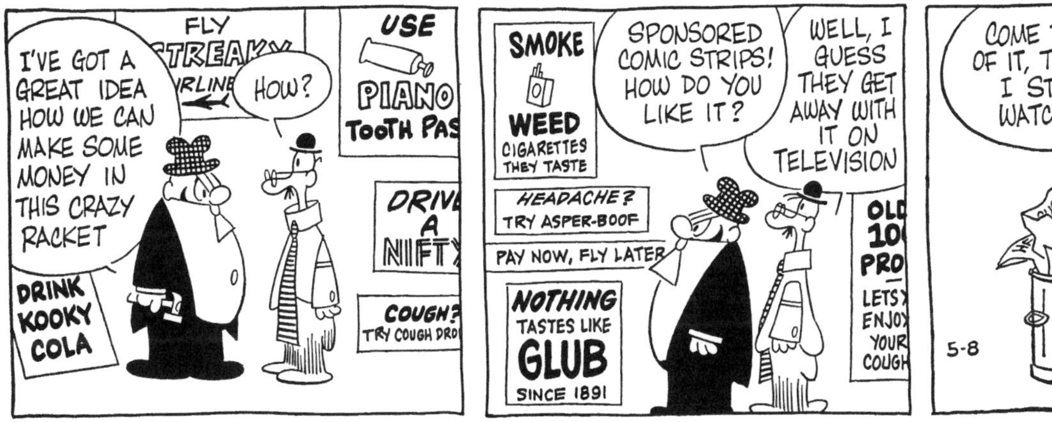
FLY STREAKY AIRLINE
I'VE GOT A GREAT IDEA HOW WE CAN MAKE SOME MONEY IN THIS CRAZY RACKET
HOW?
USE PIANO TOOTH PAS
DRIVE A NIFTY
COUGH? TRY COUGH DRO
DRINK KOOKY COLA
SMOKE WEED CIGARETTES THEY TASTE
SPONSORED COMIC STRIPS! HOW DO YOU LIKE IT?
WELL, I GUESS THEY GET AWAY WITH IT ON TELEVISION
HEADACHE? TRY ASPER-BOOF
PAY NOW, FLY LATER
NOTHING TASTES LIKE GLUB SINCE 1891
OLD 10 PRO
LETS ENJOY YOUR COUGH
COME TO THINK OF IT, THAT'S WHY I STOPPED WATCHING
USE
5-8
dumas

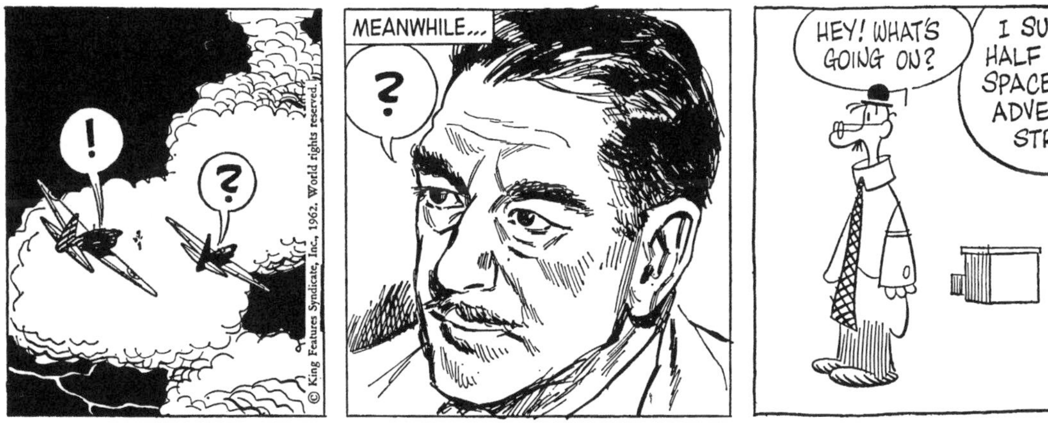
!
?
© King Features Syndicate, Inc., 1962. World rights reserved.
MEANWHILE...
?
HEY! WHAT'S GOING ON?
I SUBLET HALF OF OUR SPACE TO AN ADVENTURE STRIP
THEY NEEDED THE SPACE AND I NEEDED THE MONEY
dumas
5-9

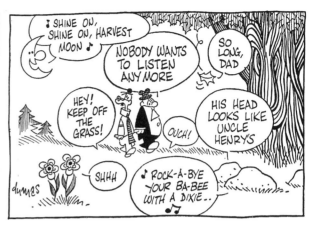

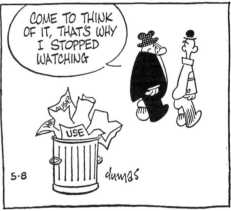

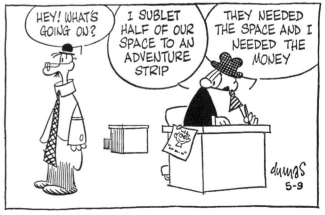

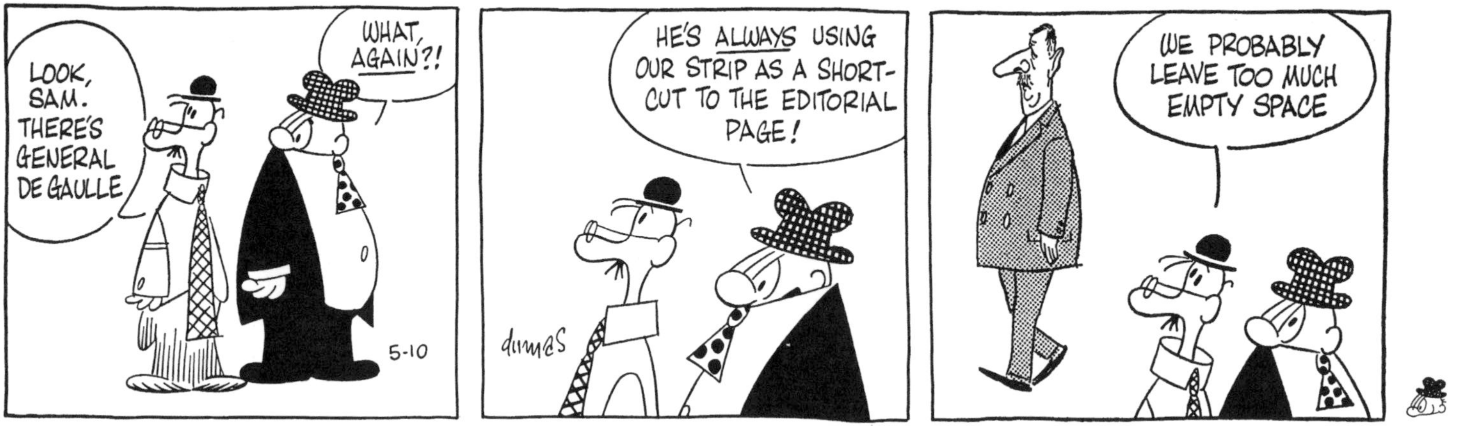
LOOK, SAM. THERE'S GENERAL DE GAULLE
WHAT, AGAIN?!
5-10
HE'S ALWAYS USING OUR STRIP AS A SHORT-CUT TO THE EDITORIAL PAGE!
dumas
WE PROBABLY LEAVE TOO MUCH EMPTY SPACE

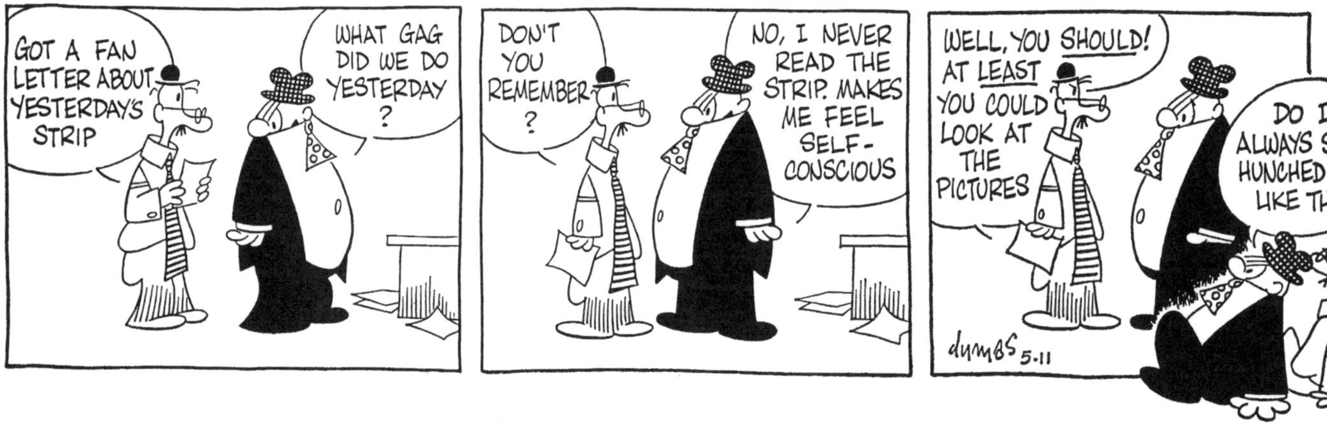
GOT A FAN LETTER ABOUT YESTERDAY'S STRIP
WHAT GAG DID WE DO YESTERDAY ?
DON'T YOU REMEMBER ?
NO, I NEVER READ THE STRIP. MAKES ME FEEL SELF-CONSCIOUS
WELL, YOU SHOULD! AT LEAST YOU COULD LOOK AT THE PICTURES
DO I ALWAYS STAND HUNCHED UP LIKE THAT?
dumas 5-11

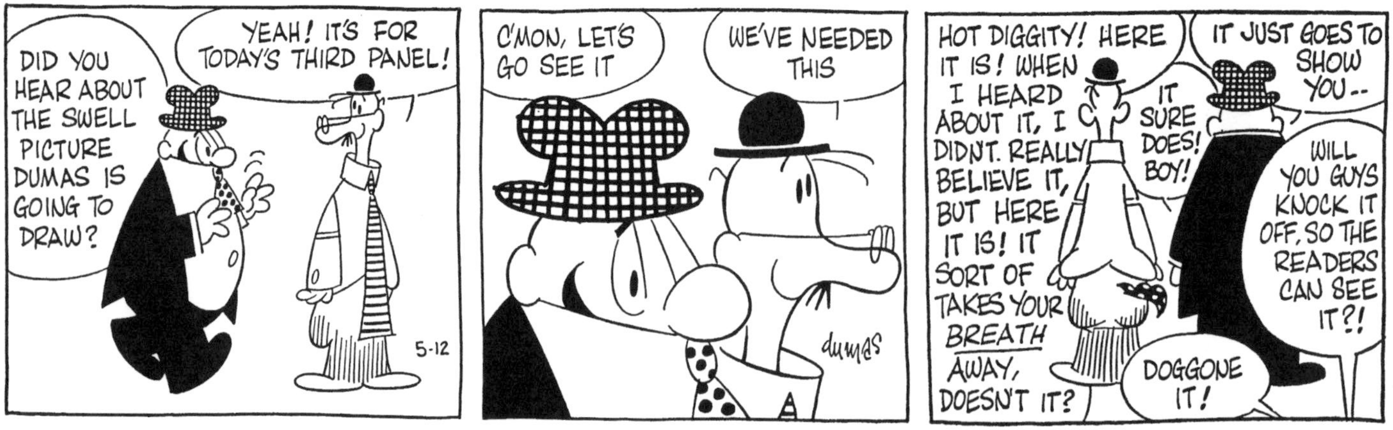
DID YOU HEAR ABOUT THE SWELL PICTURE DUMAS IS GOING TO DRAW?
YEAH! IT'S FOR TODAY'S THIRD PANEL!
5-12
C'MON, LET'S GO SEE IT
WE'VE NEEDED THIS
dumas
HOT DIGGITY! HERE IT IS! WHEN I HEARD ABOUT IT, I DIDN'T REALLY BELIEVE IT, BUT HERE IT IS! IT SORT OF TAKES YOUR BREATH AWAY, DOESN'T IT?
IT SURE DOES! BOY!
IT JUST GOES TO SHOW YOU--
WILL YOU GUYS KNOCK IT OFF, SO THE READERS CAN SEE IT?!
DOGGONE IT!

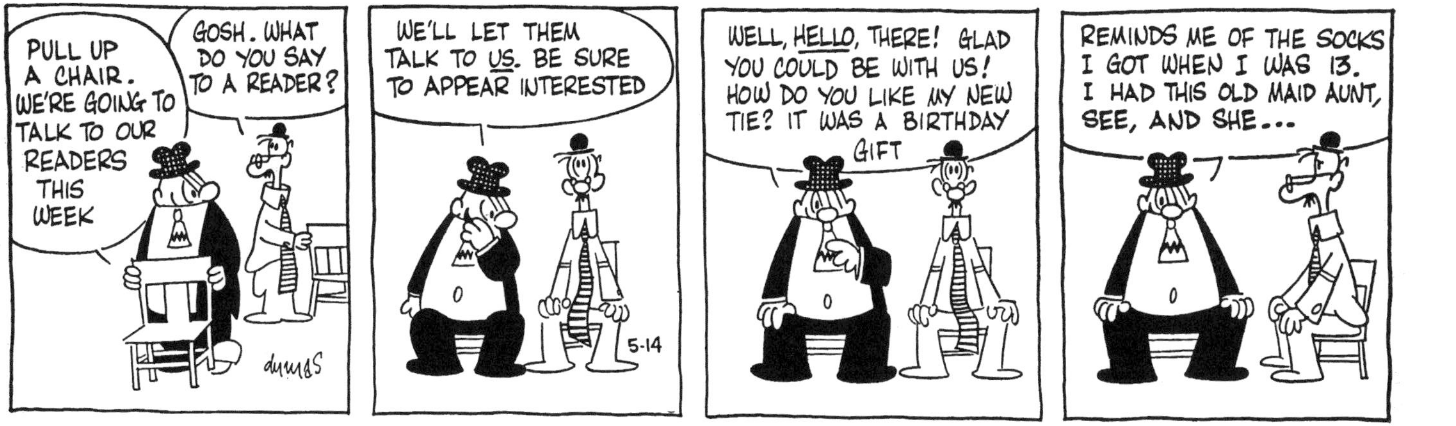
PULL UP A CHAIR. WE'RE GOING TO TALK TO OUR READERS THIS WEEK
GOSH. WHAT DO YOU SAY TO A READER?
WE'LL LET THEM TALK TO US. BE SURE TO APPEAR INTERESTED
5-14
WELL, HELLO, THERE! GLAD YOU COULD BE WITH US! HOW DO YOU LIKE MY NEW TIE? IT WAS A BIRTHDAY GIFT
REMINDS ME OF THE SOCKS I GOT WHEN I WAS 13. I HAD THIS OLD MAID AUNT, SEE, AND SHE...

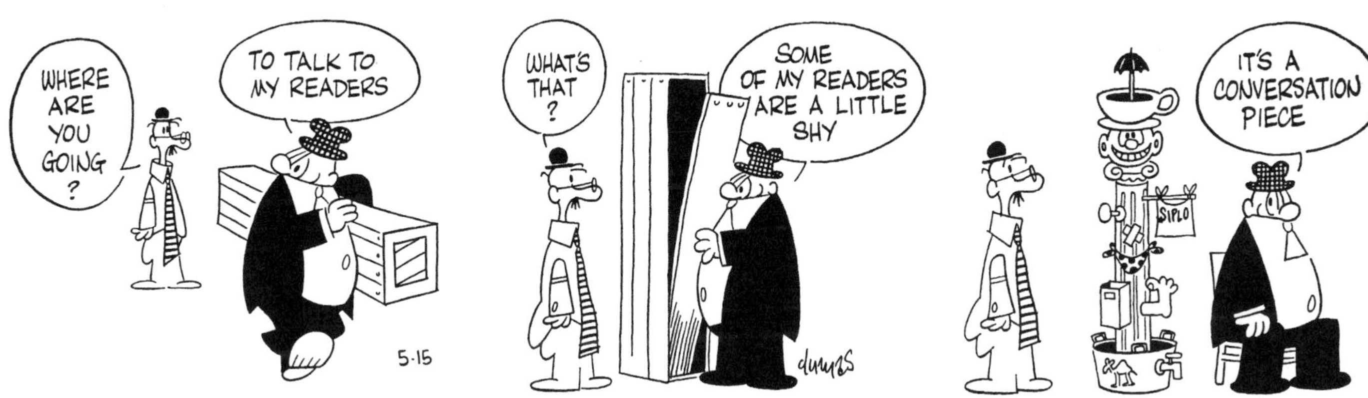
WHERE ARE YOU GOING ?
TO TALK TO MY READERS
5-15
WHAT'S THAT ?
SOME OF MY READERS ARE A LITTLE SHY
IT'S A CONVERSATION PIECE
SIPLO

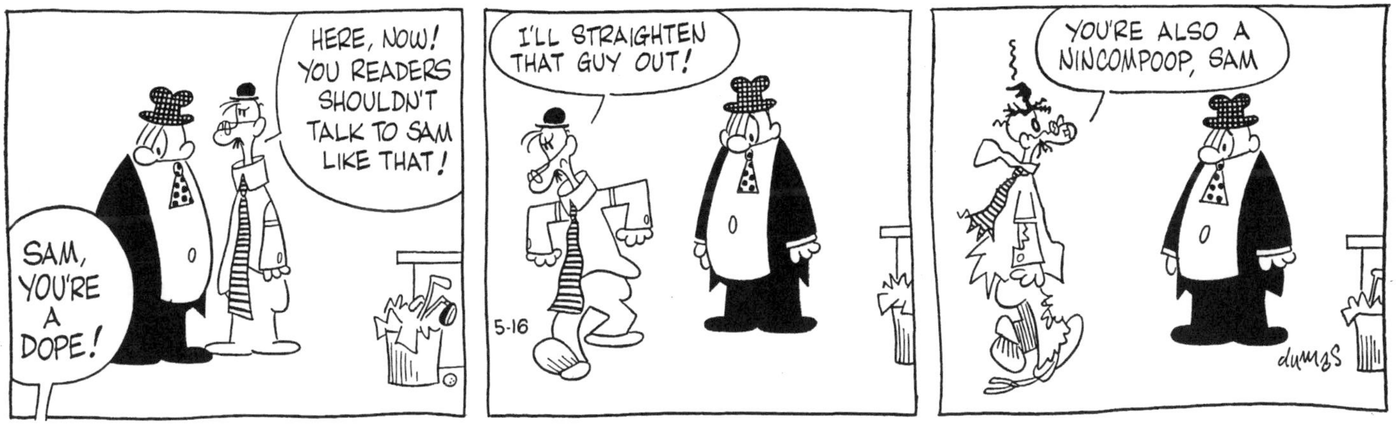
HERE, NOW! YOU READERS SHOULDN'T TALK TO SAM LIKE THAT!
SAM, YOU'RE A DOPE!
I'LL STRAIGHTEN THAT GUY OUT!
5-16
YOU'RE ALSO A NINCOMPOOP, SAM

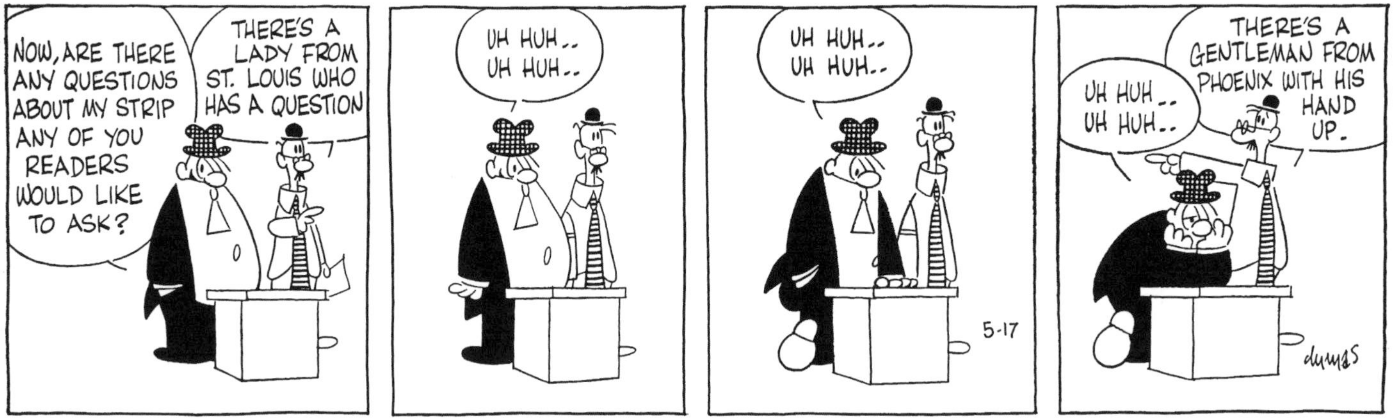
NOW, ARE THERE ANY QUESTIONS ABOUT MY STRIP ANY OF YOU READERS WOULD LIKE TO ASK?
THERE'S A LADY FROM ST. LOUIS WHO HAS A QUESTION
UH HUH.. UH HUH..
UH HUH.. UH HUH..
5-17
THERE'S A GENTLEMAN FROM PHOENIX WITH HIS HAND UP.
UH HUH.. UH HUH..
dumas

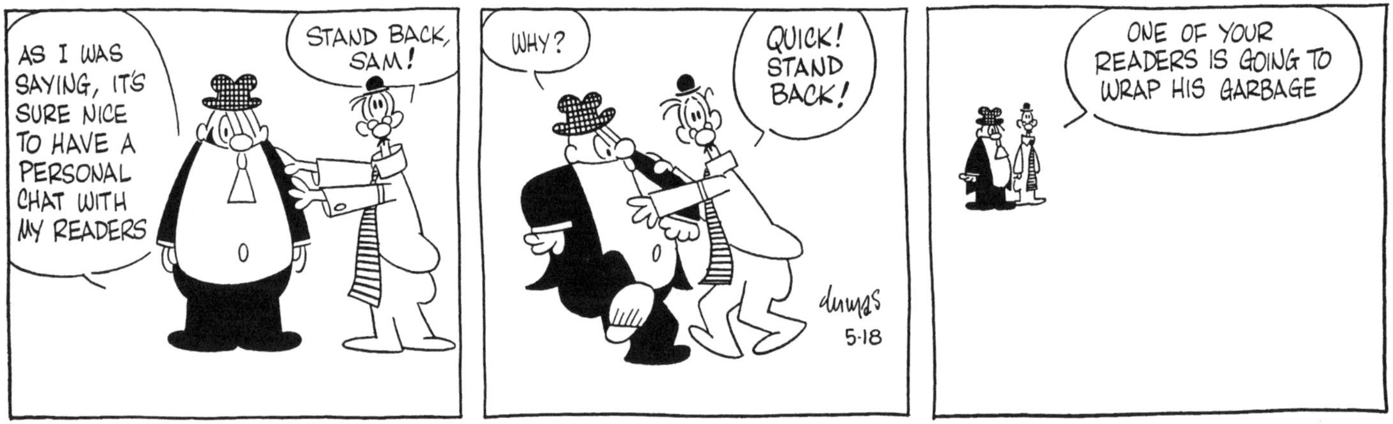
AS I WAS SAYING, IT'S SURE NICE TO HAVE A PERSONAL CHAT WITH MY READERS
STAND BACK, SAM!
WHY?
QUICK! STAND BACK!
dumas
5-18
ONE OF YOUR READERS IS GOING TO WRAP HIS GARBAGE

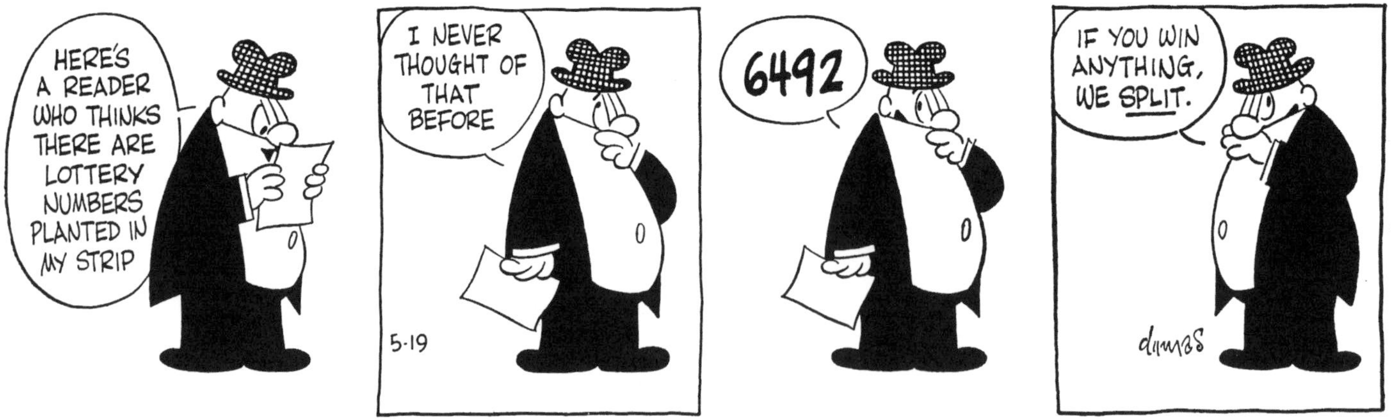
HERE'S A READER WHO THINKS THERE ARE LOTTERY NUMBERS PLANTED IN MY STRIP
I NEVER THOUGHT OF THAT BEFORE
5-19
6492
IF YOU WIN ANYTHING, WE SPLIT.
dumas

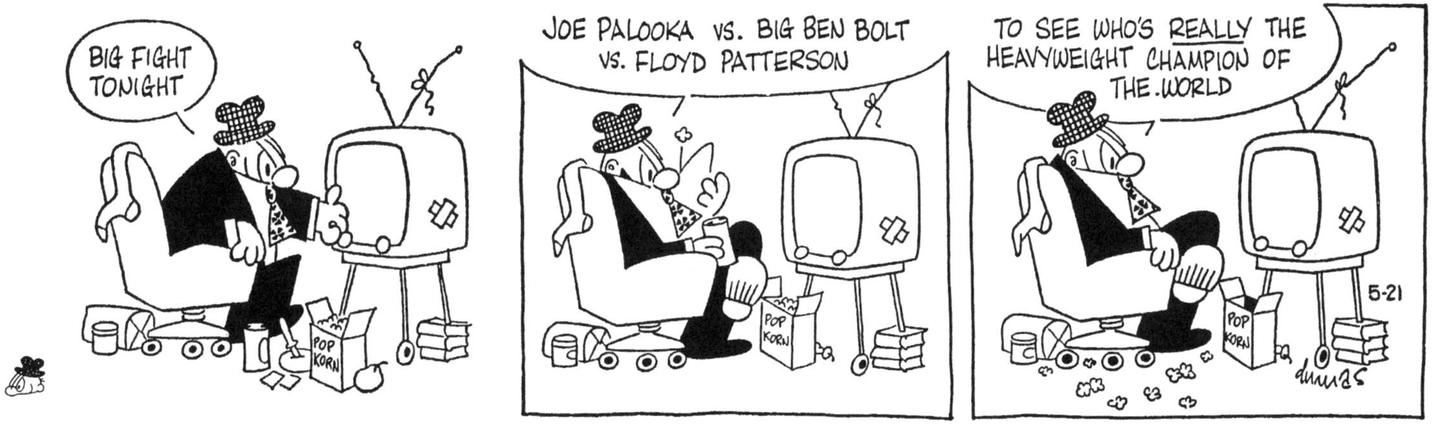
BIG FIGHT TONIGHT
POP KORN
JOE PALOOKA VS. BIG BEN BOLT VS. FLOYD PATTERSON
POP KORN
TO SEE WHO'S REALLY THE HEAVYWEIGHT CHAMPION OF THE WORLD
POP KORN
5-21
dumas

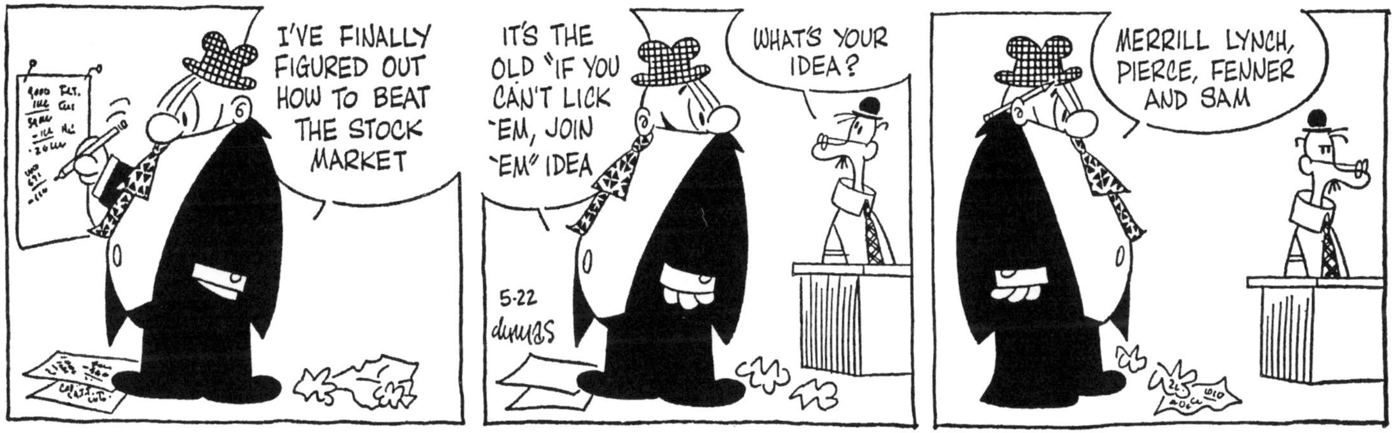
I'VE FINALLY FIGURED OUT HOW TO BEAT THE STOCK MARKET
IT'S THE OLD "IF YOU CAN'T LICK 'EM, JOIN 'EM" IDEA
WHAT'S YOUR IDEA?
5-22
dumas
MERRILL LYNCH, PIERCE, FENNER AND SAM

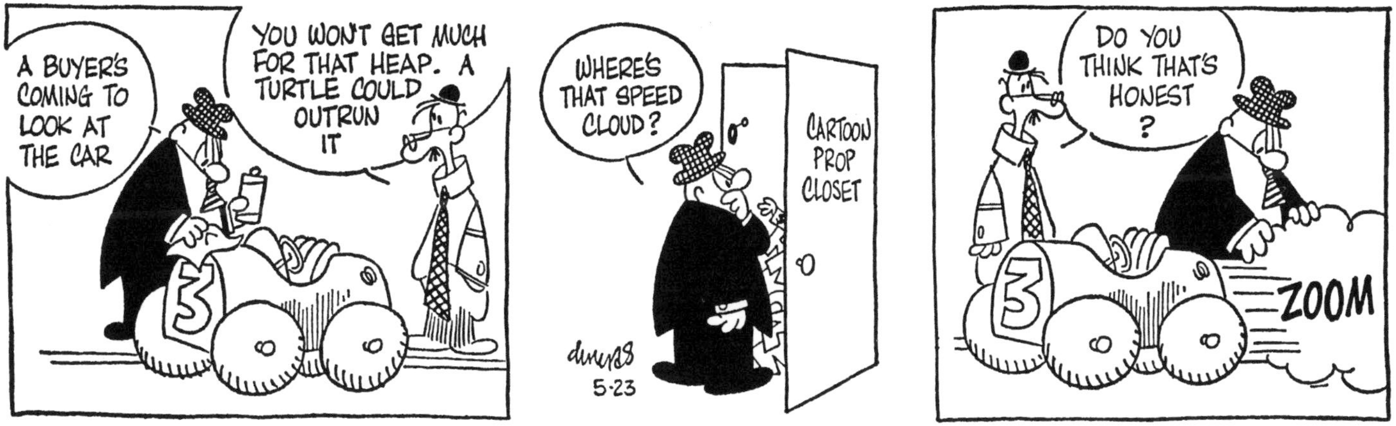
A BUYER'S COMING TO LOOK AT THE CAR
YOU WON'T GET MUCH FOR THAT HEAP. A TURTLE COULD OUTRUN IT
WHERE'S THAT SPEED CLOUD?
CARTOON PROP CLOSET
dumas
5-23
DO YOU THINK THAT'S HONEST ?
ZOOM

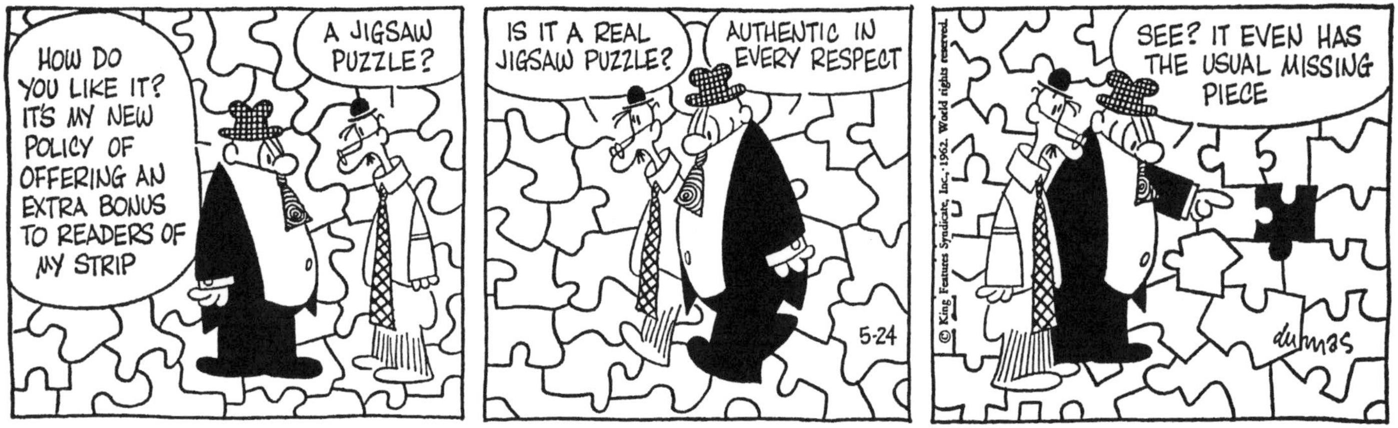
HOW DO YOU LIKE IT? IT'S MY NEW POLICY OF OFFERING AN EXTRA BONUS TO READERS OF MY STRIP
A JIGSAW PUZZLE?
IS IT A REAL JIGSAW PUZZLE?
AUTHENTIC IN EVERY RESPECT
5-24
© King Features Syndicate, Inc., 1962. World rights reserved.
SEE? IT EVEN HAS THE USUAL MISSING PIECE
dumas

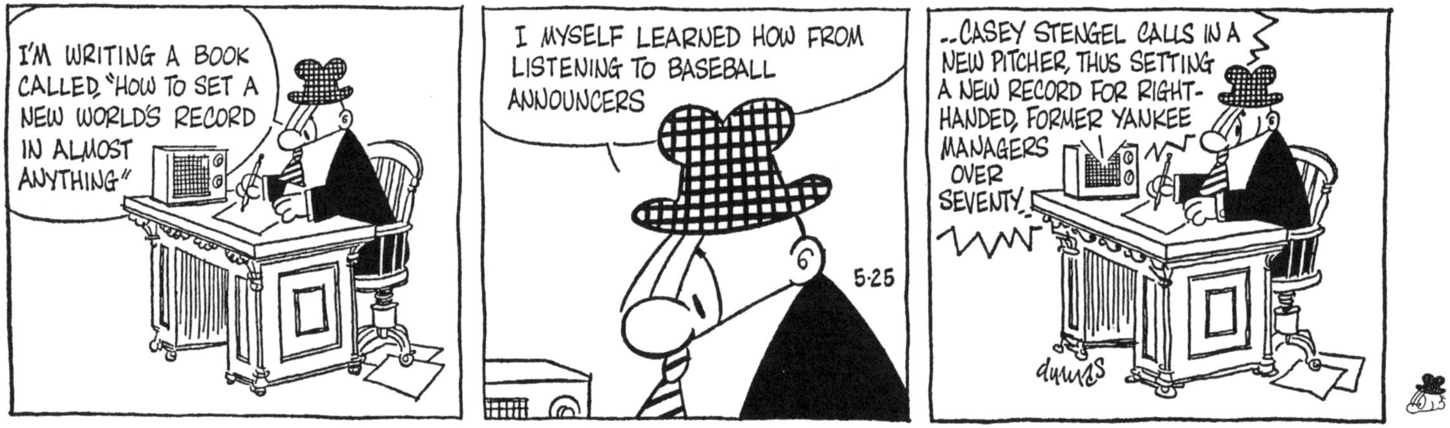
I'M WRITING A BOOK CALLED, "HOW TO SET A NEW WORLD'S RECORD IN ALMOST ANYTHING"
I MYSELF LEARNED HOW FROM LISTENING TO BASEBALL ANNOUNCERS
5-25
--CASEY STENGEL CALLS IN A NEW PITCHER, THUS SETTING A NEW RECORD FOR RIGHT-HANDED, FORMER YANKEE MANAGERS OVER SEVENTY
dumas

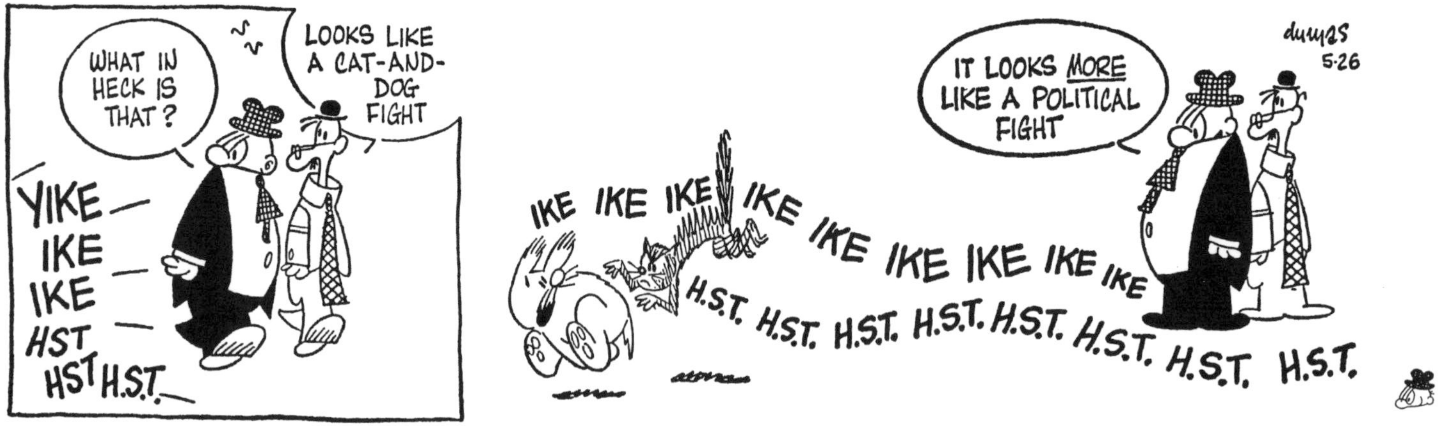
WHAT IN HECK IS THAT?
LOOKS LIKE A CAT-AND-DOG FIGHT
YIKE IKE IKE HST HST H.S.T.
dumas
5-26
IT LOOKS MORE LIKE A POLITICAL FIGHT
IKE IKE IKE IKE IKE IKE IKE IKE IKE
H.S.T. H.S.T. H.S.T. H.S.T. H.S.T. H.S.T. H.S.T. H.S.T.

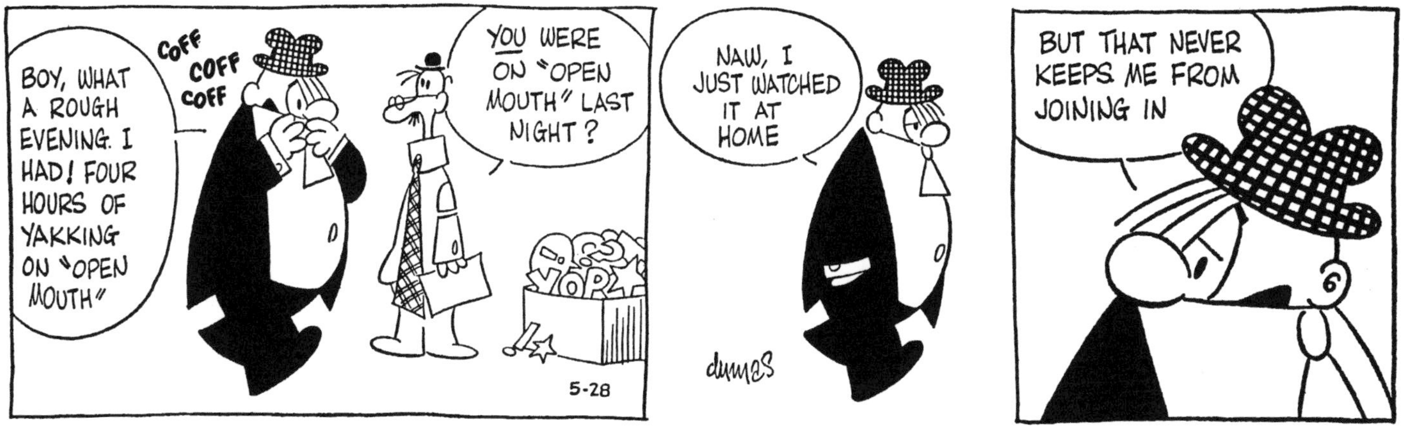
BOY, WHAT A ROUGH EVENING. I HAD! FOUR HOURS OF YAKKING ON "OPEN MOUTH"
COFF COFF COFF
YOU WERE ON "OPEN MOUTH" LAST NIGHT?
5-28
NAW, I JUST WATCHED IT AT HOME
dumas
BUT THAT NEVER KEEPS ME FROM JOINING IN

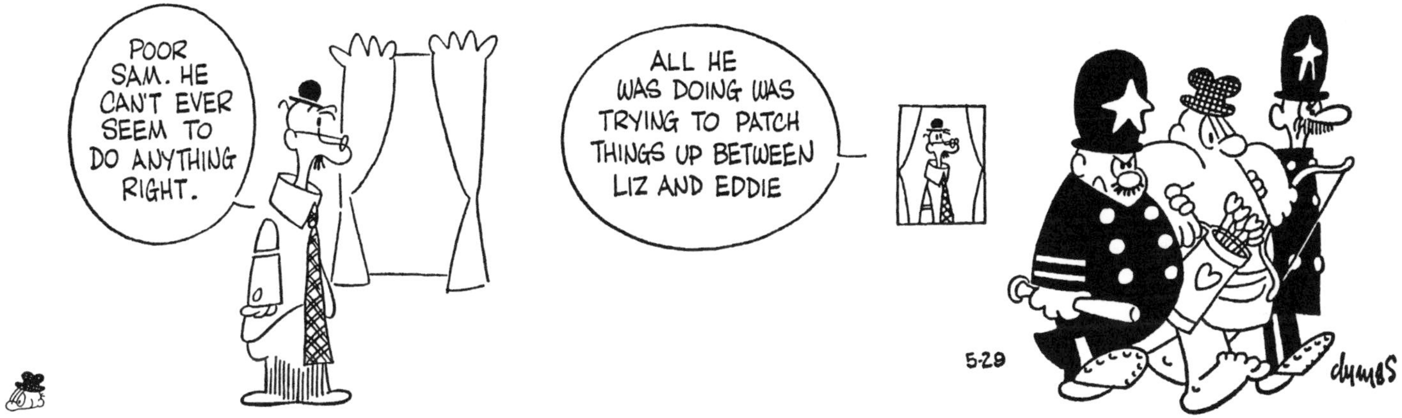
POOR SAM. HE CAN'T EVER SEEM TO DO ANYTHING RIGHT.
ALL HE WAS DOING WAS TRYING TO PATCH THINGS UP BETWEEN LIZ AND EDDIE
5-29
dumas

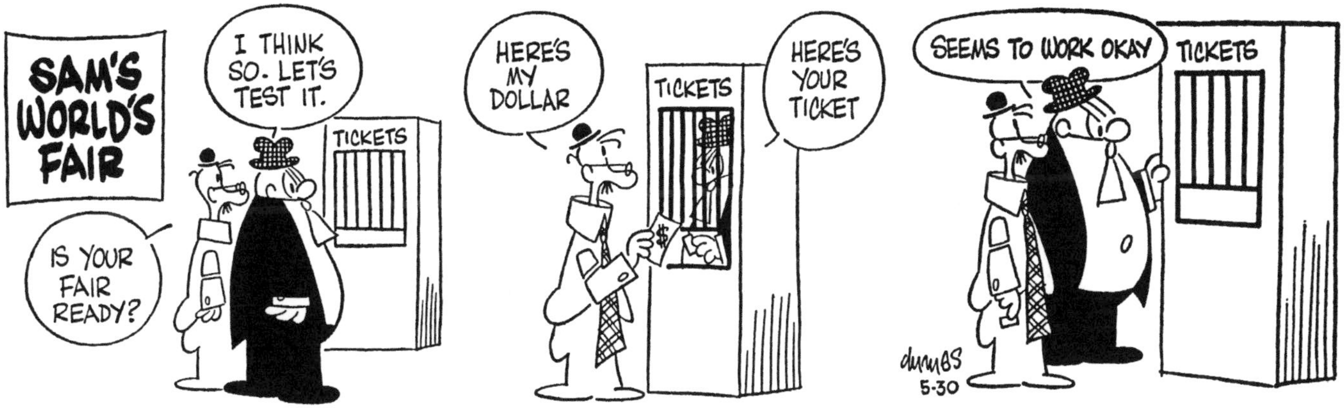
SAM'S WORLD'S FAIR
IS YOUR FAIR READY?
I THINK SO. LET'S TEST IT.
TICKETS
HERE'S MY DOLLAR
TICKETS
HERE'S YOUR TICKET
SEEMS TO WORK OKAY
TICKETS
dumas
5-30

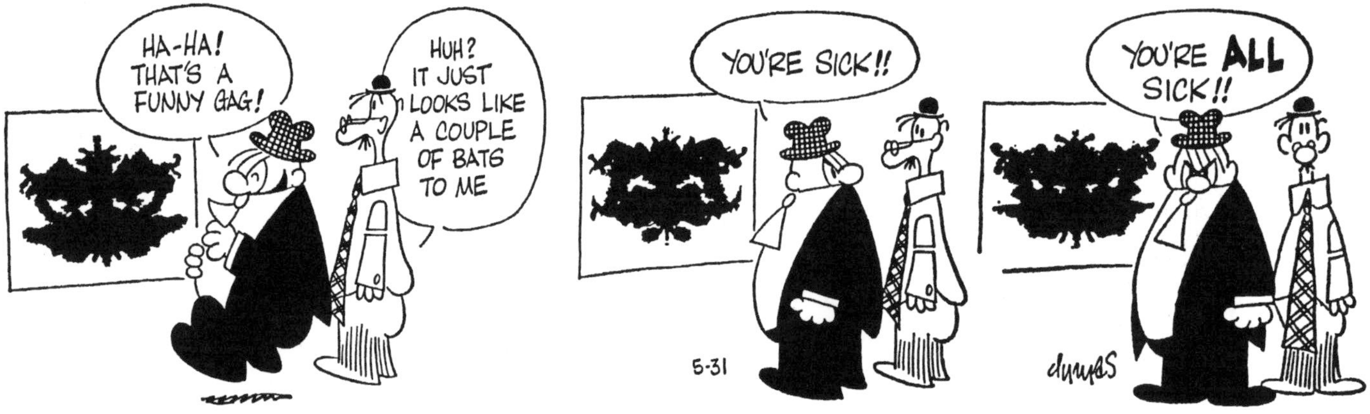
HA-HA! THAT'S A FUNNY GAG!
HUH? IT JUST LOOKS LIKE A COUPLE OF BATS TO ME
YOU'RE SICK!!
5-31
YOU'RE ALL SICK!!
dumas

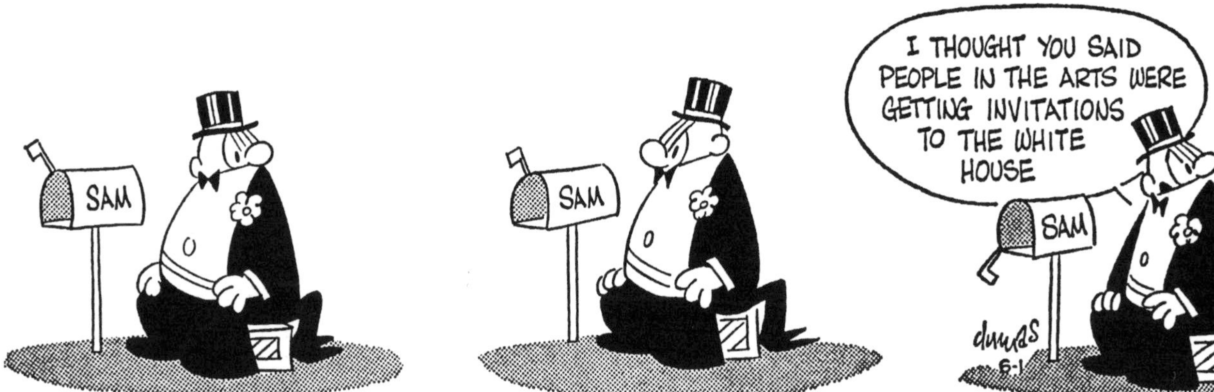
SAM
SAM
I THOUGHT YOU SAID PEOPLE IN THE ARTS WERE GETTING INVITATIONS TO THE WHITE HOUSE
SAM
dumas
6-1

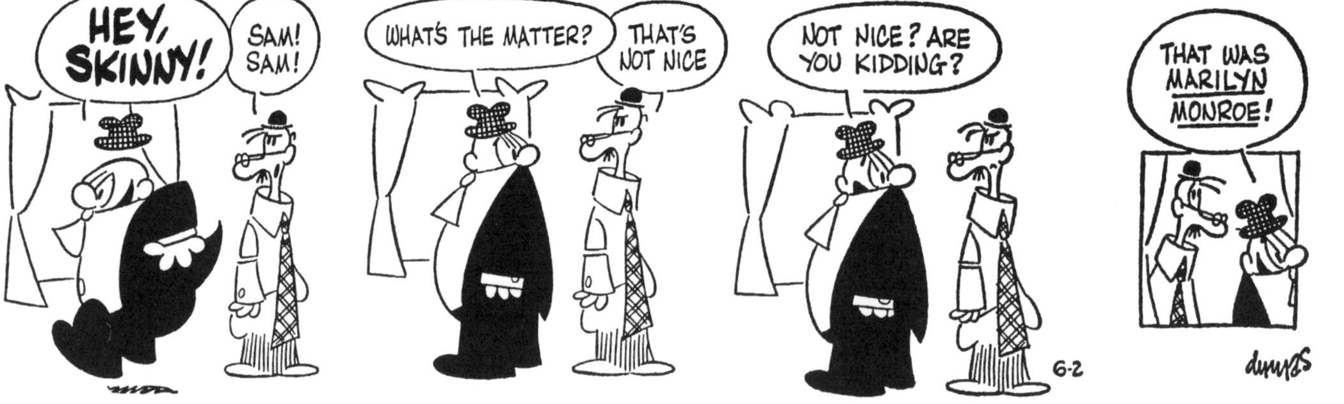
HEY, SKINNY!
SAM! SAM!
WHAT'S THE MATTER?
THAT'S NOT NICE
NOT NICE? ARE YOU KIDDING?
6-2
THAT WAS MARILYN MONROE!
dumas

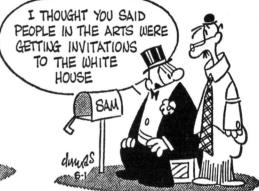

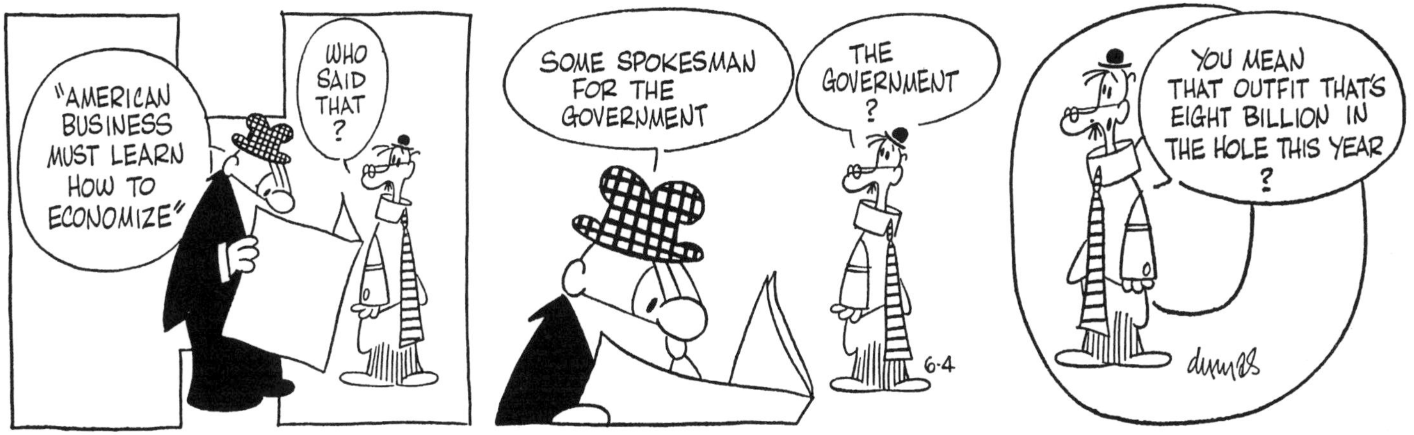
"AMERICAN BUSINESS MUST LEARN HOW TO ECONOMIZE"
WHO SAID THAT ?
SOME SPOKESMAN FOR THE GOVERNMENT
THE GOVERNMENT ?
YOU MEAN THAT OUTFIT THAT'S EIGHT BILLION IN THE HOLE THIS YEAR ?
6-4
dumas

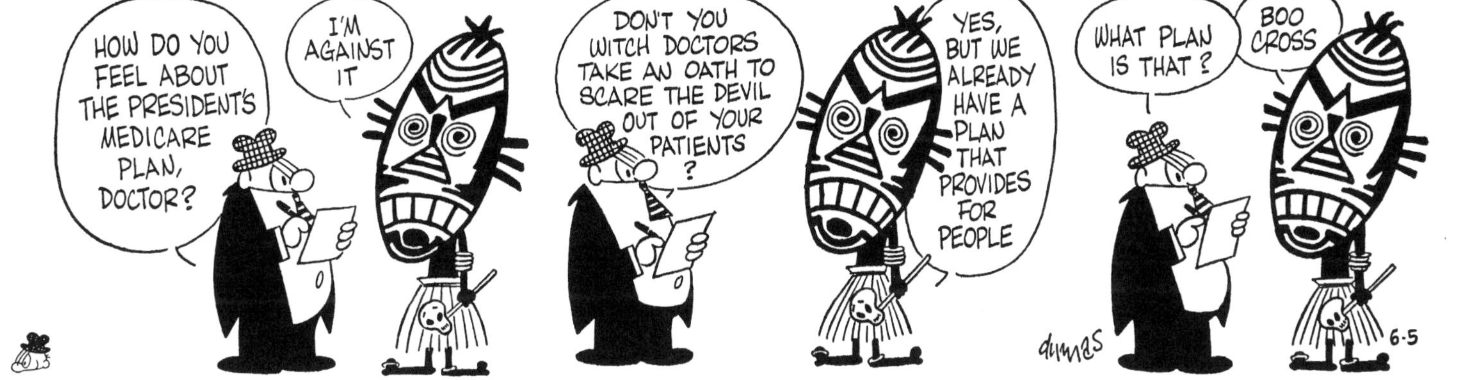
HOW DO YOU FEEL ABOUT THE PRESIDENT'S MEDICARE PLAN, DOCTOR?
I'M AGAINST IT
DON'T YOU WITCH DOCTORS TAKE AN OATH TO SCARE THE DEVIL OUT OF YOUR PATIENTS ?
YES, BUT WE ALREADY HAVE A PLAN THAT PROVIDES FOR PEOPLE
WHAT PLAN IS THAT ?
BOO CROSS
dumas
6-5

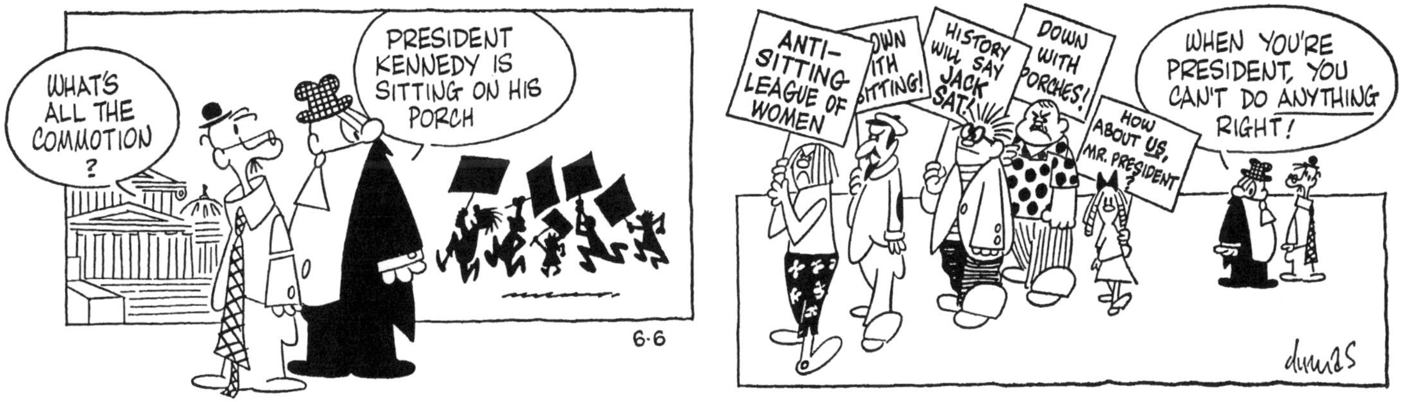
WHAT'S ALL THE COMMOTION ?
PRESIDENT KENNEDY IS SITTING ON HIS PORCH
6-6
ANTI-SITTING LEAGUE OF WOMEN
OWN ITH ITTING!
HISTORY WILL SAY JACK SAT!
DOWN WITH PORCHES!
HOW ABOUT US, MR. PRESIDENT ?
WHEN YOU'RE PRESIDENT, YOU CAN'T DO ANYTHING RIGHT!
dumas

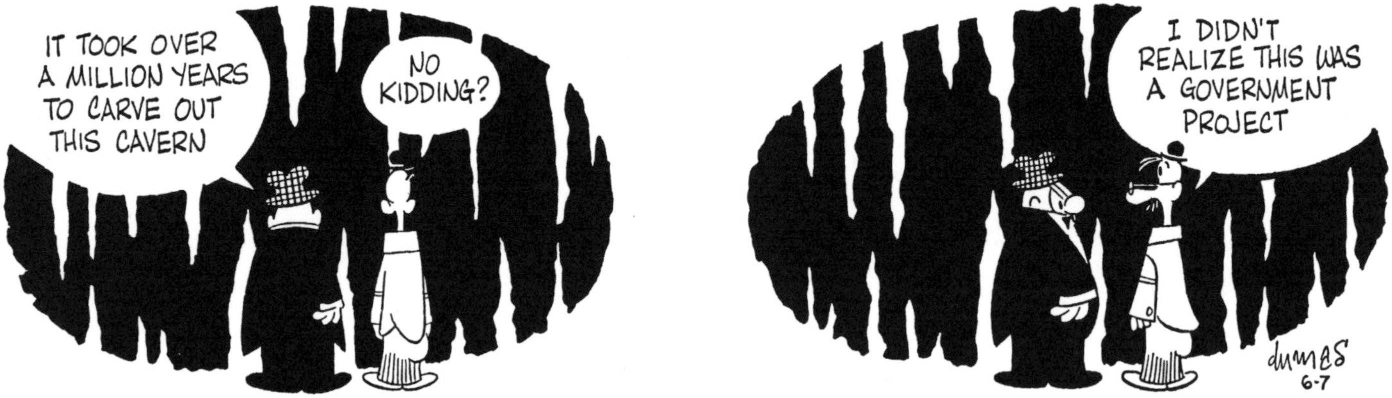
IT TOOK OVER A MILLION YEARS TO CARVE OUT THIS CAVERN
NO KIDDING?
I DIDN'T REALIZE THIS WAS A GOVERNMENT PROJECT
dumas
6-7

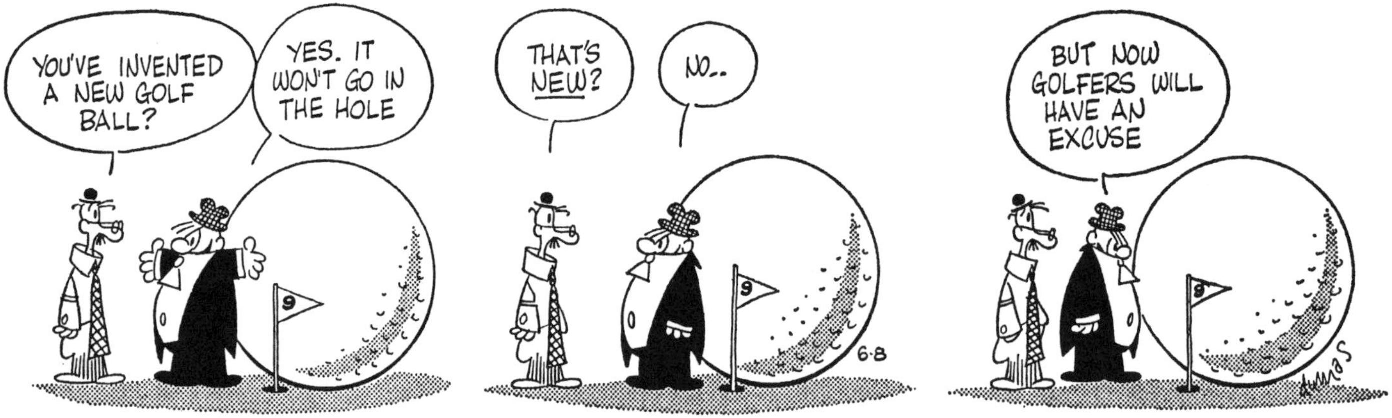
YOU'VE INVENTED A NEW GOLF BALL?
YES. IT WON'T GO IN THE HOLE
THAT'S NEW?
NO..
6-8
BUT NOW GOLFERS WILL HAVE AN EXCUSE
dumas

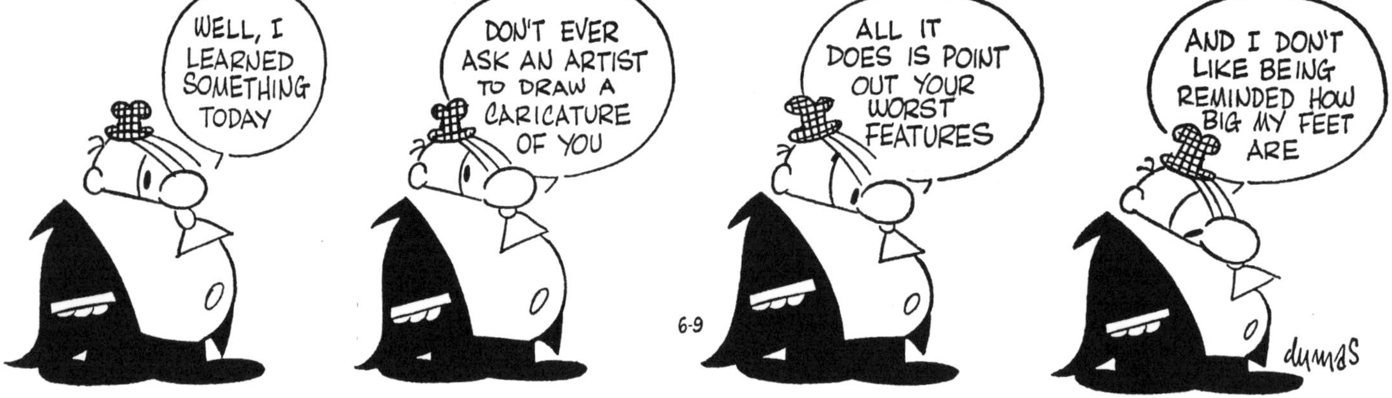
WELL, I LEARNED SOMETHING TODAY
DON'T EVER ASK AN ARTIST TO DRAW A CARICATURE OF YOU
ALL IT DOES IS POINT OUT YOUR WORST FEATURES
6-9
AND I DON'T LIKE BEING REMINDED HOW BIG MY FEET ARE
dumas

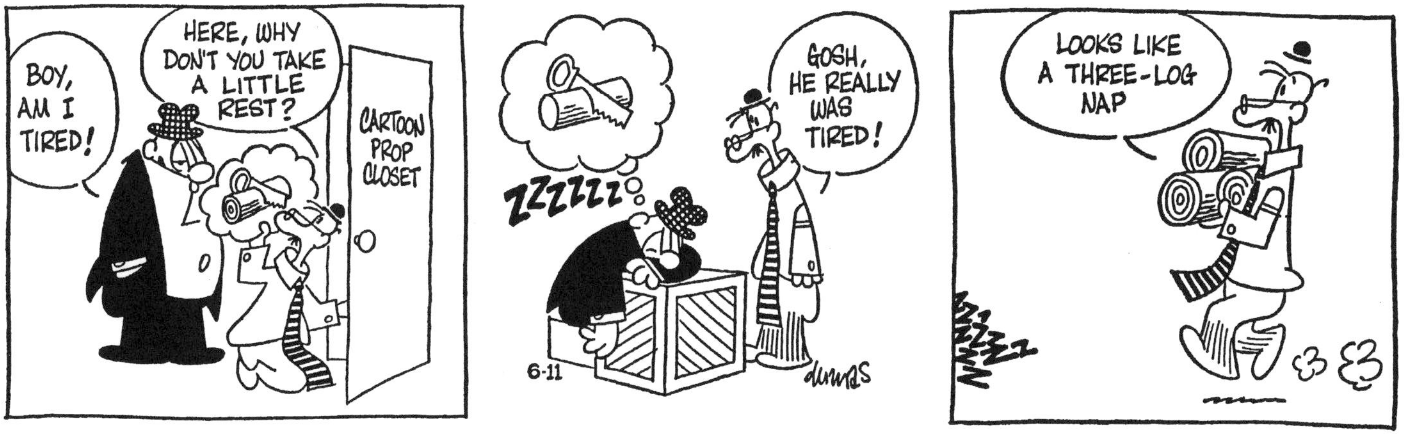
BOY, AM I TIRED!
HERE, WHY DON'T YOU TAKE A LITTLE REST?
CARTOON PROP CLOSET
ZZZZZZ
GOSH, HE REALLY WAS TIRED!
6-11
dumas
LOOKS LIKE A THREE-LOG NAP

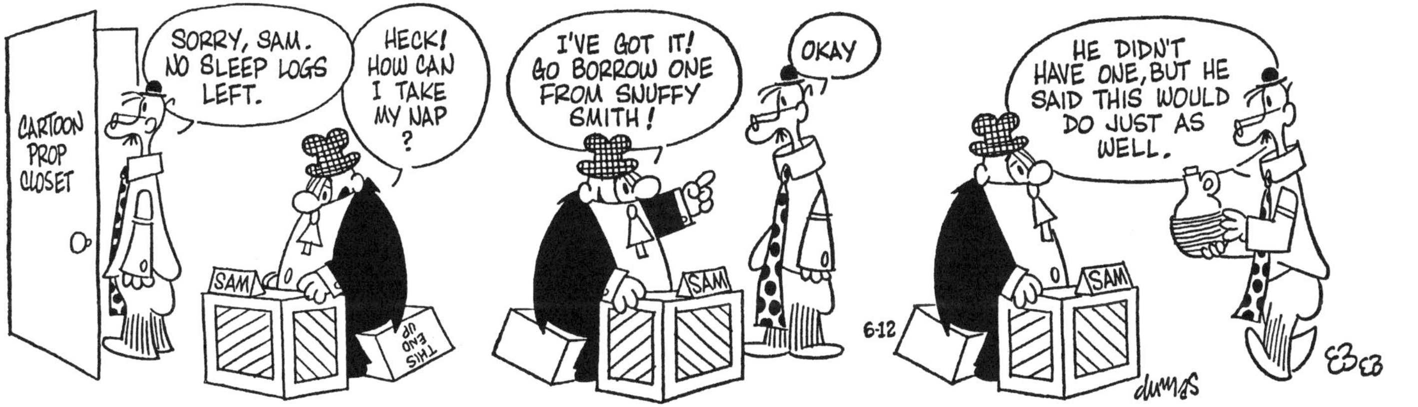
CARTOON PROP CLOSET
SORRY, SAM. NO SLEEP LOGS LEFT.
HECK! HOW CAN I TAKE MY NAP?
SAM
THIS END UP
I'VE GOT IT! GO BORROW ONE FROM SNUFFY SMITH!
OKAY
SAM
6-12
HE DIDN'T HAVE ONE, BUT HE SAID THIS WOULD DO JUST AS WELL.
SAM
dumas

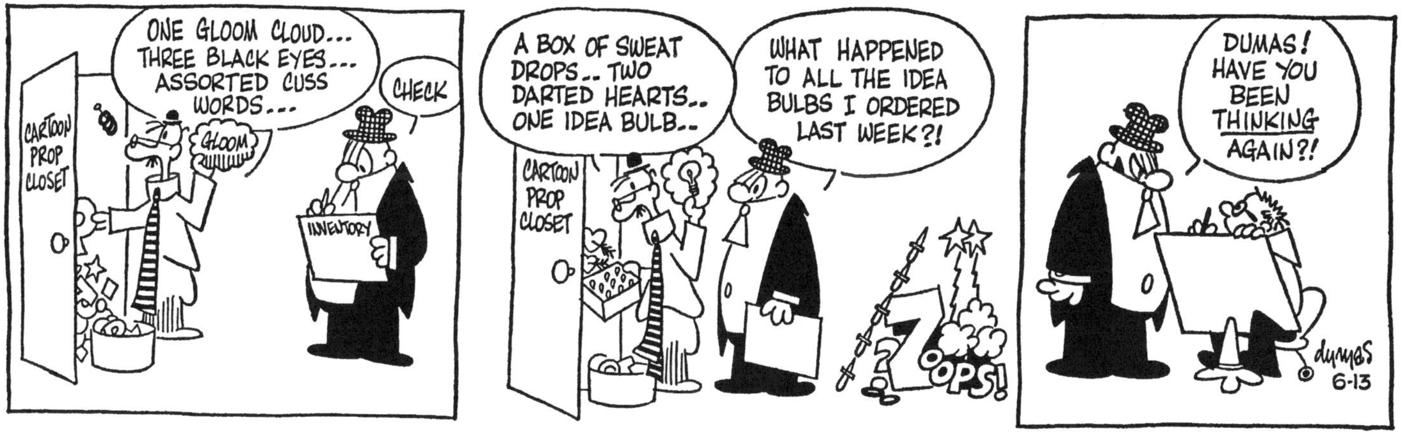
ONE GLOOM CLOUD... THREE BLACK EYES... ASSORTED CUSS WORDS...
CHECK
CARTOON PROP CLOSET
GLOOM
INVENTORY
A BOX OF SWEAT DROPS.. TWO DARTED HEARTS.. ONE IDEA BULB..
WHAT HAPPENED TO ALL THE IDEA BULBS I ORDERED LAST WEEK?!
CARTOON PROP CLOSET
OOPS!
DUMAS! HAVE YOU BEEN THINKING AGAIN?!
dumas
6-13

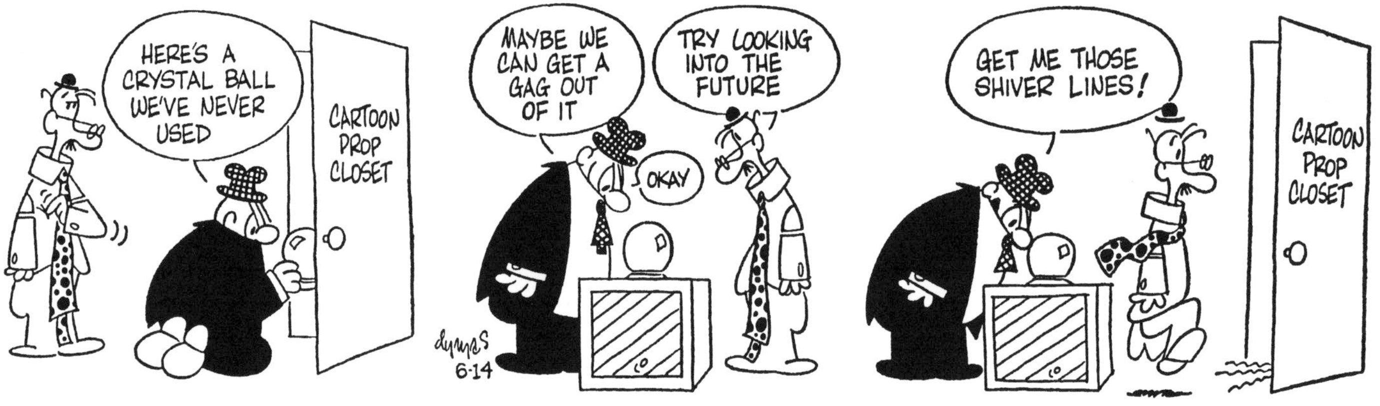
HERE'S A CRYSTAL BALL WE'VE NEVER USED
CARTOON PROP CLOSET
MAYBE WE CAN GET A GAG OUT OF IT
TRY LOOKING INTO THE FUTURE
OKAY
GET ME THOSE SHIVER LINES!
CARTOON PROP CLOSET
6-14

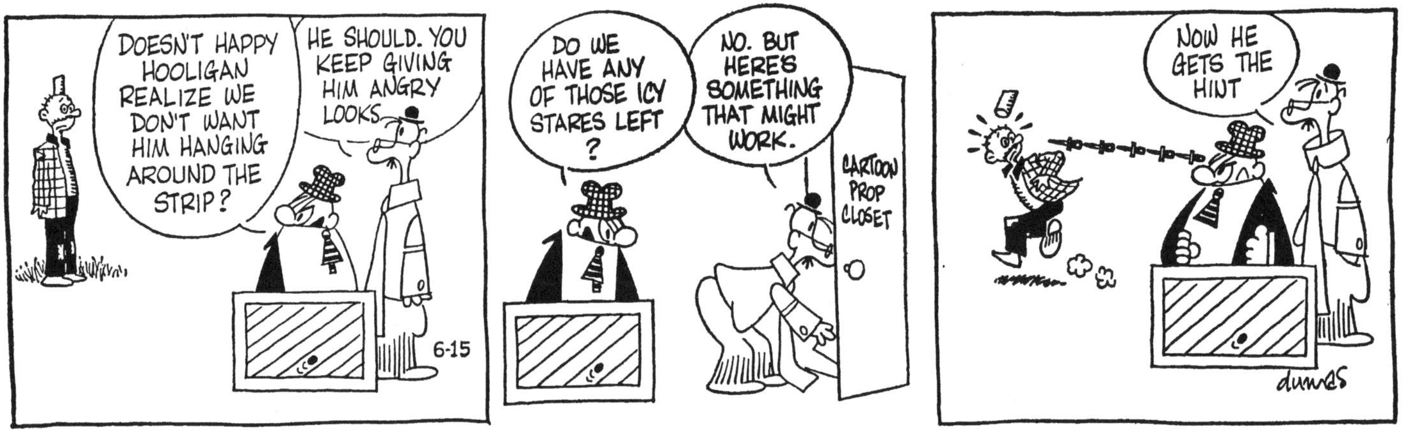
DOESN'T HAPPY HOOLIGAN REALIZE WE DON'T WANT HIM HANGING AROUND THE STRIP?
HE SHOULD. YOU KEEP GIVING HIM ANGRY LOOKS.
6-15
DO WE HAVE ANY OF THOSE ICY STARES LEFT?
NO. BUT HERE'S SOMETHING THAT MIGHT WORK.
CARTOON PROP CLOSET
NOW HE GETS THE HINT

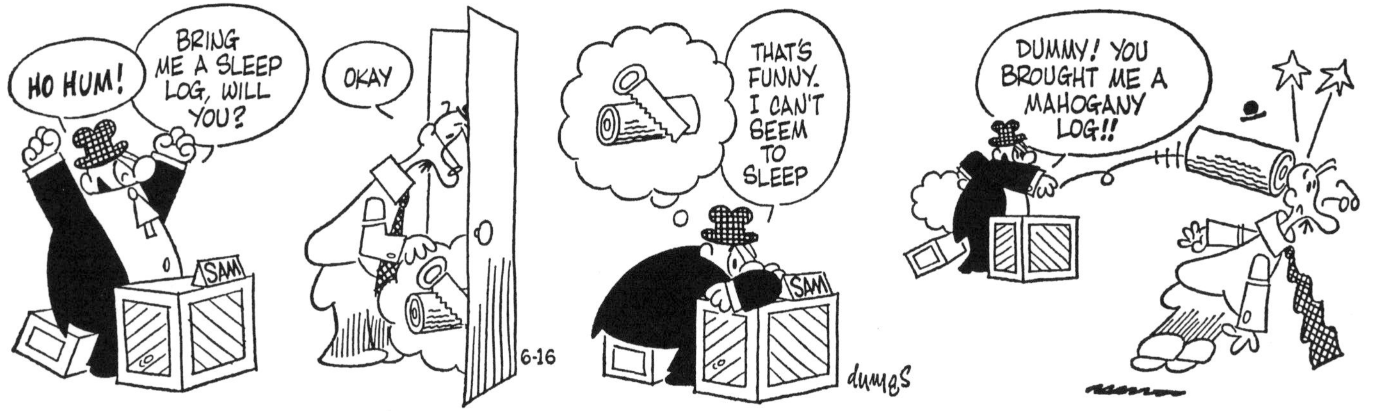
HO HUM!
BRING ME A SLEEP LOG, WILL YOU?
SAM
OKAY
6-16
THAT'S FUNNY. I CAN'T SEEM TO SLEEP
SAM
DUMMY! YOU BROUGHT ME A MAHOGANY LOG!!

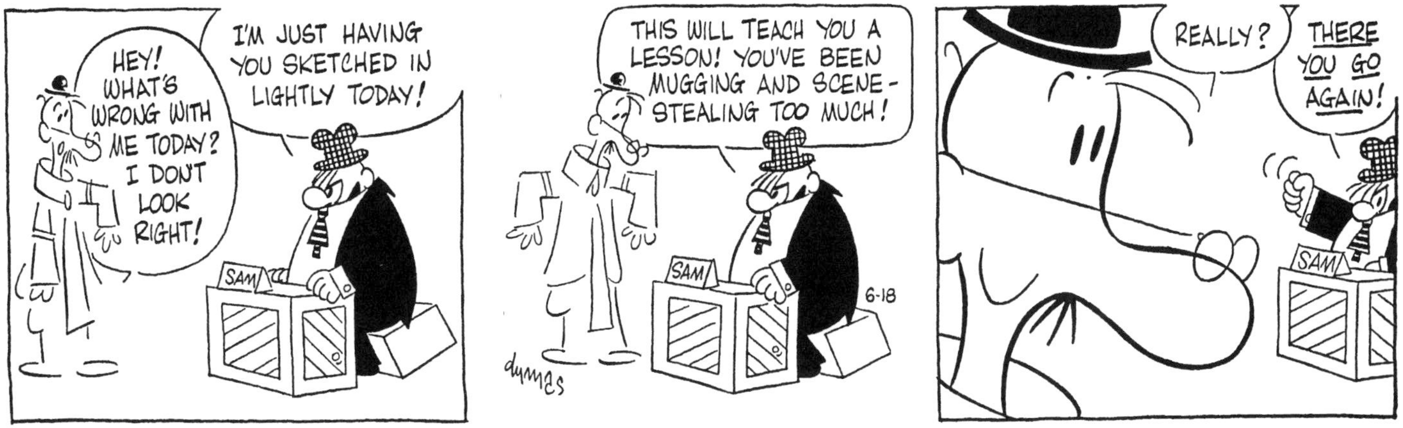
HEY! WHAT'S WRONG WITH ME TODAY? I DON'T LOOK RIGHT!
I'M JUST HAVING YOU SKETCHED IN LIGHTLY TODAY!
THIS WILL TEACH YOU A LESSON! YOU'VE BEEN MUGGING AND SCENE-STEALING TOO MUCH!
SAM
6-18
REALLY?
THERE YOU GO AGAIN!

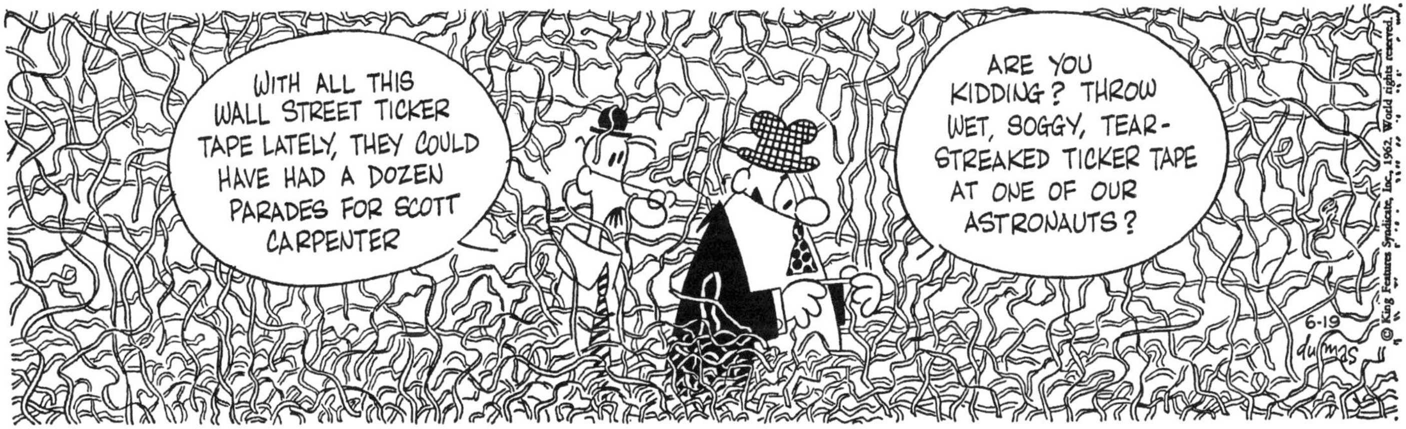
WITH ALL THIS WALL STREET TICKER TAPE LATELY, THEY COULD HAVE HAD A DOZEN PARADES FOR SCOTT CARPENTER
ARE YOU KIDDING? THROW WET, SOGGY, TEAR-STREAKED TICKER TAPE AT ONE OF OUR ASTRONAUTS?
6-19
© King Features Syndicate, Inc., 1962. World rights reserved.

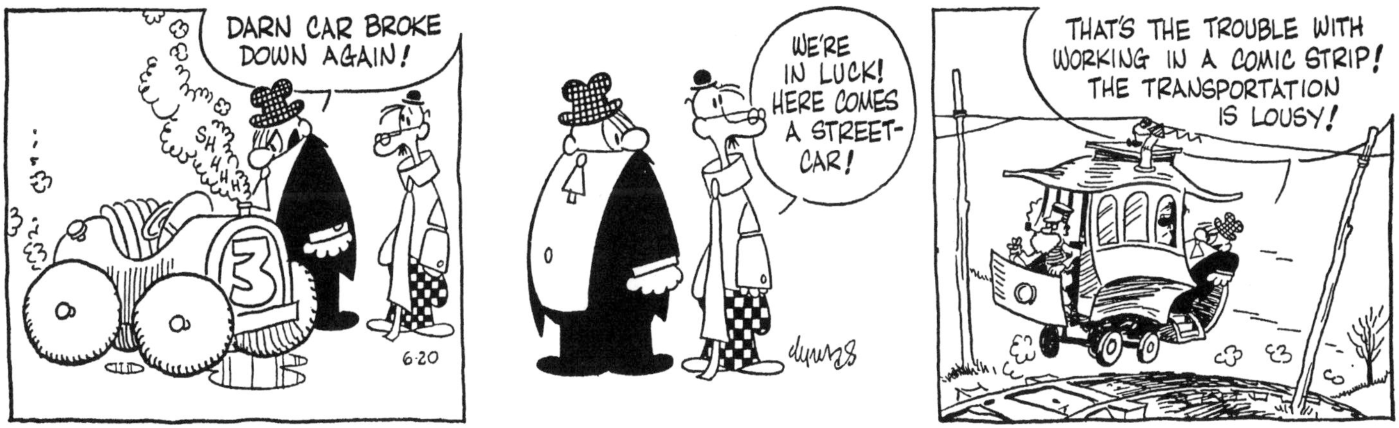
DARN CAR BROKE DOWN AGAIN!
SHHHHH
3
6-20
WE'RE IN LUCK! HERE COMES A STREET-CAR!
THAT'S THE TROUBLE WITH WORKING IN A COMIC STRIP! THE TRANSPORTATION IS LOUSY!

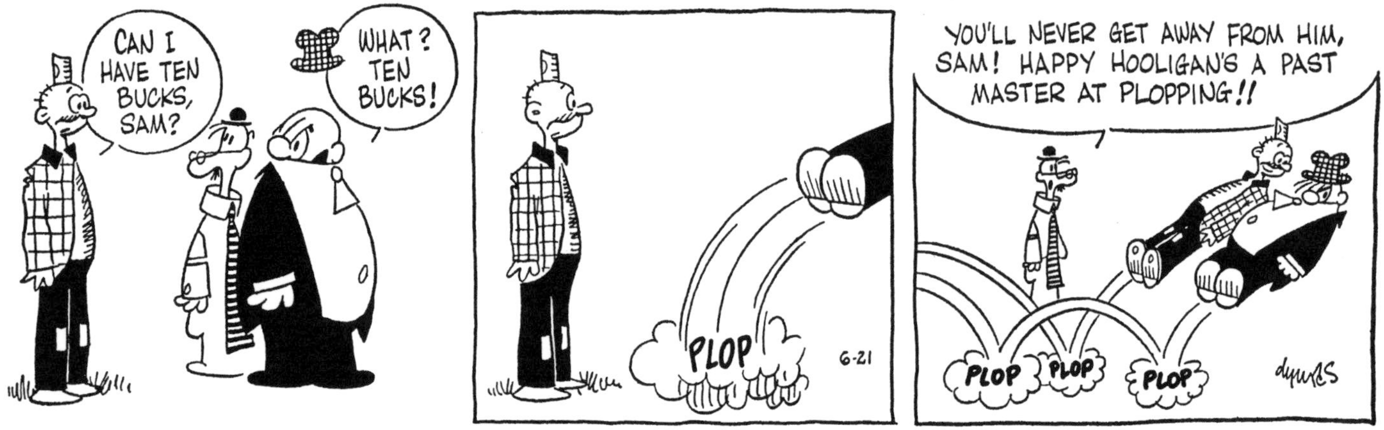
CAN I HAVE TEN BUCKS, SAM?
WHAT? TEN BUCKS!
PLOP
6-21
YOU'LL NEVER GET AWAY FROM HIM, SAM! HAPPY HOOLIGAN'S A PAST MASTER AT PLOPPING!!
PLOP
PLOP
PLOP
dumas

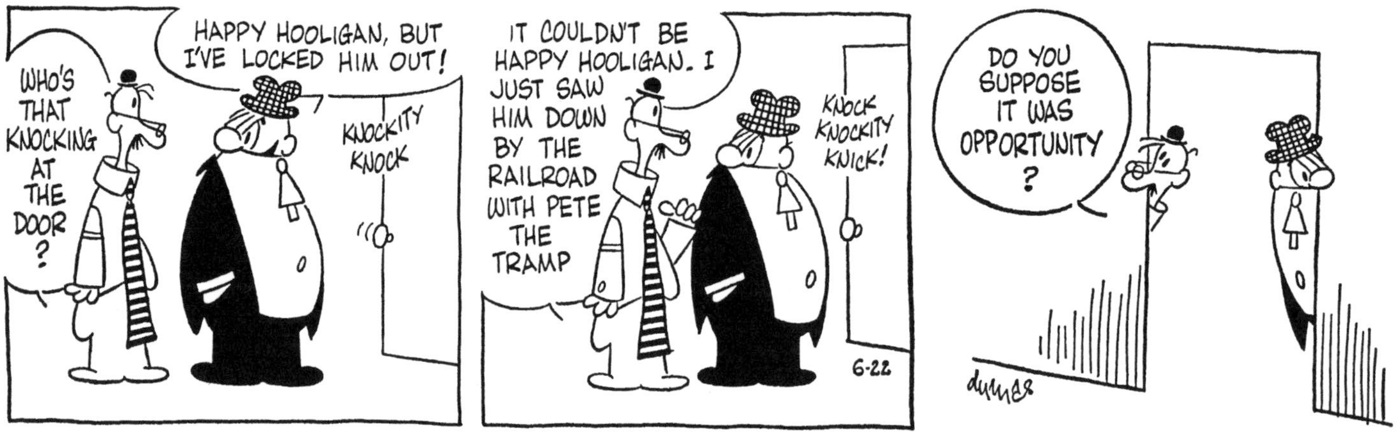
WHO'S THAT KNOCKING AT THE DOOR?
HAPPY HOOLIGAN, BUT I'VE LOCKED HIM OUT!
KNOCKITY KNOCK
IT COULDN'T BE HAPPY HOOLIGAN. I JUST SAW HIM DOWN BY THE RAILROAD WITH PETE THE TRAMP
KNOCK KNOCKITY KNICK!
6-22
DO YOU SUPPOSE IT WAS OPPORTUNITY?
dumas

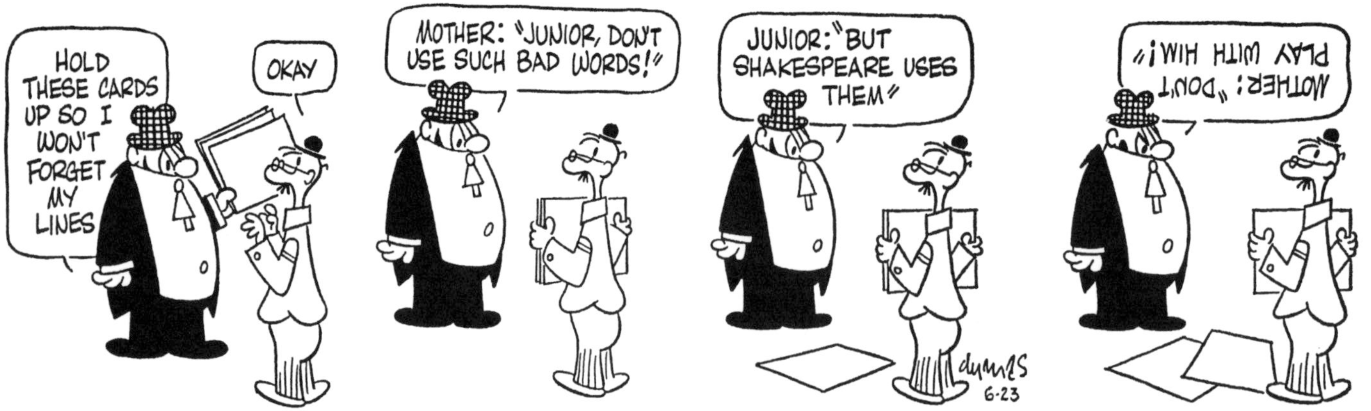
HOLD THESE CARDS UP SO I WON'T FORGET MY LINES
OKAY
MOTHER: "JUNIOR, DON'T USE SUCH BAD WORDS!"
JUNIOR: "BUT SHAKESPEARE USES THEM"
dumas
6-23
MOTHER: "DON'T PLAY WITH HIM!"

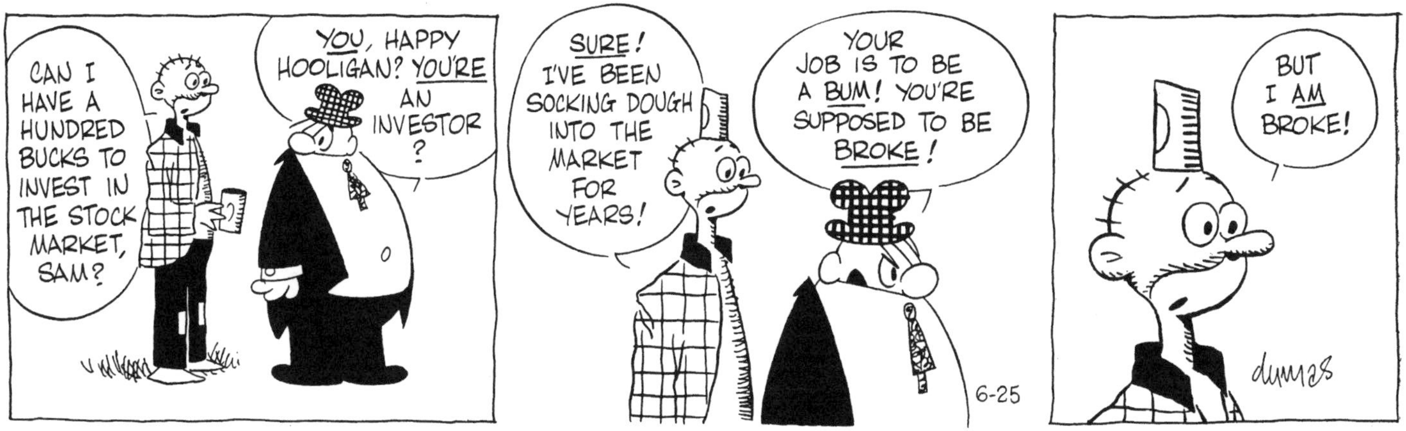
CAN I HAVE A HUNDRED BUCKS TO INVEST IN THE STOCK MARKET, SAM?
YOU, HAPPY HOOLIGAN? YOU'RE AN INVESTOR?
SURE! I'VE BEEN SOCKING DOUGH INTO THE MARKET FOR YEARS!
YOUR JOB IS TO BE A BUM! YOU'RE SUPPOSED TO BE BROKE!
6-25
BUT I AM BROKE!

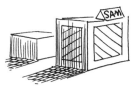

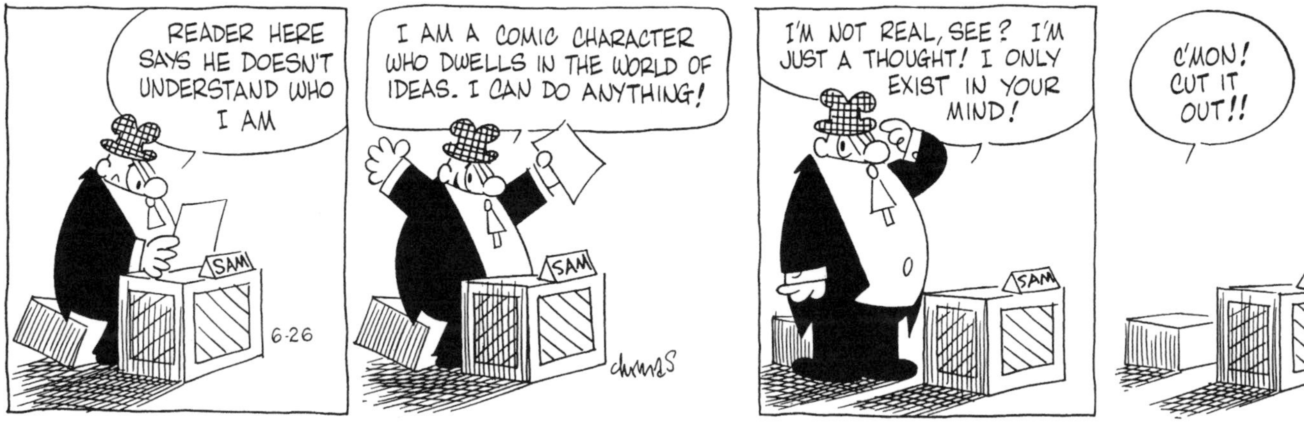
READER HERE SAYS HE DOESN'T UNDERSTAND WHO I AM
SAM
6-26
I AM A COMIC CHARACTER WHO DWELLS IN THE WORLD OF IDEAS. I CAN DO ANYTHING!
I'M NOT REAL, SEE? I'M JUST A THOUGHT! I ONLY EXIST IN YOUR MIND!
C'MON! CUT IT OUT!!

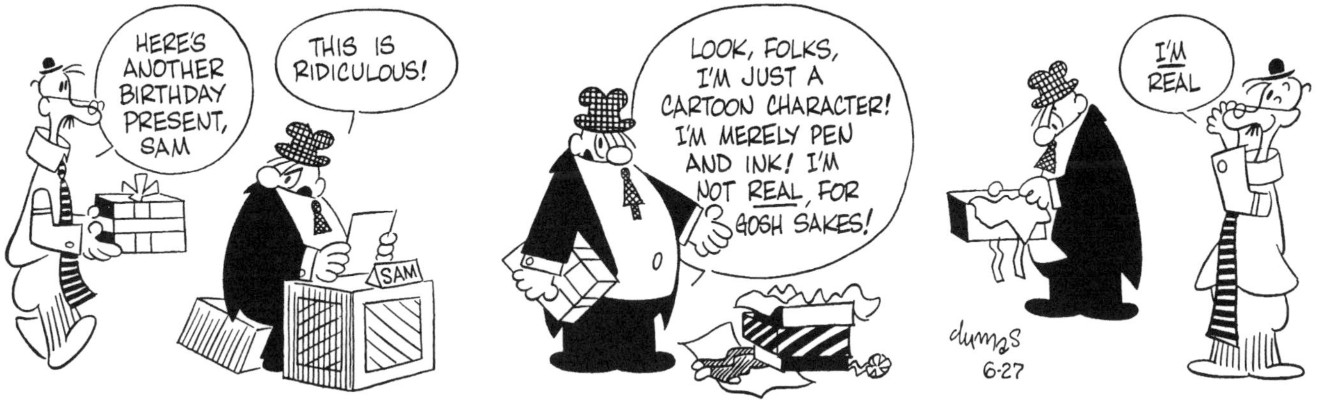
HERE'S ANOTHER BIRTHDAY PRESENT, SAM
THIS IS RIDICULOUS!
SAM
LOOK, FOLKS, I'M JUST A CARTOON CHARACTER! I'M MERELY PEN AND INK! I'M NOT REAL, FOR GOSH SAKES!
6-27
I'M REAL

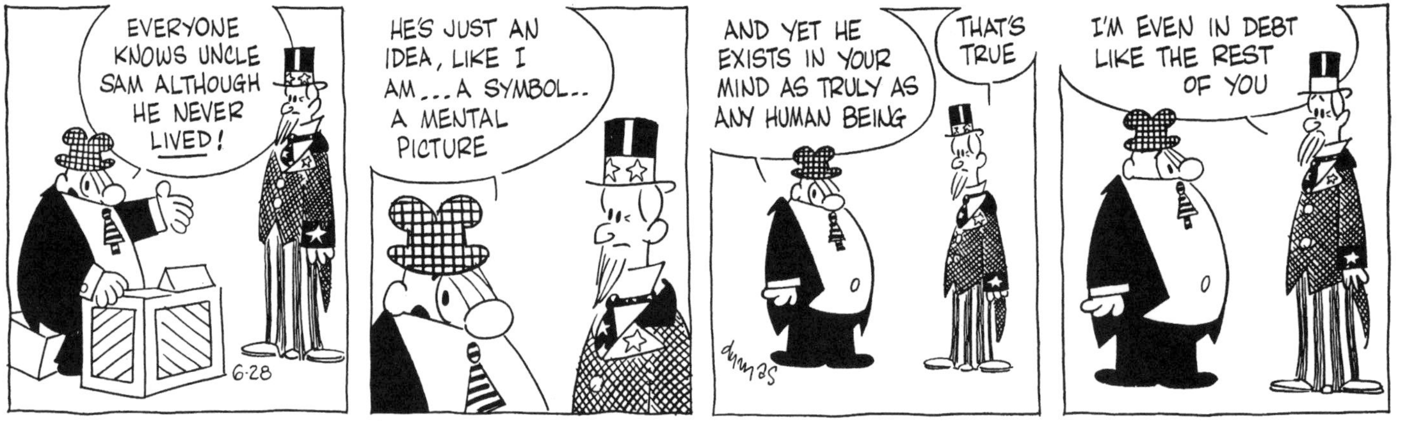
EVERYONE KNOWS UNCLE SAM ALTHOUGH HE NEVER LIVED!
6-28
HE'S JUST AN IDEA, LIKE I AM... A SYMBOL.. A MENTAL PICTURE
AND YET HE EXISTS IN YOUR MIND AS TRULY AS ANY HUMAN BEING
THAT'S TRUE
dumas
I'M EVEN IN DEBT LIKE THE REST OF YOU

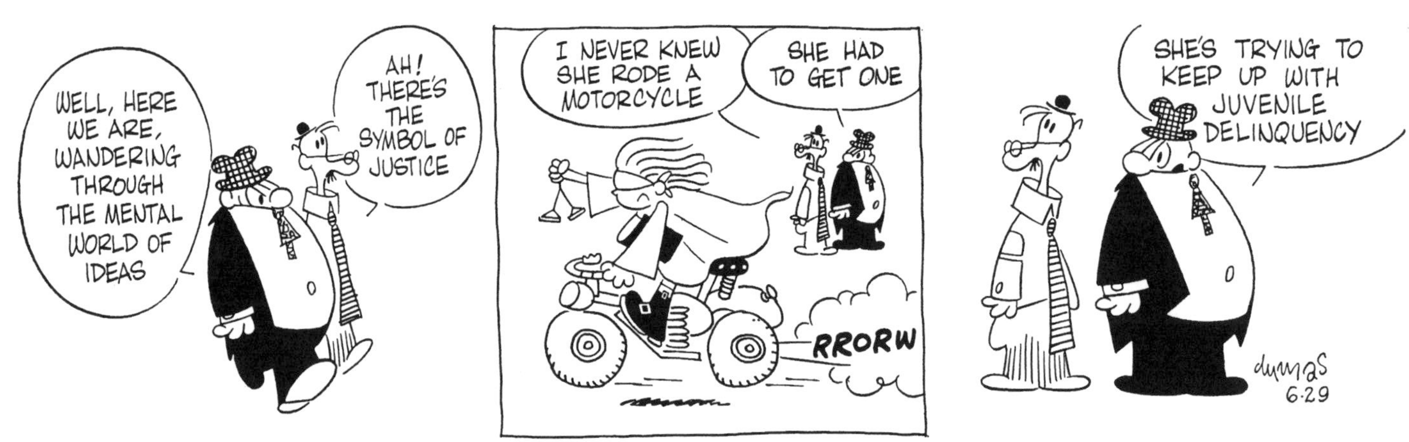
WELL, HERE WE ARE, WANDERING THROUGH THE MENTAL WORLD OF IDEAS
AH! THERE'S THE SYMBOL OF JUSTICE
I NEVER KNEW SHE RODE A MOTORCYCLE
SHE HAD TO GET ONE
RRORW
SHE'S TRYING TO KEEP UP WITH JUVENILE DELINQUENCY
dumas
6-29

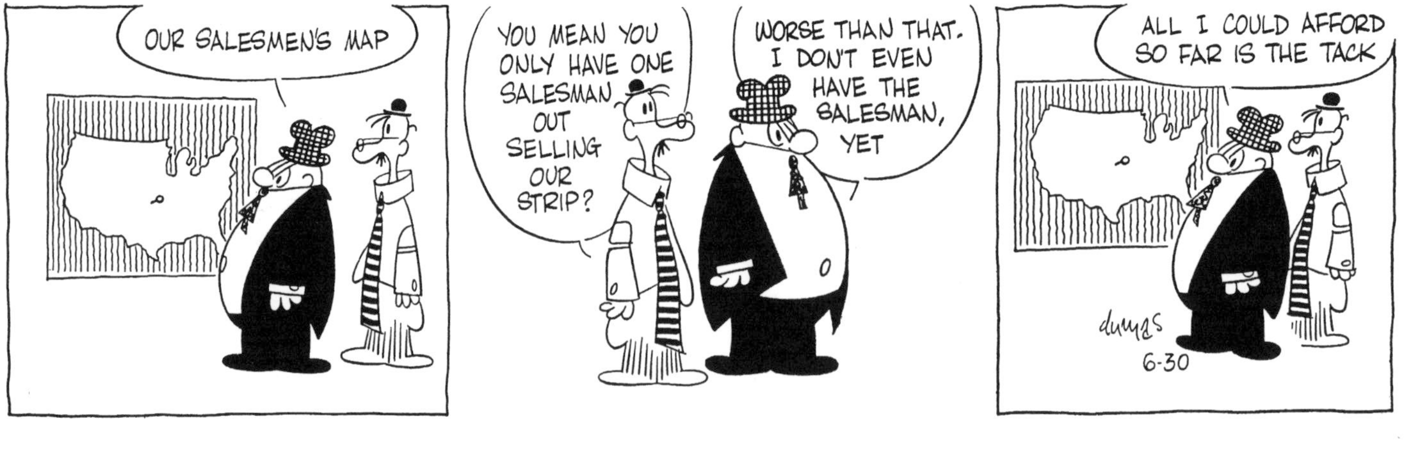
OUR SALESMEN'S MAP
YOU MEAN YOU ONLY HAVE ONE SALESMAN OUT SELLING OUR STRIP?
WORSE THAN THAT. I DON'T EVEN HAVE THE SALESMAN, YET
ALL I COULD AFFORD SO FAR IS THE TACK
dumas
6-30

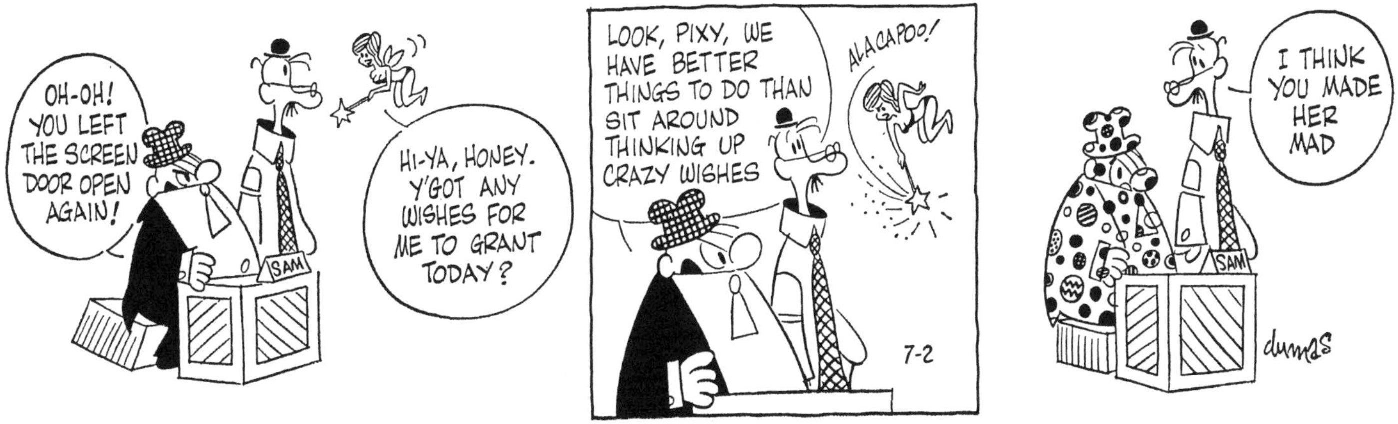
OH-OH! YOU LEFT THE SCREEN DOOR OPEN AGAIN!
SAM
HI-YA, HONEY. Y'GOT ANY WISHES FOR ME TO GRANT TODAY?
LOOK, PIXY, WE HAVE BETTER THINGS TO DO THAN SIT AROUND THINKING UP CRAZY WISHES
ALACAPOO!
7-2
I THINK YOU MADE HER MAD
SAM
dumas

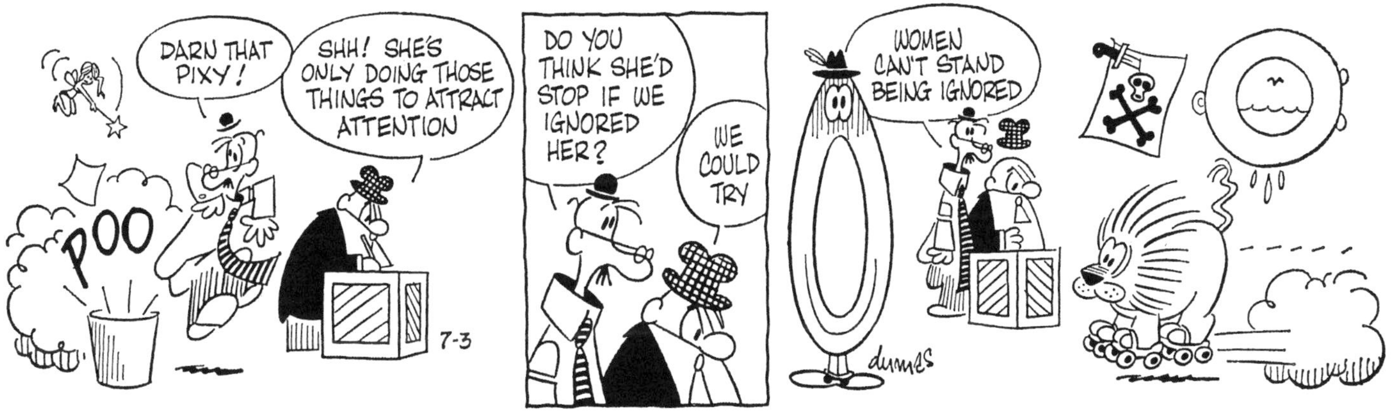
DARN THAT PIXY!
SHH! SHE'S ONLY DOING THOSE THINGS TO ATTRACT ATTENTION
POO
7-3
DO YOU THINK SHE'D STOP IF WE IGNORED HER?
WE COULD TRY
WOMEN CAN'T STAND BEING IGNORED
dumas

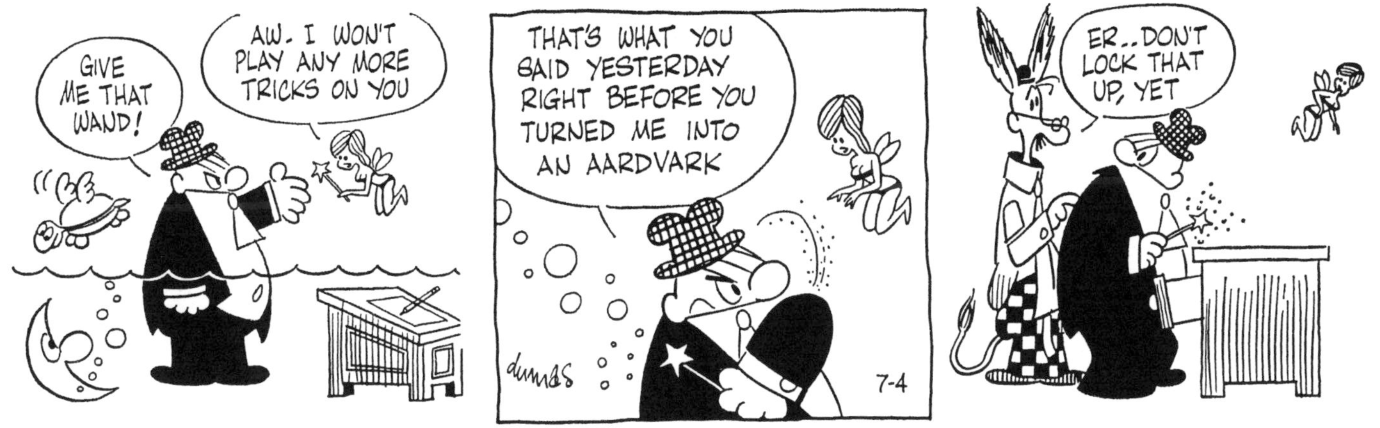
GIVE ME THAT WAND!
AW- I WON'T PLAY ANY MORE TRICKS ON YOU
THAT'S WHAT YOU SAID YESTERDAY RIGHT BEFORE YOU TURNED ME INTO AN AARDVARK
dumas
7-4
ER.. DON'T LOCK THAT UP, YET

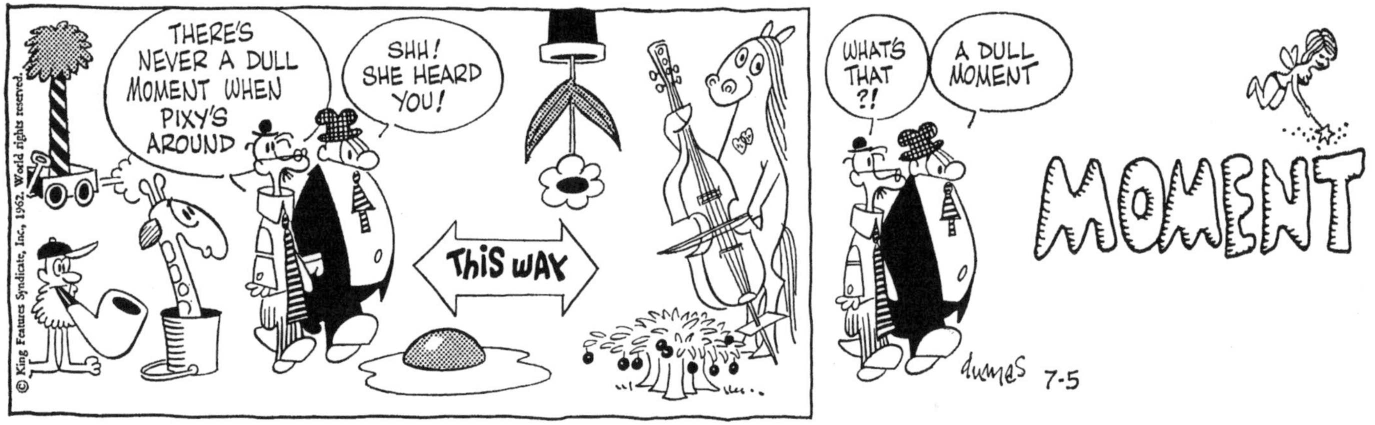
© King Features Syndicate, Inc., 1962. World rights reserved.
THERE'S NEVER A DULL MOMENT WHEN PIXY'S AROUND
SHH! SHE HEARD YOU!
THIS WAY
WHAT'S THAT ?!
A DULL MOMENT
MOMENT
dumas 7-5

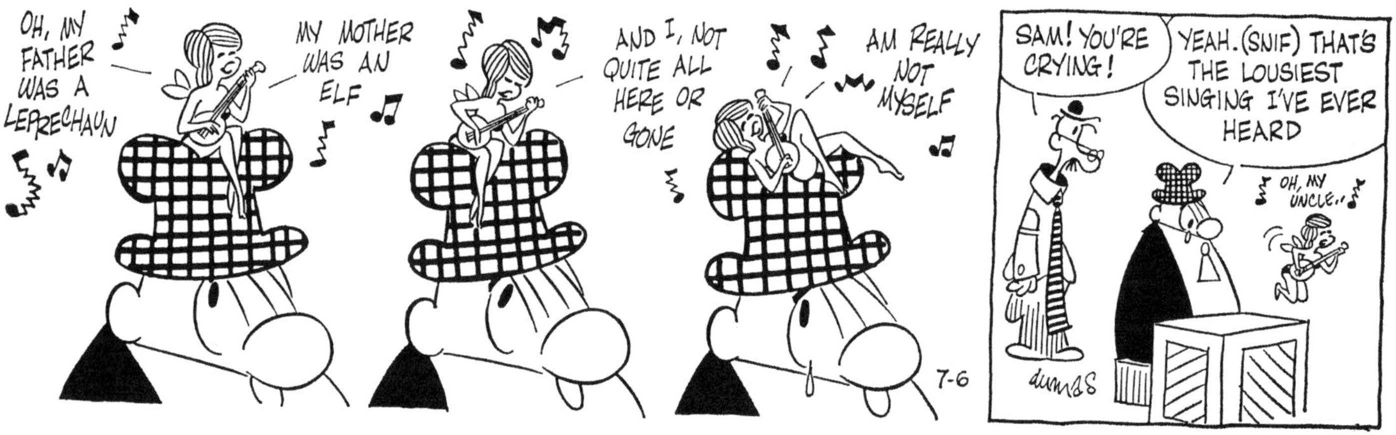
OH, MY FATHER WAS A LEPRECHAUN
MY MOTHER WAS AN ELF
AND I, NOT QUITE ALL HERE OR GONE
AM REALLY NOT MYSELF
7-6
SAM! YOU'RE CRYING!
YEAH. (SNIF) THAT'S THE LOUSIEST SINGING I'VE EVER HEARD
OH, MY UNCLE..
dumas

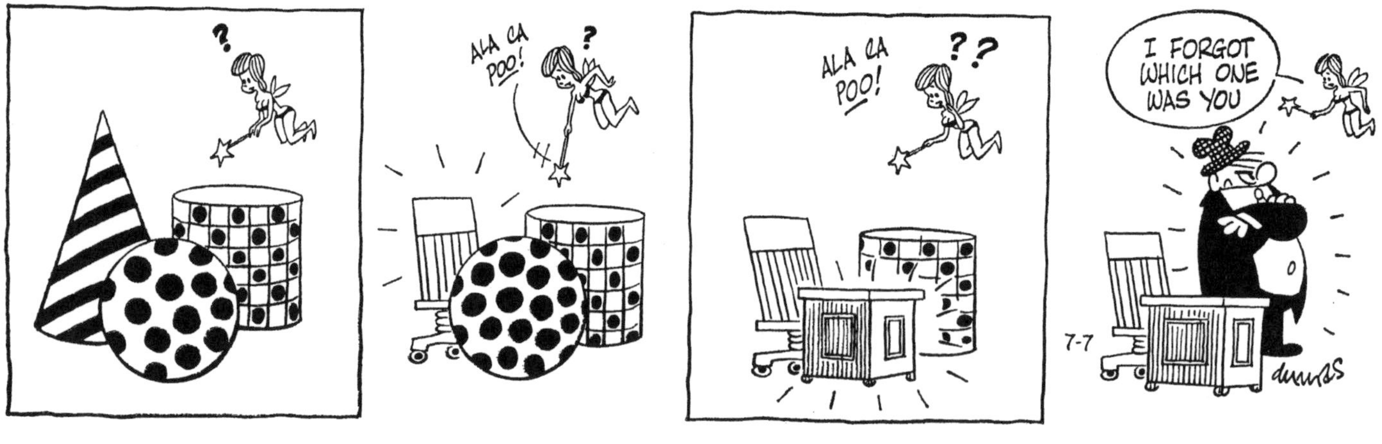
?
ALA CA POO!
?
ALA CA POO!
??
I FORGOT WHICH ONE WAS YOU
7-7
dumas

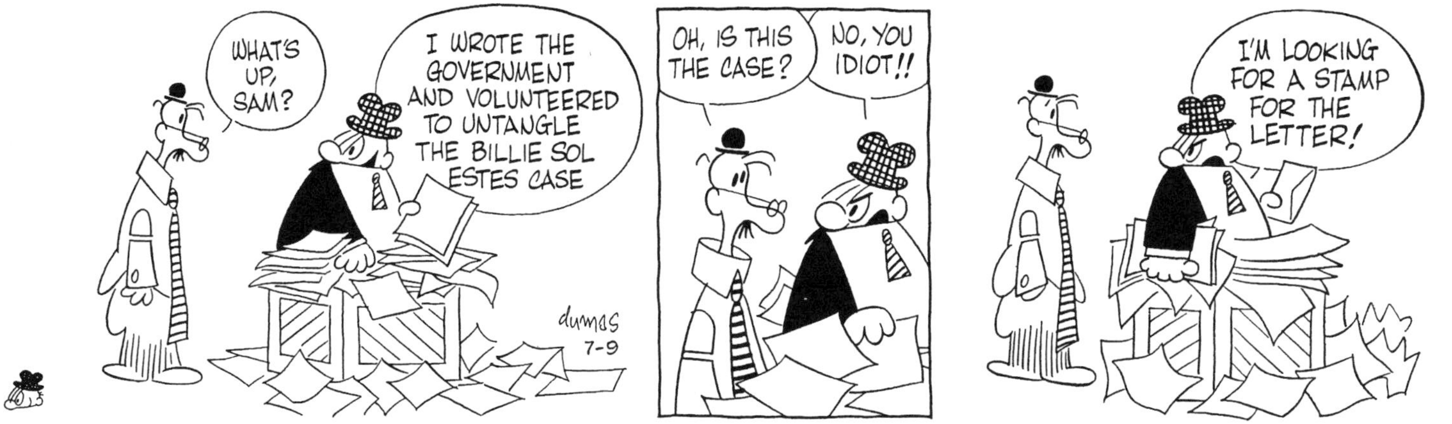
WHAT'S UP, SAM?
I WROTE THE GOVERNMENT AND VOLUNTEERED TO UNTANGLE THE BILLIE SOL ESTES CASE
dumas 7-9
OH, IS THIS THE CASE?
NO, YOU IDIOT!!
I'M LOOKING FOR A STAMP FOR THE LETTER!

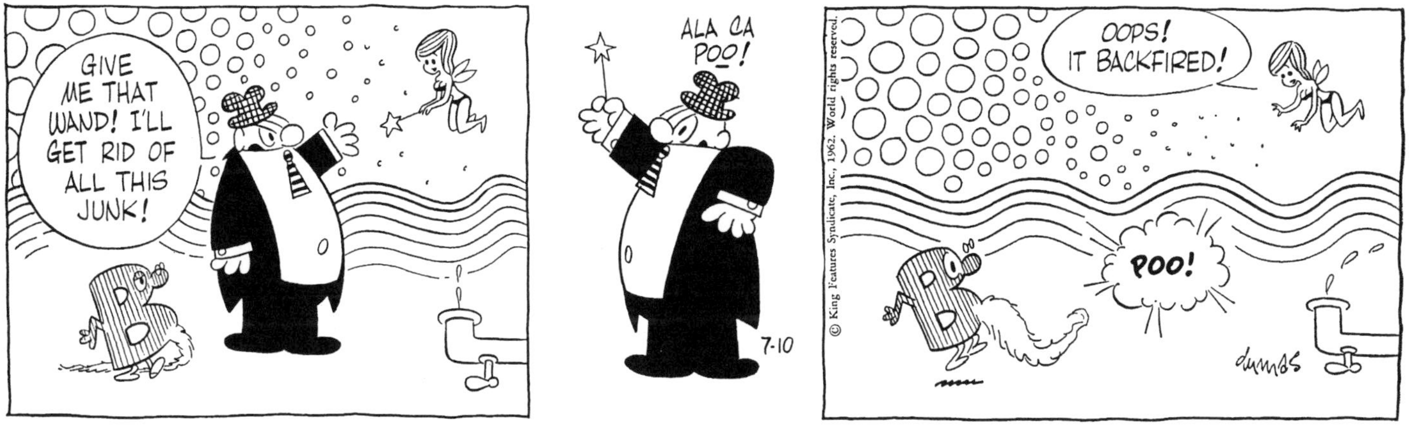
GIVE ME THAT WAND! I'LL GET RID OF ALL THIS JUNK!
ALA CA POO!
7-10
© King Features Syndicate, Inc., 1962. World rights reserved.
OOPS! IT BACKFIRED!
POO!
dumas

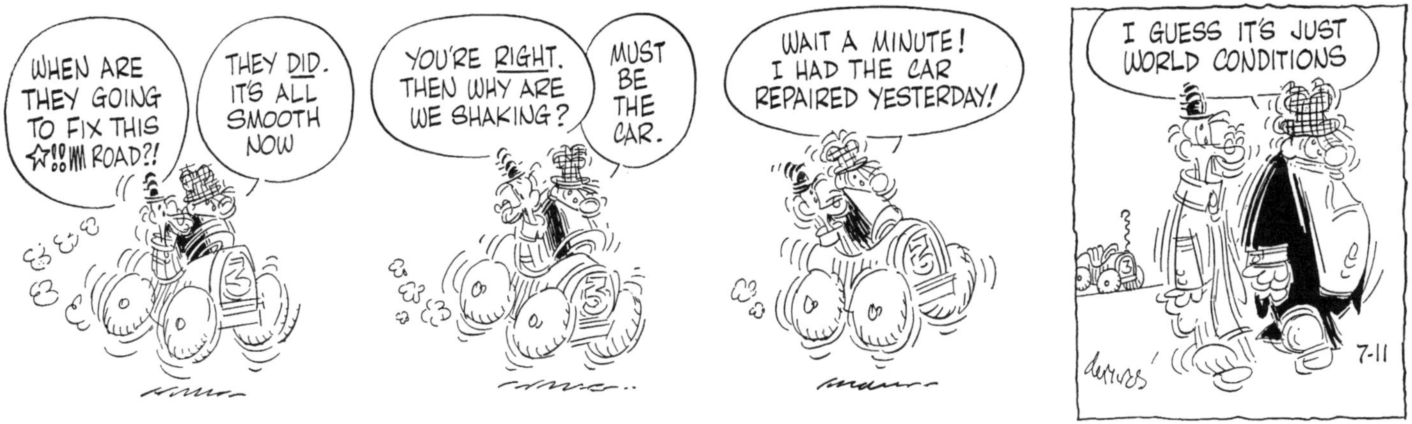
WHEN ARE THEY GOING TO FIX THIS ☆!! ROAD?!
THEY DID. IT'S ALL SMOOTH NOW
YOU'RE RIGHT. THEN WHY ARE WE SHAKING?
MUST BE THE CAR.
WAIT A MINUTE! I HAD THE CAR REPAIRED YESTERDAY!
I GUESS IT'S JUST WORLD CONDITIONS
7-11

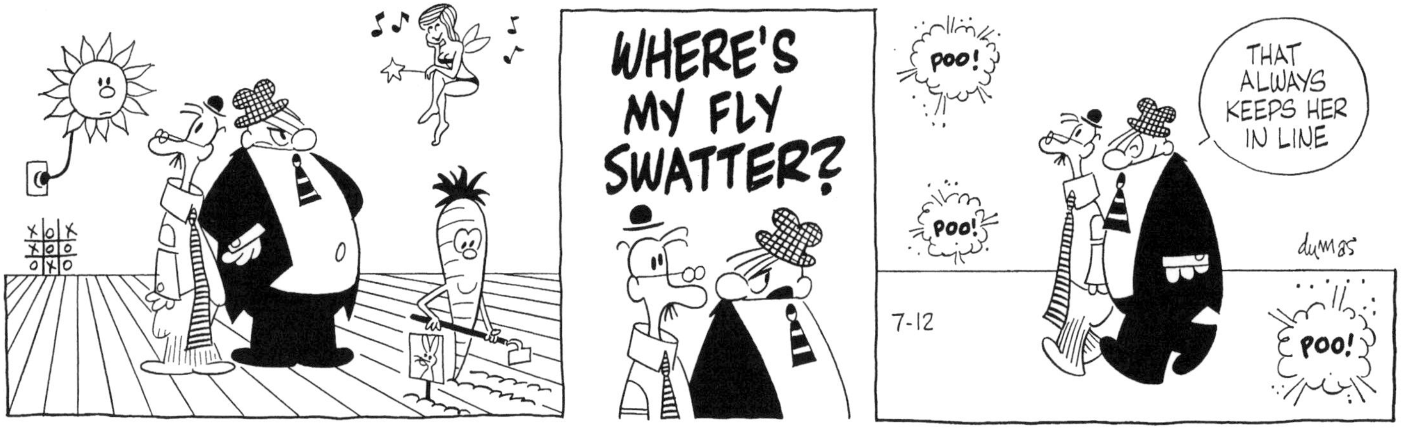
WHERE'S MY FLY SWATTER?
POO!
POO!
THAT ALWAYS KEEPS HER IN LINE
POO!
dumas
7-12

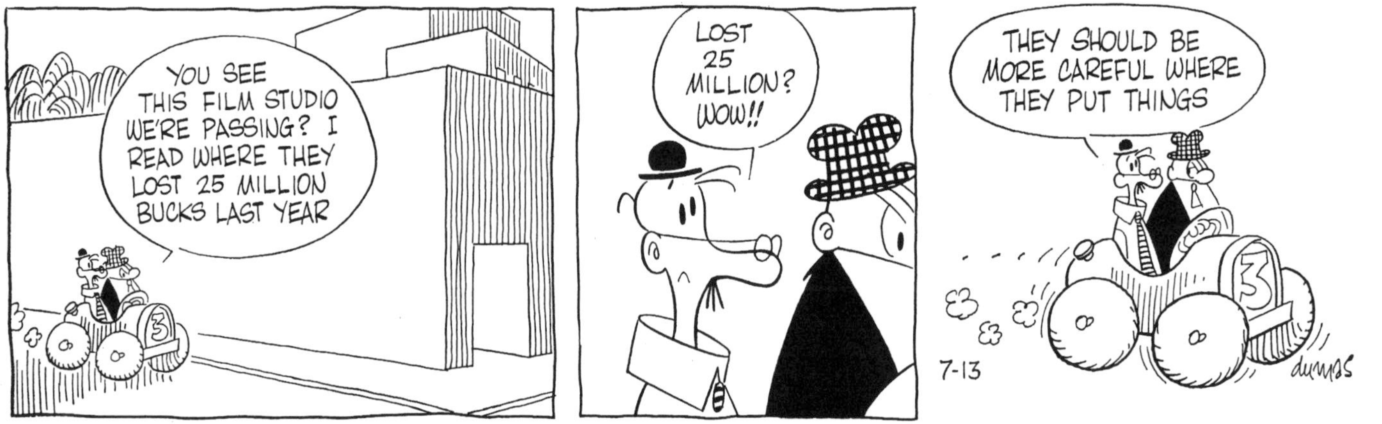
YOU SEE THIS FILM STUDIO WE'RE PASSING? I READ WHERE THEY LOST 25 MILLION BUCKS LAST YEAR
LOST 25 MILLION? WOW!!
THEY SHOULD BE MORE CAREFUL WHERE THEY PUT THINGS
7-13
dumas

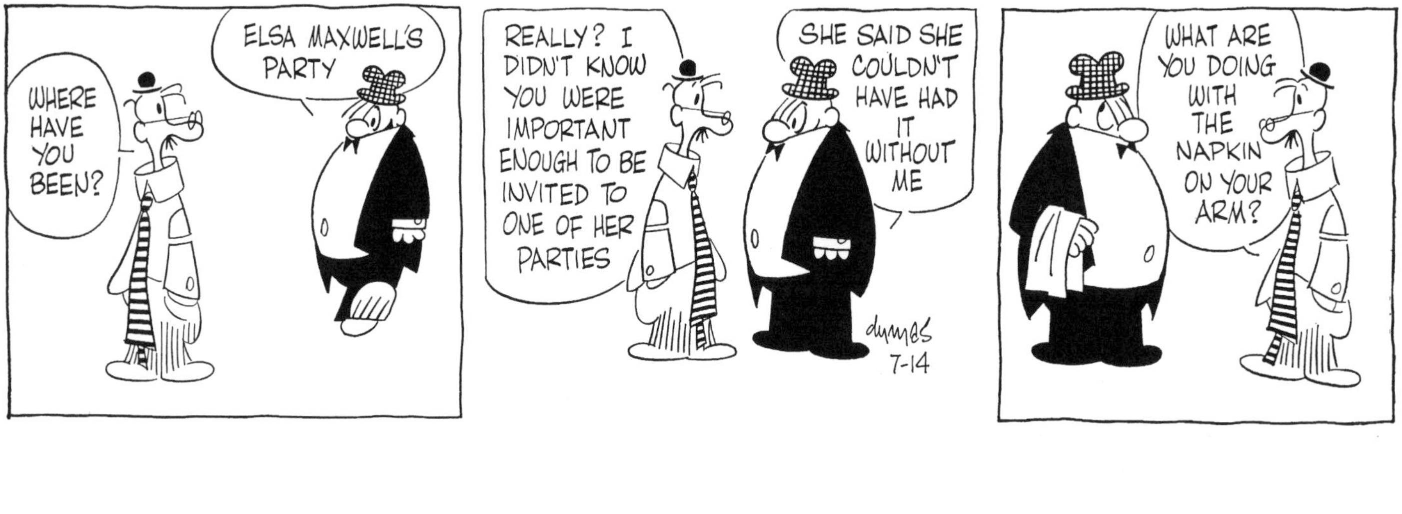
WHERE HAVE YOU BEEN?
ELSA MAXWELL'S PARTY
REALLY? I DIDN'T KNOW YOU WERE IMPORTANT ENOUGH TO BE INVITED TO ONE OF HER PARTIES
SHE SAID SHE COULDN'T HAVE HAD IT WITHOUT ME
dumas
7-14
WHAT ARE YOU DOING WITH THE NAPKIN ON YOUR ARM?

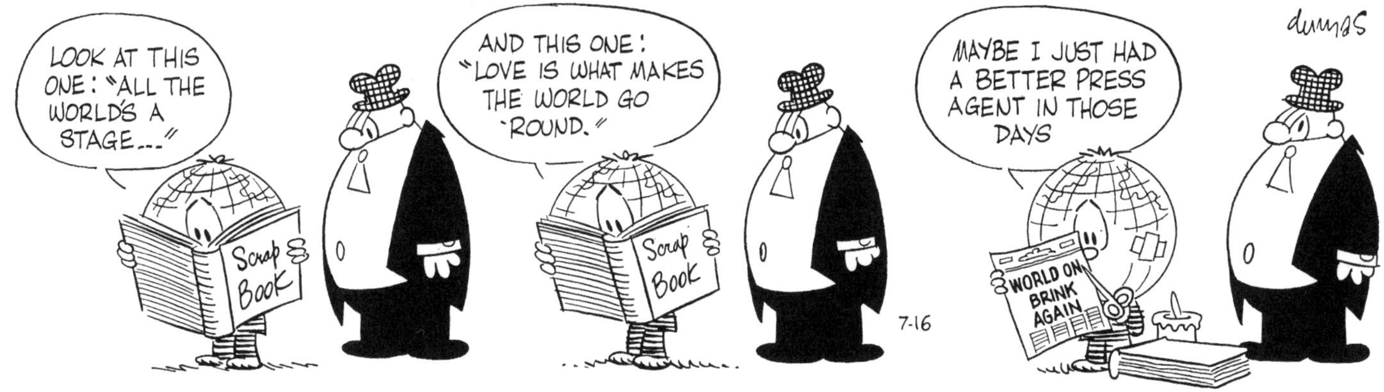
LOOK AT THIS ONE: "ALL THE WORLD'S A STAGE..."
Scrap Book
AND THIS ONE: "LOVE IS WHAT MAKES THE WORLD GO 'ROUND."
Scrap Book
7-16
dumas
MAYBE I JUST HAD A BETTER PRESS AGENT IN THOSE DAYS
WORLD ON BRINK AGAIN

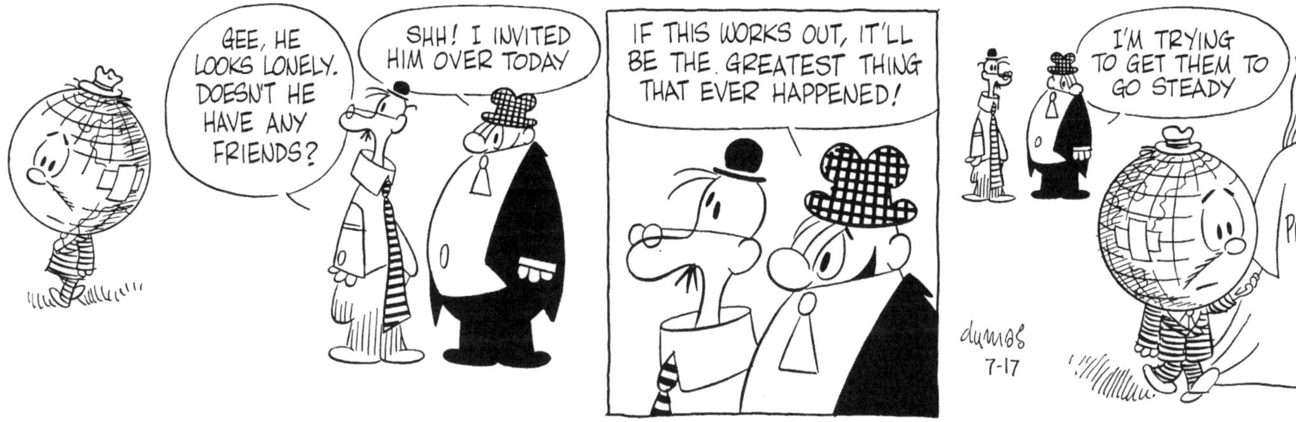
GEE, HE LOOKS LONELY. DOESN'T HE HAVE ANY FRIENDS?
SHH! I INVITED HIM OVER TODAY
IF THIS WORKS OUT, IT'LL BE THE GREATEST THING THAT EVER HAPPENED!
dumas
7-17
I'M TRYING TO GET THEM TO GO STEADY
PEACE

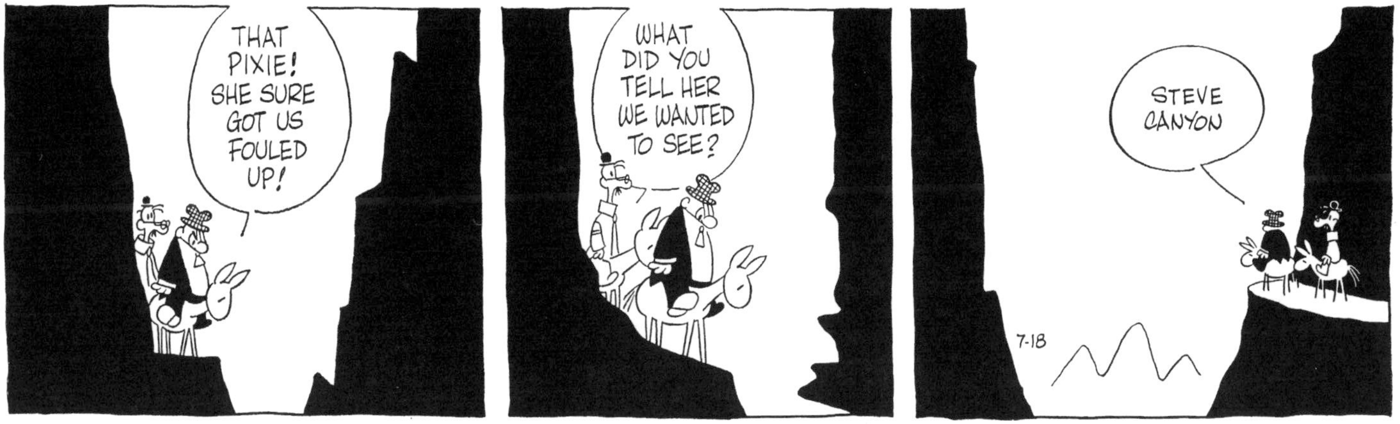
THAT PIXIE! SHE SURE GOT US FOULED UP!
WHAT DID YOU TELL HER WE WANTED TO SEE?
7-18
STEVE CANYON

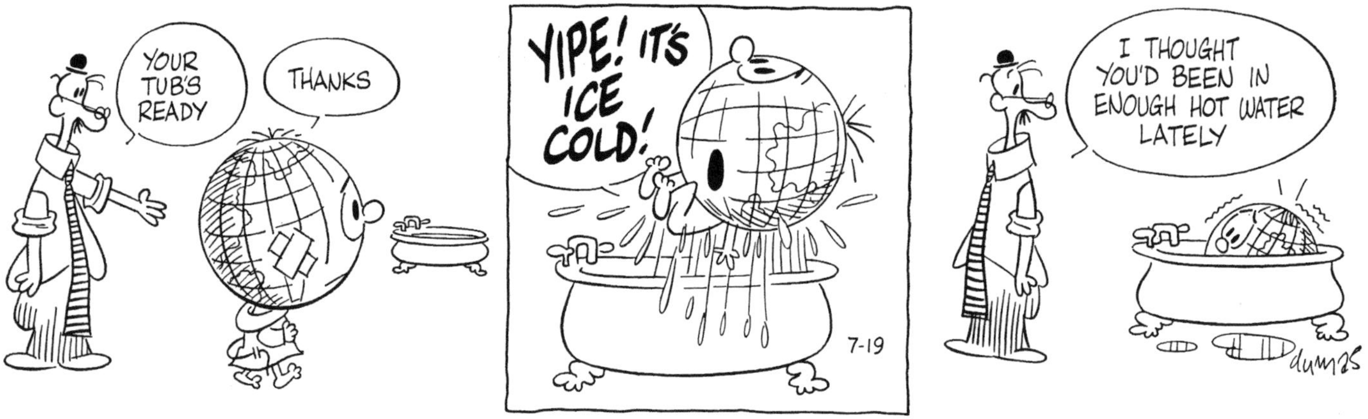
YOUR TUB'S READY
THANKS
YIPE! IT'S ICE COLD!
I THOUGHT YOU'D BEEN IN ENOUGH HOT WATER LATELY
7-19
dumas

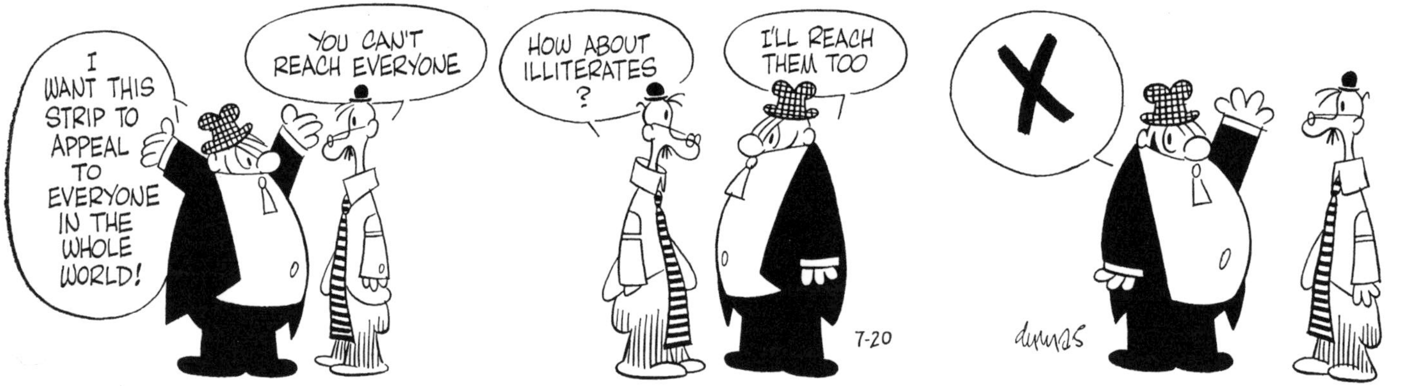
I WANT THIS STRIP TO APPEAL TO EVERYONE IN THE WHOLE WORLD!
YOU CAN'T REACH EVERYONE
HOW ABOUT ILLITERATES ?
I'LL REACH THEM TOO
X
7-20
dumas

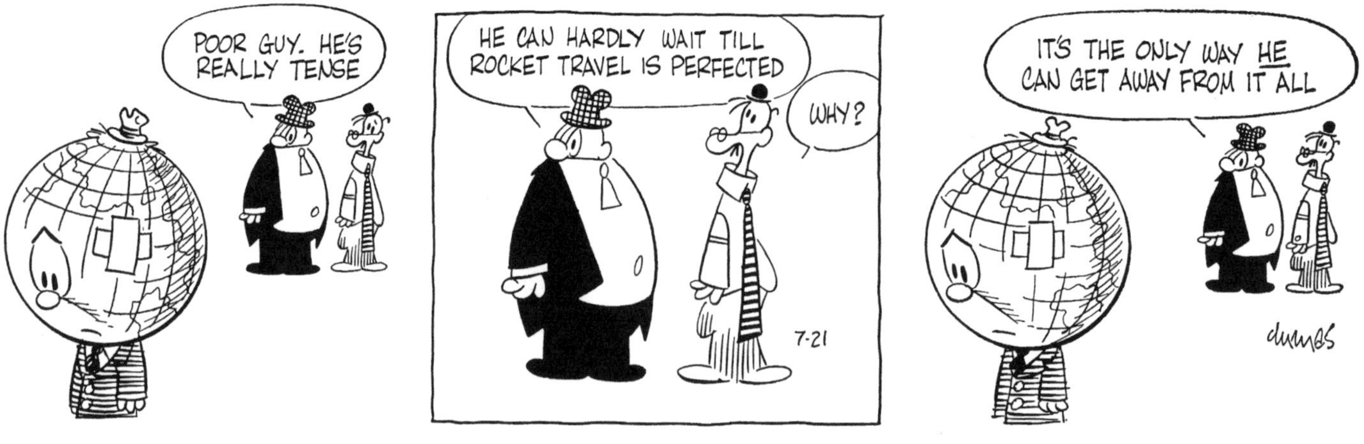
POOR GUY. HE'S REALLY TENSE
HE CAN HARDLY WAIT TILL ROCKET TRAVEL IS PERFECTED
WHY?
IT'S THE ONLY WAY HE CAN GET AWAY FROM IT ALL
7-21
dumas

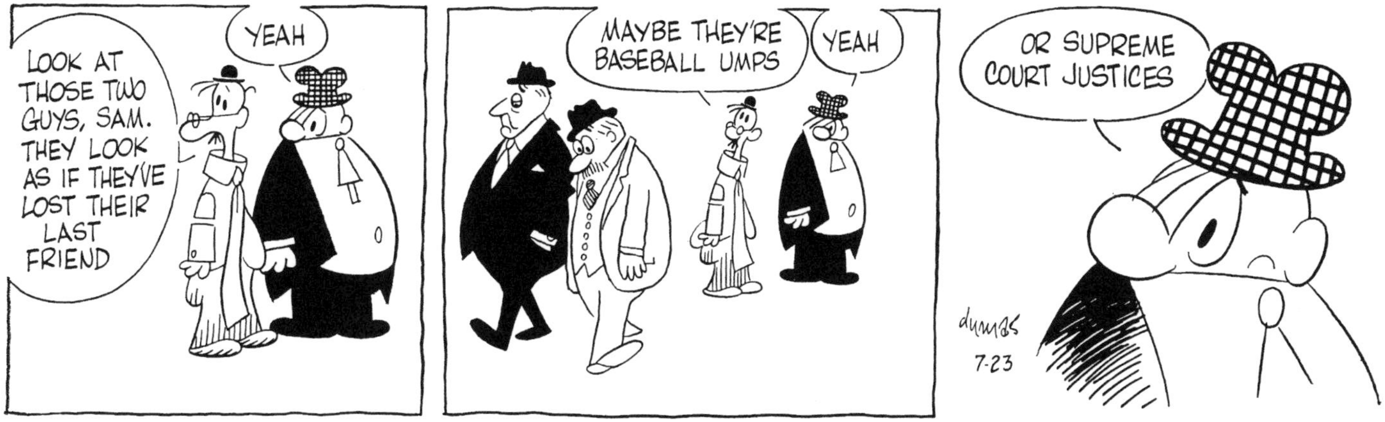
LOOK AT THOSE TWO GUYS, SAM. THEY LOOK AS IF THEY'VE LOST THEIR LAST FRIEND
YEAH
MAYBE THEY'RE BASEBALL UMPS
YEAH
OR SUPREME COURT JUSTICES
dumas
7-23

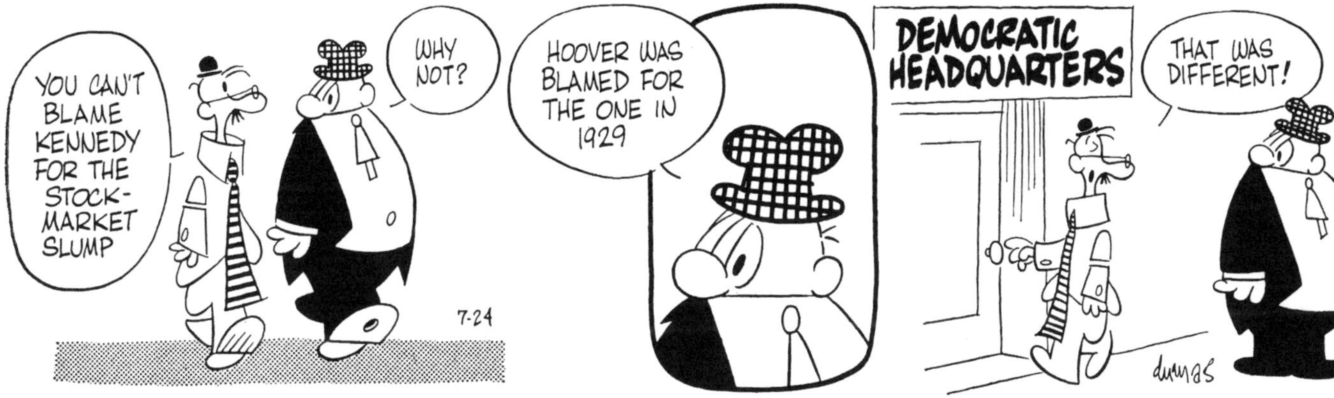
YOU CAN'T BLAME KENNEDY FOR THE STOCK-MARKET SLUMP
WHY NOT?
7-24
HOOVER WAS BLAMED FOR THE ONE IN 1929
DEMOCRATIC HEADQUARTERS
THAT WAS DIFFERENT!
dumas

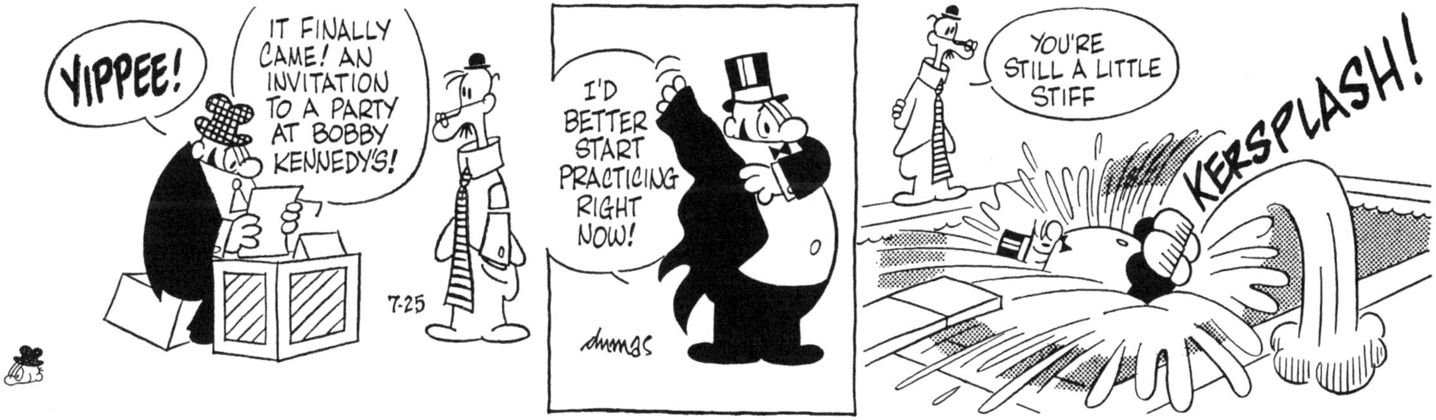
YIPPEE!
IT FINALLY CAME! AN INVITATION TO A PARTY AT BOBBY KENNEDY'S!
7-25
I'D BETTER START PRACTICING RIGHT NOW!
dumas
YOU'RE STILL A LITTLE STIFF
KERSPLASH!

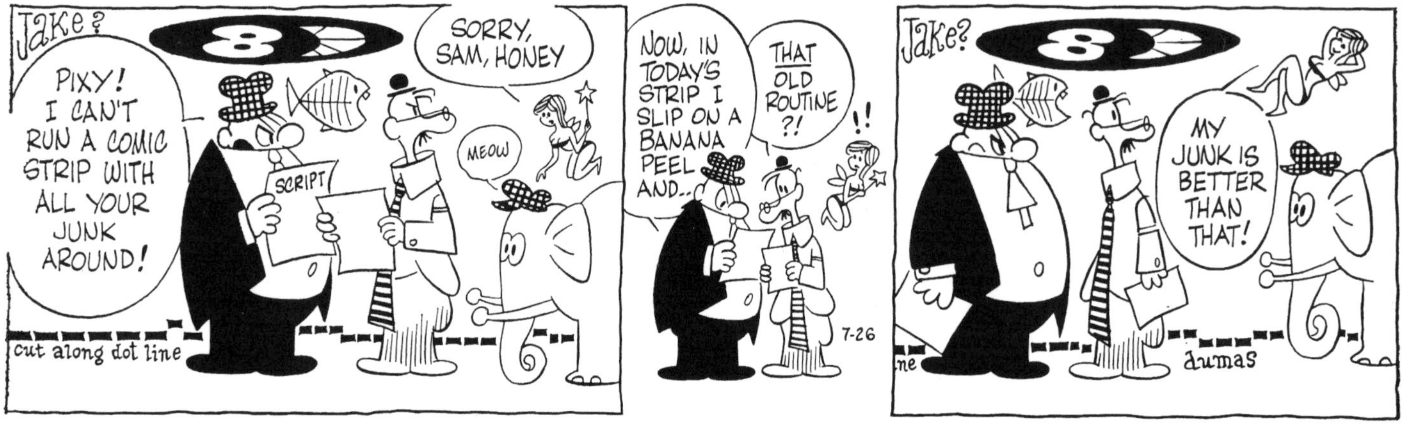
JAKE?
PIXY! I CAN'T RUN A COMIC STRIP WITH ALL YOUR JUNK AROUND!
SCRIPT
SORRY, SAM, HONEY
MEOW
cut along dot line
NOW, IN TODAY'S STRIP I SLIP ON A BANANA PEEL AND..
THAT OLD ROUTINE ?!
!!
7-26
JAKE?
MY JUNK IS BETTER THAN THAT!
dumas

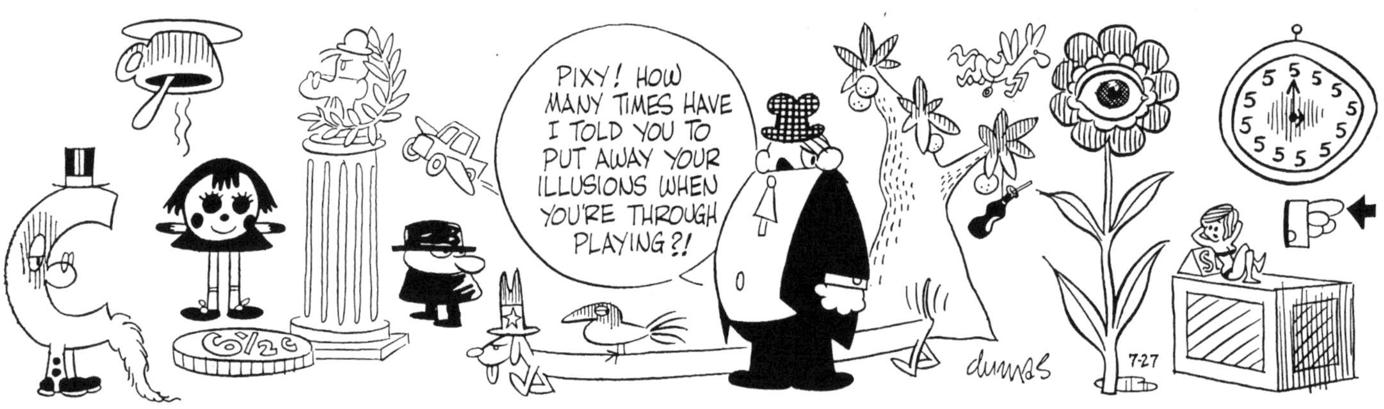
PIXY! HOW MANY TIMES HAVE I TOLD YOU TO PUT AWAY YOUR ILLUSIONS WHEN YOU'RE THROUGH PLAYING?!
dumas
7-27

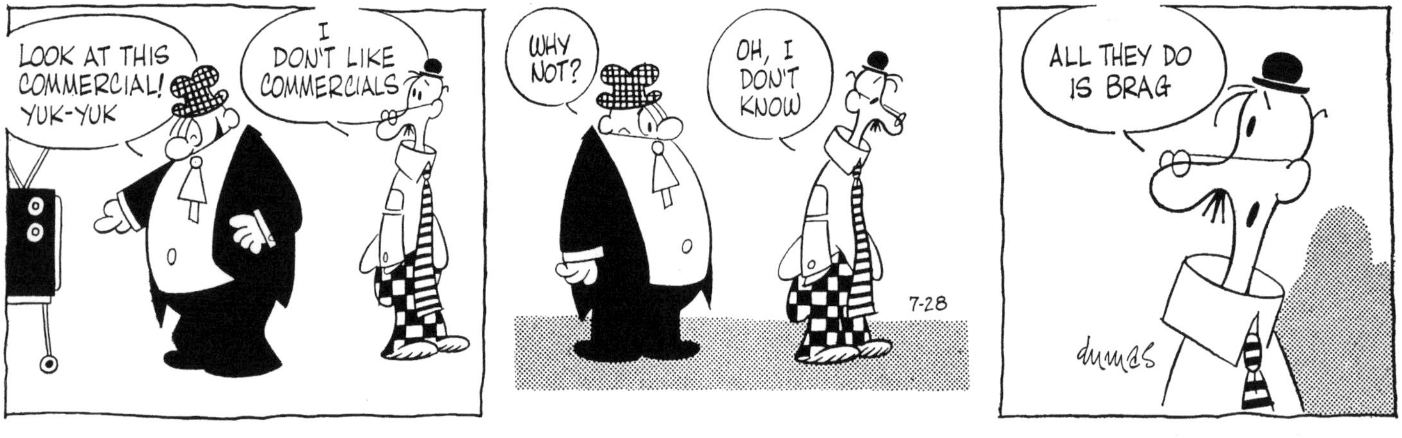
LOOK AT THIS COMMERCIAL! YUK-YUK
I DON'T LIKE COMMERCIALS
WHY NOT?
OH, I DON'T KNOW
7-28
ALL THEY DO IS BRAG
dumas

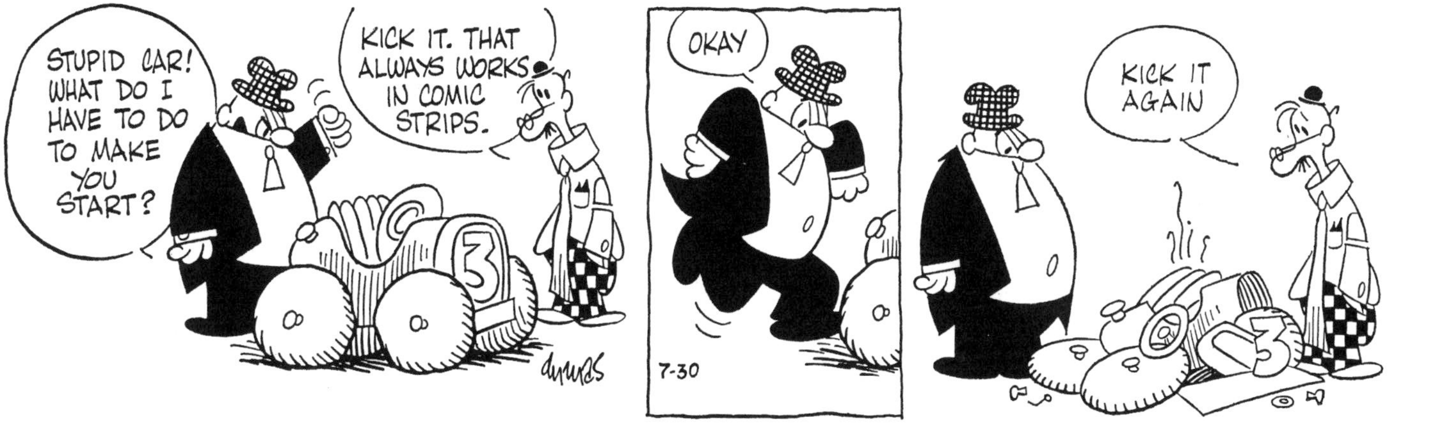
STUPID CAR! WHAT DO I HAVE TO DO TO MAKE YOU START?
KICK IT. THAT ALWAYS WORKS IN COMIC STRIPS.
dumas
7-30
OKAY
KICK IT AGAIN

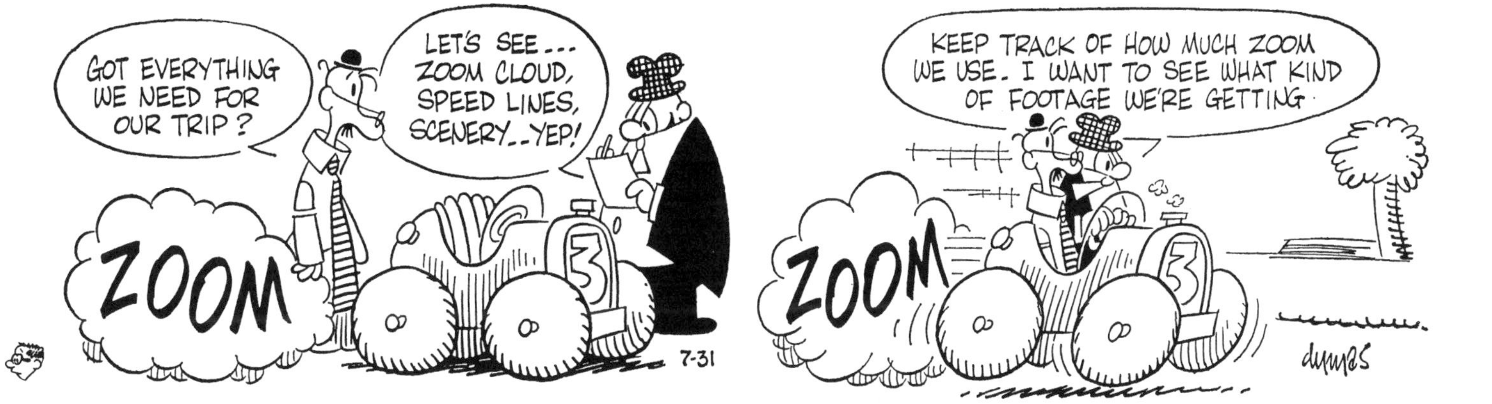
GOT EVERYTHING WE NEED FOR OUR TRIP?
LET'S SEE... ZOOM CLOUD, SPEED LINES, SCENERY...YEP!
ZOOM
7-31
KEEP TRACK OF HOW MUCH ZOOM WE USE. I WANT TO SEE WHAT KIND OF FOOTAGE WE'RE GETTING.
ZOOM
dumas

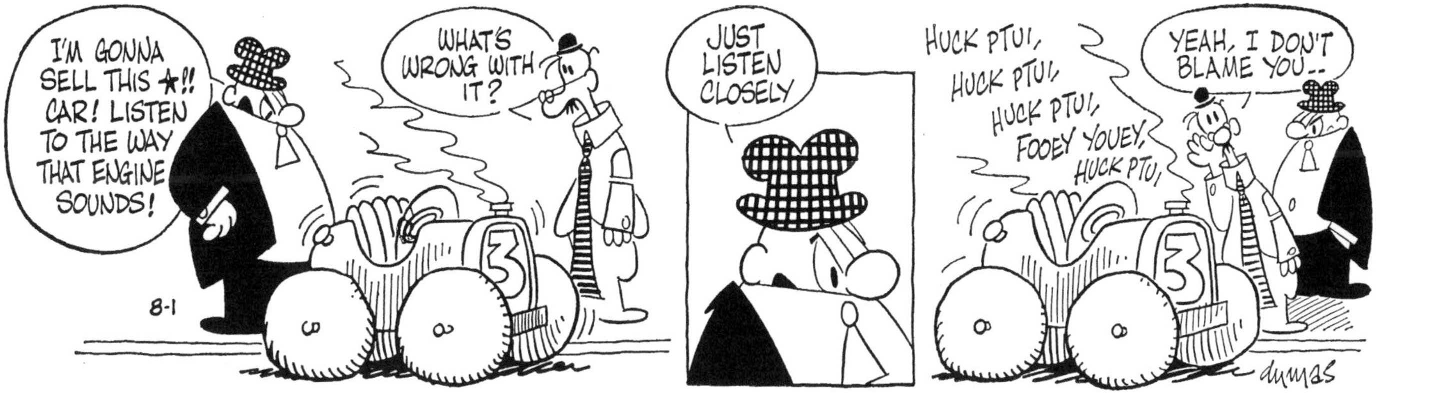
I'M GONNA SELL THIS ★!! CAR! LISTEN TO THE WAY THAT ENGINE SOUNDS!
WHAT'S WRONG WITH IT?
8-1
JUST LISTEN CLOSELY
HUCK PTUI, HUCK PTUI, HUCK PTUI, FOOEY YOUEY, HUCK PTUI
YEAH, I DON'T BLAME YOU..
dumas

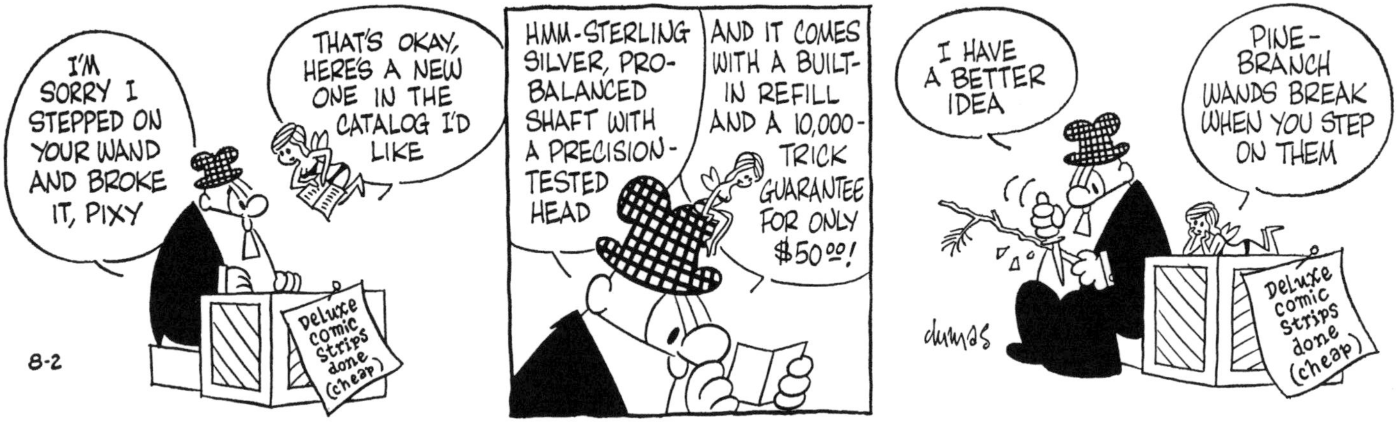
I'M SORRY I STEPPED ON YOUR WAND AND BROKE IT, PIXY
THAT'S OKAY, HERE'S A NEW ONE IN THE CATALOG I'D LIKE
Deluxe comic strips done (cheap)
8-2
HMM-STERLING SILVER, PRO-BALANCED SHAFT WITH A PRECISION-TESTED HEAD
AND IT COMES WITH A BUILT-IN REFILL AND A 10,000-TRICK GUARANTEE FOR ONLY $50⁰⁰!
I HAVE A BETTER IDEA
PINE-BRANCH WANDS BREAK WHEN YOU STEP ON THEM
Deluxe comic strips done (cheap)
dumas

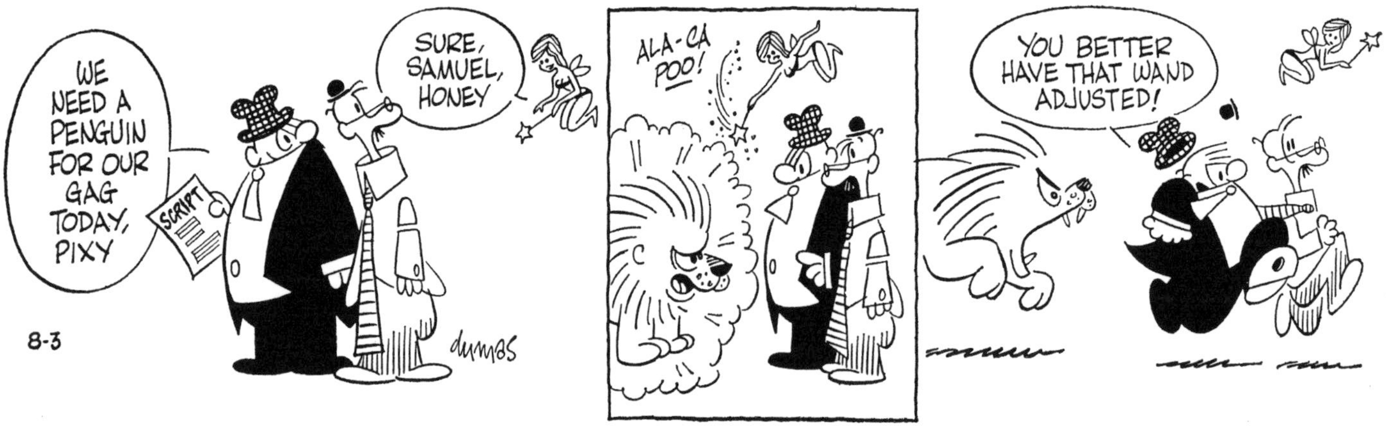
WE NEED A PENGUIN FOR OUR GAG TODAY, PIXY
SURE, SAMUEL, HONEY
SCRIPT
8-3
dumas
AL-A-CA POO!
YOU BETTER HAVE THAT WAND ADJUSTED!

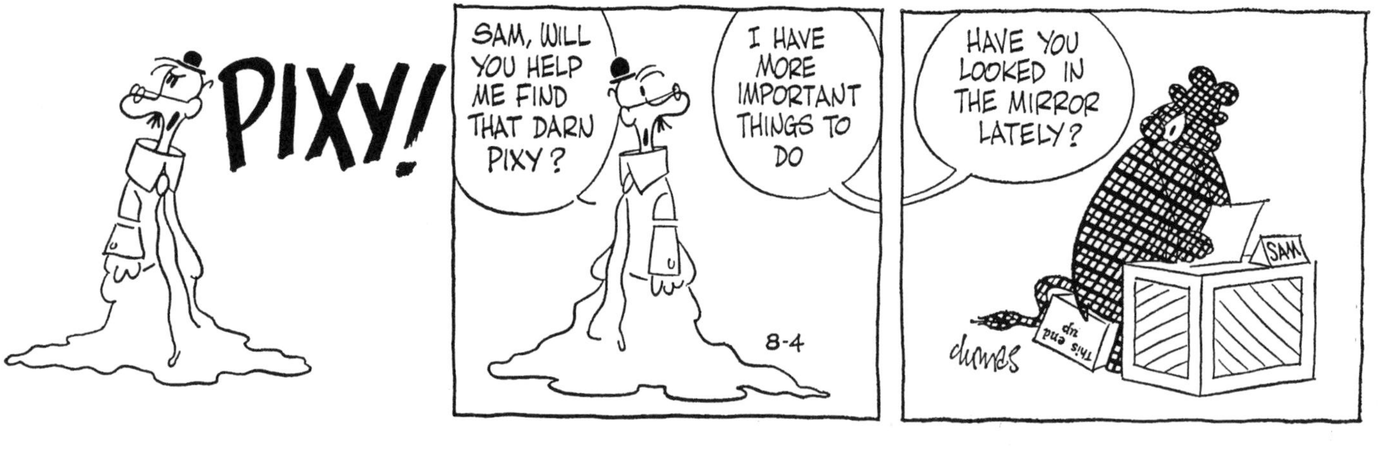
PIXY!
SAM, WILL YOU HELP ME FIND THAT DARN PIXY?
I HAVE MORE IMPORTANT THINGS TO DO
8-4
HAVE YOU LOOKED IN THE MIRROR LATELY?
SAM
This end up
dumas

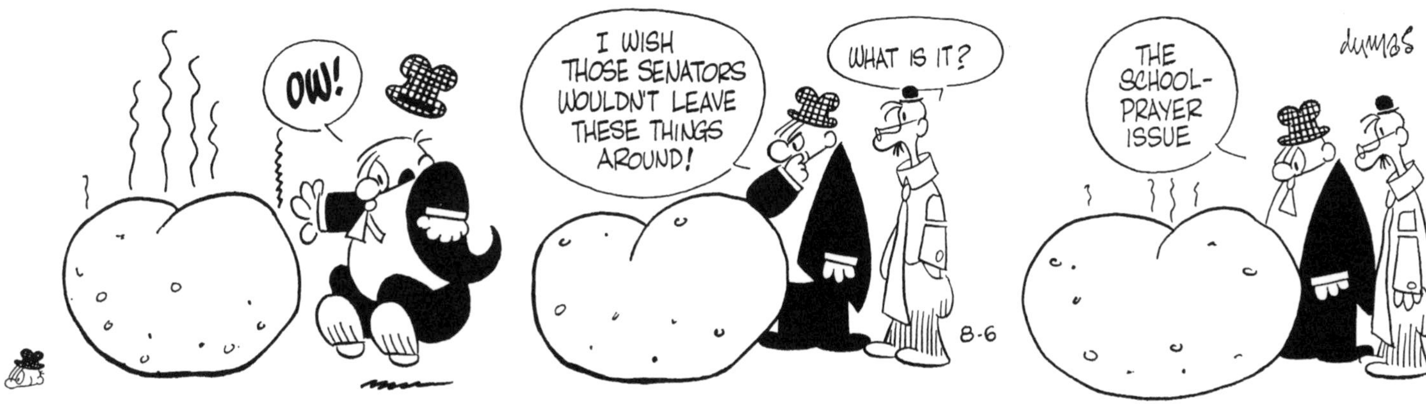
OW!
I WISH THOSE SENATORS WOULDN'T LEAVE THESE THINGS AROUND!
WHAT IS IT?
THE SCHOOL-PRAYER ISSUE
dumas
8-6

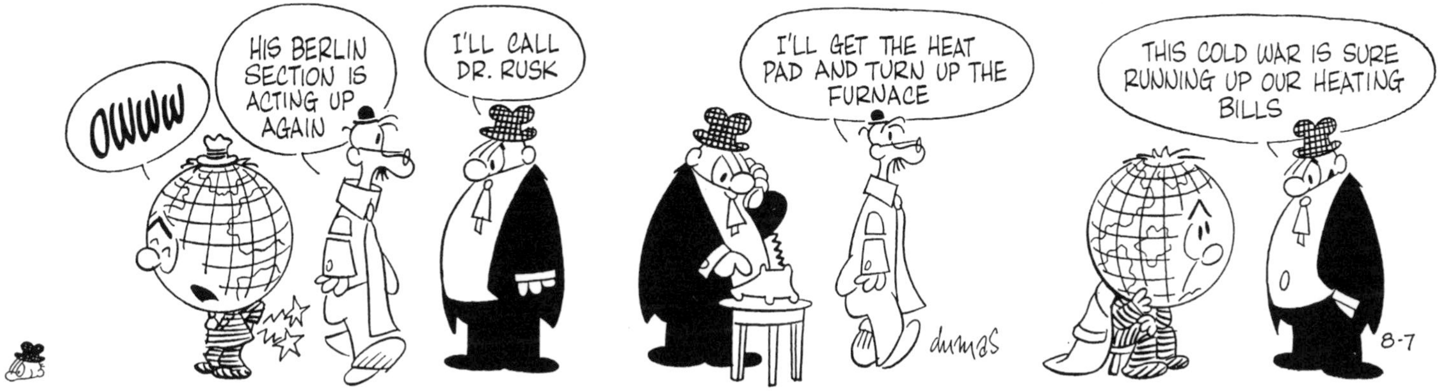
OWWW
HIS BERLIN SECTION IS ACTING UP AGAIN
I'LL CALL DR. RUSK
I'LL GET THE HEAT PAD AND TURN UP THE FURNACE
dumas
THIS COLD WAR IS SURE RUNNING UP OUR HEATING BILLS
8-7

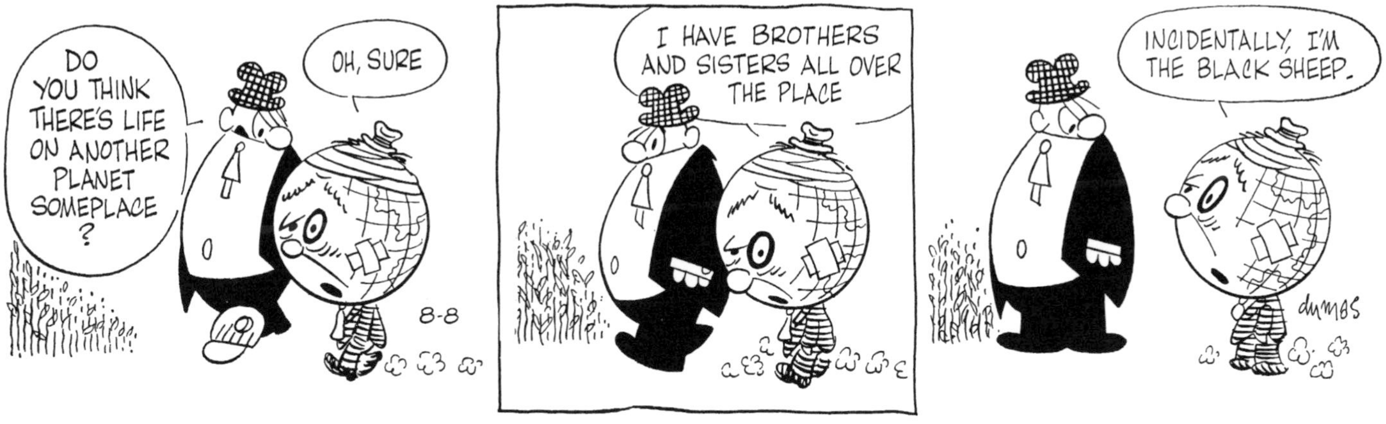
DO YOU THINK THERE'S LIFE ON ANOTHER PLANET SOMEPLACE?
OH, SURE
8-8
I HAVE BROTHERS AND SISTERS ALL OVER THE PLACE
INCIDENTALLY, I'M THE BLACK SHEEP.
dumas

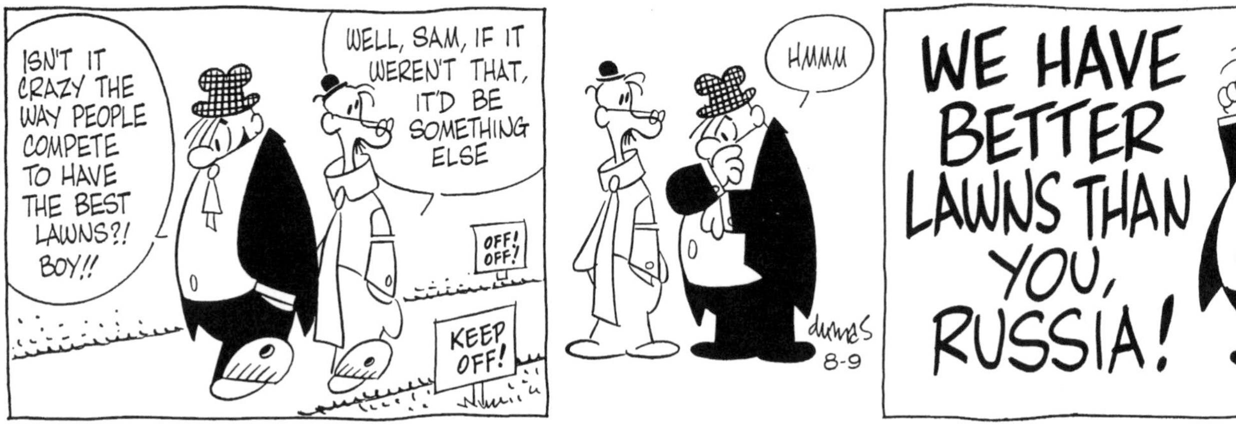
ISN'T IT CRAZY THE WAY PEOPLE COMPETE TO HAVE THE BEST LAWNS?! BOY!!
WELL, SAM, IF IT WEREN'T THAT, IT'D BE SOMETHING ELSE
OFF! OFF!
KEEP OFF!
HMMM
dumas
8-9
WE HAVE BETTER LAWNS THAN YOU, RUSSIA!

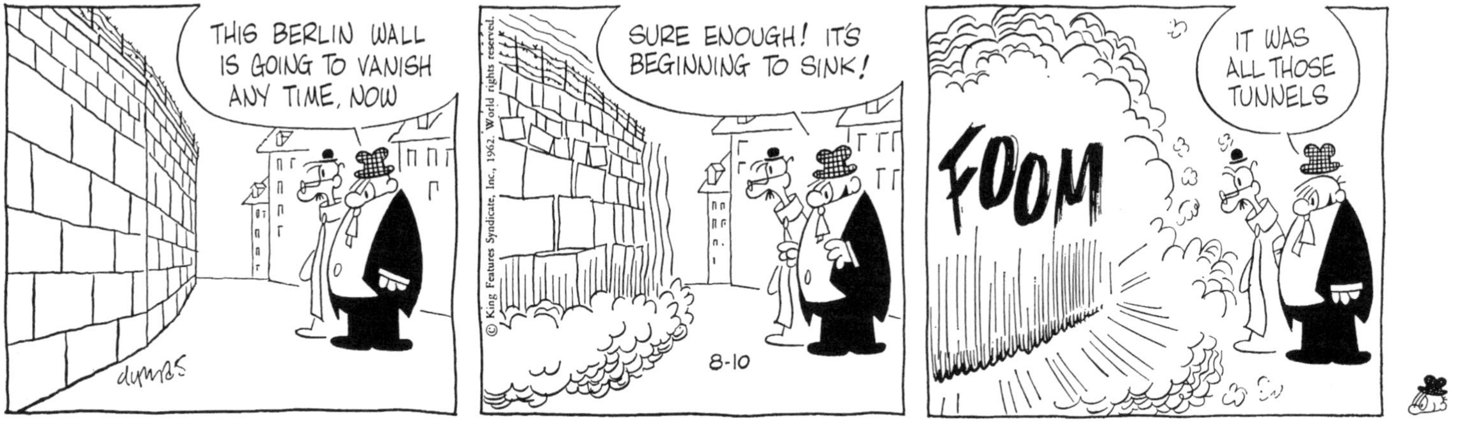
THIS BERLIN WALL IS GOING TO VANISH ANY TIME, NOW
dumas
© King Features Syndicate, Inc., 1962. World rights reserved.
SURE ENOUGH! IT'S BEGINNING TO SINK!
8-10
FOOM
IT WAS ALL THOSE TUNNELS

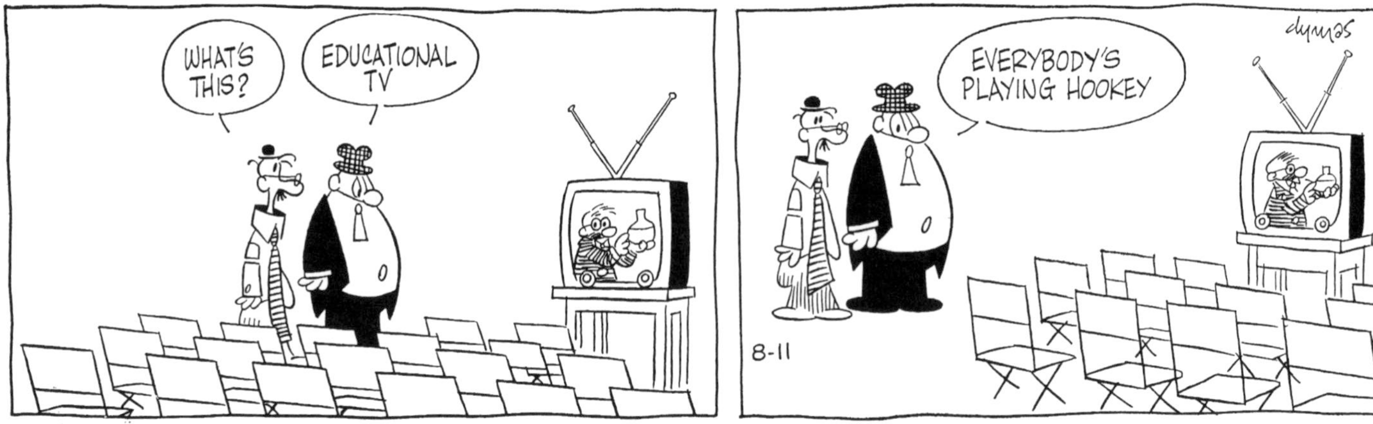
WHAT'S THIS?
EDUCATIONAL TV
dumas
EVERYBODY'S PLAYING HOOKEY
8-11

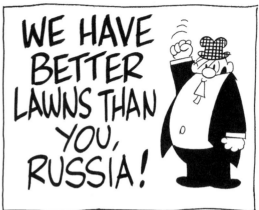

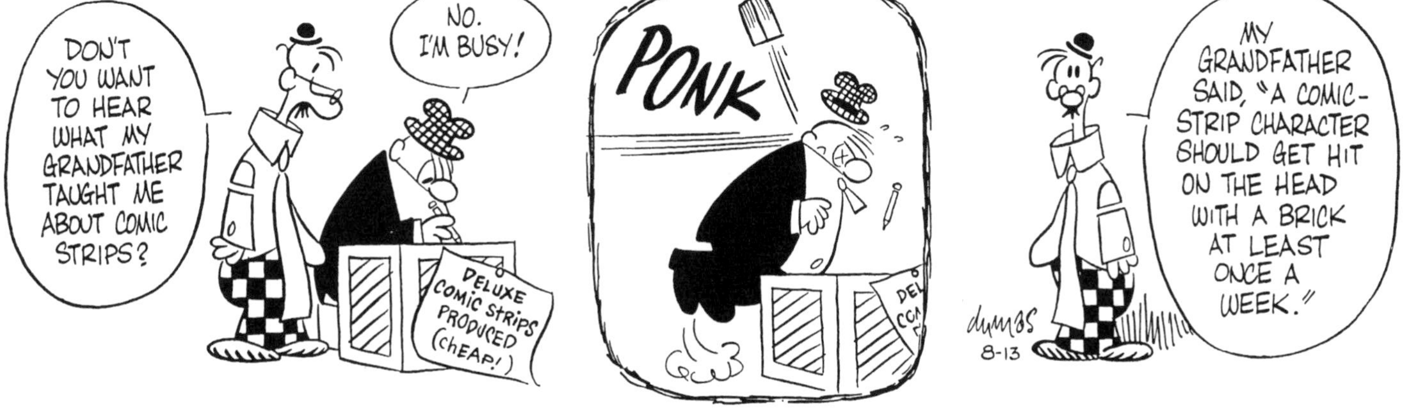
DON'T YOU WANT TO HEAR WHAT MY GRANDFATHER TAUGHT ME ABOUT COMIC STRIPS?
NO. I'M BUSY!
DELUXE COMIC STRIPS PRODUCED (CHEAP!)
PONK
MY GRANDFATHER SAID, "A COMIC-STRIP CHARACTER SHOULD GET HIT ON THE HEAD WITH A BRICK AT LEAST ONCE A WEEK."
dumas
8-13

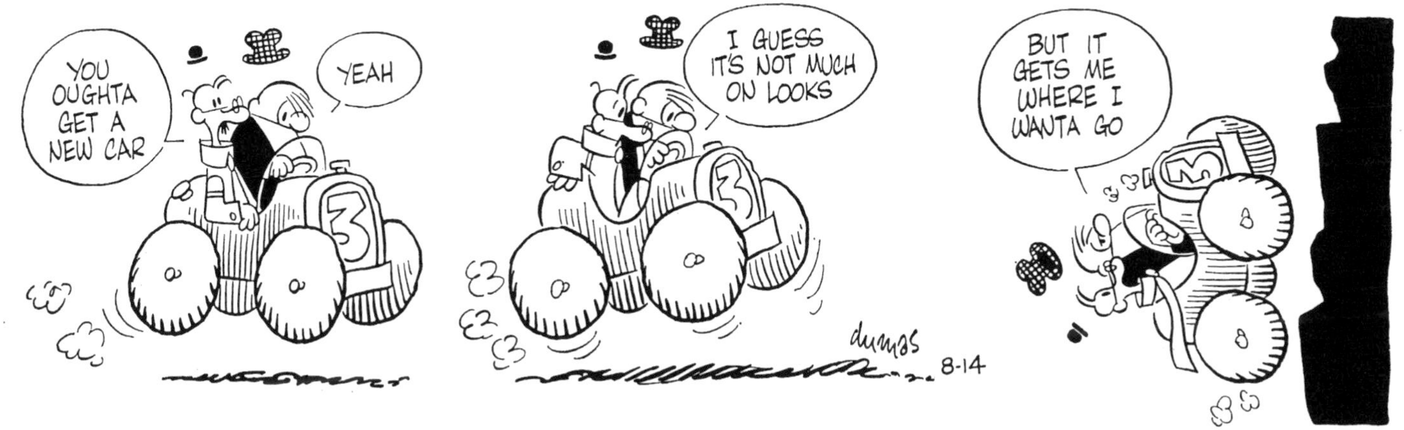
YOU OUGHTA GET A NEW CAR
YEAH
I GUESS IT'S NOT MUCH ON LOOKS
dumas
8-14
BUT IT GETS ME WHERE I WANTA GO

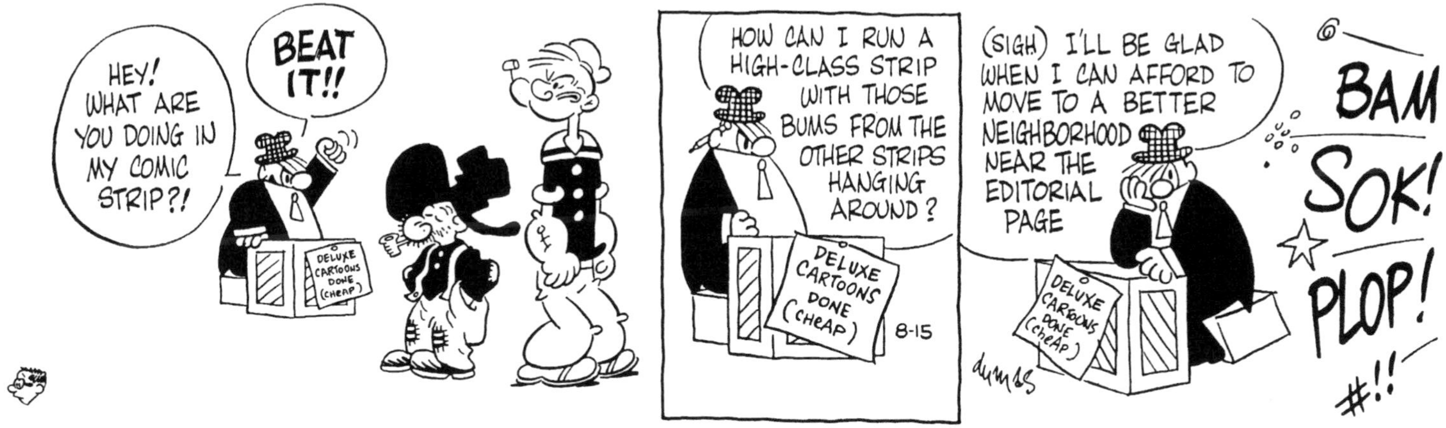
HEY! WHAT ARE YOU DOING IN MY COMIC STRIP?!
BEAT IT!!
DELUXE CARTOONS DONE (CHEAP)
HOW CAN I RUN A HIGH-CLASS STRIP WITH THOSE BUMS FROM THE OTHER STRIPS HANGING AROUND?
DELUXE CARTOONS DONE (CHEAP)
8-15
(SIGH) I'LL BE GLAD WHEN I CAN AFFORD TO MOVE TO A BETTER NEIGHBORHOOD NEAR THE EDITORIAL PAGE
DELUXE CARTOONS DONE (CHEAP)
dumas
BAM
SOK!
PLOP!
#!!

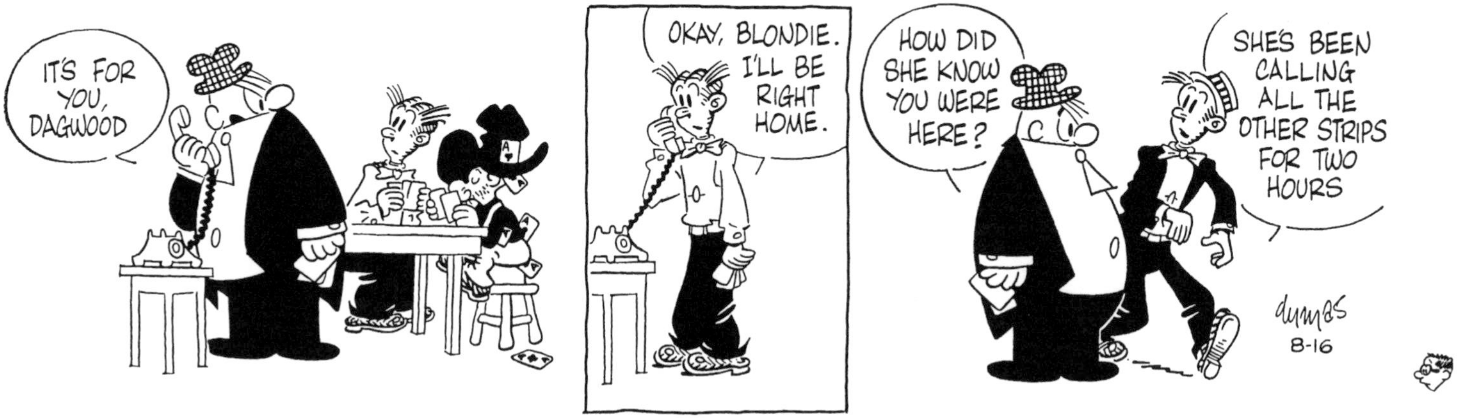
IT'S FOR YOU, DAGWOOD
OKAY, BLONDIE. I'LL BE RIGHT HOME.
HOW DID SHE KNOW YOU WERE HERE?
SHE'S BEEN CALLING ALL THE OTHER STRIPS FOR TWO HOURS
dumas
8-16

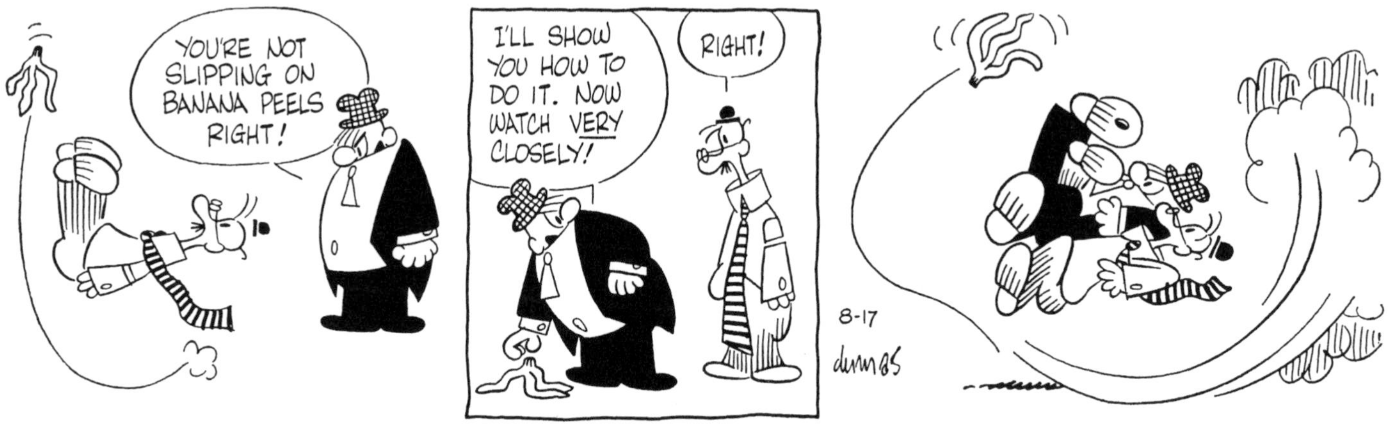
YOU'RE NOT SLIPPING ON BANANA PEELS RIGHT!
I'LL SHOW YOU HOW TO DO IT. NOW WATCH VERY CLOSELY!
RIGHT!
8-17
dumas

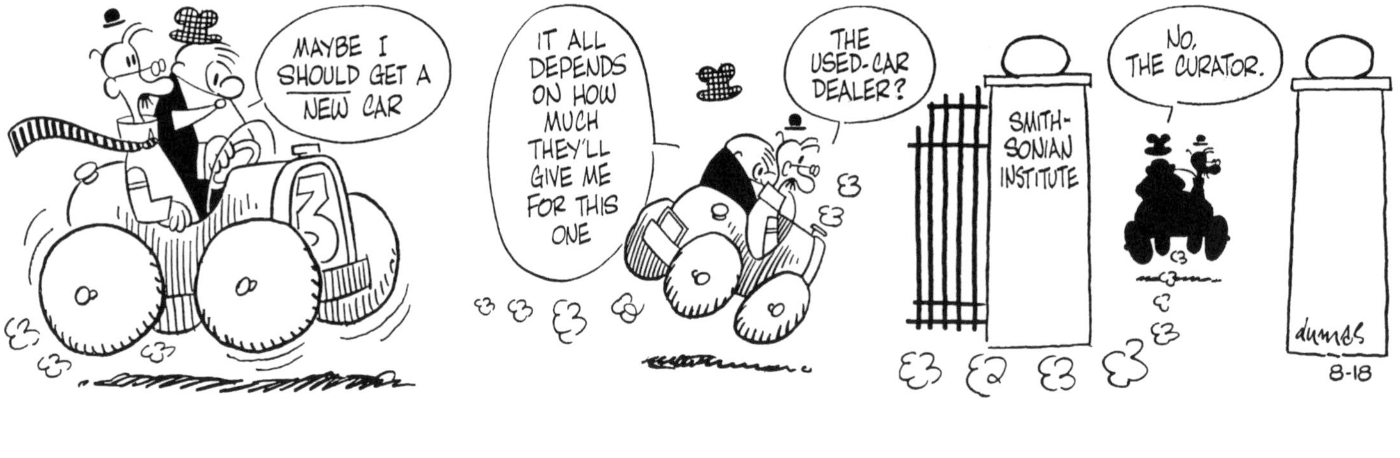
MAYBE I SHOULD GET A NEW CAR
IT ALL DEPENDS ON HOW MUCH THEY'LL GIVE ME FOR THIS ONE
THE USED-CAR DEALER?
SMITH-SONIAN INSTITUTE
NO, THE CURATOR.
dumas
8-18

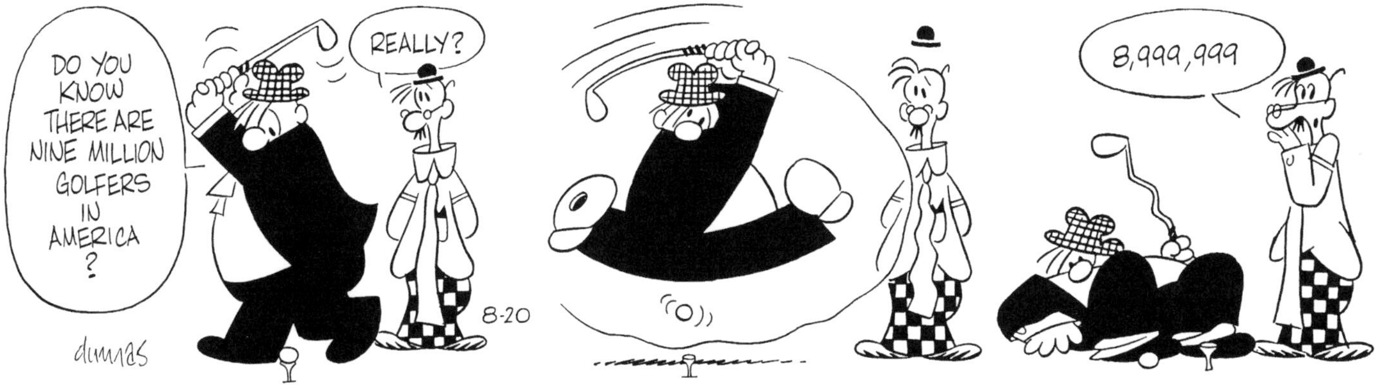
DO YOU KNOW THERE ARE NINE MILLION GOLFERS IN AMERICA ?
REALLY?
8-20
8,999,999
dumas

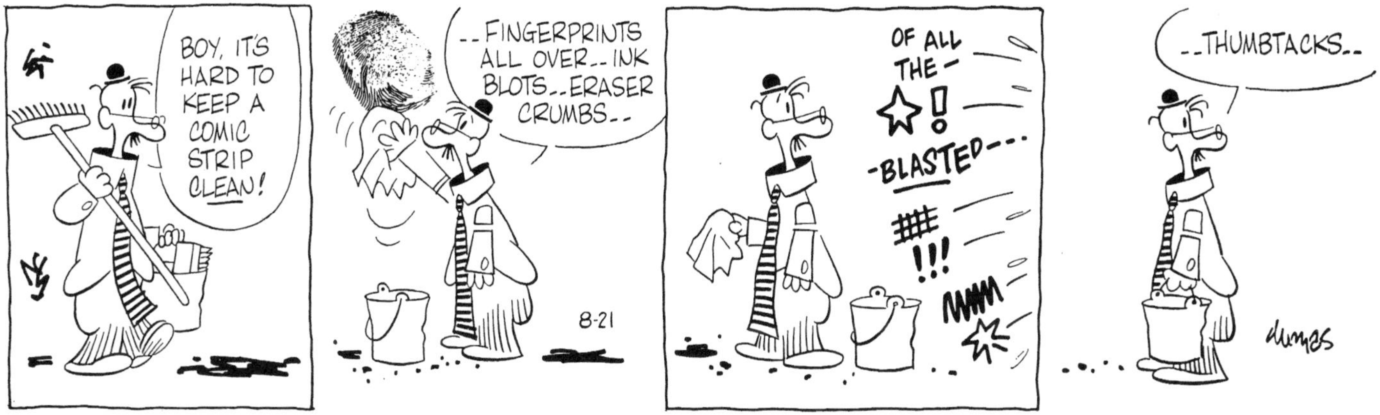
BOY, IT'S HARD TO KEEP A COMIC STRIP CLEAN!
--FINGERPRINTS ALL OVER--INK BLOTS--ERASER CRUMBS--
8-21
OF ALL THE - ☆ ! -BLASTED--- # !!!
--THUMBTACKS--
dumas

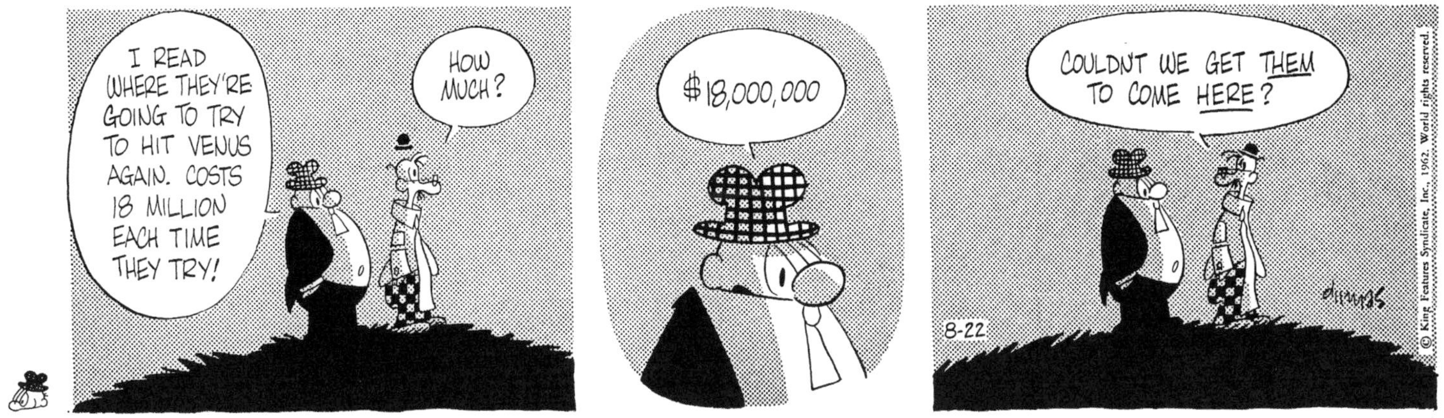
I READ WHERE THEY'RE GOING TO TRY TO HIT VENUS AGAIN. COSTS 18 MILLION EACH TIME THEY TRY!
HOW MUCH?
$18,000,000
COULDN'T WE GET THEM TO COME HERE?
8-22
dumas
© King Features Syndicate, Inc., 1962. World rights reserved.

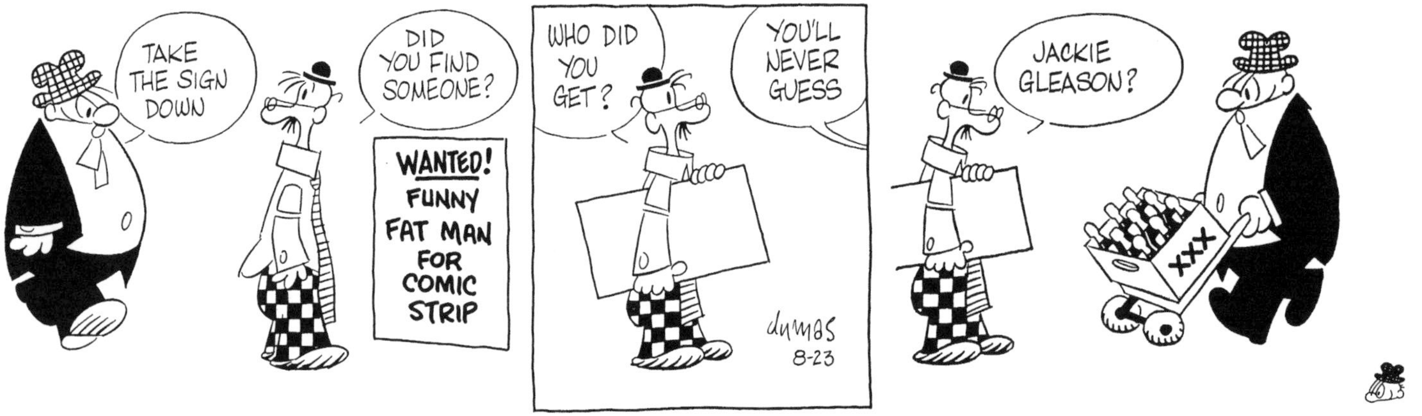
TAKE THE SIGN DOWN
DID YOU FIND SOMEONE?
WANTED! FUNNY FAT MAN FOR COMIC STRIP
WHO DID YOU GET?
YOU'LL NEVER GUESS
dumas 8-23
JACKIE GLEASON?
XXX

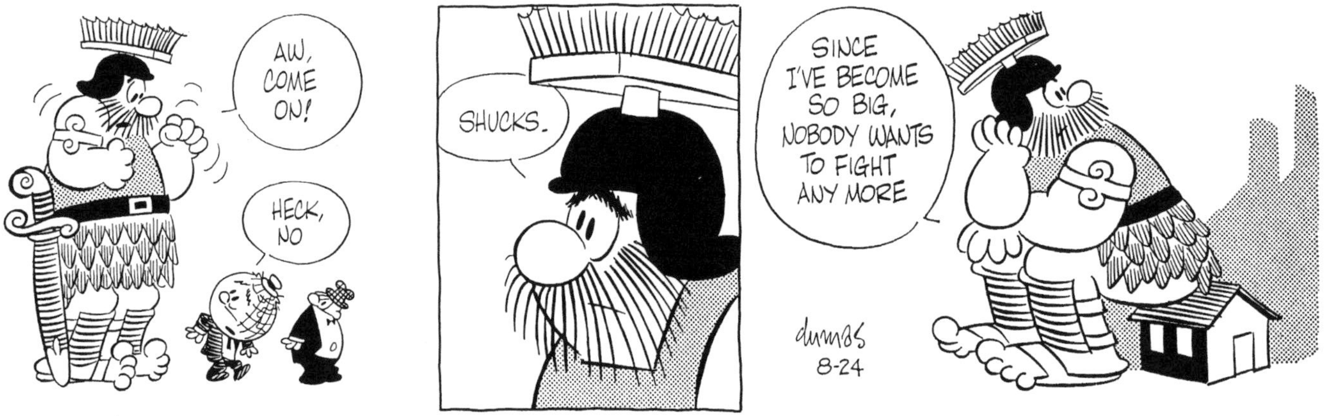
AW, COME ON!
HECK, NO
SHUCKS.
SINCE I'VE BECOME SO BIG, NOBODY WANTS TO FIGHT ANY MORE
dumas 8-24

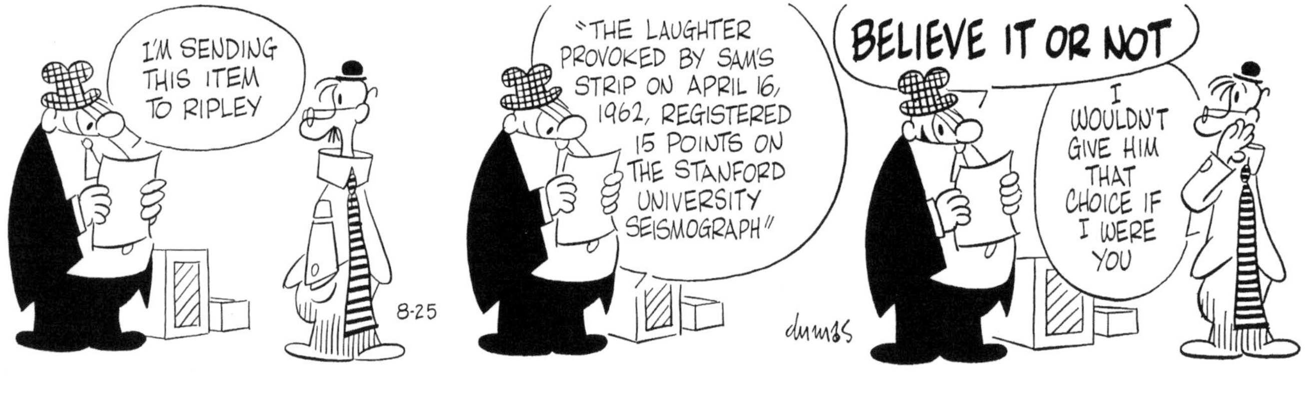
I'M SENDING THIS ITEM TO RIPLEY
8-25
"THE LAUGHTER PROVOKED BY SAM'S STRIP ON APRIL 16, 1962, REGISTERED 15 POINTS ON THE STANFORD UNIVERSITY SEISMOGRAPH"
dumas
BELIEVE IT OR NOT
I WOULDN'T GIVE HIM THAT CHOICE IF I WERE YOU

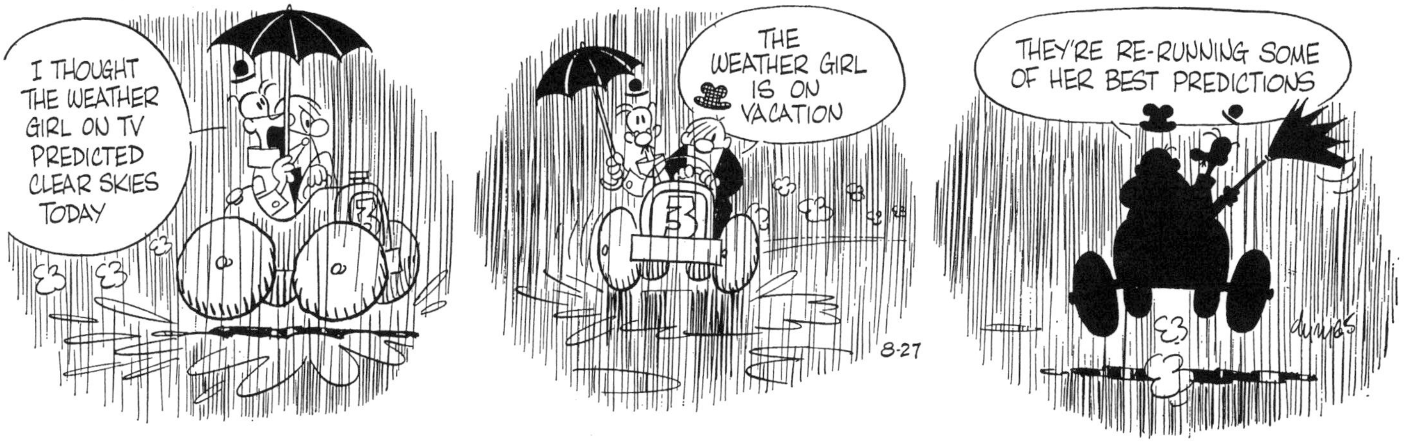
I THOUGHT THE WEATHER GIRL ON TV PREDICTED CLEAR SKIES TODAY
THE WEATHER GIRL IS ON VACATION
8-27
THEY'RE RE-RUNNING SOME OF HER BEST PREDICTIONS
dumas

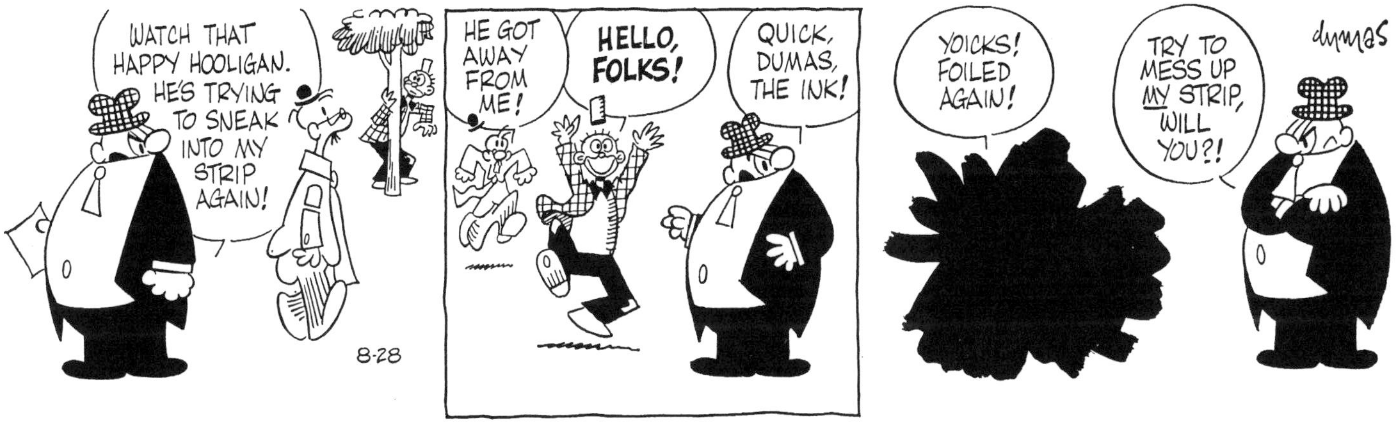
WATCH THAT HAPPY HOOLIGAN. HE'S TRYING TO SNEAK INTO MY STRIP AGAIN!
8-28
HE GOT AWAY FROM ME!
HELLO, FOLKS!
QUICK, DUMAS, THE INK!
YOICKS! FOILED AGAIN!
TRY TO MESS UP MY STRIP, WILL YOU?!
dumas

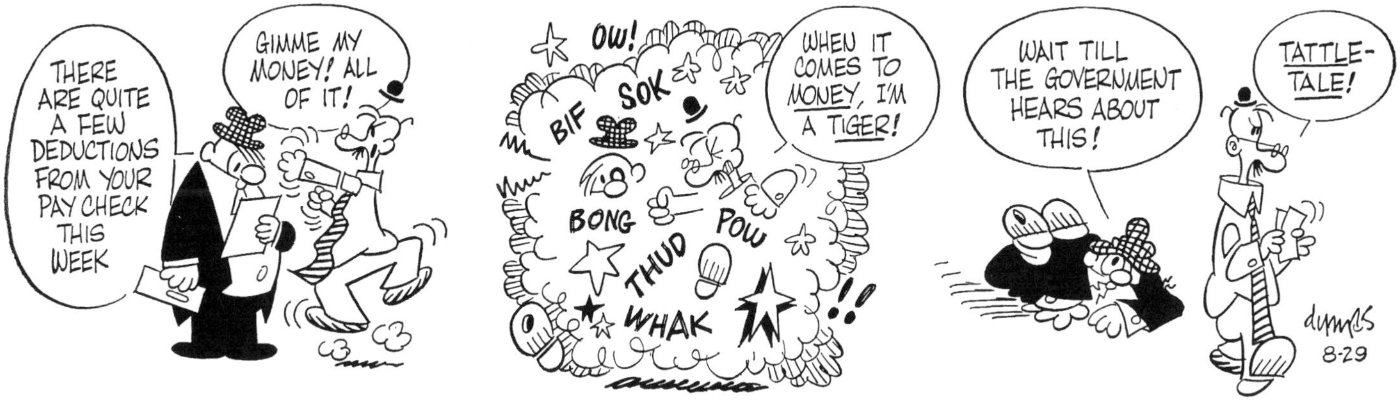
THERE ARE QUITE A FEW DEDUCTIONS FROM YOUR PAY CHECK THIS WEEK
GIMME MY MONEY! ALL OF IT!
OW!
BIF
SOK
BONG
POW
THUD
WHAK
!!
WHEN IT COMES TO MONEY, I'M A TIGER!
WAIT TILL THE GOVERNMENT HEARS ABOUT THIS!
TATTLE-TALE!
dumas
8-29

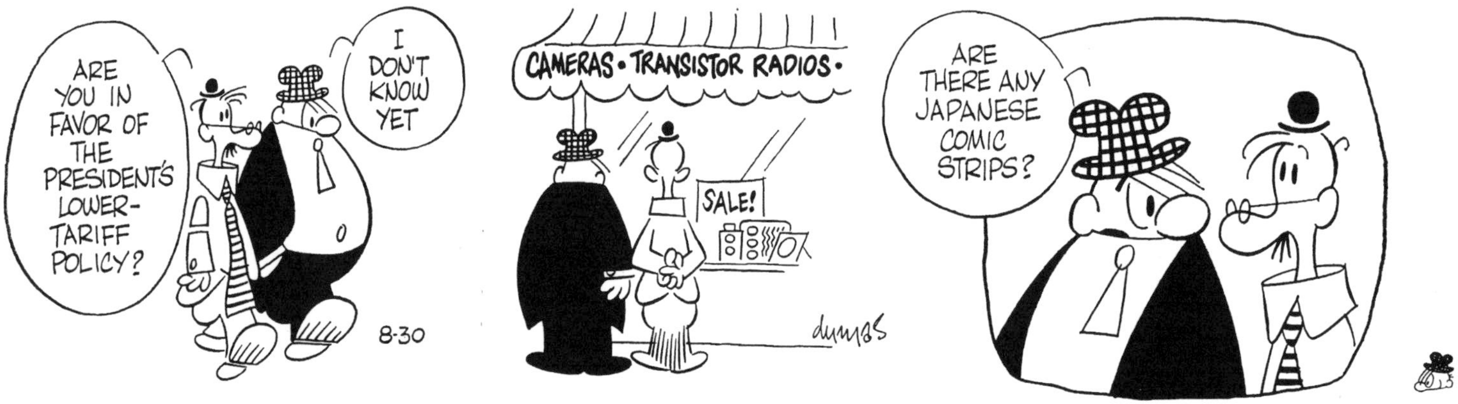
ARE YOU IN FAVOR OF THE PRESIDENT'S LOWER-TARIFF POLICY?
I DON'T KNOW YET
8-30
CAMERAS • TRANSISTOR RADIOS •
SALE!
dumas
ARE THERE ANY JAPANESE COMIC STRIPS?

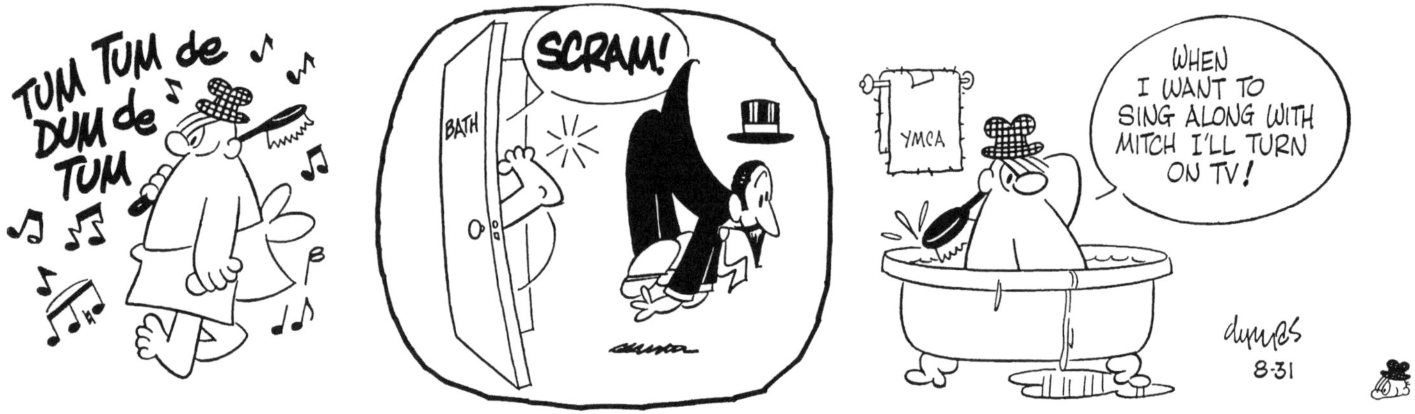
TUM TUM de DUM de TUM
SCRAM!
BATH
YMCA
WHEN I WANT TO SING ALONG WITH MITCH I'LL TURN ON TV!
dumas
8-31

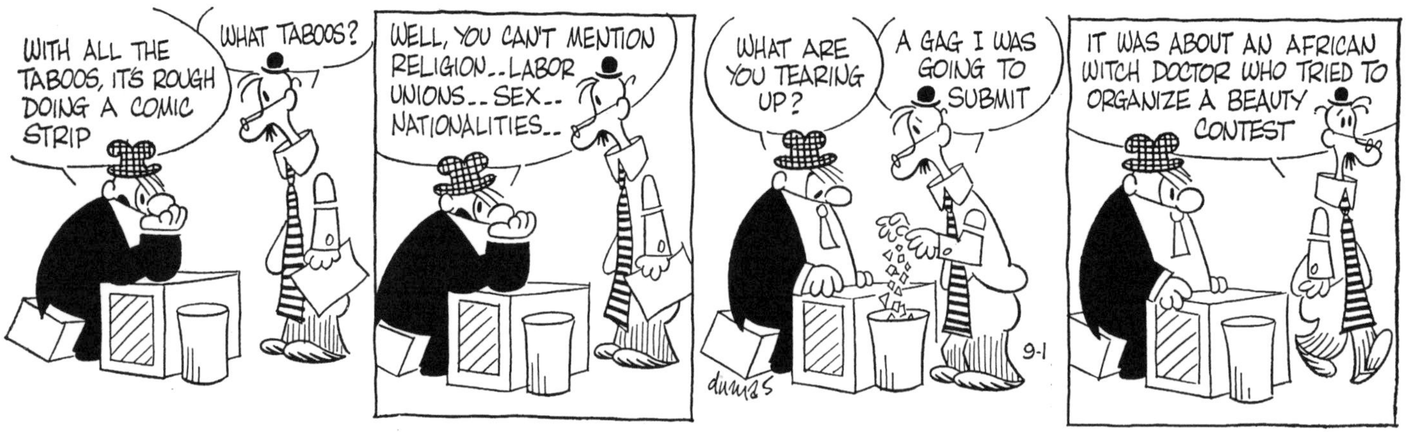
WITH ALL THE TABOOS, IT'S ROUGH DOING A COMIC STRIP
WHAT TABOOS?
WELL, YOU CAN'T MENTION RELIGION..LABOR UNIONS..SEX..NATIONALITIES..
WHAT ARE YOU TEARING UP?
A GAG I WAS GOING TO SUBMIT
dumas
9-1
IT WAS ABOUT AN AFRICAN WITCH DOCTOR WHO TRIED TO ORGANIZE A BEAUTY CONTEST

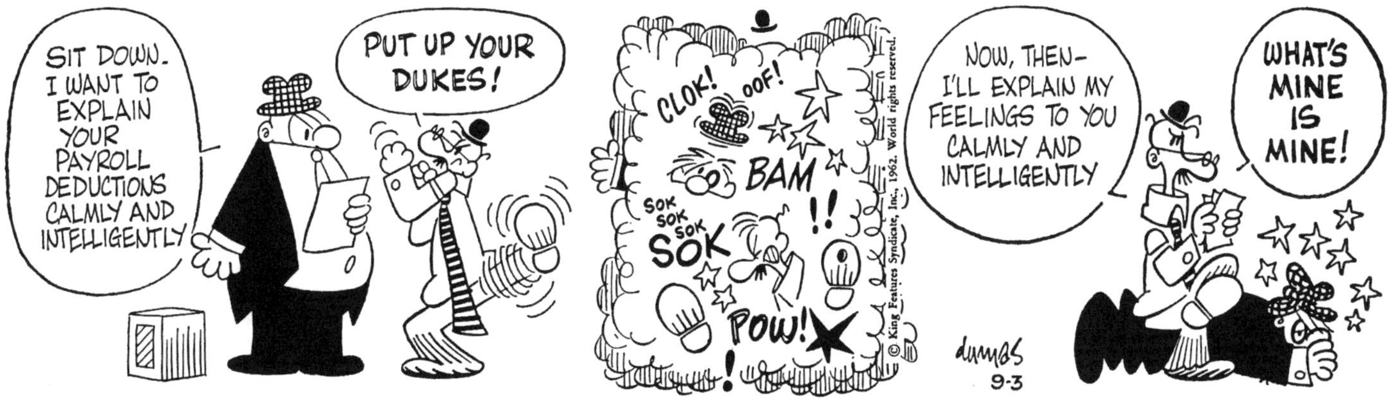
SIT DOWN. I WANT TO EXPLAIN YOUR PAYROLL DEDUCTIONS CALMLY AND INTELLIGENTLY
PUT UP YOUR DUKES!
CLOK! OOF!
BAM
SOK SOK SOK SOK
!!
POW!
!
© King Features Syndicate, Inc., 1962. World rights reserved.
NOW, THEN– I'LL EXPLAIN MY FEELINGS TO YOU CALMLY AND INTELLIGENTLY
WHAT'S MINE IS MINE!
dumas
9-3

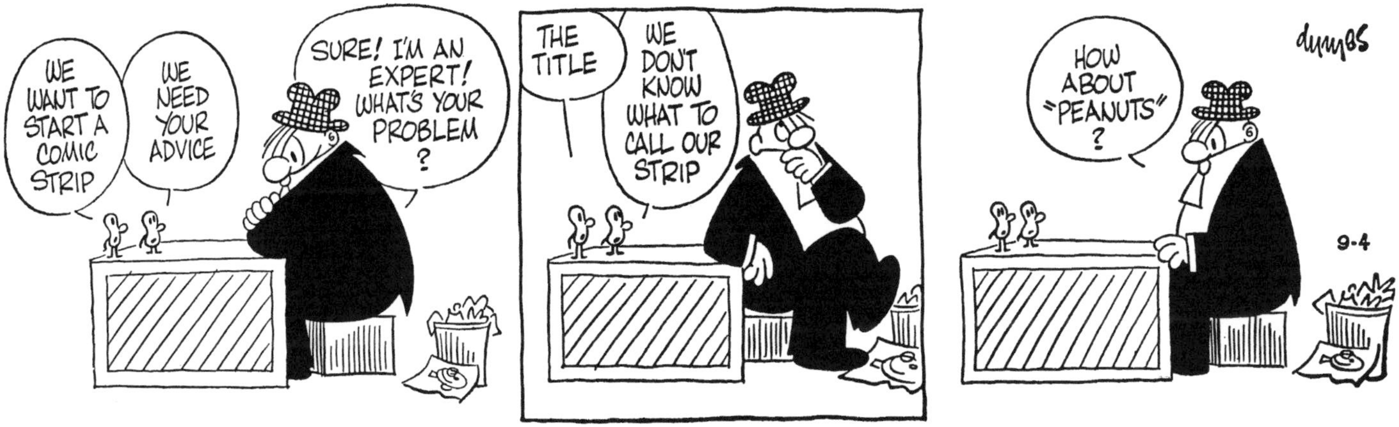
WE WANT TO START A COMIC STRIP
WE NEED YOUR ADVICE
SURE! I'M AN EXPERT! WHAT'S YOUR PROBLEM ?
THE TITLE
WE DON'T KNOW WHAT TO CALL OUR STRIP
dumas
HOW ABOUT "PEANUTS" ?
9-4

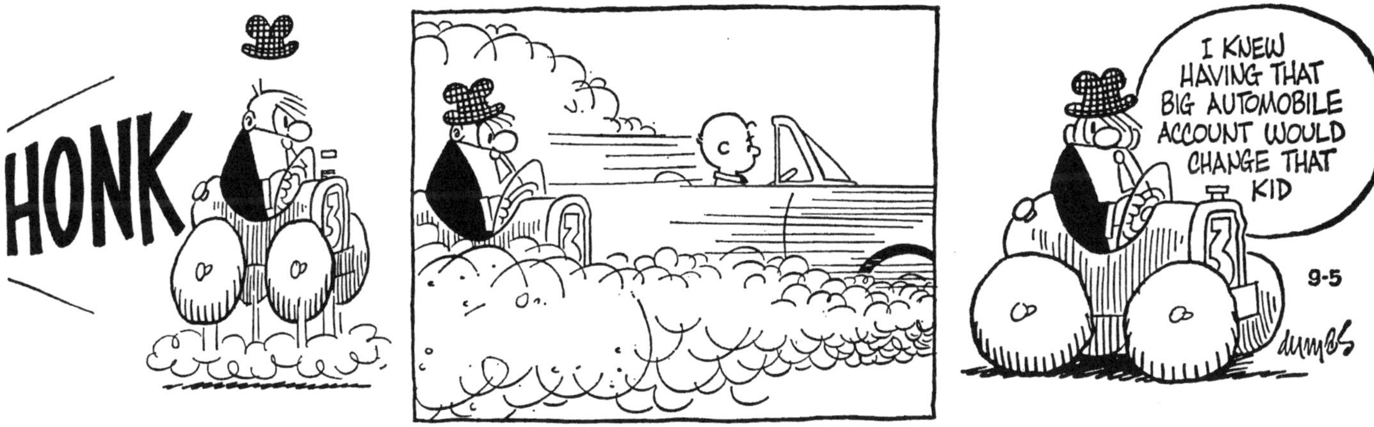
HONK
I KNEW HAVING THAT BIG AUTOMOBILE ACCOUNT WOULD CHANGE THAT KID
9-5
dumas

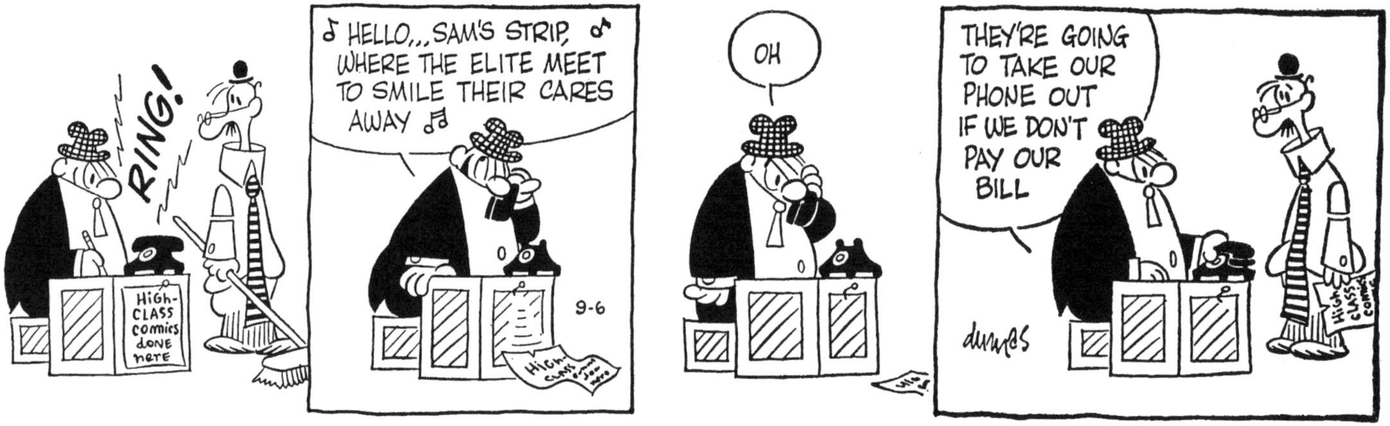
RING!
HIGH-CLASS comics done here
HELLO,,, SAM'S STRIP, WHERE THE ELITE MEET TO SMILE THEIR CARES AWAY
9-6
OH
THEY'RE GOING TO TAKE OUR PHONE OUT IF WE DON'T PAY OUR BILL
dumas
HIGH-CLASS comics

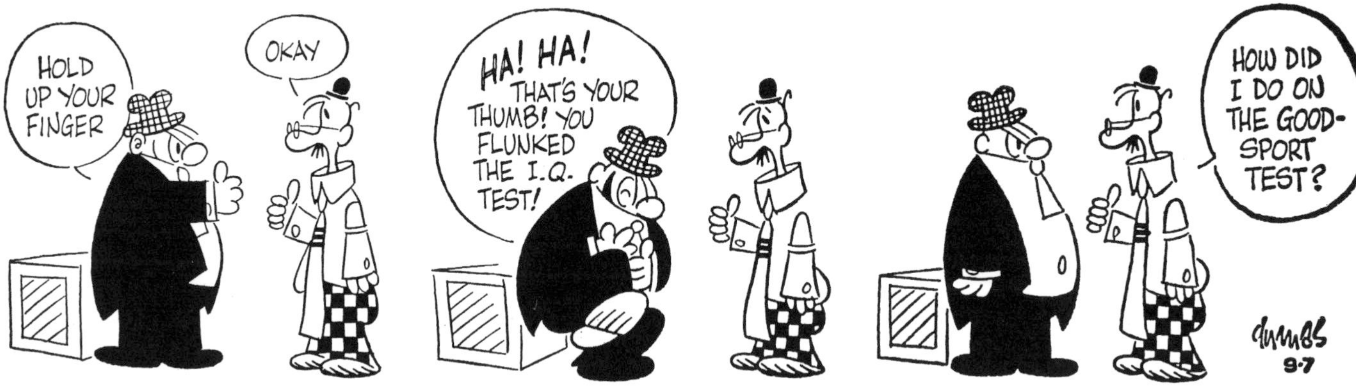
HOLD UP YOUR FINGER
OKAY
HA! HA! THAT'S YOUR THUMB! YOU FLUNKED THE I.Q. TEST!
HOW DID I DO ON THE GOOD-SPORT TEST?
dumas
9-7

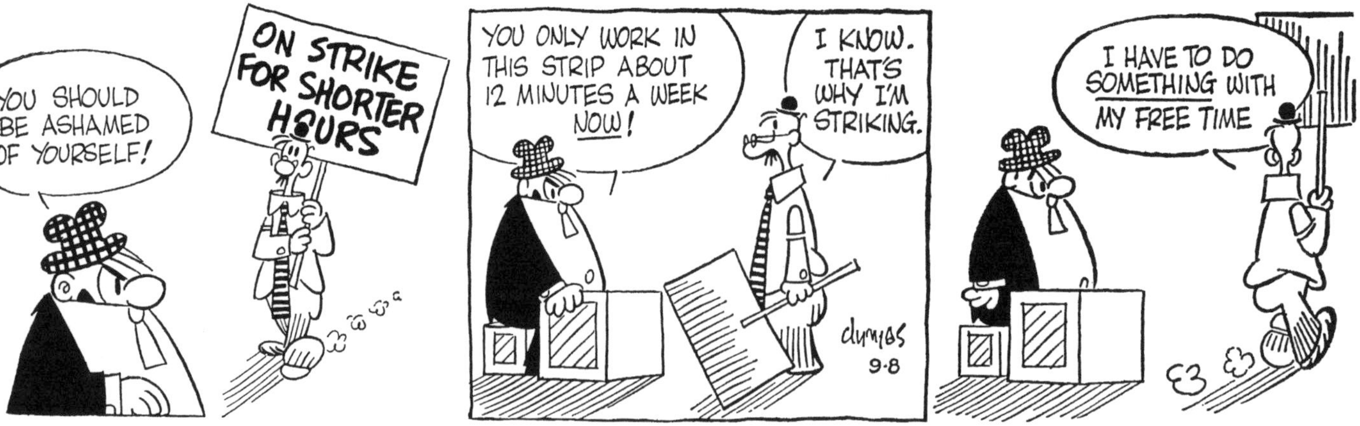
YOU SHOULD BE ASHAMED OF YOURSELF!
ON STRIKE FOR SHORTER HOURS
YOU ONLY WORK IN THIS STRIP ABOUT 12 MINUTES A WEEK NOW!
I KNOW. THAT'S WHY I'M STRIKING.
dumas
9-8
I HAVE TO DO SOMETHING WITH MY FREE TIME

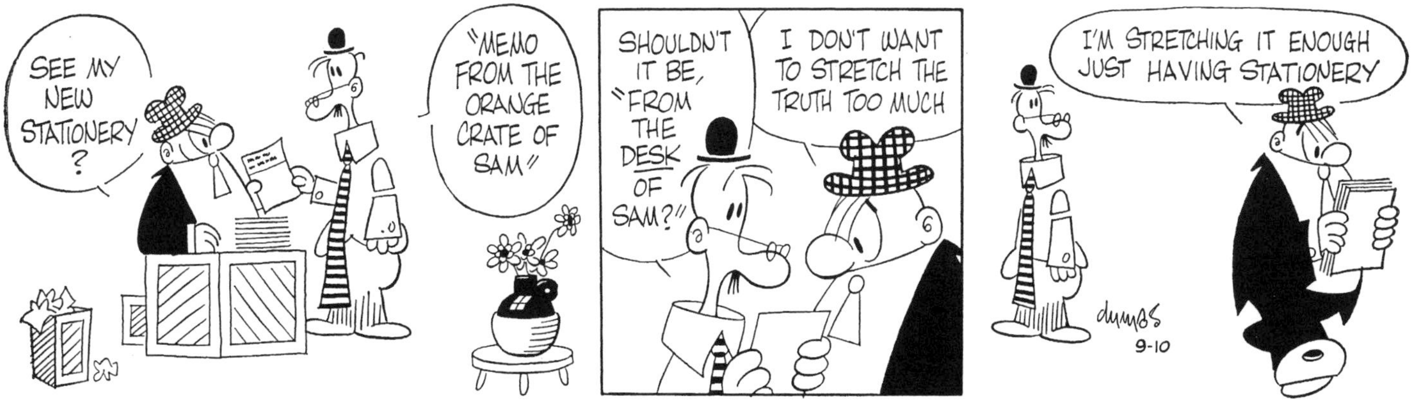
SEE MY NEW STATIONERY ?
"MEMO FROM THE ORANGE CRATE OF SAM"
SHOULDN'T IT BE, "FROM THE DESK OF SAM?"
I DON'T WANT TO STRETCH THE TRUTH TOO MUCH
I'M STRETCHING IT ENOUGH JUST HAVING STATIONERY
dumas
9-10

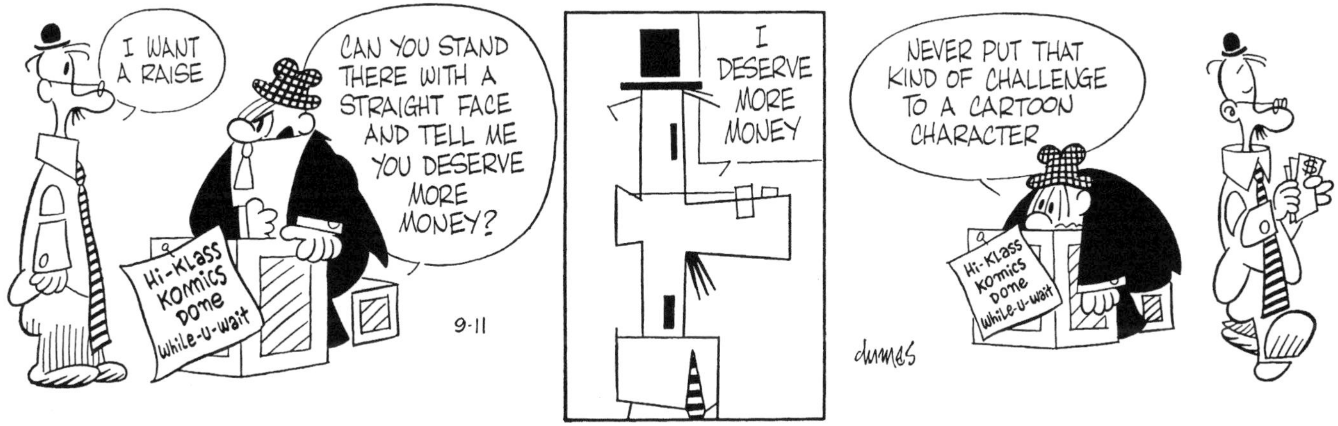
I WANT A RAISE
CAN YOU STAND THERE WITH A STRAIGHT FACE AND TELL ME YOU DESERVE MORE MONEY?
Hi-Klass Komics Done While-U-Wait
9-11
I DESERVE MORE MONEY
NEVER PUT THAT KIND OF CHALLENGE TO A CARTOON CHARACTER
Hi-Klass Komics Done While-U-Wait
dumas

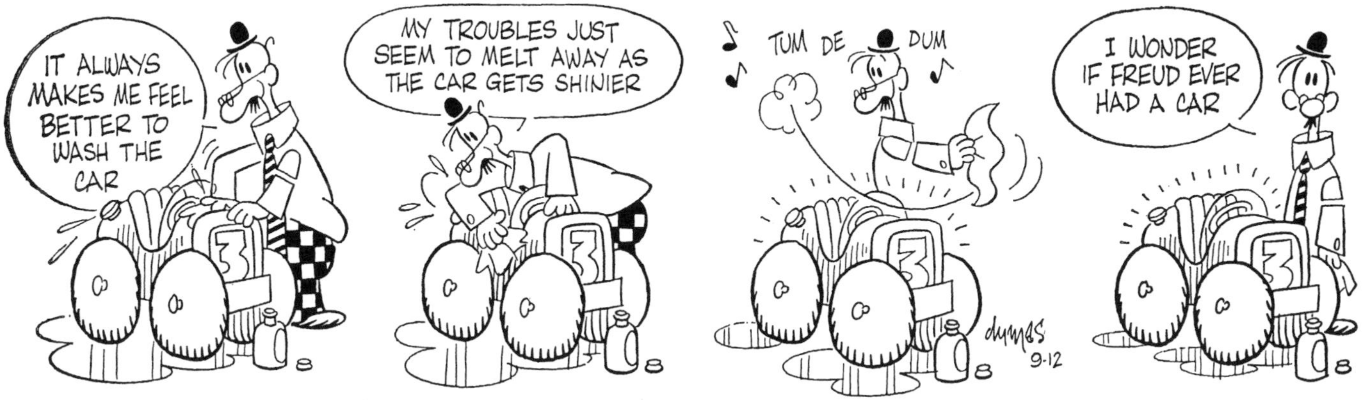
IT ALWAYS MAKES ME FEEL BETTER TO WASH THE CAR
MY TROUBLES JUST SEEM TO MELT AWAY AS THE CAR GETS SHINIER
TUM DE DUM
I WONDER IF FREUD EVER HAD A CAR
dumas
9-12

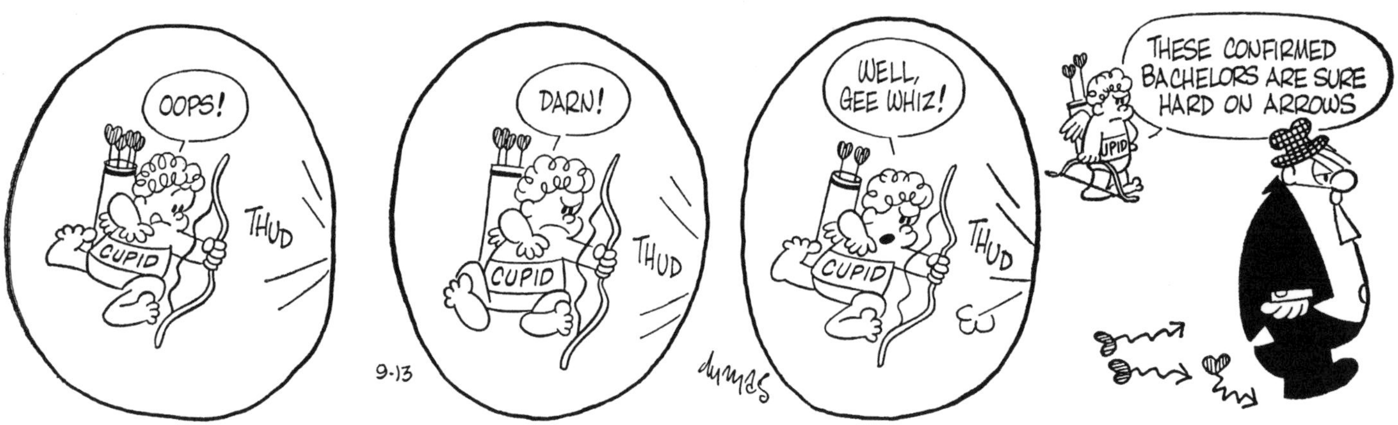
OOPS!
CUPID
THUD
9-13
DARN!
CUPID
THUD
WELL, GEE WHIZ!
CUPID
THUD
THESE CONFIRMED BACHELORS ARE SURE HARD ON ARROWS

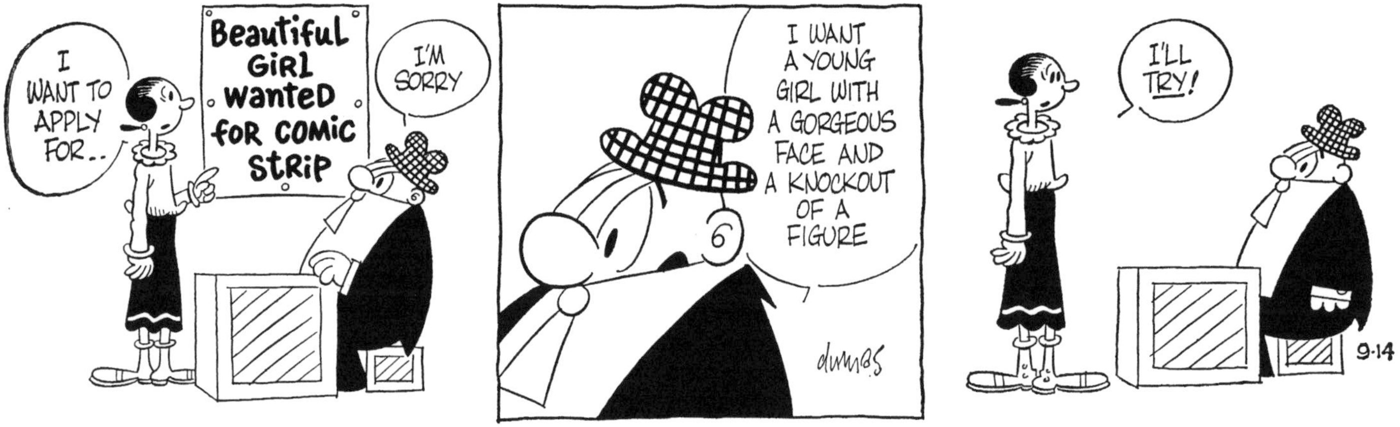
I WANT TO APPLY FOR..
Beautiful GIRL Wanted FOR COMIC STRIP
I'M SORRY
I WANT A YOUNG GIRL WITH A GORGEOUS FACE AND A KNOCKOUT OF A FIGURE
I'LL TRY!
9-14

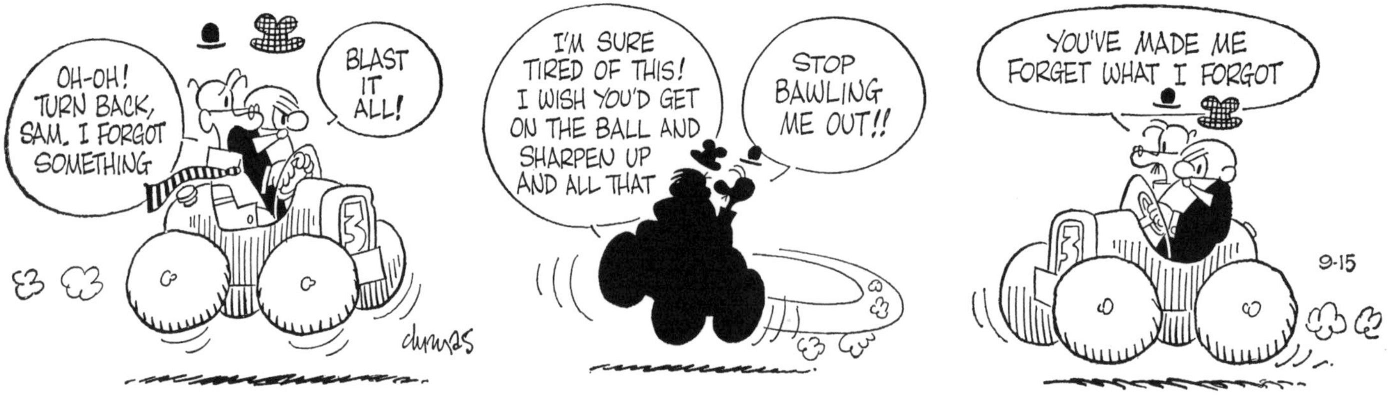
OH-OH! TURN BACK, SAM. I FORGOT SOMETHING
BLAST IT ALL!
I'M SURE TIRED OF THIS! I WISH YOU'D GET ON THE BALL AND SHARPEN UP AND ALL THAT
STOP BAWLING ME OUT!!
YOU'VE MADE ME FORGET WHAT I FORGOT
9-15

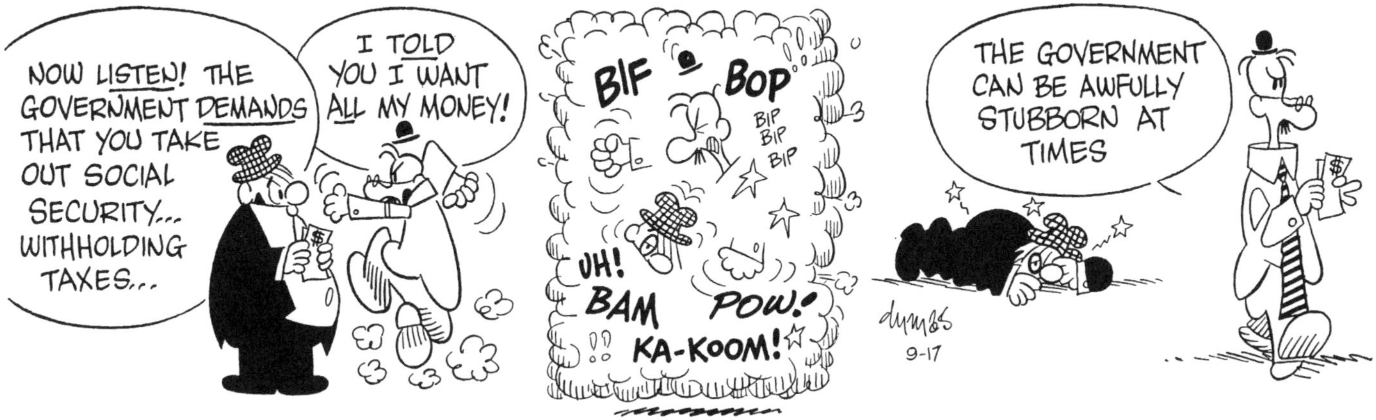
NOW LISTEN! THE GOVERNMENT DEMANDS THAT YOU TAKE OUT SOCIAL SECURITY... WITHHOLDING TAXES...
I TOLD YOU I WANT ALL MY MONEY!
BIF
BOP
BIP BIP BIP
UH!
BAM
POW!
KA-KOOM!
THE GOVERNMENT CAN BE AWFULLY STUBBORN AT TIMES
dumas
9-17

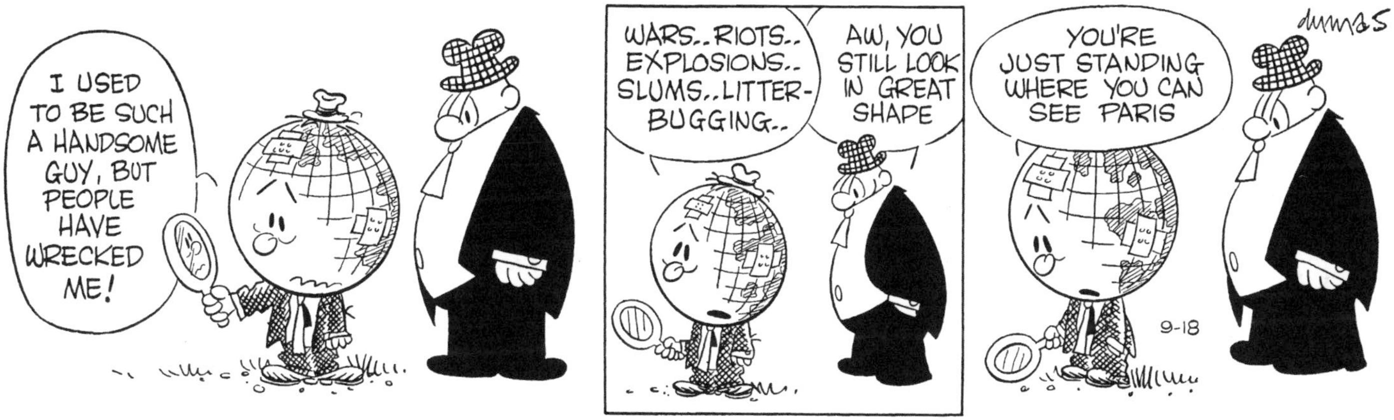
I USED TO BE SUCH A HANDSOME GUY, BUT PEOPLE HAVE WRECKED ME!
WARS.. RIOTS.. EXPLOSIONS.. SLUMS.. LITTER-BUGGING..
AW, YOU STILL LOOK IN GREAT SHAPE
YOU'RE JUST STANDING WHERE YOU CAN SEE PARIS
dumas
9-18

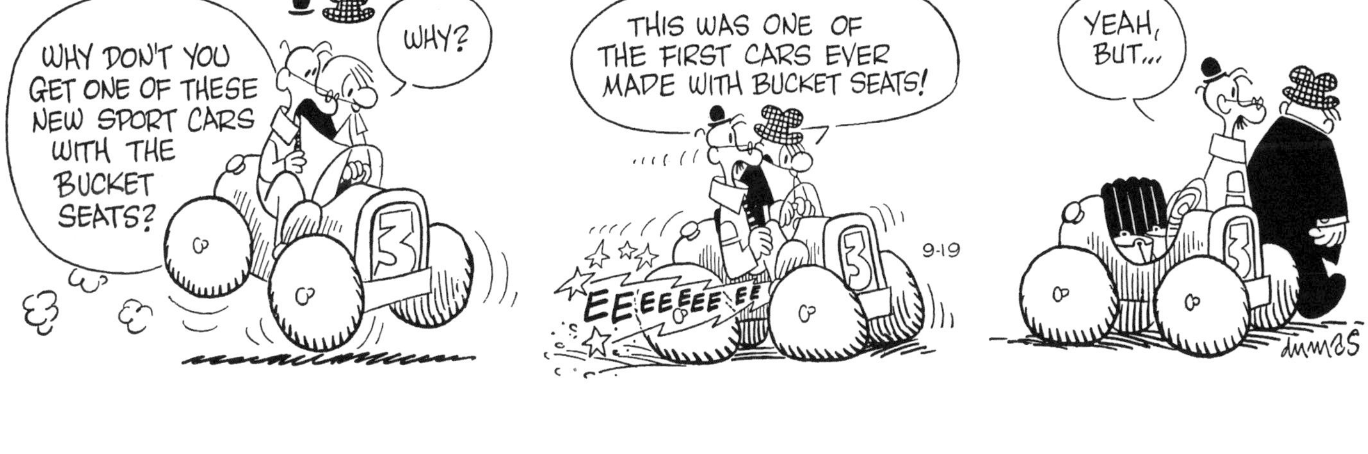
WHY DON'T YOU GET ONE OF THESE NEW SPORT CARS WITH THE BUCKET SEATS?
WHY?
THIS WAS ONE OF THE FIRST CARS EVER MADE WITH BUCKET SEATS!
EEEEEEEEE
9-19
YEAH, BUT...
dumas

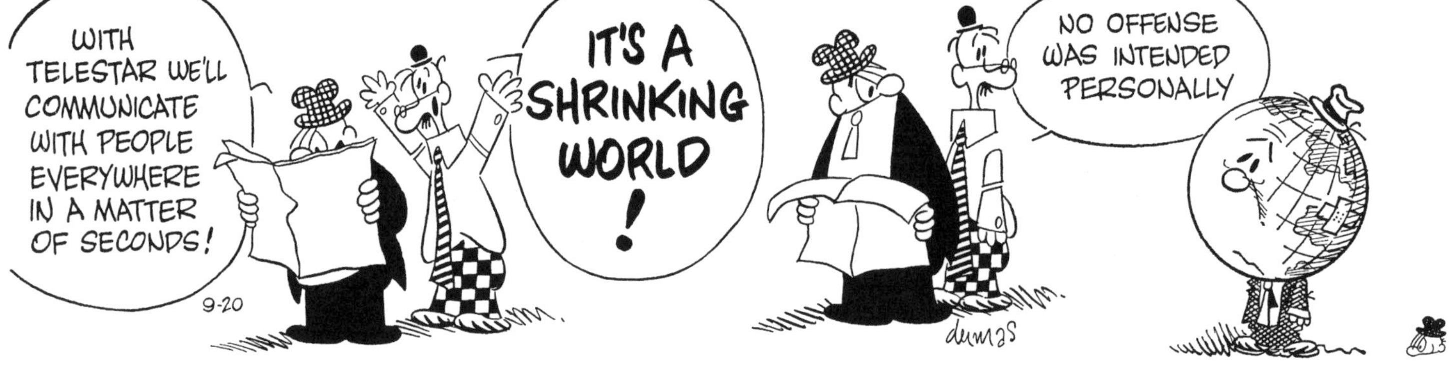
WITH TELESTAR WE'LL COMMUNICATE WITH PEOPLE EVERYWHERE IN A MATTER OF SECONDS!
9-20
IT'S A SHRINKING WORLD!
dumas
NO OFFENSE WAS INTENDED PERSONALLY

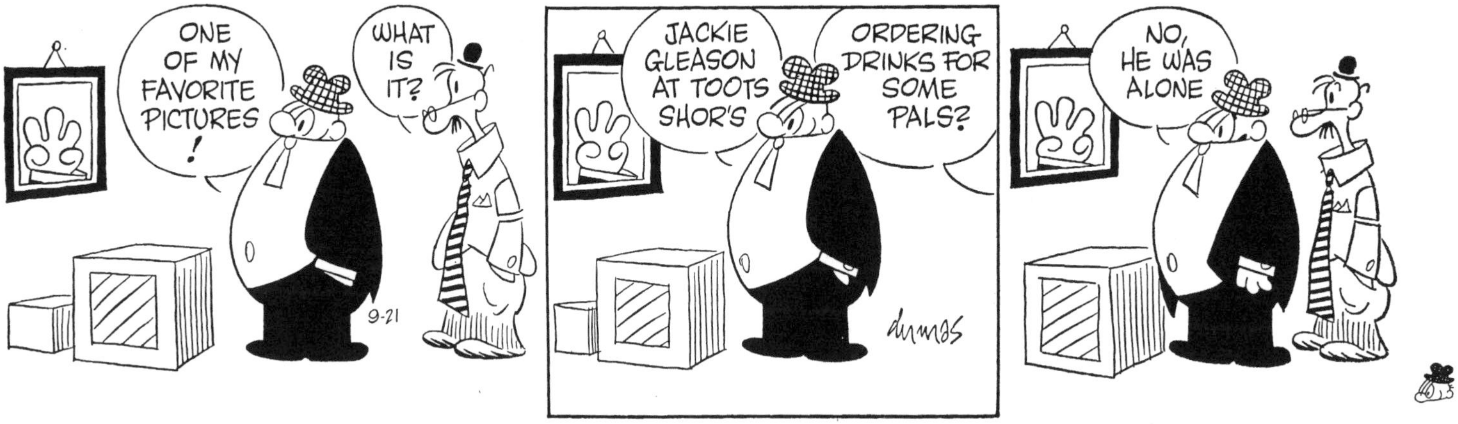
ONE OF MY FAVORITE PICTURES!
WHAT IS IT?
9-21
JACKIE GLEASON AT TOOTS SHOR'S
ORDERING DRINKS FOR SOME PALS?
dumas
NO, HE WAS ALONE

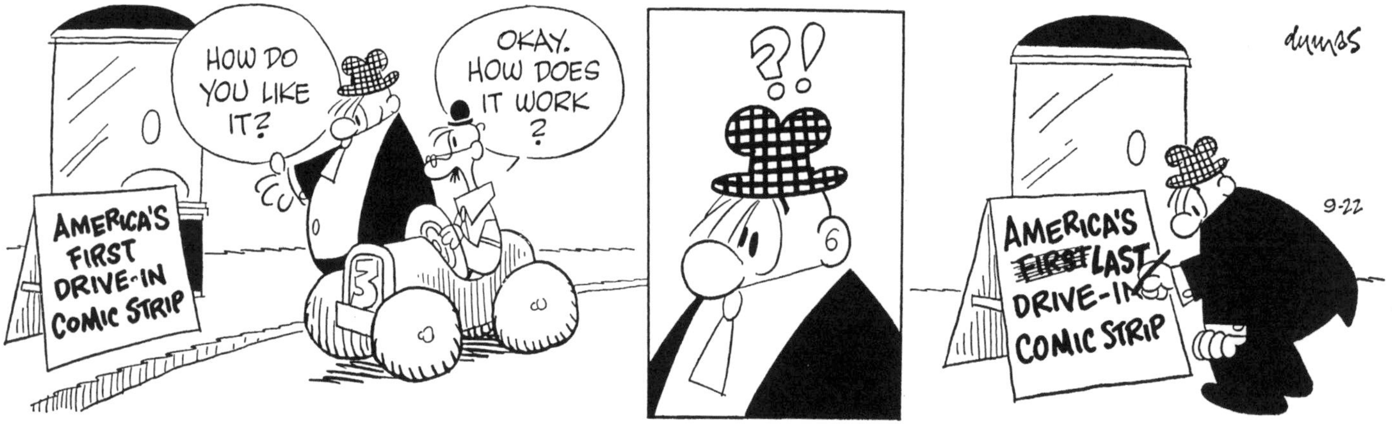
AMERICA'S FIRST DRIVE-IN COMIC STRIP
HOW DO YOU LIKE IT?
OKAY. HOW DOES IT WORK?
?!
dumas
9-22
AMERICA'S ~~FIRST~~ LAST DRIVE-IN COMIC STRIP

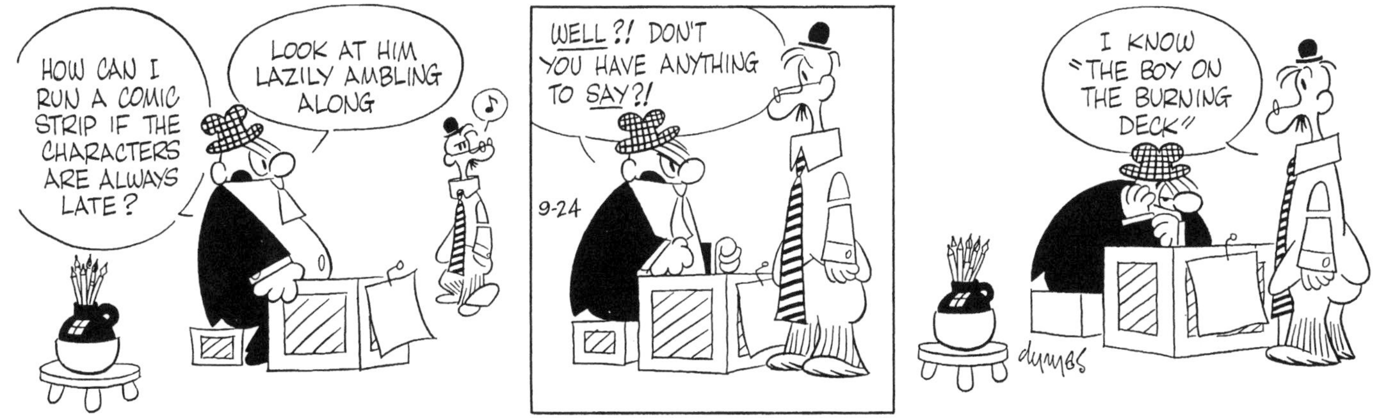
HOW CAN I RUN A COMIC STRIP IF THE CHARACTERS ARE ALWAYS LATE?
LOOK AT HIM LAZILY AMBLING ALONG
WELL?! DON'T YOU HAVE ANYTHING TO SAY?!
9-24
I KNOW "THE BOY ON THE BURNING DECK"

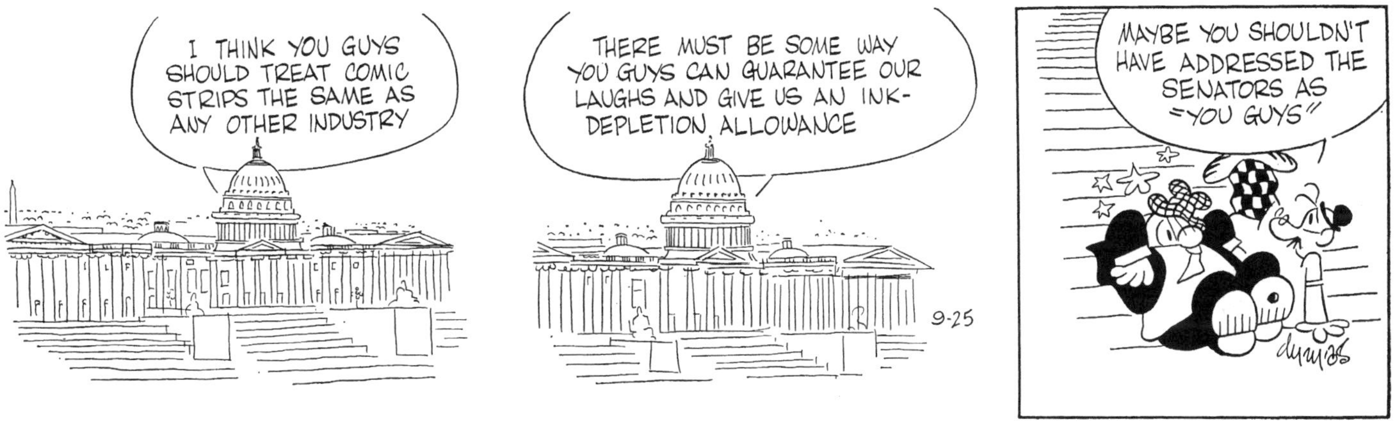
I THINK YOU GUYS SHOULD TREAT COMIC STRIPS THE SAME AS ANY OTHER INDUSTRY
THERE MUST BE SOME WAY YOU GUYS CAN GUARANTEE OUR LAUGHS AND GIVE US AN INK-DEPLETION ALLOWANCE
9-25
MAYBE YOU SHOULDN'T HAVE ADDRESSED THE SENATORS AS "YOU GUYS"

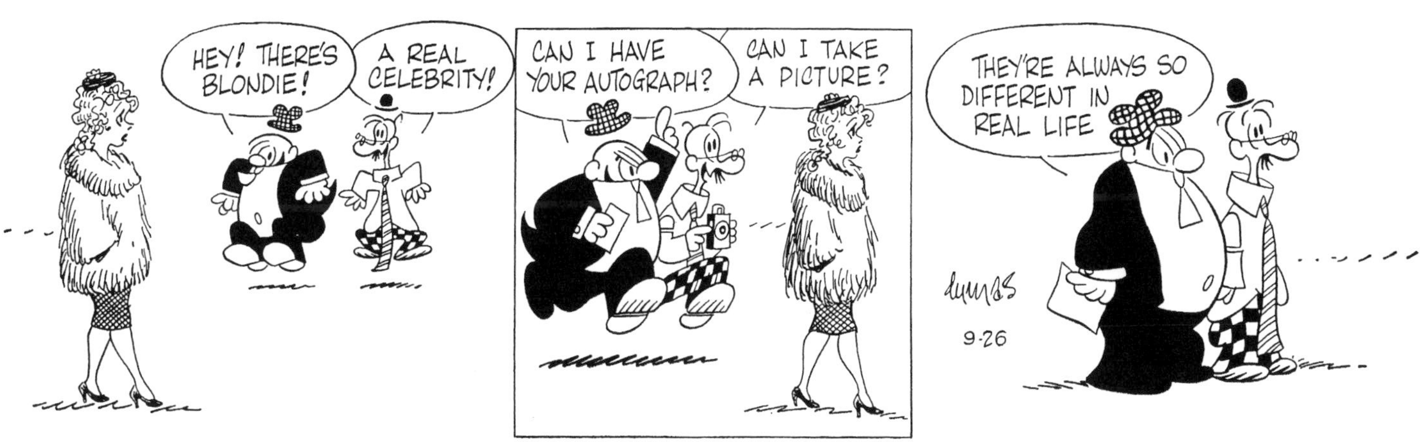
HEY! THERE'S BLONDIE!
A REAL CELEBRITY!
CAN I HAVE YOUR AUTOGRAPH?
CAN I TAKE A PICTURE?
THEY'RE ALWAYS SO DIFFERENT IN REAL LIFE
9-26

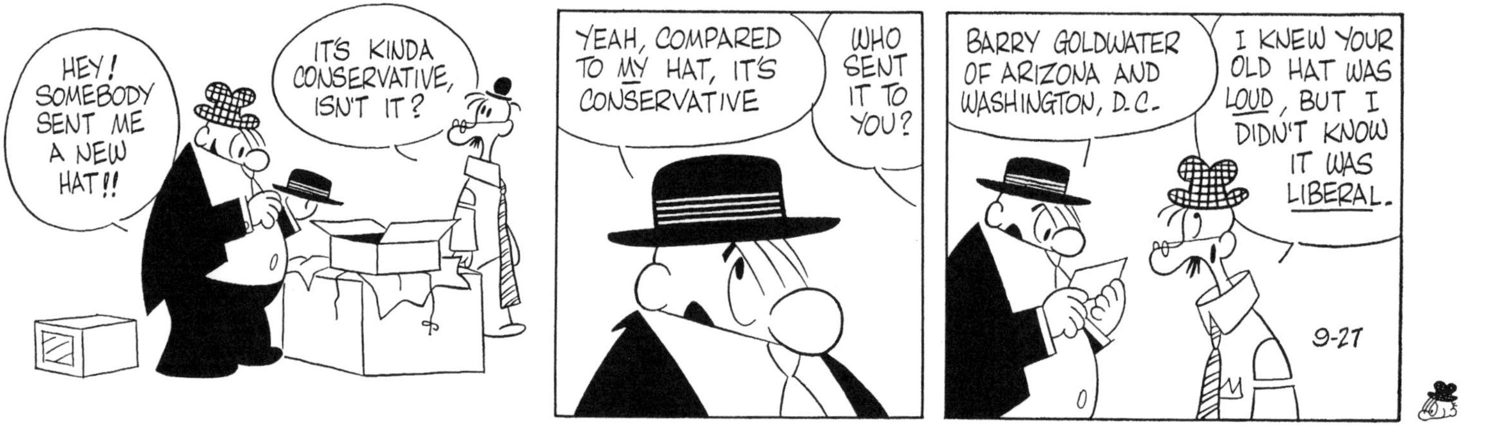
HEY! SOMEBODY SENT ME A NEW HAT!!
IT'S KINDA CONSERVATIVE, ISN'T IT?
YEAH, COMPARED TO MY HAT, IT'S CONSERVATIVE
WHO SENT IT TO YOU?
BARRY GOLDWATER OF ARIZONA AND WASHINGTON, D.C.
I KNEW YOUR OLD HAT WAS LOUD, BUT I DIDN'T KNOW IT WAS LIBERAL.
9-27

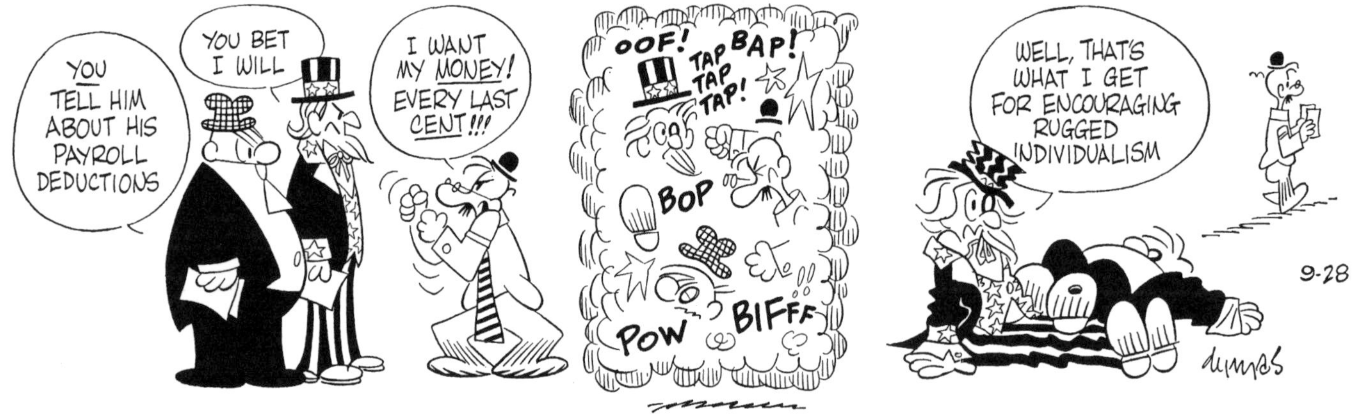
YOU TELL HIM ABOUT HIS PAYROLL DEDUCTIONS
YOU BET I WILL
I WANT MY MONEY! EVERY LAST CENT!!!
OOF! TAP TAP TAP! BAP!
BOP
POW
BIFFF
WELL, THAT'S WHAT I GET FOR ENCOURAGING RUGGED INDIVIDUALISM
9-28

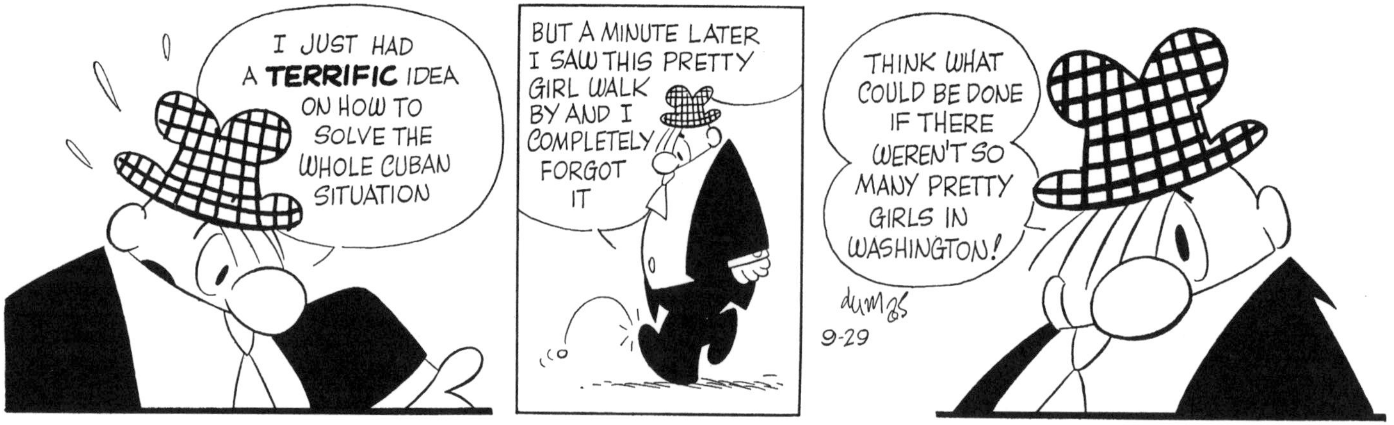
I JUST HAD A TERRIFIC IDEA ON HOW TO SOLVE THE WHOLE CUBAN SITUATION
BUT A MINUTE LATER I SAW THIS PRETTY GIRL WALK BY AND I COMPLETELY FORGOT IT
9-29
THINK WHAT COULD BE DONE IF THERE WEREN'T SO MANY PRETTY GIRLS IN WASHINGTON!

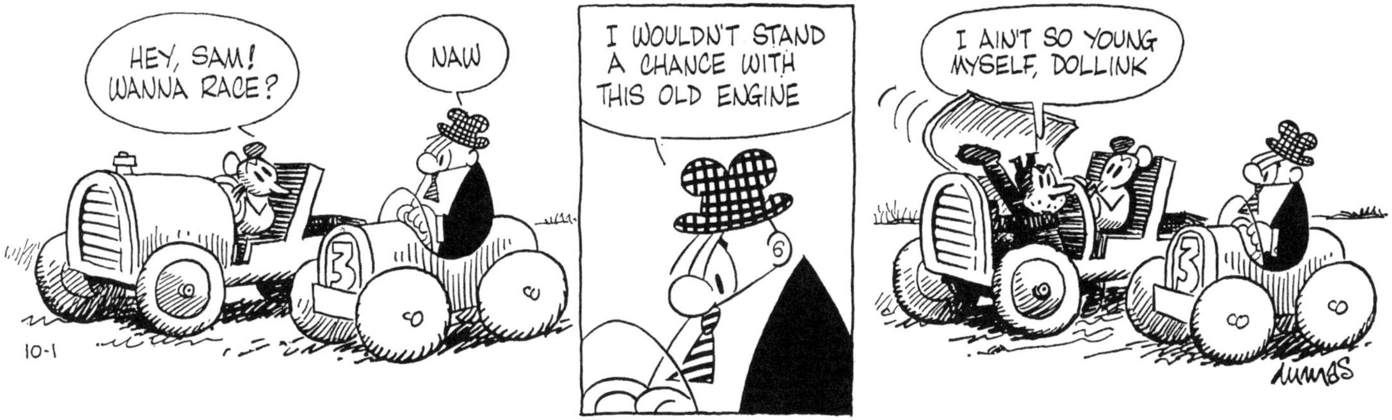
HEY, SAM! WANNA RACE?
NAW
I WOULDN'T STAND A CHANCE WITH THIS OLD ENGINE
I AIN'T SO YOUNG MYSELF, DOLLINK

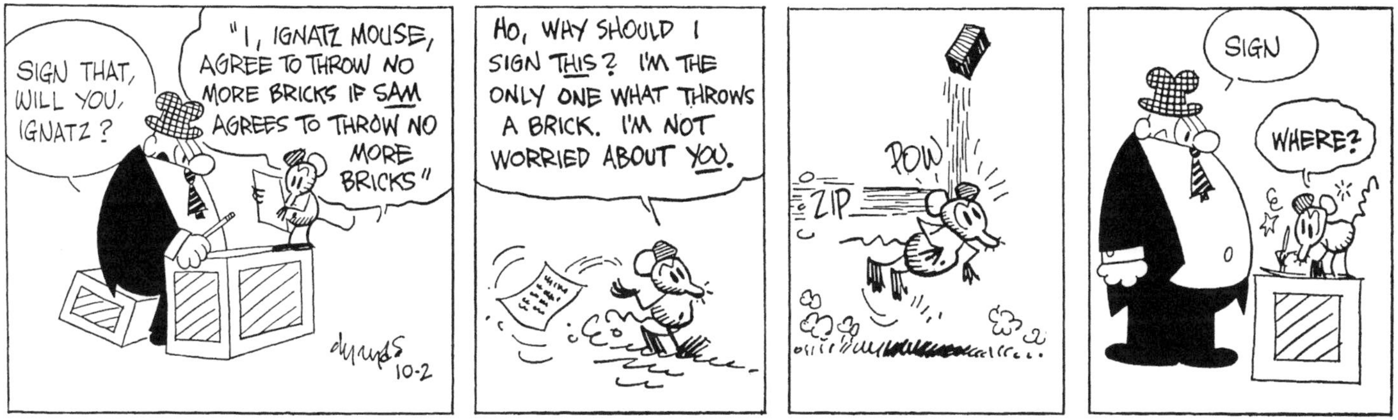
SIGN THAT, WILL YOU, IGNATZ?
"I, IGNATZ MOUSE, AGREE TO THROW NO MORE BRICKS IF SAM AGREES TO THROW NO MORE BRICKS"
HO, WHY SHOULD I SIGN THIS? I'M THE ONLY ONE WHAT THROWS A BRICK. I'M NOT WORRIED ABOUT YOU.
POW
ZIP
SIGN
WHERE?

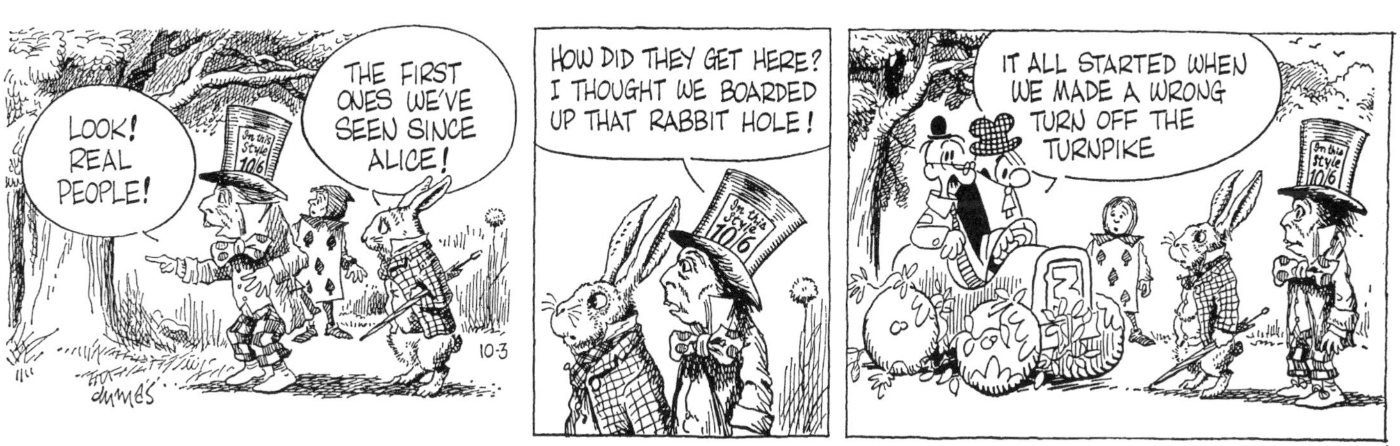
LOOK! REAL PEOPLE!
THE FIRST ONES WE'VE SEEN SINCE ALICE!
HOW DID THEY GET HERE? I THOUGHT WE BOARDED UP THAT RABBIT HOLE!
IT ALL STARTED WHEN WE MADE A WRONG TURN OFF THE TURNPIKE

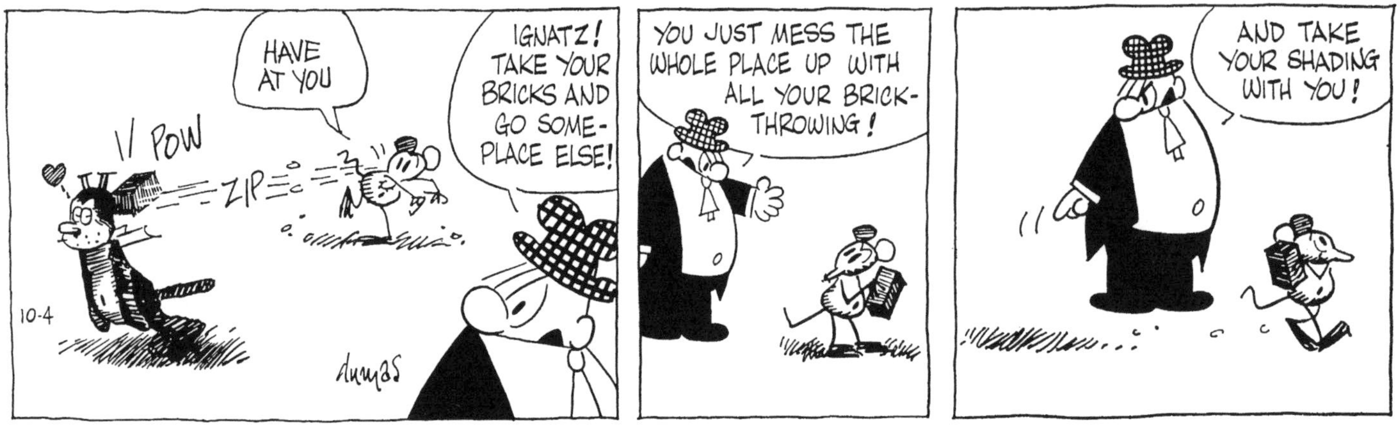
HAVE AT YOU
POW
ZIP
IGNATZ! TAKE YOUR BRICKS AND GO SOME-PLACE ELSE!
10-4
dumas
YOU JUST MESS THE WHOLE PLACE UP WITH ALL YOUR BRICK-THROWING!
AND TAKE YOUR SHADING WITH YOU!

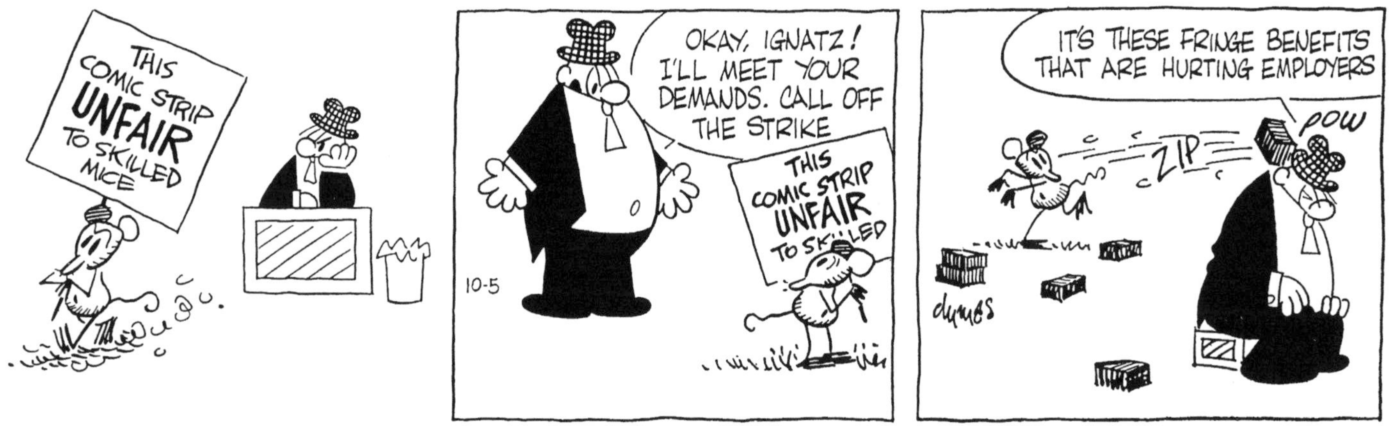
THIS COMIC STRIP UNFAIR TO SKILLED MICE
OKAY, IGNATZ! I'LL MEET YOUR DEMANDS. CALL OFF THE STRIKE
THIS COMIC STRIP UNFAIR
10-5
IT'S THESE FRINGE BENEFITS THAT ARE HURTING EMPLOYERS
ZIP
POW
dumas

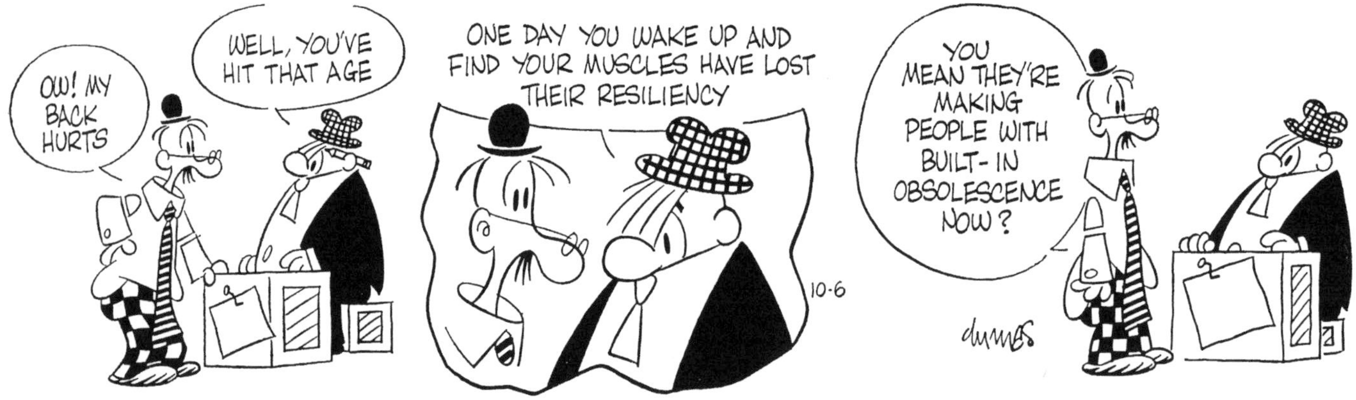
OW! MY BACK HURTS
WELL, YOU'VE HIT THAT AGE
ONE DAY YOU WAKE UP AND FIND YOUR MUSCLES HAVE LOST THEIR RESILIENCY
10-6
YOU MEAN THEY'RE MAKING PEOPLE WITH BUILT-IN OBSOLESCENCE NOW?
dumas

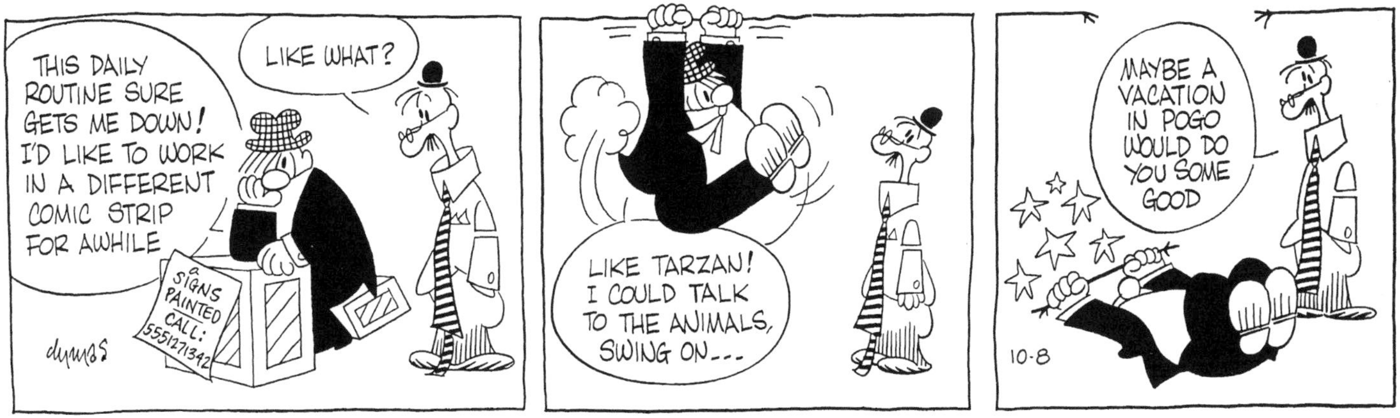
THIS DAILY ROUTINE SURE GETS ME DOWN! I'D LIKE TO WORK IN A DIFFERENT COMIC STRIP FOR AWHILE
LIKE WHAT?
SIGNS PAINTED CALL: 5551271342
LIKE TARZAN! I COULD TALK TO THE ANIMALS, SWING ON...
MAYBE A VACATION IN POGO WOULD DO YOU SOME GOOD
10-8

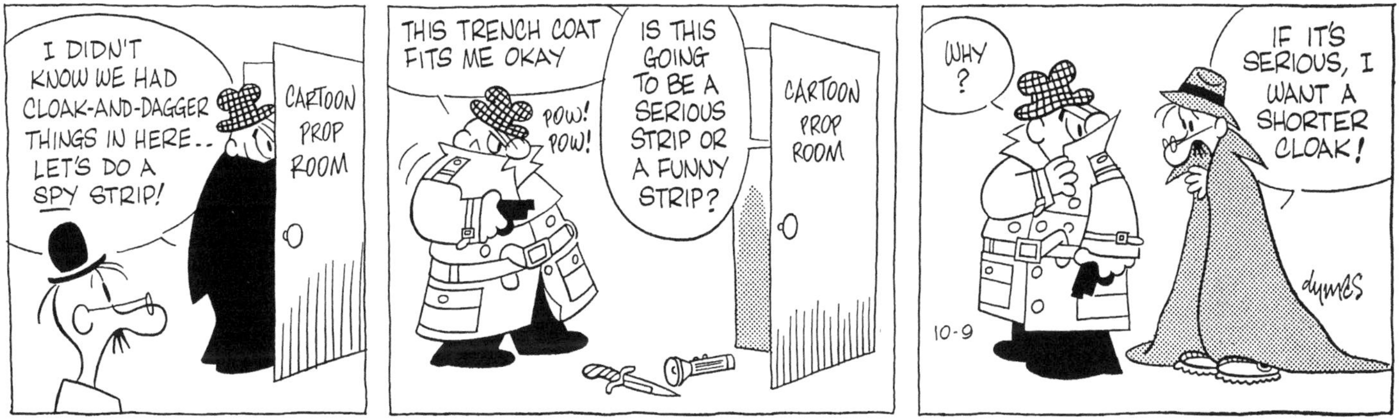
I DIDN'T KNOW WE HAD CLOAK-AND-DAGGER THINGS IN HERE.. LET'S DO A SPY STRIP!
CARTOON PROP ROOM
THIS TRENCH COAT FITS ME OKAY
POW! POW!
IS THIS GOING TO BE A SERIOUS STRIP OR A FUNNY STRIP?
CARTOON PROP ROOM
WHY?
IF IT'S SERIOUS, I WANT A SHORTER CLOAK!
10-9

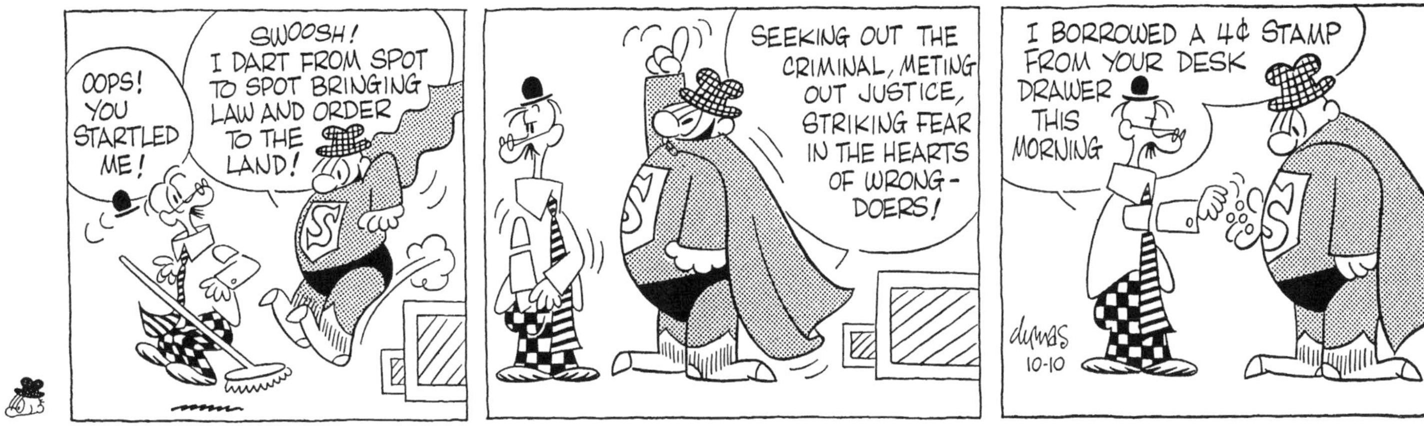
OOPS! YOU STARTLED ME!
SWOOSH! I DART FROM SPOT TO SPOT BRINGING LAW AND ORDER TO THE LAND!
SEEKING OUT THE CRIMINAL, METING OUT JUSTICE, STRIKING FEAR IN THE HEARTS OF WRONG-DOERS!
I BORROWED A 4¢ STAMP FROM YOUR DESK DRAWER THIS MORNING
10-10

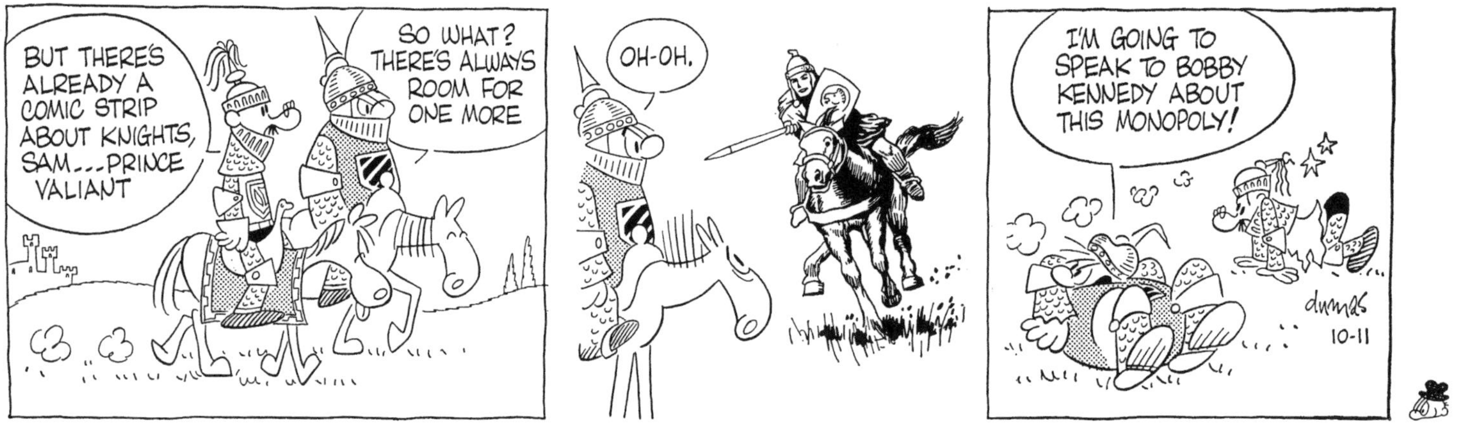
BUT THERE'S ALREADY A COMIC STRIP ABOUT KNIGHTS, SAM---PRINCE VALIANT
SO WHAT? THERE'S ALWAYS ROOM FOR ONE MORE
OH-OH.
I'M GOING TO SPEAK TO BOBBY KENNEDY ABOUT THIS MONOPOLY!
dumas
10-11

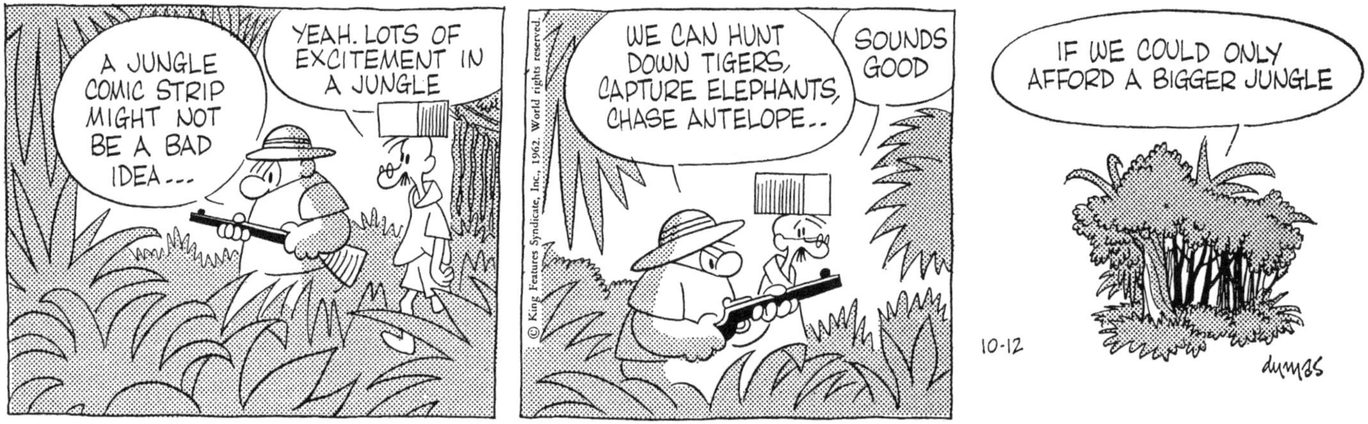
A JUNGLE COMIC STRIP MIGHT NOT BE A BAD IDEA---
YEAH. LOTS OF EXCITEMENT IN A JUNGLE
© King Features Syndicate, Inc., 1962. World rights reserved.
WE CAN HUNT DOWN TIGERS, CAPTURE ELEPHANTS, CHASE ANTELOPE..
SOUNDS GOOD
IF WE COULD ONLY AFFORD A BIGGER JUNGLE
10-12
dumas

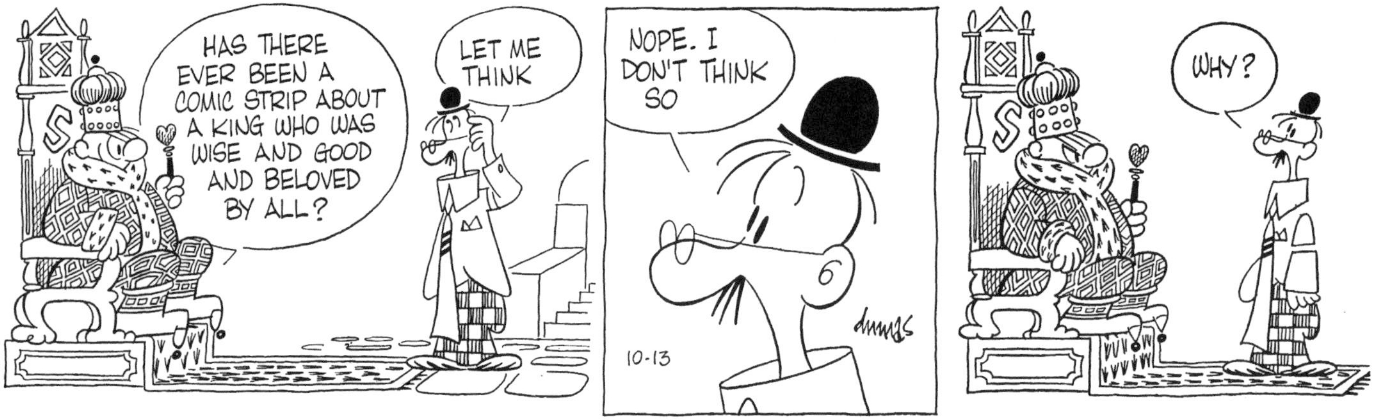
HAS THERE EVER BEEN A COMIC STRIP ABOUT A KING WHO WAS WISE AND GOOD AND BELOVED BY ALL?
LET ME THINK
NOPE. I DON'T THINK SO
dumas
10-13
WHY?

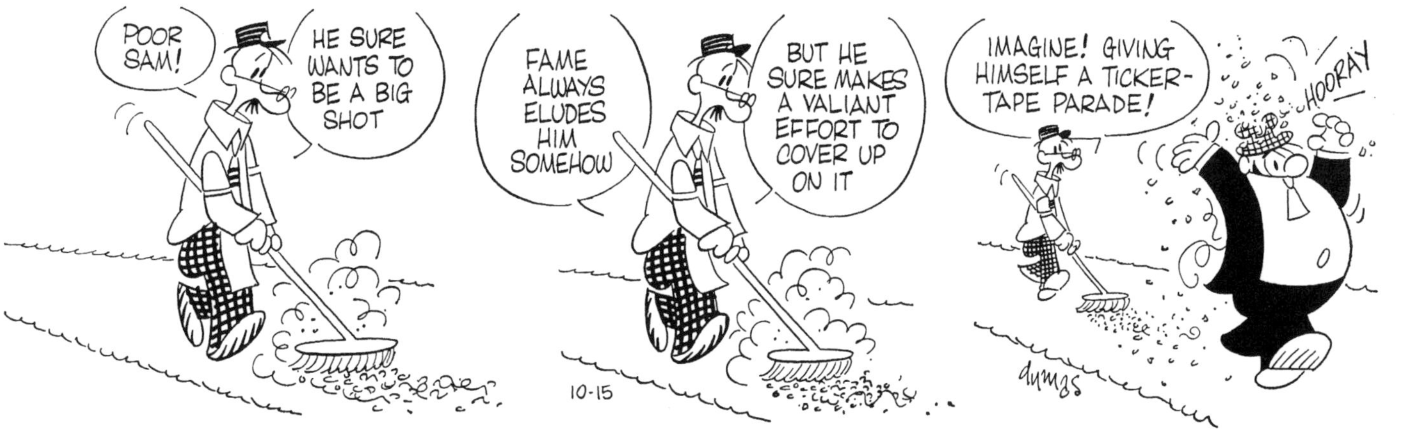
POOR SAM!
HE SURE WANTS TO BE A BIG SHOT
FAME ALWAYS ELUDES HIM SOMEHOW
BUT HE SURE MAKES A VALIANT EFFORT TO COVER UP ON IT
IMAGINE! GIVING HIMSELF A TICKER-TAPE PARADE!
HOORAY
10-15
dumas

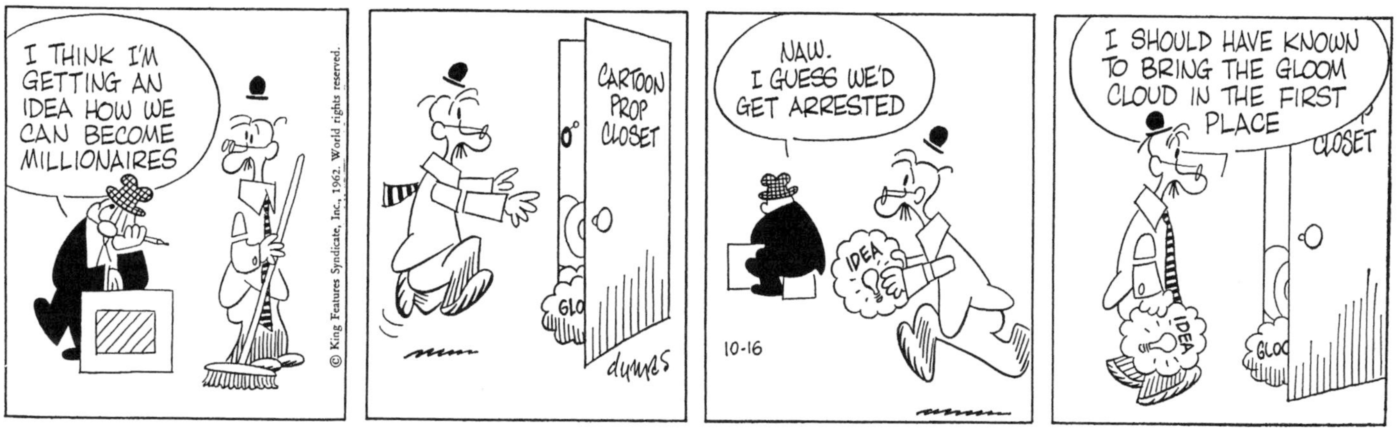
I THINK I'M GETTING AN IDEA HOW WE CAN BECOME MILLIONAIRES
CARTOON PROP CLOSET
GLO
dumas
NAW. I GUESS WE'D GET ARRESTED
IDEA
10-16
I SHOULD HAVE KNOWN TO BRING THE GLOOM CLOUD IN THE FIRST PLACE
CLOSET
IDEA
GLOO

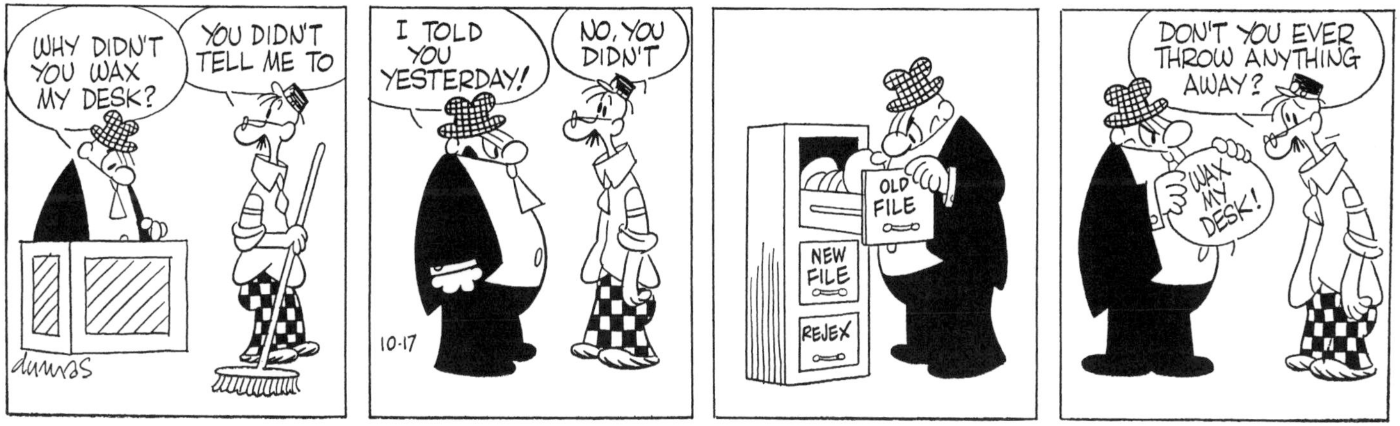
WHY DIDN'T YOU WAX MY DESK?
YOU DIDN'T TELL ME TO
dumas
I TOLD YOU YESTERDAY!
NO, YOU DIDN'T
10-17
OLD FILE
NEW FILE
REJEX
DON'T YOU EVER THROW ANYTHING AWAY?
WAX MY DESK!

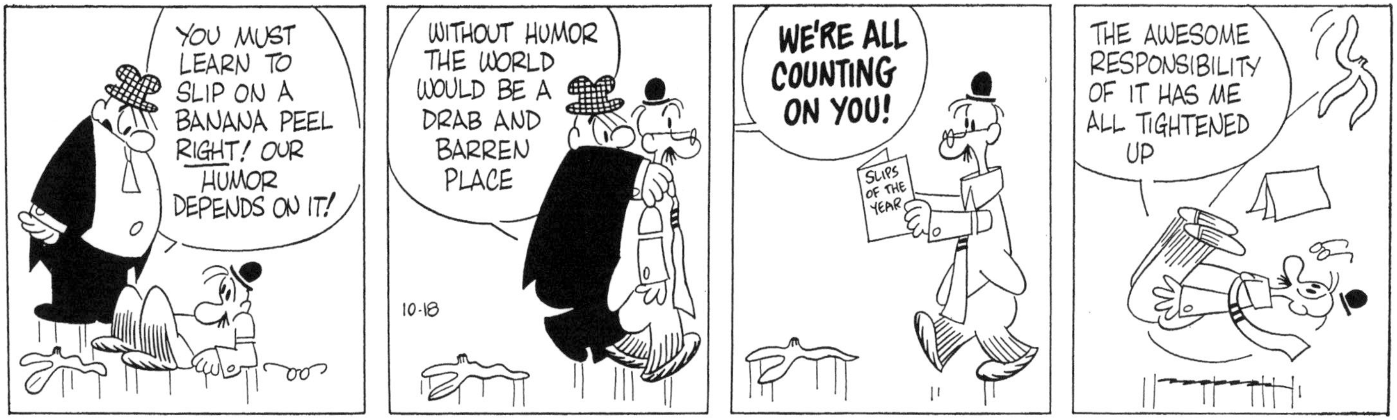
YOU MUST LEARN TO SLIP ON A BANANA PEEL RIGHT! OUR HUMOR DEPENDS ON IT!
WITHOUT HUMOR THE WORLD WOULD BE A DRAB AND BARREN PLACE
10-18
WE'RE ALL COUNTING ON YOU!
SLIPS OF THE YEAR
THE AWESOME RESPONSIBILITY OF IT HAS ME ALL TIGHTENED UP

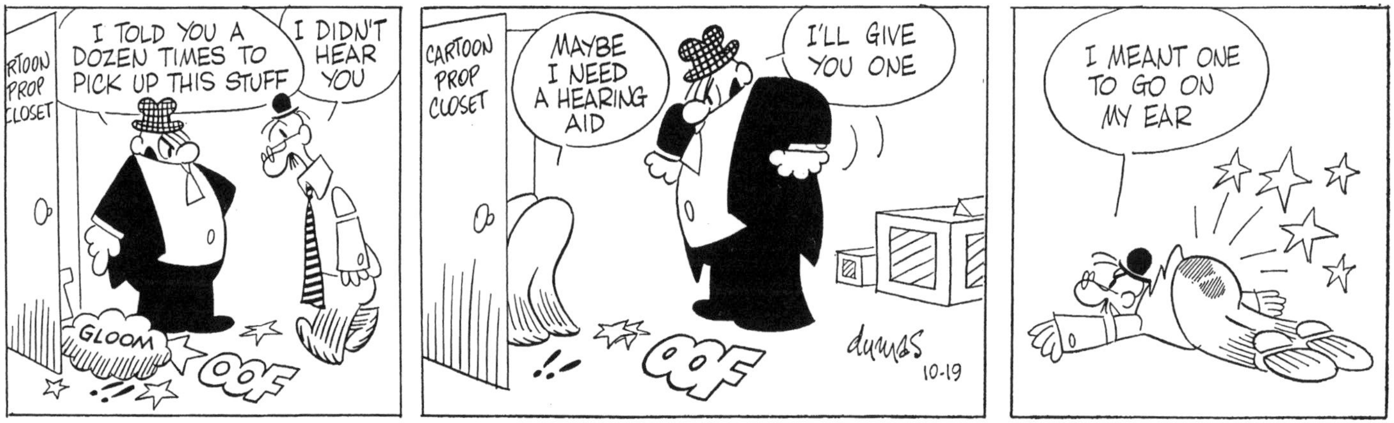
RTOON PROP CLOSET
I TOLD YOU A DOZEN TIMES TO PICK UP THIS STUFF
I DIDN'T HEAR YOU
GLOOM
OOF
CARTOON PROP CLOSET
MAYBE I NEED A HEARING AID
I'LL GIVE YOU ONE
OOF
dumas
10-19
I MEANT ONE TO GO ON MY EAR

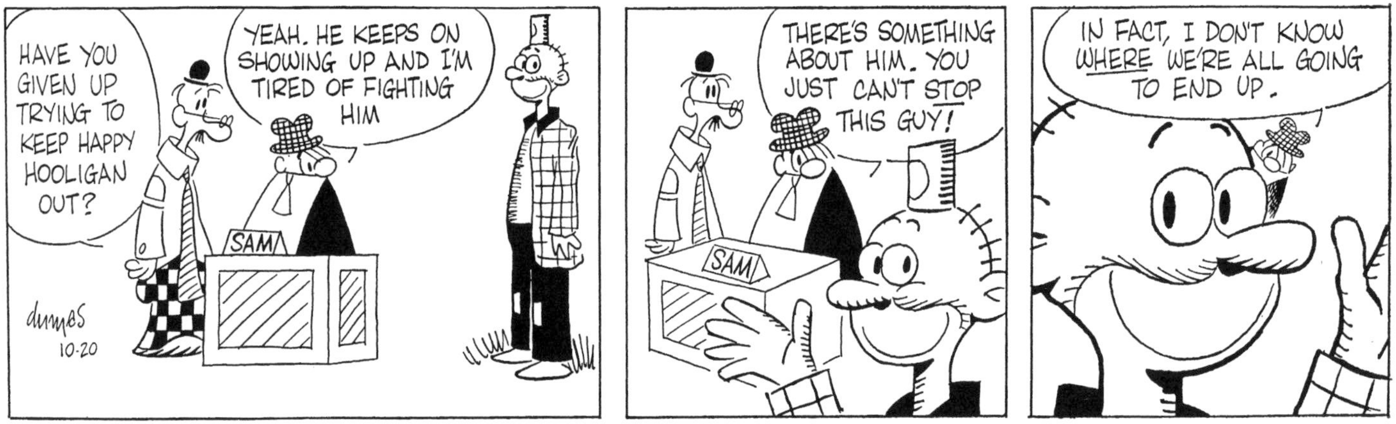
HAVE YOU GIVEN UP TRYING TO KEEP HAPPY HOOLIGAN OUT?
YEAH. HE KEEPS ON SHOWING UP AND I'M TIRED OF FIGHTING HIM
SAM
dumas
10-20
THERE'S SOMETHING ABOUT HIM. YOU JUST CAN'T STOP THIS GUY!
SAM
IN FACT, I DON'T KNOW WHERE WE'RE ALL GOING TO END UP.

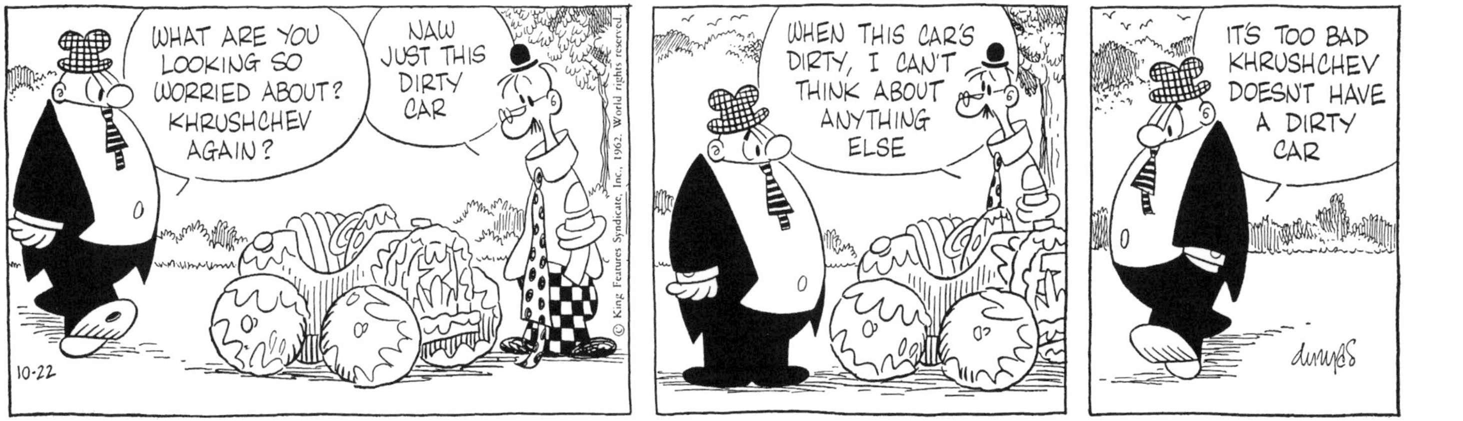
WHAT ARE YOU LOOKING SO WORRIED ABOUT? KHRUSHCHEV AGAIN?
NAW JUST THIS DIRTY CAR
© King Features Syndicate, Inc., 1962. World rights reserved.
10-22
WHEN THIS CAR'S DIRTY, I CAN'T THINK ABOUT ANYTHING ELSE
IT'S TOO BAD KHRUSHCHEV DOESN'T HAVE A DIRTY CAR
dumas

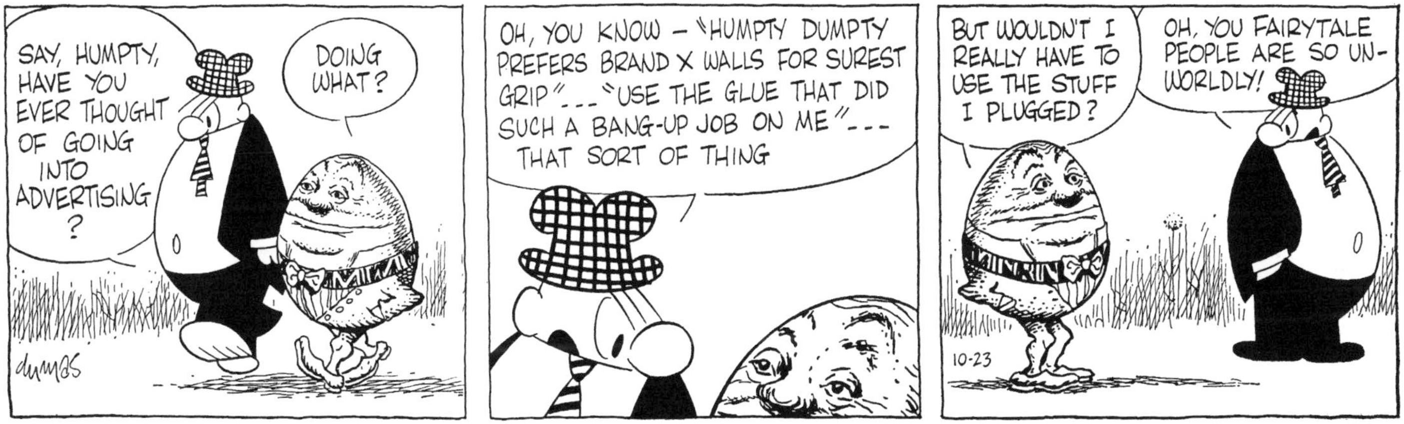
SAY, HUMPTY, HAVE YOU EVER THOUGHT OF GOING INTO ADVERTISING?
DOING WHAT?
dumas
OH, YOU KNOW – "HUMPTY DUMPTY PREFERS BRAND X WALLS FOR SUREST GRIP"... "USE THE GLUE THAT DID SUCH A BANG-UP JOB ON ME"... THAT SORT OF THING
BUT WOULDN'T I REALLY HAVE TO USE THE STUFF I PLUGGED?
OH, YOU FAIRYTALE PEOPLE ARE SO UN-WORLDLY!
10-23

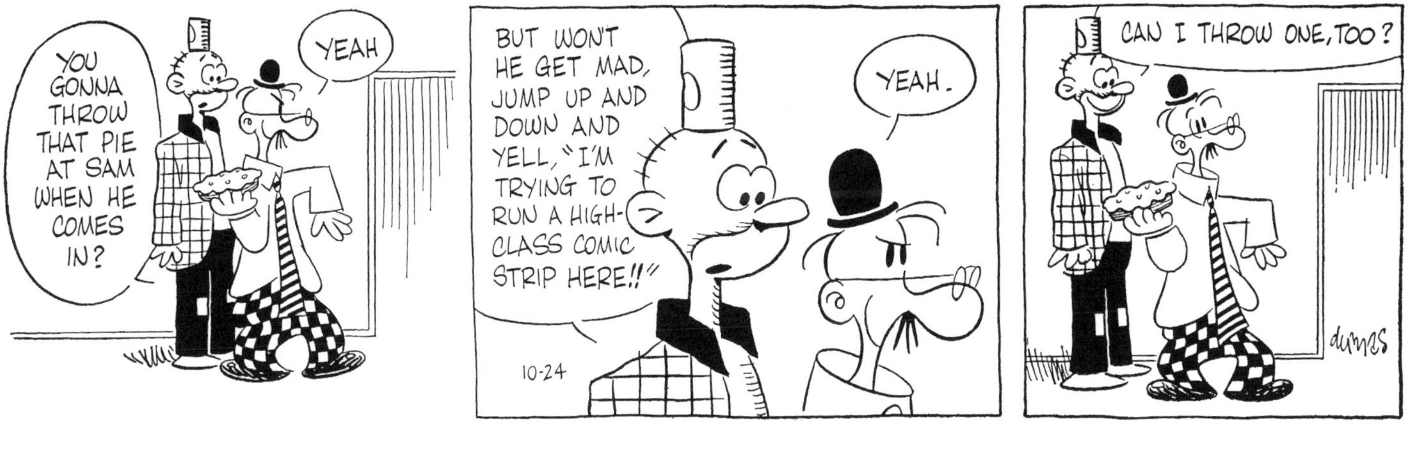
YOU GONNA THROW THAT PIE AT SAM WHEN HE COMES IN?
YEAH
BUT WON'T HE GET MAD, JUMP UP AND DOWN AND YELL, "I'M TRYING TO RUN A HIGH-CLASS COMIC STRIP HERE!!"
YEAH.
10-24
CAN I THROW ONE, TOO?
dumas

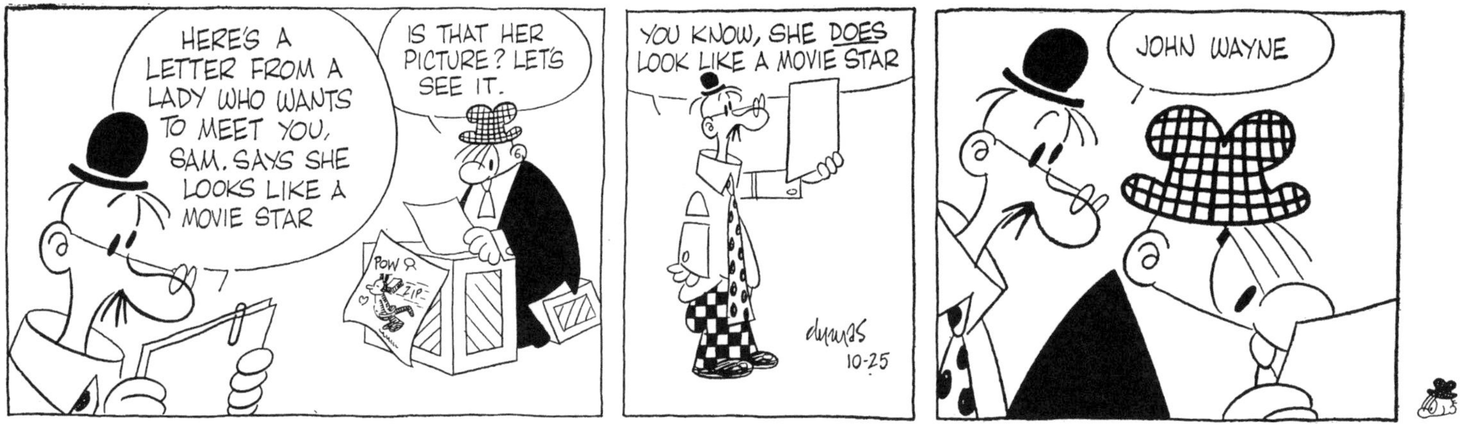
HERE'S A LETTER FROM A LADY WHO WANTS TO MEET YOU, SAM. SAYS SHE LOOKS LIKE A MOVIE STAR
IS THAT HER PICTURE? LET'S SEE IT.
POW
ZIP
YOU KNOW, SHE DOES LOOK LIKE A MOVIE STAR
dumas
10-25
JOHN WAYNE

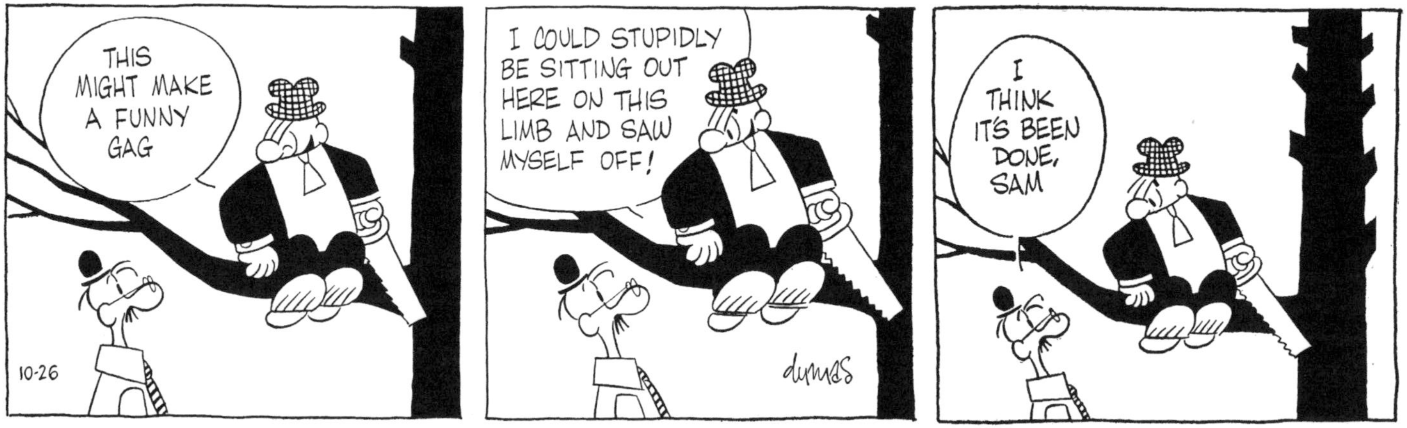
THIS MIGHT MAKE A FUNNY GAG
10-26
I COULD STUPIDLY BE SITTING OUT HERE ON THIS LIMB AND SAW MYSELF OFF!
dumas
I THINK IT'S BEEN DONE, SAM

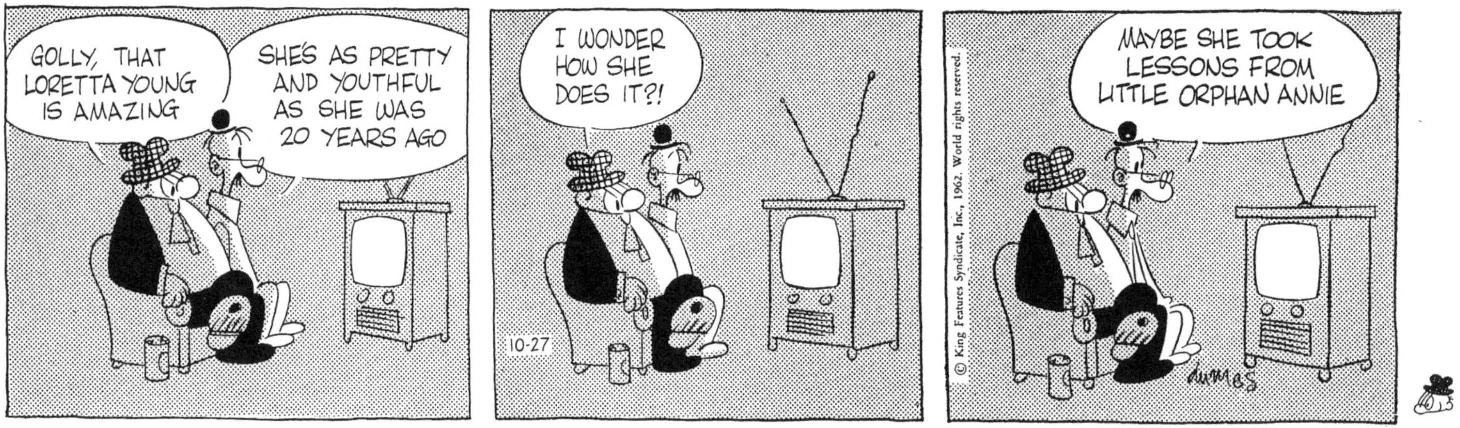
GOLLY, THAT LORETTA YOUNG IS AMAZING
SHE'S AS PRETTY AND YOUTHFUL AS SHE WAS 20 YEARS AGO
I WONDER HOW SHE DOES IT?!
10-27
MAYBE SHE TOOK LESSONS FROM LITTLE ORPHAN ANNIE
dumas

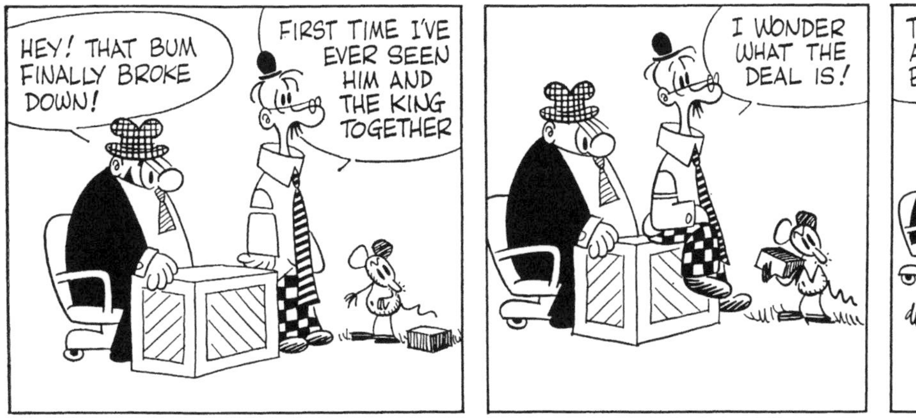
HEY! THAT BUM FINALLY BROKE DOWN!
FIRST TIME I'VE EVER SEEN HIM AND THE KING TOGETHER
I WONDER WHAT THE DEAL IS!
THEY'RE JUST GETTING A GOOD START ON BROTHERHOOD WEEK
dumas
10-29

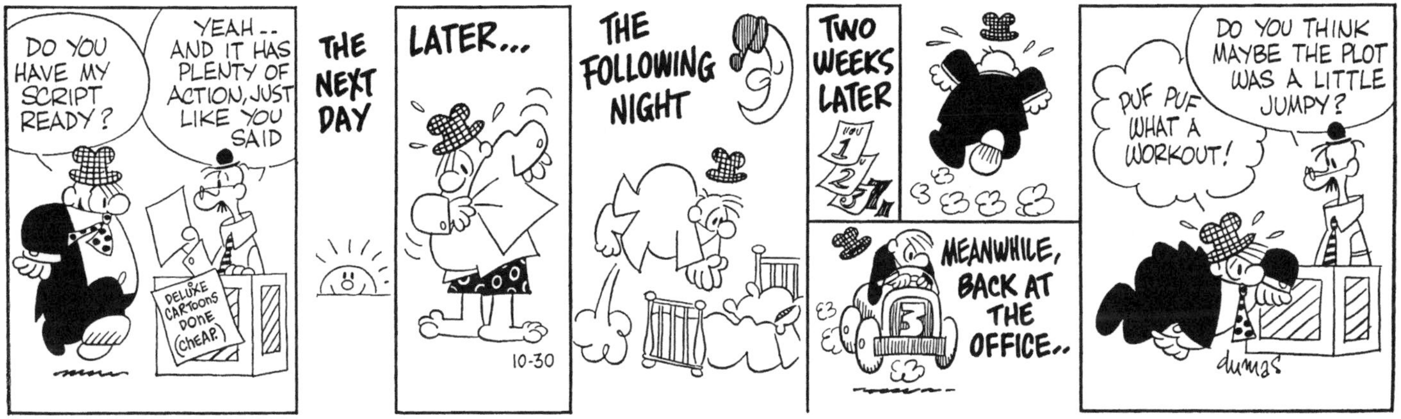
DO YOU HAVE MY SCRIPT READY?
YEAH -- AND IT HAS PLENTY OF ACTION, JUST LIKE YOU SAID
DELUXE CARTOONS DONE (CHEAP.)
THE NEXT DAY
LATER...
10-30
THE FOLLOWING NIGHT
TWO WEEKS LATER
MEANWHILE, BACK AT THE OFFICE..
PUF PUF WHAT A WORKOUT!
DO YOU THINK MAYBE THE PLOT WAS A LITTLE JUMPY?
dumas

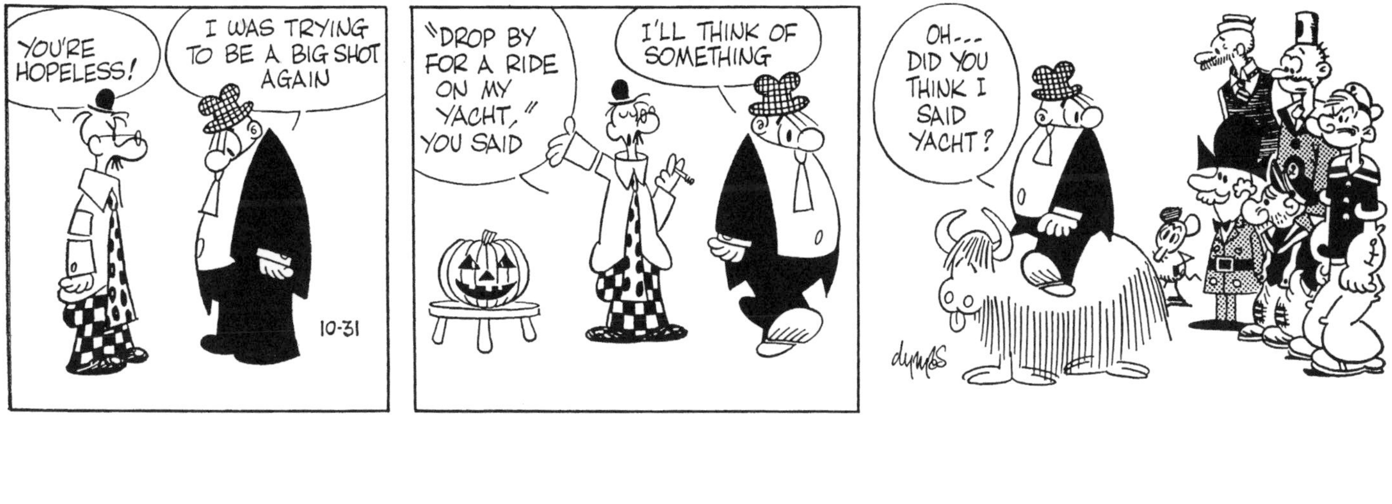
YOU'RE HOPELESS!
I WAS TRYING TO BE A BIG SHOT AGAIN
10-31
"DROP BY FOR A RIDE ON MY YACHT," YOU SAID
I'LL THINK OF SOMETHING
OH--- DID YOU THINK I SAID YACHT?
dumas

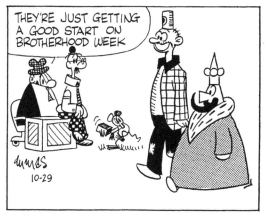

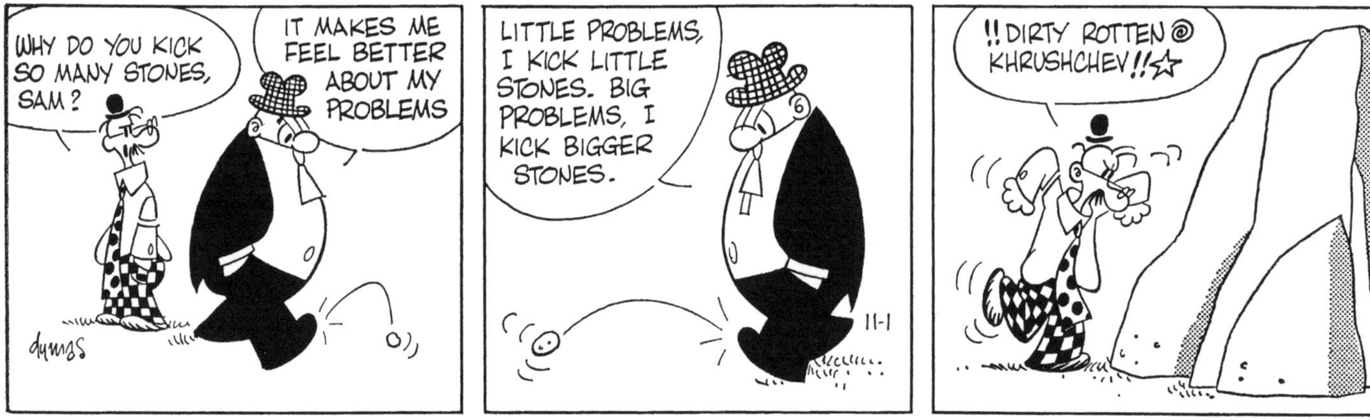
WHY DO YOU KICK SO MANY STONES, SAM?
IT MAKES ME FEEL BETTER ABOUT MY PROBLEMS
LITTLE PROBLEMS, I KICK LITTLE STONES. BIG PROBLEMS, I KICK BIGGER STONES.
!! DIRTY ROTTEN @ KHRUSHCHEV !!☆
dumas
11-1

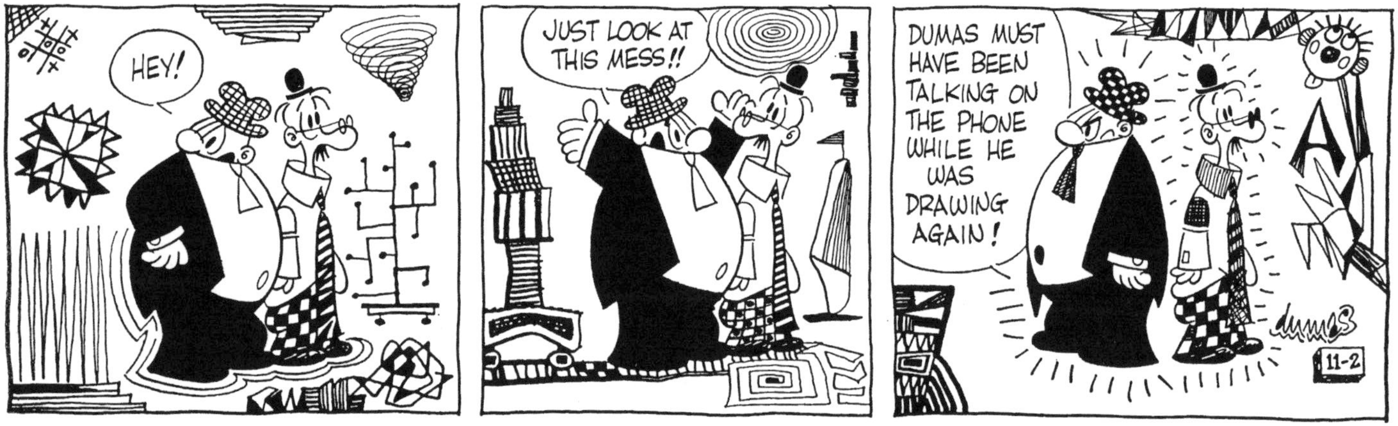
HEY!
JUST LOOK AT THIS MESS!!
DUMAS MUST HAVE BEEN TALKING ON THE PHONE WHILE HE WAS DRAWING AGAIN!
dumas
11-2

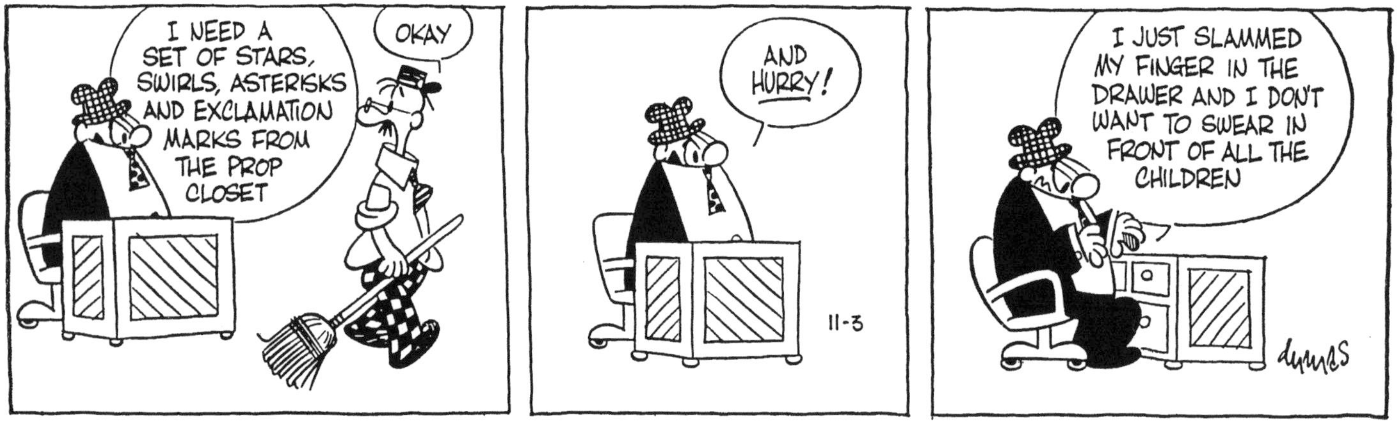
I NEED A SET OF STARS, SWIRLS, ASTERISKS AND EXCLAMATION MARKS FROM THE PROP CLOSET
OKAY
AND HURRY!
I JUST SLAMMED MY FINGER IN THE DRAWER AND I DON'T WANT TO SWEAR IN FRONT OF ALL THE CHILDREN
11-3
dumas

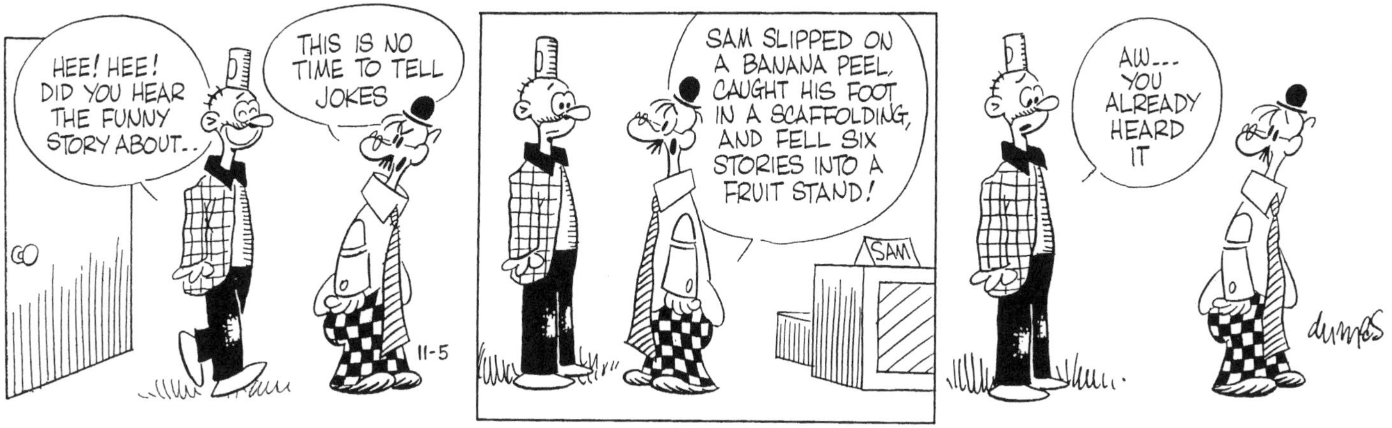
HEE! HEE! DID YOU HEAR THE FUNNY STORY ABOUT--
THIS IS NO TIME TO TELL JOKES
11-5
SAM SLIPPED ON A BANANA PEEL, CAUGHT HIS FOOT IN A SCAFFOLDING, AND FELL SIX STORIES INTO A FRUIT STAND!
SAM
AW--- YOU ALREADY HEARD IT

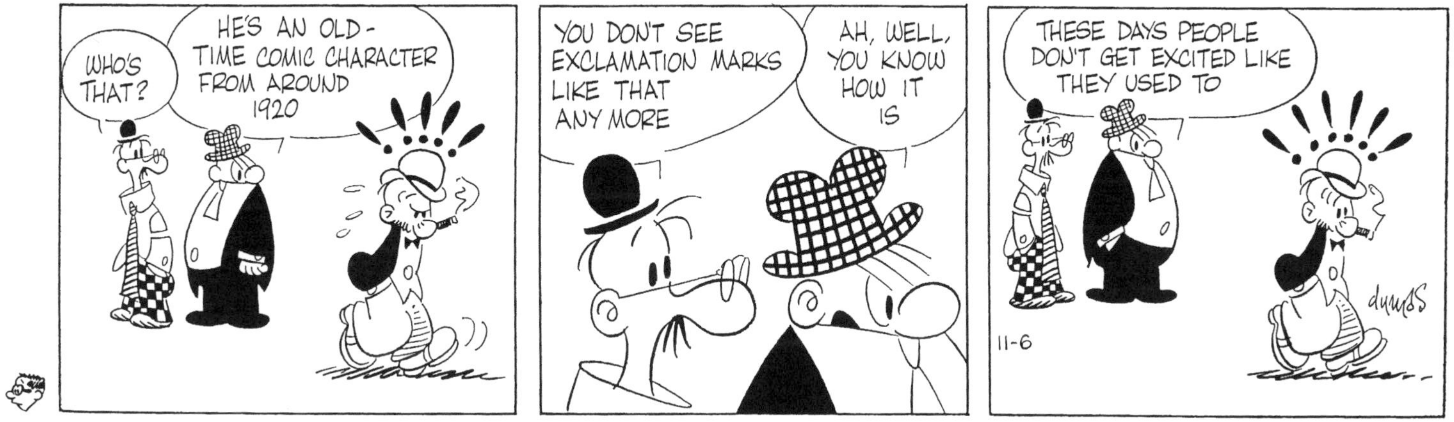
WHO'S THAT?
HE'S AN OLD-TIME COMIC CHARACTER FROM AROUND 1920
YOU DON'T SEE EXCLAMATION MARKS LIKE THAT ANY MORE
AH, WELL, YOU KNOW HOW IT IS
THESE DAYS PEOPLE DON'T GET EXCITED LIKE THEY USED TO
11-6

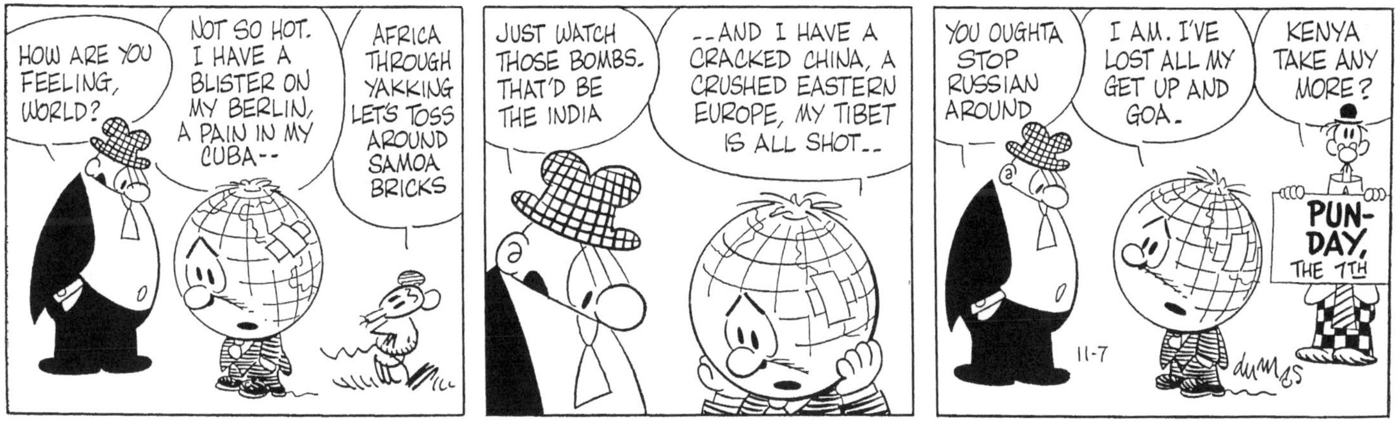
HOW ARE YOU FEELING, WORLD?
NOT SO HOT. I HAVE A BLISTER ON MY BERLIN, A PAIN IN MY CUBA--
AFRICA THROUGH YAKKING LET'S TOSS AROUND SAMOA BRICKS
JUST WATCH THOSE BOMBS. THAT'D BE THE INDIA
--AND I HAVE A CRACKED CHINA, A CRUSHED EASTERN EUROPE, MY TIBET IS ALL SHOT--
YOU OUGHTA STOP RUSSIAN AROUND
I AM. I'VE LOST ALL MY GET UP AND GOA.
KENYA TAKE ANY MORE?
PUN-DAY, THE 7TH
11-7

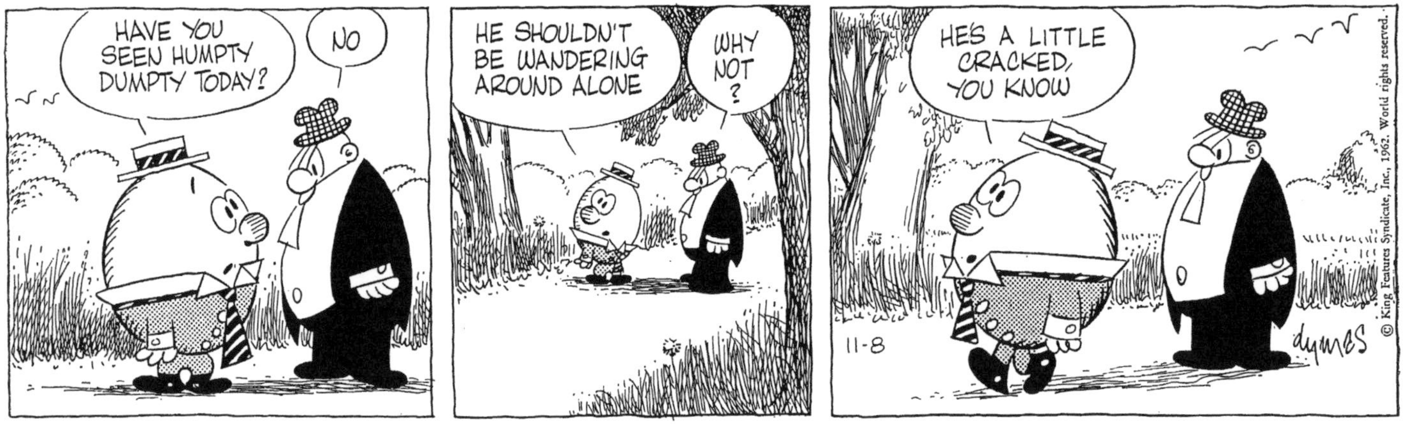
HAVE YOU SEEN HUMPTY DUMPTY TODAY?
NO
HE SHOULDN'T BE WANDERING AROUND ALONE
WHY NOT ?
HE'S A LITTLE CRACKED, YOU KNOW
11-8
© King Features Syndicate, Inc., 1962. World rights reserved.

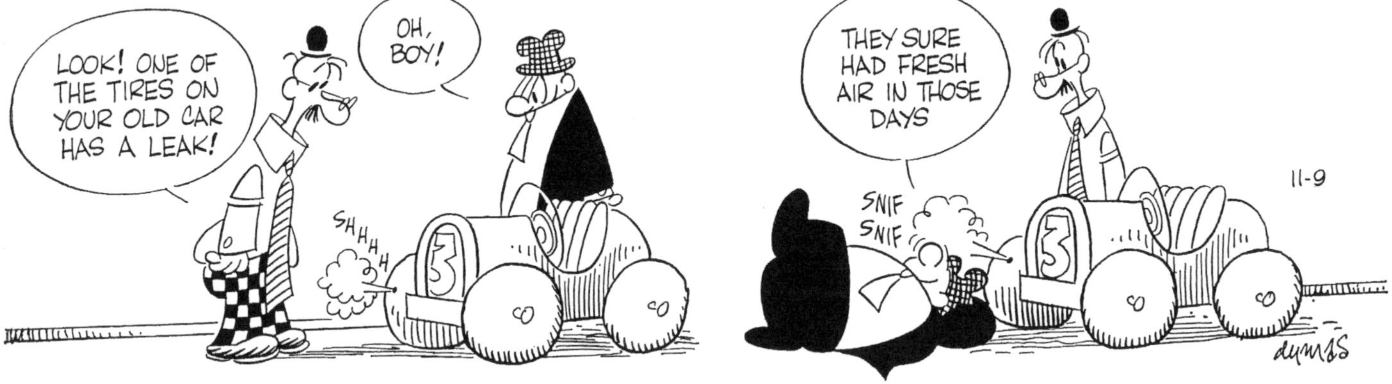
LOOK! ONE OF THE TIRES ON YOUR OLD CAR HAS A LEAK!
OH, BOY!
SHHHHH
THEY SURE HAD FRESH AIR IN THOSE DAYS
SNIF SNIF
11-9

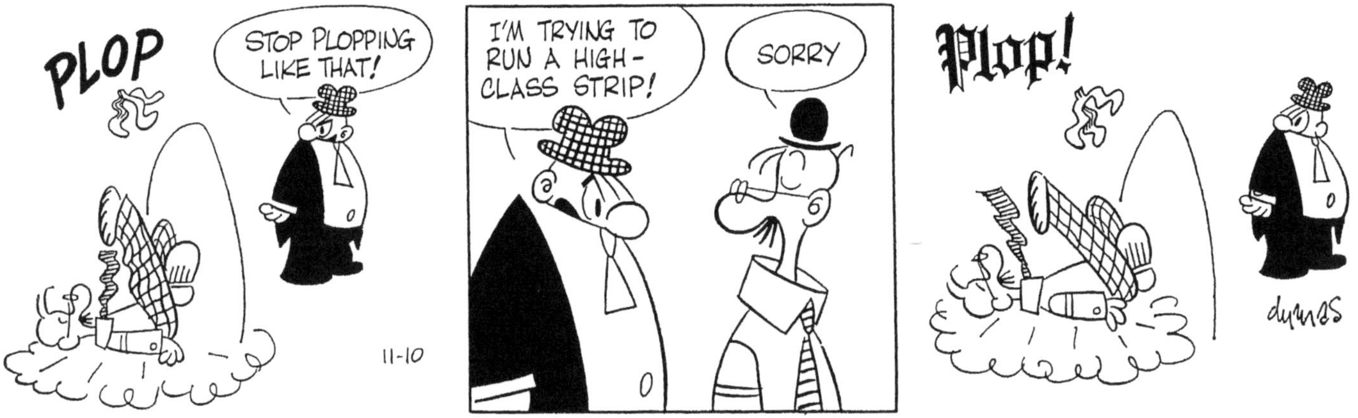
PLOP
STOP PLOPPING LIKE THAT!
11-10
I'M TRYING TO RUN A HIGH-CLASS STRIP!
SORRY
Plop!

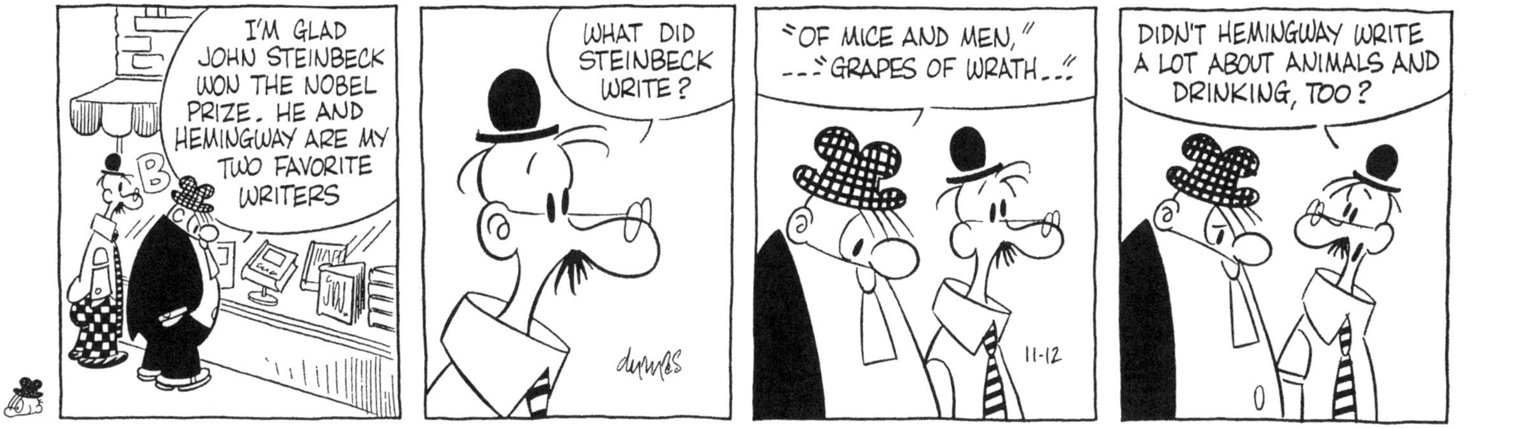
I'M GLAD JOHN STEINBECK WON THE NOBEL PRIZE. HE AND HEMINGWAY ARE MY TWO FAVORITE WRITERS
WHAT DID STEINBECK WRITE?
"OF MICE AND MEN," ..."GRAPES OF WRATH..."
DIDN'T HEMINGWAY WRITE A LOT ABOUT ANIMALS AND DRINKING, TOO?
dumas
11-12

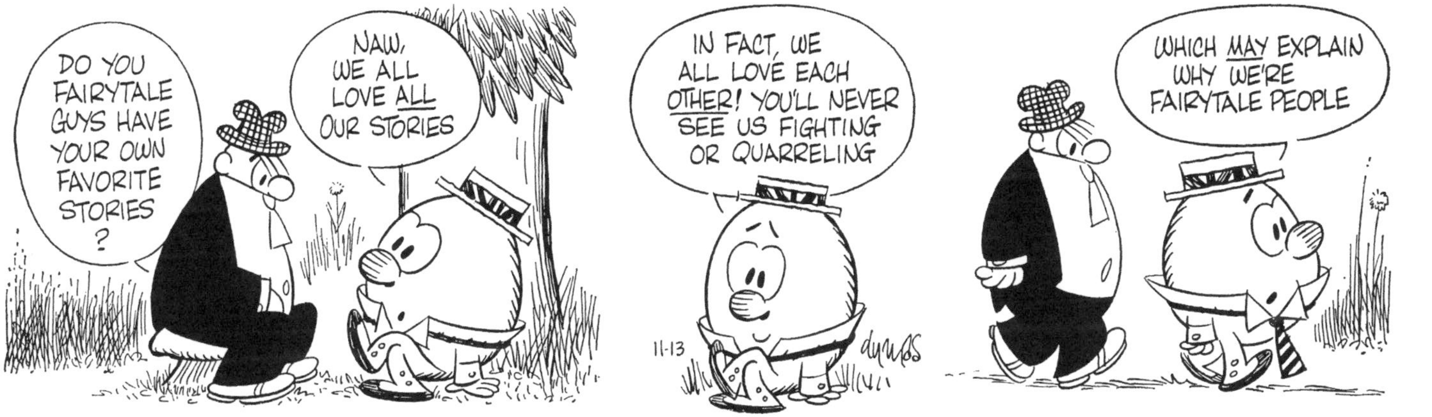
DO YOU FAIRYTALE GUYS HAVE YOUR OWN FAVORITE STORIES?
NAW, WE ALL LOVE ALL OUR STORIES
IN FACT, WE ALL LOVE EACH OTHER! YOU'LL NEVER SEE US FIGHTING OR QUARRELING
11-13
dumas
WHICH MAY EXPLAIN WHY WE'RE FAIRYTALE PEOPLE

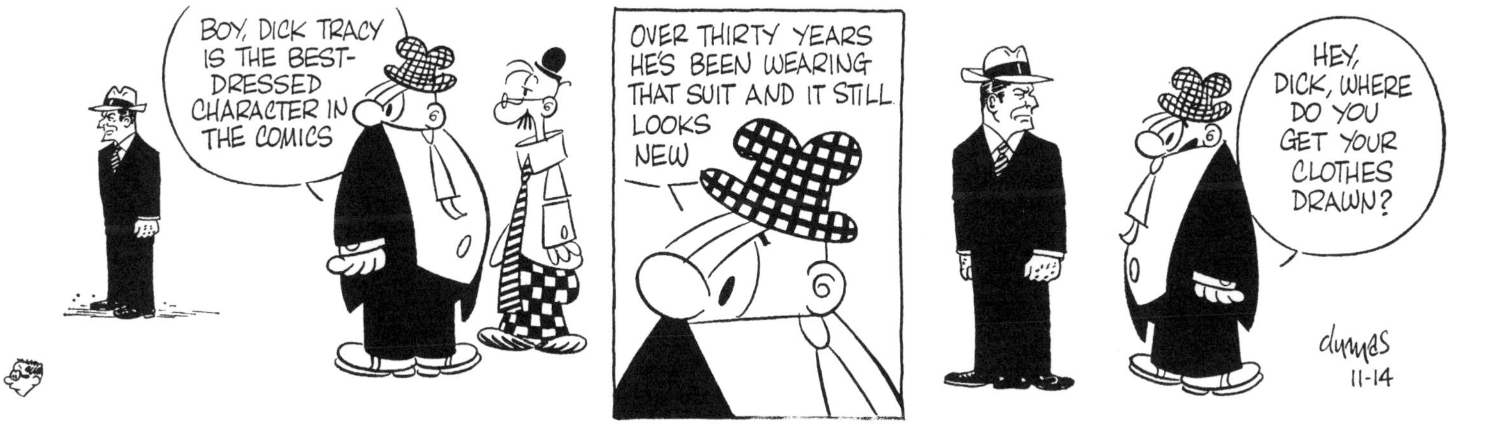
BOY, DICK TRACY IS THE BEST-DRESSED CHARACTER IN THE COMICS
OVER THIRTY YEARS HE'S BEEN WEARING THAT SUIT AND IT STILL LOOKS NEW
HEY, DICK, WHERE DO YOU GET YOUR CLOTHES DRAWN?
dumas
11-14

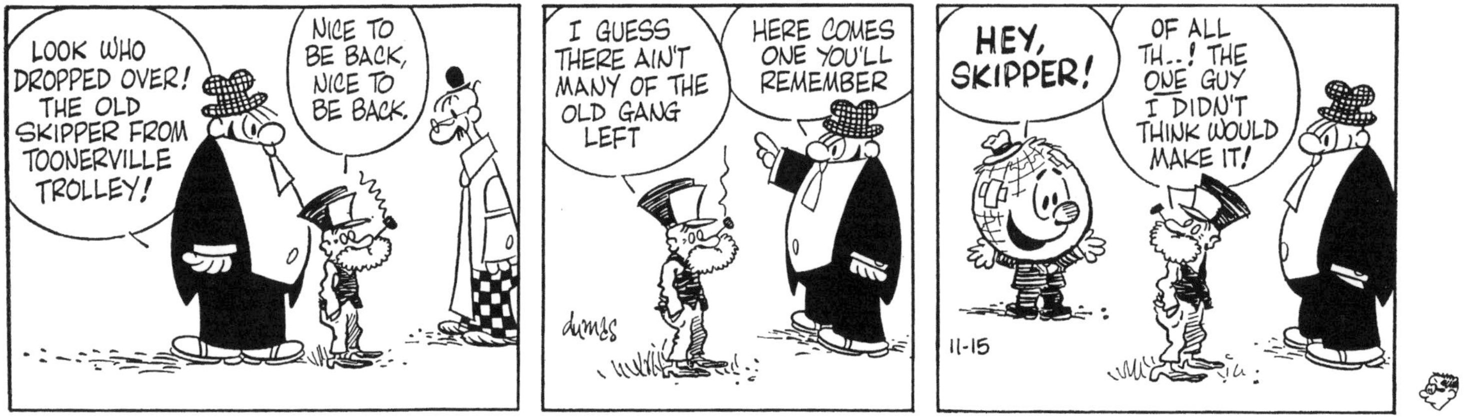
LOOK WHO DROPPED OVER! THE OLD SKIPPER FROM TOONERVILLE TROLLEY!
NICE TO BE BACK, NICE TO BE BACK.
I GUESS THERE AIN'T MANY OF THE OLD GANG LEFT
HERE COMES ONE YOU'LL REMEMBER
HEY, SKIPPER!
OF ALL TH--! THE ONE GUY I DIDN'T THINK WOULD MAKE IT!
11-15

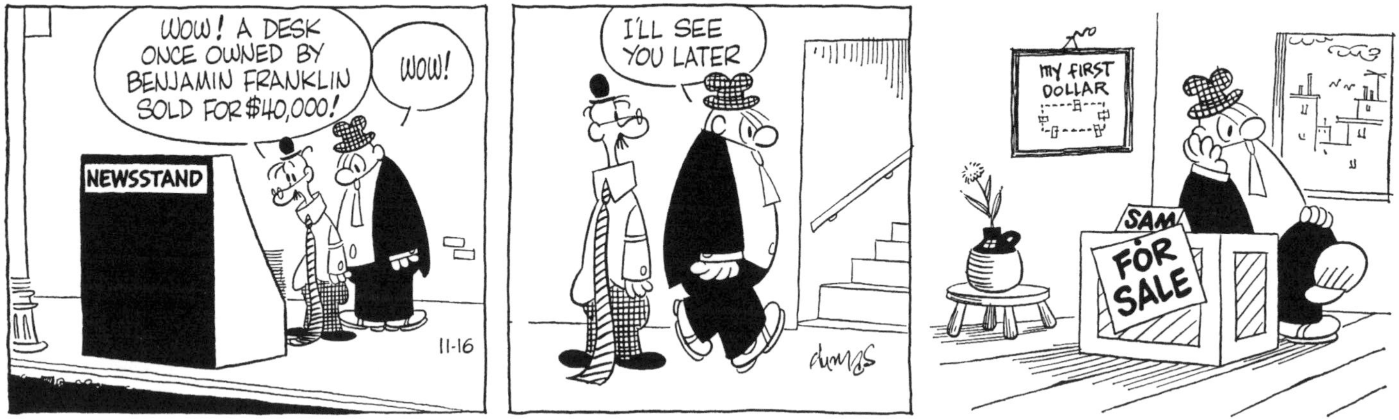
WOW! A DESK ONCE OWNED BY BENJAMIN FRANKLIN SOLD FOR $40,000!
WOW!
NEWSSTAND
11-16
I'LL SEE YOU LATER
MY FIRST DOLLAR
SAM
FOR SALE

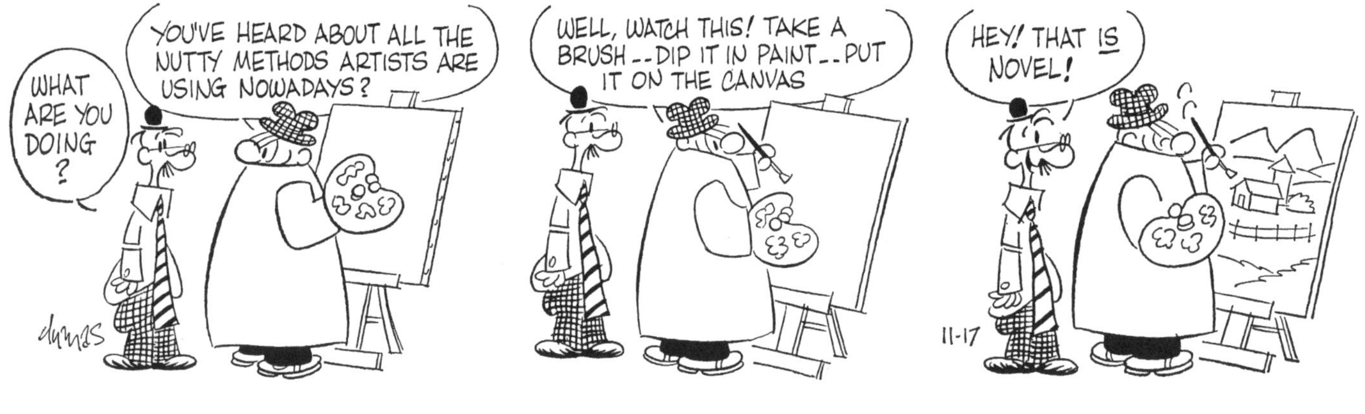
WHAT ARE YOU DOING?
YOU'VE HEARD ABOUT ALL THE NUTTY METHODS ARTISTS ARE USING NOWADAYS?
WELL, WATCH THIS! TAKE A BRUSH--DIP IT IN PAINT--PUT IT ON THE CANVAS
HEY! THAT IS NOVEL!
11-17

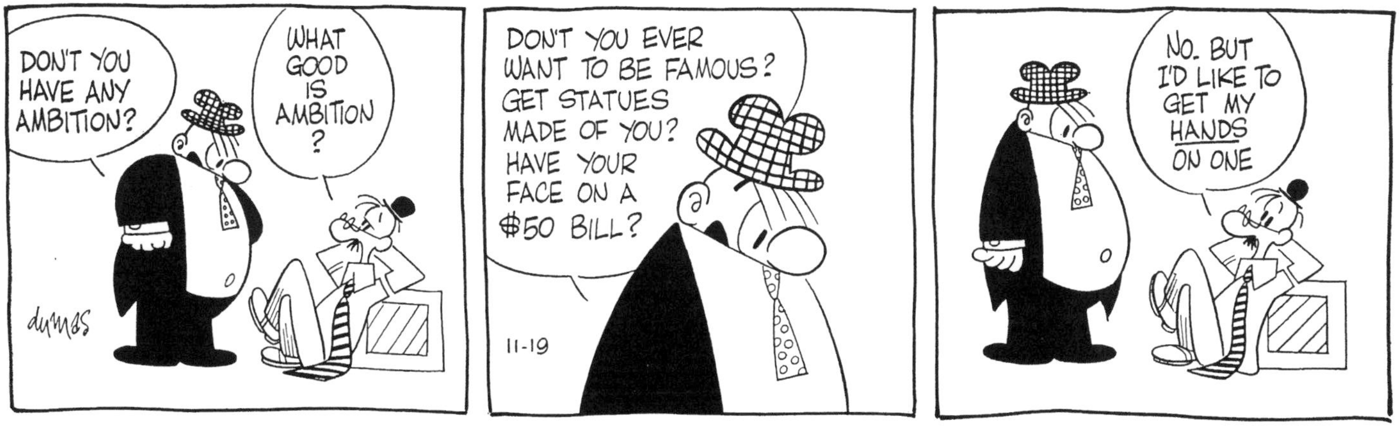
DON'T YOU HAVE ANY AMBITION?
WHAT GOOD IS AMBITION ?
dumas
DON'T YOU EVER WANT TO BE FAMOUS? GET STATUES MADE OF YOU? HAVE YOUR FACE ON A $50 BILL?
11-19
NO. BUT I'D LIKE TO GET MY HANDS ON ONE

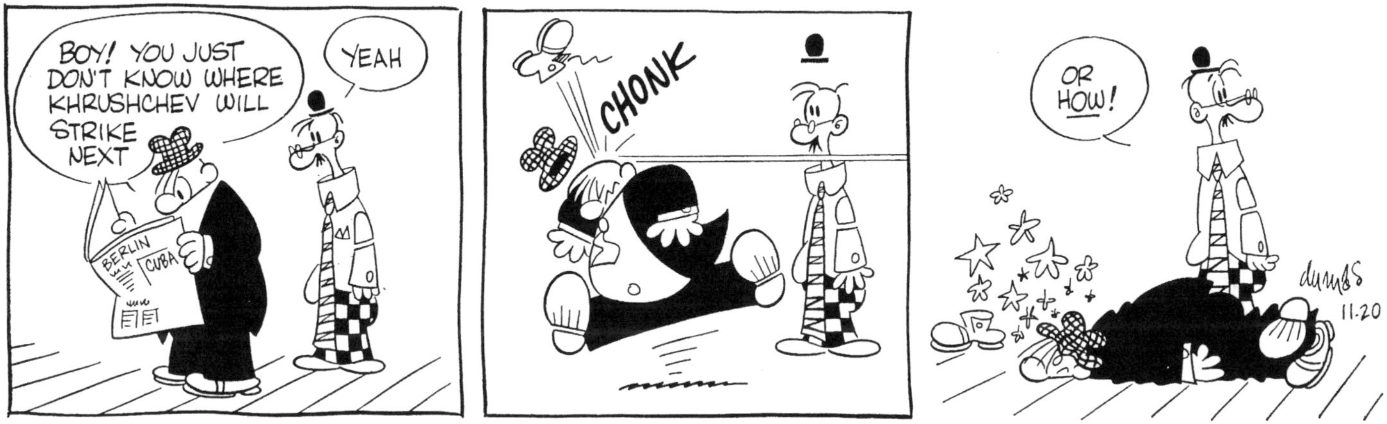
BOY! YOU JUST DON'T KNOW WHERE KHRUSHCHEV WILL STRIKE NEXT
YEAH
BERLIN
CUBA
CHONK
OR HOW!
dumas
11-20

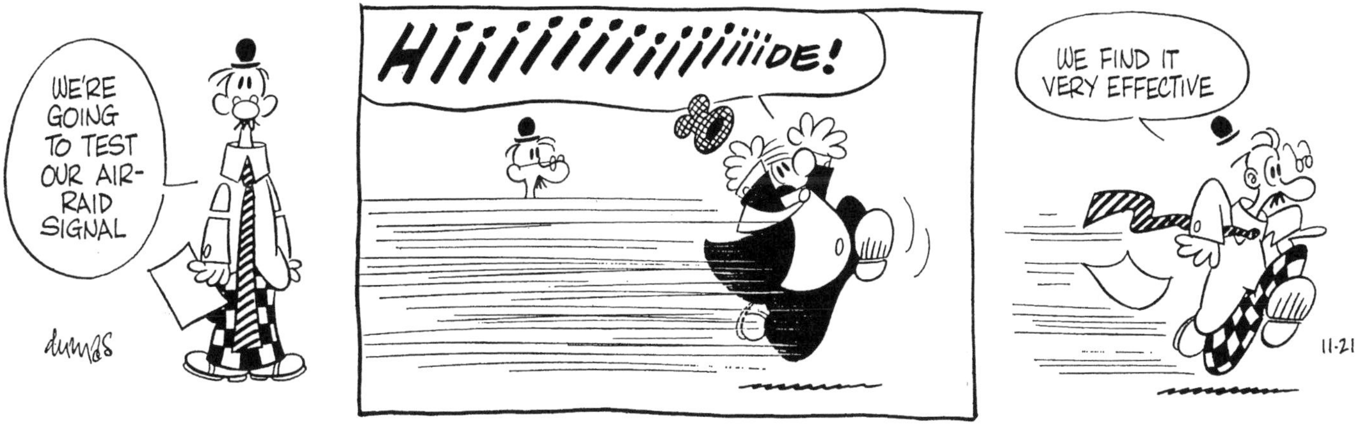
WE'RE GOING TO TEST OUR AIR-RAID SIGNAL
dumas
HIIIIIIIIIIIIIIDE!
WE FIND IT VERY EFFECTIVE
11-21

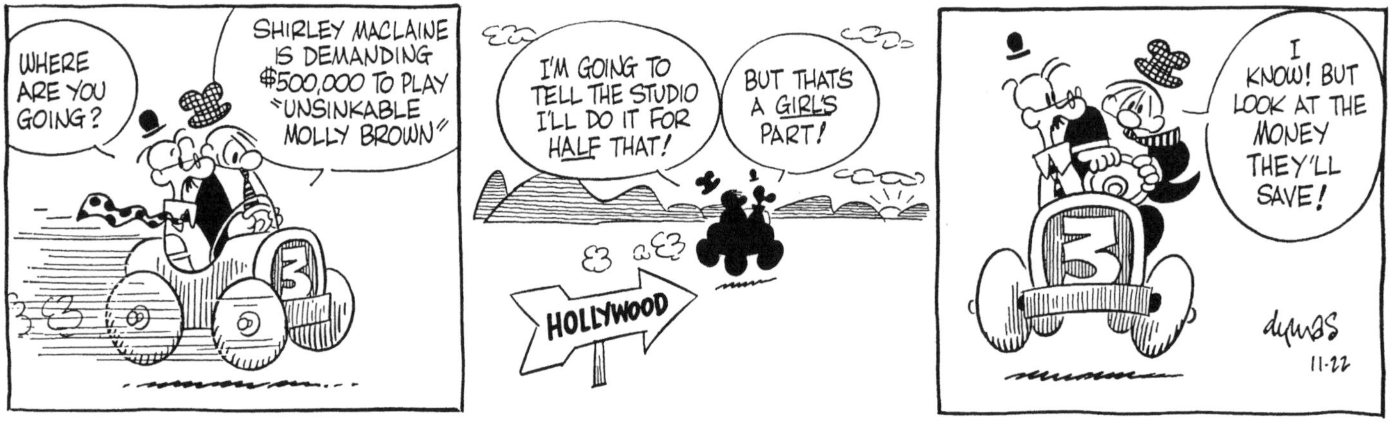
WHERE ARE YOU GOING?
SHIRLEY MACLAINE IS DEMANDING $500,000 TO PLAY "UNSINKABLE MOLLY BROWN"
I'M GOING TO TELL THE STUDIO I'LL DO IT FOR HALF THAT!
BUT THAT'S A GIRL'S PART!
HOLLYWOOD
I KNOW! BUT LOOK AT THE MONEY THEY'LL SAVE!
dumas
11-22

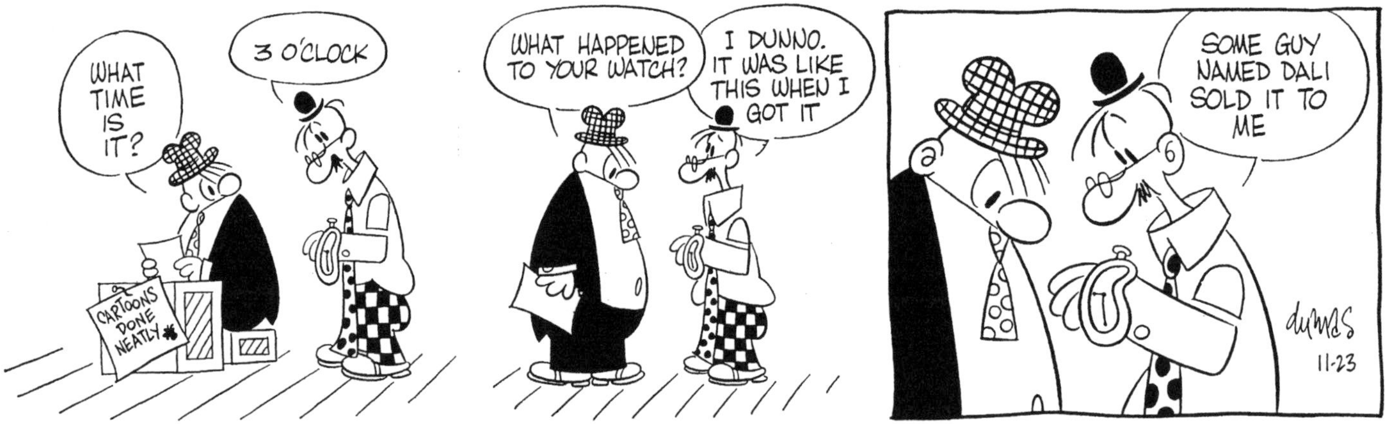
WHAT TIME IS IT?
3 O'CLOCK
CARTOONS DONE NEATLY
WHAT HAPPENED TO YOUR WATCH?
I DUNNO. IT WAS LIKE THIS WHEN I GOT IT
SOME GUY NAMED DALI SOLD IT TO ME
dumas
11-23

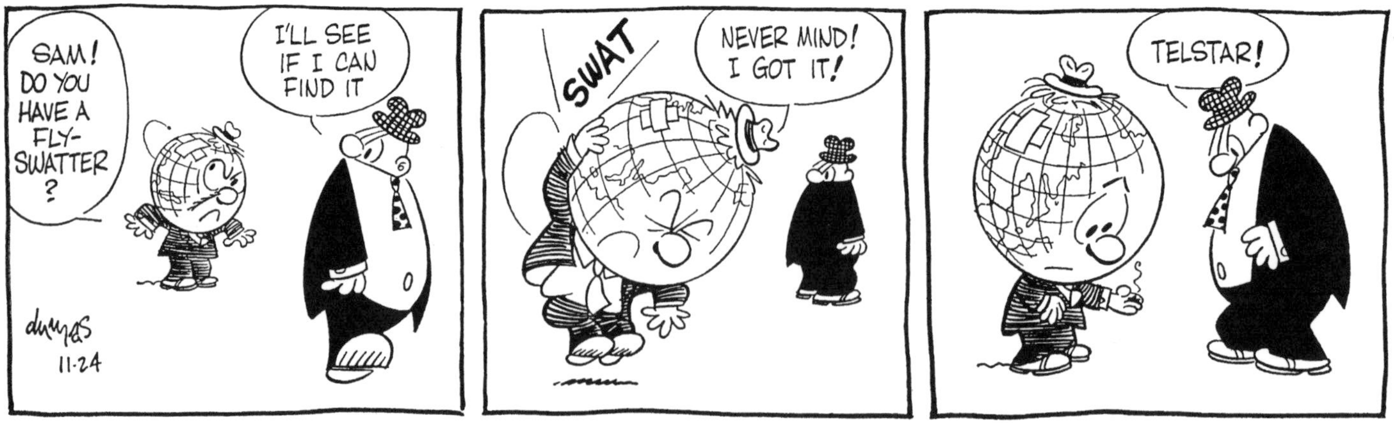
SAM! DO YOU HAVE A FLY-SWATTER?
I'LL SEE IF I CAN FIND IT
dumas
11-24
SWAT
NEVER MIND! I GOT IT!
TELSTAR!

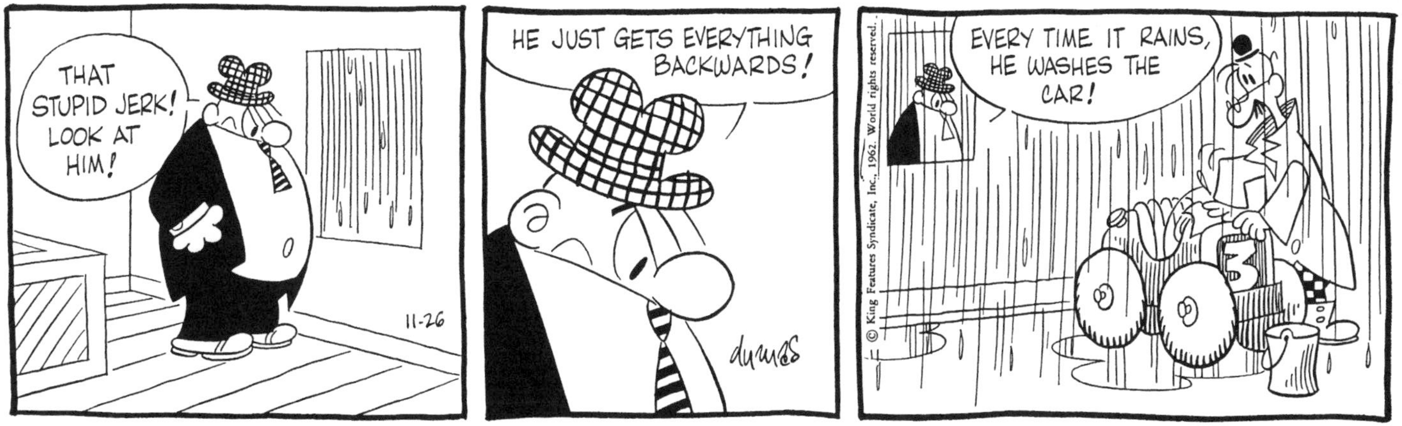
THAT STUPID JERK! LOOK AT HIM!
11-26
HE JUST GETS EVERYTHING BACKWARDS!
dumas
© King Features Syndicate, Inc., 1962. World rights reserved.
EVERY TIME IT RAINS, HE WASHES THE CAR!

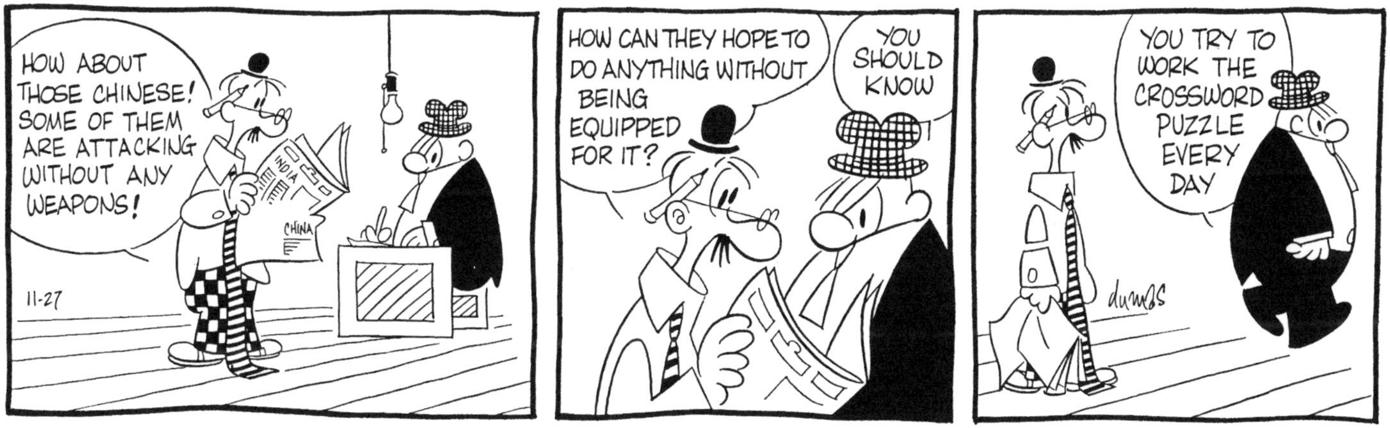
HOW ABOUT THOSE CHINESE! SOME OF THEM ARE ATTACKING WITHOUT ANY WEAPONS!
INDIA
CHINA
11-27
HOW CAN THEY HOPE TO DO ANYTHING WITHOUT BEING EQUIPPED FOR IT?
YOU SHOULD KNOW
YOU TRY TO WORK THE CROSSWORD PUZZLE EVERY DAY
dumas

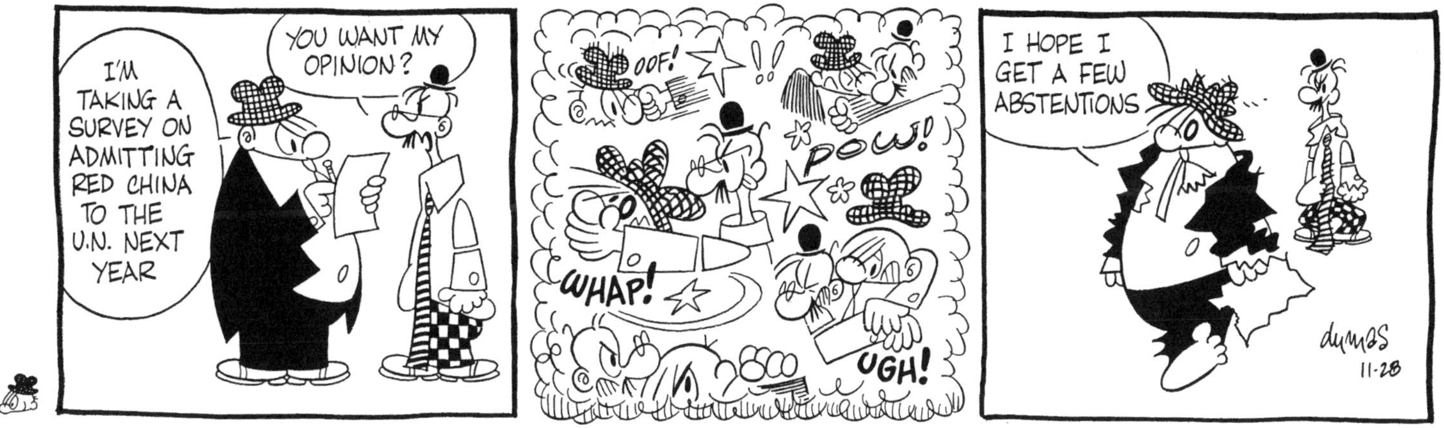
I'M TAKING A SURVEY ON ADMITTING RED CHINA TO THE U.N. NEXT YEAR
YOU WANT MY OPINION?
OOF!
!!
POW!
WHAP!
UGH!
I HOPE I GET A FEW ABSTENTIONS
dumas
11-28

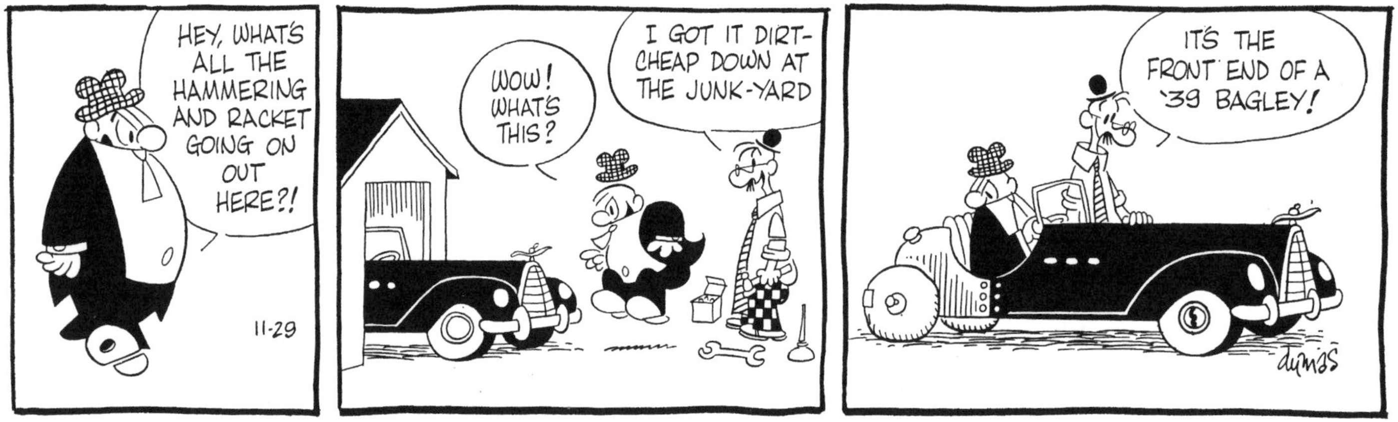
HEY, WHAT'S ALL THE HAMMERING AND RACKET GOING ON OUT HERE?!
11-29
WOW! WHAT'S THIS?
I GOT IT DIRT-CHEAP DOWN AT THE JUNK-YARD
IT'S THE FRONT END OF A '39 BAGLEY!
dumas

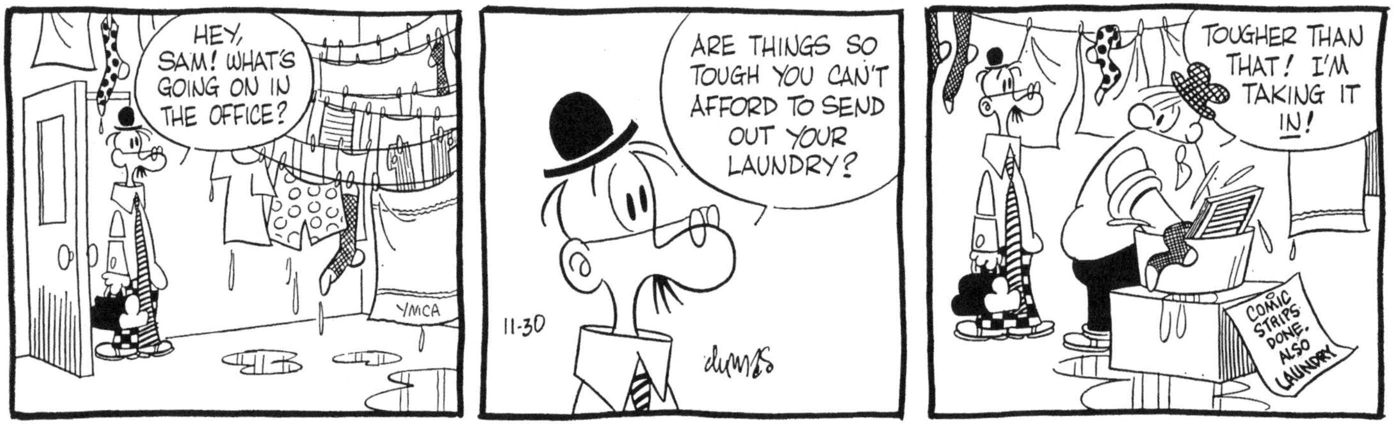
HEY, SAM! WHAT'S GOING ON IN THE OFFICE?
YMCA
ARE THINGS SO TOUGH YOU CAN'T AFFORD TO SEND OUT YOUR LAUNDRY?
11-30
dumas
TOUGHER THAN THAT! I'M TAKING IT IN!
COMIC STRIPS DONE. ALSO LAUNDRY

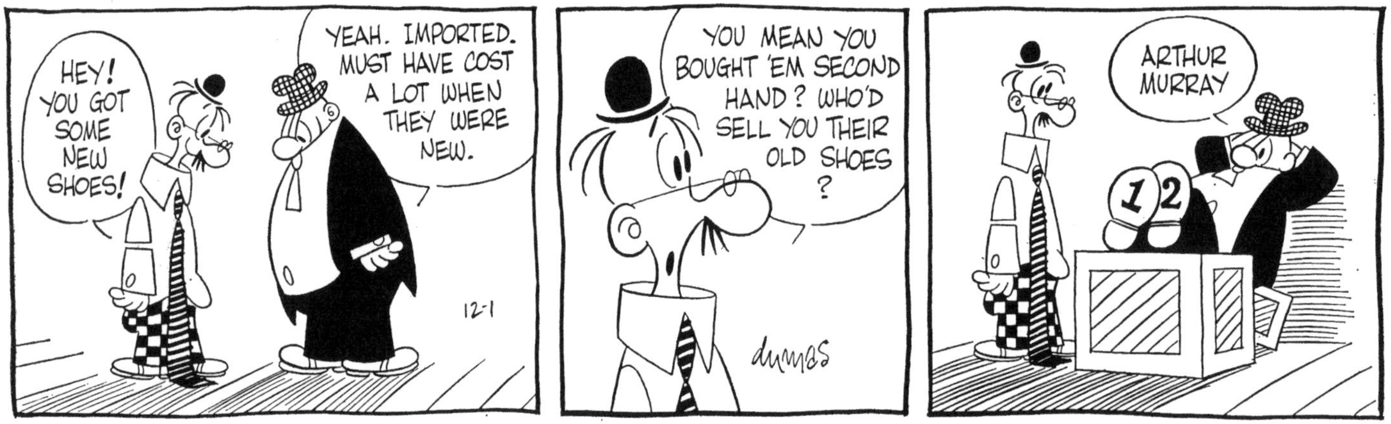
HEY! YOU GOT SOME NEW SHOES!
YEAH. IMPORTED. MUST HAVE COST A LOT WHEN THEY WERE NEW.
12-1
YOU MEAN YOU BOUGHT 'EM SECOND HAND? WHO'D SELL YOU THEIR OLD SHOES?
dumas
ARTHUR MURRAY
1
2

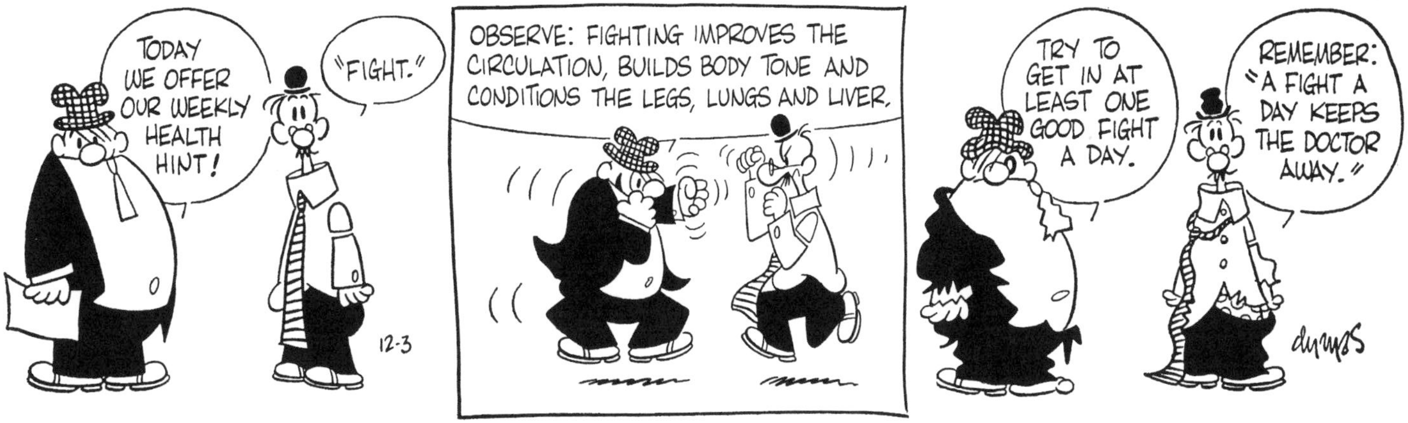
TODAY WE OFFER OUR WEEKLY HEALTH HINT!
"FIGHT."
OBSERVE: FIGHTING IMPROVES THE CIRCULATION, BUILDS BODY TONE AND CONDITIONS THE LEGS, LUNGS AND LIVER.
TRY TO GET IN AT LEAST ONE GOOD FIGHT A DAY.
REMEMBER: "A FIGHT A DAY KEEPS THE DOCTOR AWAY."
12-3

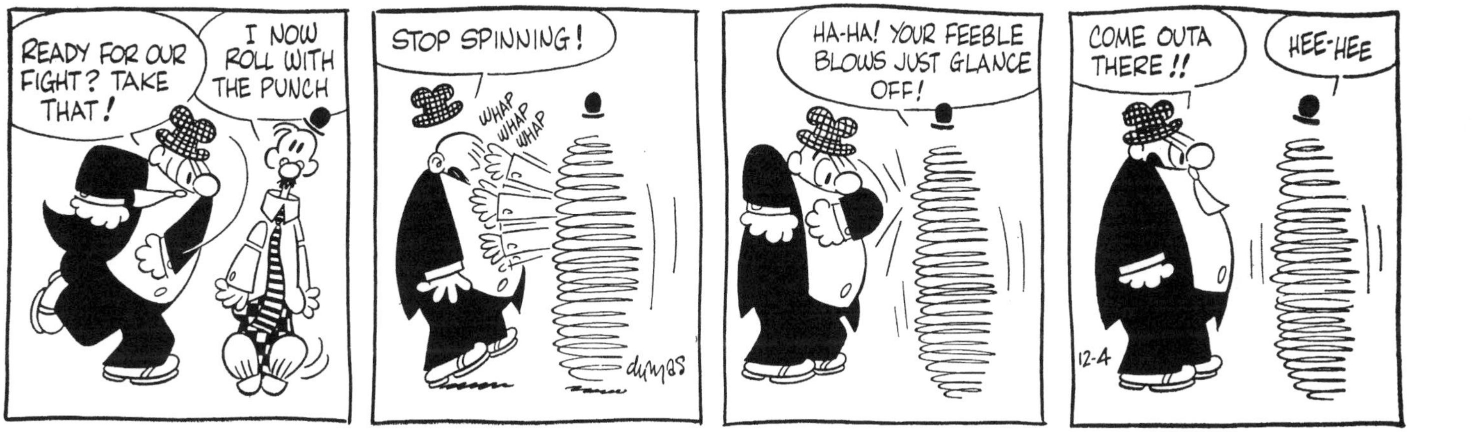
READY FOR OUR FIGHT? TAKE THAT!
I NOW ROLL WITH THE PUNCH
STOP SPINNING!
WHAP WHAP WHAP
HA-HA! YOUR FEEBLE BLOWS JUST GLANCE OFF!
COME OUTA THERE!!
HEE-HEE
12-4

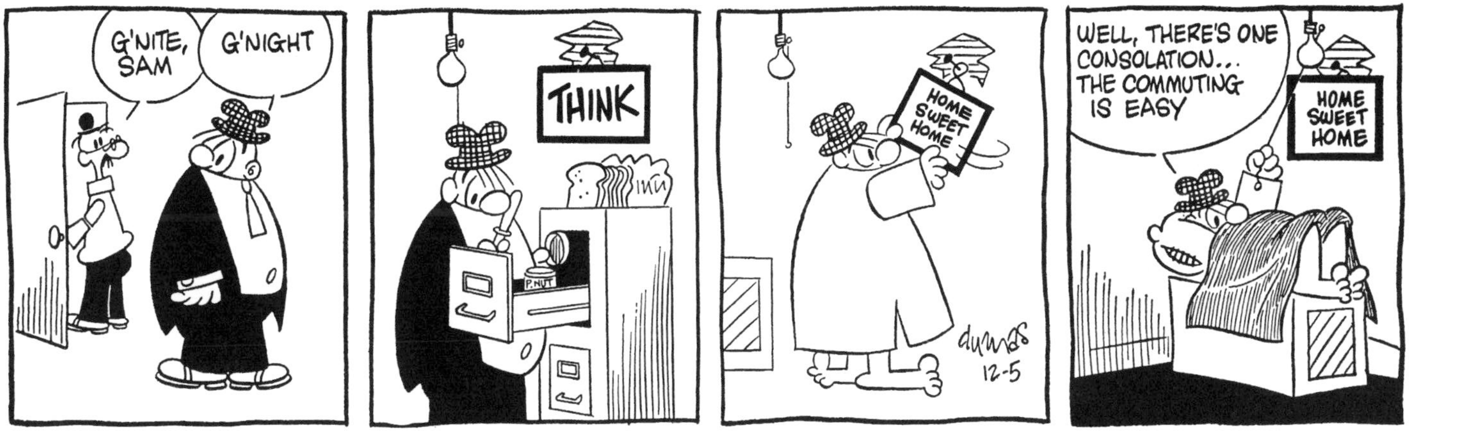
G'NITE, SAM
G'NIGHT
THINK
P. NUT
HOME SWEET HOME
12-5
WELL, THERE'S ONE CONSOLATION... THE COMMUTING IS EASY
HOME SWEET HOME

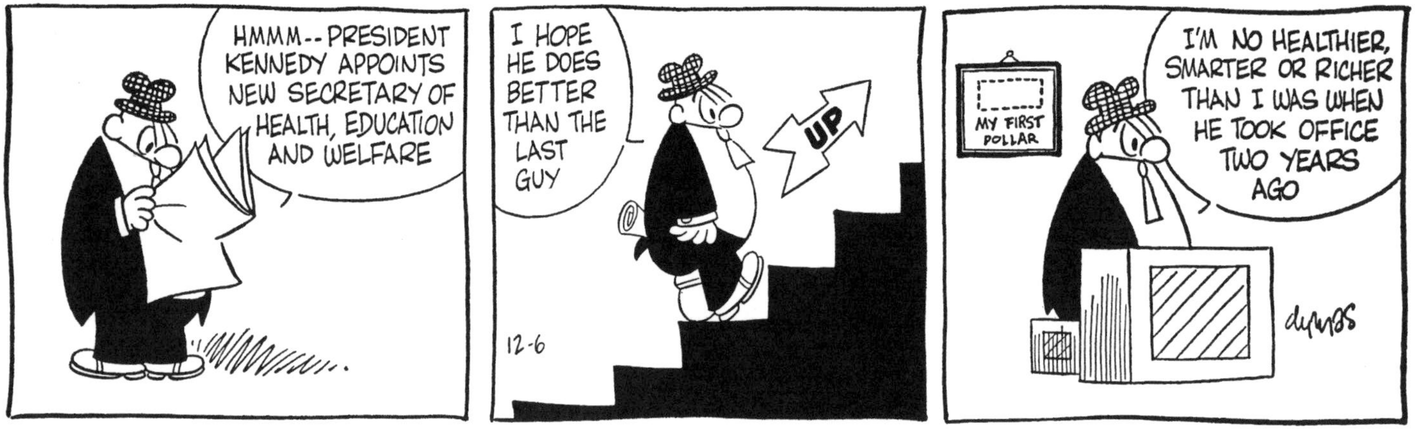
HMMM--PRESIDENT KENNEDY APPOINTS NEW SECRETARY OF HEALTH, EDUCATION AND WELFARE
I HOPE HE DOES BETTER THAN THE LAST GUY
UP
12-6
MY FIRST DOLLAR
I'M NO HEALTHIER, SMARTER OR RICHER THAN I WAS WHEN HE TOOK OFFICE TWO YEARS AGO
dumas

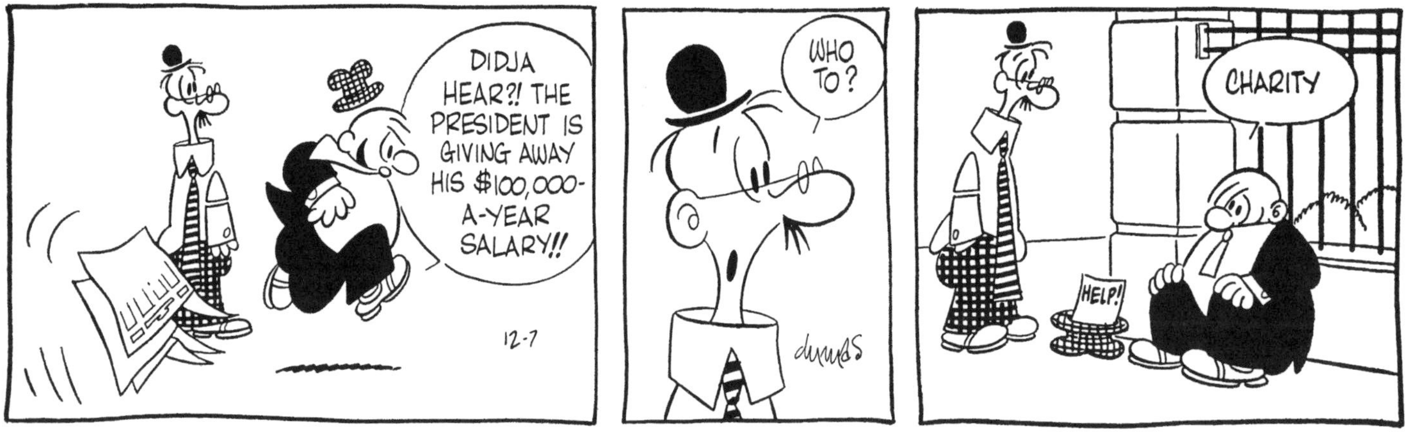
DIDJA HEAR?! THE PRESIDENT IS GIVING AWAY HIS $100,000-A-YEAR SALARY!!
12-7
WHO TO?
dumas
CHARITY
HELP!

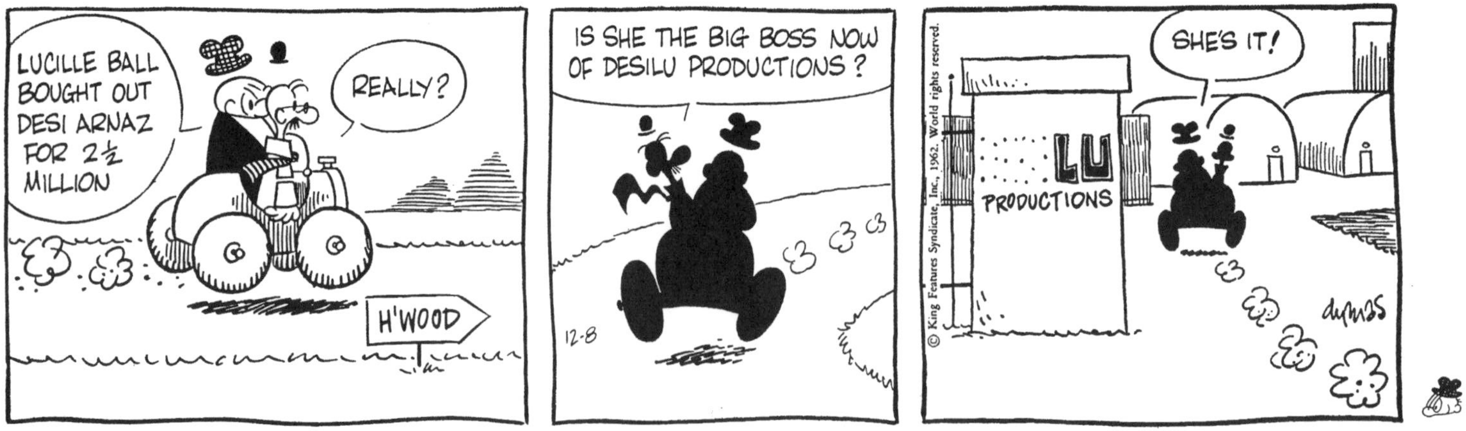
LUCILLE BALL BOUGHT OUT DESI ARNAZ FOR 2½ MILLION
REALLY?
H'WOOD
IS SHE THE BIG BOSS NOW OF DESILU PRODUCTIONS?
12-8
© King Features Syndicate, Inc., 1962. World rights reserved.
LU
PRODUCTIONS
SHE'S IT!
dumas

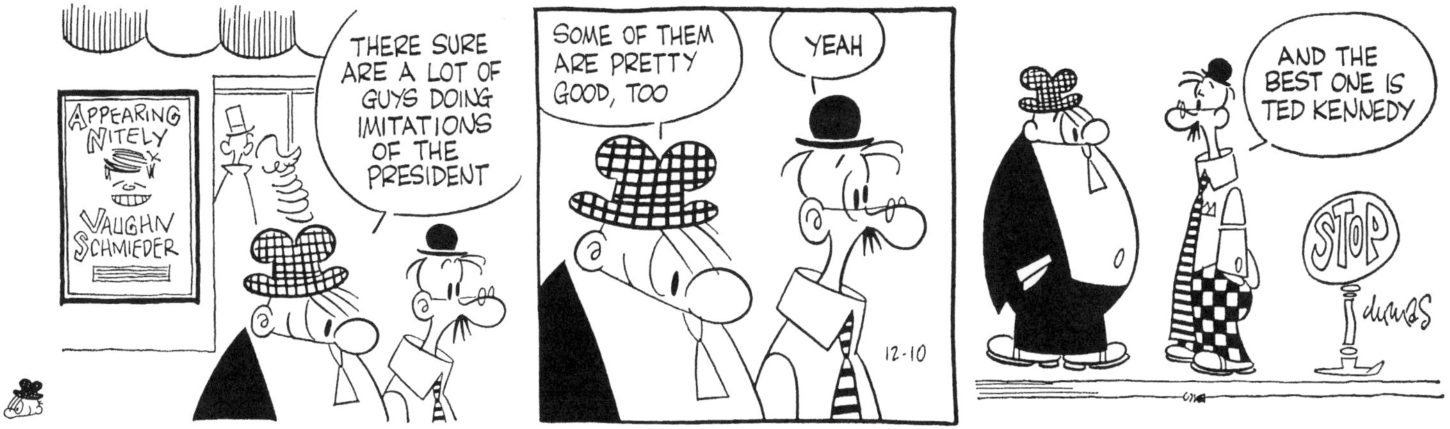
APPEARING NITELY
VAUGHN SCHMIEDER
THERE SURE ARE A LOT OF GUYS DOING IMITATIONS OF THE PRESIDENT
SOME OF THEM ARE PRETTY GOOD, TOO
YEAH
12-10
AND THE BEST ONE IS TED KENNEDY
STOP
dumas

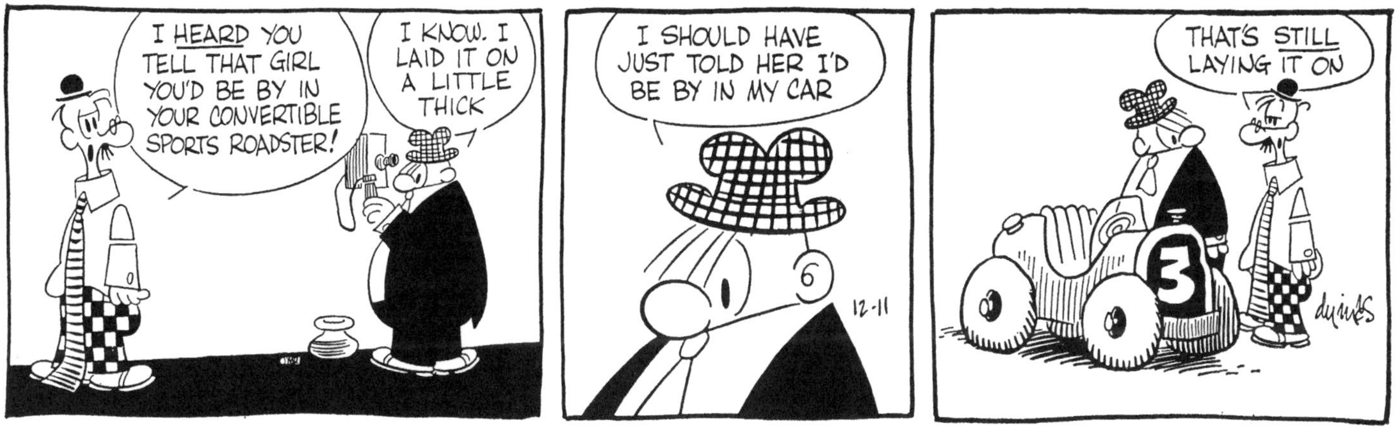
I HEARD YOU TELL THAT GIRL YOU'D BE BY IN YOUR CONVERTIBLE SPORTS ROADSTER!
I KNOW. I LAID IT ON A LITTLE THICK
I SHOULD HAVE JUST TOLD HER I'D BE BY IN MY CAR
12-11
THAT'S STILL LAYING IT ON
3
dumas

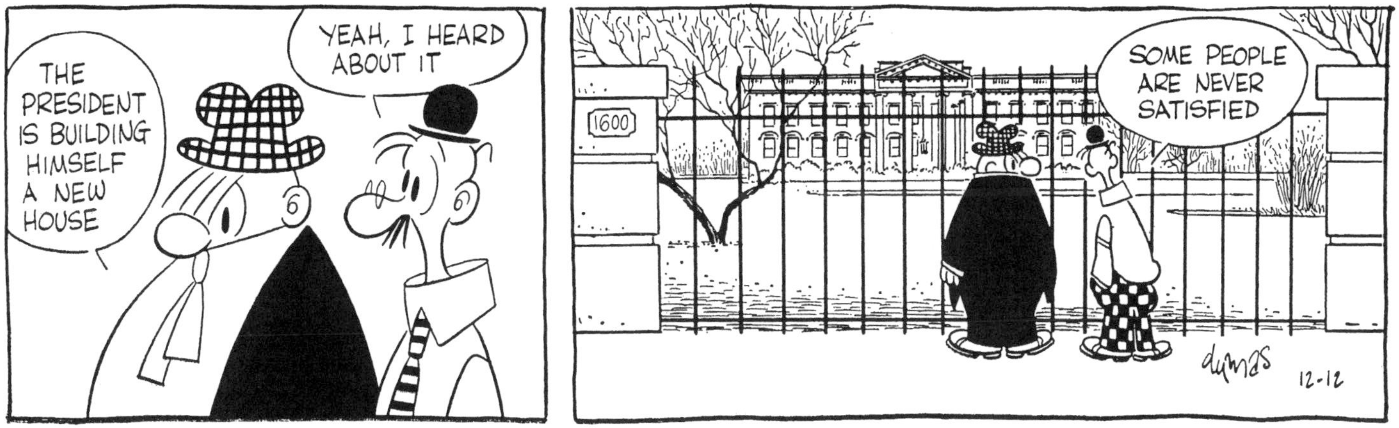
THE PRESIDENT IS BUILDING HIMSELF A NEW HOUSE
YEAH, I HEARD ABOUT IT
1600
SOME PEOPLE ARE NEVER SATISFIED
dumas
12-12

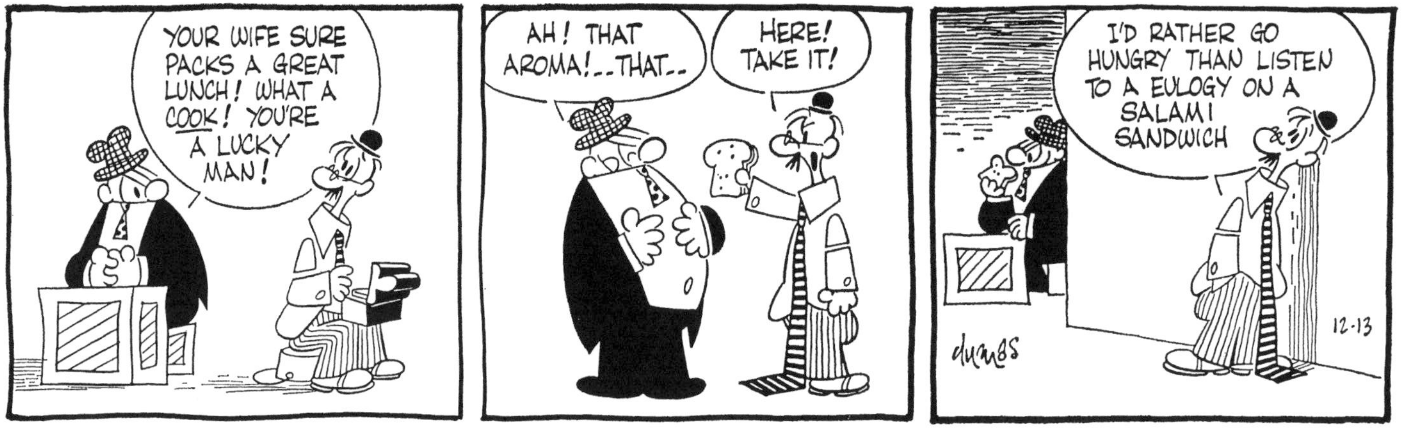
YOUR WIFE SURE PACKS A GREAT LUNCH! WHAT A COOK! YOU'RE A LUCKY MAN!
AH! THAT AROMA!--THAT--
HERE! TAKE IT!
I'D RATHER GO HUNGRY THAN LISTEN TO A EULOGY ON A SALAMI SANDWICH
dumas
12-13

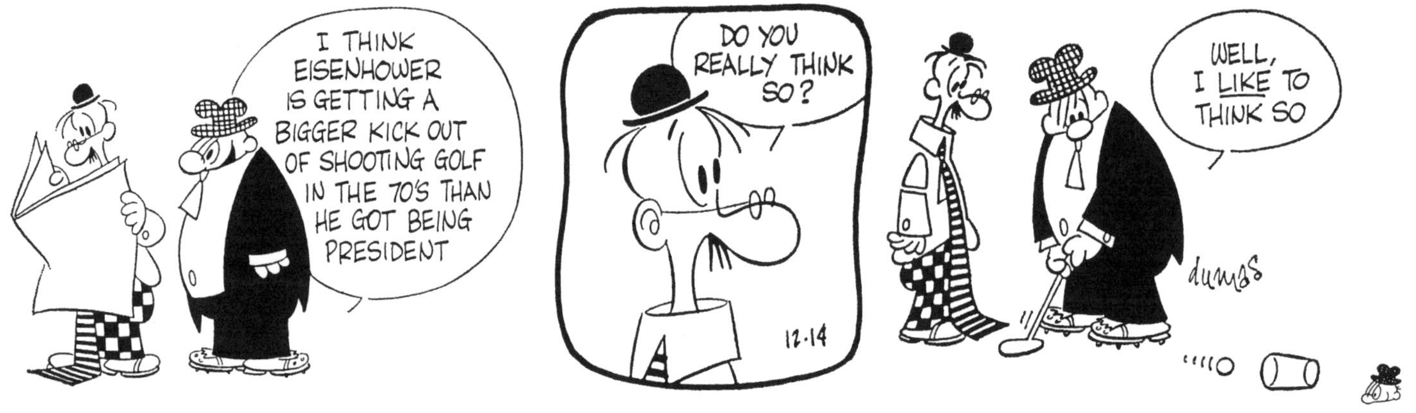
I THINK EISENHOWER IS GETTING A BIGGER KICK OUT OF SHOOTING GOLF IN THE 70'S THAN HE GOT BEING PRESIDENT
DO YOU REALLY THINK SO?
12-14
WELL, I LIKE TO THINK SO
dumas

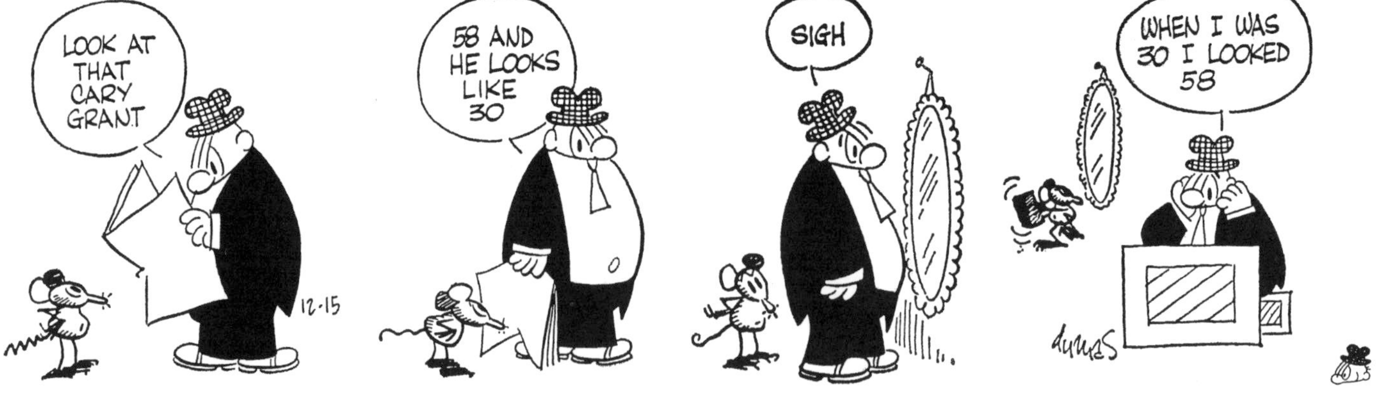
LOOK AT THAT CARY GRANT
12-15
58 AND HE LOOKS LIKE 30
SIGH
WHEN I WAS 30 I LOOKED 58
dumas

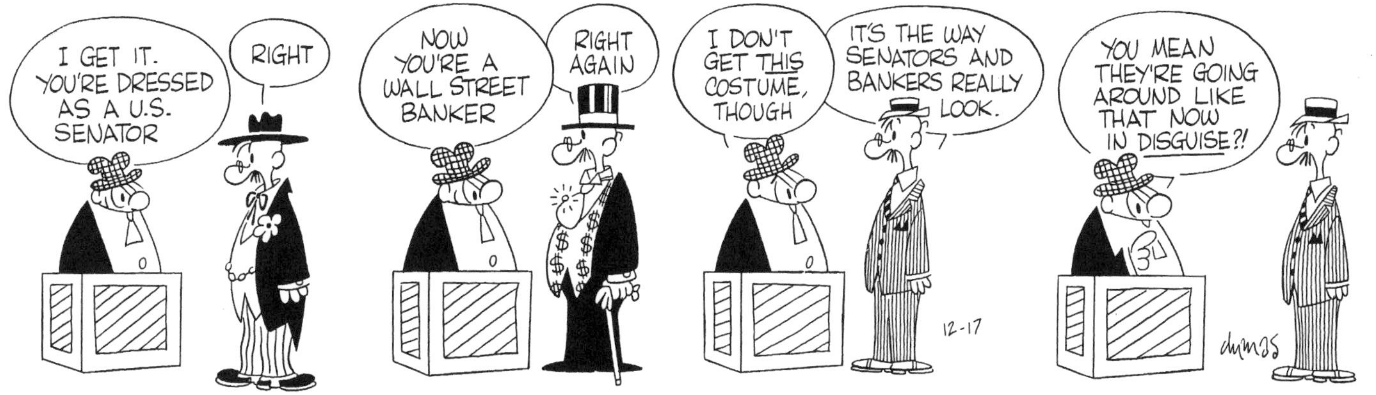

I GET IT. YOU'RE DRESSED AS A U.S. SENATOR
RIGHT
NOW YOU'RE A WALL STREET BANKER
RIGHT AGAIN
I DON'T GET THIS COSTUME, THOUGH
IT'S THE WAY SENATORS AND BANKERS REALLY LOOK.
YOU MEAN THEY'RE GOING AROUND LIKE THAT NOW IN DISGUISE?!
12-17
dumas

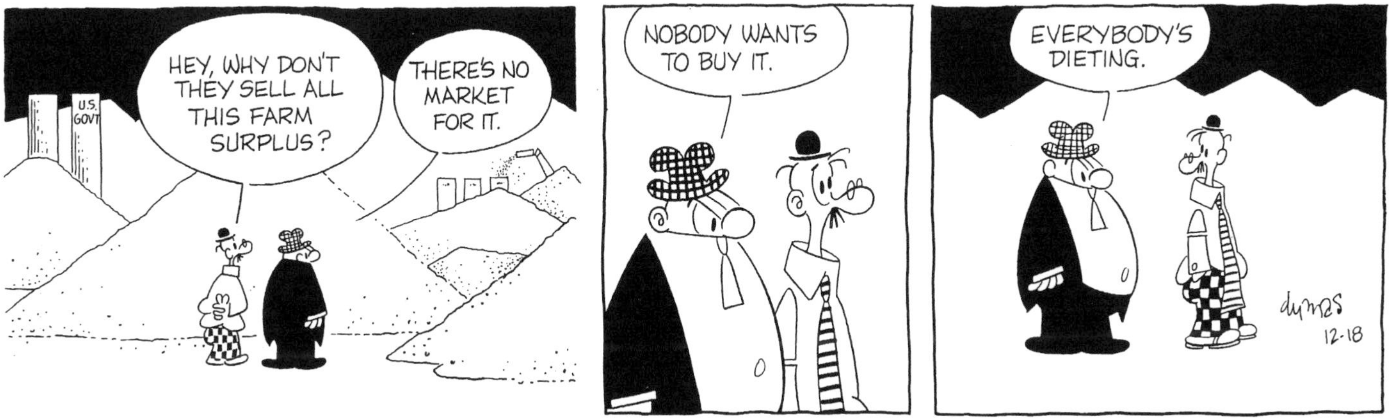

U.S. GOVT
HEY, WHY DON'T THEY SELL ALL THIS FARM SURPLUS?
THERE'S NO MARKET FOR IT.
NOBODY WANTS TO BUY IT.
EVERYBODY'S DIETING.
dumas
12-18

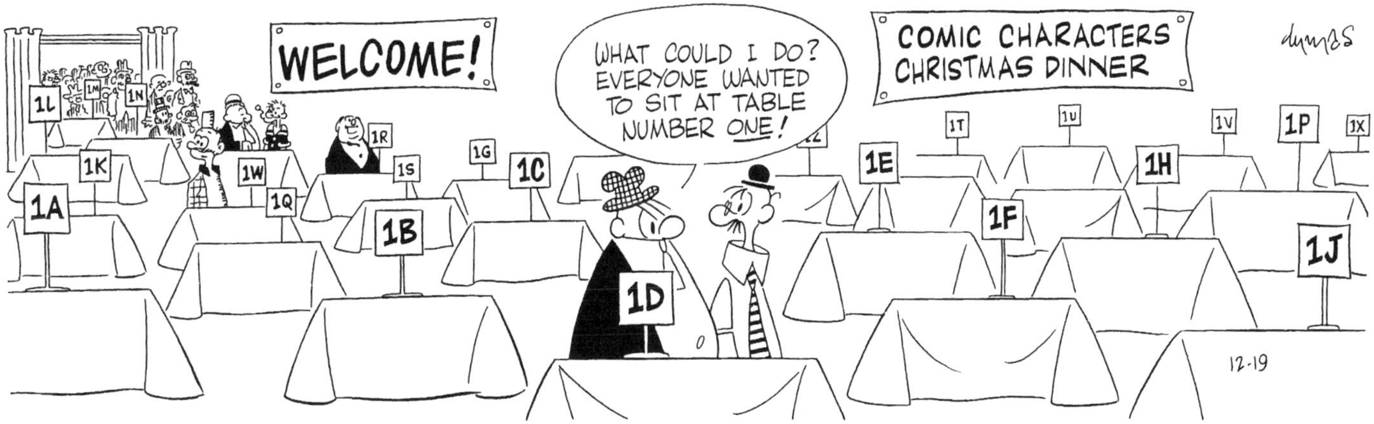

WELCOME!
WHAT COULD I DO? EVERYONE WANTED TO SIT AT TABLE NUMBER ONE!
COMIC CHARACTERS CHRISTMAS DINNER
dumas
12-19

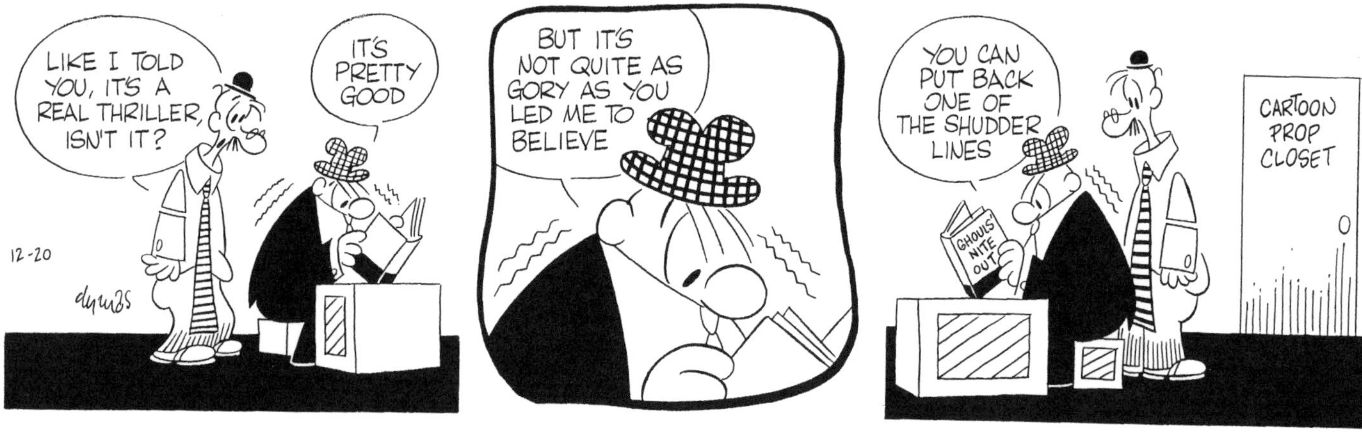
LIKE I TOLD YOU, IT'S A REAL THRILLER, ISN'T IT?
IT'S PRETTY GOOD
12-20
BUT IT'S NOT QUITE AS GORY AS YOU LED ME TO BELIEVE
YOU CAN PUT BACK ONE OF THE SHUDDER LINES
GHOULS' NITE OUT
CARTOON PROP CLOSET

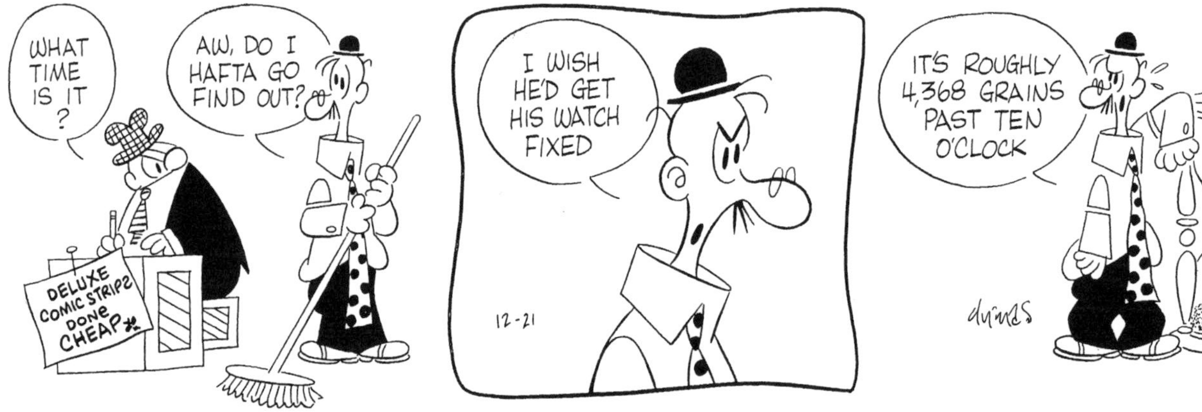
WHAT TIME IS IT ?
AW, DO I HAFTA GO FIND OUT?
DELUXE COMIC STRIPS DONE CHEAP
I WISH HE'D GET HIS WATCH FIXED
12-21
IT'S ROUGHLY 4,368 GRAINS PAST TEN O'CLOCK

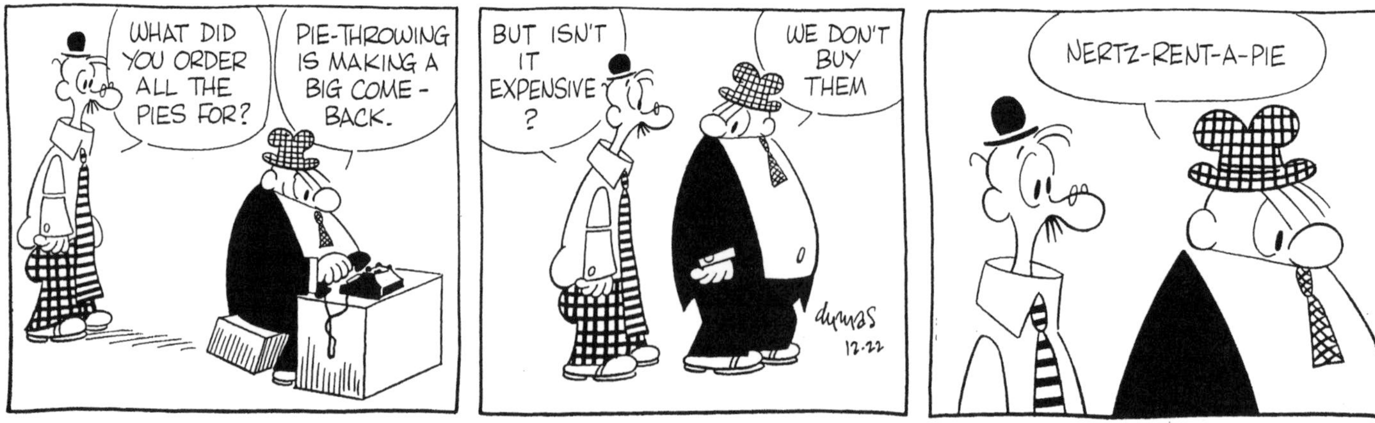
WHAT DID YOU ORDER ALL THE PIES FOR?
PIE-THROWING IS MAKING A BIG COME-BACK.
BUT ISN'T IT EXPENSIVE ?
WE DON'T BUY THEM
12-22
NERTZ-RENT-A-PIE

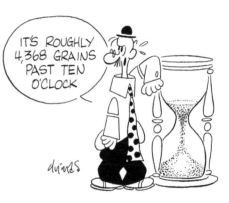

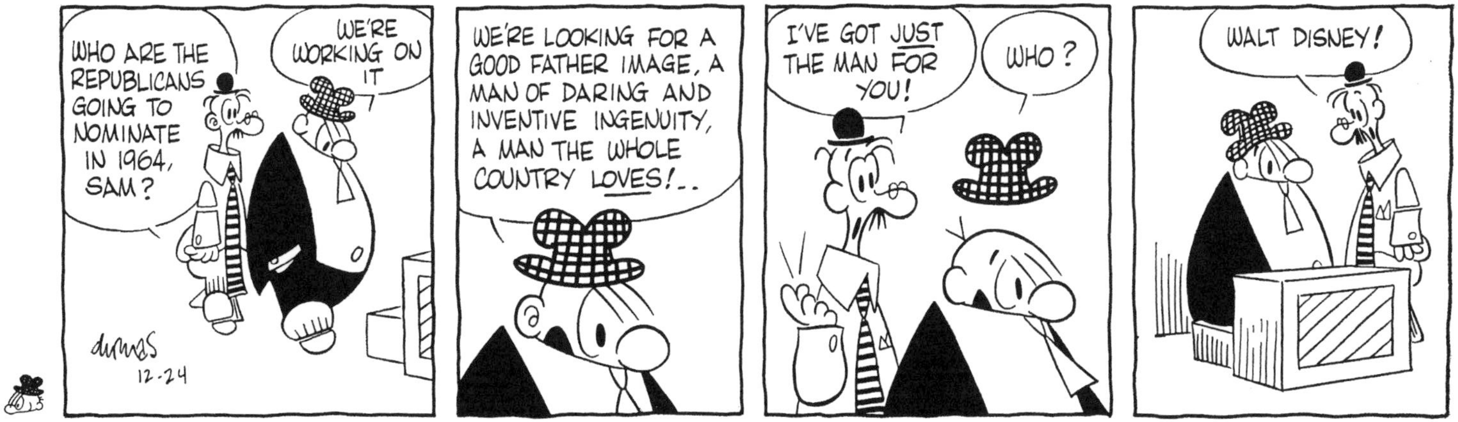
WHO ARE THE REPUBLICANS GOING TO NOMINATE IN 1964, SAM?
WE'RE WORKING ON IT
dumas
12-24
WE'RE LOOKING FOR A GOOD FATHER IMAGE, A MAN OF DARING AND INVENTIVE INGENUITY, A MAN THE WHOLE COUNTRY LOVES!..
I'VE GOT JUST THE MAN FOR YOU!
WHO?
WALT DISNEY!

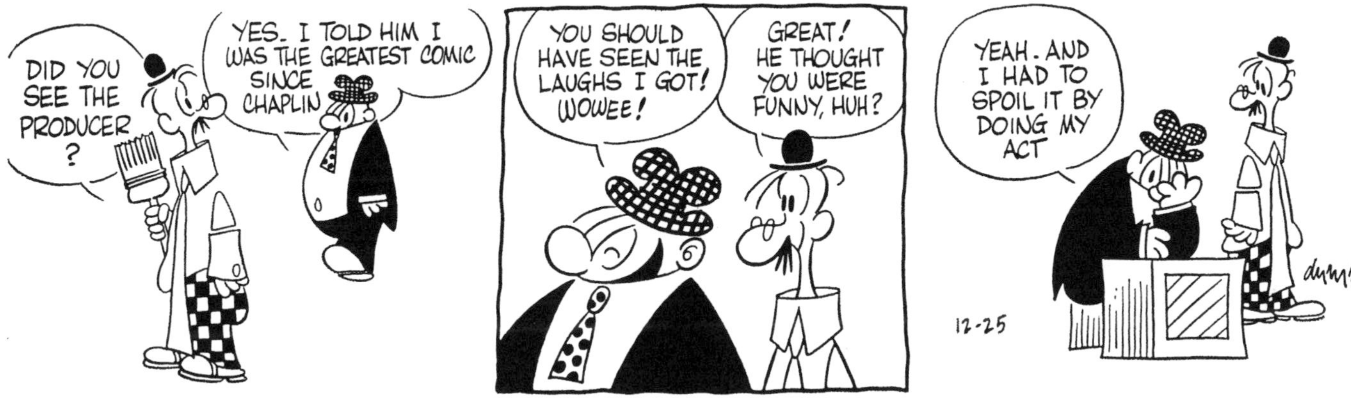
DID YOU SEE THE PRODUCER?
YES. I TOLD HIM I WAS THE GREATEST COMIC SINCE CHAPLIN
YOU SHOULD HAVE SEEN THE LAUGHS I GOT! WOWEE!
GREAT! HE THOUGHT YOU WERE FUNNY, HUH?
YEAH. AND I HAD TO SPOIL IT BY DOING MY ACT
12-25
dumas

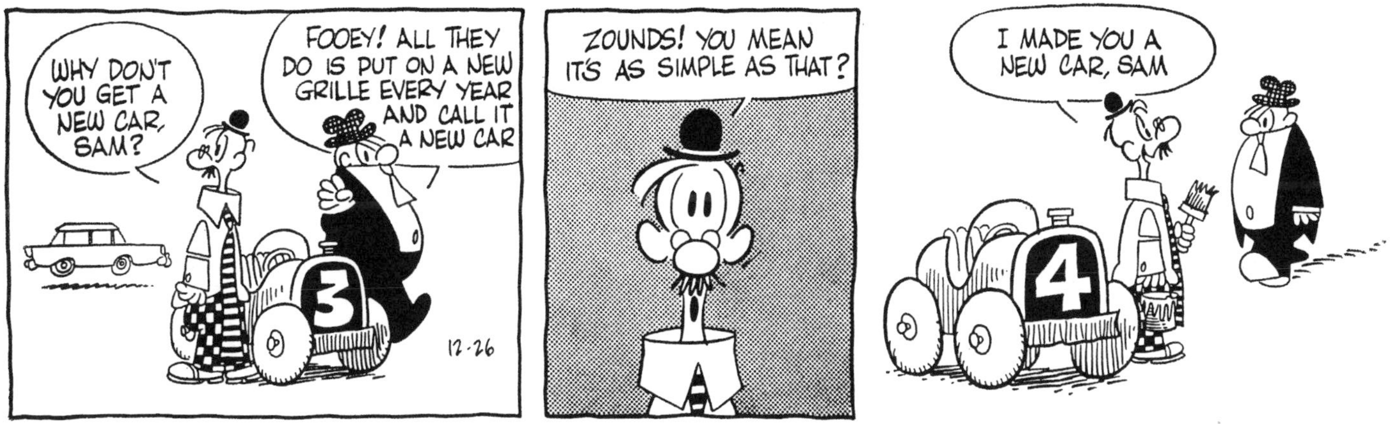
WHY DON'T YOU GET A NEW CAR, SAM?
FOOEY! ALL THEY DO IS PUT ON A NEW GRILLE EVERY YEAR AND CALL IT A NEW CAR
3
12-26
ZOUNDS! YOU MEAN IT'S AS SIMPLE AS THAT?
I MADE YOU A NEW CAR, SAM
4

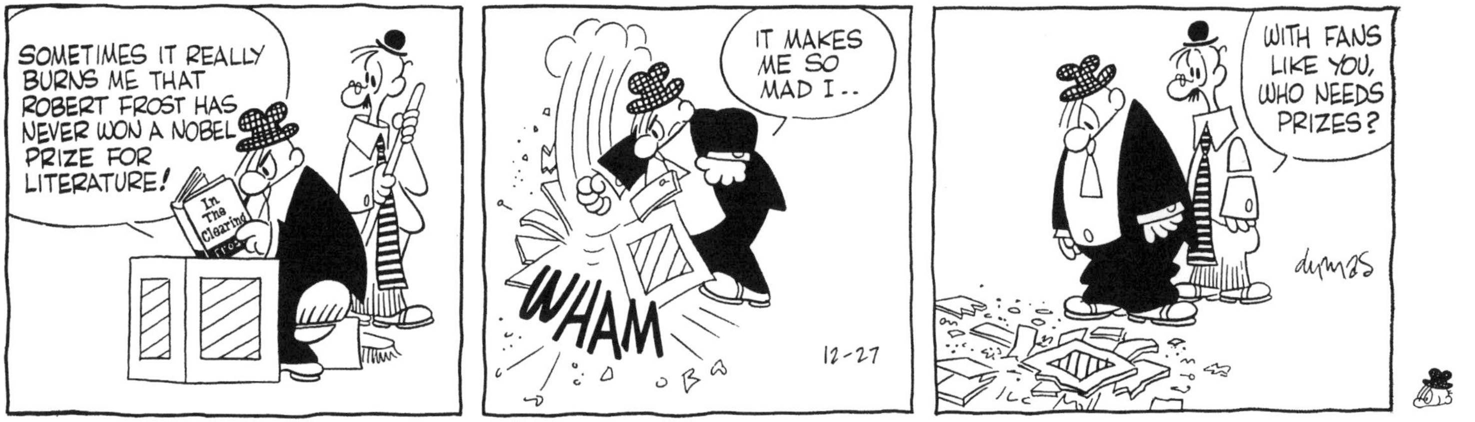
SOMETIMES IT REALLY BURNS ME THAT ROBERT FROST HAS NEVER WON A NOBEL PRIZE FOR LITERATURE!
In The Clearing
IT MAKES ME SO MAD I..
WHAM
12-27
WITH FANS LIKE YOU, WHO NEEDS PRIZES?
dumas

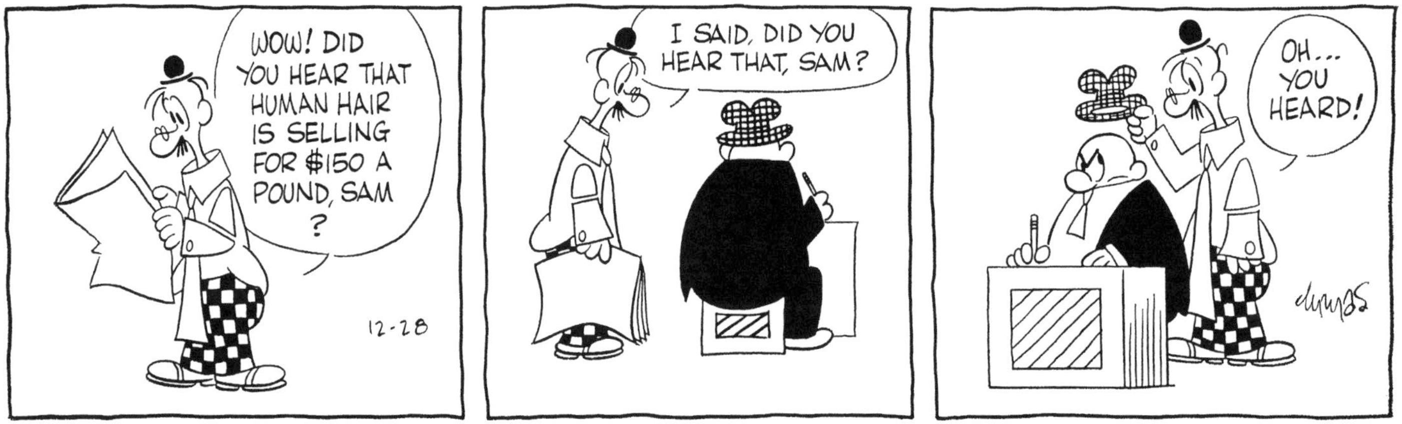
WOW! DID YOU HEAR THAT HUMAN HAIR IS SELLING FOR $150 A POUND, SAM ?
12-28
I SAID, DID YOU HEAR THAT, SAM?
OH... YOU HEARD!
dumas

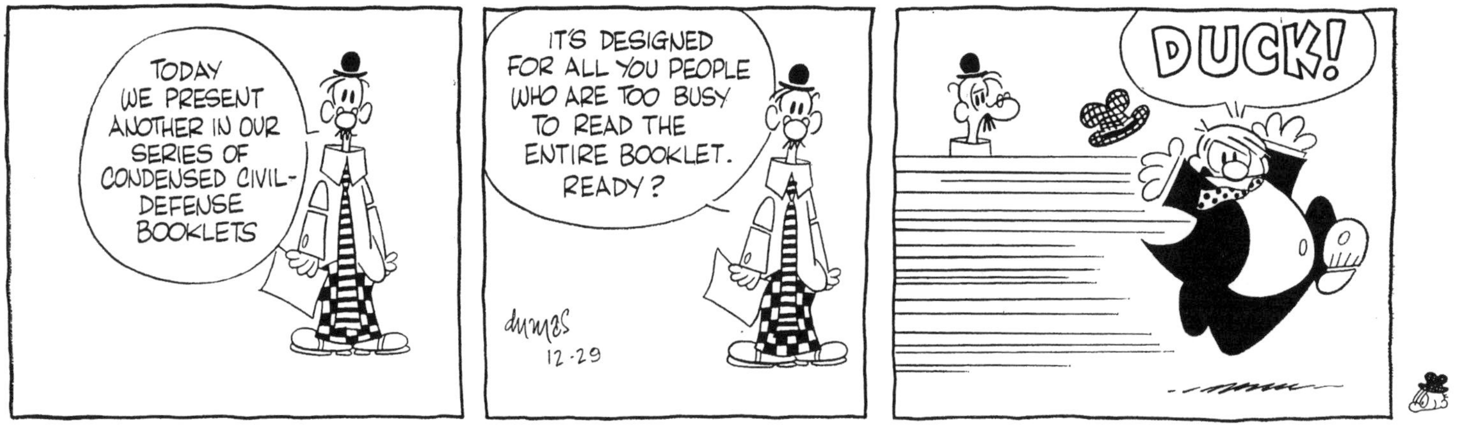
TODAY WE PRESENT ANOTHER IN OUR SERIES OF CONDENSED CIVIL-DEFENSE BOOKLETS
IT'S DESIGNED FOR ALL YOU PEOPLE WHO ARE TOO BUSY TO READ THE ENTIRE BOOKLET. READY?
dumas
12-29
DUCK!

1963

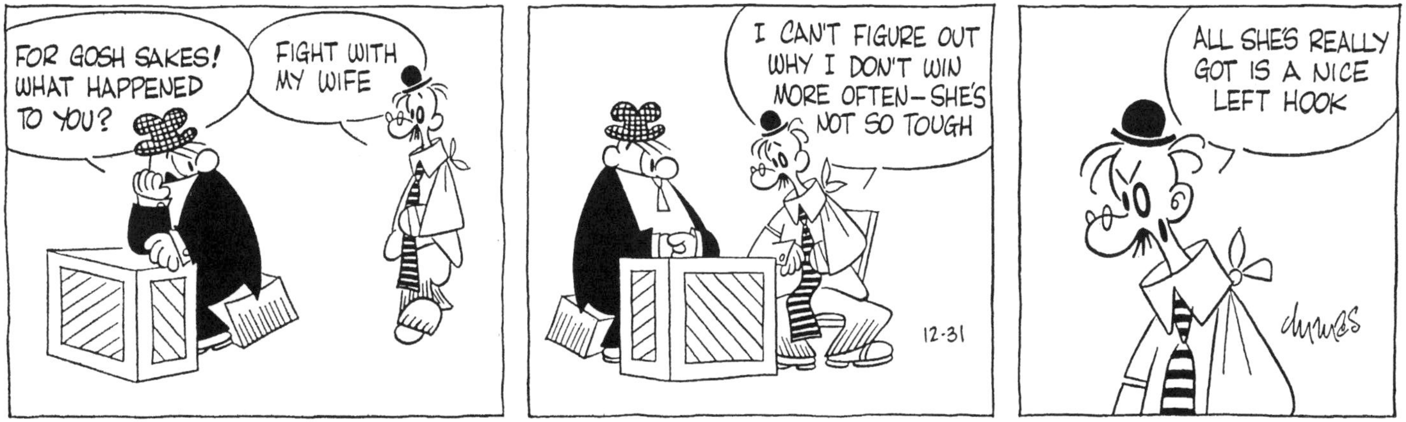

FOR GOSH SAKES! WHAT HAPPENED TO YOU?
FIGHT WITH MY WIFE
I CAN'T FIGURE OUT WHY I DON'T WIN MORE OFTEN—SHE'S NOT SO TOUGH
12-31
ALL SHE'S REALLY GOT IS A NICE LEFT HOOK

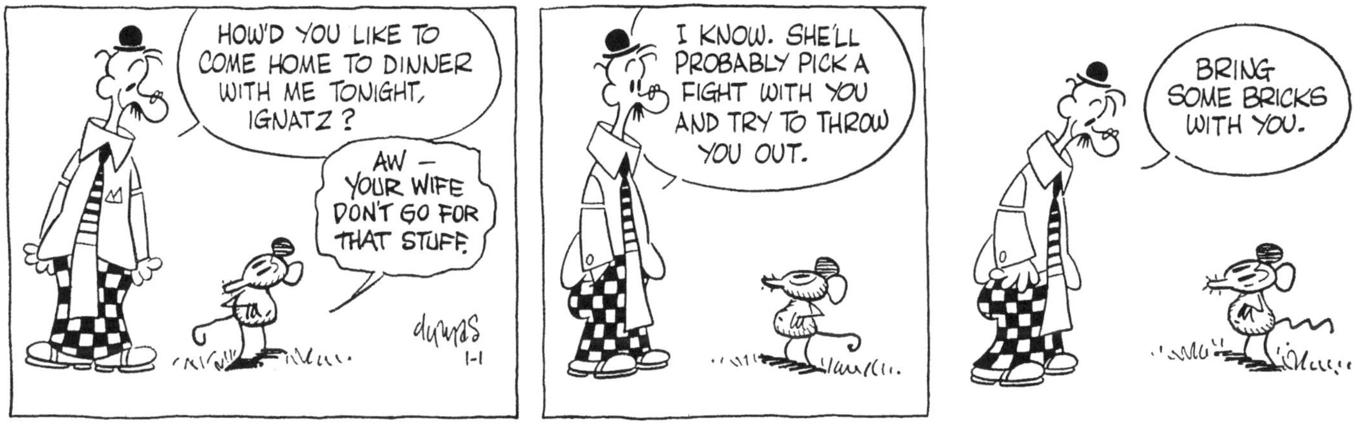

HOW'D YOU LIKE TO COME HOME TO DINNER WITH ME TONIGHT, IGNATZ?
AW — YOUR WIFE DON'T GO FOR THAT STUFF.
1-1
I KNOW. SHE'LL PROBABLY PICK A FIGHT WITH YOU AND TRY TO THROW YOU OUT.
BRING SOME BRICKS WITH YOU.

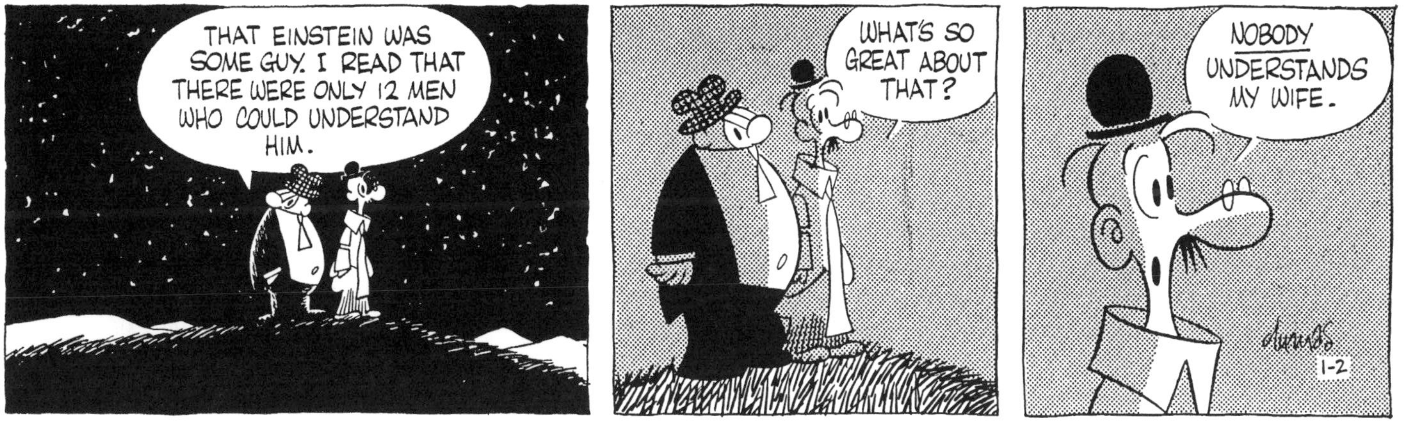

THAT EINSTEIN WAS SOME GUY. I READ THAT THERE WERE ONLY 12 MEN WHO COULD UNDERSTAND HIM.
WHAT'S SO GREAT ABOUT THAT?
NOBODY UNDERSTANDS MY WIFE.
1-2

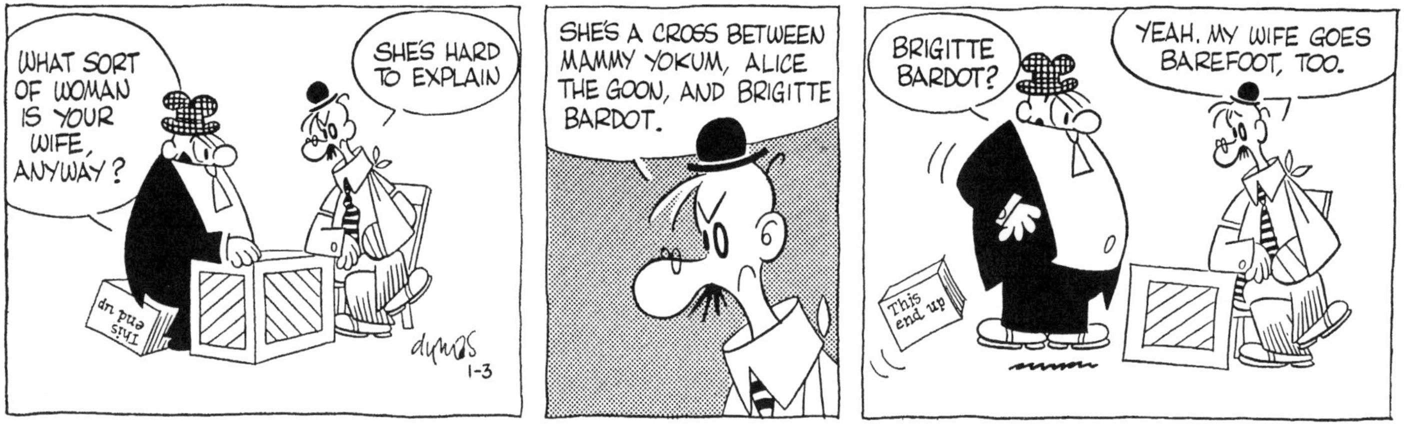
WHAT SORT OF WOMAN IS YOUR WIFE, ANYWAY?
SHE'S HARD TO EXPLAIN
This end up
1-3
SHE'S A CROSS BETWEEN MAMMY YOKUM, ALICE THE GOON, AND BRIGITTE BARDOT.
BRIGITTE BARDOT?
YEAH. MY WIFE GOES BAREFOOT, TOO.
This end up

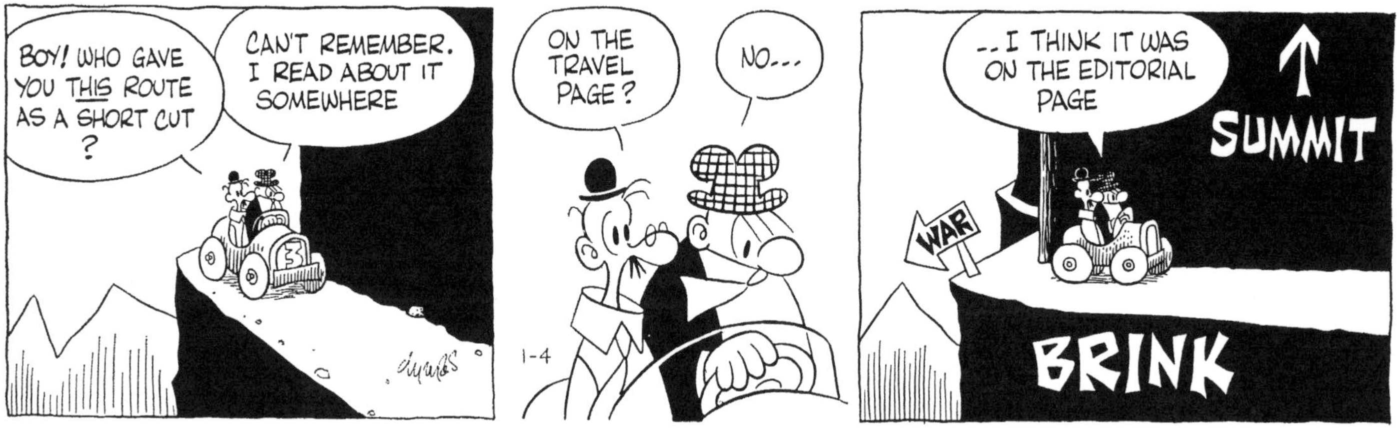
BOY! WHO GAVE YOU THIS ROUTE AS A SHORT CUT?
CAN'T REMEMBER. I READ ABOUT IT SOMEWHERE
1-4
ON THE TRAVEL PAGE?
NO...
..I THINK IT WAS ON THE EDITORIAL PAGE
SUMMIT
WAR
BRINK

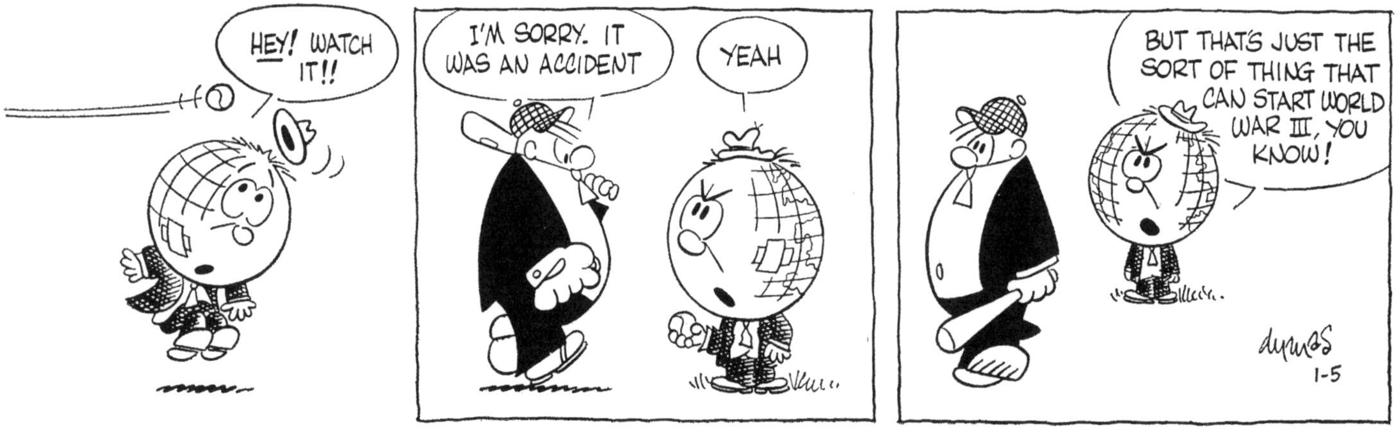
HEY! WATCH IT!!
I'M SORRY. IT WAS AN ACCIDENT
YEAH
BUT THAT'S JUST THE SORT OF THING THAT CAN START WORLD WAR III, YOU KNOW!
1-5

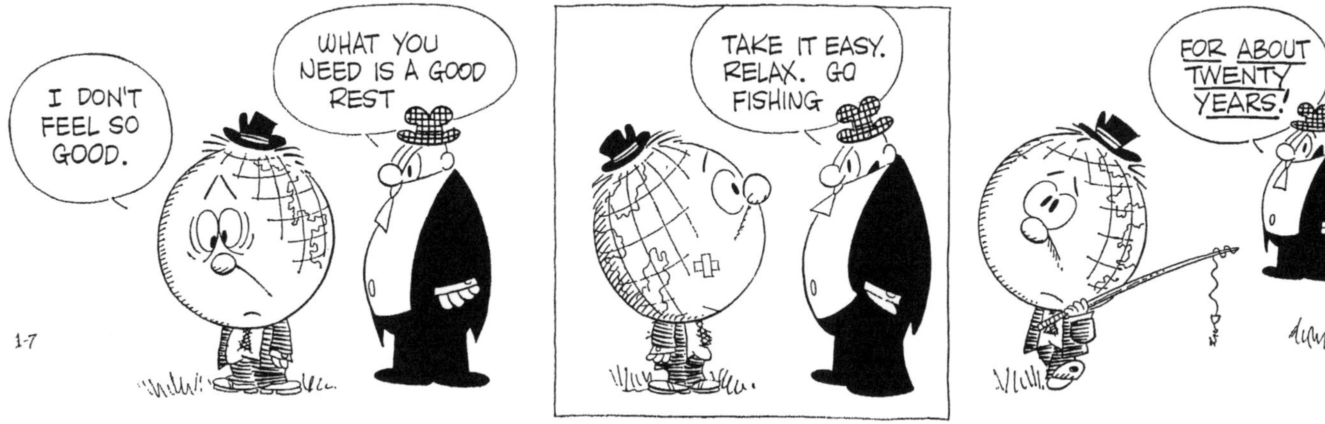
I DON'T FEEL SO GOOD.
WHAT YOU NEED IS A GOOD REST
TAKE IT EASY. RELAX. GO FISHING
FOR ABOUT TWENTY YEARS!
1-7
dumas

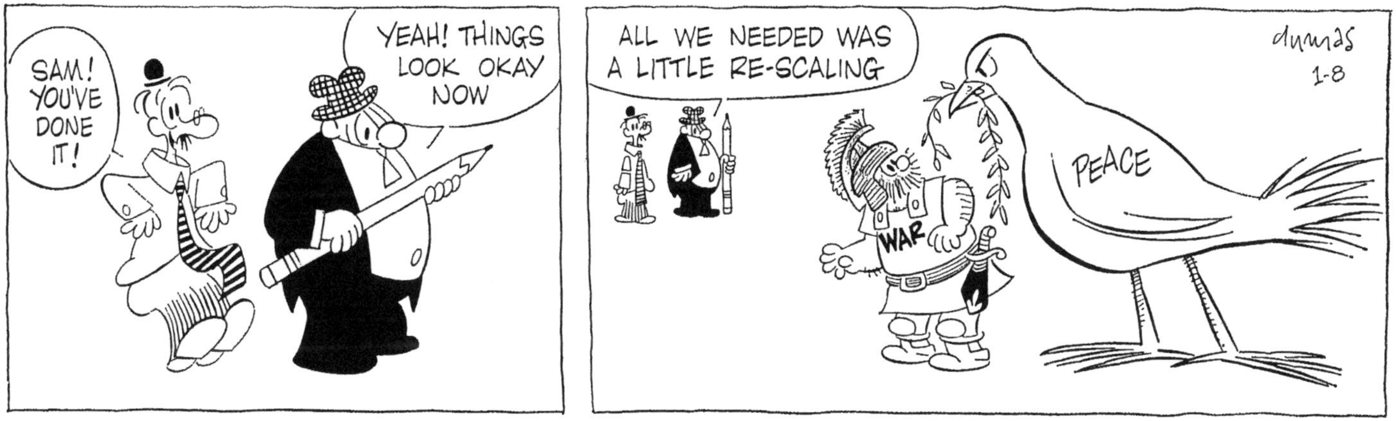
SAM! YOU'VE DONE IT!
YEAH! THINGS LOOK OKAY NOW
ALL WE NEEDED WAS A LITTLE RE-SCALING
WAR
PEACE
dumas
1-8

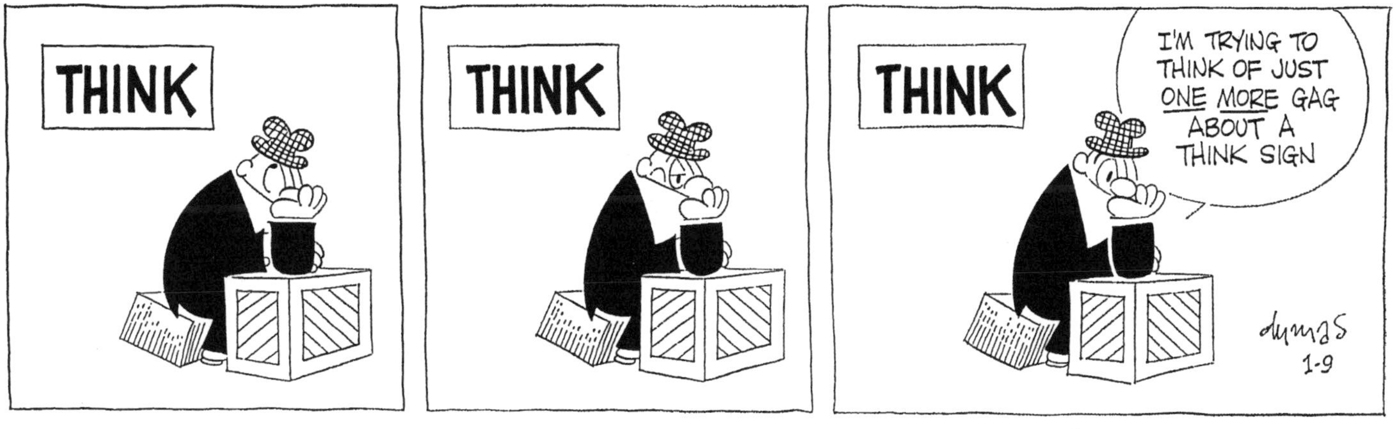
THINK
THINK
THINK
I'M TRYING TO THINK OF JUST ONE MORE GAG ABOUT A THINK SIGN
dumas
1-9

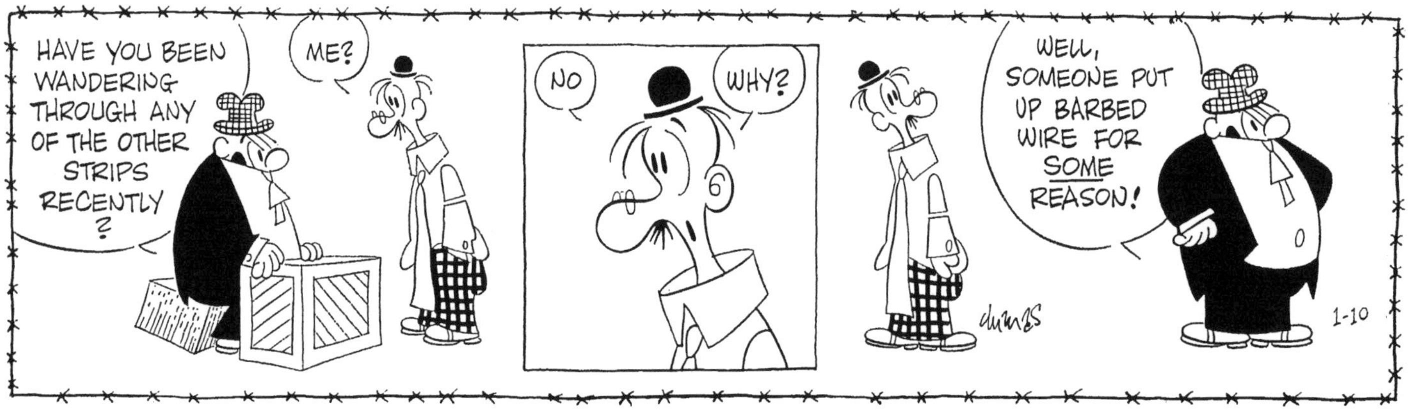
HAVE YOU BEEN WANDERING THROUGH ANY OF THE OTHER STRIPS RECENTLY?
ME?
NO
WHY?
WELL, SOMEONE PUT UP BARBED WIRE FOR SOME REASON!
dumas
1-10

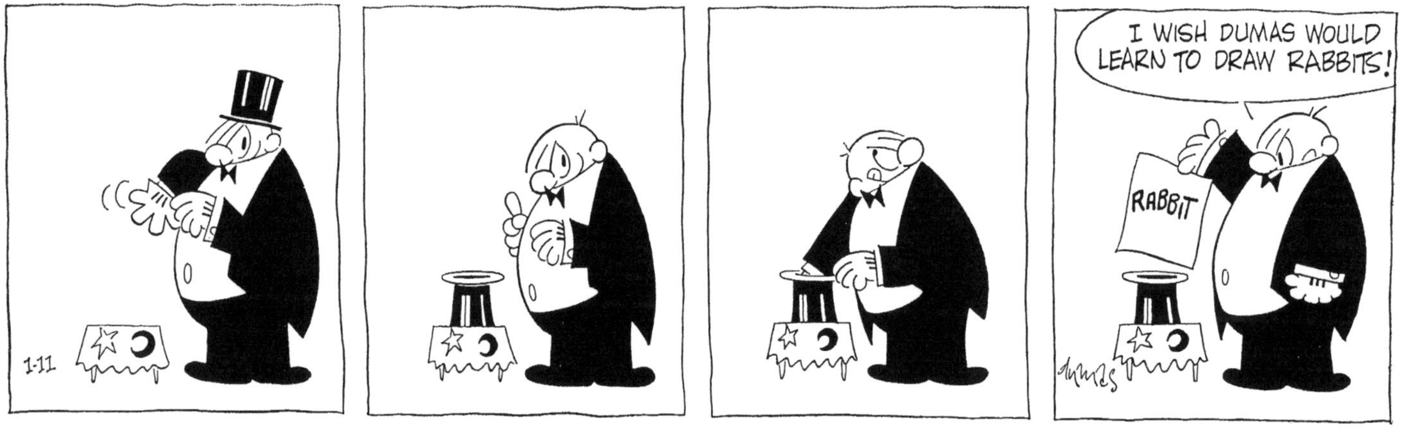
1-11
RABBIT
I WISH DUMAS WOULD LEARN TO DRAW RABBITS!
dumas

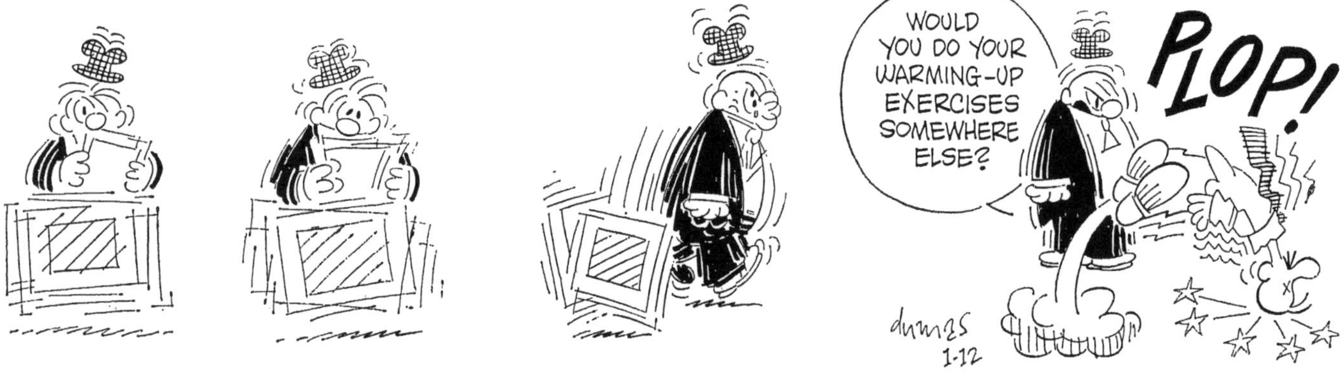
WOULD YOU DO YOUR WARMING-UP EXERCISES SOMEWHERE ELSE?
PLOP!
dumas
1-12

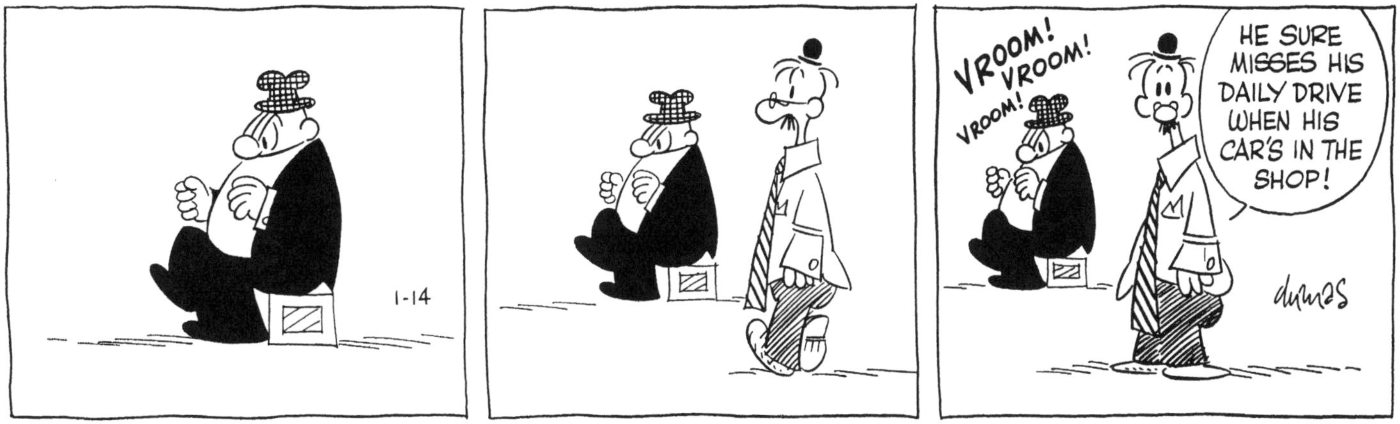
1-14
VROOM! VROOM! VROOM!
HE SURE MISSES HIS DAILY DRIVE WHEN HIS CAR'S IN THE SHOP!
dumas

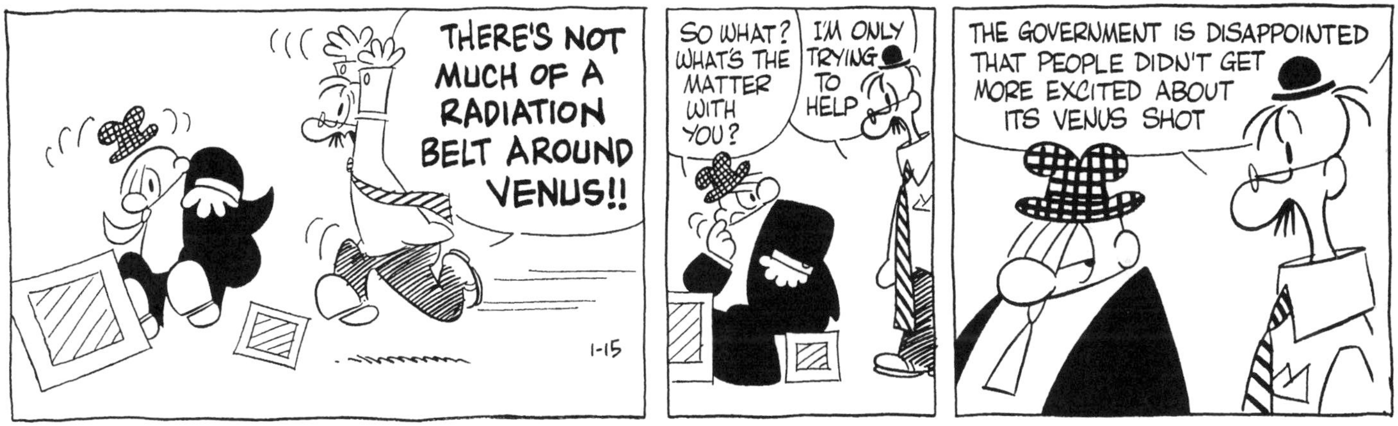
THERE'S NOT MUCH OF A RADIATION BELT AROUND VENUS!!
1-15
SO WHAT? WHAT'S THE MATTER WITH YOU?
I'M ONLY TRYING TO HELP
THE GOVERNMENT IS DISAPPOINTED THAT PEOPLE DIDN'T GET MORE EXCITED ABOUT ITS VENUS SHOT

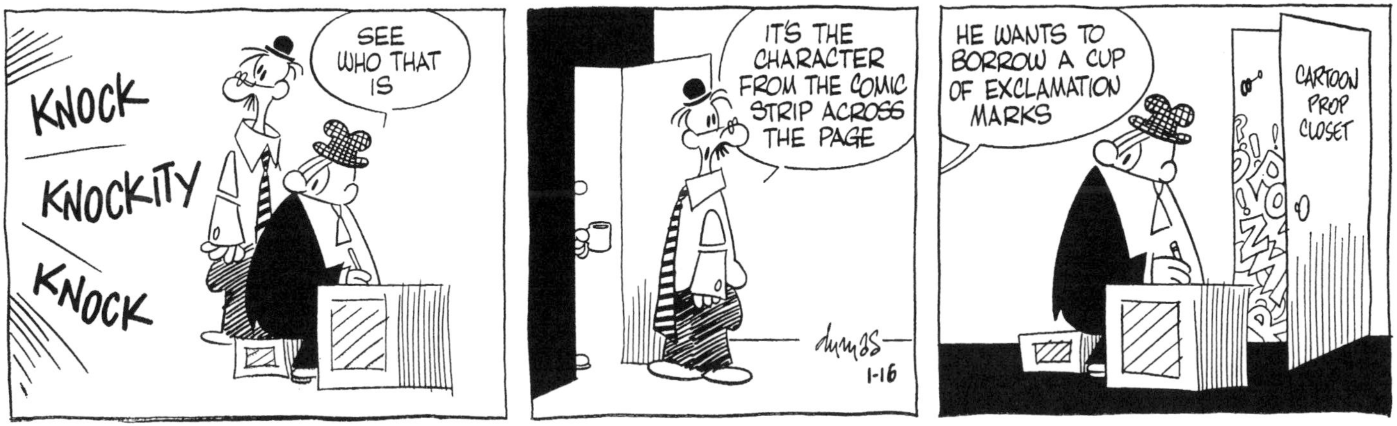
KNOCK
KNOCKITY
KNOCK
SEE WHO THAT IS
IT'S THE CHARACTER FROM THE COMIC STRIP ACROSS THE PAGE
dumas
1-16
HE WANTS TO BORROW A CUP OF EXCLAMATION MARKS
CARTOON PROP CLOSET

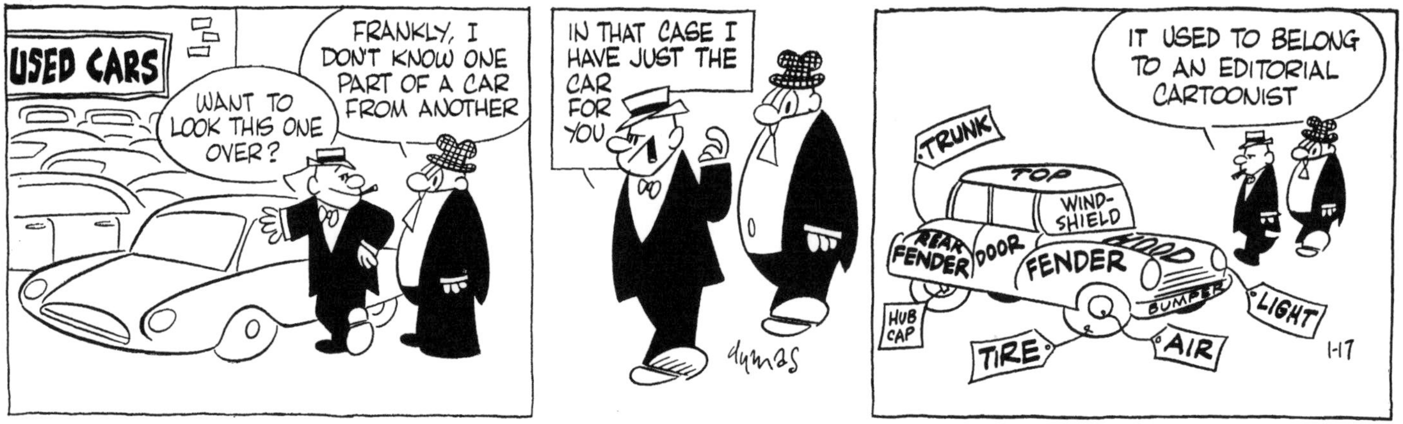
USED CARS
WANT TO LOOK THIS ONE OVER?
FRANKLY, I DON'T KNOW ONE PART OF A CAR FROM ANOTHER
IN THAT CASE I HAVE JUST THE CAR FOR YOU
IT USED TO BELONG TO AN EDITORIAL CARTOONIST
TRUNK
TOP
WIND-SHIELD
REAR FENDER
DOOR
FENDER
HOOD
BUMPER
LIGHT
HUB CAP
TIRE
AIR
dumas
1-17

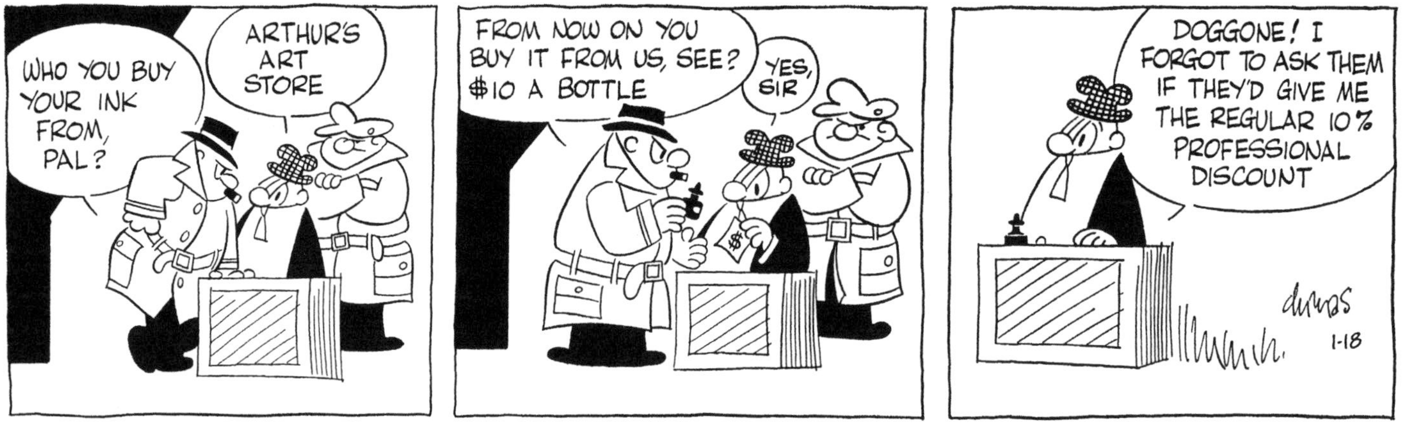
WHO YOU BUY YOUR INK FROM, PAL?
ARTHUR'S ART STORE
FROM NOW ON YOU BUY IT FROM US, SEE? $10 A BOTTLE
YES, SIR
DOGGONE! I FORGOT TO ASK THEM IF THEY'D GIVE ME THE REGULAR 10% PROFESSIONAL DISCOUNT
dumas
1-18

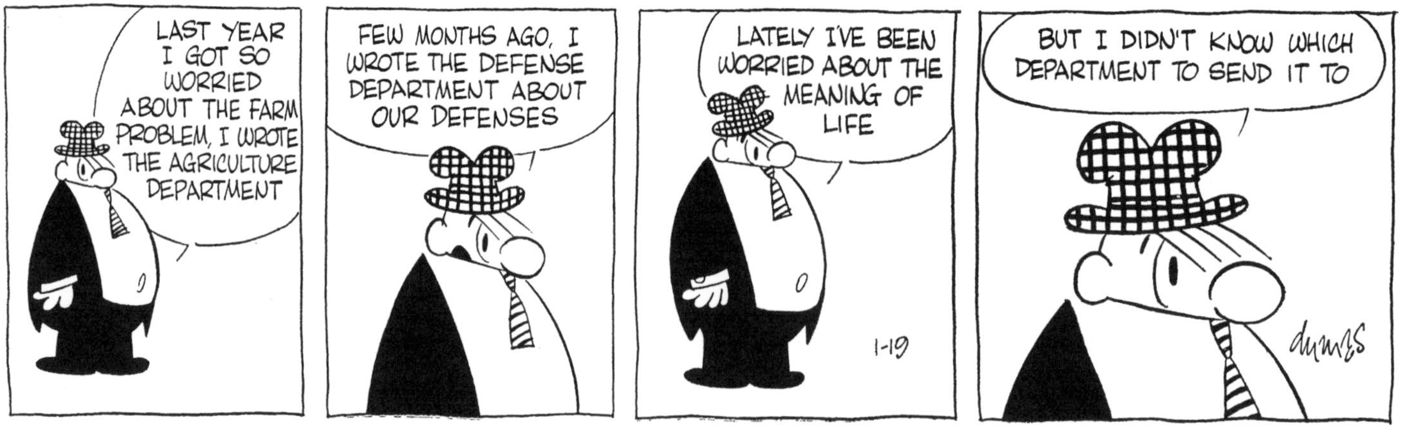
LAST YEAR I GOT SO WORRIED ABOUT THE FARM PROBLEM, I WROTE THE AGRICULTURE DEPARTMENT
FEW MONTHS AGO, I WROTE THE DEFENSE DEPARTMENT ABOUT OUR DEFENSES
LATELY I'VE BEEN WORRIED ABOUT THE MEANING OF LIFE
1-19
BUT I DIDN'T KNOW WHICH DEPARTMENT TO SEND IT TO
dumas

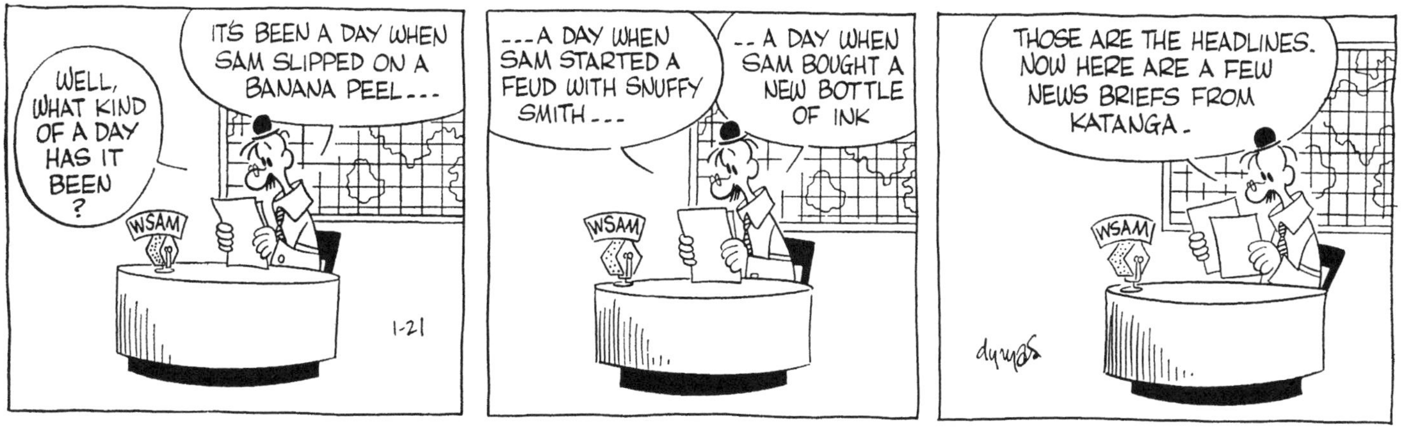
WELL, WHAT KIND OF A DAY HAS IT BEEN ?
IT'S BEEN A DAY WHEN SAM SLIPPED ON A BANANA PEEL---
WSAM
1-21
---A DAY WHEN SAM STARTED A FEUD WITH SNUFFY SMITH---
--A DAY WHEN SAM BOUGHT A NEW BOTTLE OF INK
WSAM
THOSE ARE THE HEADLINES. NOW HERE ARE A FEW NEWS BRIEFS FROM KATANGA.
WSAM
dumas

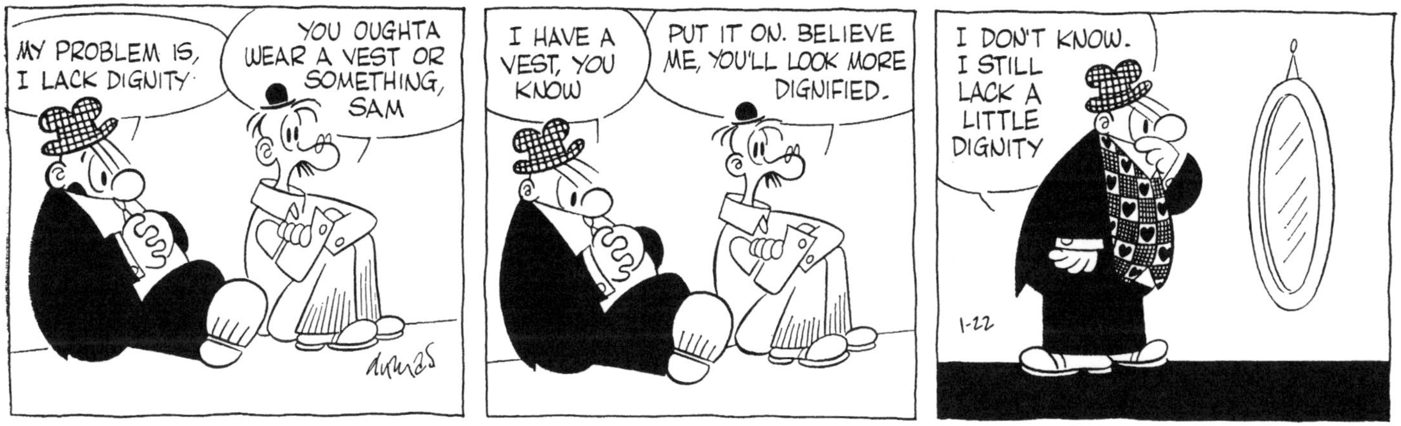
MY PROBLEM IS, I LACK DIGNITY
YOU OUGHTA WEAR A VEST OR SOMETHING, SAM
dumas
I HAVE A VEST, YOU KNOW
PUT IT ON. BELIEVE ME, YOU'LL LOOK MORE DIGNIFIED.
I DON'T KNOW. I STILL LACK A LITTLE DIGNITY
1-22

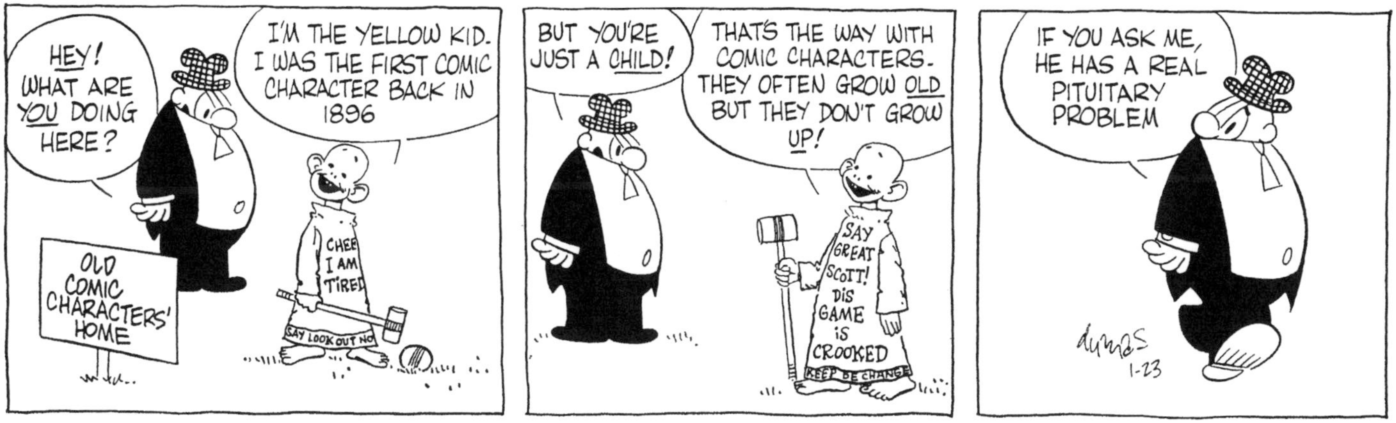
HEY! WHAT ARE YOU DOING HERE?
I'M THE YELLOW KID. I WAS THE FIRST COMIC CHARACTER BACK IN 1896
OLD COMIC CHARACTERS' HOME
CHEE I AM TIRED
BUT YOU'RE JUST A CHILD!
THAT'S THE WAY WITH COMIC CHARACTERS. THEY OFTEN GROW OLD BUT THEY DON'T GROW UP!
SAY GREAT SCOTT! DIS GAME IS CROOKED
KEEP DE CHANGE
IF YOU ASK ME, HE HAS A REAL PITUITARY PROBLEM
dumas
1-23

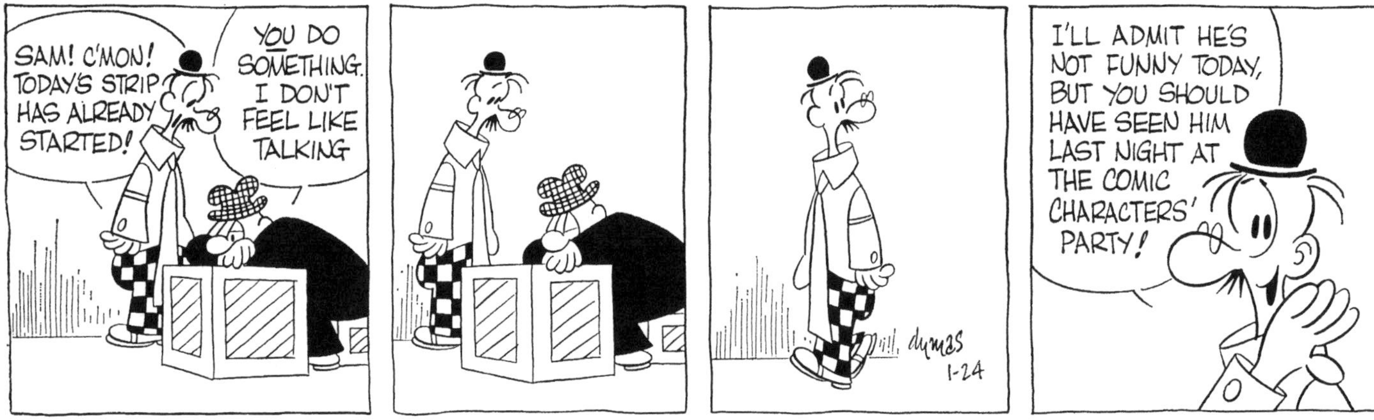
SAM! C'MON! TODAY'S STRIP HAS ALREADY STARTED!
YOU DO SOMETHING. I DON'T FEEL LIKE TALKING
I'LL ADMIT HE'S NOT FUNNY TODAY, BUT YOU SHOULD HAVE SEEN HIM LAST NIGHT AT THE COMIC CHARACTERS' PARTY!
1-24

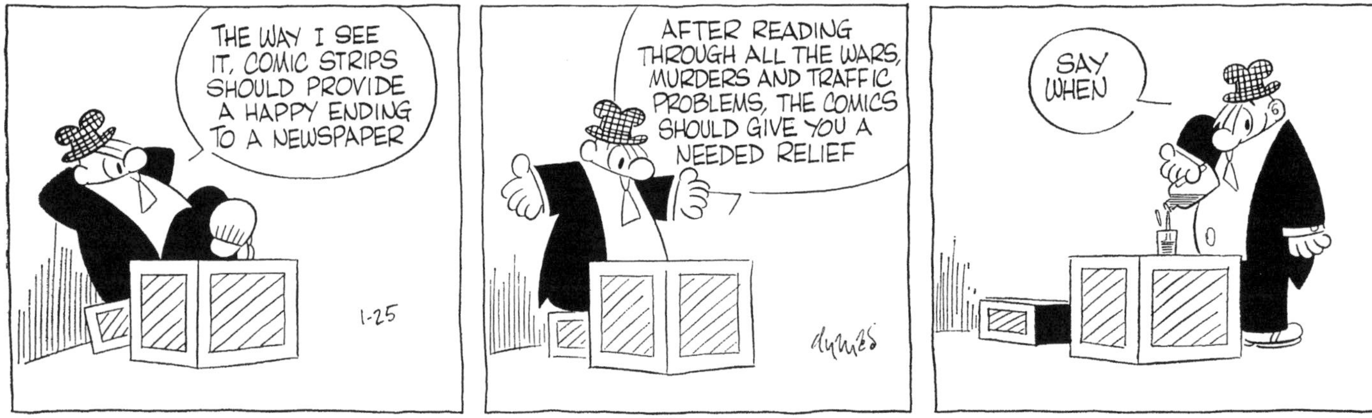
THE WAY I SEE IT, COMIC STRIPS SHOULD PROVIDE A HAPPY ENDING TO A NEWSPAPER
1-25
AFTER READING THROUGH ALL THE WARS, MURDERS AND TRAFFIC PROBLEMS, THE COMICS SHOULD GIVE YOU A NEEDED RELIEF
SAY WHEN

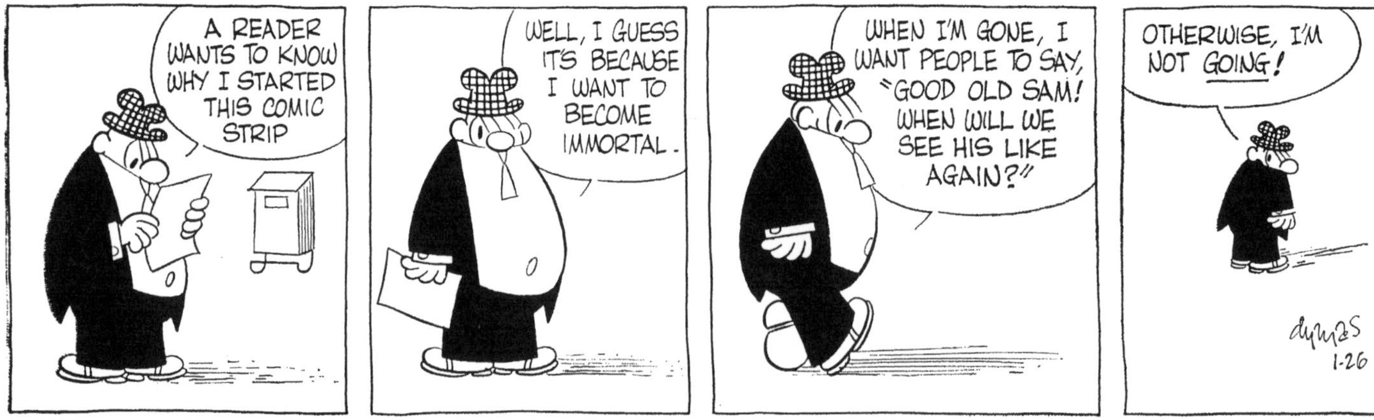
A READER WANTS TO KNOW WHY I STARTED THIS COMIC STRIP
WELL, I GUESS IT'S BECAUSE I WANT TO BECOME IMMORTAL.
WHEN I'M GONE, I WANT PEOPLE TO SAY, "GOOD OLD SAM! WHEN WILL WE SEE HIS LIKE AGAIN?"
OTHERWISE, I'M NOT GOING!
1-26

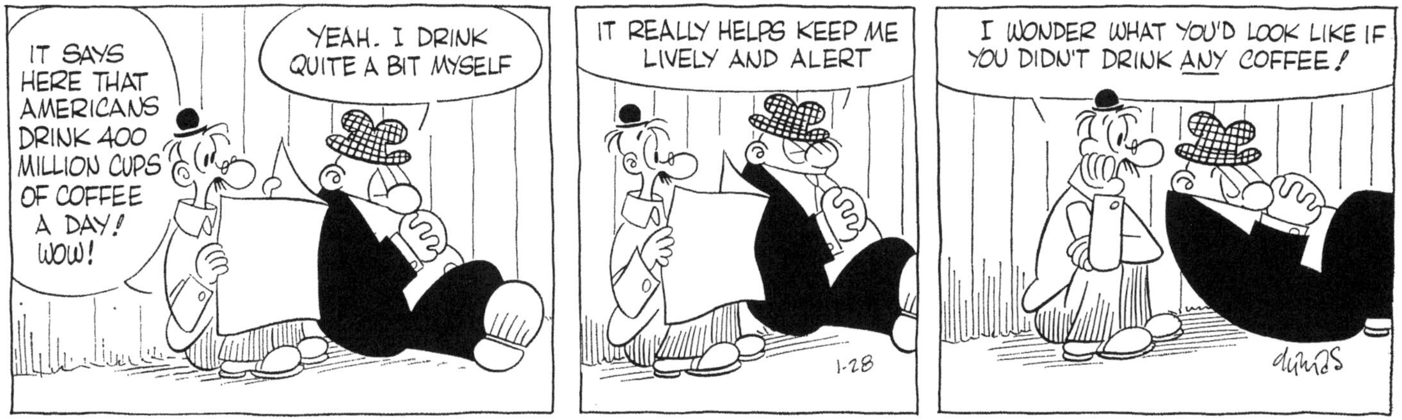
IT SAYS HERE THAT AMERICANS DRINK 400 MILLION CUPS OF COFFEE A DAY! WOW!
YEAH. I DRINK QUITE A BIT MYSELF
IT REALLY HELPS KEEP ME LIVELY AND ALERT
1-28
I WONDER WHAT YOU'D LOOK LIKE IF YOU DIDN'T DRINK ANY COFFEE!
dumas

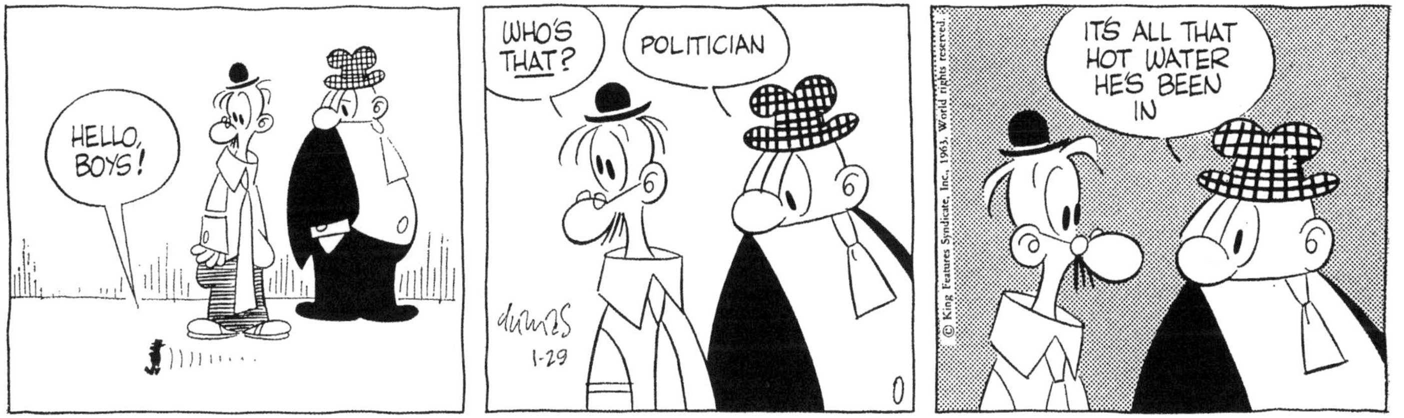
HELLO, BOYS!
WHO'S THAT?
POLITICIAN
dumas
1-29
IT'S ALL THAT HOT WATER HE'S BEEN IN
© King Features Syndicate, Inc., 1963. World rights reserved.

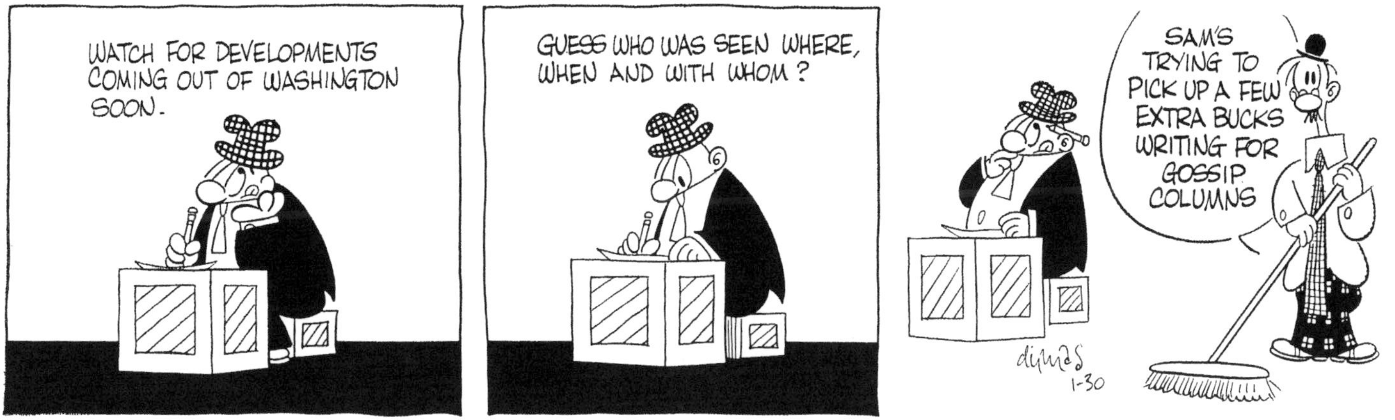
WATCH FOR DEVELOPMENTS COMING OUT OF WASHINGTON SOON.
GUESS WHO WAS SEEN WHERE, WHEN AND WITH WHOM?
SAM'S TRYING TO PICK UP A FEW EXTRA BUCKS WRITING FOR GOSSIP COLUMNS
dumas
1-30

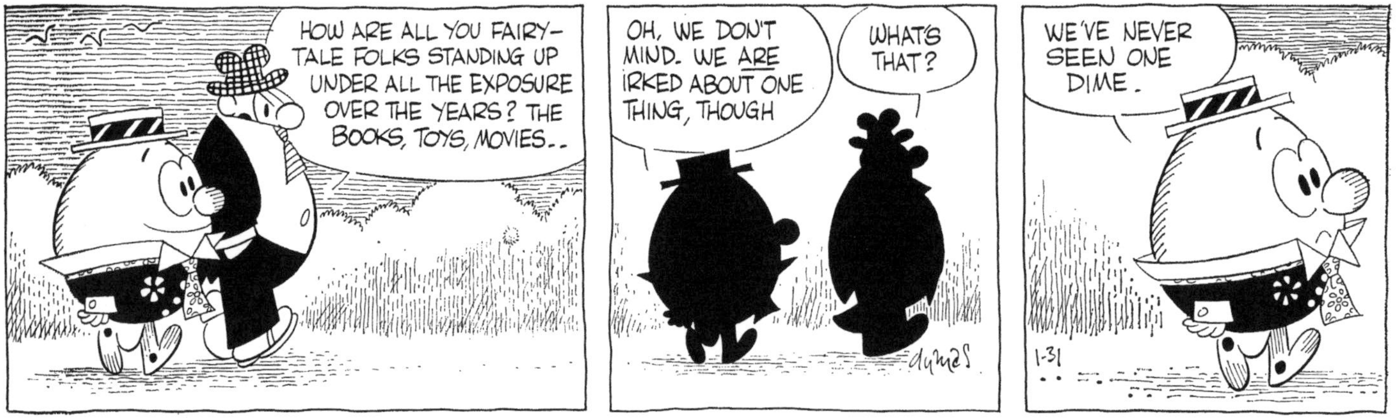
HOW ARE ALL YOU FAIRY-TALE FOLKS STANDING UP UNDER ALL THE EXPOSURE OVER THE YEARS? THE BOOKS, TOYS, MOVIES--
OH, WE DON'T MIND. WE ARE IRKED ABOUT ONE THING, THOUGH
WHAT'S THAT?
WE'VE NEVER SEEN ONE DIME.
1-31

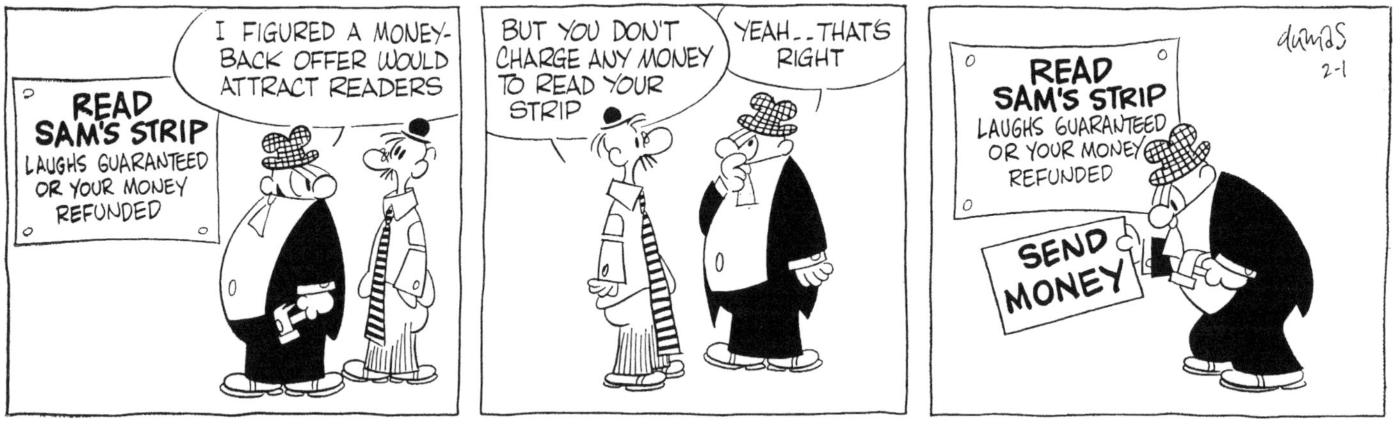
READ SAM'S STRIP LAUGHS GUARANTEED OR YOUR MONEY REFUNDED
I FIGURED A MONEY-BACK OFFER WOULD ATTRACT READERS
BUT YOU DON'T CHARGE ANY MONEY TO READ YOUR STRIP
YEAH--THAT'S RIGHT
2-1
READ SAM'S STRIP LAUGHS GUARANTEED OR YOUR MONEY REFUNDED
SEND MONEY

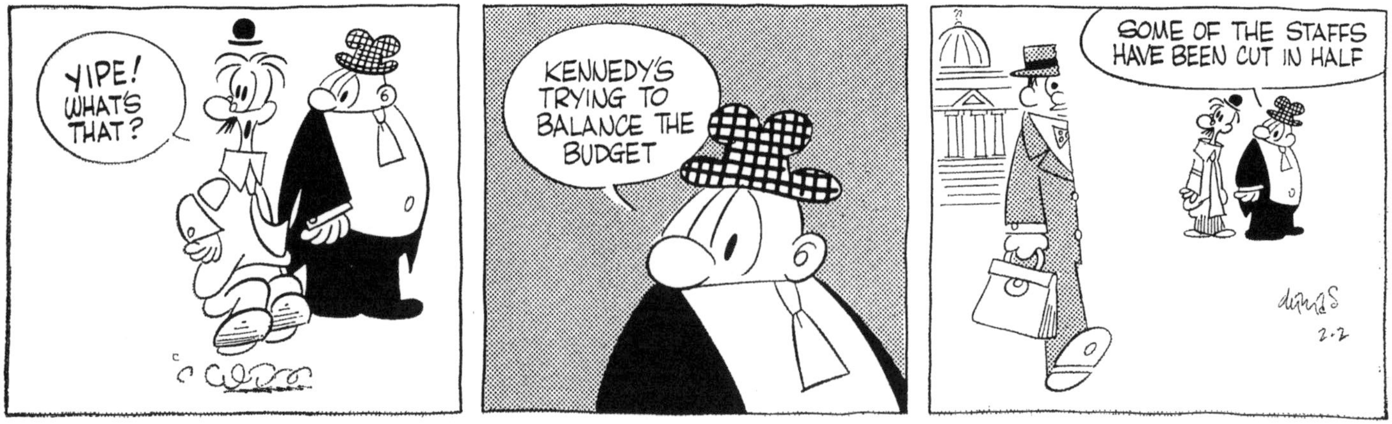
YIPE! WHAT'S THAT?
KENNEDY'S TRYING TO BALANCE THE BUDGET
SOME OF THE STAFFS HAVE BEEN CUT IN HALF
2-2

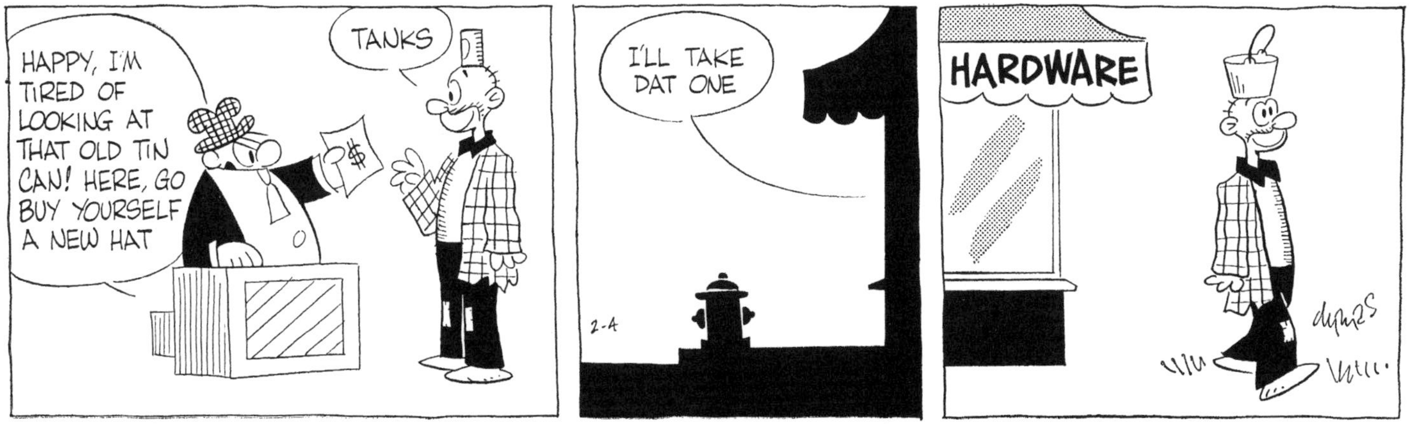
HAPPY, I'M TIRED OF LOOKING AT THAT OLD TIN CAN! HERE, GO BUY YOURSELF A NEW HAT
$
TANKS
I'LL TAKE DAT ONE
2-4
HARDWARE
dumas

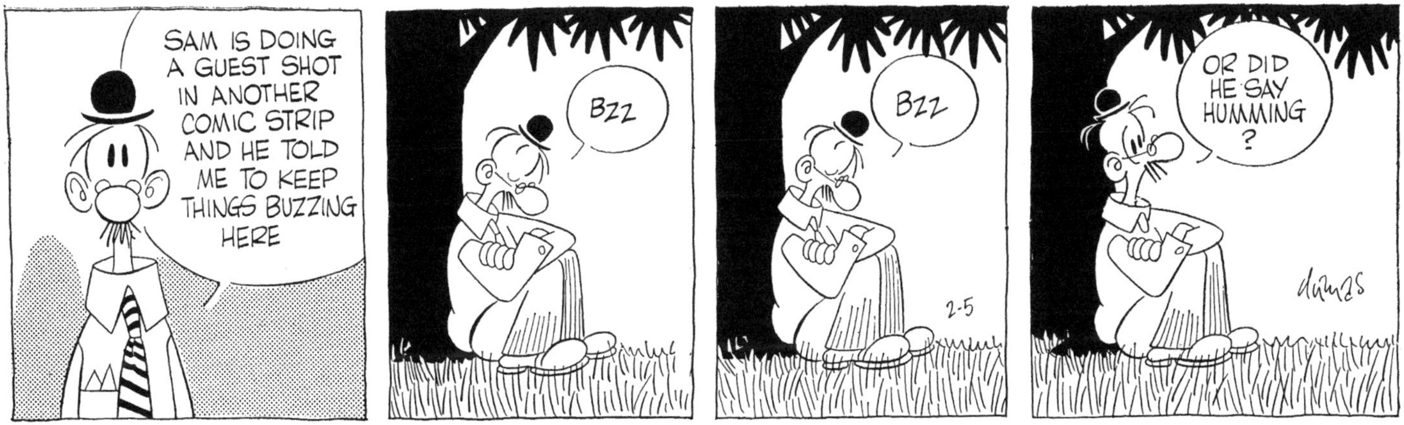
SAM IS DOING A GUEST SHOT IN ANOTHER COMIC STRIP AND HE TOLD ME TO KEEP THINGS BUZZING HERE
BZZ
BZZ
2-5
OR DID HE SAY HUMMING ?
dumas

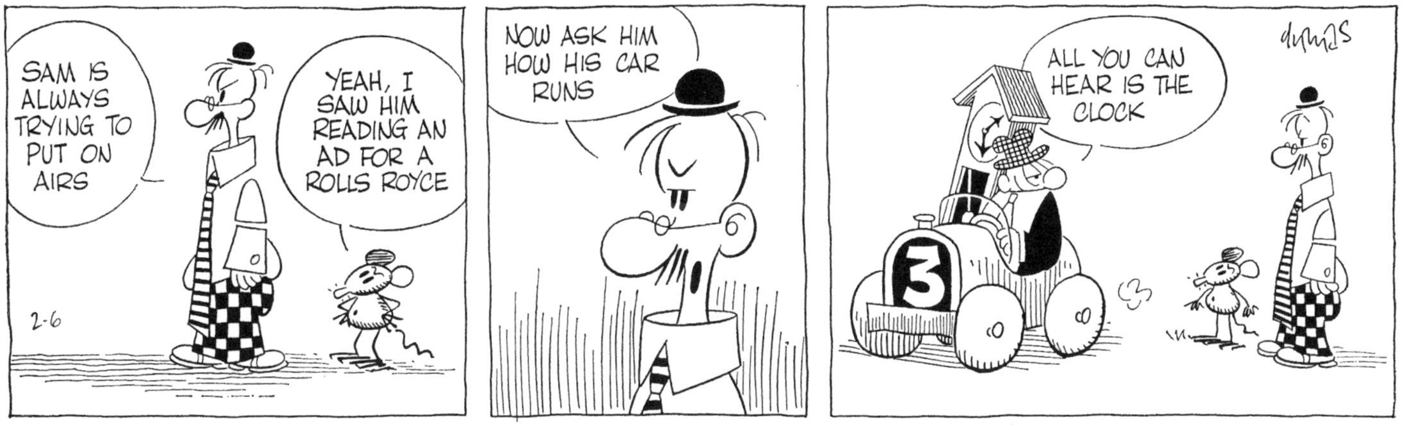
SAM IS ALWAYS TRYING TO PUT ON AIRS
YEAH, I SAW HIM READING AN AD FOR A ROLLS ROYCE
2-6
NOW ASK HIM HOW HIS CAR RUNS
dumas
ALL YOU CAN HEAR IS THE CLOCK
3

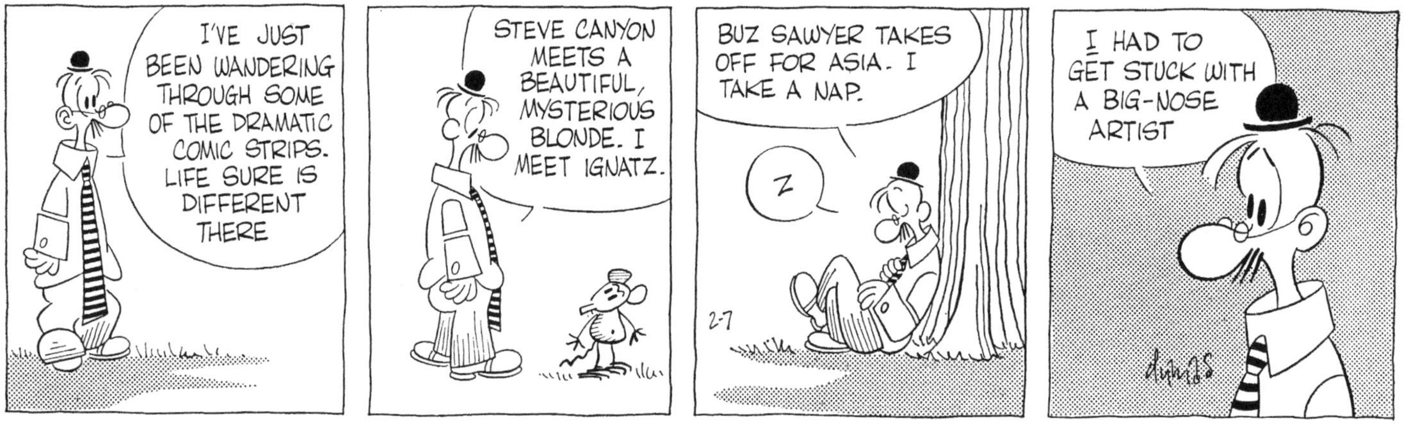
I'VE JUST BEEN WANDERING THROUGH SOME OF THE DRAMATIC COMIC STRIPS. LIFE SURE IS DIFFERENT THERE
STEVE CANYON MEETS A BEAUTIFUL, MYSTERIOUS BLONDE. I MEET IGNATZ.
BUZ SAWYER TAKES OFF FOR ASIA. I TAKE A NAP.
Z
2-7
I HAD TO GET STUCK WITH A BIG-NOSE ARTIST

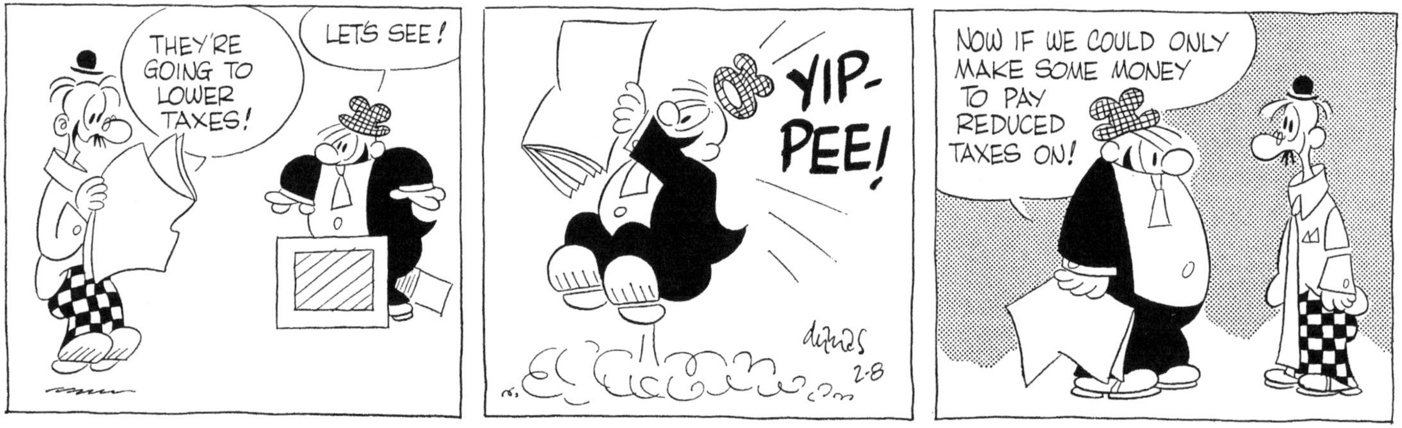
THEY'RE GOING TO LOWER TAXES!
LET'S SEE!
YIP-PEE!
2-8
NOW IF WE COULD ONLY MAKE SOME MONEY TO PAY REDUCED TAXES ON!

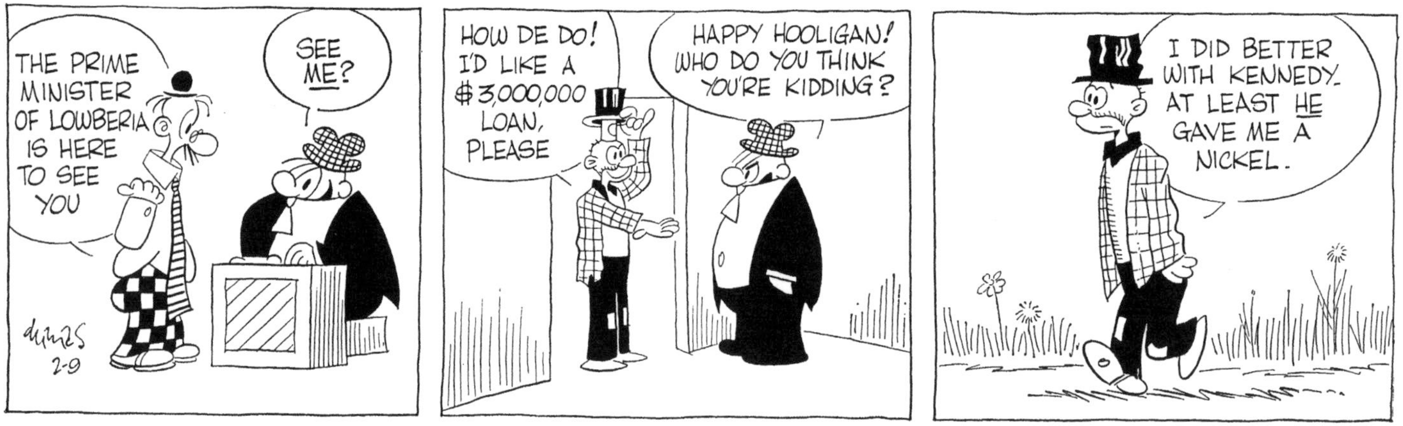
THE PRIME MINISTER OF LOWBERIA IS HERE TO SEE YOU
SEE ME?
2-9
HOW DE DO! I'D LIKE A $3,000,000 LOAN, PLEASE
HAPPY HOOLIGAN! WHO DO YOU THINK YOU'RE KIDDING?
I DID BETTER WITH KENNEDY. AT LEAST HE GAVE ME A NICKEL.

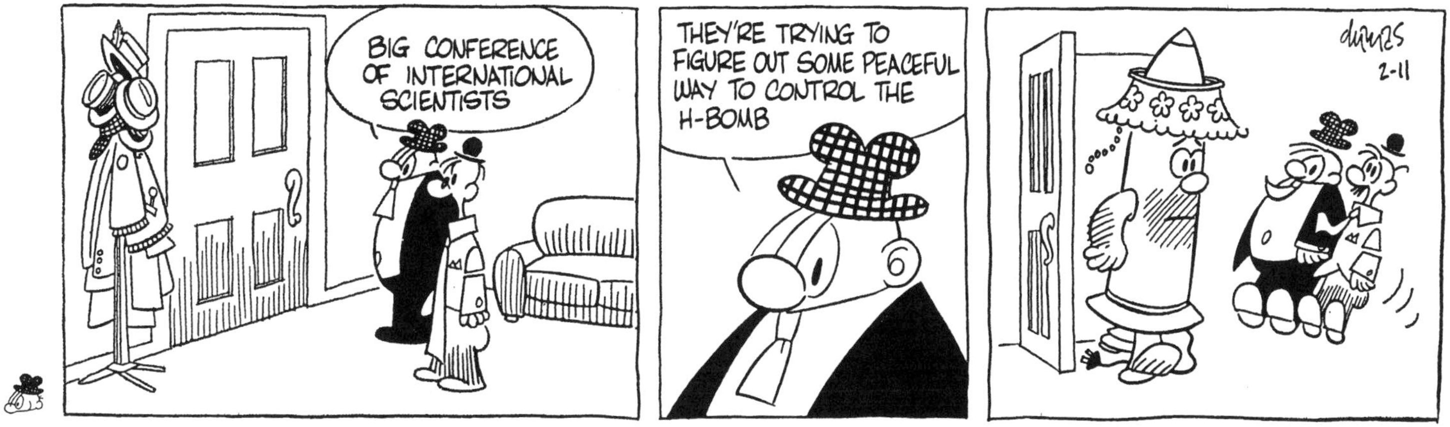
BIG CONFERENCE OF INTERNATIONAL SCIENTISTS
THEY'RE TRYING TO FIGURE OUT SOME PEACEFUL WAY TO CONTROL THE H-BOMB

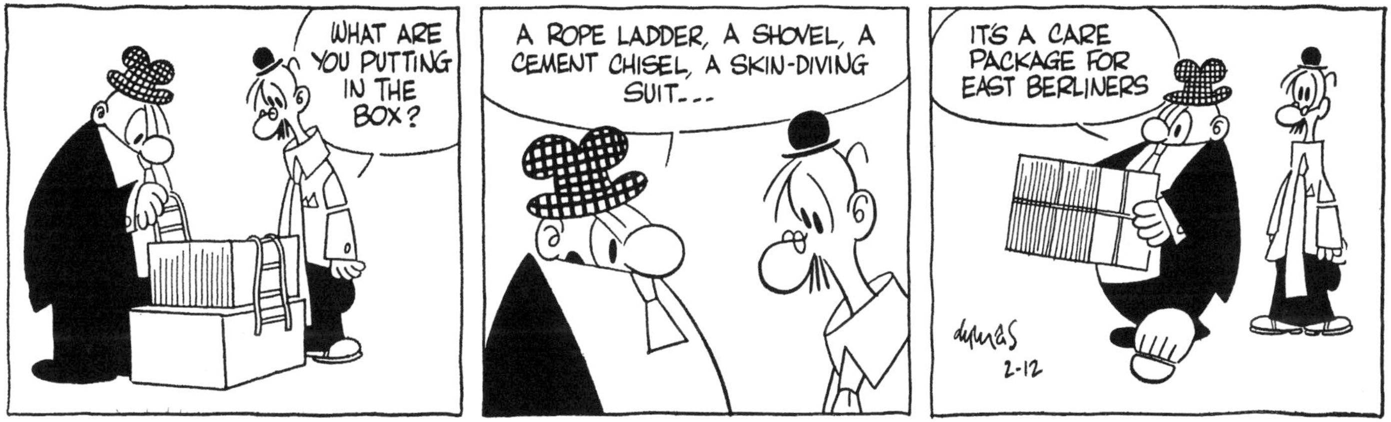
WHAT ARE YOU PUTTING IN THE BOX?
A ROPE LADDER, A SHOVEL, A CEMENT CHISEL, A SKIN-DIVING SUIT...
IT'S A CARE PACKAGE FOR EAST BERLINERS

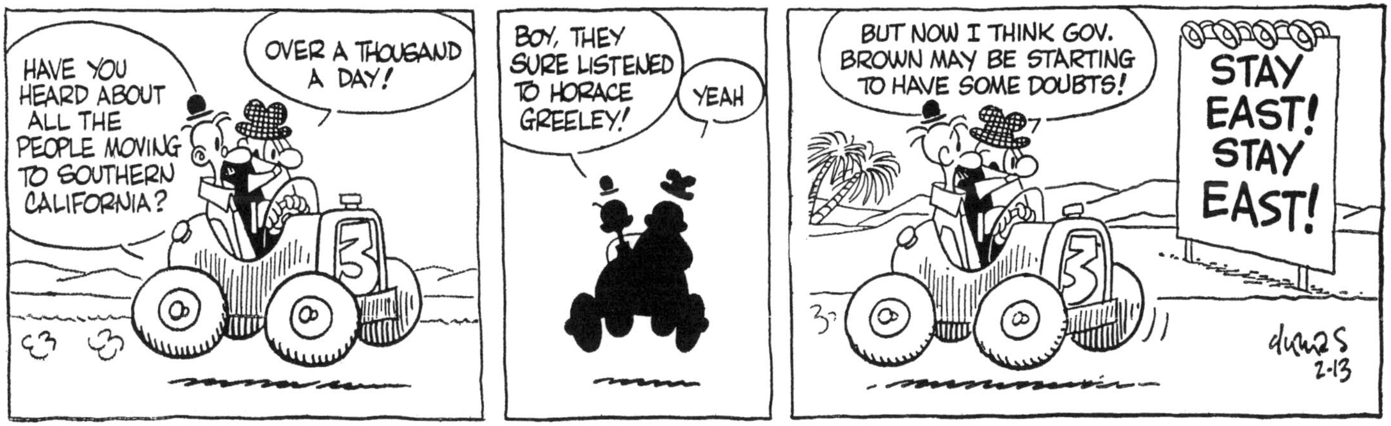
HAVE YOU HEARD ABOUT ALL THE PEOPLE MOVING TO SOUTHERN CALIFORNIA?
OVER A THOUSAND A DAY!
BOY, THEY SURE LISTENED TO HORACE GREELEY!
YEAH
BUT NOW I THINK GOV. BROWN MAY BE STARTING TO HAVE SOME DOUBTS!
STAY EAST! STAY EAST!

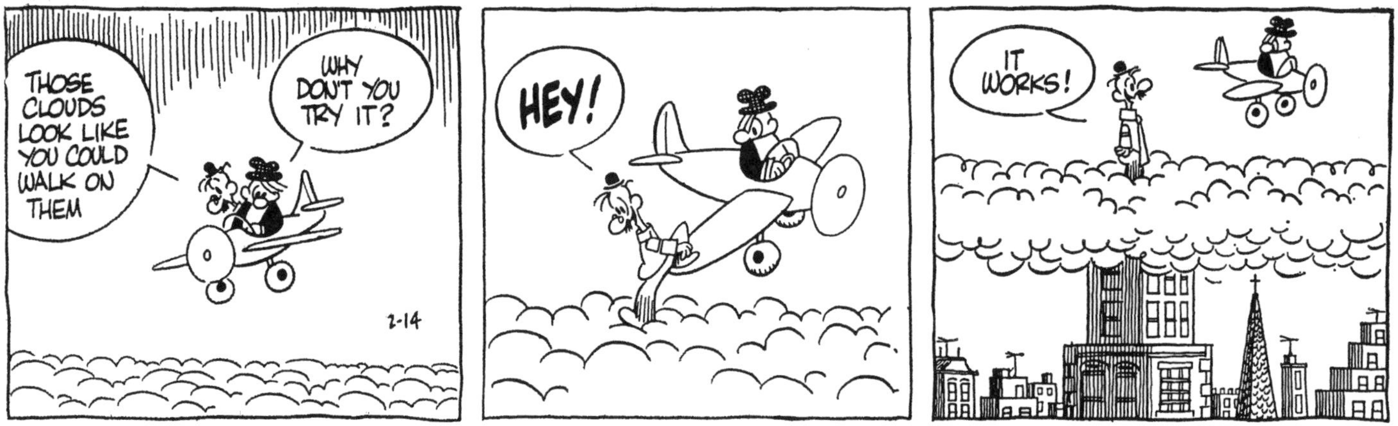
THOSE CLOUDS LOOK LIKE YOU COULD WALK ON THEM
WHY DON'T YOU TRY IT?
2-14
HEY!
IT WORKS!

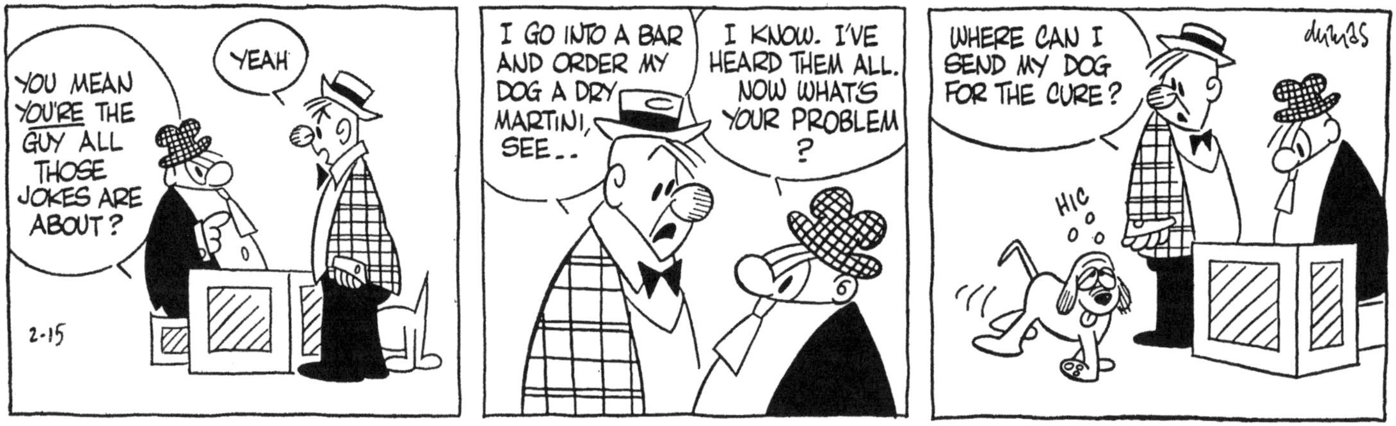
YOU MEAN YOU'RE THE GUY ALL THOSE JOKES ARE ABOUT?
YEAH
2-15
I GO INTO A BAR AND ORDER MY DOG A DRY MARTINI, SEE...
I KNOW. I'VE HEARD THEM ALL. NOW WHAT'S YOUR PROBLEM?
WHERE CAN I SEND MY DOG FOR THE CURE?
HIC

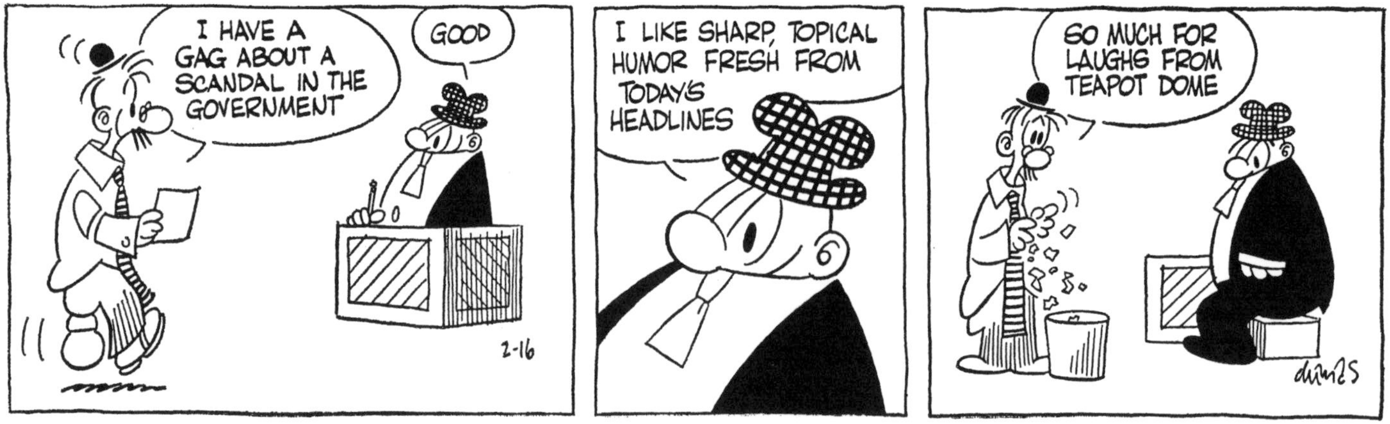
I HAVE A GAG ABOUT A SCANDAL IN THE GOVERNMENT
GOOD
2-16
I LIKE SHARP, TOPICAL HUMOR FRESH FROM TODAY'S HEADLINES
SO MUCH FOR LAUGHS FROM TEAPOT DOME

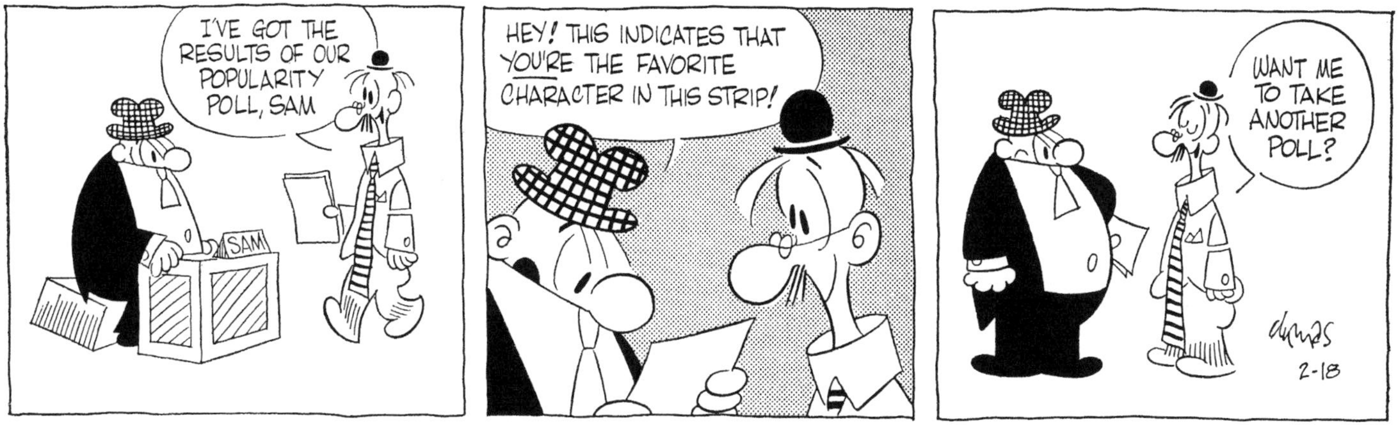
I'VE GOT THE RESULTS OF OUR POPULARITY POLL, SAM
SAM
HEY! THIS INDICATES THAT YOU'RE THE FAVORITE CHARACTER IN THIS STRIP!
WANT ME TO TAKE ANOTHER POLL?
2-18

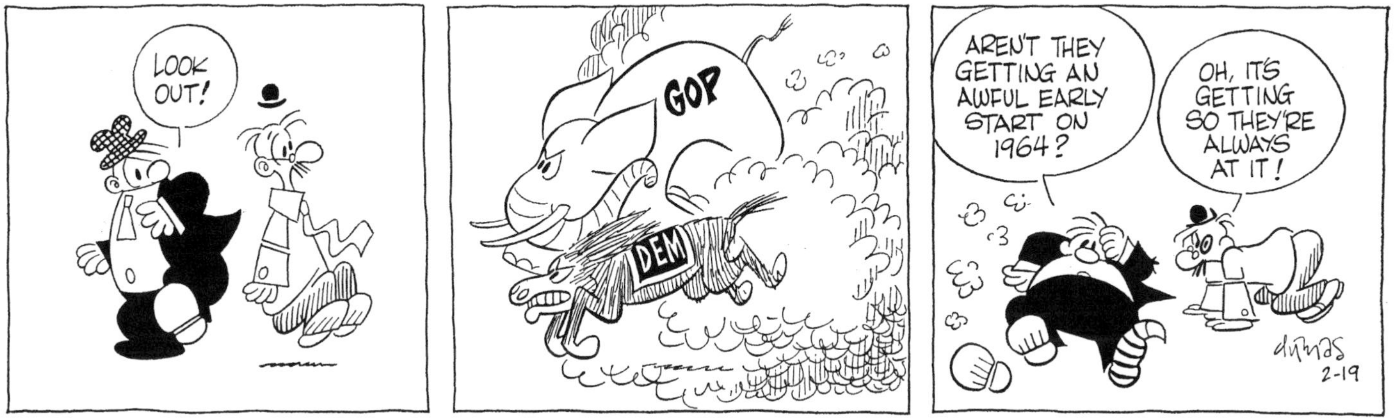
LOOK OUT!
GOP
DEM
AREN'T THEY GETTING AN AWFUL EARLY START ON 1964?
OH, IT'S GETTING SO THEY'RE ALWAYS AT IT!
2-19

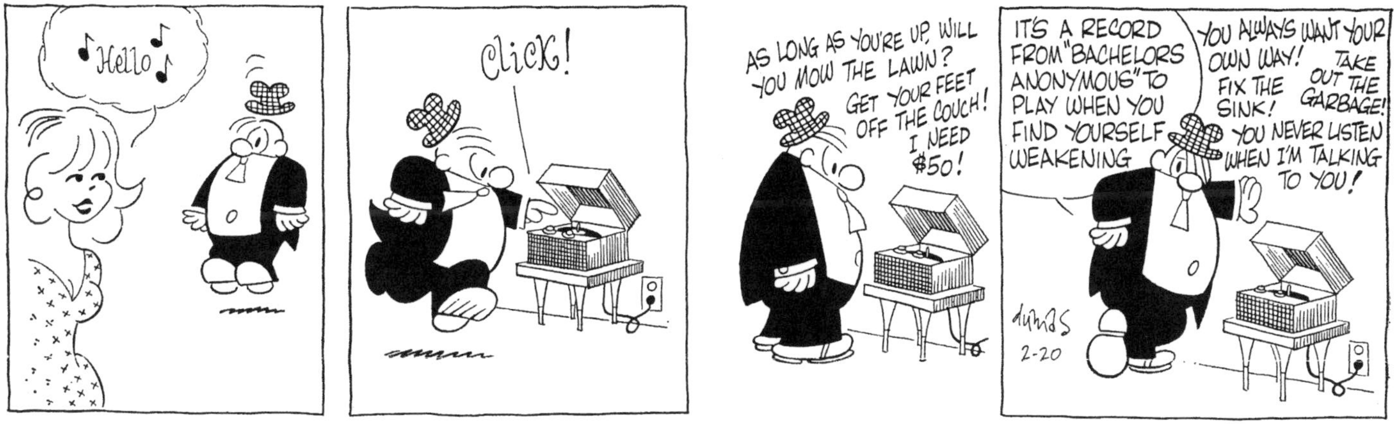
Hello
CLICK!
AS LONG AS YOU'RE UP, WILL YOU MOW THE LAWN?
GET YOUR FEET OFF THE COUCH! I NEED $50!
IT'S A RECORD FROM "BACHELORS ANONYMOUS" TO PLAY WHEN YOU FIND YOURSELF WEAKENING
YOU ALWAYS WANT YOUR OWN WAY! FIX THE SINK! TAKE OUT THE GARBAGE! YOU NEVER LISTEN WHEN I'M TALKING TO YOU!
2-20

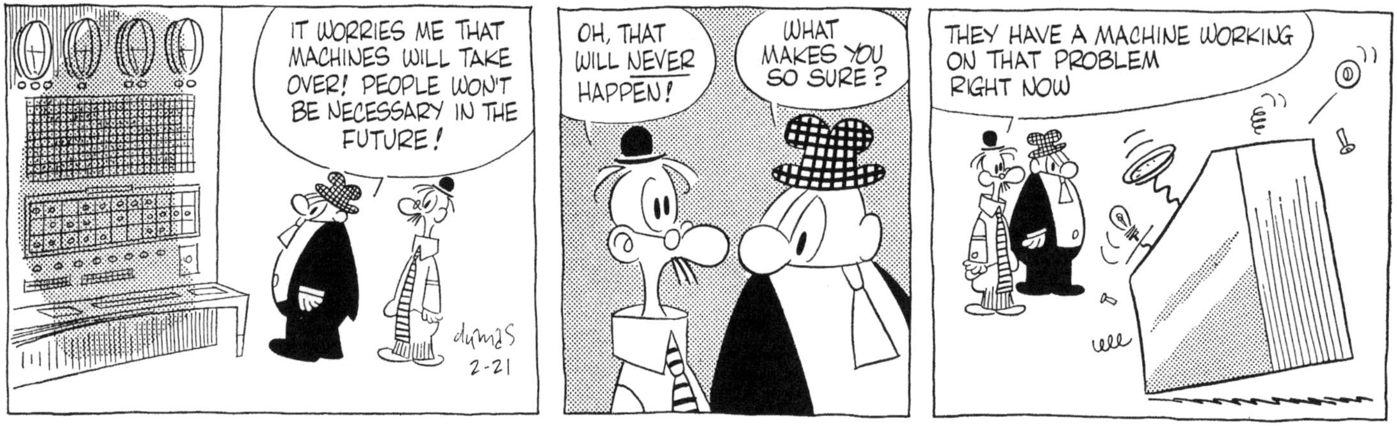
IT WORRIES ME THAT MACHINES WILL TAKE OVER! PEOPLE WON'T BE NECESSARY IN THE FUTURE!
dumas 2-21
OH, THAT WILL NEVER HAPPEN!
WHAT MAKES YOU SO SURE?
THEY HAVE A MACHINE WORKING ON THAT PROBLEM RIGHT NOW

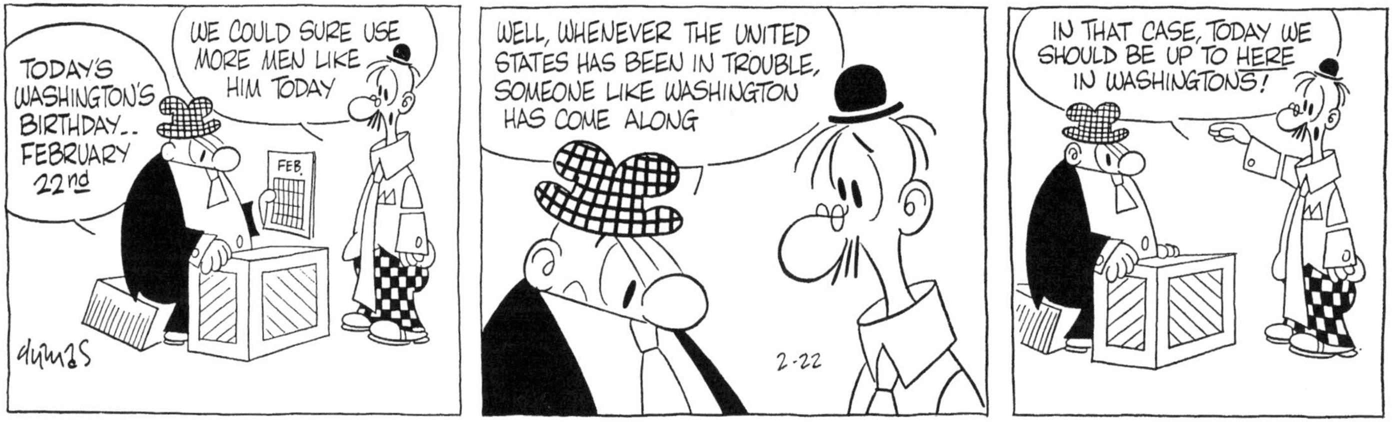
TODAY'S WASHINGTON'S BIRTHDAY.. FEBRUARY 22nd
WE COULD SURE USE MORE MEN LIKE HIM TODAY
FEB.
dumas
WELL, WHENEVER THE UNITED STATES HAS BEEN IN TROUBLE, SOMEONE LIKE WASHINGTON HAS COME ALONG
2-22
IN THAT CASE, TODAY WE SHOULD BE UP TO HERE IN WASHINGTONS!

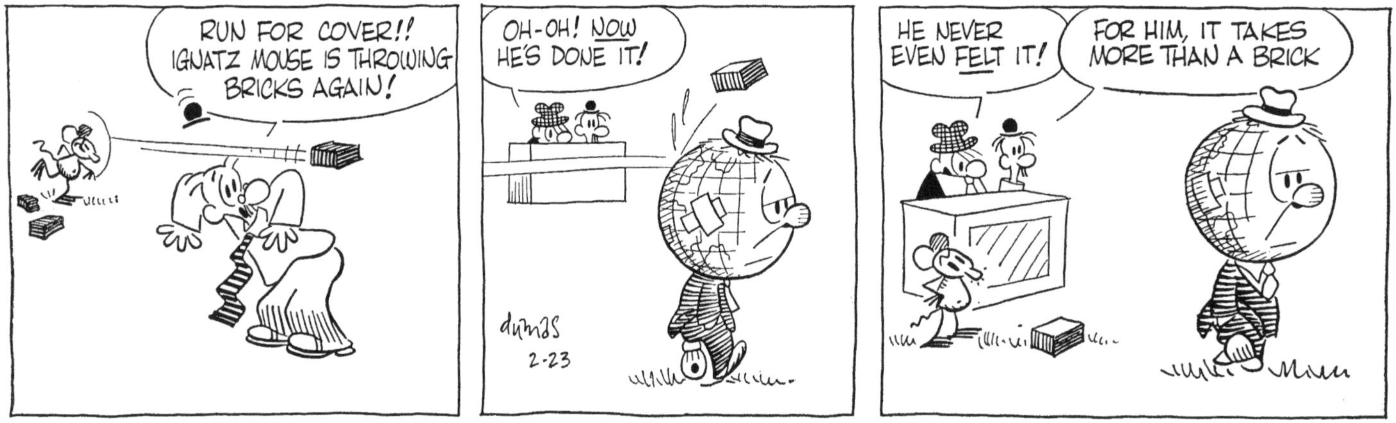
RUN FOR COVER!! IGNATZ MOUSE IS THROWING BRICKS AGAIN!
OH-OH! NOW HE'S DONE IT!
dumas 2-23
HE NEVER EVEN FELT IT!
FOR HIM, IT TAKES MORE THAN A BRICK

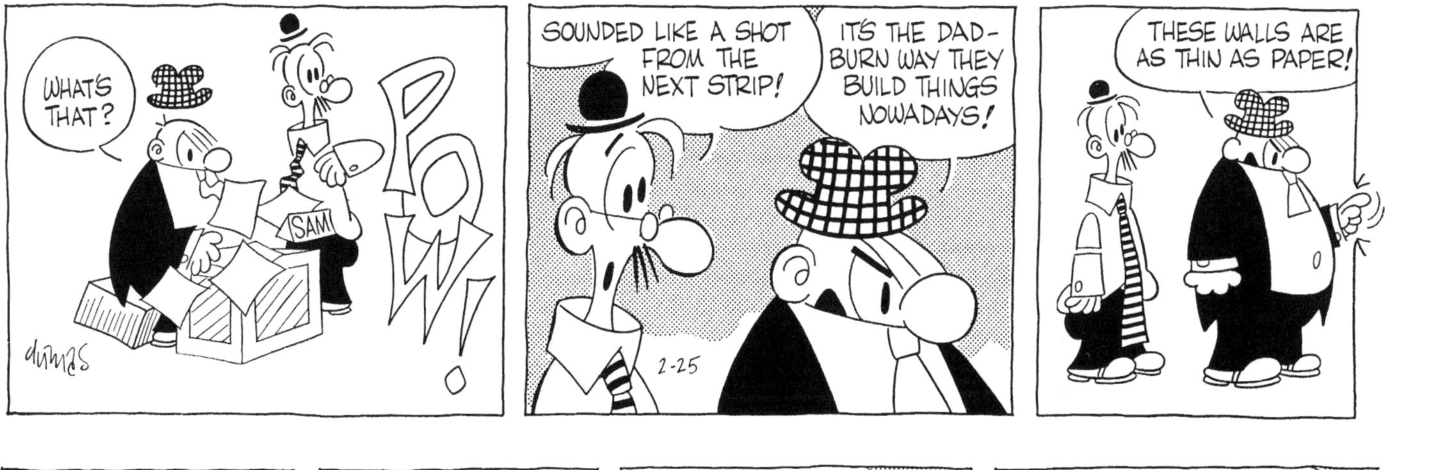
WHAT'S THAT?
SAM
POW!
SOUNDED LIKE A SHOT FROM THE NEXT STRIP!
IT'S THE DAD-BURN WAY THEY BUILD THINGS NOWADAYS!
2-25
THESE WALLS ARE AS THIN AS PAPER!

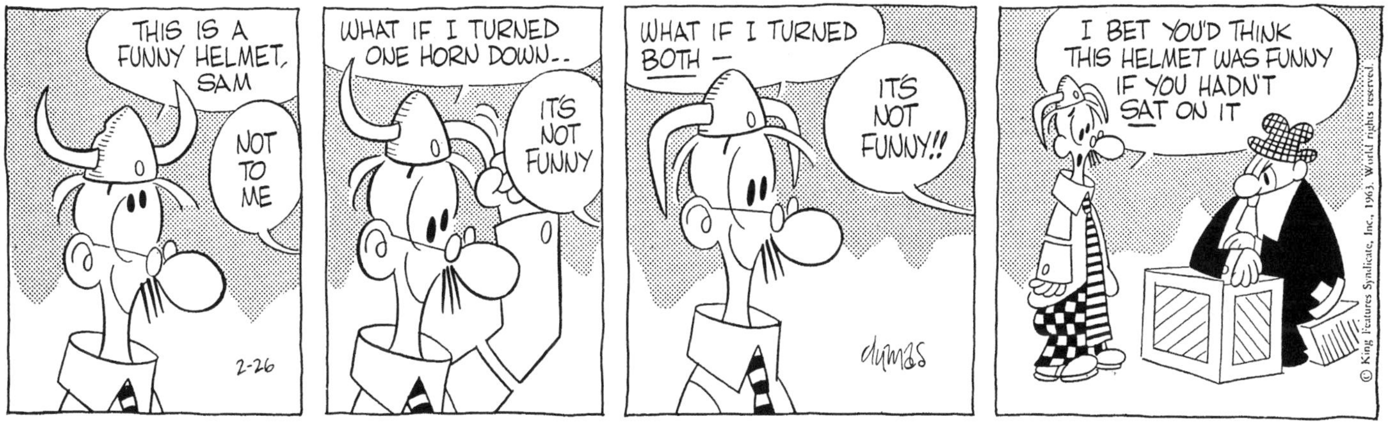
THIS IS A FUNNY HELMET, SAM
NOT TO ME
2-26
WHAT IF I TURNED ONE HORN DOWN..
IT'S NOT FUNNY
WHAT IF I TURNED BOTH —
IT'S NOT FUNNY!!
I BET YOU'D THINK THIS HELMET WAS FUNNY IF YOU HADN'T SAT ON IT
© King Features Syndicate, Inc., 1963. World rights reserved.

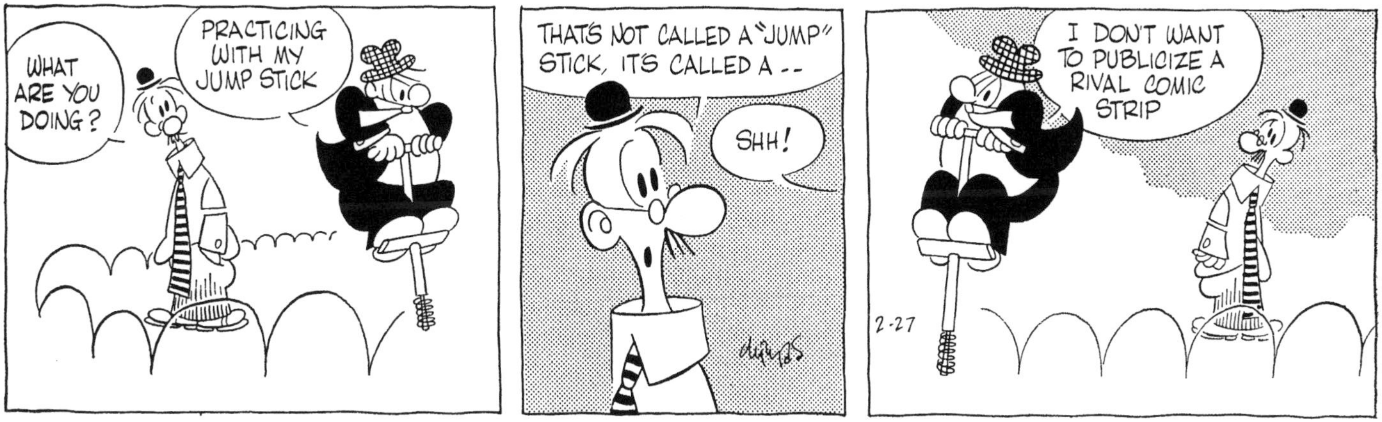
WHAT ARE YOU DOING?
PRACTICING WITH MY JUMP STICK
THAT'S NOT CALLED A "JUMP" STICK, IT'S CALLED A --
SHH!
2-27
I DON'T WANT TO PUBLICIZE A RIVAL COMIC STRIP

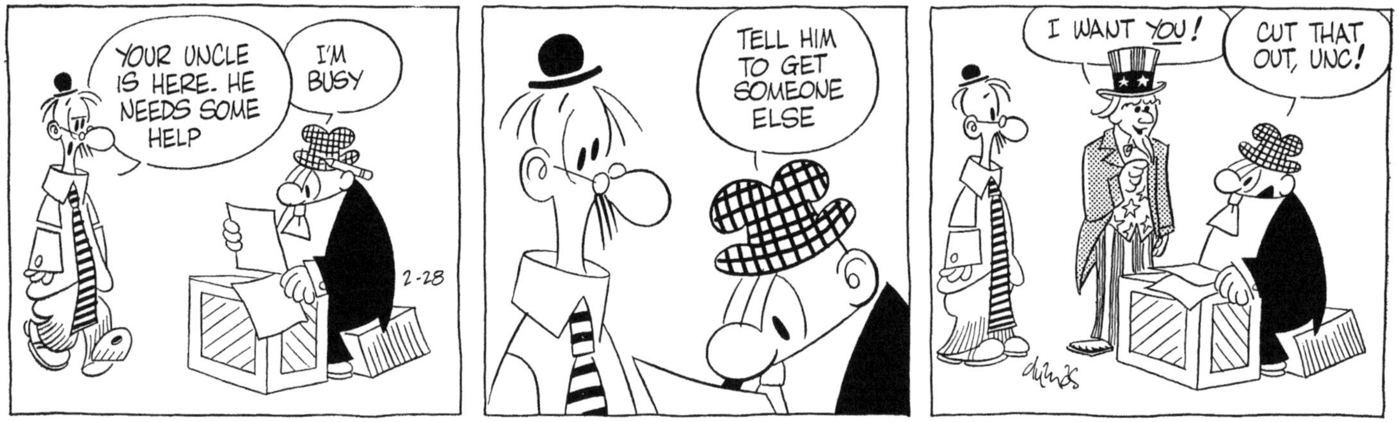
YOUR UNCLE IS HERE. HE NEEDS SOME HELP
I'M BUSY
2-28
TELL HIM TO GET SOMEONE ELSE
I WANT YOU!
CUT THAT OUT, UNC!

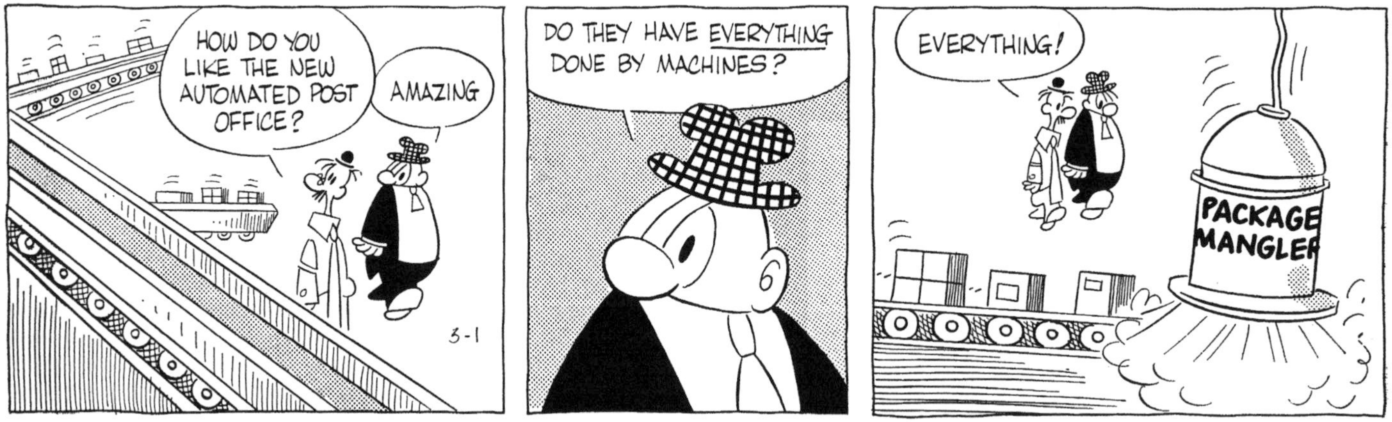
HOW DO YOU LIKE THE NEW AUTOMATED POST OFFICE?
AMAZING
3-1
DO THEY HAVE EVERYTHING DONE BY MACHINES?
EVERYTHING!
PACKAGE MANGLER

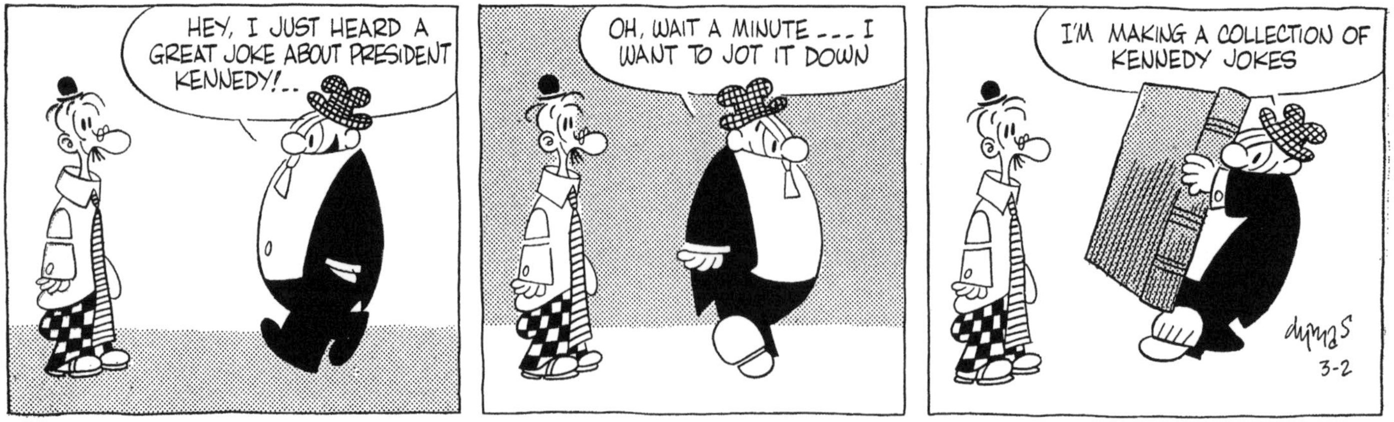
HEY, I JUST HEARD A GREAT JOKE ABOUT PRESIDENT KENNEDY!..
OH, WAIT A MINUTE --- I WANT TO JOT IT DOWN
I'M MAKING A COLLECTION OF KENNEDY JOKES
3-2

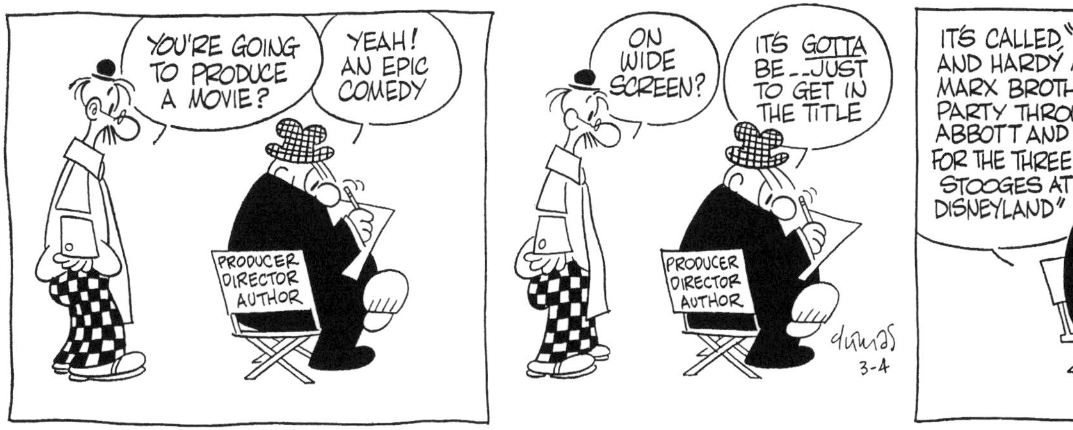
YOU'RE GOING TO PRODUCE A MOVIE?
YEAH! AN EPIC COMEDY
PRODUCER DIRECTOR AUTHOR
ON WIDE SCREEN?
IT'S GOTTA BE--JUST TO GET IN THE TITLE
PRODUCER DIRECTOR AUTHOR
dumas
3-4
IT'S CALLED "LAUREL AND HARDY MEET THE MARX BROTHERS AT A PARTY THROWN BY ABBOTT AND COSTELLO FOR THE THREE STOOGES AT DISNEYLAND"

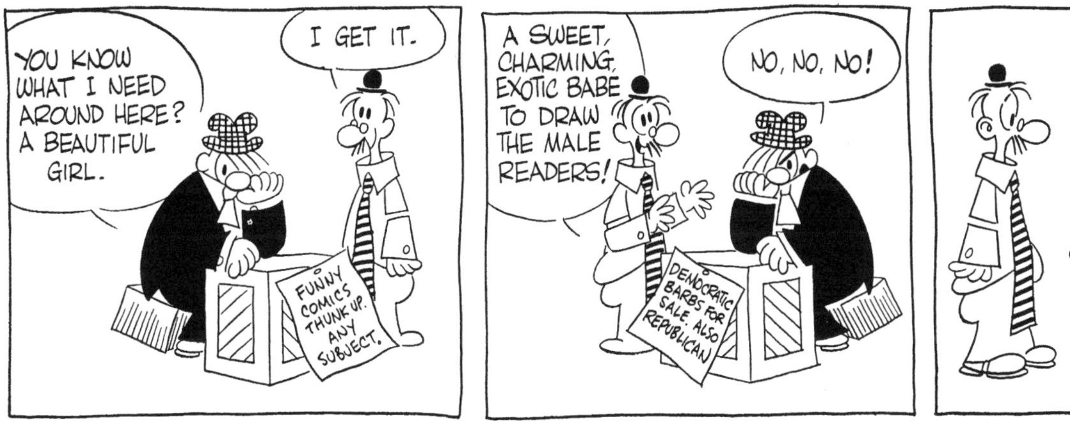
YOU KNOW WHAT I NEED AROUND HERE? A BEAUTIFUL GIRL.
I GET IT.
FUNNY COMICS THUNK UP. ANY SUBJECT.
A SWEET, CHARMING, EXOTIC BABE TO DRAW THE MALE READERS!
NO, NO, NO!
DEMOCRATIC BARBS FOR SALE. ALSO REPUBLICAN
I MEANT FOR ME! LET THEM FIND THEIR OWN!
dumas
3-5

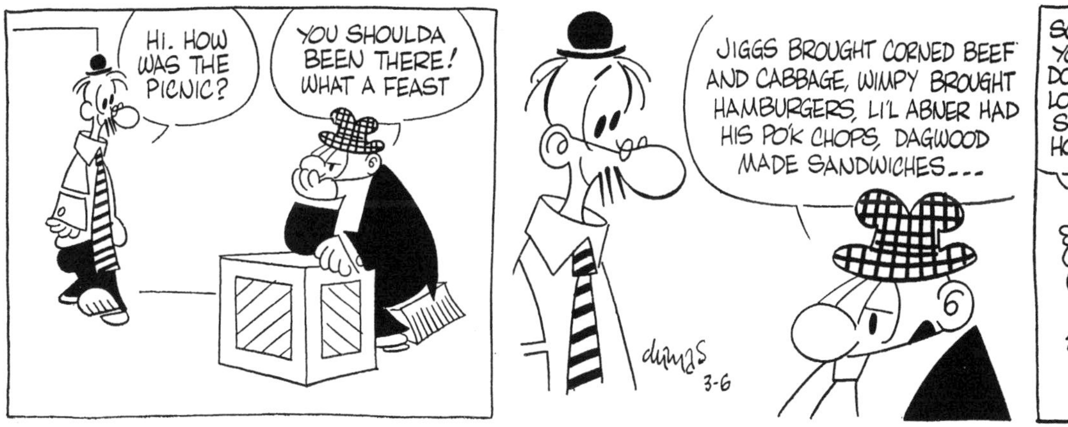
HI. HOW WAS THE PICNIC?
YOU SHOULDA BEEN THERE! WHAT A FEAST
JIGGS BROUGHT CORNED BEEF AND CABBAGE, WIMPY BROUGHT HAMBURGERS, LI'L ABNER HAD HIS PO'K CHOPS, DAGWOOD MADE SANDWICHES---
dumas
3-6
SOMEHOW YOU DON'T LOOK SO HOT
SNUFFY SMITH BROUGHT CORN SQUEEZIN'S

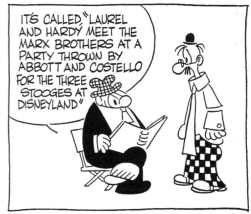

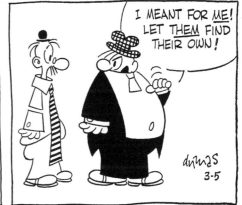

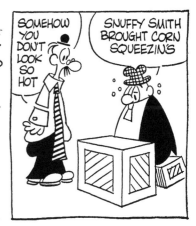

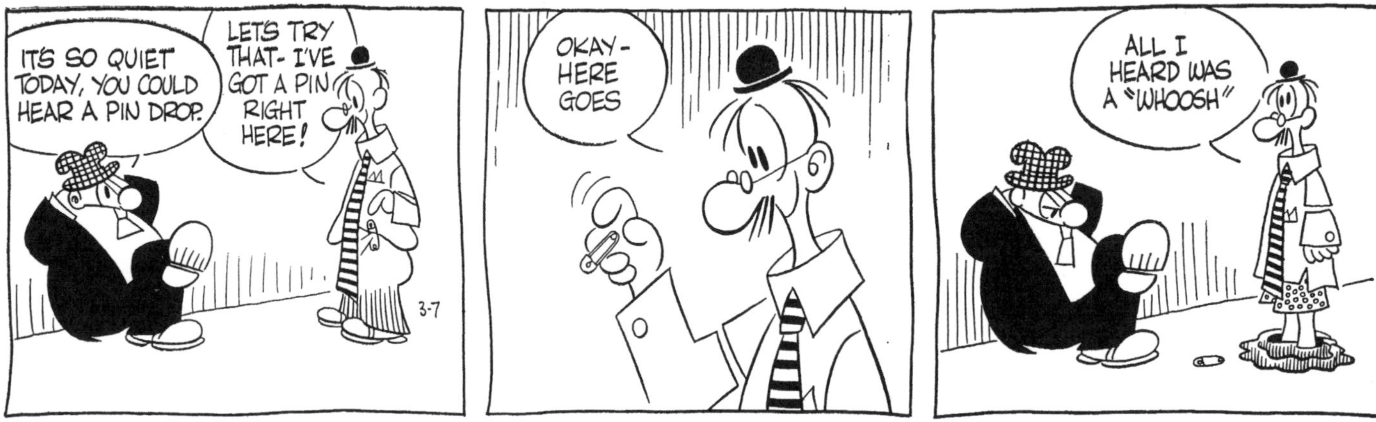
IT'S SO QUIET TODAY, YOU COULD HEAR A PIN DROP.
LET'S TRY THAT- I'VE GOT A PIN RIGHT HERE!
3-7
OKAY- HERE GOES
ALL I HEARD WAS A "WHOOSH"

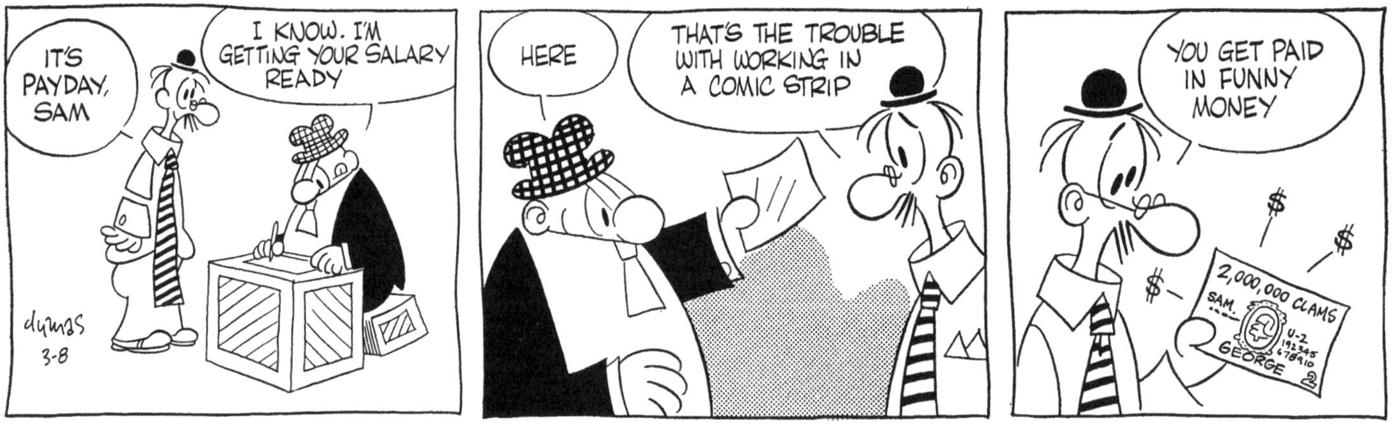
IT'S PAYDAY, SAM
I KNOW. I'M GETTING YOUR SALARY READY
dumas
3-8
HERE
THAT'S THE TROUBLE WITH WORKING IN A COMIC STRIP
YOU GET PAID IN FUNNY MONEY
$
$
$
2,000,000 CLAMS
SAM.
U-2 192345 678910
GEORGE

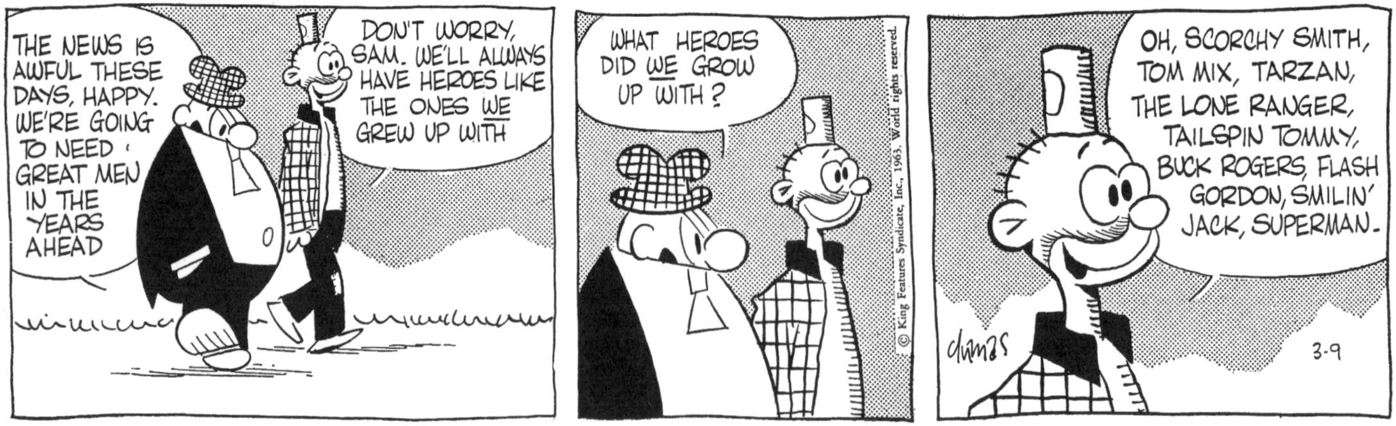
THE NEWS IS AWFUL THESE DAYS, HAPPY. WE'RE GOING TO NEED GREAT MEN IN THE YEARS AHEAD
DON'T WORRY, SAM. WE'LL ALWAYS HAVE HEROES LIKE THE ONES WE GREW UP WITH
WHAT HEROES DID WE GROW UP WITH?
OH, SCORCHY SMITH, TOM MIX, TARZAN, THE LONE RANGER, TAILSPIN TOMMY, BUCK ROGERS, FLASH GORDON, SMILIN' JACK, SUPERMAN-
dumas
3-9

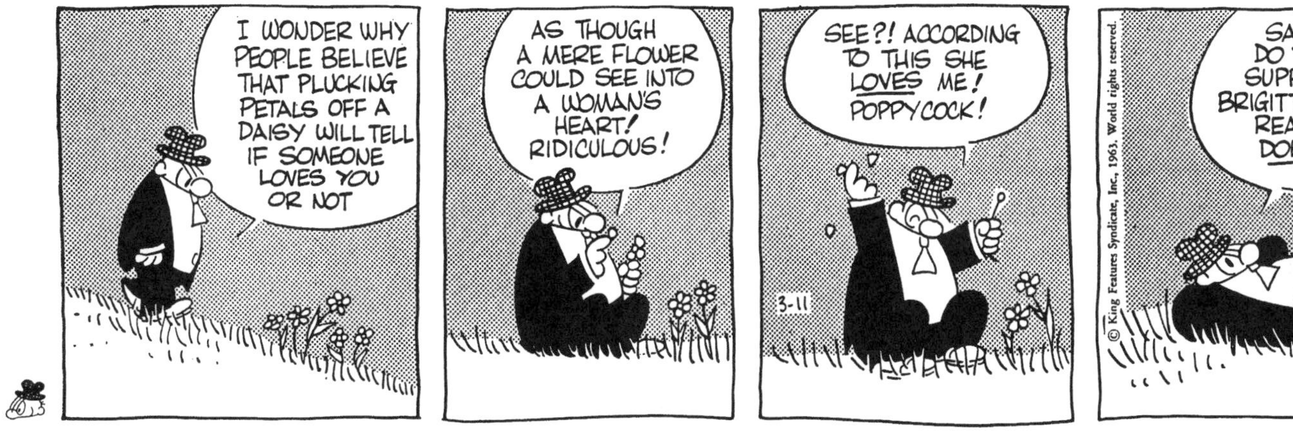
I WONDER WHY PEOPLE BELIEVE THAT PLUCKING PETALS OFF A DAISY WILL TELL IF SOMEONE LOVES YOU OR NOT
AS THOUGH A MERE FLOWER COULD SEE INTO A WOMAN'S HEART! RIDICULOUS!
SEE?! ACCORDING TO THIS SHE LOVES ME! POPPYCOCK!
3-11
SAY, DO YOU SUPPOSE BRIGITTE BARDOT REALLY DOES?!
© King Features Syndicate, Inc., 1963. World rights reserved.
dumas

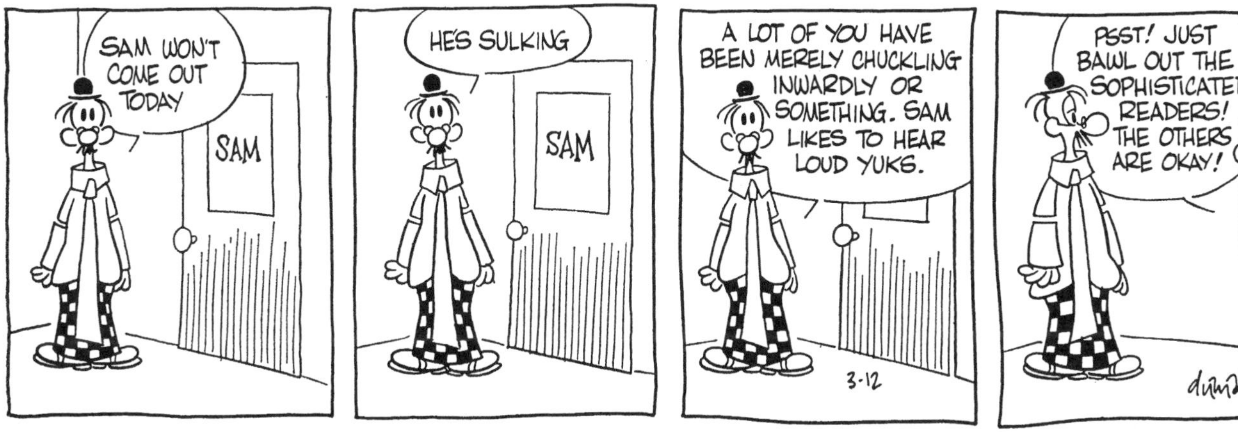
SAM WON'T COME OUT TODAY
SAM
HE'S SULKING
SAM
A LOT OF YOU HAVE BEEN MERELY CHUCKLING INWARDLY OR SOMETHING. SAM LIKES TO HEAR LOUD YUKS.
3-12
PSST! JUST BAWL OUT THE SOPHISTICATED READERS! THE OTHERS ARE OKAY!
SAM
dumas

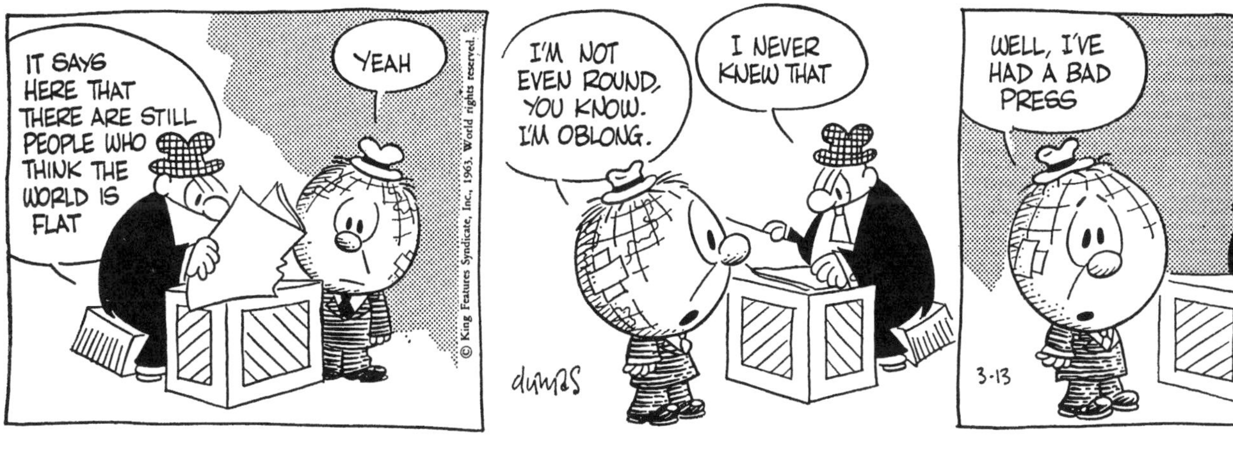
IT SAYS HERE THAT THERE ARE STILL PEOPLE WHO THINK THE WORLD IS FLAT
YEAH
© King Features Syndicate, Inc., 1963. World rights reserved.
dumas
I'M NOT EVEN ROUND, YOU KNOW. I'M OBLONG.
I NEVER KNEW THAT
WELL, I'VE HAD A BAD PRESS
3-13

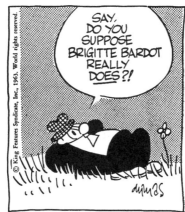

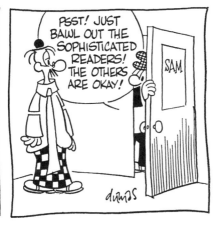

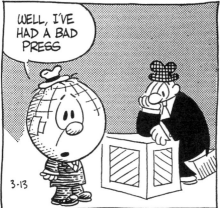

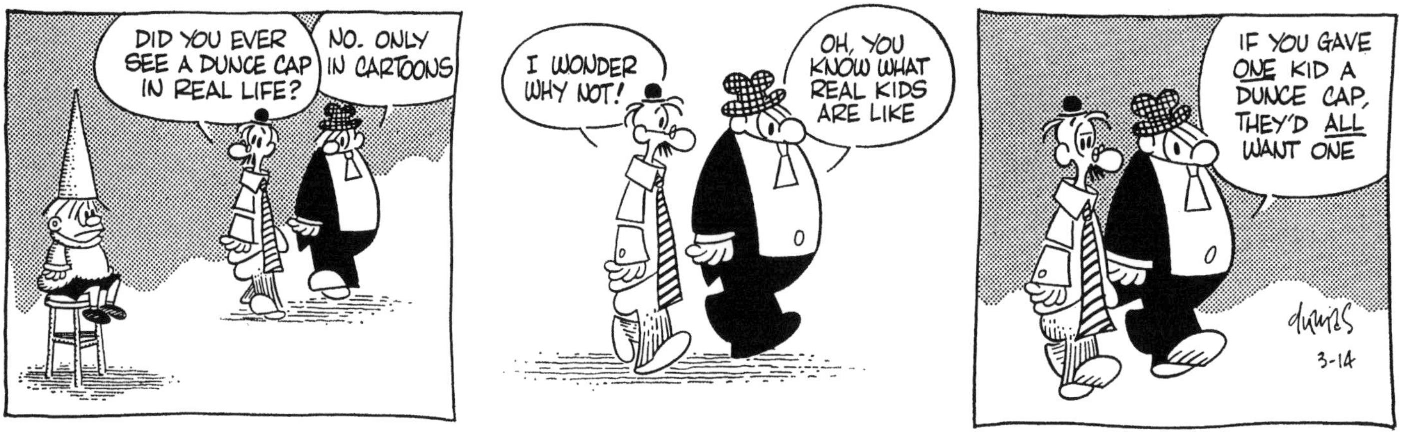
DID YOU EVER SEE A DUNCE CAP IN REAL LIFE?
NO. ONLY IN CARTOONS
I WONDER WHY NOT!
OH, YOU KNOW WHAT REAL KIDS ARE LIKE
IF YOU GAVE ONE KID A DUNCE CAP, THEY'D ALL WANT ONE
3-14

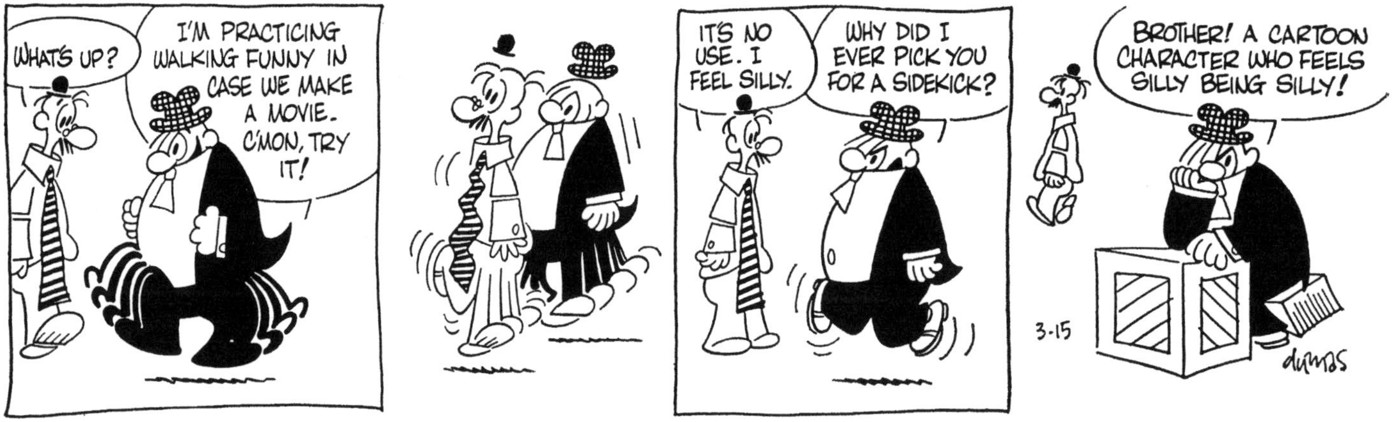
WHAT'S UP?
I'M PRACTICING WALKING FUNNY IN CASE WE MAKE A MOVIE. C'MON, TRY IT!
IT'S NO USE. I FEEL SILLY.
WHY DID I EVER PICK YOU FOR A SIDEKICK?
BROTHER! A CARTOON CHARACTER WHO FEELS SILLY BEING SILLY!
3-15

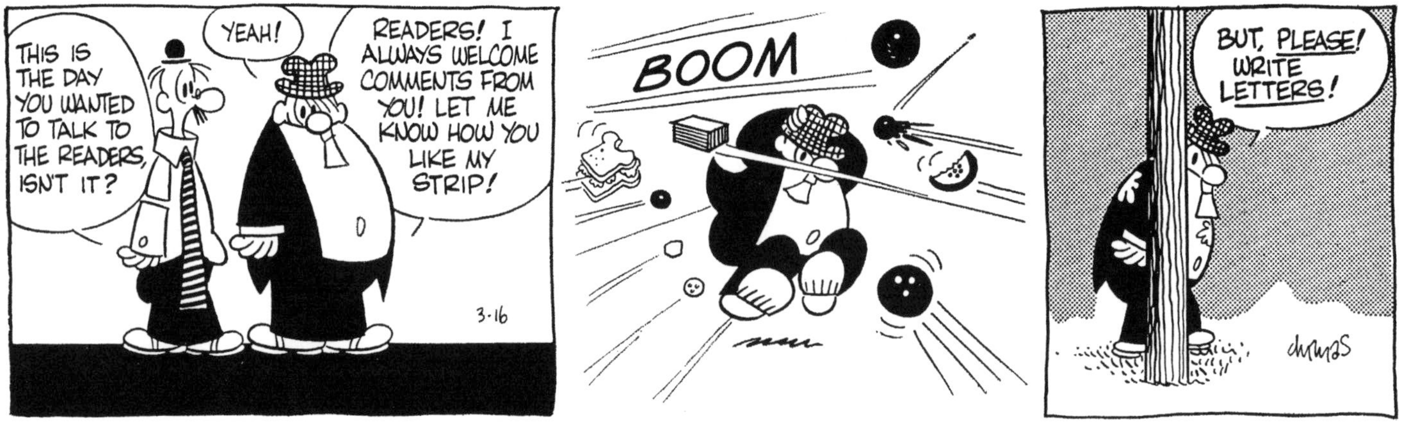
THIS IS THE DAY YOU WANTED TO TALK TO THE READERS, ISN'T IT?
YEAH!
READERS! I ALWAYS WELCOME COMMENTS FROM YOU! LET ME KNOW HOW YOU LIKE MY STRIP!
3-16
BOOM
BUT, PLEASE! WRITE LETTERS!

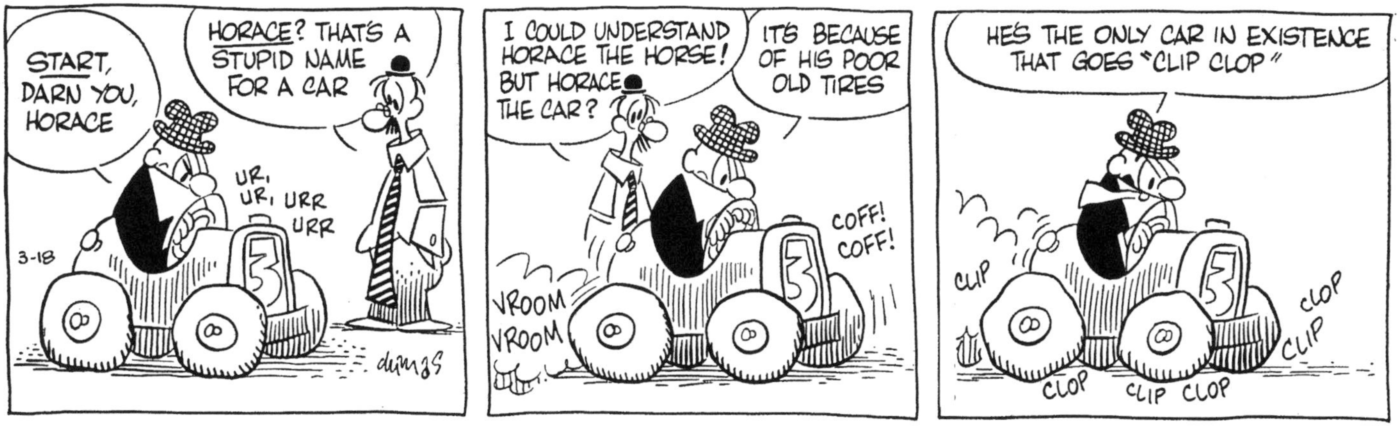
START, DARN YOU, HORACE
HORACE? THAT'S A STUPID NAME FOR A CAR
UR, UR, URR URR
3-18
dumas
I COULD UNDERSTAND HORACE THE HORSE! BUT HORACE THE CAR?
IT'S BECAUSE OF HIS POOR OLD TIRES
VROOM VROOM
COFF! COFF!
HE'S THE ONLY CAR IN EXISTENCE THAT GOES "CLIP CLOP"
CLIP
CLOP
CLIP CLOP
CLIP
CLOP

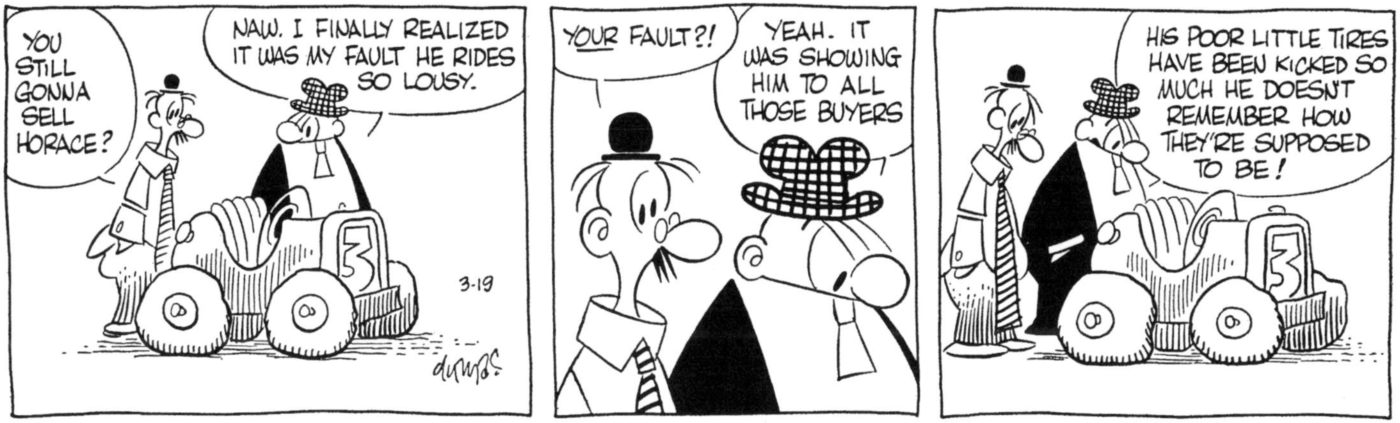
YOU STILL GONNA SELL HORACE?
NAW. I FINALLY REALIZED IT WAS MY FAULT HE RIDES SO LOUSY.
3-19
dumas
YOUR FAULT?!
YEAH. IT WAS SHOWING HIM TO ALL THOSE BUYERS
HIS POOR LITTLE TIRES HAVE BEEN KICKED SO MUCH HE DOESN'T REMEMBER HOW THEY'RE SUPPOSED TO BE!

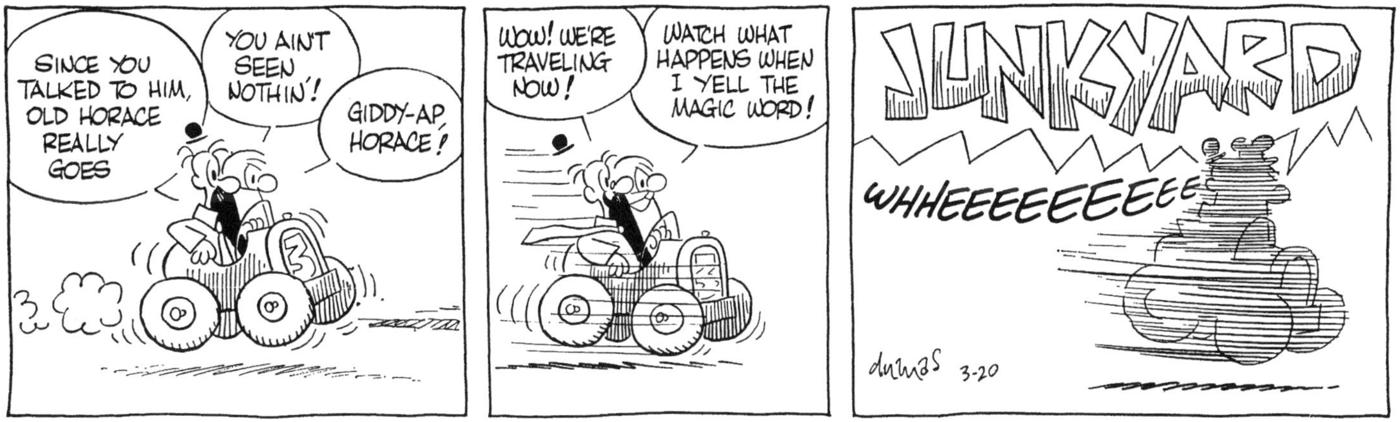
SINCE YOU TALKED TO HIM, OLD HORACE REALLY GOES
YOU AIN'T SEEN NOTHIN'!
GIDDY-AP, HORACE!
WOW! WE'RE TRAVELING NOW!
WATCH WHAT HAPPENS WHEN I YELL THE MAGIC WORD!
JUNKYARD
WHHEEEEEEEEEE
dumas 3-20

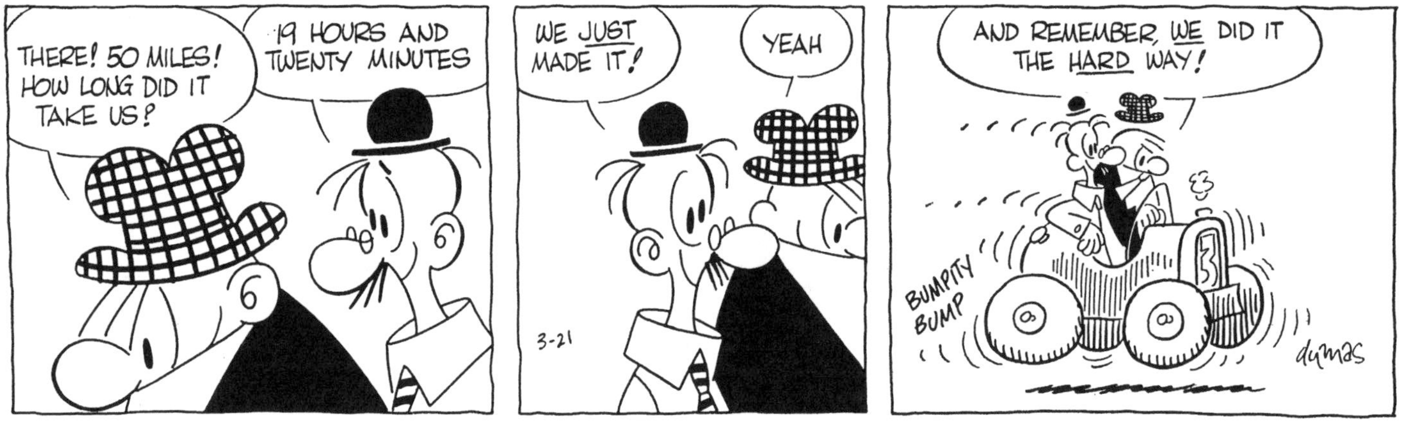
THERE! 50 MILES! HOW LONG DID IT TAKE US?
19 HOURS AND TWENTY MINUTES
WE JUST MADE IT!
YEAH
3-21
AND REMEMBER, WE DID IT THE HARD WAY!
BUMPITY BUMP
dumas

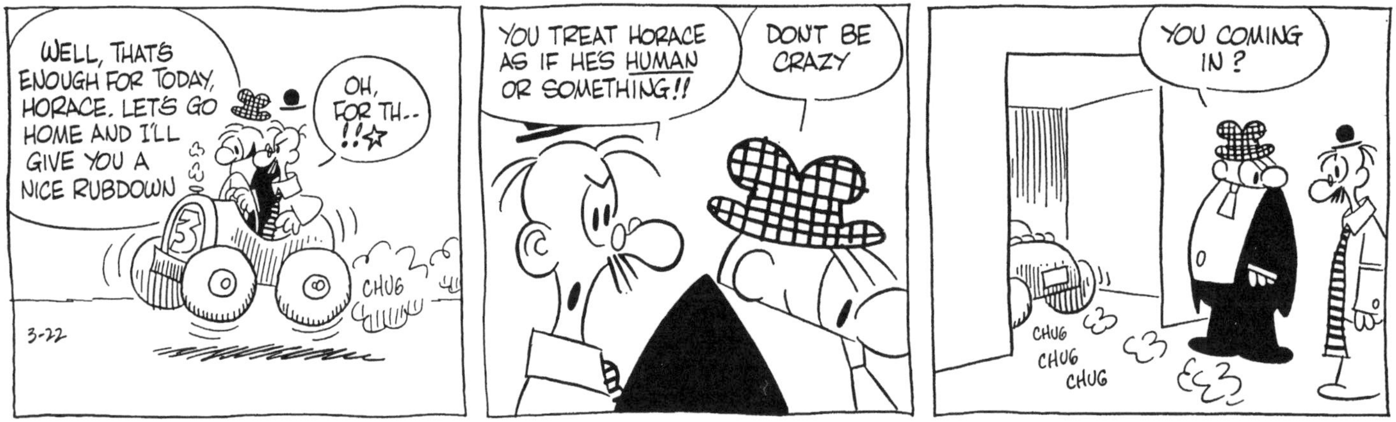
WELL, THAT'S ENOUGH FOR TODAY, HORACE. LET'S GO HOME AND I'LL GIVE YOU A NICE RUBDOWN
OH, FOR TH-- !!☆
CHUG
3-22
YOU TREAT HORACE AS IF HE'S HUMAN OR SOMETHING!!
DON'T BE CRAZY
YOU COMING IN?
CHUG
CHUG
CHUG

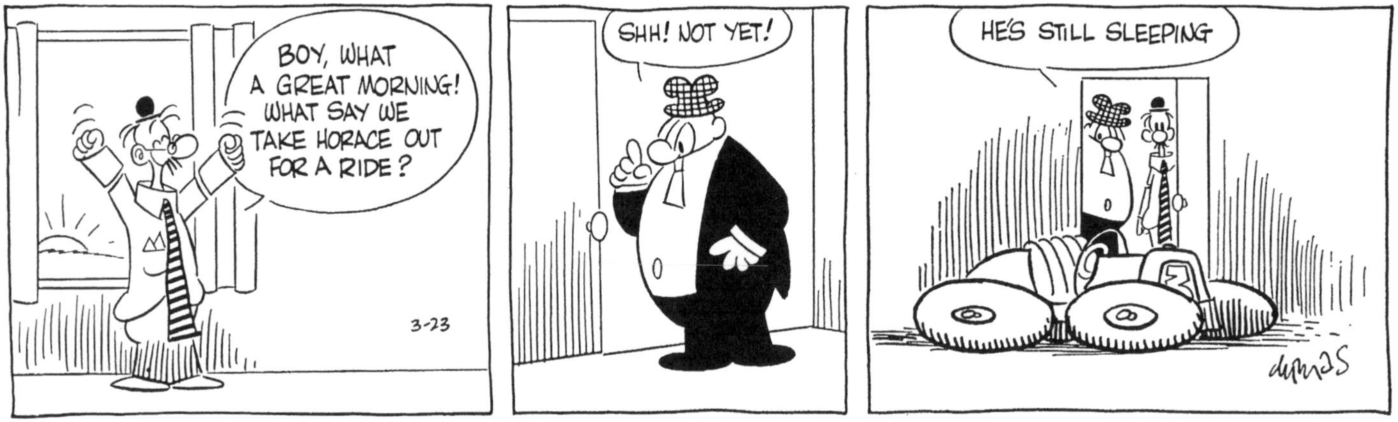
BOY, WHAT A GREAT MORNING! WHAT SAY WE TAKE HORACE OUT FOR A RIDE?
3-23
SHH! NOT YET!
HE'S STILL SLEEPING
dumas

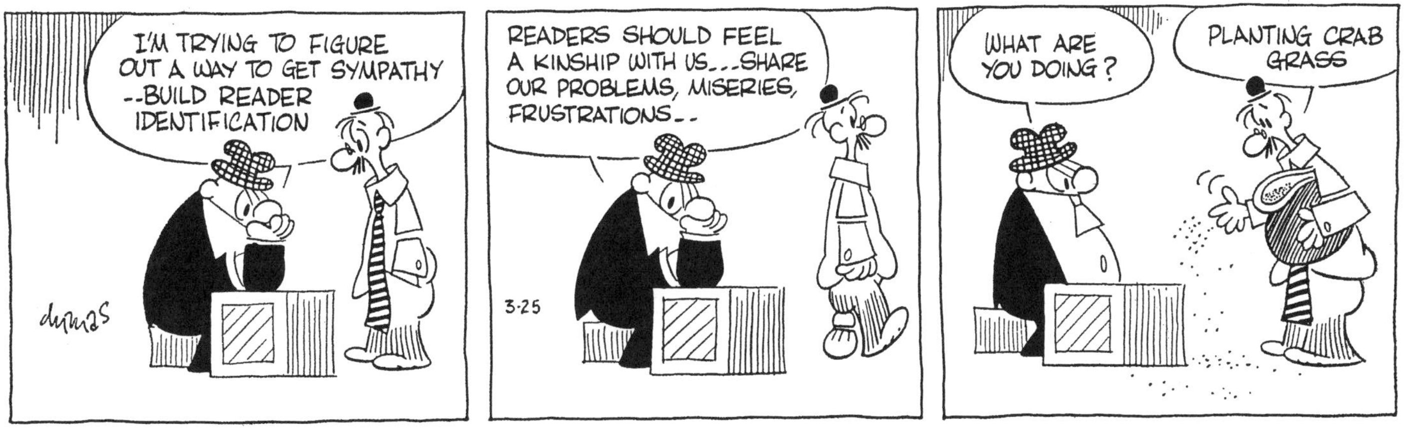
I'M TRYING TO FIGURE OUT A WAY TO GET SYMPATHY --BUILD READER IDENTIFICATION
dumas
READERS SHOULD FEEL A KINSHIP WITH US...SHARE OUR PROBLEMS, MISERIES, FRUSTRATIONS..
3-25
WHAT ARE YOU DOING?
PLANTING CRAB GRASS

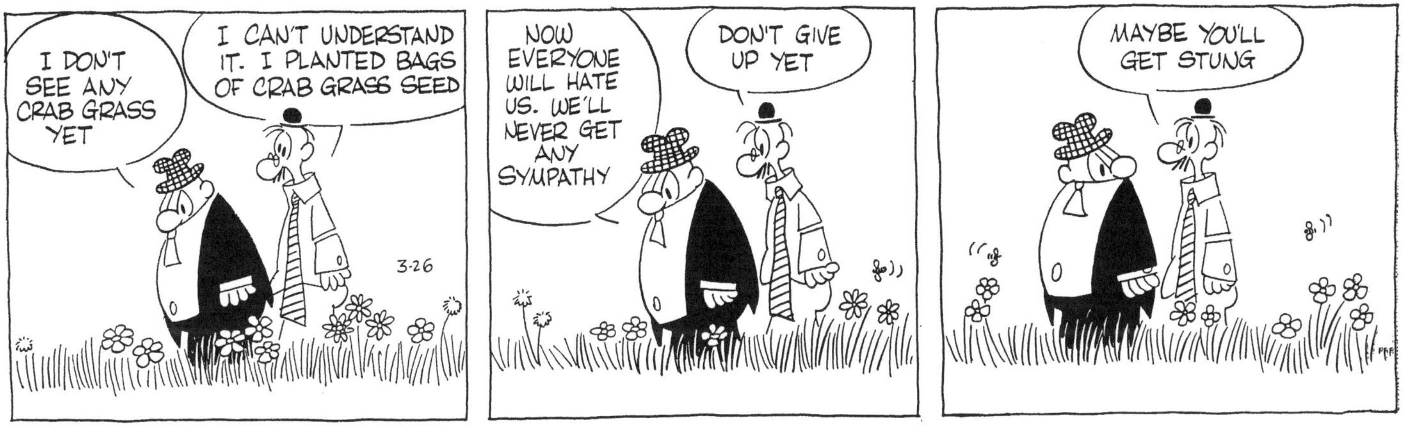
I DON'T SEE ANY CRAB GRASS YET
I CAN'T UNDERSTAND IT. I PLANTED BAGS OF CRAB GRASS SEED
3-26
NOW EVERYONE WILL HATE US. WE'LL NEVER GET ANY SYMPATHY
DON'T GIVE UP YET
MAYBE YOU'LL GET STUNG

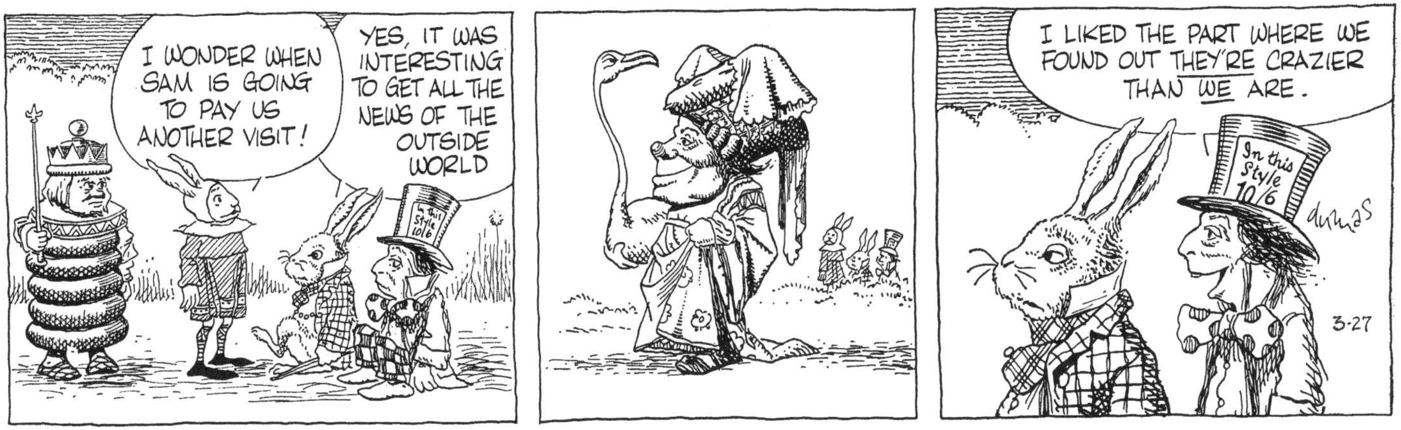
I WONDER WHEN SAM IS GOING TO PAY US ANOTHER VISIT!
YES, IT WAS INTERESTING TO GET ALL THE NEWS OF THE OUTSIDE WORLD
In this Style 10/6
I LIKED THE PART WHERE WE FOUND OUT THEY'RE CRAZIER THAN WE ARE.
In this Style 10/6
dumas
3-27

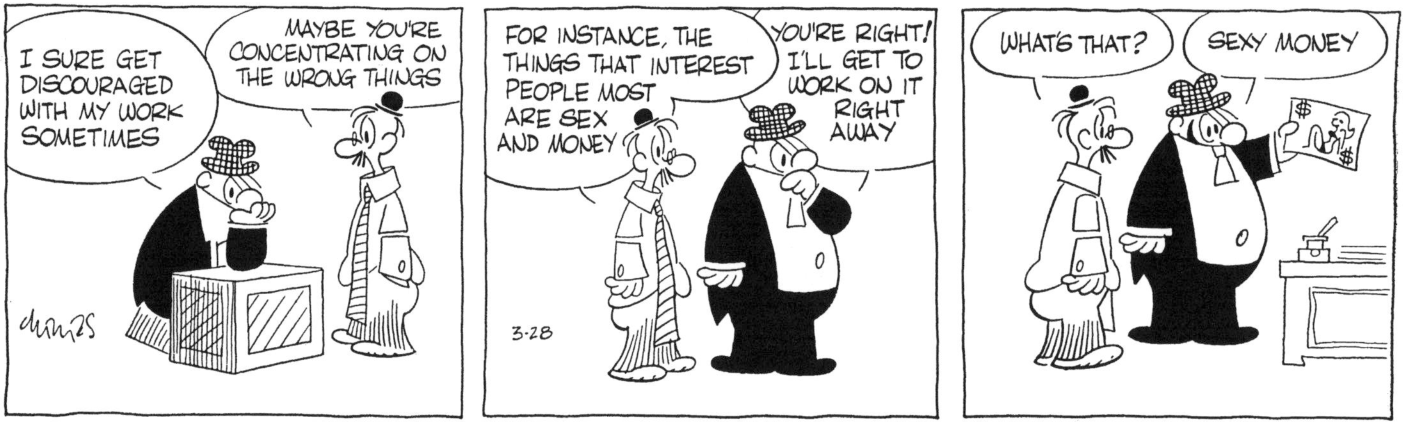
I SURE GET DISCOURAGED WITH MY WORK SOMETIMES
MAYBE YOU'RE CONCENTRATING ON THE WRONG THINGS
dumas
FOR INSTANCE, THE THINGS THAT INTEREST PEOPLE MOST ARE SEX AND MONEY
YOU'RE RIGHT! I'LL GET TO WORK ON IT RIGHT AWAY
3-28
WHAT'S THAT?
SEXY MONEY

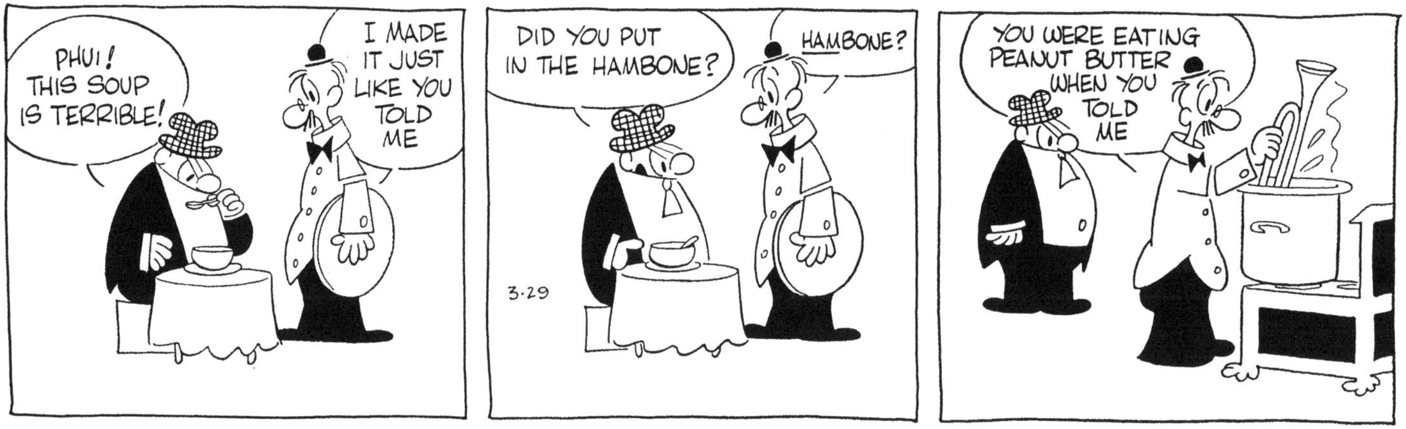
PHUI! THIS SOUP IS TERRIBLE!
I MADE IT JUST LIKE YOU TOLD ME
DID YOU PUT IN THE HAMBONE?
HAMBONE?
3-29
YOU WERE EATING PEANUT BUTTER WHEN YOU TOLD ME

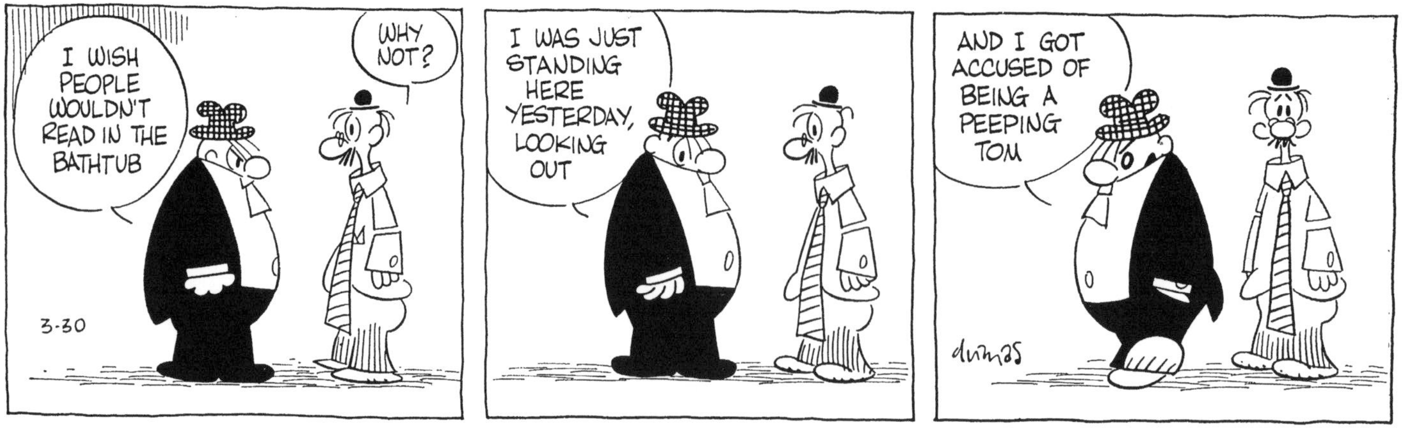
I WISH PEOPLE WOULDN'T READ IN THE BATHTUB
WHY NOT?
3-30
I WAS JUST STANDING HERE YESTERDAY, LOOKING OUT
AND I GOT ACCUSED OF BEING A PEEPING TOM
dumas

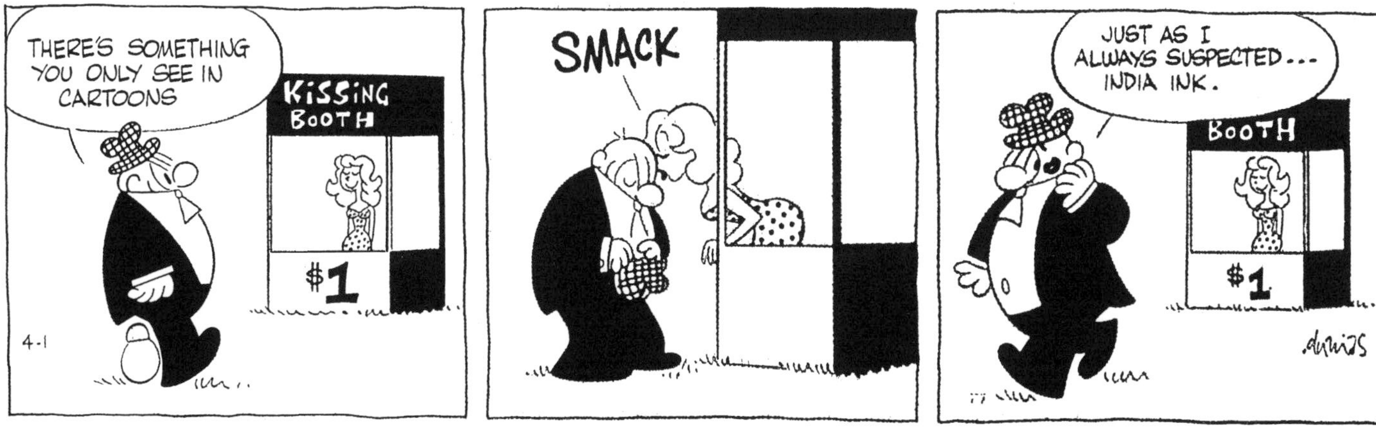
THERE'S SOMETHING YOU ONLY SEE IN CARTOONS
KISSING BOOTH
$1
4-1
SMACK
JUST AS I ALWAYS SUSPECTED... INDIA INK.
BOOTH
$1
dumas

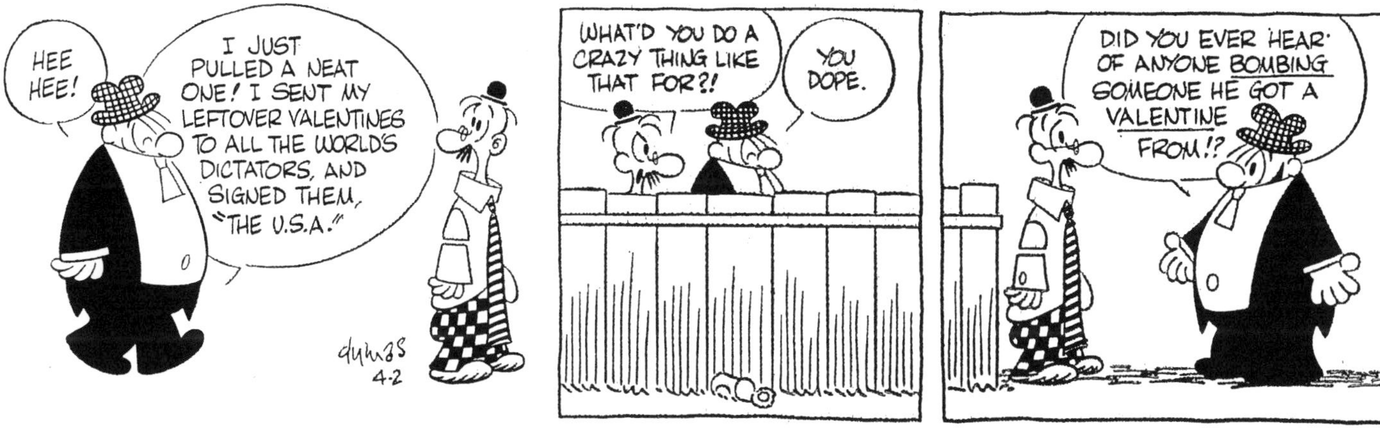
HEE HEE!
I JUST PULLED A NEAT ONE! I SENT MY LEFTOVER VALENTINES TO ALL THE WORLD'S DICTATORS, AND SIGNED THEM, "THE U.S.A."
dumas
4-2
WHAT'D YOU DO A CRAZY THING LIKE THAT FOR?!
YOU DOPE.
DID YOU EVER HEAR OF ANYONE BOMBING SOMEONE HE GOT A VALENTINE FROM!?

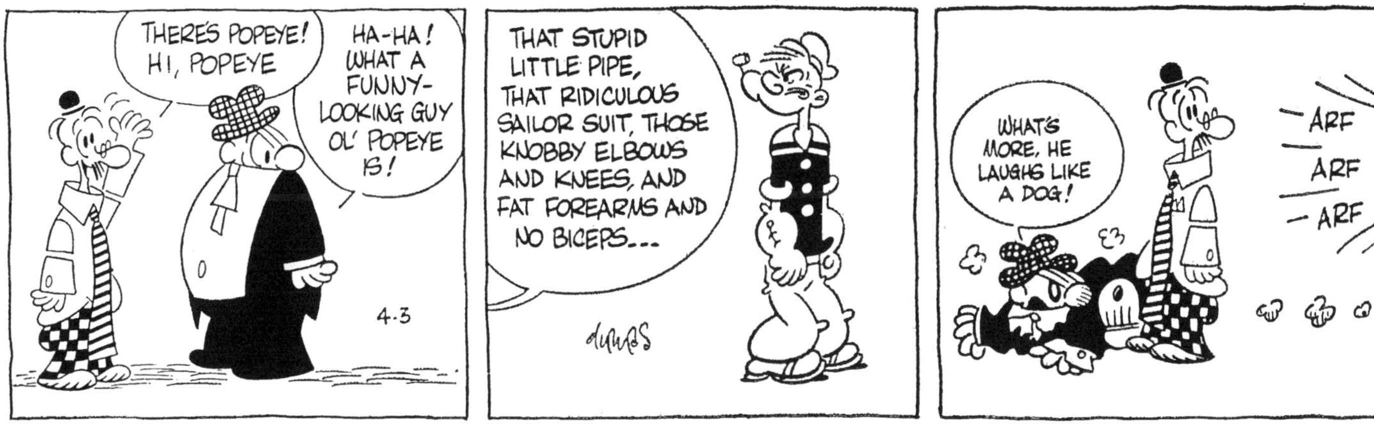
THERE'S POPEYE! HI, POPEYE
HA-HA! WHAT A FUNNY-LOOKING GUY OL' POPEYE IS!
4-3
THAT STUPID LITTLE PIPE, THAT RIDICULOUS SAILOR SUIT, THOSE KNOBBY ELBOWS AND KNEES, AND FAT FOREARMS AND NO BICEPS...
dumas
WHAT'S MORE, HE LAUGHS LIKE A DOG!
ARF
ARF
ARF

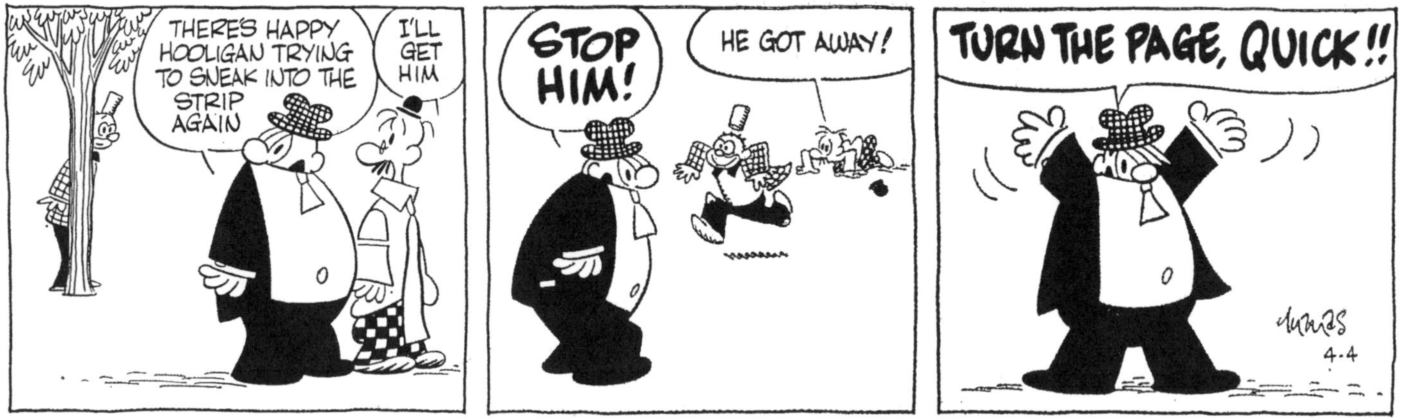
THERE'S HAPPY HOOLIGAN TRYING TO SNEAK INTO THE STRIP AGAIN
I'LL GET HIM
STOP HIM!
HE GOT AWAY!
TURN THE PAGE, QUICK!!
4·4

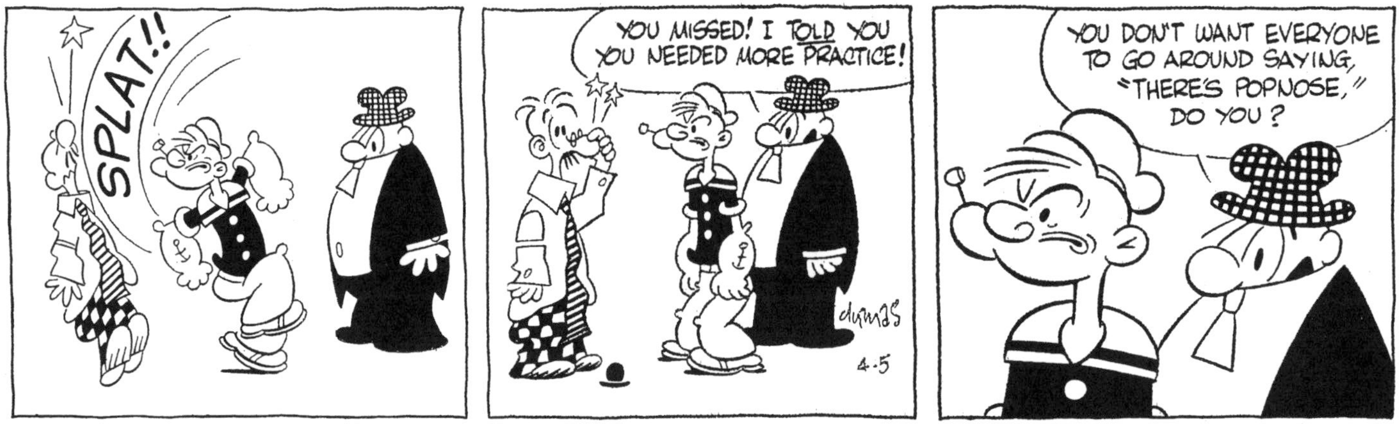
SPLAT!!
YOU MISSED! I TOLD YOU YOU NEEDED MORE PRACTICE!
4·5
YOU DON'T WANT EVERYONE TO GO AROUND SAYING, "THERE'S POPNOSE," DO YOU?

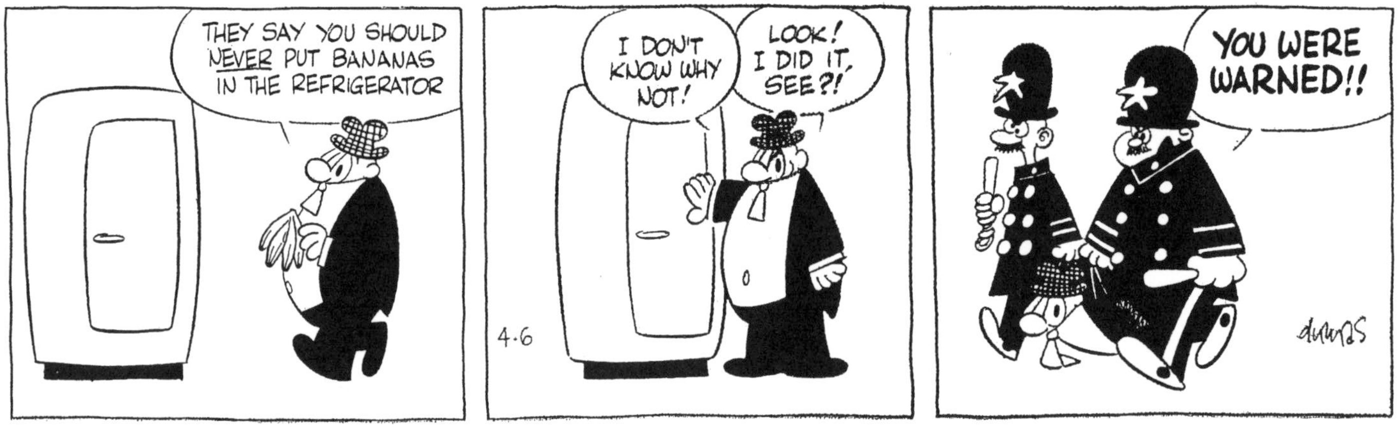
THEY SAY YOU SHOULD NEVER PUT BANANAS IN THE REFRIGERATOR
I DON'T KNOW WHY NOT!
LOOK! I DID IT, SEE?!
4·6
YOU WERE WARNED!!

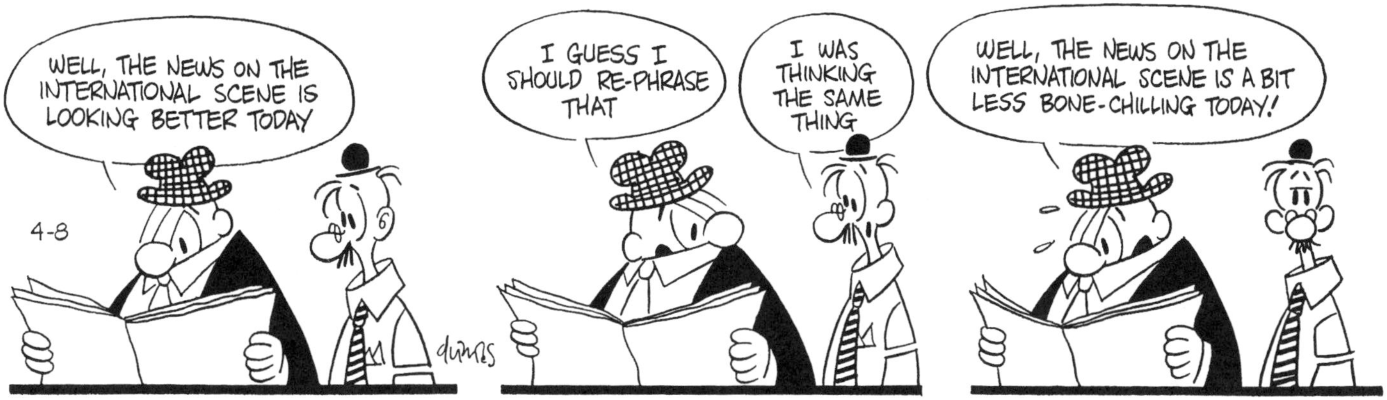
WELL, THE NEWS ON THE INTERNATIONAL SCENE IS LOOKING BETTER TODAY
4-8
I GUESS I SHOULD RE-PHRASE THAT
I WAS THINKING THE SAME THING
WELL, THE NEWS ON THE INTERNATIONAL SCENE IS A BIT LESS BONE-CHILLING TODAY!

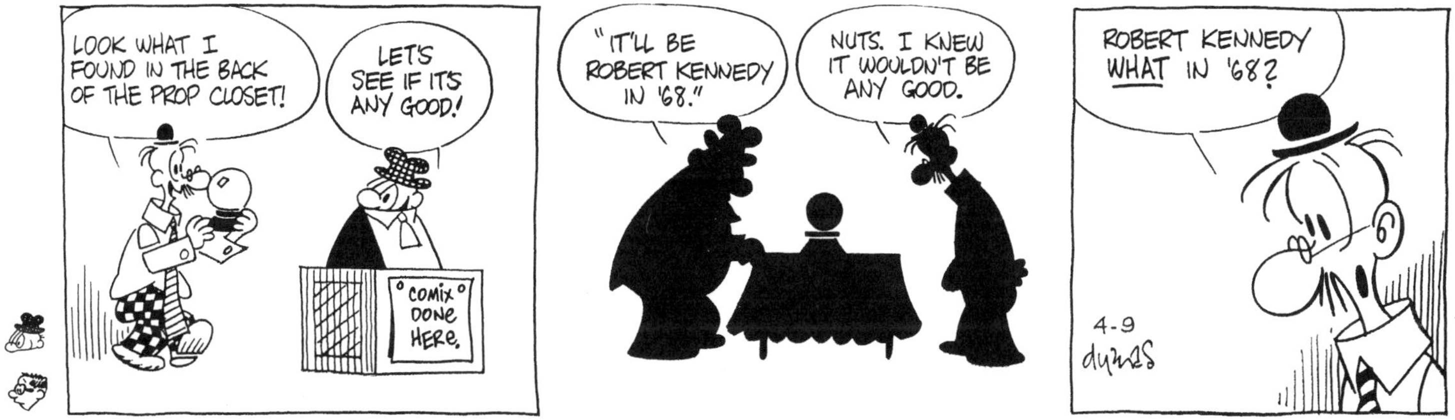
LOOK WHAT I FOUND IN THE BACK OF THE PROP CLOSET!
LET'S SEE IF IT'S ANY GOOD!
COMIX DONE HERE.
"IT'LL BE ROBERT KENNEDY IN '68."
NUTS. I KNEW IT WOULDN'T BE ANY GOOD.
ROBERT KENNEDY WHAT IN '68?
4-9

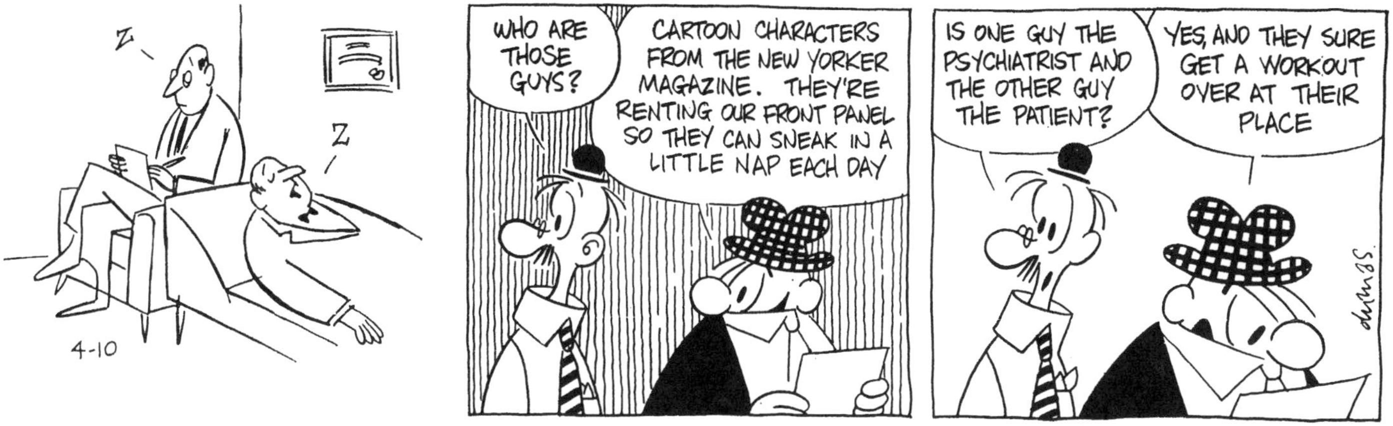
Z
Z
4-10
WHO ARE THOSE GUYS?
CARTOON CHARACTERS FROM THE NEW YORKER MAGAZINE. THEY'RE RENTING OUR FRONT PANEL SO THEY CAN SNEAK IN A LITTLE NAP EACH DAY
IS ONE GUY THE PSYCHIATRIST AND THE OTHER GUY THE PATIENT?
YES, AND THEY SURE GET A WORKOUT OVER AT THEIR PLACE

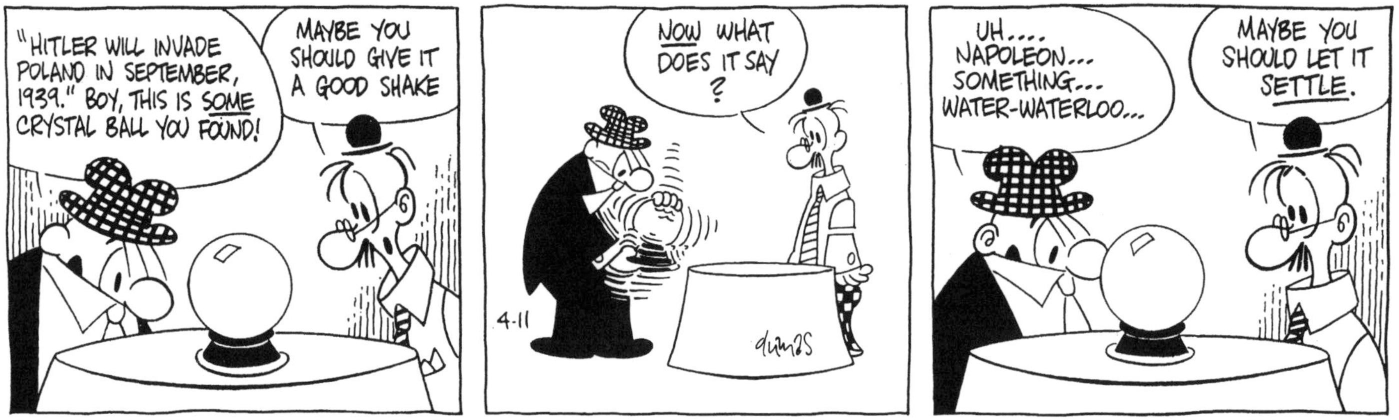
"HITLER WILL INVADE POLAND IN SEPTEMBER, 1939." BOY, THIS IS SOME CRYSTAL BALL YOU FOUND!
MAYBE YOU SHOULD GIVE IT A GOOD SHAKE
NOW WHAT DOES IT SAY ?
4-11
dumas
UH.... NAPOLEON... SOMETHING... WATER-WATERLOO...
MAYBE YOU SHOULD LET IT SETTLE.

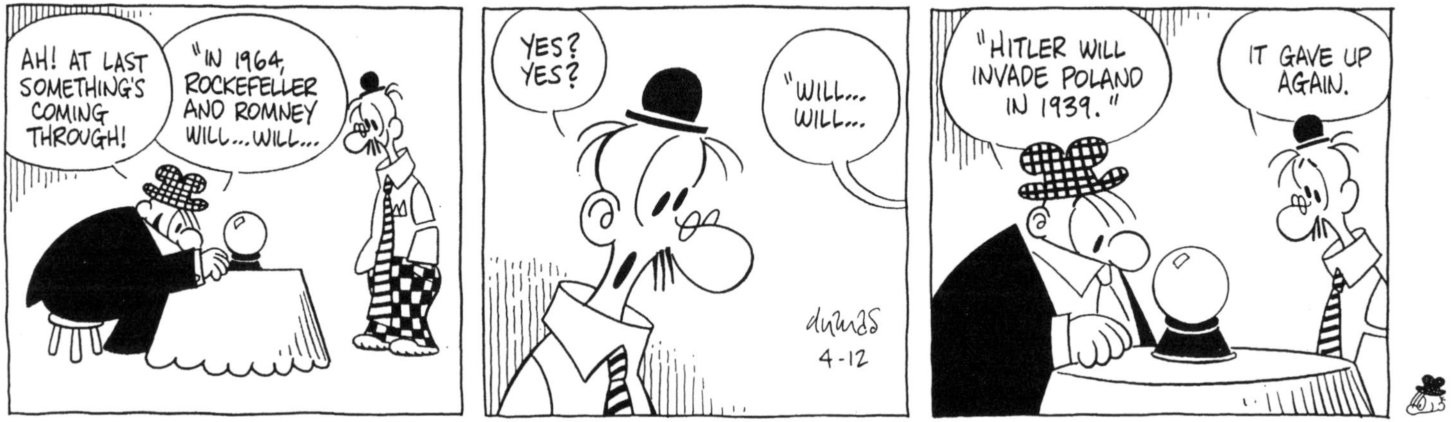
AH! AT LAST SOMETHING'S COMING THROUGH!
"IN 1964, ROCKEFELLER AND ROMNEY WILL...WILL...
YES? YES?
"WILL... WILL...
dumas
4-12
"HITLER WILL INVADE POLAND IN 1939."
IT GAVE UP AGAIN.

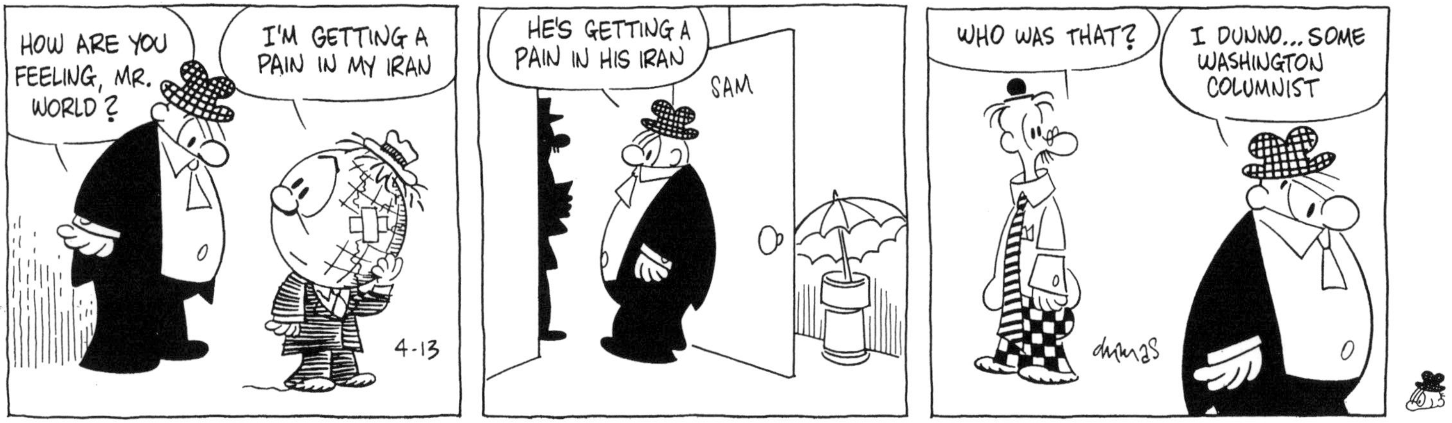
HOW ARE YOU FEELING, MR. WORLD?
I'M GETTING A PAIN IN MY IRAN
4-13
HE'S GETTING A PAIN IN HIS IRAN
SAM
WHO WAS THAT?
I DUNNO...SOME WASHINGTON COLUMNIST
dumas

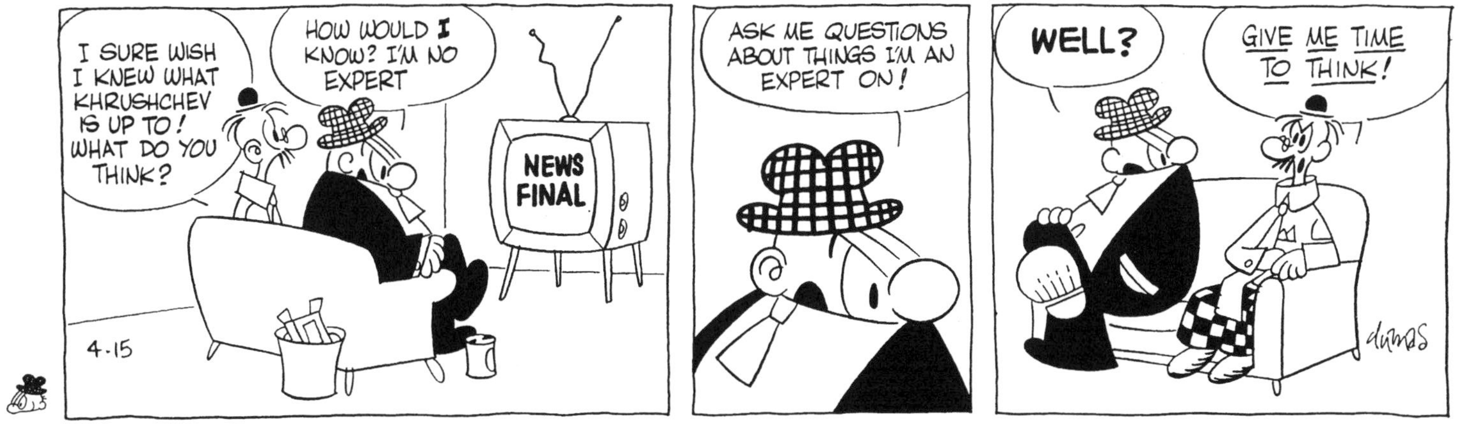
I SURE WISH I KNEW WHAT KHRUSHCHEV IS UP TO! WHAT DO YOU THINK?
HOW WOULD I KNOW? I'M NO EXPERT
NEWS FINAL
ASK ME QUESTIONS ABOUT THINGS I'M AN EXPERT ON!
WELL?
GIVE ME TIME TO THINK!
4-15
dumas

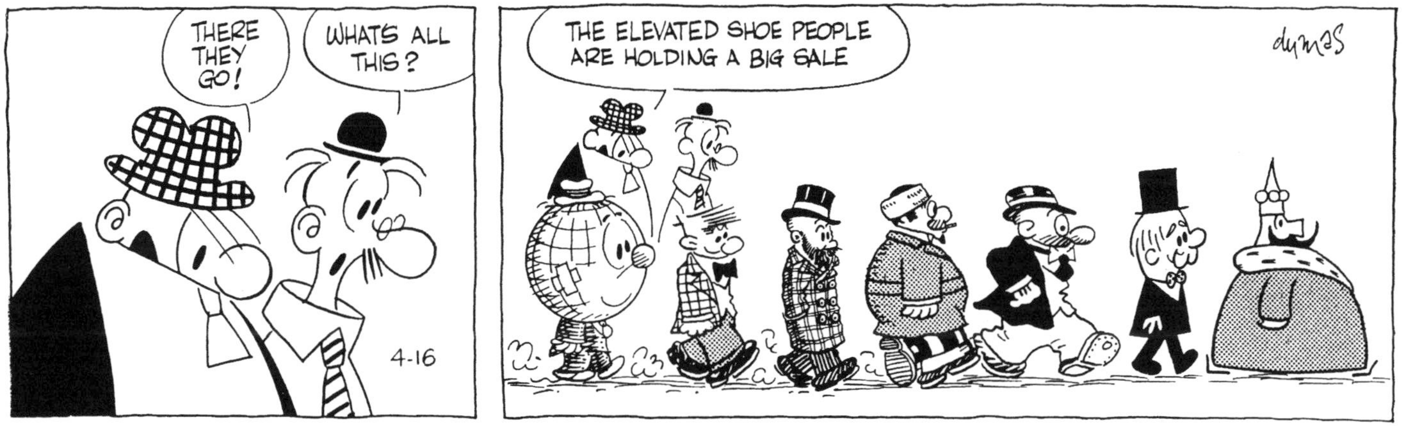
THERE THEY GO!
WHAT'S ALL THIS?
4-16
THE ELEVATED SHOE PEOPLE ARE HOLDING A BIG SALE
dumas

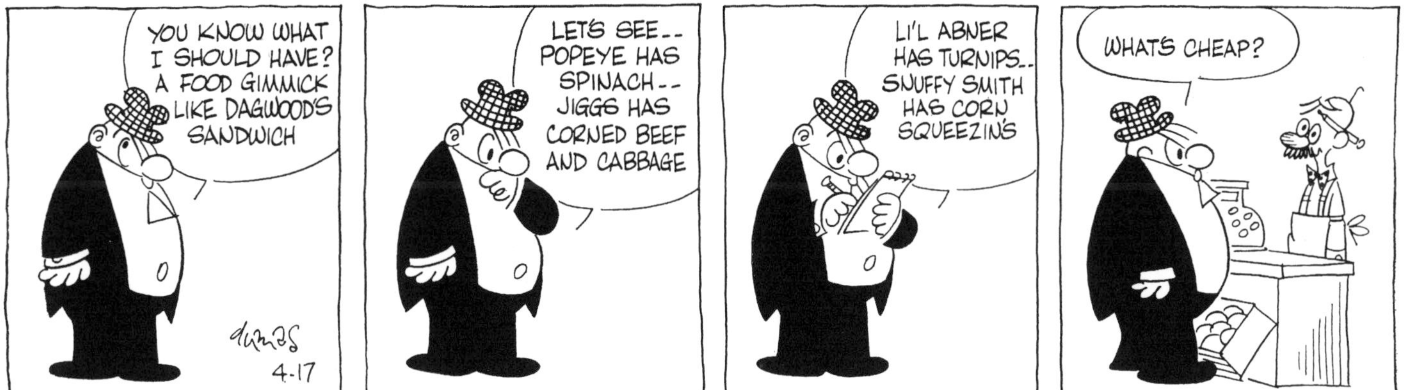
YOU KNOW WHAT I SHOULD HAVE? A FOOD GIMMICK LIKE DAGWOOD'S SANDWICH
dumas
4-17
LET'S SEE-- POPEYE HAS SPINACH-- JIGGS HAS CORNED BEEF AND CABBAGE
LI'L ABNER HAS TURNIPS-- SNUFFY SMITH HAS CORN SQUEEZIN'S
WHAT'S CHEAP?

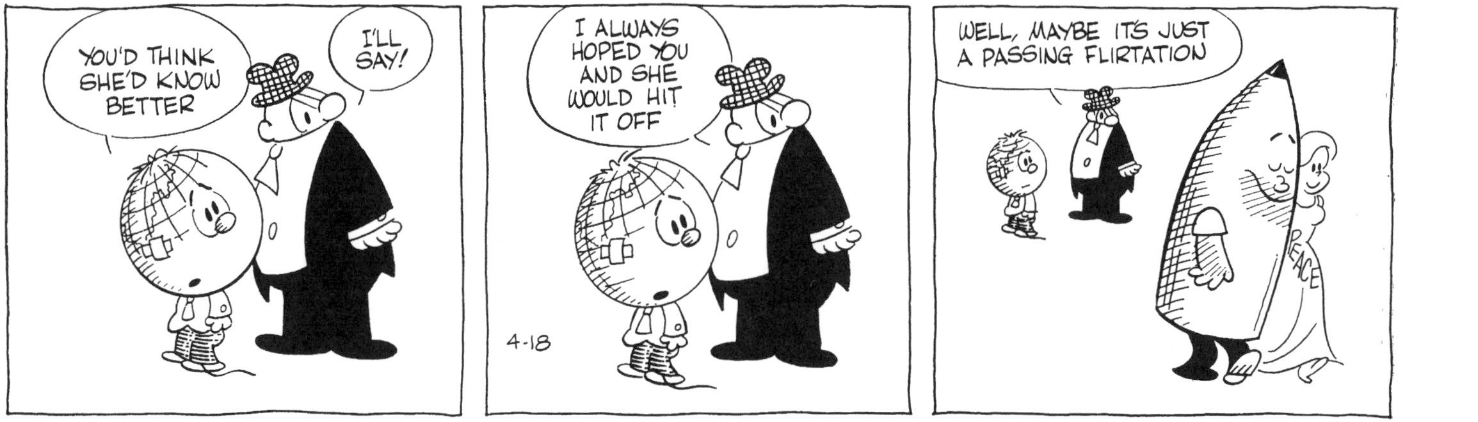
YOU'D THINK SHE'D KNOW BETTER
I'LL SAY!
I ALWAYS HOPED YOU AND SHE WOULD HIT IT OFF
4-18
WELL, MAYBE IT'S JUST A PASSING FLIRTATION
PEACE

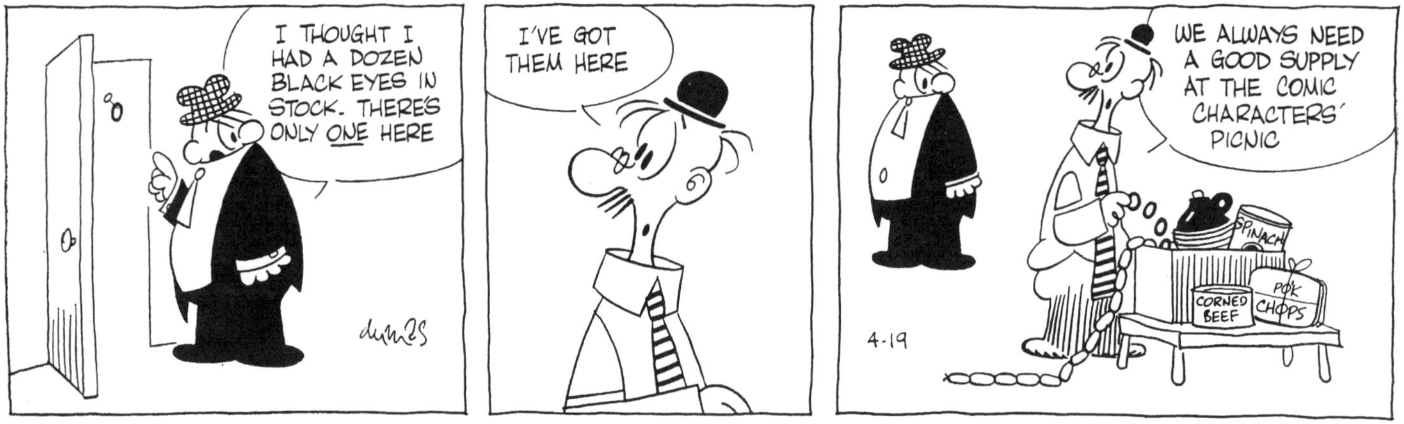
I THOUGHT I HAD A DOZEN BLACK EYES IN STOCK. THERE'S ONLY ONE HERE
dumas
I'VE GOT THEM HERE
WE ALWAYS NEED A GOOD SUPPLY AT THE COMIC CHARACTERS' PICNIC
SPINACH
CORNED BEEF
POK CHOPS
4-19

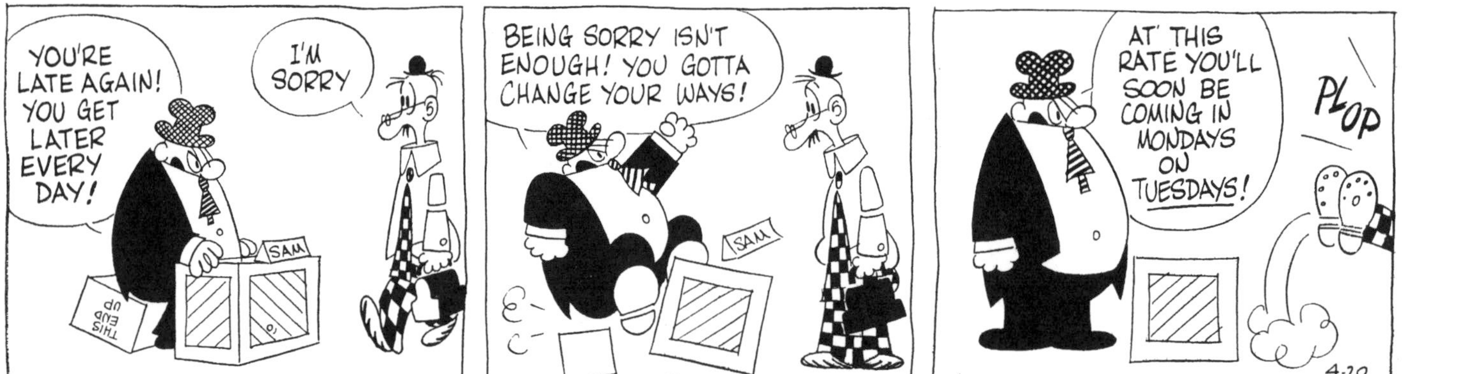
YOU'RE LATE AGAIN! YOU GET LATER EVERY DAY!
I'M SORRY
SAM
THIS END UP
BEING SORRY ISN'T ENOUGH! YOU GOTTA CHANGE YOUR WAYS!
SAM
AT THIS RATE YOU'LL SOON BE COMING IN MONDAYS ON TUESDAYS!
PLOP
dumas
4-20

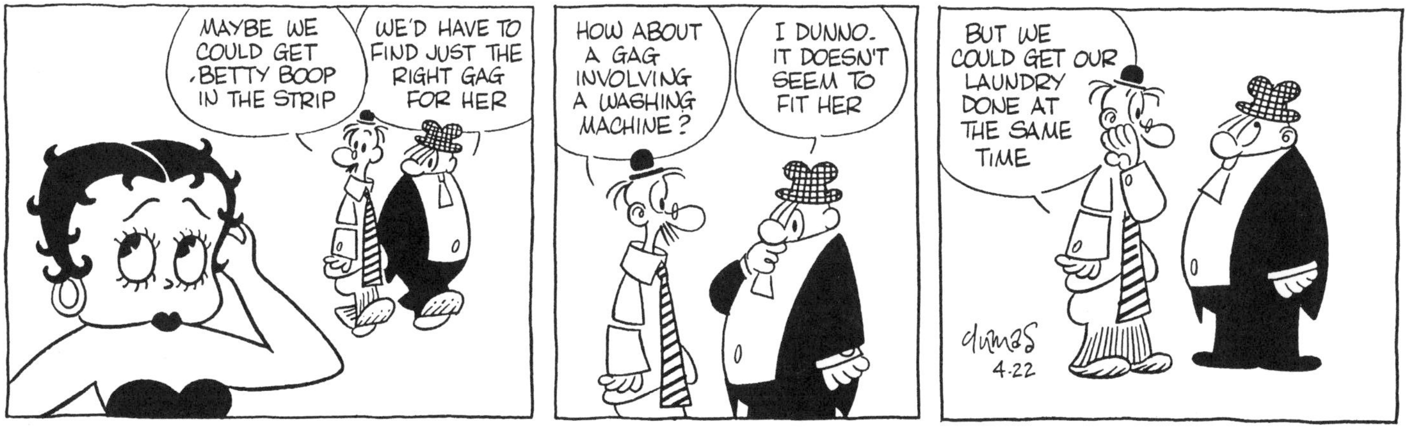
MAYBE WE COULD GET BETTY BOOP IN THE STRIP
WE'D HAVE TO FIND JUST THE RIGHT GAG FOR HER
HOW ABOUT A GAG INVOLVING A WASHING MACHINE?
I DUNNO- IT DOESN'T SEEM TO FIT HER
BUT WE COULD GET OUR LAUNDRY DONE AT THE SAME TIME
dumas
4-22

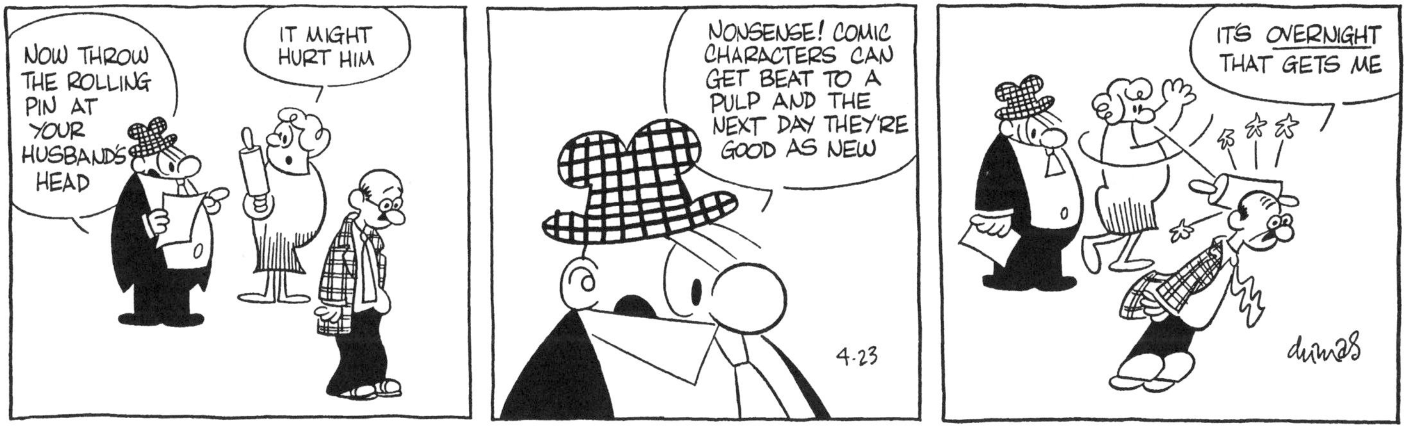
NOW THROW THE ROLLING PIN AT YOUR HUSBAND'S HEAD
IT MIGHT HURT HIM
NONSENSE! COMIC CHARACTERS CAN GET BEAT TO A PULP AND THE NEXT DAY THEY'RE GOOD AS NEW
4-23
IT'S OVERNIGHT THAT GETS ME
dumas

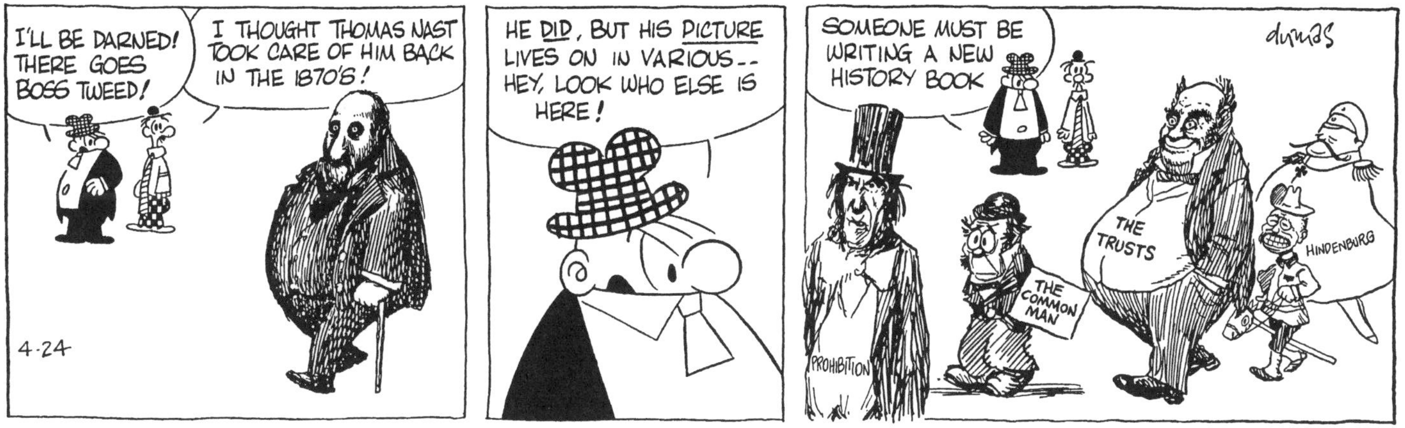
I'LL BE DARNED! THERE GOES BOSS TWEED!
I THOUGHT THOMAS NAST TOOK CARE OF HIM BACK IN THE 1870'S!
4-24
HE DID, BUT HIS PICTURE LIVES ON IN VARIOUS-- HEY, LOOK WHO ELSE IS HERE!
SOMEONE MUST BE WRITING A NEW HISTORY BOOK
dumas
THE TRUSTS
HINDENBURG
THE COMMON MAN
PROHIBITION

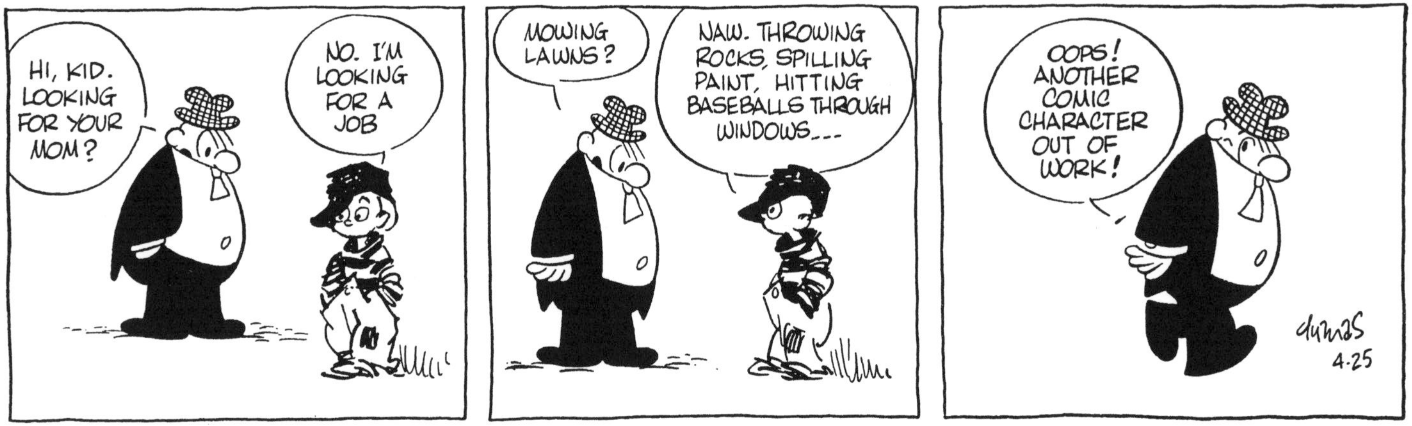
HI, KID. LOOKING FOR YOUR MOM?
NO. I'M LOOKING FOR A JOB
MOWING LAWNS?
NAW. THROWING ROCKS, SPILLING PAINT, HITTING BASEBALLS THROUGH WINDOWS...
OOPS! ANOTHER COMIC CHARACTER OUT OF WORK!
dumas
4-25

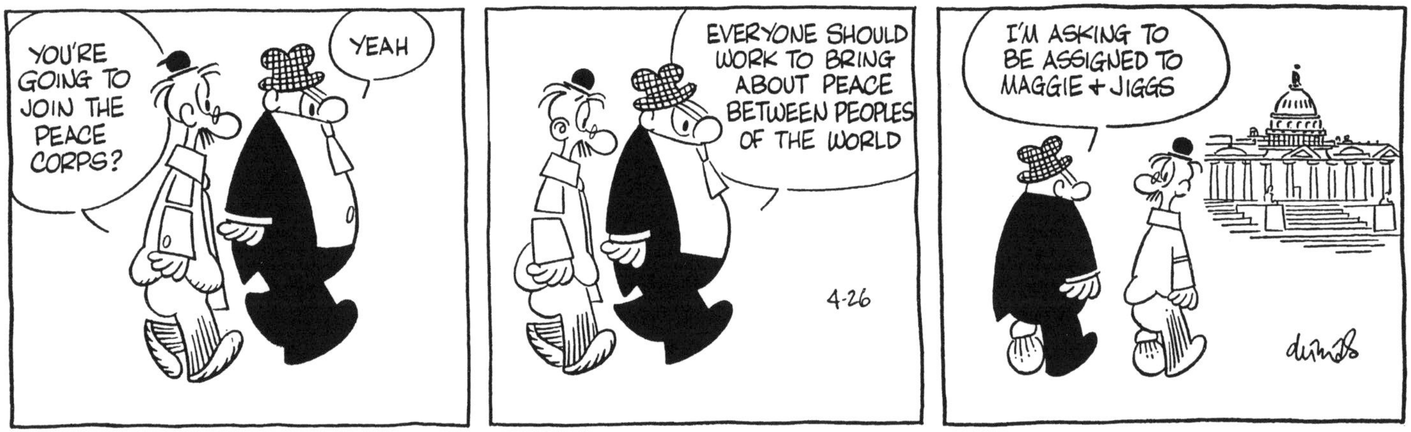
YOU'RE GOING TO JOIN THE PEACE CORPS?
YEAH
EVERYONE SHOULD WORK TO BRING ABOUT PEACE BETWEEN PEOPLES OF THE WORLD
4-26
I'M ASKING TO BE ASSIGNED TO MAGGIE + JIGGS
dumas

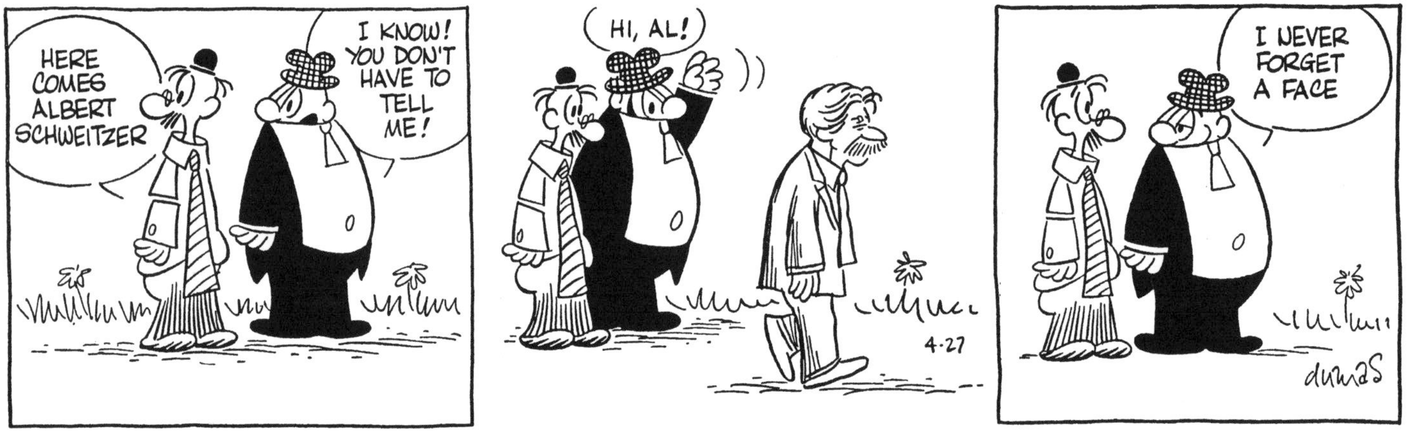
HERE COMES ALBERT SCHWEITZER
I KNOW! YOU DON'T HAVE TO TELL ME!
HI, AL!
4-27
I NEVER FORGET A FACE
dumas

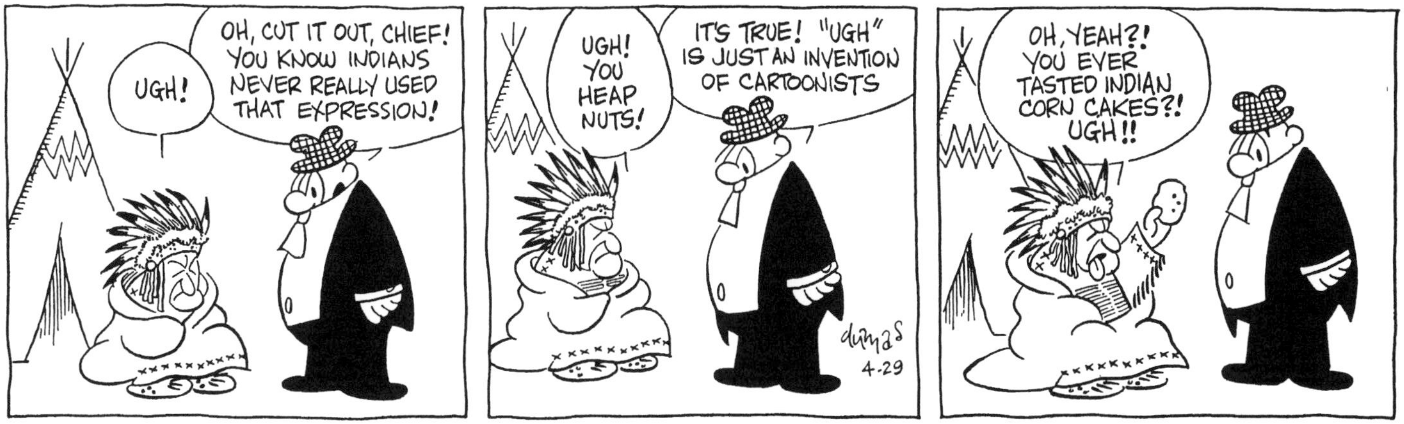
UGH!
OH, CUT IT OUT, CHIEF! YOU KNOW INDIANS NEVER REALLY USED THAT EXPRESSION!
UGH! YOU HEAP NUTS!
IT'S TRUE! "UGH" IS JUST AN INVENTION OF CARTOONISTS
OH, YEAH?! YOU EVER TASTED INDIAN CORN CAKES?! UGH!!
dumas
4-29

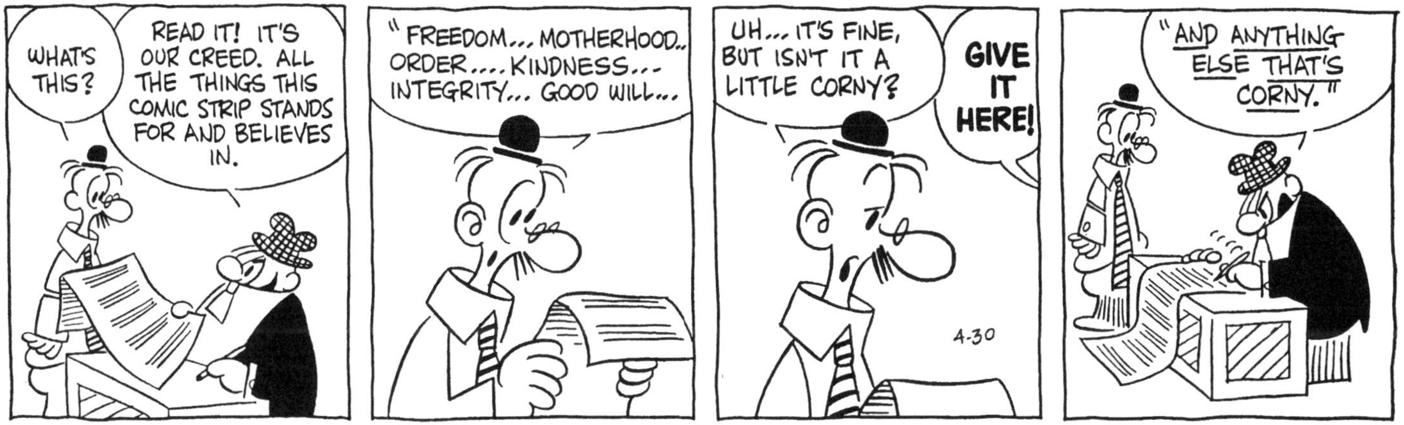
WHAT'S THIS?
READ IT! IT'S OUR CREED. ALL THE THINGS THIS COMIC STRIP STANDS FOR AND BELIEVES IN.
"FREEDOM... MOTHERHOOD.. ORDER.... KINDNESS... INTEGRITY... GOOD WILL...
UH... IT'S FINE, BUT ISN'T IT A LITTLE CORNY?
GIVE IT HERE!
4-30
"AND ANYTHING ELSE THAT'S CORNY."

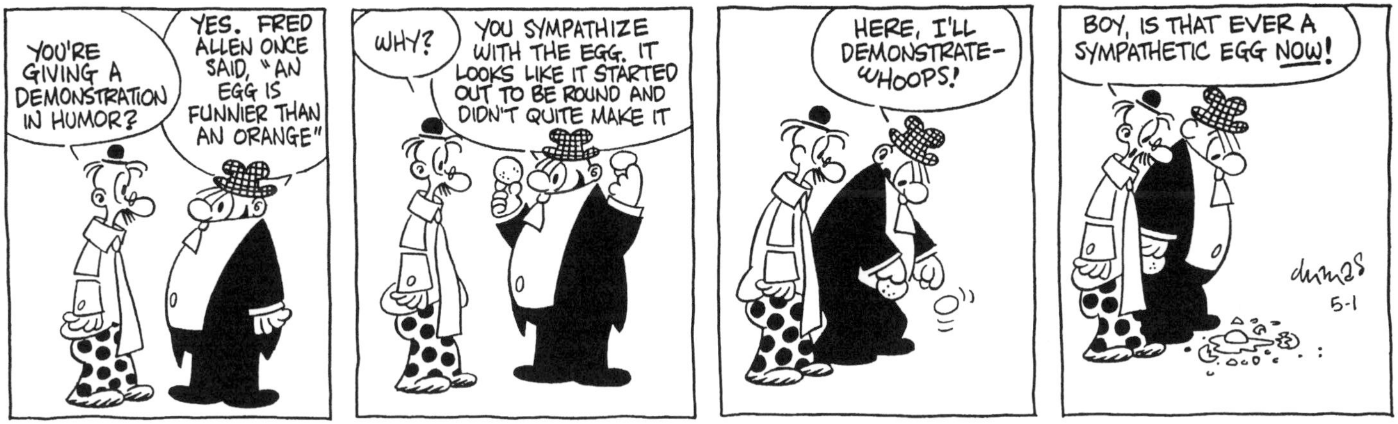
YOU'RE GIVING A DEMONSTRATION IN HUMOR?
YES. FRED ALLEN ONCE SAID, "AN EGG IS FUNNIER THAN AN ORANGE"
WHY?
YOU SYMPATHIZE WITH THE EGG. IT LOOKS LIKE IT STARTED OUT TO BE ROUND AND DIDN'T QUITE MAKE IT
HERE, I'LL DEMONSTRATE- WHOOPS!
BOY, IS THAT EVER A SYMPATHETIC EGG NOW!
dumas
5-1

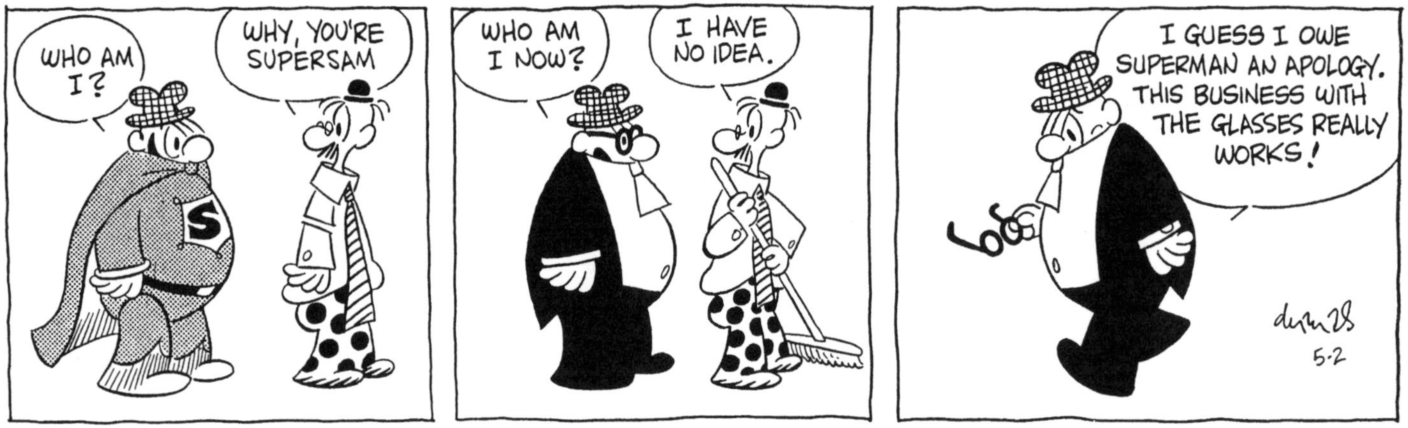
WHO AM I?
WHY, YOU'RE SUPERSAM
WHO AM I NOW?
I HAVE NO IDEA.
I GUESS I OWE SUPERMAN AN APOLOGY. THIS BUSINESS WITH THE GLASSES REALLY WORKS!
5-2

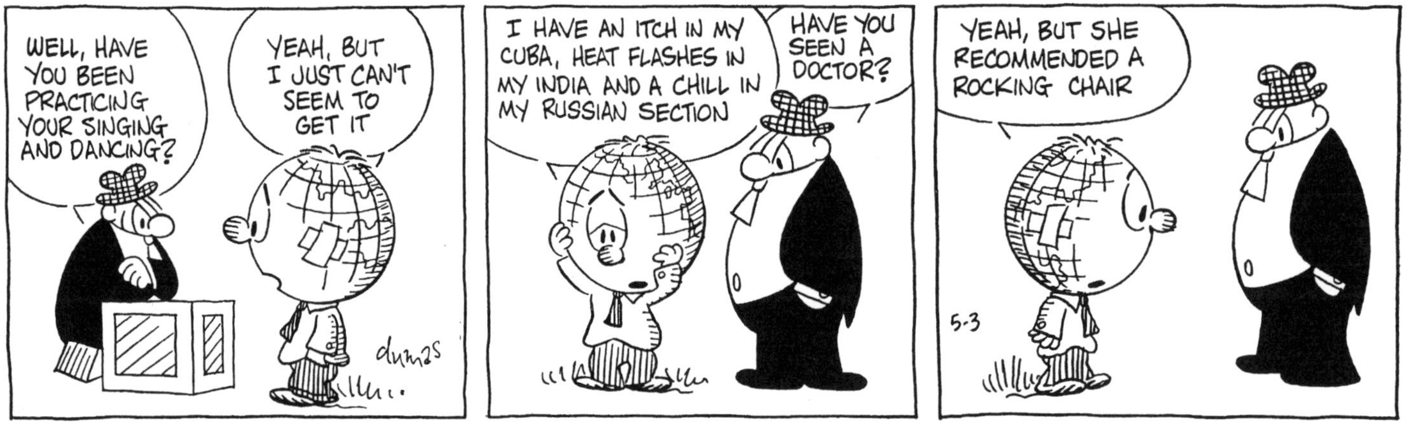
WELL, HAVE YOU BEEN PRACTICING YOUR SINGING AND DANCING?
YEAH, BUT I JUST CAN'T SEEM TO GET IT
I HAVE AN ITCH IN MY CUBA, HEAT FLASHES IN MY INDIA AND A CHILL IN MY RUSSIAN SECTION
HAVE YOU SEEN A DOCTOR?
YEAH, BUT SHE RECOMMENDED A ROCKING CHAIR
5-3

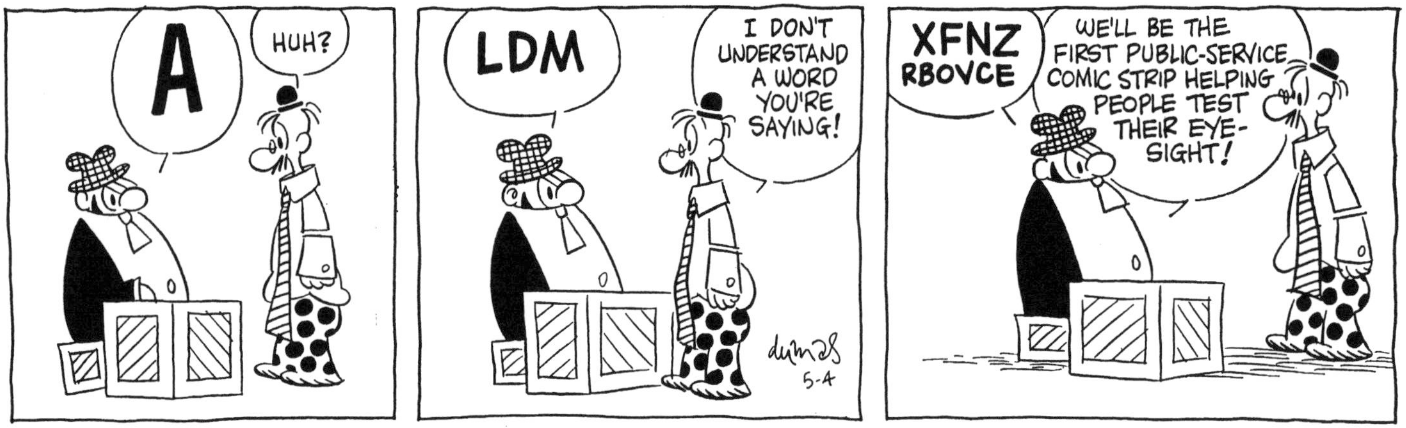
A
HUH?
LDM
I DON'T UNDERSTAND A WORD YOU'RE SAYING!
5-4
XFNZ
RBOVCE
WE'LL BE THE FIRST PUBLIC-SERVICE COMIC STRIP HELPING PEOPLE TEST THEIR EYE-SIGHT!

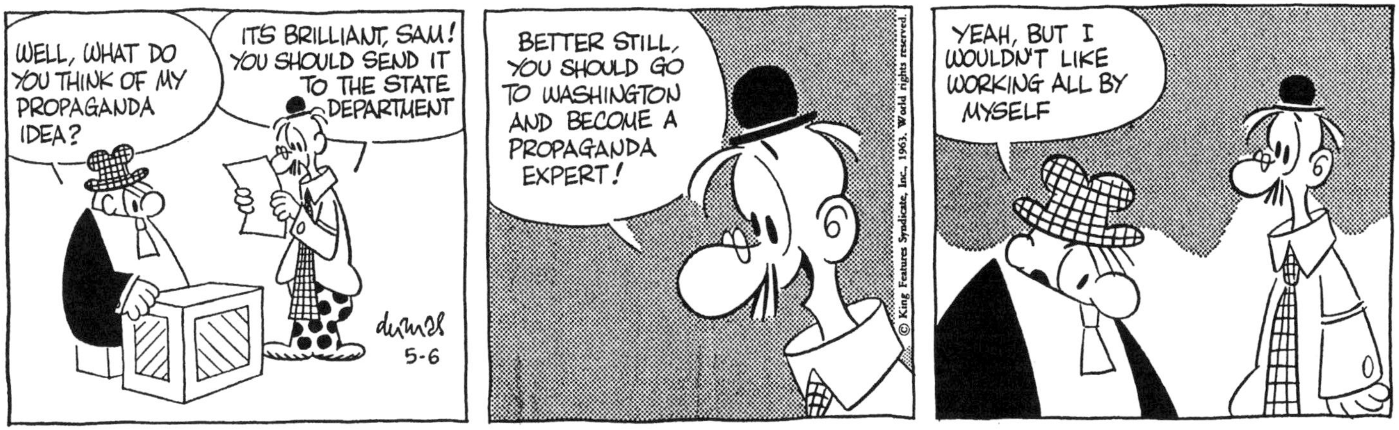
WELL, WHAT DO YOU THINK OF MY PROPAGANDA IDEA?
IT'S BRILLIANT, SAM! YOU SHOULD SEND IT TO THE STATE DEPARTMENT
dumas 5-6
BETTER STILL, YOU SHOULD GO TO WASHINGTON AND BECOME A PROPAGANDA EXPERT!
© King Features Syndicate, Inc., 1963. World rights reserved.
YEAH, BUT I WOULDN'T LIKE WORKING ALL BY MYSELF

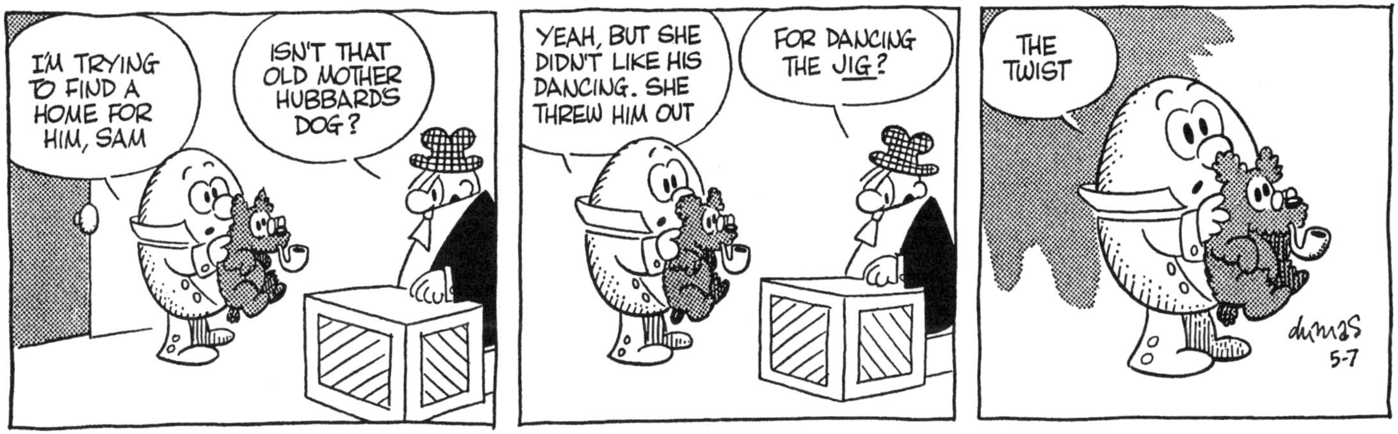
I'M TRYING TO FIND A HOME FOR HIM, SAM
ISN'T THAT OLD MOTHER HUBBARD'S DOG?
YEAH, BUT SHE DIDN'T LIKE HIS DANCING. SHE THREW HIM OUT
FOR DANCING THE JIG?
THE TWIST
dumas 5-7

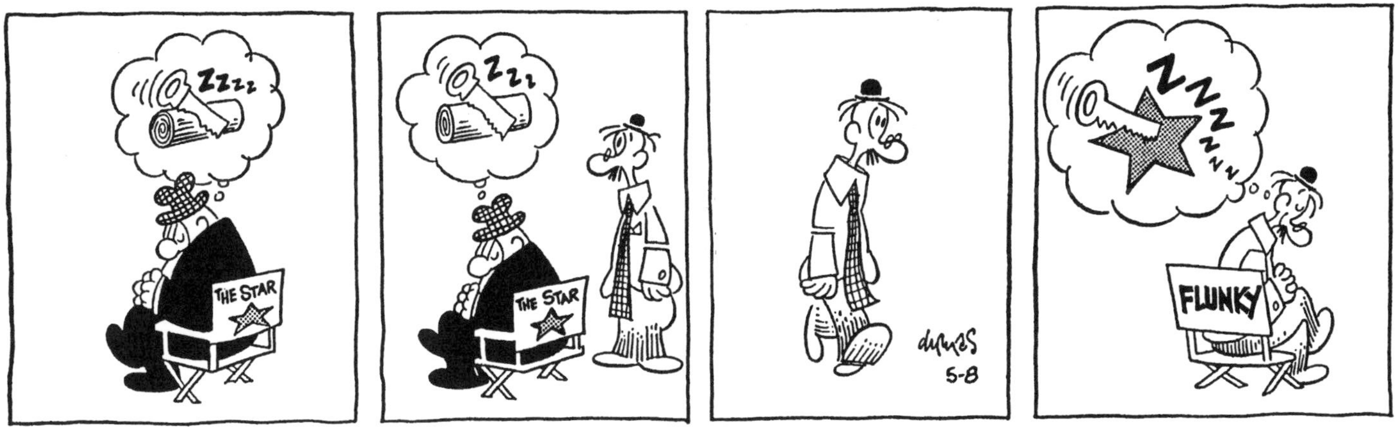
ZZZZ
THE STAR
ZZZ
THE STAR
dumas 5-8
ZZZZZZZ
FLUNKY

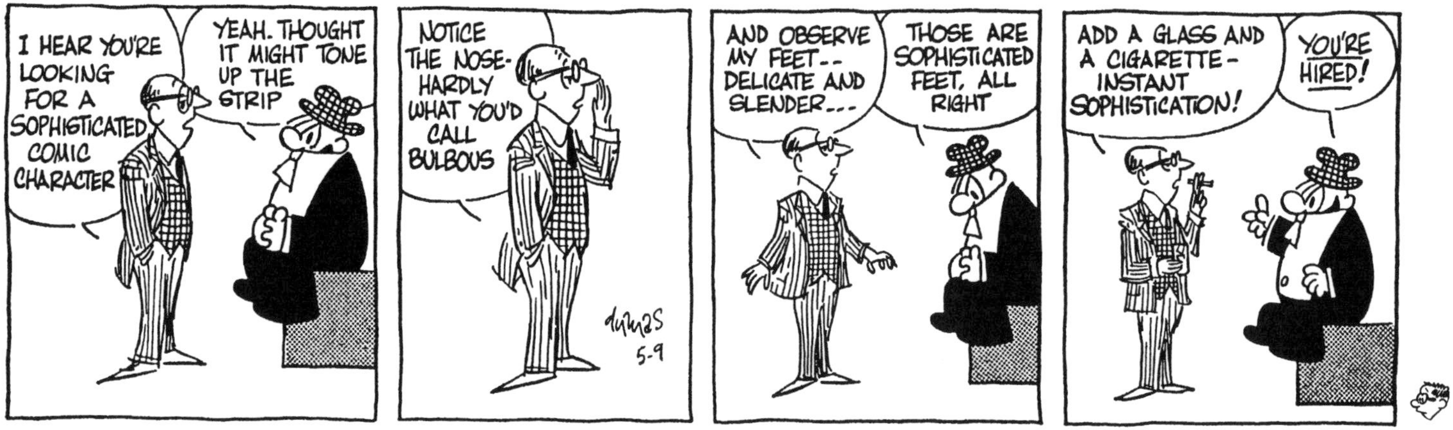
I HEAR YOU'RE LOOKING FOR A SOPHISTICATED COMIC CHARACTER
YEAH. THOUGHT IT MIGHT TONE UP THE STRIP
NOTICE THE NOSE- HARDLY WHAT YOU'D CALL BULBOUS
dumas
5-9
AND OBSERVE MY FEET-- DELICATE AND SLENDER...
THOSE ARE SOPHISTICATED FEET, ALL RIGHT
ADD A GLASS AND A CIGARETTE- INSTANT SOPHISTICATION!
YOU'RE HIRED!

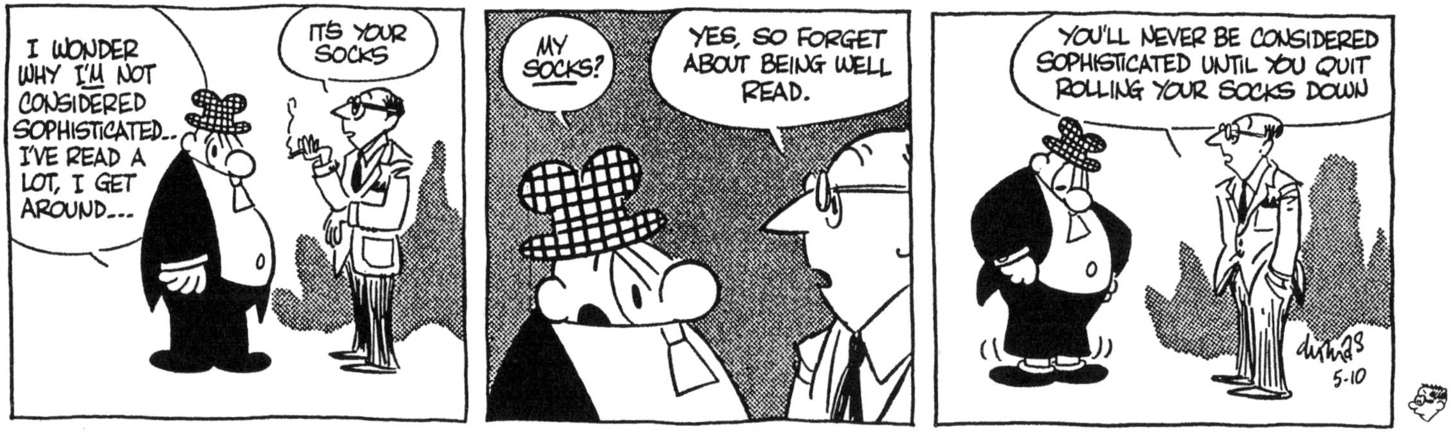
I WONDER WHY I'M NOT CONSIDERED SOPHISTICATED.. I'VE READ A LOT, I GET AROUND...
IT'S YOUR SOCKS
MY SOCKS?
YES, SO FORGET ABOUT BEING WELL READ.
YOU'LL NEVER BE CONSIDERED SOPHISTICATED UNTIL YOU QUIT ROLLING YOUR SOCKS DOWN
dumas
5-10

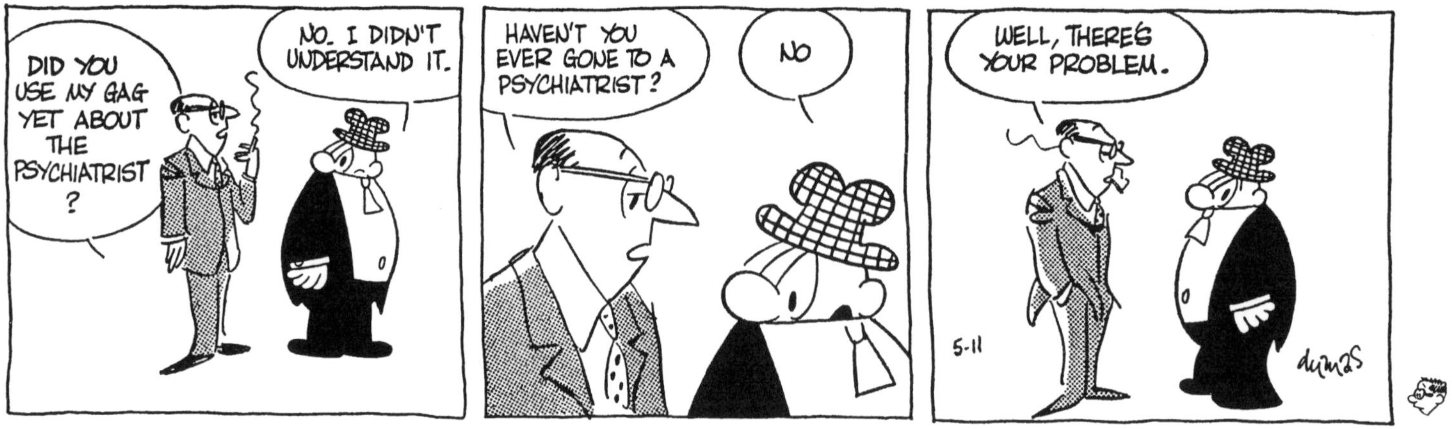
DID YOU USE MY GAG YET ABOUT THE PSYCHIATRIST ?
NO. I DIDN'T UNDERSTAND IT.
HAVEN'T YOU EVER GONE TO A PSYCHIATRIST?
NO
WELL, THERE'S YOUR PROBLEM.
5-11
dumas

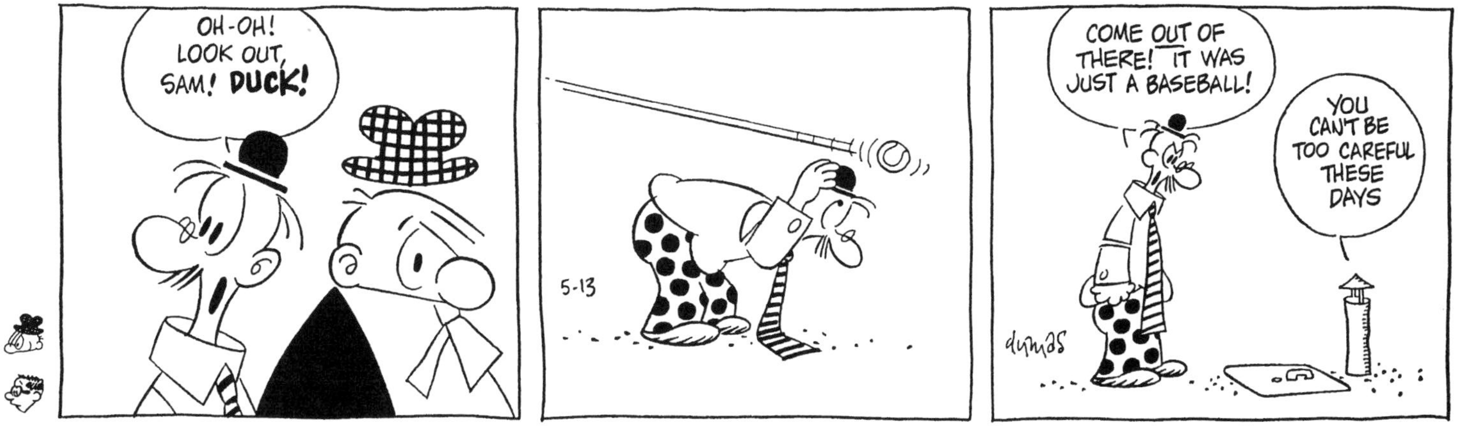
OH-OH! LOOK OUT, SAM! **DUCK!**
5-13
COME OUT OF THERE! IT WAS JUST A BASEBALL!
YOU CAN'T BE TOO CAREFUL THESE DAYS
dumas

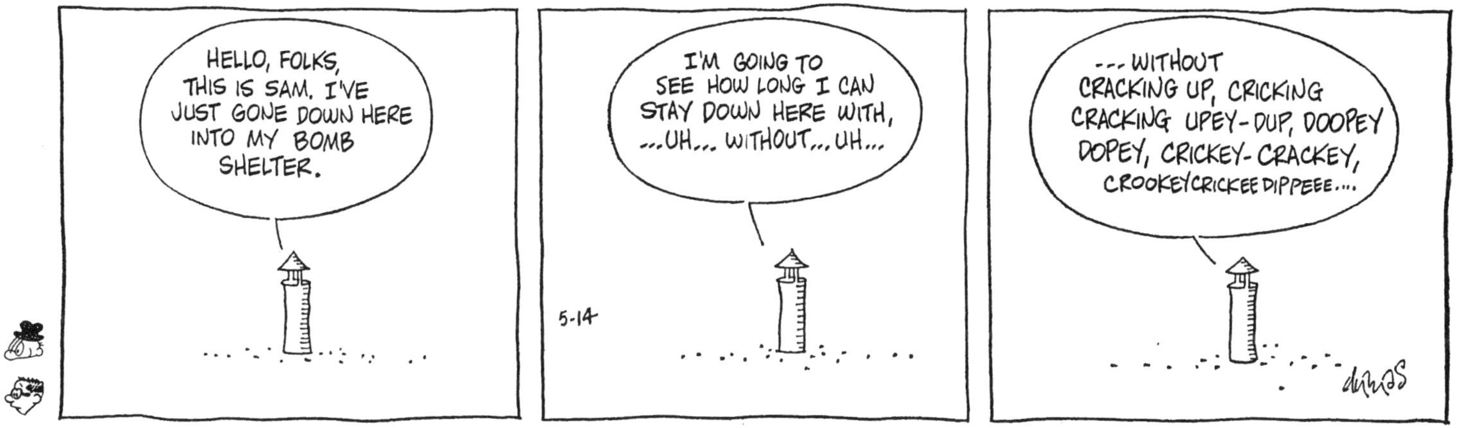
HELLO, FOLKS, THIS IS SAM. I'VE JUST GONE DOWN HERE INTO MY BOMB SHELTER.
I'M GOING TO SEE HOW LONG I CAN STAY DOWN HERE WITH, ...UH... WITHOUT... UH...
5-14
---WITHOUT CRACKING UP, CRICKING CRACKING UPEY-DUP, DOOPEY DOPEY, CRICKEY-CRACKEY, CROOKEYCRICKEE DIPPEEE....
dumas

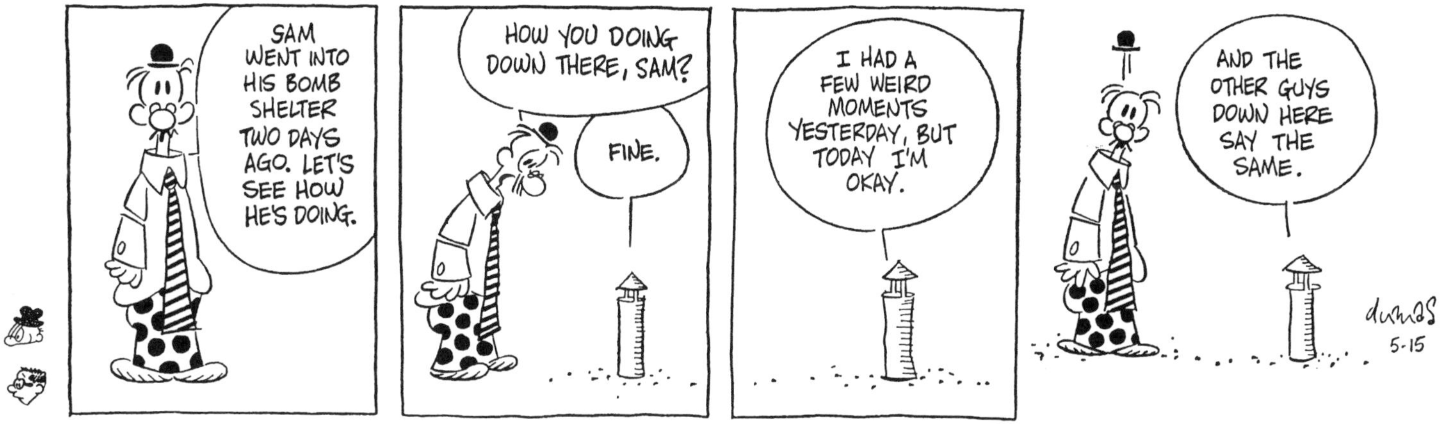
SAM WENT INTO HIS BOMB SHELTER TWO DAYS AGO. LET'S SEE HOW HE'S DOING.
HOW YOU DOING DOWN THERE, SAM?
FINE.
I HAD A FEW WEIRD MOMENTS YESTERDAY, BUT TODAY I'M OKAY.
AND THE OTHER GUYS DOWN HERE SAY THE SAME.
dumas
5-15

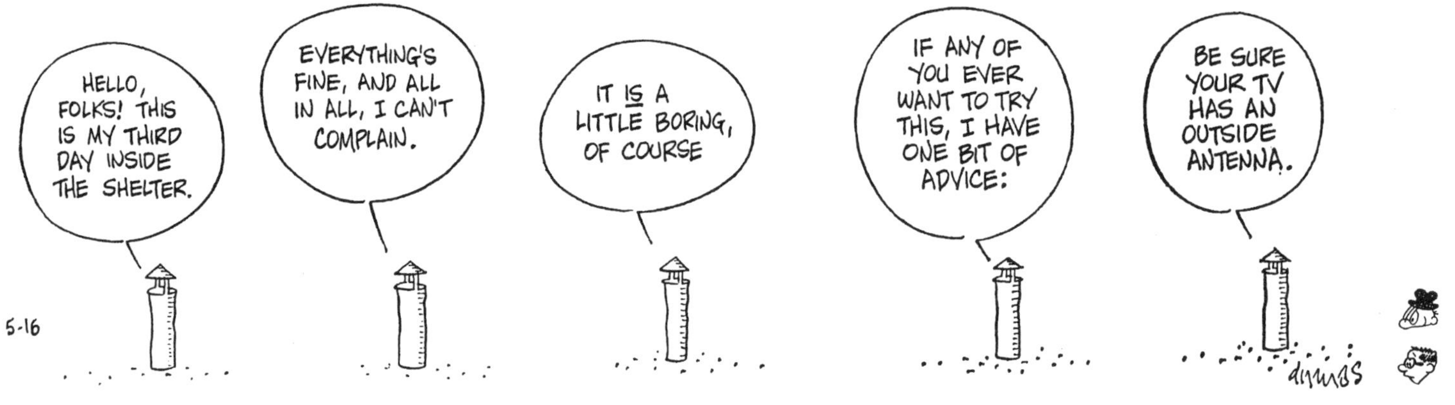
HELLO, FOLKS! THIS IS MY THIRD DAY INSIDE THE SHELTER.
EVERYTHING'S FINE, AND ALL IN ALL, I CAN'T COMPLAIN.
IT IS A LITTLE BORING, OF COURSE
IF ANY OF YOU EVER WANT TO TRY THIS, I HAVE ONE BIT OF ADVICE:
BE SURE YOUR TV HAS AN OUTSIDE ANTENNA.
5-16

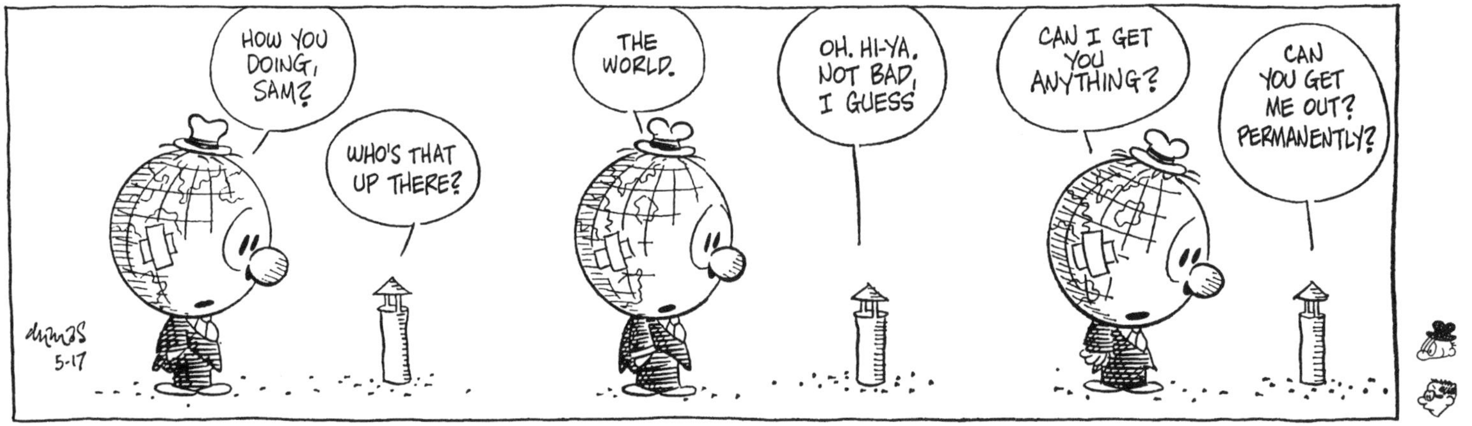
HOW YOU DOING, SAM?
WHO'S THAT UP THERE?
THE WORLD.
OH. HI-YA. NOT BAD, I GUESS
CAN I GET YOU ANYTHING?
CAN YOU GET ME OUT? PERMANENTLY?
5-17

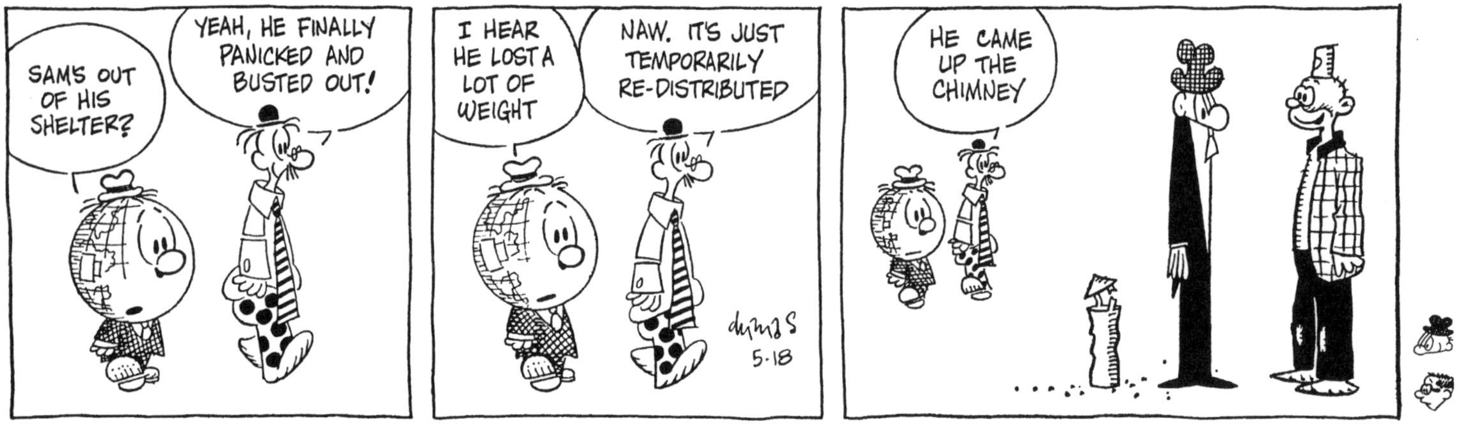
SAM'S OUT OF HIS SHELTER?
YEAH, HE FINALLY PANICKED AND BUSTED OUT!
I HEAR HE LOST A LOT OF WEIGHT
NAW. IT'S JUST TEMPORARILY RE-DISTRIBUTED
5-18
HE CAME UP THE CHIMNEY

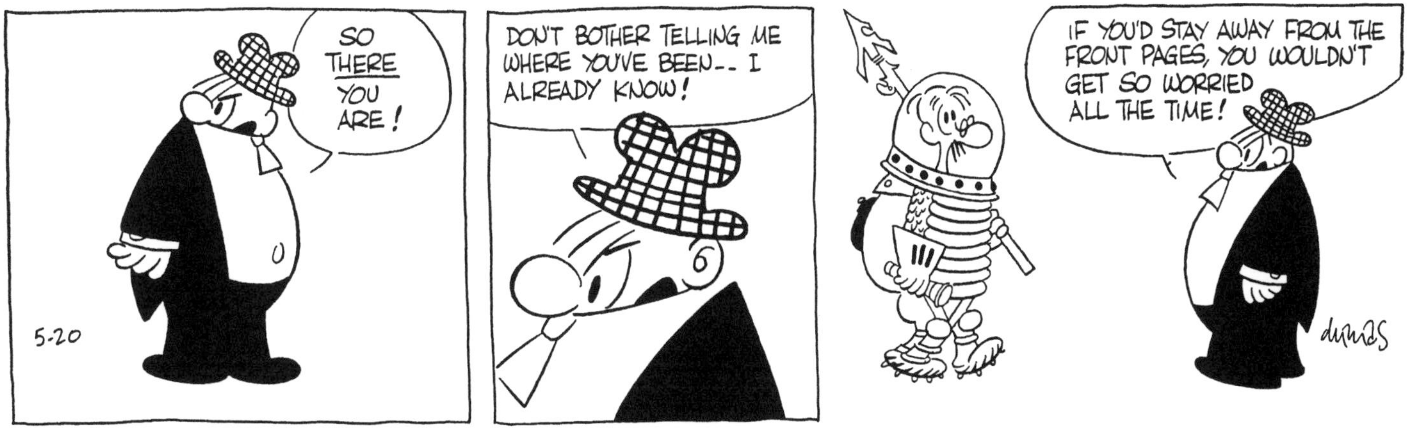
SO THERE YOU ARE!
5-20
DON'T BOTHER TELLING ME WHERE YOU'VE BEEN-- I ALREADY KNOW!
IF YOU'D STAY AWAY FROM THE FRONT PAGES, YOU WOULDN'T GET SO WORRIED ALL THE TIME!
dumas

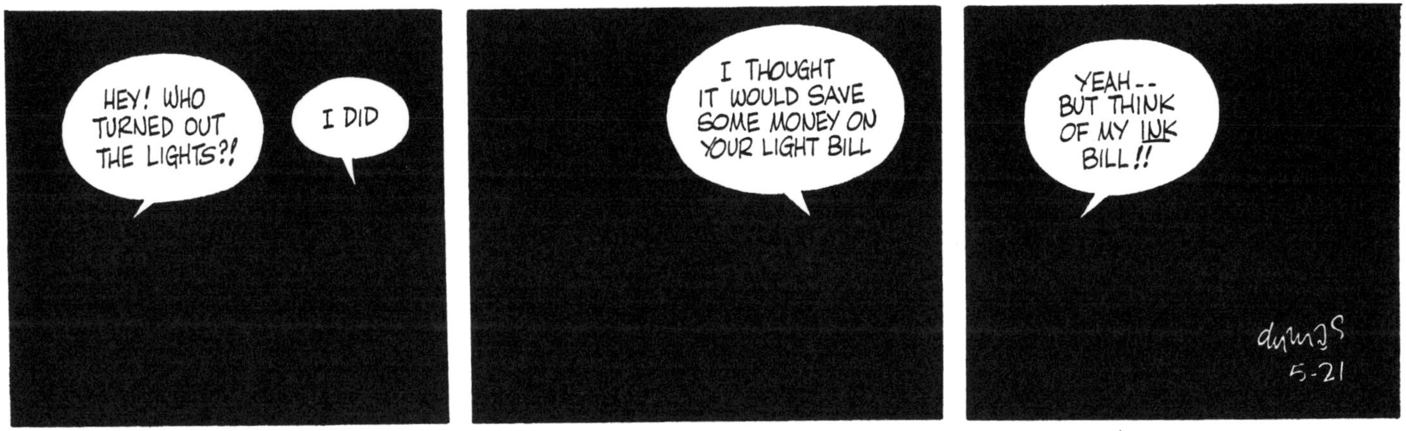
HEY! WHO TURNED OUT THE LIGHTS?!
I DID
I THOUGHT IT WOULD SAVE SOME MONEY ON YOUR LIGHT BILL
YEAH-- BUT THINK OF MY INK BILL!!
dumas
5-21

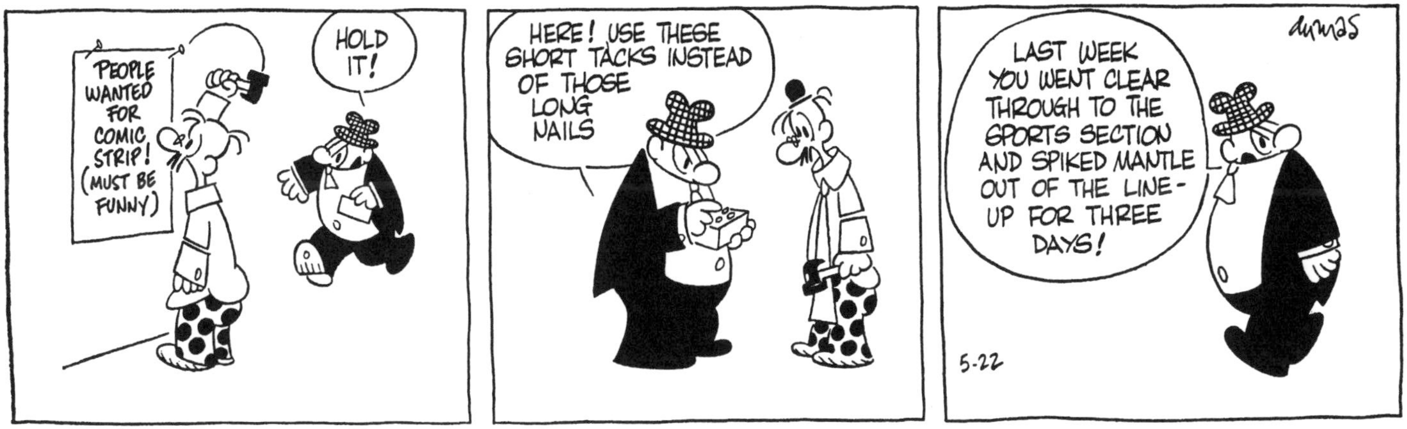
PEOPLE WANTED FOR COMIC STRIP! (MUST BE FUNNY)
HOLD IT!
HERE! USE THESE SHORT TACKS INSTEAD OF THOSE LONG NAILS
dumas
LAST WEEK YOU WENT CLEAR THROUGH TO THE SPORTS SECTION AND SPIKED MANTLE OUT OF THE LINE-UP FOR THREE DAYS!
5-22

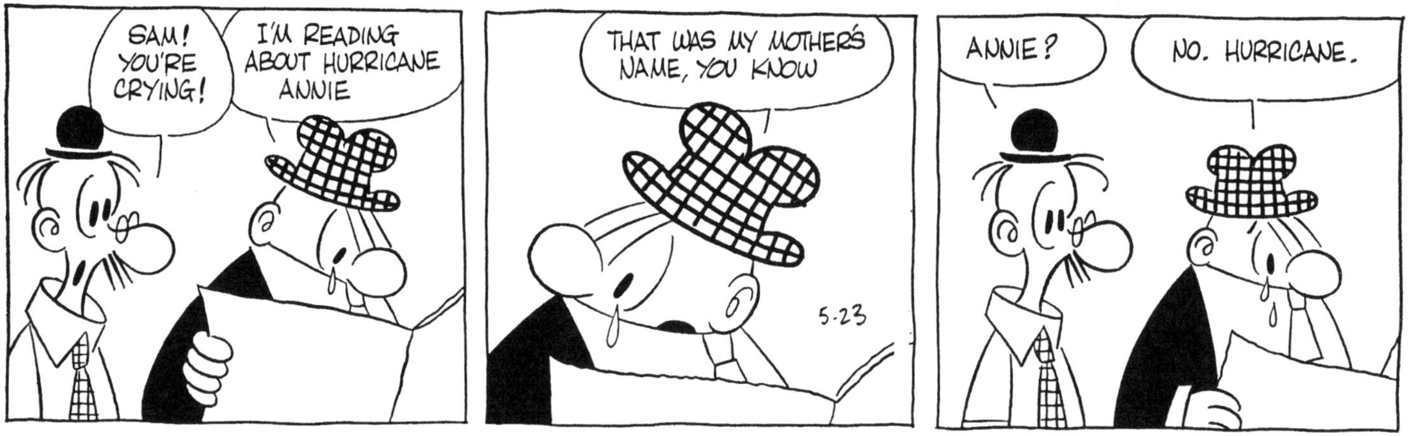
SAM! YOU'RE CRYING!
I'M READING ABOUT HURRICANE ANNIE
THAT WAS MY MOTHER'S NAME, YOU KNOW
5-23
ANNIE?
NO. HURRICANE.

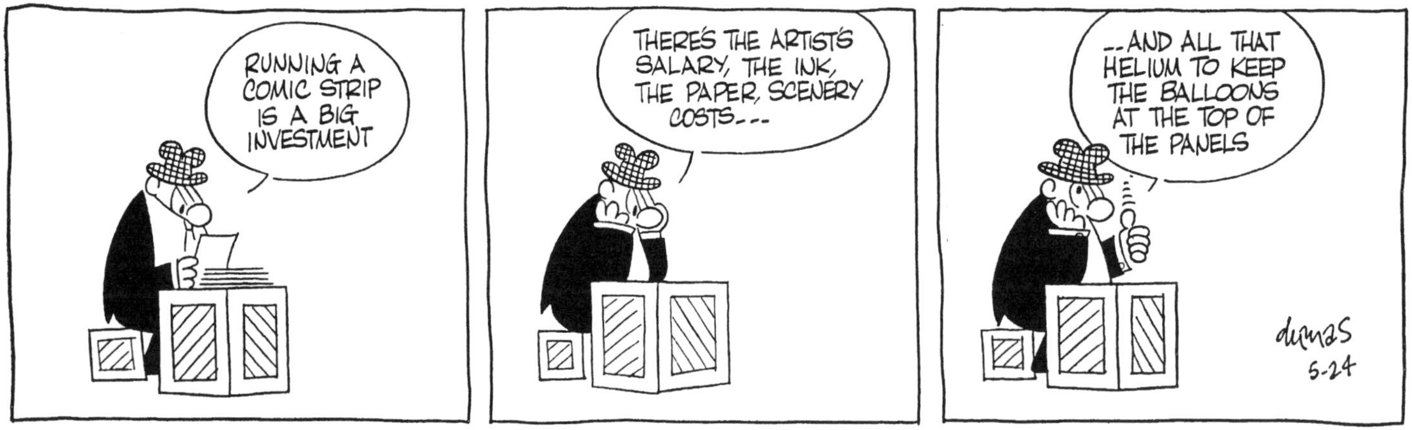
RUNNING A COMIC STRIP IS A BIG INVESTMENT
THERE'S THE ARTIST'S SALARY, THE INK, THE PAPER, SCENERY COSTS---
--AND ALL THAT HELIUM TO KEEP THE BALLOONS AT THE TOP OF THE PANELS
5-24

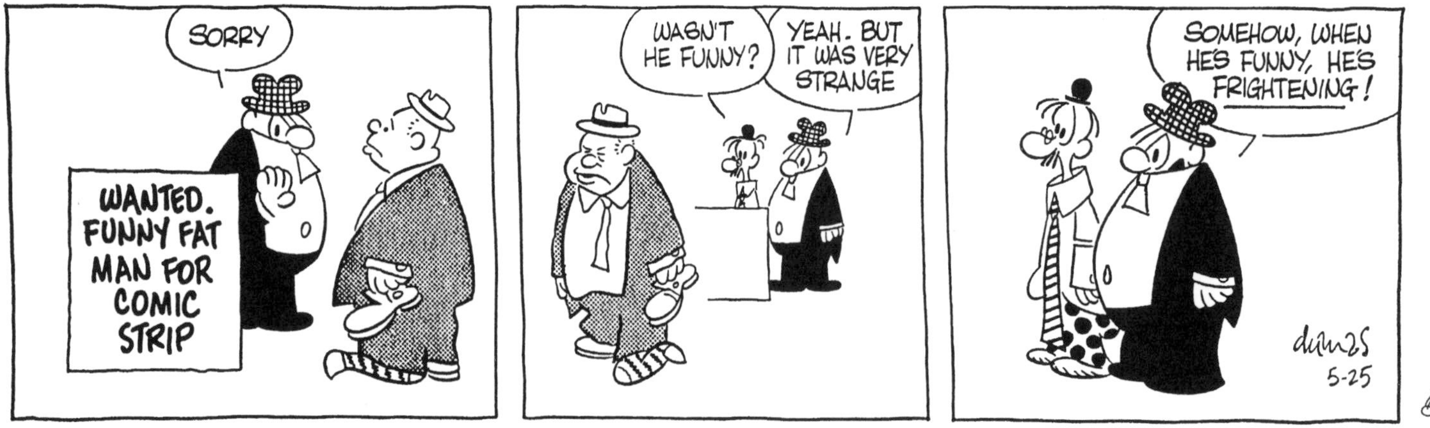
SORRY
WANTED. FUNNY FAT MAN FOR COMIC STRIP
WASN'T HE FUNNY?
YEAH. BUT IT WAS VERY STRANGE
SOMEHOW, WHEN HE'S FUNNY, HE'S FRIGHTENING!
5-25

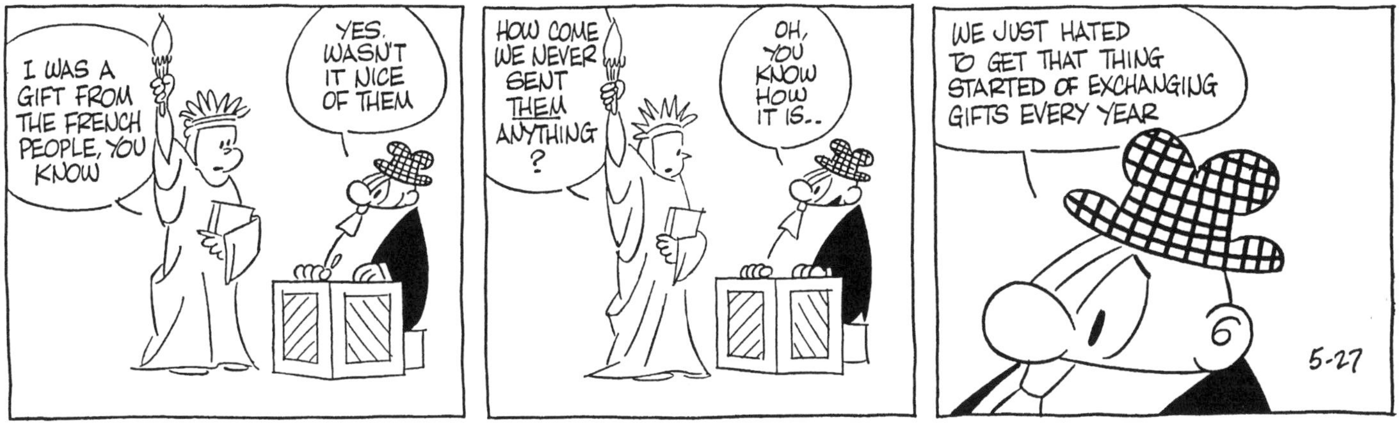
I WAS A GIFT FROM THE FRENCH PEOPLE, YOU KNOW
YES. WASN'T IT NICE OF THEM
HOW COME WE NEVER SENT THEM ANYTHING ?
OH, YOU KNOW HOW IT IS..
WE JUST HATED TO GET THAT THING STARTED OF EXCHANGING GIFTS EVERY YEAR
5-27

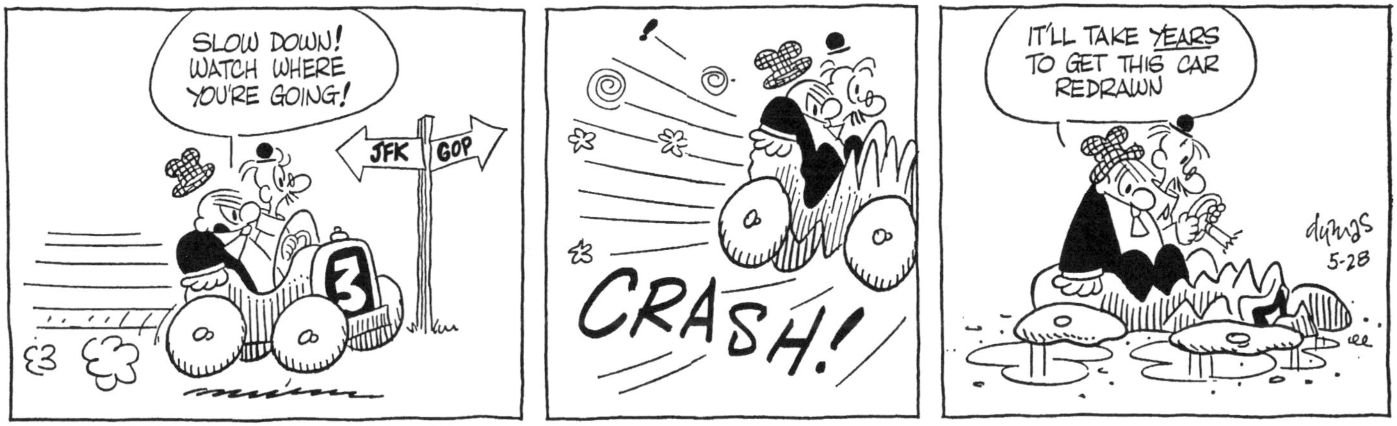
SLOW DOWN! WATCH WHERE YOU'RE GOING!
JFK
GOP
3
CRASH!
IT'LL TAKE YEARS TO GET THIS CAR REDRAWN
dumas
5-28

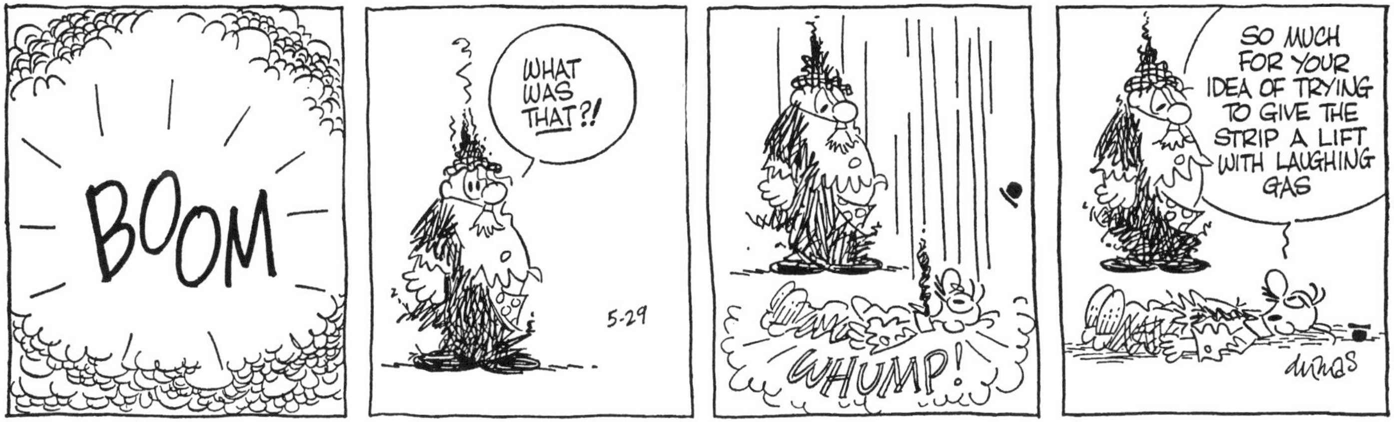
BOOM
WHAT WAS THAT?!
5-29
WHUMP!
SO MUCH FOR YOUR IDEA OF TRYING TO GIVE THE STRIP A LIFT WITH LAUGHING GAS
dumas

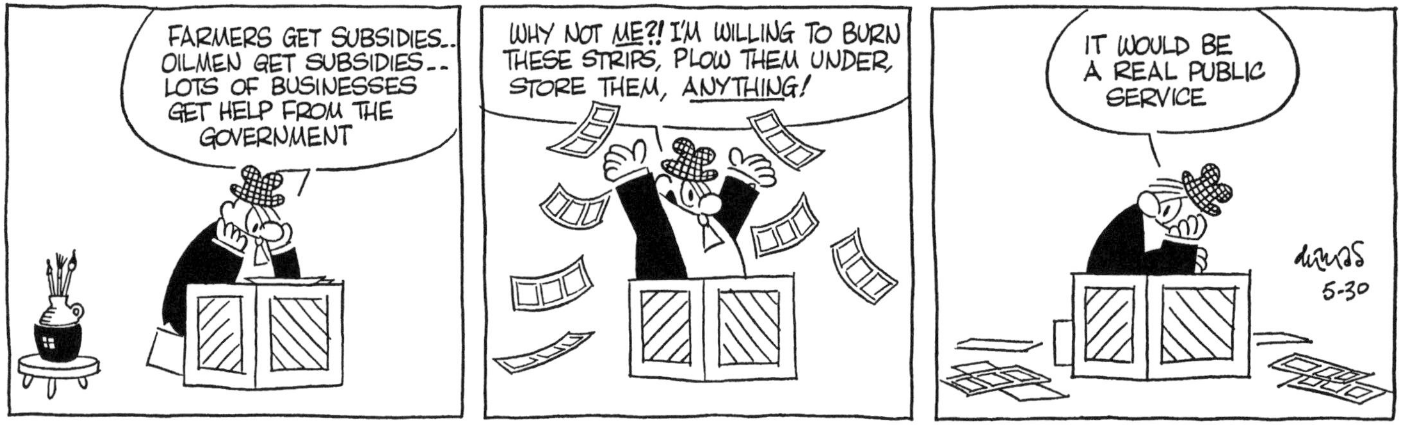
FARMERS GET SUBSIDIES.. OILMEN GET SUBSIDIES-- LOTS OF BUSINESSES GET HELP FROM THE GOVERNMENT
WHY NOT ME?! I'M WILLING TO BURN THESE STRIPS, PLOW THEM UNDER, STORE THEM, ANYTHING!
IT WOULD BE A REAL PUBLIC SERVICE
5-30

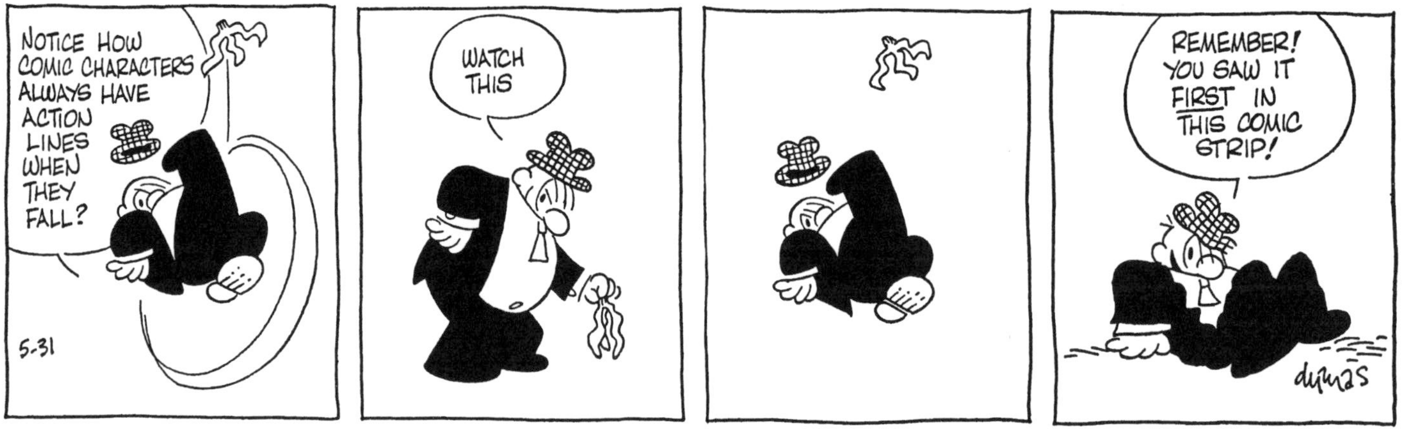
NOTICE HOW COMIC CHARACTERS ALWAYS HAVE ACTION LINES WHEN THEY FALL?
5-31
WATCH THIS
REMEMBER! YOU SAW IT FIRST IN THIS COMIC STRIP!

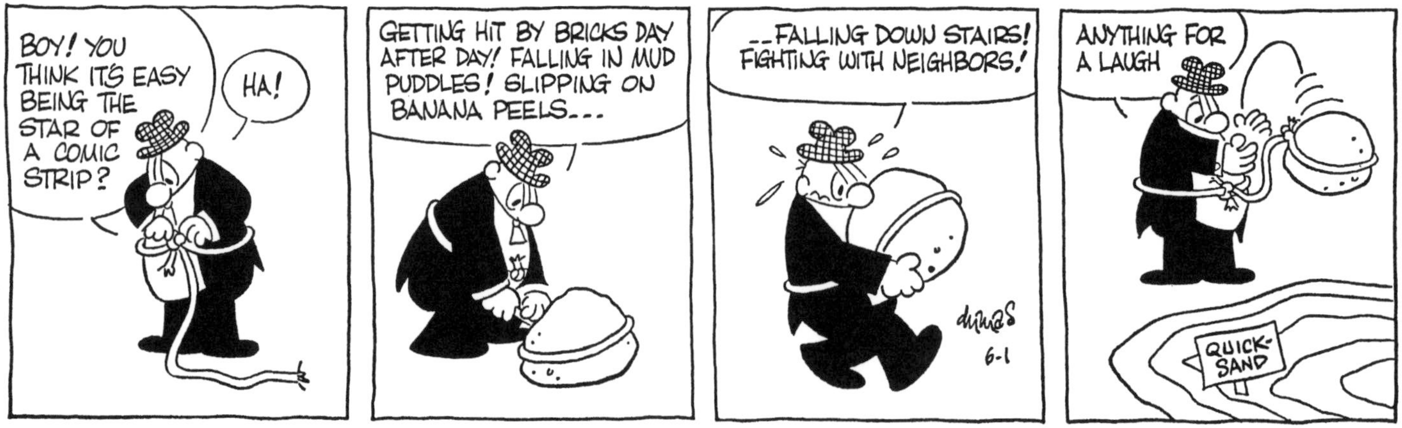
BOY! YOU THINK IT'S EASY BEING THE STAR OF A COMIC STRIP?
HA!
GETTING HIT BY BRICKS DAY AFTER DAY! FALLING IN MUD PUDDLES! SLIPPING ON BANANA PEELS---
--FALLING DOWN STAIRS! FIGHTING WITH NEIGHBORS!
6-1
ANYTHING FOR A LAUGH
QUICK-SAND

STRIP COMMENTS

by JERRY DUMAS

I have not looked at most of these strips for a very long time. Now, seeing them again after 47 years, some of the strips, both gag and art, look fine, others are just OK, while others fill me with dismay. A few are pretty bad; space is not well used, composition is faulty, and the sidekick character who became "Silo" in *Sam and Silo* is not constructed as well as he could be. A good dozen of the drawings I would happily consign to oblivion.

The two very best weeks, in my opinion, where *Sam's Strip* became all that it could be, were the weeks of April 30 to May 5, 1962 (the comic characters convention), and the week of October 1 to 6, 1962 (with Krazy Kat and Ignatz and Tenniel's *Alice in Wonderland* characters).

The six daily strips for comics convention week took me three weeks to draw (not counting writing time). That is how long it took for research, penciling and inking (using Higgins ink and a Gillotte 170 pen point). It must have taken Mort most of a morning to ink the lettering. It's obvious that this kind of week could not be drawn very often; we would never have been able to keep up with the deadline, which was tough enough already doing fairly normal strips.

Readers and fellow cartoonists thought then, and apparently still think today, that there was a lot of cutting and pasting and early copy machine work going on. But every single strip was penciled and inked from scratch, with intensive copying of famous characters. And it wasn't just out-and-out copying; sometimes heads had to be turned, expressions and gestures altered, positions reversed. After a

MAYBE I NEED A FOOD GIMMICK LIKE DAGWOOD'S SANDWICH
LET'S SEE.. POPEYE HAS SPINACH.. JIGGS HAS CORNED BEEF AND CABBAGE..
LI'L ABNER LIKES TURNIPS.. SNUFFY SMITH LIKES HIS CORN SQUEEZIN'S
WHAT'S CHEAP ?

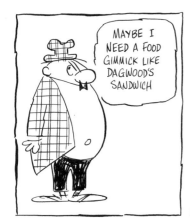

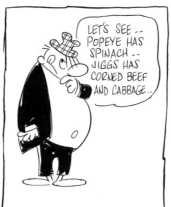

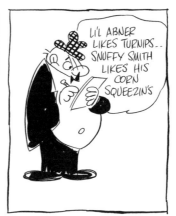

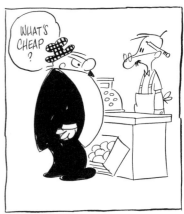

Jerry explains: "This is one of the first 'exploratory' strips, inked by Mort [above]. We had already decided on the basic look of Sam's face. "Now what are we going to do with the rest of him?' we wondered. The idea was to make it look like we were **drawing**. Mort wrote this gag. And this is the first appearance of Sam's sidekick, who never had a name in *Sam's Strip*, but who became Silo in *Sam and Silo*. The redrawn version of this strip [opposite] was published on April 17, 1963."

couple of years I could see that I might not want to be still scratching away at all this thirty years hence.

I did learn a lot from carefully copying the drawing of George Herriman, John Tenniel and some of the others, Thomas Nast and Billy DeBeck in particular. Their drawings were complete, they were solid, there was nothing empty or unfinished about them; their drawings were sculptural. I have the *Alice in Wonderland* original strip, where Sam takes a wrong turn off the turnpike (October 3, 1962), matted and framed and on my wall today. For many years it hung in my wife's parents' home in Phoenix, Arizona, and when they died the strip came back to Connecticut. It is in mint condition, thanks to Higgins ink and good paper, and I enjoy looking at this one a lot. But it's not me that makes it sing, it's Tenniel's White Rabbit, Mad Hatter and solid line work in the trees and leaves.

Oddly enough, a strip with the least work in it will catch a reader's eye first when he turns to the comics page. There is nothing like a patch of white space to make a reader say, "What's going on here?" One of the most famous *Sam's Strip* gags is the one where for three panels you see in large letters the words, "CLOSED FOR REPAIRS" (January 19, 1962). In the last panel, Sam pulls aside a curtain and says to us, "Ink blot." It attracted the eye, it summed up what the strip was all about, and it could not have taken more than fifteen minutes to do.

So here are my thoughts about a random selection of strips:

October 18, 1961 (page 1): This John Steinbeck gag, the third strip ever published, is one of my top favorites. I don't like my drawing of the sidekick, but the gag, by Mort, goes deeper than others and has something to say about our culture.

December 13, 1961 (page 17): Charles Addams' old lady popping out of the cake. All the cartoonists I knew admired the work of Charles Addams. He was in and out of Greenwich, Connecticut (where I live) socially, but spent most his time in New York City and Long Island. He should have won the Reuben Award early on, but he was not a member of The National Cartoonists Society, and in those days members tended not to think outside the box. I don't know why Mort and I didn't write gags about James Thurber's cartoon characters; we should have. I knew Thurber's widow, Helen, and she once had our family up to Cornwall, Connecticut for lunch. I sat in Thurber's wingchair and she showed me how he tried to draw on a large pad of paper, one scrawl to a page, when he was nearly blind.

YOU KNOW WHAT I SHOULD HAVE? A FOOD GIMMICK LIKE DAGWOOD'S SANDWICH
4-17
© King Features Syndicate, Inc., 1963. World rights reserved.
LET'S SEE-- POPEYE HAS SPINACH-- JIGGS HAS CORNED BEEF AND CABBAGE
LI'L ABNER HAS TURNIPS-- SNUFFY SMITH HAS CORN SQUEEZIN'S
WHAT'S CHEAP?

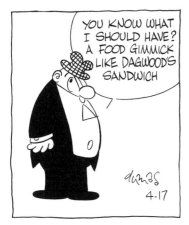

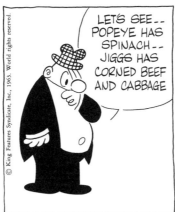

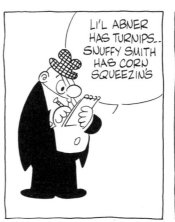

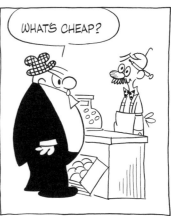

He wasn't a happy man in his last years, but he sure was funny when he was young.

December 20, 1961 (page 19): Sam brings in a little orphan girl and her dog and says it would make a great strip, with her traveling around the country. When shown *Little Orphan Annie*, he says "Oh!...we could throw out the dog and give her a monkey." Now, Harold Gray was still doing his strip – he would die in 1968 – but I never met him, never saw him at any parties or at any N.C.S. meeting. I heard that he was a loner. But about four months after our "monkey" strip appeared, a strange thing happened. A new *Little Orphan Annie* sequence began, with Annie traveling around the country – with a monkey. I never phoned or wrote him, I don't know why, but I'm certain this was his way of playing a quiet little game with us. He lived in Westport, Connecticut, only a few minutes from Greenwich, and many of our cartoonist friends also lived there and read *Sam's Strip*, so Mort and I were pretty sure he did too. I wonder if he wondered if we read his strip.

January 4, 1962 (page 24): Four panels and in each panel "Silo" is completely white – skin, shirt, pants, shoes, all white against a white background. I have no idea why I did that. He looks unfinished, like a child's coloring book. The best cartoon figures stand out from the background, they don't blend into it.

Back in the beginning of *Beetle Bailey* the uniforms were gray, accomplished with the use of all the tiny Ben Day dots. Then, for about twenty years, all the uniforms were white. On a day when there were no backgrounds, the whole strip was white; there was no sculptural solidity to the characters, and things looked somewhat unfinished. The reason for that was this:

Once a year, a *Beetle Bailey* paperback was published with the best 125 strips or more of the year. For a while things were fine. Then somehow, the collections began to be published by a publisher who had only a glancing familiarity with quality. The paper was bad, the printing was bad. The lines were fuzzy, the Ben Day mushed together and all the uniforms came out black. The strips looked fine in the newspapers, but terrible in paperback. Mainly for that reason the use of Ben Day was stopped. I felt that *Beetle* often looked empty, and from time to time I would urge Mort to return to the use of Ben Day, and force King Features to switch to a different publisher. Finally, *Beetle* went back to its original look. With the advent of computers, installing gray wherever you wanted it became much easier than the old painstaking blue-watercolor-and-razor-blade technique.

January 30, 1962 (page 31): Sam reads a note from a reader who asks, "...what kind of pants do you wear?" and the sidekick (now Silo) replies, "These are comic strip pants." This is the sort of gag that was the foundation of the strip, and the kind we would have liked to do every day. As time went on, we probably would have been able to continue with variations, but it wasn't easy day by day, week

WHY ARE WE DRESSING UP LIKE THIS, SAM ?
I THOUGHT A STRIP ABOUT PIRATES MIGHT CLICK. THERE'S NEVER BEEN ONE
10-16
WHAT DO WE DO NOW? WE DON'T HAVE ANY JOKES ABOUT PIRATES
I DUNNO
©1961 KING FEATURES SYNDICATE, INC., WORLD RIGHTS RESERVED
LET'S GO BOWLING
dumas

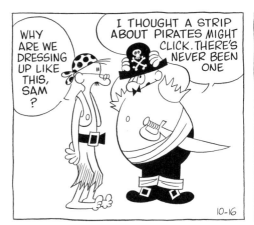

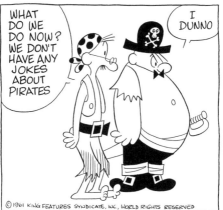

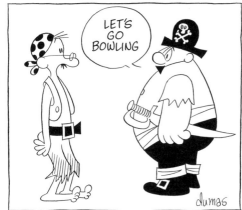

Jerry writes: "Back at the start, we sometimes did multiple versions of the same gag. Mort did all of the lettering on all of the strips, including this one. We were still adjusting to the art, including the proper size of the lettering. Oddly, the version with the larger, more readable balloons, shown here, was not the one we decided on. Compare this to the published version [opposite], from October 21, 1961."

by week. When we resorted to more conventional gags, even gags about the Cold War and political cartoon figures, the strip didn't seem to me to be as interesting. Incidentally, the drawing of the car in the second panel isn't very good. As with the sidekick's head, compared to Silo's head forty years later, the construction of the car is not as solid, as interesting, as in later years.

Drawing is a personal thing, and I began to notice as time went along that I preferred a slightly wavering, jumpy, line to a smooth sweep of a line. In the 1960s, '70s and '80s, when I inked *Beetle Bailey*, I liked to pencil the static background areas of the strip by using a triangle to make straight lines for things like windows, doorways, floor lines, steps, but then ink those penciled straight lines freehand, to give the look of a panel a more relaxed feeling. That's why the tires on the *Sam and Silo* car look the way they do.

February 10, 1962 (page 34): My least favorite strip. Terrible artwork. Somebody should have taken my cartoonist's license away.

March 7, 1962 (page 41): Jiggs, Donald Duck, Popeye, Snuffy Smith and Beetle are all in a bathtub with Sam. Along with the characters from *Peanuts*, these were fairly easy people to copy, I'm not sure why. Krazy Kat, Ignatz the mouse and Happy Hooligan were also easy for me to draw, but by far the most difficult was Blondie and to some extent Dagwood. With them, if you make one slight mistake, everything is thrown off. Every line has to be just so, unlike George Herriman's work, where if you attack the paper with vigor and confidence, things will all work out all right, even if the characters vary from panel to panel.

April 30, 1962 (page 57): This strip, with all the comic characters arriving for "Comics Week," is probably the most famous of all the strips. It has been used on invitations, greeting cards, stationery, T-shirts and other clothing. This may be the only strip where I drew Thurber's characters (the man and woman on the extreme left and the seal on the top of the sign). The seal is from Thurber's famous "I thought I heard a seal bark" cartoon, which shows a man and wife in bed, and the seal on top of the headboard. Thurber had been trying to draw a seal on a rock, but the rock turned out to look more like a bed's headboard, and that's how this gag came to be. A cartoonist once barged into the founding editor's office at *The New Yorker* and asked Harold Ross, "How can you reject my stuff while you publish the work of a fifth-rate cartoonist like James Thurber?"

WHY ARE WE DRESSING UP LIKE THIS, SAM?
I THOUGHT A STRIP ABOUT PIRATES MIGHT CLICK. THERE'S NEVER BEEN ONE
WHAT DO WE DO NOW? WE DON'T HAVE ANY JOKES ABOUT PIRATES
I DUNNO
10-21
LET'S GO BOWLING
dumas

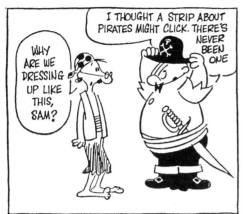

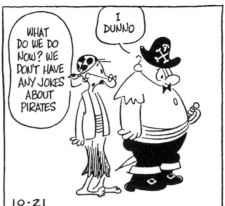

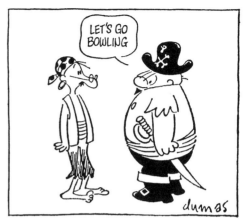

"Third-rate," Ross defended.

I was sorry that Ross died by the time I started at *The New Yorker*. I missed him by just eight years; anything of mine they published was done during the long reign of the great William Shawn. (Any editor is great if he likes your stuff.)

May 2, 1962 (page 57): One of my favorites. It says something about human pomposity. I like the way all the heads are looking to the left in the first panel, and suddenly have turned to the right in the second. In its own way there is more action here than in a gag showing characters running around. Fans have noticed that there are few "realistic" comic characters in most of the strips, Prince Valiant being one exception. We never included Superman, Batman, Captain America, The Phantom, Buz Sawyer or any of the others. Partly this was because even as a child I felt that the word "comic" ought to be restricted to characters and strips that were funny. To me, there was nothing comic about action heroes who were heavily involved in blood, guts, death and a paucity of wit. Still, my favorite strip as a boy in the 1940s was Roy Crane's *Buz Sawyer*. I never missed reading the dailies and copied, diligently, many of them. My favorite Sunday page was *Prince Valiant*. Somewhere back in the 1960s I had drinks with Roy Crane but I couldn't get him to talk much; Hal Foster was quite a bit more entertaining.

The other reasons action figures were largely absent were: (1) Space — it was necessary to use short characters who did not take up a lot of room (Barney Google, Pogo, Ignatz, Mickey Mouse) and, if you were going to use a lot of them, with just a few taller ones in the rear (Andy Gump, Happy Hooligan, Casper Milquetoast); and (2) To us, it looked like more fun to show a line-up of humor characters interacting rather than a line-up of serious-minded fighters for truth and justice. I suppose it all comes down to my personal likes and Mort's background...we were always more interested in humorous newspaper comic strips than we were in comic book superheroes.

May 3, 1962 (page 58): All the comic characters seated at the long dais. On the second floor of The Lambs' Club on 44th Street in New York City, where the monthly National Cartoonists Society meetings were held for many years, there was a long, raised dais with room for ten or fifteen chairs. In the early days, 150 to 200 cartoonists would look from their tables to see, side by side on the dais, Rube Goldberg, Harry Hershfield, Walt Kelly, Hal Foster, Russell Patterson, Otto Soglow, Milton Caniff and many other early greats. Exhilarating talk, with free-flowing comments and rejoinders from all across the room could be heard. Otto Soglow actually preferred to sit at a table at the rear of the room. He had a large, handsome head, but he was barely five feet tall. It was a "standing" joke when, during the question period, members voiced business concerns, Otto would raise his hand and upon being recognized ask, "Why don't we ever have soup?" Someone always cried out, "Stand up Otto!" Otto

WANTED
FUNNY FAT
MAN FOR
COMIC STRIP
SEE SAM
OH! THINK
YOU'RE TOO GOOD
FOR THE
COMICS, EH?!
WANTED
FUNNY FAT
MAN FOR
COMIC STRIP
SEE SAM

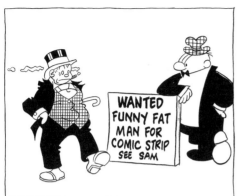

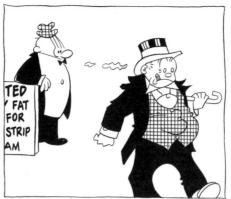

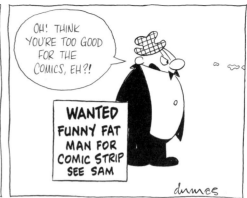

Jerry laments: "I wish I had taken a little more care with some of the strips. In the episode shown here, Sam is supposed to be looking at Jiggs. But he looks as if he is gazing off to the side. I always believe that when possible, characters should be depicted doing what they are supposed to be doing. Redrawn, with heavier lettering, the finished version of this strip [opposite] was published on March 2, 1962."

would always snap back, "I AM standing." Otto was a funny, Buster Keaton-sort-of-guy, and would have made an excellent 1930s Hollywood character actor. I grew up reading his *The Little King*, but I liked better talking with him about early days at *The New Yorker*.

July 26, 1962 (page 82): I never liked the Pixy gags much, nor the drawing. The strips are filled with endless odds and ends, all of it very busy and crowded, none of it, as I view it now, funny. Pixy was cute, but no comedian.

July 31, 1962 (page 83): We did a fair amount of gags involving ZOOM clouds behind the car. One day a huge box arrived at the door, containing about 24 boxes of ZOOM cereal, with thanks from the company. It was decent cereal, I guess, but I never saw it in a store anywhere. I suggested that if companies were going to send us their products simply for mentioning them in the strip, we ought to make the car a Cadillac. But we didn't, because we thought it would be a touch blatant.

August 15 and 16, 1962 (page 87-88): In these strips we see Snuffy Smith, Popeye and Dagwood. Over the years people have asked if any creator ever complained about our unauthorized use of their characters. Nobody ever did, not even Walt Disney or Charles M. Schulz. In fact, both Schulz and the Disney Company asked for and received the originals when their characters appeared in *Sam's Strip*. Much later, both had a change of minds. Disney began to threaten legal action when someone made free with Donald Duck and Sparky Schulz did not like others drawing his people either, and I can't blame him.

November 6, 1962 (page 111): This small comic character "from around 1920" with four exclamation marks above his head in the first panel, and five in the third, has obviously been reincarnated as Mayor McGuffey in *Sam and Silo*. It's generally a good idea to have a little guy holding a position of power, from a humor standpoint. From a structural standpoint, it's good to have a small person in a comic strip because then an artist has more room for the words. And, as in real life, it's less boring when people are not all the same size.

November 14, 1962 (page 113): This Dick Tracy gag, written by Mort, is a long-time fan favorite, and seems just right in every way. Sam's innocently brash personality reminds me of the time my five-year-old son John called out loudly in the barber shop, "Hey Dad! Why is the bald guy getting a hair cut?"

WANTED
FUNNY FAT
MAN FOR
COMIC STRIP
SEE SAM
OH! THINK
YOU'RE TOO GOOD
FOR THE
COMICS, EH?!
WANTED
FUNNY FAT
MAN FOR
COMIC STRIP
SEE SAM
3-2
dumas

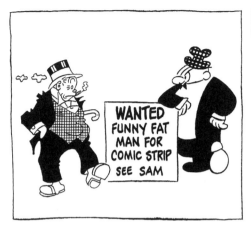

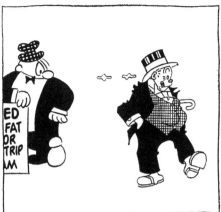

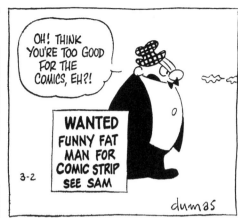

November 15, 1962 (page 114): We used the *Toonerville Trolley* characters several times. Fontaine Fox had retired by then, but I met him one day and was surprised that he was living right in Greenwich, Connecticut. We used to hang around with each other and talk about old cartooning days at our Y.M.C.A. One night I invited him to dinner and also invited Mort and Dik Browne and their wives. Fontaine was also a loner and was from another era. Mort and Dik had never seen him and didn't know what he looked like. I gave him a different name and introduced him as a neighbor. We talked baseball all evening, which Fox knew a lot about since he had played minor league ball in Louisville. I don't know how much our wives enjoyed it, but Fox was tickled with the whole charade and it was a memorable moment when his true identity was revealed to Mort and Dik, whose work was much admired by Fontaine Fox.

April 9, 1963 (page 155): Sam looks in a crystal ball and reads, "It'll be Robert Kennedy in '68." In the third panel Sam's partner asks, "Robert Kennedy WHAT in '68?" The answer to "Silo's" question would prove to be that Robert Kennedy gets killed in '68. And Sam was prescient in that Robert Kennedy probably would have won the Democratic nomination in '68. Maybe even the presidency. Remember that this strip appeared in April, 1963, before John F. Kennedy had been shot.

May 9 to 11, 1963 (page 164): Here are three of the gags we did, having fun with "sophisticated" cartoon characters, in *The New Yorker* style. I published my first cartoon in *The New Yorker* in 1959, and my last in 1980, so I was very familiar with the cartoons and the cartoonists. (My alternate universe.) The sophisticates seen here are not drawn in my own *New Yorker* style, but they are a combination of styles of many of the cartoonists. Here you see hints of Frank Modell, Mischa Richter and Robert Weber and my all-time favorite and friend, Chuck Saxon. The drawings I did for magazines like *The New Yorker* and *Connoisseur* were closer to faded old photographs with a dash of humor than anything else, and were a pleasant change from syndicated comic strips.

May 13 to 18, 1963 (pages 165-166): This was the week that Sam went into his bomb shelter, and little drawing was required. Not a particularly funny week, but it was restful and easy on the eyes. Many years later, my wife, Gail, and I went to dinner at John Cullen Murphy's house. We saw Jack and his wife, Joan, often over more than fifty years. Jack, at that time, had stopped doing *Big Ben Bolt* (beautiful artwork) and had taken over *Prince Valiant* from Hal Foster. Over wild rice and chicken, Jack chuckled and said, a bit enviously, "You probably did that whole week in less time than it took me to draw a porticullis." •

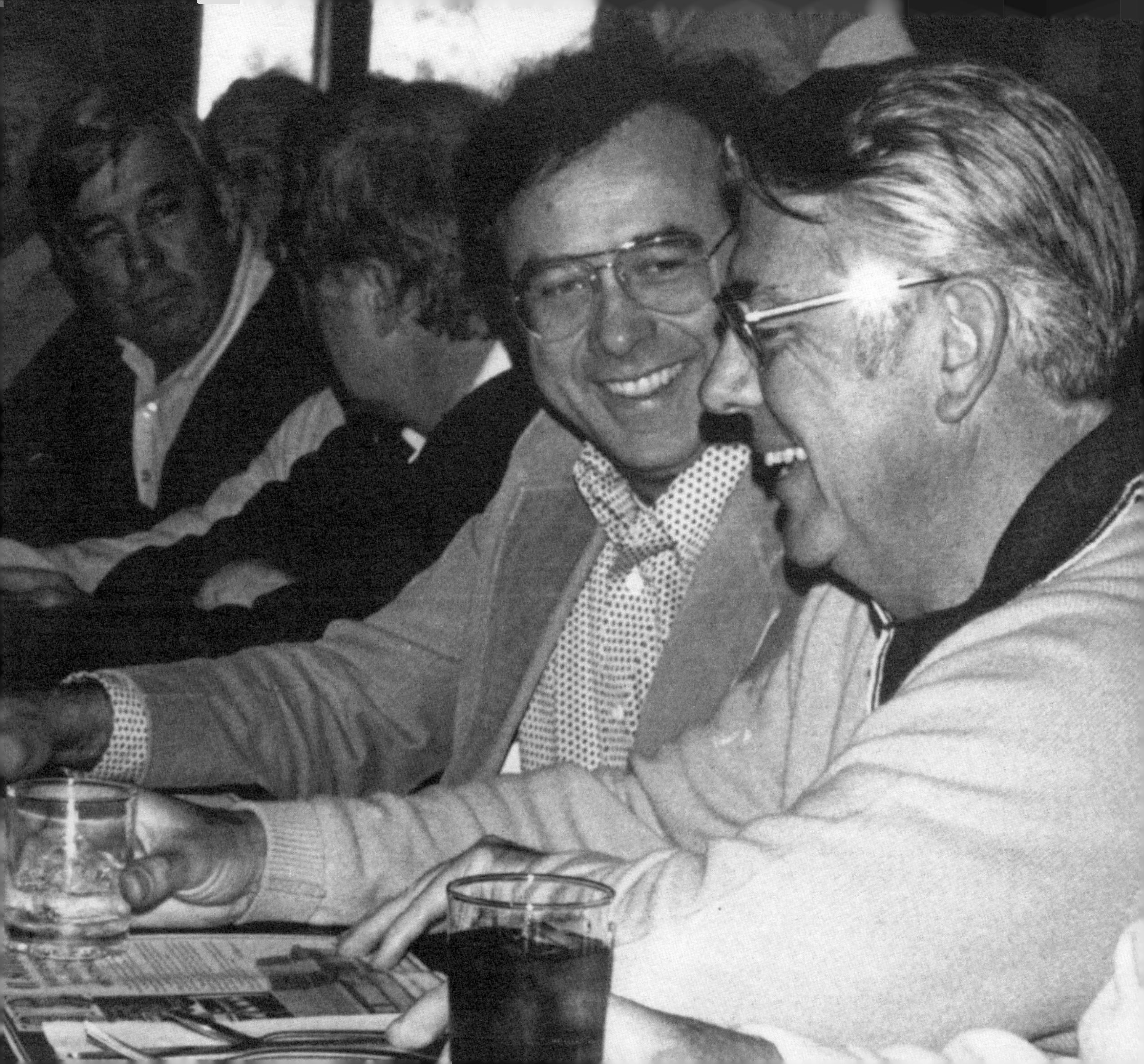

SAM'S SIXTIES

by BRIAN WALKER

The early 1960s in America was a time of both optimistic faith in human progress and anxious tension about international relations. There was a new president in the White House, the Cold War was in deep freeze and television dominated popular culture. Mort Walker and Jerry Dumas reflected the mood of this era in *Sam's Strip* and used current events as a source of humor. Many of the names and phrases of the period may not be familiar to today's readers. The following information is intended to provide some background about the people, places and happenings that are mentioned in the panels of *Sam's Strip*.

October 18, 1961 (page 1): American author **John Steinbeck** won the Pulitzer Prize for *Grapes of Wrath* in 1939 and the Nobel Prize for literature in 1962.

October 25, 1961 (page 3): **John F. Kennedy** was President of the United States between January 20, 1961 and his assassination on November 22, 1963.

OPPOSITE: A photo of Jerry and Mort from 1977, the year that *Sam & Silo* was launched.

October 27, 1961 (page 4): **Mr. Dry**, a character popularized in the cartoons of Rollin Kirby, represented the Prohibition era, from 1920 to 1933.

November 1, 1961 (page 5): **Adlai Stevenson**, a liberal intellectual, was the U.S. Ambassador to the United Nations from 1961 to 1965.

November 16, 1961 (page 10): **Nikita Khrushchev** was the First Secretary of the Communist Party of the Soviet Union from 1953 to 1964.

November 20, 1961 (page 11): John F. Kennedy hired **Pierre Salinger** as his press secretary when he was elected President in 1961.

November 21, 1961 (page 11): The **New York World's Fair** opened on April 22, 1964.

November 23, 1961 (page 12): The term **New Frontier** was first used by John F. Kennedy in 1960 and became a label for his administration's domestic and foreign policies.

November 30, 1961 (page 14): **Jimmy Durante**, a popular comedic personality from the 1920s to the 1970s, was famous for mangling the English language.

December 11, 1961 (page 17): The construction of the **Berlin Wall**, which separated the communist and democratic sections of the city, began on August 13, 1961.

December 15, 1961 (page 18): John F. Kennedy was honored as a hero during World War II for saving the crew of **PT 109**.

December 19, 1961 (page 19): **Bing Crosby**, a popular singer from 1926 to 1977, was known for his unique, rhythmic vocal intonation.

December 21, 1961 (page 20): American cartoonist **Rube Goldberg** is best remembered for inventing wildly complicated contraptions to perform the simplest of tasks.

December 26, 1961 (page 21): **Jim Bishop** wrote a column that was syndicated by King Features from 1957 to 1983.

January 3, 1962 (page 23): The term "sex kitten" was first used to describe French actress **Brigitte Bardot** in 1958.

January 5, 1962 (page 24): Frank Sinatra nicknamed **Marlon Brando** "Mumbles" for his method acting style on the set of the 1955 movie, *Guys and Dolls*.

January 9, 1962 (page 25): **Elizabeth Taylor** won the Academy Award for Best Actress in 1960.

January 24, 1962 (page 29): Many communities were forced to relocate during the construction of the **New York State Thruway** in the 1950s.

February 1 and 2, 1962 (page 32): "**The Twist**" by Chubby Checker was a number-one hit song in September, 1960 and, again, in January, 1962.

February 6, 1962 (page 33): **Jack Paar** was the host of *The Tonight Show* from 1957 to 1962.

February 13, 1962 (page 35): **Richard Nixon** lost the presidential election to John F. Kennedy in 1960.

March 5, 1962 (page 41): The **Harlem Globetrotters** exhibition basketball team made news in 1962 by losing a rare game to the Washington Generals.

March 8, 1962 (page 42): First Lady **Jackie Kennedy** became a fashion icon by wearing the clothes of Christian Dior and other European designers.

March 12, 1962 (page 43): Chuck Yeager was the first pilot to break the **sound barrier** on October 14, 1947.

March 15, 1962 (page 44): Between 1961 and 1989, an estimated 133 people were killed trying to escape from **East Germany** by crossing the Berlin Wall.

March 17, 1962 (page 44): **Dr. Benjamin Spock's** 1946 book, *Baby and Child Care*, was an indispensable manual for baby boom parents during the 1950s and '60s.

March 19 to 24, 1962 (pages 45-46): During his administration, John F. Kennedy promoted good health with his **President's Council on Physical Fitness**.

April 2, 1962 (page 49): **John Glenn**, **Alan Shepard** and **Gus Grissom** were among the original seven Mercury astronauts selected by NASA in 1959.

April 5, 1962 (page 50): In February 1962, the U.S. launched an economic embargo against **Cuba** after Fidel Castro established formal ties with the Soviet Union.

April 9 to 19, 1962 (pages 51-54): A group of '60s actors that included Frank Sinatra, Dean Martin, Sammy Davis, Jr., Peter Lawford and Joey Bishop were know as the **Rat Pack**.

April 24, 1962 (page 55): **Pete Martin** was an editor and writer for the *Saturday Evening Post* who co-wrote the autobiographies of Bing Crosby and Bob Hope.

May 10, 1962 (page 60): **Charles de Gaulle** was a general and statesman who served as President of France from 1959 to 1969.

May 21, 1962 (page 63): **Floyd Patterson** was the world heavyweight boxing champion from 1956 to 1959 and from 1960 to 1962.

May 25, 1962 (page 64): Former Yankees manager **Casey Stengel** was the skipper of the New York Mets from 1962 to 1965.

May 26, 1962 (page 64): Past presidents **Harry S. Truman** and **Dwight "Ike" Eisenhower** were still influential in their respective political parties during the 1960s.

May 29, 1962 (page 65): Actress **Elizabeth Taylor** and singer **Eddie Fisher** had a stormy marriage that lasted from 1959 to 1964.

June 2, 1962 (page 66): After singing "Happy Birthday, Mr. President" to John F. Kennedy on May 19, 1962, **Marilyn Monroe** was found dead at her home on August 5, 1962.

June 5, 1962 (page 67): John F. Kennedy's Medical Health Bill for the Aged was eventually signed into law as **Medicare** in 1965 during the Johnson administration.

June 19, 1962 (page 71): **Scott Carpenter** became the fourth American astronaut in space and the second to orbit the earth on May 24, 1962.

July 9, 1962 (page 77): **Billy Sol Estes**, a Texas financier who had ties to Vice President Lyndon Johnson, was indicted on April 5, 1962 on 57 counts of fraud.

July 14, 1962 (page 78): Gossip columnist **Elsa Maxwell** earned the title as the "hostess with the mostest" for her high society parties.

July 25, 1962 (page 81): JFK's brother, **Bobby Kennedy**, was the United States Attorney General from 1961 to 1964.

August 6, 1962 (page 85): The **school prayer issue** heated up in the early 1960s when a number of court cases redefined the separation of church and state.

August 7, 1962 (page 85): **Dean Rusk** served in the Kennedy and Johnson administrations as the United States Secretary of State from 1961 to 1969.

August 10, 1962 (page 86): The demolition of the **Berlin Wall** didn't begin until November 9, 1989.

August 22, 1962 (page 89): The first U.S. space probe of **Venus**, Mariner 1, was aborted after it launched on July 22, 1962. Mariner 2 orbited Venus on December 14, 1962.

August 23, 1962 (page 90): A hard-drinking star of early television, **Jackie Gleason**, uttered his famous phrase, "How sweet it is!" in the 1962 film *Papa's Delicate Condition*.

August 30, 1962 (page 92): The Trade Expansion Act of 1962 granted the White House unprecedented authority to reduce **tariffs** up to 50%.

August 31, 1962 (page 92): **Mitch Miller's** popular television program, *Sing Along with Mitch*, ran from 1961 to 1964.

September 20, 1962 (page 98): The first active communications satellite, **Telstar**, was launched on July 10, 1962.

September 21, 1962 (page 98): The owner of one of the most famous restaurants in New York City, **Toots Shor**, was also a regular drinking buddy of Jackie Gleason's.

September 27, 1962 (page 100): "Mr. Conservative" **Barry Goldwater** was a five-term U.S. Senator from Arizona and the Republican Party nominee for president in 1964.

September 29, 1962 (page 100): A major confrontation between the Soviet Union and the United States culminated in the **Cuban Missile Crisis** in October, 1962.

October 10, 1962 (page 103): The U.S. **postage rate** for a first-class letter went up to 4¢ in 1958 and increased to 5¢ on January 7, 1963.

October 11, 1962 (page 104): During his tenure as U.S. Attorney General, **Bobby Kennedy** investigated organized crime and corrupt union officials.

October 25, 1962 (page 108): In 1962, **John Wayne** starred in the classic western *The Man Who Shot Liberty Valance* directed by John Ford.

October 27, 1962 (page 108): An Academy Award-winning film actress, **Loretta Young** was also an Emmy Award-winning host of her own television show from 1955 to 1964.

November 12, 1962 (page 113): **Ernest Hemingway** won the Nobel Prize for Literature in 1954 and **John Steinbeck** won the same award in 1962.

November 22, 1962 (page 116): **Shirley MacLaine** starred in *Irma la Douce* (1963), while Debbie Reynolds starred in the film version of *The Unsinkable Molly Brown* (1964).

November 28, 1962 (page 117): The People's Republic of China was often referred to as **Red China** by Westerners, until relations improved in the 1970s.

December 1, 1962 (page 118): **Arthur Murray** was the founder of a successful dance studio and instruction course. *The Arthur Murray Party* TV show ran from 1950 to 1960.

December 8, 1962 (page 120): **Lucille Ball** became the first female head of a major Hollywood studio when her ex-husband, **Desi Arnaz**, resigned from Desilu in 1962.

December 10, 1962 (page 121): **Ted Kennedy** was elected to his first term as a U.S. Senator from Massachusetts in November 6, 1962, filling his brother John's vacant seat.

December 14, 1962 (page 122): Former president **Dwight D. Eisenhower** has a tree named after him on the 17th hole of the Augusta National Golf Club, home of The Masters.

December 15, 1962 (page 122): The ageless leading man **Cary Grant** starred in *That Touch of Mink* with Doris Day in 1962 and *Charade* with Audrey Hepburn in 1963.

December 24, 1962 (page 125): American film director, television producer and theme park designer, **Walt Disney**, passed away in 1966.

December 27, 1962 (page 126): The popular American poet, **Robert Frost**, who died in 1963, received four Pulitzer Prizes during his lifetime.

December 29, 1962 (page 126): **Civil defense** booklets, such as *Fallout Protection*, were published to warn of the dangers of nuclear attack during the Cold War.

February 11, 1963 (page 139): In the 1960s, scientists began talks to limit the use of **hydrogen bombs** after rockets were developed to deliver H-bombs anywhere in the world.

March 11, 1963 (page 147): In 1963, **Brigitte Bardot** appeared in the critically acclaimed film *Contempt*, directed by Jean-Luc Godard.

April 9, 1963 (page 155): **Robert Kennedy** campaigned for the Democratic nomination for president in 1968 but was assassinated on June 5, 1968.

April 12, 1963 (page 156): **Nelson Rockefeller** and **George Romney** were among the Republican candidates being considered for the 1964 presidential election.

April 13, 1963 (page 156): In 1963, Ayatollah Ruhollah Khomeini was in prison for criticizing the autocratic rule of the U.S. supported Shah of **Iran**, Mohammad Reza Pahlavi.

April 15, 1963 (page 157): **Nikita Khrushchev** lost support in the Communist Party after the Cuban Missile Crisis and was replaced as Soviet leader by Leonid Brezhnev in 1964.

April 26, 1963 (page 160): President Kennedy established the **Peace Corps** in 1961, an organization that provides American volunteers to work in developing countries.

April 27, 1963 (page 160): A Nobel Peace Prize-winning physician, theologian and humanitarian, **Albert Schweitzer** died on September 4, 1965.

May 13 to 18, 1963 (pages 165-166): Many Americans built **bomb shelters** during the Cold War to protect themselves from the radioactive fallout of a potential nuclear explosion.

May 25, 1963 (page 168): On October 12, 1960, at a meeting of the United Nations General Assembly, **Nikita Khrushchev** took off his shoe and pounded it on the table. •

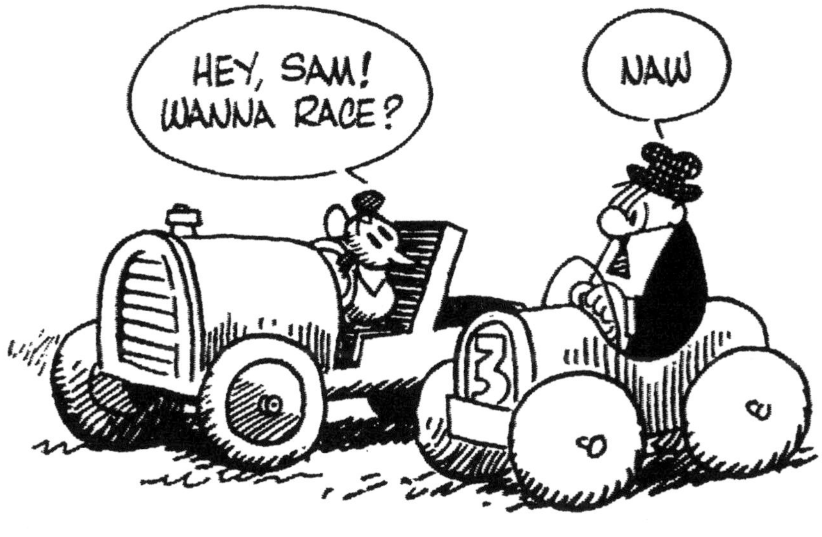
HEY, SAM! WANNA RACE?
NAW
3

SAM & SILO

by JERRY DUMAS *and* MORT WALKER

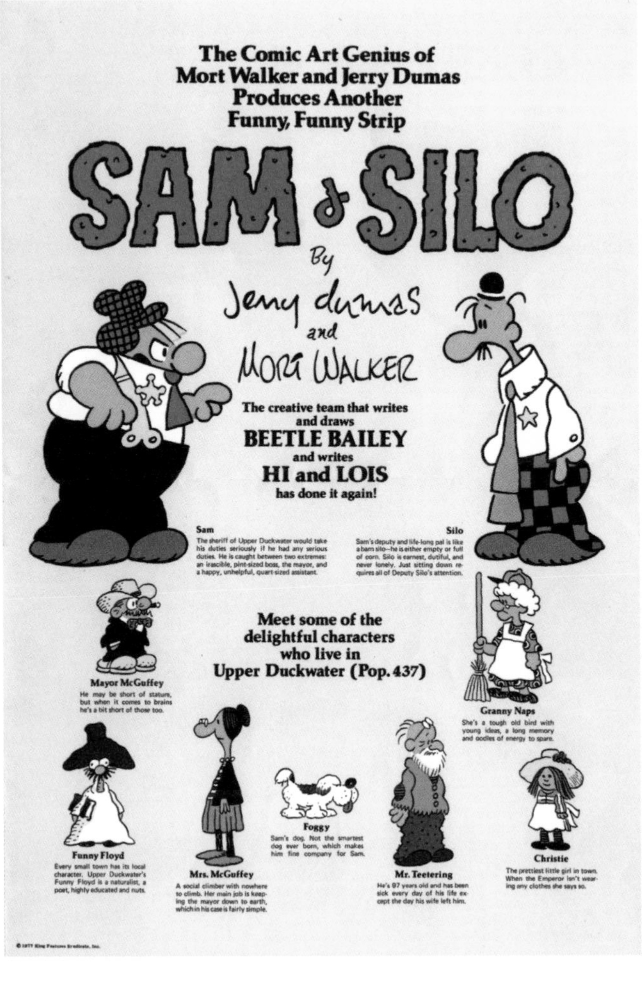

The Comic Art Genius of
Mort Walker and Jerry Dumas
Produces Another
Funny, Funny Strip
SAM & SILO
By
Jerry dumas
and
MORT WALKER
The creative team that writes
and draws
BEETLE BAILEY
and writes
HI and LOIS
has done it again!
Sam
The sheriff of Upper Duckwater would take his duties seriously if he had any serious duties. He is caught between two extremes: an irascible, pint-sized boss, the mayor, and a happy, unhelpful, quart-sized assistant.
Silo
Sam's deputy and life-long pal is like a barn silo—he is either empty or full of corn. Silo is earnest, dutiful, and never lonely. Just sitting down requires all of Deputy Silo's attention.
Meet some of the
delightful characters
who live in
Upper Duckwater (Pop. 437)
Mayor McGuffey
He may be short of stature, but when it comes to brains he's a bit short of those too.
Granny Naps
She's a tough old bird with young ideas, a long memory and oodles of energy to spare.
Funny Floyd
Every small town has its local character. Upper Duckwater's Funny Floyd is a naturalist, a poet, highly educated and nuts.
Mrs. McGuffey
A social climber with nowhere to climb. Her main job is keeping the mayor down to earth, which in his case is fairly simple.
Foggy
Sam's dog. Not the smartest dog ever born, which makes him fine company for Sam.
Mr. Teetering
He's 97 years old and has been sick every day of his life except the day his wife left him.
Christie
The prettiest little girl in town. When the Emperor isn't wearing any clothes she says so.

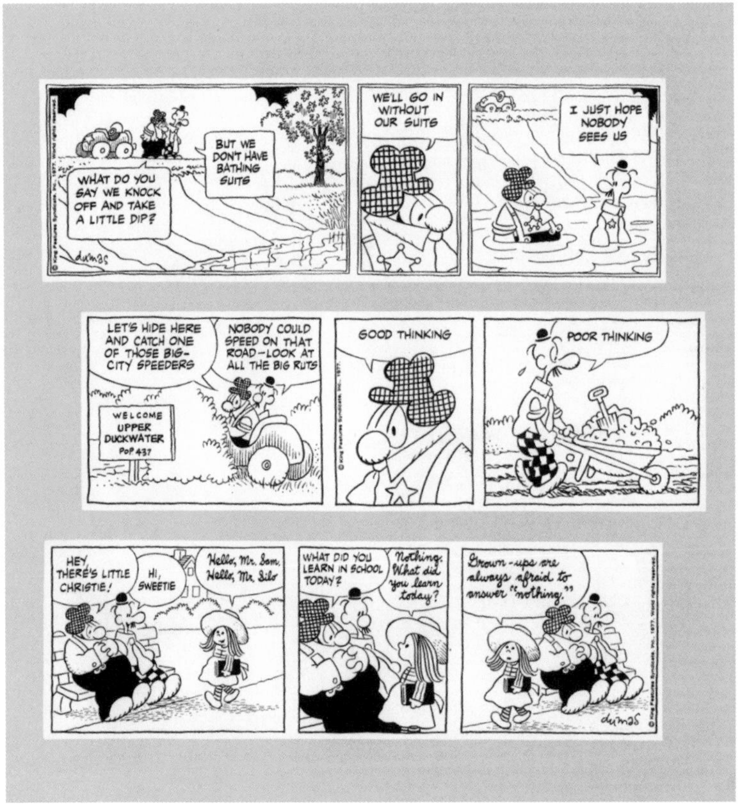

WHAT DO YOU SAY WE KNOCK OFF AND TAKE A LITTLE DIP?
BUT WE DON'T HAVE BATHING SUITS
WE'LL GO IN WITHOUT OUR SUITS
I JUST HOPE NOBODY SEES US
LET'S HIDE HERE AND CATCH ONE OF THOSE BIG-CITY SPEEDERS
NOBODY COULD SPEED ON THAT ROAD—LOOK AT ALL THE BIG RUTS
WELCOME
UPPER DUCKWATER
POP 437
GOOD THINKING
POOR THINKING
HEY, THERE'S LITTLE CHRISTIE!
HI, SWEETIE
Hello, Mr. Sam. Hello, Mr. Silo
WHAT DID YOU LEARN IN SCHOOL TODAY?
Nothing. What did you learn today?
Grown-ups are always afraid to answer "nothing."

The cast of *Sam & Silo* was introduced in this artwork from the sales brochure produced by King Features for the strip's launch on April 18, 1977.

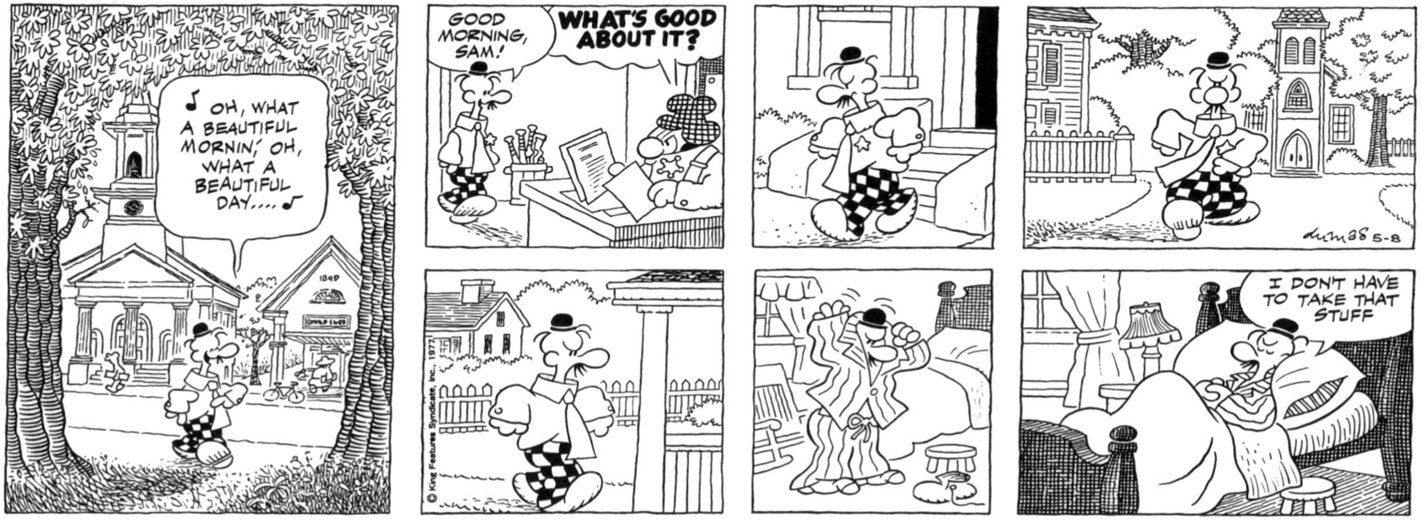
♪ OH, WHAT A BEAUTIFUL MORNIN', OH, WHAT A BEAUTIFUL DAY.... ♪
1849
GOOD MORNING, SAM!
WHAT'S GOOD ABOUT IT?
dumas 5-8
© King Features Syndicate, Inc., 1977.
I DON'T HAVE TO TAKE THAT STUFF

Sam & Silo Sunday page, May 8, 1977. This was reproduced in the original sales brochure.

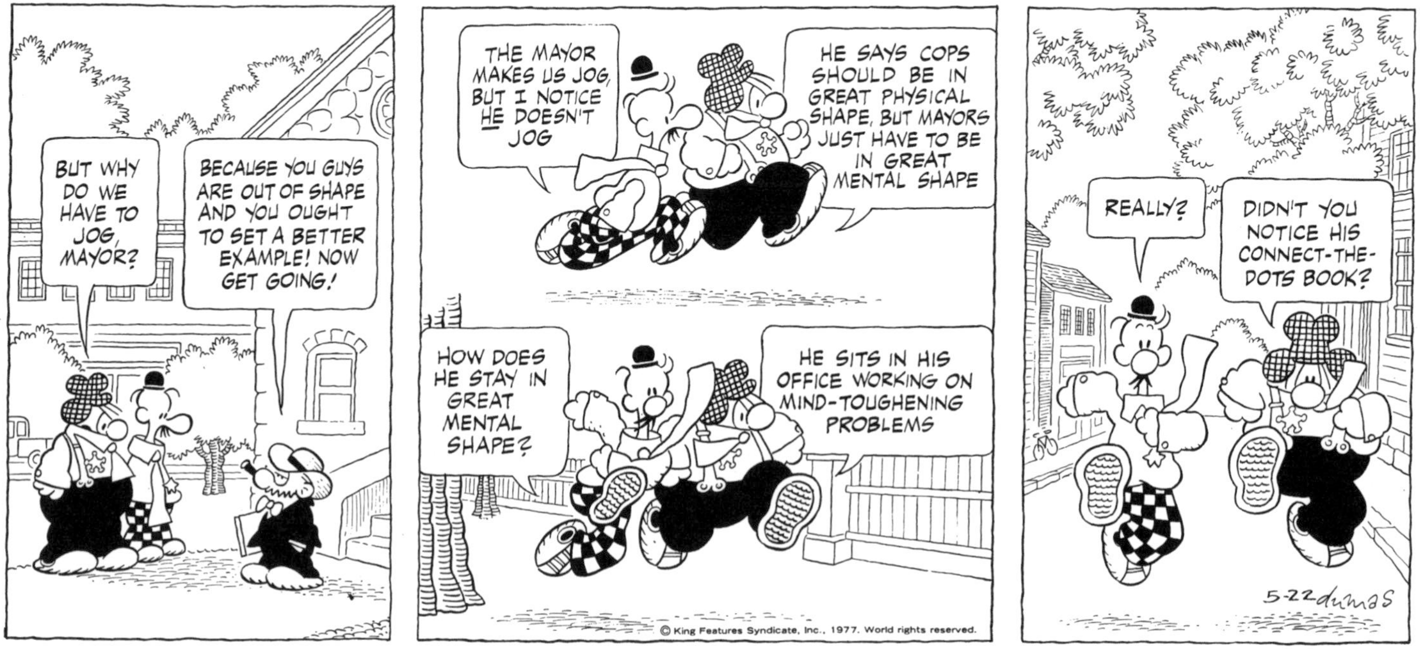
BUT WHY DO WE HAVE TO JOG, MAYOR?
BECAUSE YOU GUYS ARE OUT OF SHAPE AND YOU OUGHT TO SET A BETTER EXAMPLE! NOW GET GOING!
THE MAYOR MAKES US JOG, BUT I NOTICE HE DOESN'T JOG
HE SAYS COPS SHOULD BE IN GREAT PHYSICAL SHAPE, BUT MAYORS JUST HAVE TO BE IN GREAT MENTAL SHAPE
HOW DOES HE STAY IN GREAT MENTAL SHAPE?
HE SITS IN HIS OFFICE WORKING ON MIND-TOUGHENING PROBLEMS
© King Features Syndicate, Inc., 1977. World rights reserved.
REALLY?
DIDN'T YOU NOTICE HIS CONNECT-THE-DOTS BOOK?
5-22 dumas

Sam & Silo Sunday page, May 22, 1977. Jerry remembers this early example: "Today I can't stand to look at the size of Silo's nose. It's a wonder he can keep his head up. A lot of the backgrounds were influenced by real locations I visited in Maine and Martha's Vineyard."

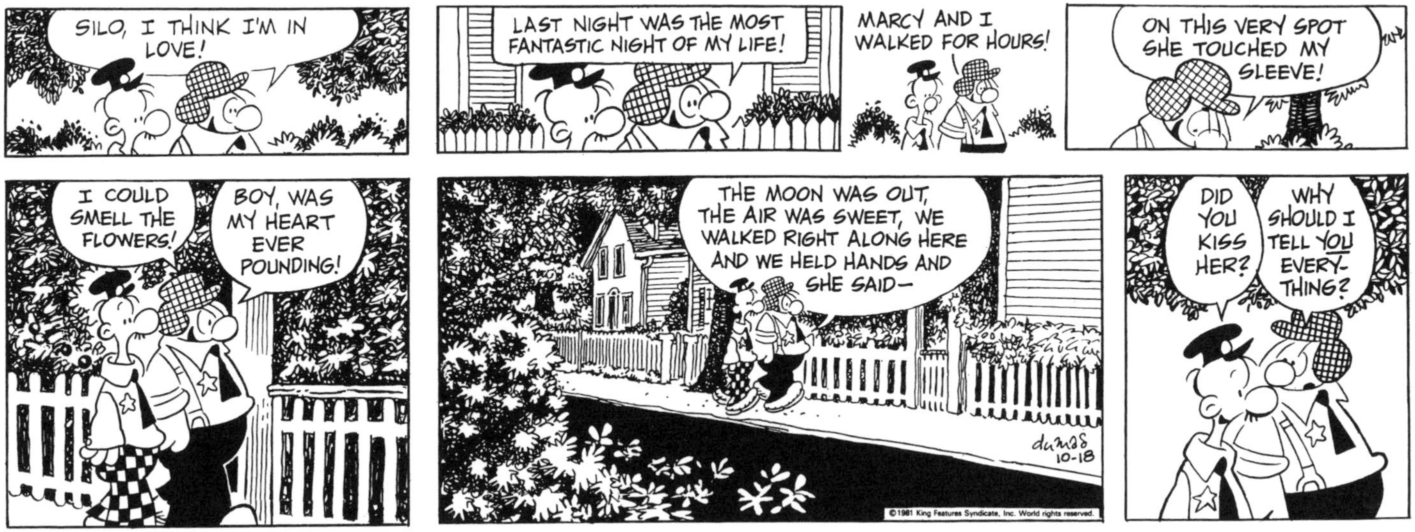
SILO, I THINK I'M IN LOVE!
LAST NIGHT WAS THE MOST FANTASTIC NIGHT OF MY LIFE!
MARCY AND I WALKED FOR HOURS!
ON THIS VERY SPOT SHE TOUCHED MY SLEEVE!
I COULD SMELL THE FLOWERS!
BOY, WAS MY HEART EVER POUNDING!
THE MOON WAS OUT, THE AIR WAS SWEET, WE WALKED RIGHT ALONG HERE AND WE HELD HANDS AND SHE SAID—
dumas 10-18
©1981 King Features Syndicate, Inc. World rights reserved.
DID YOU KISS HER?
WHY SHOULD I TELL YOU EVERYTHING?

Sam & Silo Sunday page, October 18, 1981. Waxing nostalgically, Jerry says: "I'd like to live on a street like this, if it were 1905, there were no crazed, barking dogs and everybody went quietly to bed around eleven."

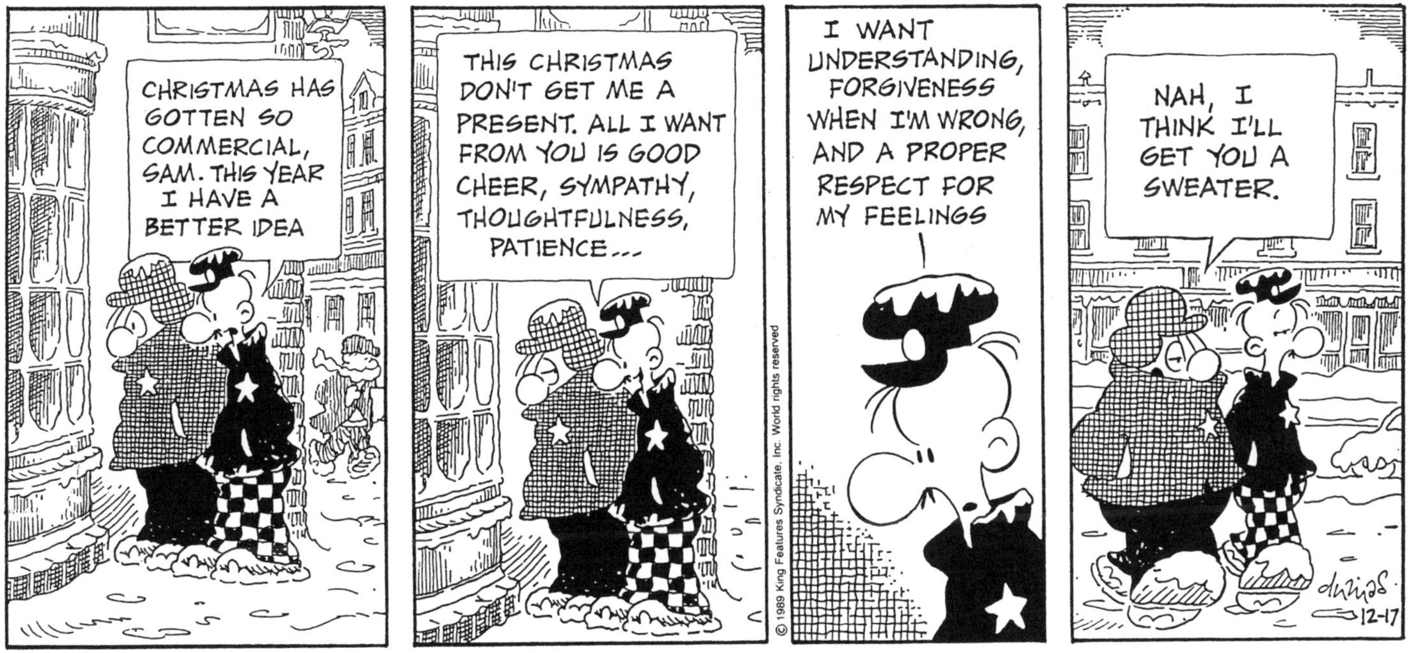
CHRISTMAS HAS GOTTEN SO COMMERCIAL, SAM. THIS YEAR I HAVE A BETTER IDEA
THIS CHRISTMAS DON'T GET ME A PRESENT. ALL I WANT FROM YOU IS GOOD CHEER, SYMPATHY, THOUGHTFULNESS, PATIENCE...
© 1989 King Features Syndicate, Inc. World rights reserved
I WANT UNDERSTANDING, FORGIVENESS WHEN I'M WRONG, AND A PROPER RESPECT FOR MY FEELINGS
NAH, I THINK I'LL GET YOU A SWEATER.
dumas 12-17

Sam & Silo Sunday page, December 17, 1989. Jerry comments: "I liked the scene in the first panel so much, I used it in a half-dozen Christmas Sunday pages. This is Silo at his best – solid and well-balanced. You would have trouble tipping him over. This is how I should have drawn him in *Sam's Strip*."

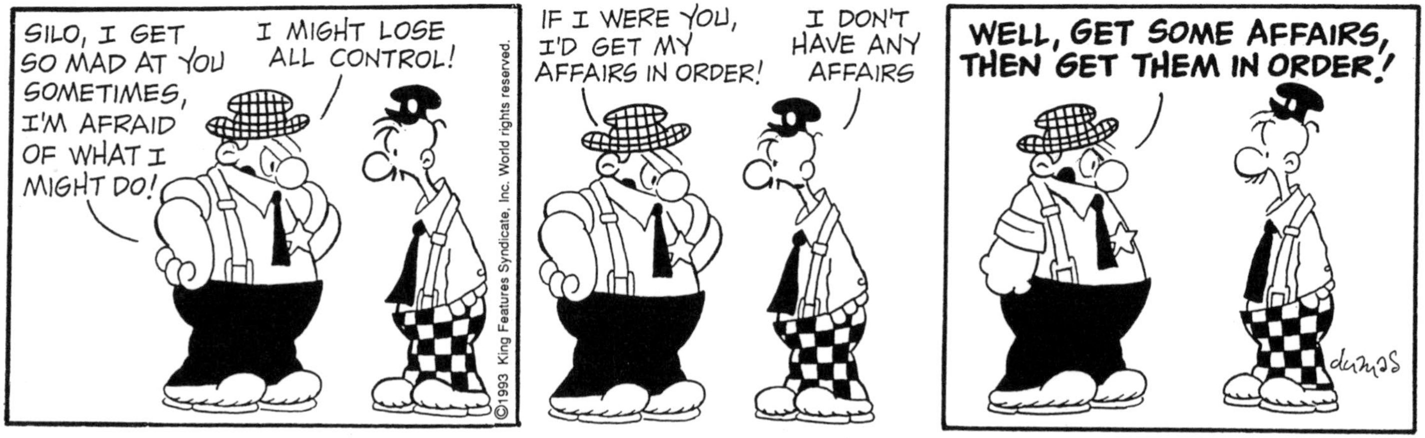
SILO, I GET SO MAD AT YOU SOMETIMES, I'M AFRAID OF WHAT I MIGHT DO!
I MIGHT LOSE ALL CONTROL!
©1993 King Features Syndicate, Inc. World rights reserved.
IF I WERE YOU, I'D GET MY AFFAIRS IN ORDER!
I DON'T HAVE ANY AFFAIRS
WELL, GET SOME AFFAIRS, THEN GET THEM IN ORDER!
dumas

Sam & Silo daily strip, 1993. Jerry explains: "In this strip Sam has evolved a little, but Silo has changed greatly. He is now more fun to draw. He is better composed, more balanced. Before, his nose was out of all proportion to his skull. Cartooning is exaggeration, but Silo's head was probably too extreme; I'm surprised he didn't keep toppling over."

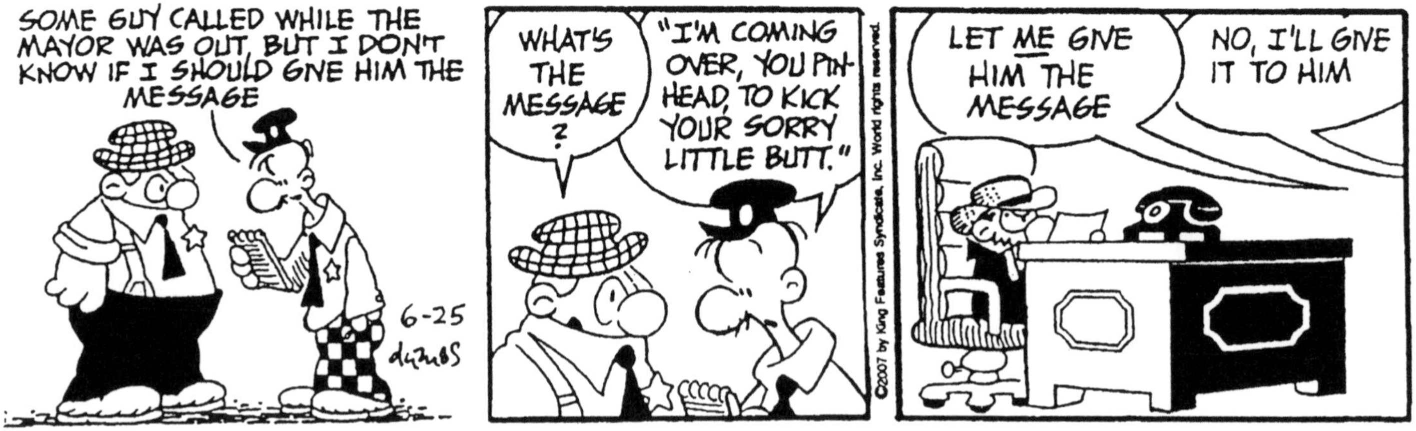
SOME GUY CALLED WHILE THE MAYOR WAS OUT, BUT I DON'T KNOW IF I SHOULD GIVE HIM THE MESSAGE
6-25
dumas
WHAT'S THE MESSAGE ?
"I'M COMING OVER, YOU PIN-HEAD, TO KICK YOUR SORRY LITTLE BUTT."
©2007 by King Features Syndicate, Inc. World rights reserved.
LET ME GIVE HIM THE MESSAGE
NO, I'LL GIVE IT TO HIM

Sam & Silo daily strip, June 25, 2007. Jerry adds: "This recent strip shows how the characters in *Sam and Silo* have changed. The character from *Sam's Strip* with the exclamation marks over his head has morphed into the mayor. The checkered pants from *Alphonse and Gaston* became Silo's pants, permanently (but not pressed)."

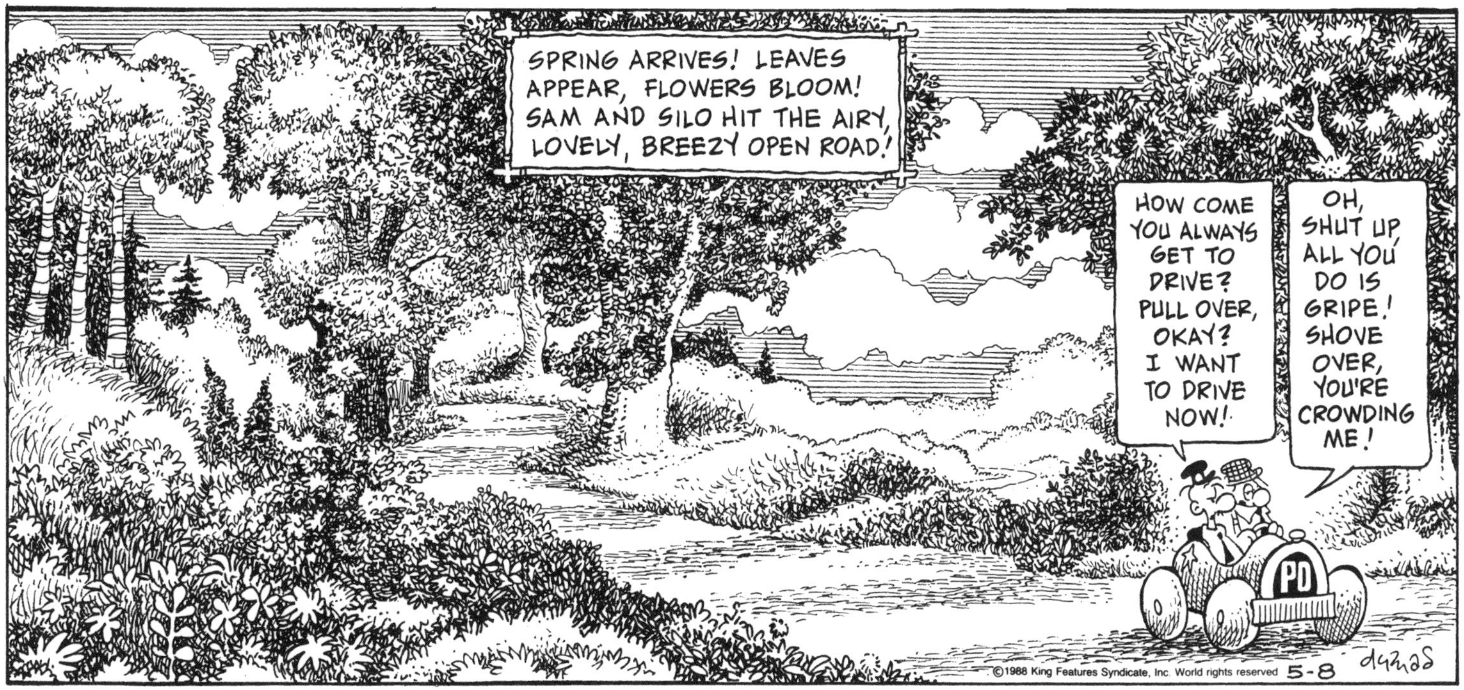
SPRING ARRIVES! LEAVES APPEAR, FLOWERS BLOOM! SAM AND SILO HIT THE AIRY, LOVELY, BREEZY OPEN ROAD!
HOW COME YOU ALWAYS GET TO DRIVE? PULL OVER, OKAY? I WANT TO DRIVE NOW!
OH, SHUT UP, ALL YOU DO IS GRIPE! SHOVE OVER, YOU'RE CROWDING ME!
PD
©1988 King Features Syndicate, Inc. World rights reserved 5-8
drumas

A READER WANTS TO KNOW WHY I STARTED THIS COMIC STRIP
WELL, I GUESS IT'S BECAUSE I WANT TO BECOME IMMORTAL.
WHEN I'M GONE, I WANT PEOPLE TO SAY, "GOOD OLD SAM! WHEN WILL WE SEE HIS LIKE AGAIN?"
OTHERWISE, I'M NOT GOING!
1-26

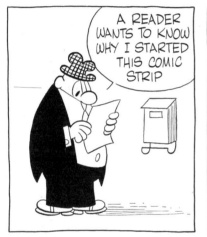

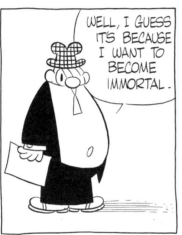

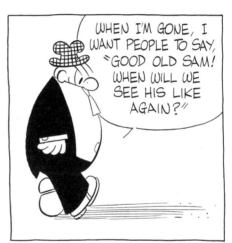

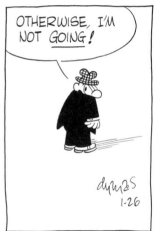